The Chinese Communist Party in Power, 1949–1976

We will build a new world, a red
world, the world of the thought
of Mao Tse-tung.

Chieh-fang-chün pao,
August 5, 1967

The Chinese Communist Party in Power, 1949–1976

JACQUES GUILLERMAZ

Translated by Anne Destenay

WESTVIEW PRESS
Boulder, Colorado

First published 1972 as *Le parti communiste chinois au pouvoir* by Payot, Paris.

©1972 Payot, Paris

This edition was revised and updated by the author to include the period from 1972 through 1976.

Copyright of English translation © 1976 by Westview Press, Inc. The English language edition was edited by Mervyn Adams Seldon.

Published in 1976 in the United States of America by

>   Westview Press, Inc.
>   1898 Flatiron Court
>   Boulder, Colorado 80301
>   Frederick A. Praeger, Publisher and Editorial Director

Library of Congress Cataloging in Publication Data

Guillermaz, Jacques.
   The Chinese Communist Party in power, 1949-1976.

   Translation of Le parti communiste chinois au pouvoir.
   Bibliography: p. 581
   Includes index.
   1. Chung-kuo kung ch'an tang—History. I. Title.
JQ1519.A5G8513   329.9'51   76-7593
ISBN 0-89158-041-7

Printed and bound in the United States of America.

FOR KIRSTI

Contents

Tables

Maps

Figures

Prologue

Like the hero of a Greek tragedy, struck down by fate in the last scene of the play, Mao Tse-tung, the central figure of this book, died just as it was being completed. As circumstances would have it, Chou En-lai and Chu Teh, his two closest and most constant companions in the political and military fields, died just a few months earlier.

In the preface to this book I tried to set out the political context in which this momentous event would take place, and similarly the delicate question of the transfer of power from one outstanding man to a group whose unity would inevitably be fragile, or to a fraction of the party, or to one man more ambitious and resolute than the rest. I also tried to reach beyond the men and foresee the difficulties lying ahead of the second generation of Chinese leaders.

Thus far this analysis and these views have not been affected by the circumstances of Mao Tse-tung's death. No change is apparent in the conditions existing before September 9, 1976, the day on which the Great Helmsman died. The problems are the same, as are their main components. Nevertheless, Mao Tse-tung's gigantic shadow often cast a veil over the reality (including human reality) which he adapted to suit his own vision of the revolution, and new elements may emerge at any moment, in addition to those we already know, to sketch the features of the China of tomorrow.

A great new page in Chinese history has been completed and turned. Its theme, the theme of this book, now takes on its full significance and relevance.

J.G.
Les Avenières
September 11, 1976

Preface

If the study of classical China has long remained a European domain, that of contemporary China owes its best and most numerous works to the younger field of American sinology. This is particularly true in the area of monographs and specialized research. Nevertheless, it is hoped that the American public will also pay heed to a book written by a European, by a Frenchman whose diverse diplomatic, military, academic, and even journalistic activities over forty years have resulted in a continuous association with Chinese history.

This long and direct experience has led me to encompass more than a quarter of a century in a single study—the period from the establishment of the new regime in Peking on October 1, 1949, to the beginning of 1976. It so happens that this quarter of a century more or less corresponds to the rule of the first generation of Chinese Communists, the generation that gained power in twenty-five years through a combination of political and military action. This generation is coming to an end. In a short space of time some of its most remarkable representatives—Chou En-lai, Tung Pi-wu, K'ang Sheng—have died, leaving behind only Mao Tse-tung (aged eighty-three), Chu Teh (ninety), Teng Hsiao-p'ing (seventy-two), Yeh Chien-ying (seventy-seven), Li Hsien-nien (seventy-one), and several others who are at least in their seventies.

And already there is a changing of the guard. An unknown, Hua Kuo-feng, marches in as the new premier and deputy premier of the Central Committee. He clearly occupies position number one after Mao Tse-tung. Teng Hsiao-p'ing has been relegated to the rank and file. Behind him a few veterans hang onto their positions, but apparently certain elements and their followers who came to the fore during the cultural revolution are crowding in. We recognize Chang Ch'un-ch'iao, Wang Hung-wen, Yao Wen-yuan, and even Mao's wife. A three-pronged problem already disturbs diplomats and analysts. Who will emerge as the true heirs of Mao Tse-tung?

Of course, this book does not attempt to predict what lies ahead. But it does seek to assemble and organize as much information as possible about conditions today, and in this sense it casts light on the future. Even if that future remains obscure, it is at least possible to identify the huge and complex problems that already condition it and that will continue to bedevil the new leaders, whoever they may be and whatever individual orientations they may have within the common ideology.

Among China's problems, the demographic problem is certainly the most important and the one about which the least is known. However incredible it may seem, within a margin of 50 to 100 million people no one is sure just what China's population is. The 583 million people counted on the mainland at the time of the official census of 1953 became 656 million in about 1957, and the approximate figure of 800 million is frequently cited today. In 1973, however, Chou En-lai noted that the rate of population increase was about 2 percent. Noted demographers, including John Aird of the U.S. Department of Commerce, have estimated the 1976 population at about 953 million Chinese, which means that the 1990 figure would be around 1.3 billion. In view of the limited amount of arable land available in China and the attendant limitations on agricultural yield, and considering China's industrial backwardness, the country must rapidly reduce its rate of demographic growth and stabilize its population at the level of about a billion people, well before the end of the century.

The second problem, closely linked with the first, is that of economic development. This is particularly important in the field of agriculture, as measured by grain production, for the Chinese diet is almost entirely vegetarian. The current grain production of 280 million tons a year translates into a per capita yield of about 0.3 tons, which is roughly what it was in 1957; thus, the rise in production has about kept pace with the increase in population. Nevertheless, since 1960 the Chinese have found it necessary to import grain. We know that the norms of the twelve-year plan for agriculture (1956-1967) were achieved in only a third of the districts (*hsien*) in 1975. The plan, which should have produced between 350 and 450 million tons of grain starting in 1967, is thus at least 100 million tons and eight or nine years behind where it should be. China has only another fifteen or twenty years to win the race between population pressure and food production.

As for Chinese industry, there has been considerable progress, and new, modern sectors have been created in the last twenty-five years. Nevertheless, the degree of industrialization remains far behind that of the "superpowers" and is extremely low in the light of the country's population. The weakness of the industrial sector is visible in the figures for foreign trade and for the gross national product. Moreover, since 1949 China has been searching for a development policy that would suit its circumstances. From 1953 to 1957 it adopted the Soviet model, which was based on rigorous planning, and placed top priority on heavy industry. In 1958, with the Great Leap Forward and the people's communes, Peking pushed for rapid development in all sectors simultaneously, mobilizing—both physically and psychologically—its rural and urban manual labor force. From 1959 to 1962, or even 1966, it returned to more moderate policies, giving agriculture first priority: development of heavy industry was slowed down, and light industry was developed insofar as it served agriculture. At present, following the disorders and reverses of the Cultural Revolution, China is trying to set in motion a semidecentralized policy of industrialization, one that is at last realistic. But the ideal road apparently has not yet been found and the possibility of a new radical thrust—though such a movement seems less likely now than a more moderate direction—remains a threat to the economy.

Will slower population growth and the discovery of vast oil resources, which may be able to transform the foreign trade situation, allow China's industry to take up the slack in agriculture, thereby ensuring adequate food for the population (as was the case in Japan and Great Britain)? No one knows the answer to this question, all of whose elements, including political and ideological ones, will have to be followed very closely during these coming years, a period crucial for China's future.

The third problem is that of the "new society." This problem, which we are beginning to perceive clearly in the West, has been faced more or less consciously in China, primarily by elites, since the middle of the nineteenth century, i.e., since modern Western civilization began to impinge on China's traditional civilization. Since 1949 the problem has become one of extreme urgency. It has developed rapidly, mainly under the influence of Chairman Mao Tse-tung.

During the first stage, it was a question of transforming:

1 Organization, socio-economic structures, social relations, and production relations.

2 Moral values and mental and intellectual habits.

3 Customs and the content and forms of expression of culture, starting with the writing system, despite its originality, and moving on to art and social studies.

The second stage would involve:

1 The abolition of class distinctions and even socio-productive categories.

2 The end of value distinctions, and even practical distinctions, between manual and intellectual work.

3 The removal of differences between city and countryside, whether in production, remuneration or even landscape.

4 Total equality of persons based on the mystique of the sacrifice of the individual to the whole.

The dimensions and difficulties of this problem can only be properly understood if one recalls that traditional Chinese civilization has a continuous history of thirty to forty centuries, that the ancient Chinese world, as a result of Confucianism, was marked by inveterate conservatism and even a yearning for some past golden age, characteristics which have far from disappeared, and that 80 to 85 percent of the population remain rural. Even if the restructuring of society can be aided by certain resemblances or convergences between former regimes and that of today, the enterprise is still an immense one and will require several generations before its results can become irreversible. The frequent rectification campaigns, the current campaigns against Confucianism and for the study of the theory of the proletarian dictatorship, the emphasis on the pursuit of class struggle under a socialist regime, and the announcement that cultural revolutions will recur from time to time prove that the solution to the problem of the "new society" is still a long way off and continues to preoccupy the Chinese leadership, especially Mao Tse-tung. It is, of course, primarily a question of placing one's bet on man, whom one would like to see rid of all individualistic traits. The old materialistic core of the Chinese, their apparent flexibility, and their attachment to family values raise doubts as to whether this wager can ever be won.

There remains the problem of "power." It has only been seriously faced since the summer of 1966, during the Cultural Revolution, when Mao, with the aid of the red guards and revolutionary rebels, delivered a powerful blow against the Party and against constitutional legality. This blow led to a long crisis for China's political and administrative institutions. Only the army more or less managed to retain its cohesion, and for five or six years it had to fill in for the Party under the guise of the revolutionary committees.

In spite of the meeting of the reconstituted Tenth Party Congress (August 1973) and the holding of the National People's Congress, which adopted a new state constitution (January 1975), the problem of power has not been finally settled. The so-called moderates, represented until recently by Chou En-lai, hold sway in the most important hierarchies of the state (general administration, the economy, and military forces), but the radicals continue to display a great deal of strength in the Party apparatus. Clearly, the Cultural Revolution has left disunity and ferment at the levels of ordinary Party membership and local functionaries as well as in the institutions of Party and state. The death of Chou En-lai (January 8, 1976) and the violent clashes in Peking (April 5, 1976) finally gave the radicals, supported by Mao Tse-tung, a chance to get rid of Teng Hsiao-p'ing. Still, the beneficiary of a compromise is not a man of their persuasion, but Hua Kuo-feng, a provincial bureaucrat from Hunan—and other Hua Kuo-feng's may follow.

Thus, the question of power, which has not been resolved in a fundamental way, may run into new and dangerous developments at two points in the future. The first is at the death of Mao Tse-tung, whose personality remains powerful and is an important factor in all possible political combinations or realignments. The collective leadership that was put into effect at the Tenth Party Congress in 1973 (and not abrogated by Hua Kuo-feng in April 1976), by associating the pragmatists concerned about economic construction with the radicals capable of assuring the survival and triumph of the spirit of the Cultural Revolution, may not be enough to forestall a succession crisis. From a long-range point of view, it must be noted that nothing in the Chinese historical tradition or even in the history of the Chinese revolutionary movement, whether Kuomintang or Communist, prepared the Communist Party for a genuine and lasting collective leadership. In short, a "strong man" like Mao or Brezhnev could emerge from an initial collective leadership. Thereafter, the problem of power would probably remain settled for a long time.

These, in brief, are the major problems that the second generation of Chinese leaders will face. According to the law of revolutionary history, it is likely that this generation will be closer to concrete issues than to ideology, that it will be more materialistic than voluntaristic, and more conscious than its predecessor of the need to solve once and for all the problem of economic imbalance. Its foreign policy is likely to move even further away from messianic goals, if not from revolutionary oratory, for well-understood reasons of national interest and pragmatism.

Whatever the future may hold, much ground has already been won. China's vast population, its geographic location, and especially the fact that its continuing development of nuclear weapons will give it the same kind of "sanctuary" as the United States and the Soviet Union mean that China, in spite of its great poverty, will become a first-rank military power, a "super-power." Because of the "balance of terror," it will have the same freedom as others in foreign policy. For that very reason, China's destiny directly affects that of the entire Western world, which is a decisive reason for gaining a better understanding of the country. It is to be hoped that this book will contribute to that goal.

Paris
April 26, 1976

Foreword to the French Edition

Should a history of the Party be a history of the regime? This is the first difficulty to arise, and it is present throughout this book, which is the second volume of my history of the Chinese Communist Party. The purpose of the book is rather to trace the history of the Party's behavior toward itself, and the way it has created and developed the regime, basing its choices on its own experience, on the state of affairs at home and abroad, and on a compelling ideology dominated by the giant-like personality of Mao Tse-tung. If this implies that all the important incidents are referred to, it means also that only the significant details are mentioned.

The second difficulty encountered in writing the book is that of obtaining objective information in China or about China. Until 1959, the Chinese government published a few basic figures concerning population and production along with the first two five-year plans. At the same time, it showed great caution as regards statistics, a strong tendency to prevent its publications from leaving the country, and an attitude toward foreigners wishing to travel within the country that could hardly be described as liberal.

From 1959 on, the disappointments arising from the Great Leap Forward and the people's communes brought about an almost complete retraction. All statistics in firm figures have disappeared. Apart from two or three daily papers, the Chinese press—particularly the provincial newspapers and specialized magazines—has become virtually inaccessible to foreigners.

A few years later, from 1966 to 1968, the troubles provoked by the Cultural Revolution made a vast body of fragmented information available to observers of China in the form of tracts, posters, newspapers, and wall newspapers, written by red guards and "revolutionary rebels." Though these were often childish in their presentation, they were rich in meaning and sometimes made it possible to deduce underlying events with comparative ease. Between the summers of 1966 and 1967 in particular, light was suddenly thrown upon different nooks and crannies of a society which until then had been plunged in darkness. The flames of revolution lit up some details at least of the endangered structure. Considerable amounts of information were collected in this way, contributing to a more thorough knowledge of China. Statistics were absent from this harvest, however (and the Chinese authorities themselves no doubt find it hard to obtain accurate figures). Darkness has now fallen upon the Chinese continent once more; now, more than ever before, the study of it has to be based on efforts to reconstruct and interpret the facts. Obviously these efforts have to be founded on a thorough acquaintance with the Chinese press, which, under the cover of apparent uniformity and conventionality of language, still reveals the wishes and fears of the leaders, on a thorough knowledge of the China of yesterday, and on real practical experience with the China of today. Theoretical works on China by sociologists and economists are also extremely useful insofar as they do not attempt to force this wholly unique country into the same mold as other countries, or to use the terminology created mainly for modern nations.

The third difficulty arises from languages. Our vocabulary, whether scientific or descriptive, generally refers to developed societies, which share the same cultural heritage and have living conditions of a comparable, although not equal, standard. To apply the same terms to a world that is unique in every respect—in its mentality, its traditional structures, its standard of living, and its chief problems—is to create a source of perpetual confusion. Ordinary words like "liberty," "family," and "state," evoke entirely different ideas, attitudes, and duties in a Westerner and a Chinese. In the same way, the basic national purposes are totally dissimilar. If the Western goal is to raise our standard of living, for the Chinese, it is one of survival; this can change everything, even political morality.

For these reasons, I have tried as far as possible to adopt a viewpoint situated within the Chinese system, not in order to justify it and still less to find examples to follow, but to share the ideas and reasoning of its leaders and to understand the feelings and the behavior of the masses.

Lastly, because this book is intended to provide a synthesis for readers who want to increase their knowledge and understanding without having to undertake specialized research, I have tried to limit the use of Chinese names, as well as quotations and references. On the other hand, the bibliography, arranged according to subjects, will refer readers to more detailed information on any given topic.

Paris, March 1, 1972

Translator's Note

The transcription of Chinese names

As in the first volume, the Wade-Giles transcription has been used for the names of persons and Chinese terms, rather than the new Chinese system, *p'in yin tzu mu*, which is not yet well known in the West and has not been used in Chinese publications in foreign languages. It is also confusing for those who are not students of Chinese. The postal system has been used for place names.

Notes on passages quoted

Most of these have been taken from the English translations published by the Foreign Languages Press in Peking. Others are translations into English of the author's own translation.

Part 1

New Democracy in China
1949 – 1953

Behold, New China is within sight. Let us all hail her! Her
masts have already risen above the horizon. Let us all cheer
in welcome! Raise both your hands. New China is ours!

Mao Tse-tung, "On New Democracy"

1 China in 1949

An immense task awaited the Communist Party when it came to power. Since the fall of the Empire in 1911, China had been split up between numerous politico-military groups supported by persistent provincial particularism. This situation gave rise to frequent, complicated civil wars involving little loss of life but enormous loss to the economy. These wars were followed by ten years of Communist insurrections and revolts within the Nationalist movement between 1927 and 1937, eight years of war against Japan (which took Manchuria as early as 1931) between 1937 and 1945, and lastly, from 1946 onward, a final struggle between the Nanking central government and the Communist Party. In 1949, at the end of the Third Civil War, the Communist Party, now equal to its adversary in the military field, won victory at last.[1]

The political fragmentation, the civil wars, and the war with Japan all hindered the successive Chinese governments, particularly the Kuomintang government, created on April 18, 1927, from guiding the general development of the country toward the modern world, whether in the realm of developing the economy, of administrative structures and practices, or of the transformation of customs and ideas. The Kuomintang, influenced by the syncretism of Sun Yat-sen who was little known among the rural population, was more inclined to encourage cautious changes than to provoke sudden transformations. This state of affairs was reflected in the country's foreign relations, for it prevented the Chinese governments from being on an equal footing with the foreign powers who for the century from 1842 to 1943 continued to benefit from the important privileges granted to them by the Unequal Treaties.

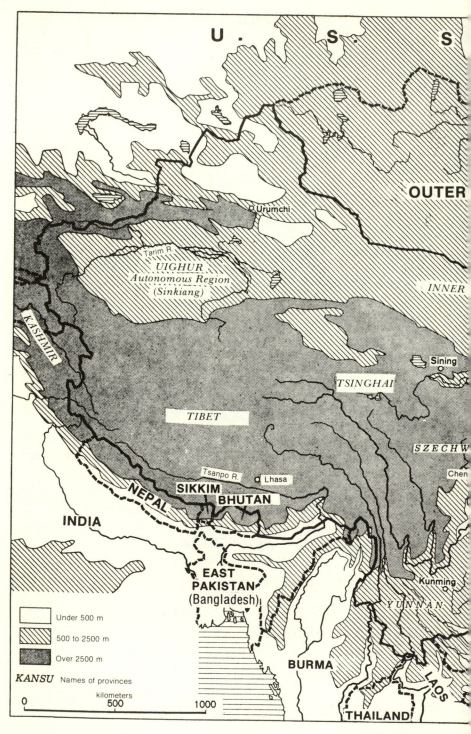

Map 1   Physical ma

China and Provinces

In the autumn of 1949, the general situation appeared to be worse than ever. The administrative system of the former government had collapsed in a few months. This left a void, which the Communists, whose armies had fallen like a curtain from Manchuria across North China to the Yangtze Valley and as far as Canton and who saw the population under their control suddenly increase from 200 million to nearly 600 million, could not fill by appointing experienced staff everywhere, as they had neither the time nor the means. Although completely at ease when in charge of the rural bases, they knew little of the more intricate difficulties presented by the towns, which were largely under the influence of the industrial and business bourgeoisie, and their ignorance worried them.[2] Twelve years later, when Field Marshal Montgomery asked Mao Tse-tung what had concerned him the most after the establishment of the new regime, Mao replied that it was the extent to which both the Communist Party and himself were lacking in experience in the face of the enormous problems ahead.[3]

The industrial economy was seriously disorganized by what was going on and above all by difficulties in obtaining supplies, both at home and abroad. Its equipment in Manchuria had been dismantled by the Russians in 1945 and 1946. Large factories were paralyzed or slowed down. The production figures for 1949—a bad year to use as a reference, it is true, because of military operations and the transfer of power—were 53 percent below those of the best prewar years, if the Communists are to be believed, when production amounted to 61,880,000 tons of coal, 923,000 tons of steel, and 6,000 million kilowatt hours of electricity.[4] Agricultural output which had reached a prewar maximum of 138.7 million tons for food crops and 850,000 tons for cotton, also fell by 25 percent in the case of food crops and soybeans, and by 48 percent in the case of cotton.[5]

Railway transport, which was inadequate at the outset—about 26,000 kilometers of line for a country covering 9.6 million square kilometers— had been largely restored. By late 1949, 21,715 kilometers of line were open, but most of the rolling stock had been requisitioned by the army.[6] Civilian motor transport was virtually nonexistent: there were only 20,000 to 30,000 vehicles and 131,000 kilometers of roads in good condition. Almost all commercial ships had gone to Taiwan.

The country's finances were in ruins. The currency of the central government had collapsed during the hyperinflation of 1946-49. The Communist currency, the jen-min-pi, now the yuan, had no foreign market value. China survived because its economy was mainly based on agriculture and handicrafts. Urban and rural craftsmen produced three-quarters of the consumer goods, while more than 80 percent of the total population, then estimated at 475 million, was engaged in agriculture, farming more than 100 million hectares. In 1949, in terms of the 1952 yuan, production amounted to 32,590 million yuan in agriculture, 14,020 million yuan in industry, and 3,240 million yuan in handicrafts.[7]

Serious specific problems existed alongside the general decay of the economy. These included returning several million refugees to their native regions; taking command of the Nationalist armies; preventing the flight of capital (currency and precious metal) and even of equipment to Hong Kong, Singapore, and Southeast Asia; and collecting taxes, not to mention continuing the war against the former government, whose fleet and air force partially blockaded the large coastal ports, and who still had 400,000 disbanded soldiers on the mainland in June 1950.

The first aims of the new regime were naturally to create and establish new political and administrative institutions; to take in hand a weary, indifferent, and illiterate population and bring about their ideological conversion; and to restore the economy to its general prewar level—that of 1936. It was essential to achieve these aims, not only to ensure the continued existence of the nation, but also to secure the establishment of a modern socialist economy, which was the chief *raison d'être* of the regime.

Several positive factors were to help the Communists in this colossal task. First of all, after an interval of nearly forty years, political unity (including the outer provinces) had been achieved once more, the administration was again centralized, it was possible to move freely from one end of the country to the other, and order had been restored. For the first time since 1911, a Chinese government was in a position to determine what changes were necessary and to put them into effect on a national scale. The people's government was to bring about all that the imperial government and the Kuomintang central government had been unable to undertake, the former through lack of imagination, and the latter through lack of authority.

To direct this work, which was without historical precedent in scope and difficulty, the Communist Party had leaders and cadres of proven worth. These people had survived rigorous selection in the field and at their work; they were tempered by twenty years of experience as military commanders, administrators, and leaders of the population. They belonged to a solid, coherent hierarchy, united by a centralized political system, which had maintained a certain degree of initiative and flexibility at the local level, because of the distances separating the red bases and the variety of problems involved. The methods used could both take into account the feelings of the population among whom the Party had had to settle, and also, when

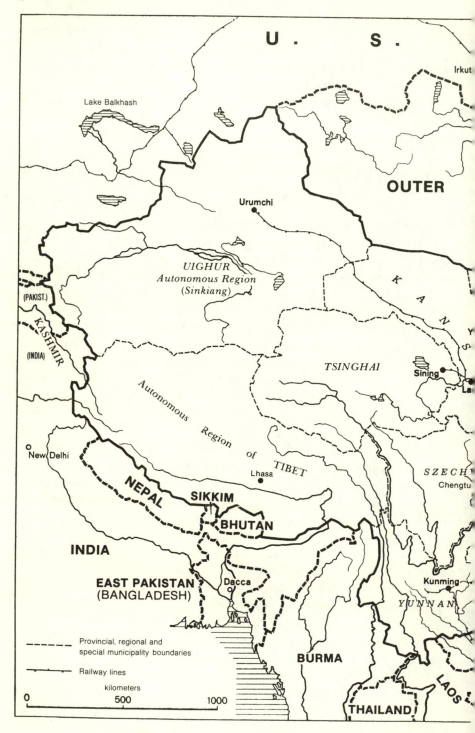

U. S.

Irkut

Lake Balkhash

OUTER

Urumchi

UIGHUR
Autonomous Region
(Sinkiang)

(PAKIST.)

K A N S

KASHMIR

(INDIA)

TSINGHAI

Sining

La

Autonomous   Region   of   *TIBET*

Lhasa

New Delhi

SZECH
Chengtu

NEPAL

SIKKIM

BHUTAN

INDIA

EAST PAKISTAN
(BANGLADESH)

Dacca

Kunming

YUNNAN

Provincial, regional and
special municipality boundaries

Railway lines

kilometers

0   500   1000

BURMA

LAOS

THAILAND

Map 2   Administrative

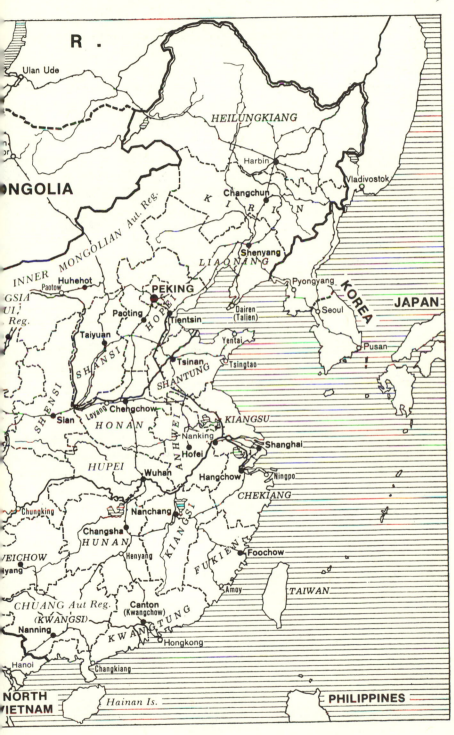

Map of China

necessary, set aside any humanitarian scruples or useless precautions, in the name of the liberation of the masses and national salvation.

In general, the state of mind and attitude of the Chinese people was also to be a positive element for the Communist Party. Few regrets followed the former government to Taiwan. In spite of initial successes and the personal popularity of Marshal Chiang Kai-shek right up to 1945, the Nationalist Party and its government had not been able to stand up to the test of war. The administration, which was unsure of itself and often corrupt, was not firmly rooted in the people. Unlike the old imperial regime, it was no longer based on a traditional moral order that ensured, from the village and family level upward, the stability and durability of structures and customs and consequently the continuity of social and economic life even during periods when the central power was weak or absent.

A weak, fragmented, liberal opposition had already played into the Communists' hands, either by joining forces with them during the war against Japan, or by forming small parties incapable of gaining power or winning confidence. Whether through propaganda or through the experience of their friends and relations, both the urban bourgeoisie and workers and the rural artisans and peasants knew of the strict austerity reigning in the red zones and of the constant intervention by the Party in the family and professional life of every individual. They accepted the new system with no illusions and no enthusiasm; their dislike of the old system, their political insignificance, and their fears made them all the more ready to accept it. This readiness, which the Communists skillfully put to use, was not born of circumstances but was linked with traditional attitudes. The Chinese people accepted dynastic changes, considering it natural and just for a vigorous race to replace an exhausted one, and they had a long acquaintance in the still recent past with the totalitarian order of the Empire, which was founded on a single ideology of Confucian inspiration. On the so-called blank page for the year 1949, the Communists drew up a Common Program appealing to all social categories—peasants, workers, petty bourgeoisie, national bourgeoisie—through its apparent moderation and national ambitions.

These ambitions were first of all economic in character. They could hardly be anything else. It was absolutely imperative to develop the Chinese economy, because of the time lost since the nineteenth century, because of unparalleled demographic pressure, and because of the desperate poverty of the people—almost all economists estimate China's national annual income at less than $50 per head in 1949 or thereabouts.[8]

A priori, it did not look as if a liberal regime, by allowing the situation to develop as circumstances dictated, could accomplish so great a task. Examples would have to be found elsewhere, among countries that were undergoing total renewal and were using ideology as a pretext to make the individual serve the higher interest of the state: Japan in the Meiji era, Italy under Mussolini and, above all, Russia in 1928. When they quoted a doctrine founded on a scientific theory of production, and cited, as proof of their future success, the economic achievements and military victories of the Soviet Union, which closely resembled China in size and initial lack of development, the Chinese Communists showed themselves in a favorable light that would ensure them of widespread support in principle.

Although the new regime came up against the same difficulties as its predecessors in science, technology, and finance, at least it had all the country's natural resources at its disposal. These are comparable to those of the Soviet Union and of the United States and, if well used, guarantee China a role as a great power. By 1949, Manchuria, which had been developed by Japan, had been recovered and could quickly be restored to working order. As a result of the war of 1937-1945, several industrial centers had been moved to the western provinces and transport routes had been created to serve them. Equipment supplied by the Americans between 1946 and 1949 for the rebuilding of the country had been inherited from the former government, and help from the Soviet Union seemed a certainty. Technological progress in the world as a whole could speed up the various stages in development of backward countries. China's industrial development, or more accurately, China's modernization, was on the way to becoming a reality.

Alongside these elements working in the Communists' favor, the most difficult problem of all to solve was that of agriculture, and particularly that of the imbalance between land and population, which reduced family holdings to about one hectare of arable land. In the early 1950s, there were about 120 million rural families and between 107 and 120 million hectares of land under cultivation. Agricultural development, and consequently the accumulation of capital for the modernization of all sectors of the economy, was also hampered by the almost total absence of chemical fertilizers, by poor tools, the lack of draft animals, resistance to innovation on the part of the peasants, and transport difficulties over both long and short distances? The Communists were to prove unable to break out entirely from the vicious circle thus created—the use of agriculture to develop industry and of industry to develop agriculture: it is interesting to note that the most serious mistakes made by the movement were in the domain of agriculture, in spite of its considerable experience of the countryside.

Although they affirmed their intention to evolve toward socialism and acknowledged the value of the Soviet example, the Chinese Communists were extremely cautious at first, making assurances that the transition to socialism would be a slow one and that a full generation would be needed to bring about basic industrialization. This attitude was to be modified little by little. From 1953 onward, with the beginning of the first five-year plan, progress toward collectivization of agriculture and state ownership of industry was to speed up. In 1949, however, it was still a question of restoring, transforming, or building the political, economic, educational, and cultural foundations that were essential for these great changes.

Notes

[1] On China between the two world wars, see Jacques Guillermaz, *A History of the Chinese Communist Party 1921-1949* (New York: Random House, 1972), and also Lucien Bianco, *The Origins of the Chinese Revolution, 1915-1949* (Stanford, Calif.: Stanford University Press, 1971).

[2] See Guillermaz, *A History of the Chinese Communist Party*, p. 432-33.

[3] See the interview with Field Marshal Montgomery in the *Sunday Times (Magazine Section)*, London, (October 15, 1961).

[4] See *Ten Great Years* (Peking: Foreign Languages Press, 1959).

[5] *Ibid.*

[6] It consisted of 3,335 locomotives, 4,212 passenger carriages, 44,401 freight cars. The transport capacity was 18,400 million ton/kilometers. A kilometer is .62 miles; a square kilometer is .3861 square miles.

[7] See *Ten Great Years*, p. 16. The figures are in new yuan; from March 1, 1955 on, 1 new yuan equalled 10,000 old yuan. A hectare is 2.47 acres.

[8] It was about $12 at the 1933 rate between 1931 and 1936, according to the economist Ou Pao-san, quoted by Yuan-li Wu, *An Economic Survey of Communist China* (New York: Bookman Associates, 1956). Alexander Eckstein has estimated the GNP at $50 per head in 1949, only 20 percent of which represented the modern sector. This income appears to him to be lower than that of preindustrial England. See Alexander Eckstein, Walter Galenson, and Ta-chung Liu, *Economic Trends in Communist China* (Chicago: Aldine, 1968). The figure of 46,610 million yuan for 1949, quoted above, gives about 93 yuan ($46 at the rate of 2.44 yuan to the dollar) reckoned on the basis of 500 million inhabitants; the total for the tertiary sector is not included, however.

[9] Chao Kuo-chün, in *Agrarian Policy of the Chinese Communist Party 1921-1959* (London and New Delhi: Asia Publishing House, 1960), notes that between 1929 and 1933 the yields were as follows: rice, 60 percent of that of Italy; wheat, 48 percent of that of Japan; potatoes. 40 percent of that of Great Britain. In 1930, productivity in China was one-fourteenth that of the United States.

2 Political and Administrative Reconstruction: The Ideological Training of the Population— The First Mass Campaigns

The elimination of the old political order and the building of the new were to be effected in two different ways and at two different levels. First, new institutions would be created at the central and regional levels, while the traditional local institutions of the province and district were adapted for the new regime. Second, procedures would be set in motion, sometimes gradually and sometimes abruptly, to control the masses, particularly by periodically launching vast "campaigns" on a national scale.

The new political institutions

From its foundation on July 1, 1921, until it rose to power in 1949, the Chinese Communist Party was principally concerned with leading the revolutionary movement for which it was responsible. From the Kiangsi period (1927-1934) onward, however, it had constituted a state authority in the territories under its control. On November 7, 1931, a Chinese soviet government was created; although its jurisdiction extended theoretically over the whole of China, in fact it controlled about ten districts and less than 10 million people.[1] Bereft of its chief territorial bases during the Long March, this government was not reconstituted during the Sino-Japanese War, because this had engendered a further period of collaboration with the Kuomintang. During the Third Civil War, the alternating periods of hostilities and negotiations, and the short-lived possibilities of a coalition government had led the Communists to delegate their state authority in regions under Communist control to a Revolutionary Military Committee.

The failure of all attempts to form a coalition government, the retreat of the Nationalist government to Taiwan, and the occupation of China as a whole, necessitated the creation of a government with adequate legal foundations. The Communist Party methodically and skillfully carried out this delicate operation in several stages: first a Chinese People's Political Consultative Conference was called. Drawing its members from different social categories, it met in Peking from September 21 to 30, 1949. It adopted a Common Program, which was a sort of charter of the new regime. It also adopted two organic laws, one concerning the Political Consultative Conference, and the other concerning the Central People's Government. The Central People's Government was then created and its members appointed.

The Political Consultative Conference was inspired by old precedents, for the National government had intended to pass through a transitional phase after the Kuomintang period of tutelage, and a similar conference had been held from January 10 to 31, 1946. It now had 662 members, of whom 585 were full members and 77 were alternate members, divided as follows:

Groups represented	Full members	Alternate members
Political parties (CCP and small parties)	142	23
Regional representatives	102	14
Army representatives	60	11
Miscellaneous (professions, cultural associations, overseas Chinese, minority races, etc.)	206	29
Guests	75	0
Total	585	77

The range of this representation, the adroitness of the new leaders in refusing to claim the majority, which in fact they did not need, and the recall of a certain number of liberals who had sought refuge in Hong Kong, all helped the Party to transform the illusion of the united front, which it had created and maintained during the years of civil war, into the legal and institutional forms of state. This illusion was prolonged still further by maintaining eight small parties with no real influence or authority, in which certain categories of the bourgeoisie who were hostile to the former government found a place; some of their leaders were appointed to posts in technical ministries.[2]

For some time—until the constitution of 1954 came into force—the Political Consultative Conference took on the role of a national assembly. It was called every three years; between sessions it delegated its power to a National Committee convened every six months, which in turn appointed a Standing Committee to act on its behalf. The Political Consultative Conference outlasted the 1954 constitution, symbolizing the maintenance of the united front. It still exists today.

The organic law of the government set up a new and complex structure whose smooth working was nevertheless assured by the Communist Party acting through committees appointed at each different level.

At the summit, the People's Central Government Council was responsible for the general line and for domestic and foreign policy; it promulgated laws and decrees, ratified and abrogated treaties, and approved the budget. It consisted of a chairman (Mao Tse-tung), six vice-chairmen, and fifty-six members, and it met twice a month. Below the Central Government Council came the State Administrative Council, the supreme administrative authority, which was responsible for putting the decisions of the Central Government Council into effect. The State Administrative Council, which was presided over by Chou En-lai, controlled about thirty ministries and other bodies, all grouped under four committees, with certain exceptions. The Political and Legal Affairs Committee was presided over by Tung Pi-wu, formerly a scholar in the old imperial tradition, a veteran of all the Chinese revolutions, and a future vice-president of the Republic. The Economy and Finance Committee was presided over by the economist Ch'en Yün, while the Culture and Education Committee was headed by the writer, poet, and archaeologist Kuo Mo-jo, who was not yet a member of the Party. The Control Committee, which recalled similar imperial or Nationalist institutions was chaired by T'an P'ing-shan, an old militant of the Kuomingtang. The Ministry of Foreign Affairs, the Overseas Chinese Committee and the Information Department all came directly under the control of the Premier, who was Foreign Minister until 1958.

Two extremely important institutions within this structure were directly responsible to the Central Government Council: the People's Revolutionary Military Council, presided over by Mao Tse-tung, which had functions roughly equivalent to those of a National Defense Ministry, since the Military Committee of the Party was the highest authority in this domain, and the Supreme People's Court and related Supreme People's Procuratorate. The territorial administration underlying the government structure was a compromise between the former state of affairs, the situation created by the military operations, and the preparations for a new order. China was divided into six large administrative regions, corresponding to the zones of action of the four field armies or equivalent military commands. The Northeastern Region included the provinces of Manchuria and Jehol; Kao Kang was chairman. The Northern Region included the provinces of Hopei, Shansi, Chahar, Suiyuan, and Pingyuan, and the municipalities of Peking and Tientsin. The region was controlled by the North China Administrative Committee formed in December 1951 and presided over by Liu Lan-t'ao. The Eastern Region—the provinces of Kiangsu, Chekiang, Anhwei, Fukien, and Shantung, and the municipalities of Nanking and Shanghai—corresponded to the zone of the former Third Field Army. Ch'en Yi was its first chairman; he was succeeded by Jao Shu-shih. The Central-South Region included the provinces of Hupei, Hunan, Honan, Kiangsi, Kwangtung, and Kwangsi, and the municipalities of Canton and Hankow. It corresponded to the Fourth Field Army zone; its chairman was Lin Piao. The Southwestern Region consisted of the provinces of Szechwan, Kweichow, and Yunnan, and the municipality of Chungking, which corresponded to the zone of the Second Field Army; its chairman was Liu Po-ch'eng. The Northwestern Region—the provinces of Shensi, Kansu, Ninghsia, Tsinghai and Sinkiang, and the municipality of Sian—was presided over by P'eng Teh-huai.[3]

Alongside the People's Government of the Northeast and the North China Administrative Committee were four regional governments called military administrative committees, headed by the commander of each of the four field armies. Because these men were also regional Party secretaries, they had considerable power. The chief function of the committees, however, was to coordinate and control. On November 15, 1952, the military and administrative functions in these regions were separated. The regional division was itself abolished in 1954, only to return in another guise and within another system—that of the Party—in January 1961, as regional delegations of the Central Committee. The political consequences of this measure were to be particularly important during the Cultural Revolution.

After the regions came the traditional provinces which remained almost exactly as they were. With a few exceptions, no changes were made in their boundaries. The weight of administrative traditions and local particularism was great enough to bring about the reconsideration of

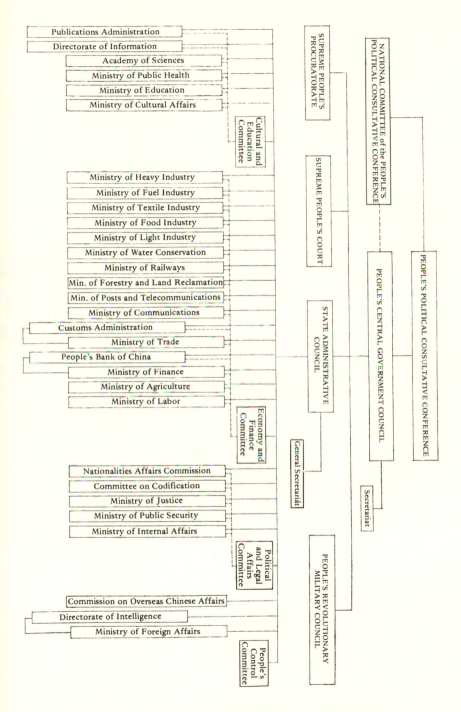

Figure 2.1   Organization Chart of the Central Government
of the People's Republic of China

measures that had already been decided and put into effect. Eventually, China was divided into twenty-two provinces, five autonomous regions inhabited by minority races, and three special municipalities.[4]

After the province came the *hsien* or district. Both before and after 1949, the *hsien*, which had been in existence for two thousand years, was the most important administrative division. In 1949, more than 2,000 *hsien* existed, from 50 to 200 to a province. Their size and population varied enormously from region to region, ranging from approximately 2,000 to 5,000 square kilometers and 200,000 to 400,000 inhabitants. The regime made appreciable modifications in the boundaries and number of *hsien*. The last atlas, published in 1974, shortly after the Cultural Revolution, showed 2,135 *hsien* in the true sense of the word, or equivalent administrative divisions.

Although the *hsien* was about the lowest level to which the imperial administration as such extended, it lost this distinction under the Communist regime to the *hsiang*, sometimes known as administrative village.

A *hsiang* consisted of several hamlets or villages. Many changes cut down their numbers regularly, reducing them from more than 220,000 in 1954 to about 70,000 in 1958 when the people's communes were formed.

Other administrative divisions supplemented the traditional ones— their function was to act as relay posts among the rest and to coordinate their activities. One such division was the "special district" (*chuan ch-ü*); it linked the the province and the *hsien*, of which it contained about ten. Lastly, "districts" (*ch'ü*) were created between the *hsien* and the *hsiang;* their number varied from two to twenty, according to the *hsien*.

Before the 1954 Constitution and while the Provisional Constitution was in force, "local conferences of representatives from all walks of life" were convened. Members were chosen either by appointment or by a feigned election based on Article 14 of the Common Program. These conferences, in turn, appointed local executive bodies to head an administrative structure known as "people's government councils."[5] This system was put into operation step by step, taking into account the preparation of each territorial division; it was adopted and given formal status by articles 53 to 56 of the 1954 Constitution.

The Common Program

The chief purpose of the Common Program adopted by the Political Consultative Conference on September 29, 1949, was to win for the

Communist Party both the political allegiance and the loyalty of the Chinese population, and to give concrete, legal expression to the principle of the united front. This principle had been constantly affirmed, if not put into effect, during the Party's fight for power. The Common Program was therefore addressed to the nation as a whole; its policy was apparently democratic in politics, liberal as regards the economy, and relatively tolerant regarding cultural matters and the treatment of the minority races. These aspects recall the "New Democracy" of 1940 and serve as an interesting starting point and a useful reference by which to gauge the progress of the regime toward a clearly stated socialist goal. Although the Common Program was deliberately reassuring in tone and omitted all details of the pace and timing of future transformations, it did not allow the slightest compromise on basic principles; every trace of liberalism was accompanied almost immediately by a reservation.

The preamble stressed the continued existence of the united front of the four traditional classes, two of which were implicitly condemned to an eventual disappearance. Article 5 confirmed the rights of the citizen to freedom of thought, speech, publication, assembly, and communication with others and acknowledged personal freedom, freedom in the choice of residence, and freedom of movement, as well as freedom of religious beliefs. Article 7, however, hastened to add that all counterrevolutionaries, accomplices of imperialism, traitors, and opponents of the work of the regime would be severely punished. Although Article 3 guaranteed the economic interests and private property of workers, peasants, the petty bourgeoisie, and the national bourgeoisie and Article 26 mentioned private interests alongside work interests, Article 28 stated that all enterprises making a contribution to the national economy or the livelihood of the people should be managed by the state. Articles 29 and 30 encouraged both the semisocialist economy of the cooperatives and private businesses. On the other hand, Article 27 gave wholehearted support to the rights of ownership won by the peasants in places where the agrarian reform had already been carried out.

The cultural and educational policy was described as "new-democratic," "national," and "scientific." Nothing heralded the severe persecutions that intellectuals were to suffer as early as 1951. Articles 50 and 53 revealed an understanding attitude toward minority races (more than 35 million people) as regards culture and administrative autonomy, though any ideas of independence or self-determination were, naturally, out of the question.

To all Chinese who were ill-informed about Communist goals or methods, or had no knowledge of the great contemporary texts of Mao

Tse-tung—"On the People's Democratic Dictatorship" (June 30, 1949), for instance—the Common Program could appear as a reasonable, well-ordered whole with acceptable aims. There seemed to be no intention to enforce stringent policies and encourage class struggle; class struggle was not even mentioned in the program. Nothing gave any indication of the brutal surgery the new leaders would shortly impose on Chinese society.

Taking the population in hand

In fact, during the first few months after its rise to power the Party showed restraint, moderation, and deliberation, examining all situations and probing at length before making decisions or taking action. This attitude did not last beyond the summer of 1950. With the beginning of the great campaigns of information, criticism, and self-criticism, with the application of the land reform of June 28, 1950, and with the publication of the law of February 21, 1951, on the repression of counterrevolutionaries, a climate of fear, and later one of real terror, was to spread to the whole of China.

The methods used for dealing with the masses between 1949 and 1953 were aimed at ensuring the transformation of the ideology of the population while at the same time destroying in advance all organized opposition and all hostile, mistrustful, or merely lukewarm reactions on the part of individuals. The advance of the Chinese Communist armies was followed everywhere by propaganda and information meetings. In every branch of the administration, every school, every enterprise, every quarter, street, and village, the Party—or rather the Army Political Department—organized sessions of information and pseudo-discussions, which were compulsory for at least one member of each family. The sessions provided a methodical training in popular Marxism, approached generally from a scientific point of view: the theory of evolution (evolutionism), Darwinism, the role of work in the physical and mental development of the individual and society, the transformation of society thanks to new methods of production, and so on. Next came the modern themes, primarily the denunciation of feudalism, imperialism, and bureaucratic capitalism, "three mountains crushing the Chinese people," which the Party wanted to eliminate for good. Finally, the construction of a new society was announced.

This piece of information—one worth noting in the case of China—was addressed to the individual. For the first time, individuals were the object of direct personal attention, being initiated into political life, which had been reserved until then to a few elements of the bourgeoisie, whether intellectuals, businessmen, or landowners. Simultaneously, a vast social and national undertaking, which caught an individual's interest straightaway, was proposed. This information, however, was also placed within a clearly defined, rigid framework—mass organizations (involving young people, students and women), trade unions, miscellaneous associations, groups belonging to an urban street or quarter, or rural peasant associations born of the land reform of 1950.[6]

In the China of 1949, as in all totalitarian countries, huge demonstrations, meetings, and parades were constantly organized to strengthen a sense of solidarity among participants and make them conscious of their power. A more original and specifically Chinese practice was soon added to these methods—nationwide mass campaigns. The mechanism behind the mass campaigns was simple. The Party leadership chose various watchwords and slogans on the selected theme and quickly and discreetly sent them out to the provincial Party apparatus. These members, backed by the cadres in the administrative system and mass organizations, stirred up vast demonstrations in which the participants pressed the government to take action and sent circular letters and telegrams to neighboring provinces and localities urging them to take part, an old practice inherited from the Republican era. Soon, the whole country was in tumult, so that the Party and the government could intervene officially, seeming to reply to the indignation and wishes of the population.

The mass campaigns always had a target. Sometimes they attacked categories of society whose destruction was essential, while also serving to crystallize and heighten revolutionary ardor; at other times, they sought to transform the existing structure or habits of thought; on still other occasions, they underlined normal administrative measures, to ensure their success in practice by a mixture of constraint, terror, and enthusiasm. The campaigns were many and varied. Between 1950 and 1953 one or two were almost constantly in operation, ranging from the elimination of the black market, the "voluntary" surrender of silver and money to the authorities, and the destruction of insects, sparrows, flies, and rats, to resistance to America and aid to Korea. Although several of them took on a spectacular, cruel character, they were also of the greatest importance for the consolidation and development of the regime. Chief among these were the Campaign for the Elimination of Counterrevolutionaries, and the Three- and Five-Anti campaigns.

The elimination of counterrevolutionaries

The Campaign for the Elimination of Counterrevolutionaries grew out of the terrible law of February 21, 1951, which provoked a vast wave of arrests and trials by the people. Thereafter, and throughout the whole of 1951, "counterrevolutionaries" or suspects were hunted out, condemned, and executed at an alarming rate. Sometimes two-thirds of the articles in the press were devoted to the subject, often with titles like "How to Organize a Meeting Against the Counterrevolutionaries," or "How to Hunt out Counterrevolutionaries." The public was invited to join in the manhunt. Pictures, caricatures, anecdotes, and news items were all used to develop the taste for it. The Party praised young heroes who denounced their parents. Conversely, severe disciplinary action was taken against Communists who were unable to break the ties of class and tried to save their families. "Committees for the extermination of counterrevolutionaries" were created in all branches of the administrative system, at every level in the hierarchy, in all public and private organizations, in factories, schools, and in the different quarters of the towns. They cooperated with the police and the public security service. Town-dwellers were panic-stricken; it was not the number of arrests that frightened them so much as the arbitrary way they were made and the wave of denunciations that occurred.

Although at first the campaign was limited to obvious and active "reactionaries" (secret agents, members of secret societies, "despots," those who had a "blood-debt" toward the revolution), the repression quickly spread to wider categories: former active members of the Kuomintang or its trade unions, journalists, writers and teachers reputed to be accomplices of "foreign cultural aggressors," freemasons on the Anglo-Saxon model, collaborators of Western or Japanese firms, or simply "anti-social elements."[7]

Arrests were often sudden and carried out on a large scale; at least 10,000 people were arrested in Shanghai during the night of terror of April 27-28, 1950, or 25,000 to 30,000, according to the Nationalists, who reckoned the total was 300,000 in Shanghai between April 27 and May 31. The accused were dragged before a jury of several thousands and a crowd of several tens of thousands of spectators. They were not tried individually; "type-cases" were chosen, and the same punishment was meted out to hundreds of other accused, without giving them a hearing. P'eng Chen, the mayor of Peking, presided over the mass trials there (seventeen years later, he was tried in the same way during the Cultural Revolution), while men later expelled from the Party, like Jao Shu-shih, presided in Shanghai. Those condemned to death were hustled straightaway to execution grounds where they were shot through the head, under the eyes of a crowd, including children, which had been invited to file past the bodies of the victims.

Although it is hard to estimate the exact numbers of executions, the press bears witness to the fact that accusation meetings were held on several different occasions in all large towns. Sometimes, as in Wuhan, the names of those killed were posted in their streets. Sometimes figures were given— 376 executions in Nanking on April 29, 50 in Hangchow on April 30, 293 in Shanghai on the same day, 32 in Shanghai and 40 in Soochow on May 6, 221 in Peking on May 23, and 208 in Shanghai once more on May 31. These incomplete statistics do not take into account those sentenced to death with suspended sentences (two years in general) and those sentenced to forced labor. Chou En-lai was to give a figure of 28,332 executions out of a total of 89,701 people arrested in the space of ten months in the province of Kwangtung alone; he deplored the fact that too many counterrevolutionaries had escaped punishment, or had been punished without the participation of the masses.[8]

The Campaign for the Elimination of Counterrevolutionaries did more than eliminate former adversaries of Communism—it frightened the bourgeoisie in the towns and cities and smothered in advance all open or potential opposition to the far-reaching reforms that were introduced shortly afterward, particularly in the economic structures.

The Three- and Five-Anti campaigns

The Three- and Five-Anti campaigns (*san fan* and *wu fan*) caused less bloodshed than the one just described but produced equally important results. The first, the Three-Anti, was launched in December 1951 after careful preparation and a trial run organized by Kao Kang in Manchuria. It applied to civil servants and cadres of all kinds and attacked corruption, waste, and bureaucratism.

The aims were to give the new administration a new style of work and new ethics, to correct the cadres inherited from the former regime, to save the new ones from the temptations of power and above all from the two contradictory tendencies toward "authoritarianism" and slovenliness, both of which involved the danger of turning the Party and the regime away from the masses. This two-fold consideration was to recur from time to time and constituted one of the chief themes of the Cultural Revolution. To those who know how easily a Chinese political cadre—whether an imperial civil servant or a Kuomintang or Communist cadre—may misuse or abuse his authority, the concern may not appear unjustified. The disdain of the scholar for the ignorant, the lack of control by the lowest strata, the dispersion of authority and the difficulties of liaison with the higher levels in the hierarchy, the weight of old habits, and the legendary patience of a docile and even pliable population toward the excesses of its governors ("Even an honest prefect can amass a hundred thousand beautiful silver taels in his three years in office," as one proverb goes) furnish a partial explanation for this movement of purge and rectification involving prison sentences and often executions. The campaign lasted until April 30, 1952.

The Three-Anti Campaign gave place to the Five-Anti. This campaign was directed against bribes, fraud, tax evasion, embezzlement of state property, and the illegal obtaining of state economic secrets. The Five-Anti Campaign was not therefore aimed at civil servants and cadres, but at those who might corrupt them: the industrial and commercial bourgeoisie. The latter were to be discredited politically by the revelation of some of their practices, while their economic influence on various state or provincial bodies was to be destroyed. This campaign, known as the "tiger hunt," with its secret denunciations and public accusation meetings, was accompanied by thousands of condemnations and caused hundreds of people to commit suicide in the large towns. The enormous fines and confiscations it inflicted greatly helped the finances of the regime and facilitated the launching of the first five-year plan in 1953.[9] The campaign came to an end on June 13, 1952. According to Po I-po, then minister of finance, 450,000 firms were checked in only seven large towns; 76 percent of them were guilty of irregular practices, some more serious than others.[10]

On the whole, after several months of indescribable disorder in economic affairs, the Three- and Five-Anti campaigns achieved their targets. An uprightness hitherto unknown became the rule in all commercial dealings and in the administration. The "national bourgeoisie" was terror-stricken. The other, greater bourgeoisie, known as "bureaucratic," had already moved to Taiwan, Hong Kong, or countries in Southeast Asia. As in the case of the Campaign for the Elimination of Counterrevolutionaries, the political effects of the Three- and Five-Anti campaigns were considerable. They gave notice of and prepared the way for the nationalization of all industry and almost all commerce, and consequently for the disappearance of the industrial and commercial bourgeoisie. At the same time, the intellectual bourgeoisie, which was also urged to transform itself, proved more difficult to handle; matter is more pliable than mind.

Notes

[1] See Guillermaz, *A History of the Chinese Communist Party*, Chapter 17.

[2] Kuomingtang Revolutionary Committee (Li Chi-sen), Democratic League (Chang Lan, and Shen Chün-ju), Association for Democratic Construction (Huang Yen-p'ei and Chang Nai-ch'i), Association for the Development of Democracy (Ma Hsü-lun and Madame Lu Hsün), Workers' and Peasants' Democratic Party (Chang Po-chün), Chih Kung Tang or Freemasons (Ch'en Ch'i-yu), the Chiu San Society (Hsü Te-heng), and the League for the Democratic Autonomy of Taiwan.

[3] Inner Mongolia was also a region but was independent of the six others.

[4] For the sake of clarity, the variations occurring between 1949 and 1973 have been omitted. Map 2 tallies with the most recent known official documents.

[5] A general rule on the meetings of representatives of all social categories at the provincial level was drawn up on December 2, 1949. Another rule concerning the creation of local governments was drawn up on January 6, 1951.

[6] The *Guide to New China* for 1952 gave the following figures: Association of Democratic Women, 76 million; Democratic Youth, 7 million; Student Federation, 1.6 million; Sino-Soviet Friendship Association, 18 million; General Workers' Confederation, 6.13 million.

[7] Two foreigners—one Italian and one Japanese—were executed in Peking.

[8] On the basis of this figure, a total of 600,000 executions over ten months can be estimated for the whole country. This is well below the true figure if victims of the land reform and other campaigns are included. The total was probably in the region of 5 million for the whole of China between 1949 and 1952. Some external, non-Communist sources quote instructions by Mao Tse-tung to restrict the number of executions to 0.6 percent of the population in rural areas and 0.8 percent in the towns. This proportion was probably exceeded.

[9] A. Doak Barnet, *Communist China: The Early Years* (New York: Praeger, 1964), estimates that the Three- and Five-Anti campaigns probably brought in the equivalent of $1,700 million for the government.

[10] *People's Daily* (October 1, 1952). On the same subject, see also an article by Hsi-en Chen and Wen-hui Chen, "The Three- and Five-Anti Movements in Communist China," *Pacific Affairs* XXVI, No. 1 (March 1953).

3 The Restoration of the Economy

The agrarian reform law of June 28, 1950

The agricultural vocation of China, the numerical importance of the peasantry, the revolutionary role played by a fraction of them, the Party's long experience of agricultural policy, the differences between the old and the recently liberated areas as regards land statutes, the desire to increase production in the domain to which the state looked for almost all of its resources (in 1949, production of food crops was 25 percent below that of the best prewar years)—all these reasons encouraged the government to draw up a new land law without delay.[2] The law passed on June 28, 1950 was to serve as a basis and a source of reference for all later transformations.

The law of June 28, 1950, on which Liu Shao-ch'i wrote an introductory report, had two complementary aspects: one was purely economic; the other, more important aspect was political and social in content. Three documents accompanied it, at least two of which were to endure: "Decisions Concerning the Differentiation of Class Status in the Countryside" (August 4, 1950), "General Regulations Governing the Organization of Peasant Associations" (July 14, 1950), and "General Regulations on the Organization of People's Tribunals" (July 20, 1950).

Essentially, the new law gave each individual aged sixteen or older a minimum of two to three *mou* of land, depending on the region.[3] In practice, a family of five was to have nearly one hectare. The granting of land, legalized by title deeds, gave new owners the right to use the land as they wished and to purchase, sell, or rent it (Article 30). The land redistributed in this way was taken first from corporately owned land: ancestral temples belonging to clans, Taoist and Buddhist temples and monasteries, Christian churches and other bodies; and then from individual landowners, whose land, animals, agricultural tools and grain stores were confiscated without compensation. The owners retained the right to receive two or three *mou* of land like everyone else. All their nonagricultural enterprises—small factories, workshops, and shops—were left untouched (Article 4). Apart from certain exceptional cases mentioned by the law, land belonging to rich peasants was "protected" (Article 6); land belonging to middle peasants, including the most well-off among them, could not be touched at all. In order to disturb production as little as possible, redistribution was carried out by increasing or decreasing the size of existing lots.

The land reform of 1950 was far from egalitarian from an economic point of view. Although it established an essential minimum for each person, it showed caution, primarily, in its treatment of rich peasants, who were often better equipped, better organized, and more hard-working than the rest. Production had to be protected above all; this consideration, strikingly evident in the introductory report by Liu Shao-ch'i, was also—in spite of statements made during the Cultural Revolution—the policy of the Party as a whole and of Mao Tse-tung. Mao had declared it at the Third Session of the Seventh Central Committee on June 6, 1950:

> This is why our policy toward the rich peasants ought to be changed. Their excess land must no longer be confiscated, but their life must be preserved to speed up the restoration of production in rural areas.

By freeing millions of peasants of the burden of paying rent to landlords and by enabling them to invest in their new plots, the regime hoped to increase production, but it gave little thought as to how these measures might be the basis for opposition to collectivization in the future.

In all, 700 million *mou* of land (46 million hectares out of a total of 107 or 108 million hectares) changed hands. Three hundred million poor peasants had their plots of land enlarged and instead of being tenant farmers, at least in a partial sense, became for a short time owners of small independent holdings, subject to a tax of 17 to 19 percent of the value of their harvest. From a technical point of view, the 1950 land reform, the largest of many in Chinese history, had been prepared carefully and methodically. It had also been preceded by studies and local experiments and was helped by the training of several hundred thousand provincial cadres, who were responsible for setting it in motion and seeing that it was correctly applied from one *hsien* to another. Its flexibility allowed it to be adapted to the widely differing situations of a vast country with a great variety of basic crops.

By the end of 1952, or at least by the spring of 1953, land reform had been more or less completed, except among the minority races, where changes had to be made cautiously and slowly, partly because of their customs, and partly because they often had a pastoral economy. Reference to official figures shows that reform had a beneficial effect on agriculture, for in 1952 production was well ahead of the best prewar figure, except in the case of soybeans. The following table gives results and comparisons in millions of tons for cereals,[4] cotton, and soybeans.

Products	Highest Prewar figure	1952
Cereals	138.7	154.4
Cotton	0.85	1.3
Soybeans	11.31	9.52

These statistics should be accepted with reservation. The land reform could not fail to produce some negative results: disturbances in production owing to changes in ownership, the breaking up of estates, the efforts of many peasants to avoid inclusion in the discredited categories of landlords and rich peasants, interruptions in the commercial circuits and the working of the private agricultural credit system, and discord in the inner relationships of a rural world with complicated family and clan ties.

On the other hand, the return to political unity, to peace within the country, and to financial stability, combined with the restoration of the transport system and the completion of extensive irrigation work created conditions that encouraged economic development.

The results of the year 1952, which were little improved by those of 1953, fell well below the production needed for the consumer market and industrial construction, according to Teng Tzu-hui, who was in charge of agriculture. Analyzing the figures for 1952, he estimated that an annual production of 275 to 300 million tons of cereals was essential and would be possible "after one or two plans of five years or a little more."[5] The future was to belie his hopes sadly, for nearly twenty years later, according to official figures, production was still only 240 million tons.

From a political and ideological point of view, the land reform was a mass movement intended to heighten the revolutionary consciousness of hundreds of millions of Chinese peasants, organizing them under the authority of the Party and giving them a spiritual link with the regime. For this reason, it was never allowed to be settled peaceably, according to the natural inclinations of the Chinese, but had to be effected boldly, in an atmosphere of accusation meetings, the paying off of old scores, and mass trials. It also had to be preceded by the assignment of each person to categories clearly defined by official texts. This was indispensable in order to carry out class struggle in the countryside. Behind the land reform was the same spirit of violence that had moved Mao Tse-tung in 1927 when speaking of the peasant movements in Hunan:

> A revolution is not a dinner party, or writing an essay, or painting a picture, or doing embroidery; it cannot be so refined, so leisurely and gentle. . . . A rural revolution is a revolution by which the peasantry over-throws the power of the feudal landlord class. . . . The rural areas need a mighty revolutionary upsurge, for it alone can rouse the people in their millions to become a powerful force. . . . To put it bluntly, it is necessary to create terror for a while in every rural area.[6]

People's Courts were created in every district:

> . . . to judge and punish, according to the law, despots guilty of odious crimes, cursed and brought to justice by the great masses of the people, as well as all criminals infringing or undermining the law and rulings of the Land Reform.[7]

The reform instituted a legal reign of terror. By setting up peasant associations open to poor and middle peasants only, it installed class dictatorship in the villages and replaced old injustices with new ones.

The great wave of terror accompanying the land reform of 1950 was responsible for the death of several million people, whether by execution or suicide (landlords and their agents who were grouped together by law, leaders of rural militia, and the like). It also created a class of political outcasts that was still being attacked twenty years later. It struck fear in advance into all enemies of collectivization—almost all the peasants who had become small landowners. In this sense, it was important in preparing the way, both ideologically and psychologically, for the progressive changes which in some regions at least began as early as 1951.

The land reform brought about far-reaching modifications in the shape of society in the countryside. For the first time, the old rule of the Communist movement as regards land policy—"Look to the poor peasants for support, form an alliance with the middle peasants, neutralize the rich peasants, eliminate landlords"—was applied to the country as a whole. The disappearance of the landlords and the weakening of the moral and economic position of the rich peasants reduced the inner solidarity of the clans, which embraced families of different financial resources. The land reform attacked the ideas and practices of traditional life, just as the marriage law was doing in the same social context at the same time. Although the village was made more aware of regional, national, and even international political life, the reform destroyed some measure of local unity in the face of the state and the Party. The individual was more emancipated—land ownership was conferred on individuals—and came of age at sixteen as a worker and small landowner, but he stood alone in his relations with authority, the Party and above all the peasant associations, without the protecting screen afforded by family, clan, and village, represented by their respective headmen.

Nearly fifty years earlier, Sun Yat-sen had identified the redistribution of the land with his third principle, "the people's livelihood" (*min-sheng*), as the membership oath of the T'ung-meng-hui of 1905 bears witness: "Drive out the Manchu and rehabilitate China, found a republic, share out the land equally." The central Nanking government, heir to Sun's authority and repository of his thought, had not had the time, the means, or even a genuine desire to accomplish a wish so contrary to the interest of its supporters. Measures for reducing land rent—and in particular the laws of June 30, 1930 and of April 29, 1946 on landed property—had remained dead letters, whereas a last proposal laid before the Legislative Yuan on September 21, 1948 came too late to bear any fruit. The Communists carried out this long awaited operation easily and successfully because they had the necessary determination, strength and experience. Above all, they intended to do more than bring about a mere transfer of land; their aim was to revolutionize the countryside, to replace traditional influences by the authority of their Party, and Confucian ethics by revolutionary ethics. The peasants, however, regarded the land reform of June 28, 1950 as an end in itself; the Communists considered it as a beginning. The principal difficulties of the regime were to arise from this misunderstanding.

The rehabilitation of industry

Modern industry had first of all to be restored so that its potential could be realized. In 1949, as in 1937 on the eve of the Sino-Japanese war,[8] several characteristics predominated, which Chinese economists and their Soviet advisers had to take into account, sometimes trying to correct them. Light industry—particularly textiles and food—played a much greater role in the economy than heavy industry. Some branches of modern industry— engines, machine tools, precision instruments, copper and petroleum products—did not exist. Little capital was invested in industry; it seldom exceeded an average figure of $50,000 per enterprise? The geographical distribution of industrial centers was still uneven; 80 percent of those that were not in Manchuria were near the coast. Technicians and skilled labor were lacking in both quality and quantity. Some regions had none at all. Tables 3.1 and 3.2 summarize the situation of Chinese industry at the end of 1947; the figures serve as a point of reference by which to measure the economic development of the regime. Communist statistics for the same period are largely similar (see Chapter 1).

The Communists, anxious to preserve this weak industrial capital, and convinced that they would soon be victorious, gave orders early enough to the technicians and workers in the government zones to protect all establishments. Large-scale sabotage was forbidden, and as far as possible an effort was made to prevent the Nationalist authorities from evacuating equipment to Taiwan or destroying it. Frightened industrialists were encouraged to return from Hong Kong and various countries in Southeast Asia, while students finishing their studies abroad were recalled.[10] Industrial production and commerce were hardly interrupted when towns were occupied. The few strikes that occurred were short. Care was taken to reassure heads of firms, treat them with caution, and safeguard their authority.

This sound and sensible policy, in strong contrast to the liquidation of landlords who were no more and no less "bourgeois" than the industrialists and tradespeople, was pursued by the Party until the Five-Anti Campaign in 1952. The policy was resumed after that crisis and remained in effect until the changes of 1955 and 1956 and even later still, because the heads of firms were entirely at the mercy of authorities as regards raw materials, state orders, and controls of every kind. During the Cultural Revolution, Liu Shao-ch'i was said to be the originator of this capitalist policy "of exploitation." "Exploitation has its merits" was a phrase put into his mouth in dozens of caricatures and satires. Some of his remarks encouraging the industrialists were taken out of context and quoted with no reference to the needs of the times, or to the fact that the policy was then that of the Party as a whole and of its chairman, Mao Tse-tung.

Official statistics reveal that the value of industrial production and handicrafts rose from 14,020 million to 34,330 million yuan between 1949

Table 3.1
The situation of Chinese industry in 1947 (firms,
employees, and workers)

Products	Factories	Employees and workers
Metal manufactures	181	49,716
Tools	2,001	74,762
Metal workshops	830	29,830
Electrical industry	261	16,829
Chemical industry	2,760	172,915
Textiles	3,270	394,337
Clothing	934	62,118
Food	3,824	131,182
Paper	533	24,889
Miscellaneous	527	14,384
Totals	15,121	971,962 (138,000 of whom were employees)

Source: *China Year Book 1950* (New York: Rockport
Press), Chapter 14.

Notes: Out of the above total, 493 factories, comprising 177,000 workers and employees, belonged to the
state.
   The energy available to industry amounted to 559,268
hp and 2,132,333 kW. The total electricity production
in 1943 was 3795 million kWh, or, to put it another
way, 6 kWh per inhabitant.
   The textile industry had 4,556,000 spindles and 64,000
looms for cotton.
   Industrial capital amounted to 1078 million Chinese
dollars (CNC).

and 1952; industrial production figures are shown in Table 3.3. The share
of modern industry (i.e., Western type industry as opposed to indigenous
technology and handicrafts) in the total industrial and agricultural
production rose from 23.2 percent to 32.7 percent between 1949 and 1952.
   By the end of 1952, rail and road transport had been restored everywhere
and its capacity had been increased. The 21,715 kilometers of railways in
use in 1949 had risen to 24,232 kilometers; the new lines were almost all

Table 3.2
Production during the best prewar years

Products	China proper	Manchuria (1943)	Total
	(millions of tons)		
Coal	33	25.63	58.63
Pig iron	0.290	1.7	1.990
Steel	0.05	0.843	0.893
Cement	0.608	1.532	2.14
	(millions of kWh)		
Electricity	2,425	4,475	6,900
	(millions of bales)		
Cotton (spun)	2.1		
	(millions of bolts)		
Cotton (fabrics)	30		

Source: Statistics compiled from various sources by
W. W. Rostow and Alexander Eckstein, *The Prospects for
Communist China* (New York: Wiley, 1955), p. 229.

Table 3.3
Modern industrial production in 1949 and 1952

Products	1949	1952	Unit
Steel	158	1,349	thousands of tons
Pig iron	252	1,929	thousands of tons
Coal	32,430	66,490	thousands of tons
Crude oil	121	436	thousands of tons
Cement	660	2,860	thousands of tons
Fertilizers	27	181	thousands of tons
Electric power	4,310	7,260	millions of kWh

Source: *Ten Great Years* (Peking, 1960).

built in the western part of the country where most of the construction had been begun by the preceding government. The most important of these were the Tienshui-Lanchow line (354 kilometers) from Shensi to Kansu, the line from Laipin (Kwangsi) to the frontier of Vietnam (419 kilometers), and the Chungking-Chengtu line (505 kilometers) in Szechwan. The rolling stock was once again made in the workshops in Taiyuan in Shansi, and in Mukden and Dairen in Manchuria. Roads, often built for political and strategic reasons rather than economic ones, had above all been pushed into regions inhabited by minority races: Tsinghai, Yunnan, and Tibet. In terms of tons per kilometer, they carried 180 times less goods than the railway for a price four times as high and were used mainly for transport by draft animals, or even men. Water transport retained traditional methods and characteristics.[12]

Foreign trade, which was directed more and more toward the socialist countries (70 percent in 1952) expanded steadily, increasing from the index number 100 in 1949 to 155.5 in 1952, or in value from 4,150 to 6,460 million yuan.[13] Quality, however, was affected by the United Nations embargo of May 17, 1951 on the exportation of strategic equipment to China. The purely conventional value of the yuan compared to the dollar (2.44 yuan to $1.00), the fact that several different rates of exchange existed for the rouble and the yuan, the preferential tariffs allowed for transport by the Trans-Siberian railway, and the question of military supplies make it almost impossible to calculate Chinese foreign trade figures with any accuracy. Table 3.4 cites Yuan-li Wu's estimates for the years 1950 to 1952 as a rough indication.[14]

Table 3.4
China's foreign trade 1950–1952

Years	Imports	Exports	Total
	(millions of U.S. dollars)		
1950	436.4	466.5	902.9
1951	1,033.3	672.4	1,705.7
1952	717.01	478.0	1,195.01

Financial recovery

The government published its financial decisions after two important national conferences, the Tax Conference of November 1949 that resulted in the law of January 31, 1950, which simplified and unified the taxation system, and the Financial Conference of November 1950, which reorganized the financial apparatus of the state, separating the Government Treasury from the administration.[15] In March 1950, the currency was more or less stable, after a brief period of distinct inflation. The budget, which at first showed a deficit, was balanced and from then on, at least until 1956, the state was able to keep its receipts and expenses in equilibrium, while the index of the cost of living has risen little in the intervening years.

Financial recovery was the fruit of numerous measures depending for their success on a highly authoritarian political context. The methods used and the respective effects do not appear to have been studied until now and would require the analysis of a sociologist, political scientist, and economist. The chief methods may be summarized as follows:

Exchange of old currency against the new at a rate that was advantageous to the state.

Acquisition of capital and extensive property at the expense of certain social categories or of firms owned by Chinese or foreigners by means of confiscation, surrender, donation, and above all obligatory gifts.

Compulsory handing over of gold, silver coins, and foreign currency.

Creation of a "parity unit" based on the price of essential foodstuffs in large towns, and varying from region to region. It usually consisted of a pound of grain, a pound of coal, an ounce of oil and sometimes of salt, and a foot of fabric.

Control of prices by the creation of state buying agencies, which dominated the market.

The issuance of indexed Victory Bonds paying 5 percent interest, with assessment based on the appearance of wealth; purchase was generally compulsory.[16]

Reduction of state expenses by numerous austerity campaigns and the fight against waste, corruption, and bureaucracy, of which the Three-Anti Campaign is the best example.

A general inventory of the property and deposits of the former government and of the property abandoned by owners who had fled the country, which were then either sold or appropriated by the state.

The institution of taxes in kind, controlled by the government alone, to the exclusion of local authorities.

These measures were strictly applied and proved extremely effective; the Communist currency, converted on March 1, 1955, on the basis of 1 new yuan for 10,000 old yuan, was to remain remarkably stable, in spite of the expenses entailed by the Korean War, military aid to Korea and Vietnam, and the colossal budgets of the first five-year plan.

By the end of 1952, although weaknesses and mistakes in the original plans for recovery had made them only 85 percent successful, according to official sources, many things had been achieved.[17] The land reform was almost completed, industry was running again, transport had been restored and developed, the budget had been balanced, the currency stabilized, and production figures were equal to those of the best prewar years in every field. The end of the Korean War and the obtaining of considerable help from the Soviet Union, which was costly but essential, were to enable the regime to enter on an era of planning and collectivization; the building of socialism could begin.

Notes

[1] On the land statutes and the agrarian policy of the Chinese Communist Party before 1949, see Guillermaz, *A History of the Chinese Communist Party*, pp. 9-10. On Chinese history as a whole, see Henri Maspero, *Etudes Historiques*, vol. 2, *Les Regimes fonciers en Chine des origines aux temps modernes*, (Paris: Presses Universitaires de France, 1967).

[2] According to Communist statistics, total Chinese population for 1949 was distributed as follows: 30.1 percent industry and handicrafts, 69.6 percent agriculture. See *Ten Great Years*, p. 17.

[3] One *mou* is equivalent to 0.06 hectare, or 0.165 acre.

[4] By cereals the Chinese mean rice, wheat, cereals of secondary importance (barley, millet, sorghum, maize, and so on), and potatoes and sweet potatoes, which count for a quarter of their weight. The 1952 figures, in millions of tons, were as follows: rice, 68.4; wheat, 18; secondary cereals, 51.5; potatoes and sweet potatoes, 16.35. The total value of agricultural production (including subsidiary activities) rose between 1949 and 1952 from 32,590 to 48,390 million yuan. See *Ten Great Years*, p. 16.

[5] See the *People's Daily* (July 23, 1953).

[6] Mao Tse-tung, *Selected Works*. 4 vols. (Peking: Foreign Language Press, 1961-65), vol. 1, pp. 28-29.

[7] Text creating revolutionary courts in the *People's Daily*. (July 21, 1950).

[8] For a general view of Chinese industry before 1949, see Yuan-li Wu, *An Economic Survey of Communist China*, and J. K. Chang, *Industrial Development in Pre-Communist China* (Chicago: Aldine, 1969).

[9] On Chinese industrial capital before the war, see D. K. Lieu (Liu Ta-chun), *China's Economic Stabilization and Reconstruction* (New Brunswick: Rutgers University Press, 1948).

[10] On October 6, 1954 the Hsinhua Agency reported that, since 1949, 178,000 Overseas Chinese had returned to take part in reconstruction and production.

[11] *Ten Great Years.*

[12] In 1952, goods traffic, in terms of millions of tons per kilometer, rose to 60,160 for the railways, 770 for the roads, and 10,610 for inland waterways. See *Ten Great Years*, p. 148.

[13] *Ibid.*, p. 175.

[14] Y. L. Wu, *An Economic Survey of Communist China.* For a general work on Chinese foreign trade from 1950 to 1966, see Sydney Klein, *Politics Versus Economics: The Foreign Trade and Aid Policies of China* (Hong Kong: International Studies Group, 1968).

[15] On all these questions, see François J. Durand, *Le Financement du budget en Chine populaire* (Paris: Editions Sirey, 1965).

[16] At the start, 200 million units were quoted on January 6, 1950, at 14,055 yuan (jen-min-pi); in January 1954, they were worth 24,893 yuan.

[17] The State Statistical Bureau, in one of its reports, attributed this to overhastiness, insufficient knowledge of the complicated problems involved, bad management planning, and defects in the chain of authority.

4 Social Changes: The Marriage Law of May 1, 1950

If the Westernization of ideas and customs had affected certain elements of Chinese society—the population of large ports and industrial centers, and the southern coastal provinces to which many emigrants were returning—it had scarcely touched the peasant masses or the people in small and middle-sized inland towns. In 1949, living standards, habits and customs, and attitudes remained those of Imperial China for three-quarters of the population.[1]

This unchanging world was to be awakened by mass campaigns in the towns, land reform in the villages, and intensive and permanent use of propaganda everywhere. The awakening did not become a reality until the late 1950s, when great changes in social structures and in production relations came to overthrow the old society. Meanwhile, the regime had to clear away obstacles that its predecessors had been unable to overcome. Consequently, the marriage law published on May 1, 1950, was the first proclaimed by the regime, except for the organic laws of 1949. It was also the most far-reaching in its effects, given the strength of the idea of the family and the role of the family in Chinese society at the time. Nevertheless, although the new law set out to free the individual from the restraints of the family unit, its chief aim was to put him in a new position, standing alone with no one to screen him or mediate between him and the Party. The regime wanted to ensure the transfer of his efforts, and his traditional devotion and loyalty from the family or clan community to the large communities soon to be constituted in the form of new production units and, through them, to the Party and the regime.

It was not an easy undertaking. Resistance to it existed within the Party itself, and the task has probably not yet been completed. To estimate its scope, many things must be taken into consideration: the inner characteristics of the Chinese family, the exact position of the individual, and especially women, within it, and the leading role of the family, not only in society, but in the economy and the state. The issue is therefore an important one. The following brief account applies first of all to the authentically traditional family, though it is valid in the case of families in a state of transition, which have begun to appear in several places in the last generation or two.

The traditional family

The characteristics and the vitality of the traditional family have a religious derivation. The family was the center of a cult of veneration addressed to the ancestors by their male descendants; this cult affirmed and encouraged the continuity of the species, associating the living and the dead in the same concept. At the same time, it diminished the importance of the individual, who was lost in the sequence of generations and, as one author puts it, it became an homage rendered to the immortality of the race rather than to the immortality of the soul.[2] In this respect, Paul Valéry has probably summed up its effects better than anyone else:

> Here each man feels that he is both son and father, between a thousand and ten thousand, and sees himself as held fast among the race around him, and the race dead before him, and the race yet to come, like the brick in a brick wall.[3]

The family cult remained deeply rooted in the population until the arrival of the Communists. This was particularly true in the countryside, where both the need for labor to ensure the economic survival of the family and the high rate of mortality gave it further meaning. The outward signs of the cult were a family altar in each home, with tablets bearing the names of the five last heads of the family; various rites had to be performed at certain moments in the family's life. Births, deaths, marriages, success in examinations, and other advancements were announced to the ancestors with all due ceremony, with prostrations and offerings of incense and food. Anniversaries of ancestral births and deaths were also celebrated with all possible solemnity. The need to preserve the continuity of ancester worship and all it symbolized explained certain extremely widespread habits, which were important for their demographic and social implications: early marriages, childhood betrothals, adoption, double inheritance, concubinage, and so on.

In addition to their family ancestors, some families also venerated the ancestors of their clan. These clans had often produced several families, which bore the same name and sometimes formed entire villages called after them. Countless Wang family or Li family villages exist. Often the clan had been endowed by some of its members and had temples or shrines housing tablets of the dead beyond the fifth generation. Sometimes—particularly in the southern provinces—it owned large amounts of landed property. The fact of common origins and name created special moral and material obligations among clan members building up among them a web of complex relationships that transcended class and economic levels.

Apart from these primary religious and ritual characteristics, the Chinese family contained other elements that strengthened its unity. It was a patriarchal family. The authority of the head of the family, often helped by a family council in the case of rich and large families, was considerable. Its boundaries were the society's traditional customs, morality, and prejudices; in practice, no appeal was possible. By inclination, the family stayed grouped around its property, particularly when it owned large amounts, sometimes living in the same residence consisting of pavilions built around several courtyards and constituting a budgetary and economic unit: "Six generations under the same roof, nine generations without splitting up the land," as a proverb had it. Needless to say, large families of this kind had become rare and in 1949 were to be found mainly among the gentry and landowner descendants of the old "scholar-officials," and among the rich merchants. Families of poor or middle peasants were more like European rural families, with between four and eight members and scarcely any relations. Because statistics are lacking and field research is impossible, only a rough idea is to be had of the size of the Chinese family.

Alongside the patriarchy, another characteristic of Chinese domestic order was the separation of the sexes from childhood onward. Based on ancient moral concepts, and originally arising also from the sexes' different economic functions, such separation was in opposition to the practical, legal emancipation of women. The moral solidarity linking all members was another strong characteristic of the Chinese family and often of the clan as well. It was partly due to a solidarity in the face of penal measures, which lasted until modern times. The penal code of the last dynasty gives minute details of the punishments to which a criminal's next of kin were liable: death, banishment, slavery, corporal punishment. Balancing this, the group had considerable responsibilities to fulfil toward any one of its members, whether in coming to his aid or helping him advance. This obligation, which was particularly important in the case of one's elders, had precedence over all duties to the sovereign, the state, the town, the profession, and to one's neighbors. To those subject to it, it provided justification for nepotism, extortion, and every kind of egoism. In the eyes of public opinion,* it served as an extenuating circumstance for the guilty, from whom blame was withheld except when the fault was so great that it exceeded the usefulness of the principle.

The prevailing characteristic of relationships within the family was filial piety. The behavior of each member was dictated by strict rules of propriety and obedience determined by his or her position in the family in relation to all the others. The importance and often the richness of the ceremonies, their complexity, their length, the long period of mourning, the terrible punishments awaiting the parricide, even if he was insane, the preponderance of family relationships in the Five Cardinal Relationships, and even the strict definitions of ties of kinship, all bear witness to the spirit of filial piety, which found expression in strong paternal or marital authority.

The woman's place in this traditional family structure was inferior and yet at the same time often important, for her sex was not despised, but rather the contrary. Her marriage was arranged by her parents—or even by the whole family—through a professional intermediary whose discreet, often anonymous role prevented mistakes, false moves, and wounds to self-esteem. She did not see her husband before the day of the ceremony when she was borne to her new family in a sedan chair colored red for happiness. Here at least she was on an equal footing with her husband who had also had no choice in the matter, and for whom marriage was also a social, not a personal, affair. The wife owed obedience to her new family and, above all, to her mother-in-law. All the normal conjugal virtues were expected of her, and sometimes she had to accept or tolerate the existence of secondary wives and concubines. Should she become a widow, and want to marry again, she came up against strong prejudice and many practical obstacles. On the other hand, although grounds for divorce were many—among them a tendency toward excessive gossiping—numerous impediments stood in the way of a husband trying to get rid of his wife.[4] The wife acted as mother to all her husband's children, and concubines were subordinate to her. As the old proverb put it, "The wife fears the husband, the husband fears the concubine, and the concubine fears the wife." In practice, the wife had great influence, particularly after the first children were born, and she finished by dealing out the same tyrannical treatment to her daughters-in-law as she had received herself, and by ensuring the ruling of the household from within.

The traditional family in the context of society

In pre-Communist society, the social and political importance of the family arose not only from its solid structure and unity, but also from two marked characteristics of society: insufficient administration and the role of ethics in human relationships. The imperial administration stopped at the level of the *hsien* or district, leaving the responsibility for the villages in the hands of the most influential heads of families, and the responsibility for the individual in the hands of the family itself, always providing that certain appearances and customs were respected. This almost discretionary power could not fail to reinforce administrative and political conservatism and, at the same time, the authority of the heads of families.

Ethics were more effective than legal constraint in ensuring fundamental order in society or in the family. Through two thousand years of history, Confucian principles adapted as popular precepts had permeated the entire population, reaching even the most simple elements. At this level, family ethics either replaced or merged with civic ethics. In more educated circles, to govern one's family well was to take a share in the highest responsibilities of all, as confirmed by many admirably concise sayings: "To govern the state is to put one's family in order first of all," or this rule summarizing an entire philosophy of universal harmony: "To fashion oneself, to rule one's family, to govern the state, to pacify the world."

The evolution of the traditional family

The Chinese family had been evolving slowly since the end of the Empire. The chief cause was naturally the disappearance of the old order, the former institutions and, above all, the mandarinate, which was the depository and guardian of Confucian ethics. Another cause was the educational reform of 1905, whose effects were gradually diffused. It aimed not only at the suppression of the old examination system but also at a far-reaching revision of the content of education. Gradually, moral sayings or maxims of filial piety drawn from the classics gave way to reality and everyday experience, which was influenced by Western learning and new ideas to a large extent. Little by little, principles, values and behavior that had remained intact through thousands of years were questioned. Customs imposed by the family began to weaken, such as foot-binding, for instance, which was so deeply rooted in certain classes that girls were not considered marriageable without it.

Changes varied greatly from one social category and one region to another. They naturally came about more quickly and were more striking among the nascent industrial and commercial bourgeoisie and even among the landed bourgeoisie whose children often studied abroad or attended foreign schools (missionary schools in particular). They were also more apparent in the large coastal towns (Shanghai, Tsingtao, Tientsin, Canton) or in towns accessible by large rivers or by railway than in inland towns, while the foreign concessions exercised great influence on the evolution of ideas and customs through their example and the easy contacts they offered. To a certain extent, the millions of Overseas Chinese returning to their own country also played a part in the transformation.

Even so, the size of the country, which was both vast and compact, the difficulties of travel, illiteracy, the minute percentage of bourgeoisie in the total population, resistance on the part of heads of families, and the massive force of habit in a world looking to the past rather than to the future, all contributed to slow down changes and confine them to limited areas, in spite of the efforts of the rulers. The civil code of 1930, for example, proclaimed freedom of marriage and equal rights of inheritance for both parties and even allowed divorce by mutual consent, but all kinds of social prejudice and material difficulties impeded its application.[5]

In 1934, the New Life Movement attempted to diffuse modern ideas on morality, civic sense, and even hygiene; its success was restricted by lack of time and conviction on the part of its originators and, above all, by lack of an organization sufficiently powerful and well rooted among the population to enable it to spread and win obedience. The destruction of the old system could only be brought about by an all-embracing revolutionary movement supported by massive and ceaseless propaganda, and ready to impose all necessary constraints. Even this movement was only partially successful, at the cost of huge difficulties.

The marriage law

The new marriage law, promulgated on May 1st, 1950, after one year and five months of preparation, contained twenty-seven articles accompanied by two more or less official documents.[6] As was to be expected, the law first of all denounced the arbitrary character of the traditional form of marriage which was imposed by families, and forbade bigamy, concubinage (in the sense of polygamy), and the practice of adopting little girls who later married one of the sons of the adoptive family. It also tried to do away with the prejudice against the remarriage of widows, and with marriages arranged by intermediaries (Articles 1 to 3).

The minimum age for marriage was fixed at twenty for men and eighteen for women (Article 4). This measure aimed at removing children still further from the pressure exerted by parents and grandparents anxious to ensure their descent and the survival of the ancestor cult, with the additional aim, left unstated, of reducing the birthrate. (The latter preoccupation is still so acute today that men are encouraged to put off marriage until the age of twenty-eight or thirty, and women until twenty-five.)

It now became compulsory for all couples to register their marriages (Article 6); this important innovation was designed to make it easier to obtain statistics on which to base a demographic policy and allowed for political intervention, as marriage was supposed to be founded on similar points of view on ideological matters. Among the duties and rights of the couple (Articles 7 to 12), Article 8 mentioned the duty to "strive jointly . . . for the building up of the new society." Article 11 confirmed the practice allowing married women to retain their own surnames.

Concerning the relationship between parents and children (Articles 13 to 16), Article 13 contains a specific prohibition, which reveals the frequency of a certain form of infanticide: "Infanticide by drowning . . . [is] strictly prohibited."[7]

The provisions regarding divorce did much to encourage it, as it was possible to obtain a divorce by mutual consent simply by putting the request on record and asking for a certificate (Article 17). The emphasis was on depopulation and on correcting the arbitrary character of marriages, which still persisted. Women were given preferential treatment, because they were presumed to be the victims of the old society as far as the material consequences of divorce were concerned, such as debts and support of the party who did not remarry (Articles 24 and 25).

As might be expected, the new law made an exception in the case of minority races; marriage ceremonies and the state of marriage were to be governed by special arrangements or by amendments to the law of May 1st, 1950 (Article 26).

Taken as a whole, the new law, like that of 1930, had the appearance of a law of emancipation. It was more liberal, more flexible, and more understanding than that passed in 1944 by the Soviet Union, which put several obstacles in the way of divorce. As Mme Chou En-lai pointed out, the two countries had not reached the same stage, particularly as regards the liberation of women. At the same time—quite apart from the question of lowering the birthrate—the old system, linked to a type of society whose time was past, had to be eradicated completely and as quickly as possible.

The new marriage law, once applied, came up against many obstacles and the official commentators readily admitted it. Although the law set out "to free women without doing the least injustice to men," it was unfavorable to them in their capacities of father, husband, and even brother. The Communists and their supporters were affected in these three ways as much as everyone else, and sometimes more so. Their situation, as far as their families were concerned, was often more complicated than that of most people. Most cadres came from urban or rural bourgeois families; some had been married early by their families, as in the case of Mao Tse-tung himself. Often the wandering life of the revolutionaries and their flight to the Communist base had led them to found a second family while the first still existed or while their children—now scattered—were left in the charge of peasants. Their difficult situations, and the natural dislike of the Chinese for meddling with someone else's family affairs, made them feel little interest in applying the new law, which in any case they found hard to understand: "Even among the cadres of the people's government and the members of the Communist Party there are some who do not show enough respect for their wives," exclaimed Teng Ying-ch'ao (Mme Chou En-lai).[8] In towns, where many divorces were asked for, mainly by women, the people's courts (generally organized or taken over by the army's Political Department) mainly showed understanding toward the women. This reversal of prejudice sometimes aroused masculine resentment.[9]

Painful situations existed nonetheless. It was not always possible to send secondary wives away from the family when they were fond of their husbands, or separate them from their children, or leave them without means of livelihood. Sometimes the only solution was to turn a blind eye and make the best of long-existing situations. Marriages arranged by intermediaries still had to be tolerated because they protected the parties' self-esteem and afforded certain safeguards, and traditional ceremonies had to be allowed because they were so firmly rooted in popular customs that people believed that a marriage unaccompanied by them would be neither happy nor fertile. Class considerations also affected the decisions of cadres and people's courts, since they hesitated to provoke the discontent of poor peasants, artisans, or workers by stripping them of their paternal or marital authority, or causing them material loss.

The government twice had to take vigorous steps to ensure a better application of the law of 1950, first in September 1951 and again in January 1953. After a government decision of September 26, 1951, a real mass campaign was organized on a national scale to oppose old prejudices and promote the correct and rapid execution of the law.[10] Cadres were asked to study the texts once more, to undertake their own reeducation, and to set a good example. The mass organizations (trade unions and various federations) were mobilized. The themes discussed in the newspapers revealed the nature and the extent of the problem. It was said, for instance, that "without putting love above all else," couples ought to be allowed to meet before marriage without running the risk of being mocked or gossiped about. Women were strongly encouraged to fight against their apathy and ignorance, to aspire to a higher status, and above all to heighten their political consciousness by taking an active part in all kinds of constructive work.

In January 1953 the People's Government again realized that the law was not being applied everywhere in a fully satisfactory way. "Feudal" marriages, "arranged" marriages, business marriages, and cases of bigamy persisted. There were still child brides. Many people committed suicide. Women's rights were often ignored. Cadres and sometimes even magistrates took no interest in marriage problems or, if they did intervene, did so awkwardly. A committee of twenty-nine members, presided over by Shen Chün-ju, a former scholar-official under the Empire and a member of the Democratic League, was formed to keep a closer watch on the situation. Mme Chou En-lai, aware that much still had to be done in spite of three years of progress, announced that a new, large campaign for ideological reeducation would take place on World Women's Day. Government directives were published soon afterwards, and large-scale propaganda methods (including theatrical troupes) were brought into play. In addition to the usual themes, the campaign strongly defended the new marriage law, with commentaries reassuring the public that it was not directed against the family and did not encourage divorce.

In spite of lasting suspicion and the persistence of old practices even today, the marriage law of 1950 has had far-reaching and relatively rapid effects. This success is due to the dynamic energy of the Communist Party, which had had lengthy experience in handling the population, particularly in country areas, and which had to break down the family unit in order to organize and indoctrinate individuals more easily. It is also due to structural changes which the new regime was soon to put into effect. Once the 1950 land reform was over, the advance toward collectivization began, with mutual aid teams, elementary and then socialist cooperatives, and finally people's communes as the different stages. All these changes, by eliminating landed property, except for individual houses, and by gradually organizing a collective way of life, were to help weaken the idea of the family. The "big family," which was what the production teams aimed at becoming, tried to wipe out the "small family," confining it to a purely biological role. With the failure of the people's communes and of the Great Leap Forward, the leaders were forced to realize that they had been too hasty and to recognize that the Chinese family would not disappear under the Communism of Fourier any more than under that of Marx or Mao.

However, in 1950 the Party acted with moderation and reserve. The marriage law appeared chiefly as an open break with the old society and as an essential starting point for the building of the new one. The same was true of the land reform law, also adopted in 1950. The former was seen as liberating the rural world, the latter as liberating the world of women; both seemed to bring more justice to China, while bringing the country nearer to modern times. No voice of authority was to oppose them, either within China or abroad.

Notes

[1] On this subject, see Guillermaz, *A History of the Chinese Communist Party*, pp. 8-10.

[2] Ch'u Chai and Winberg Chai, *The Changing Society of China* (New York: New American Library, Mentor Books, 1962). Following a similar idea, another author points out that, whereas in the West the family is centered around the couple, husband and wife, in China it is centered around the relationship between father and son. F. L. K. Hsü, *Americans and Chinese, Two Ways of Life* (New York: Schuman, 1958).

[3] Paul Valery, *Regards sur le monde actuel* (Paris: Gallimard, 1945).

[4] Particularly, as the classics state, in the case of mourning for one or both parents of the husband, or when the latter after some difficulties achieves certain honors, or when the wife cannot be taken back into her own family.

[5] See *The Civil Code of the Republic of China* (Shanghai, 1930). The Communists had also published a marriage law in Kiangsi in 1931, but it was to be short lived. Mao Tse-tung several times expressed his opposition to the "power of the family," particularly through marriage, which he linked with the power of the landowners, adding that the true emancipation of women depended on the success of the socialist revolution.

[6] A text in English was published by the Foreign Languages Press (Peking, 1950).

[7] A careful analysis of the way the articles are formulated could give a revealing picture of the real state of Chinese society in 1950.

[8] Teng Ying-ch'ao, Report of May 14, 1950.

[9] According to fragmentary statistics available for four provinces in North China during the last six months of 1950, between 50.21 and 68.52 percent of civil trials were motivated by divorce.

[10] See the *People's Daily* of September 29, 1951. Chou En-lai emphasized the strength of old habits, the numerous suicides due to enforced marriages: 10,000 in one year in the Central-Southern region, and 1,245 in the province of Shantung alone, for example.

5 Cultural Changes

> Bourgeois intellectuals cannot be banished or destroyed, they must be overcome, transformed, assimilated and re-educated.
>
> *Lenin*

During the process of reconsidering every question on a national scale, and with an eye to the rebuilding of the country, the new regime could not delay dealing with the question of literature and the arts, and that of intellectuals in general and their education.[1] One of the first concerns of 1949 was that of transforming the intellectuals, or "recasting," "remolding," or "brainwashing" them, as the contemporary expressions put it.

The Common Program defined an educational and cultural policy in its fifth chapter. Although it was set out in rather vague terms compared with the clarity of earlier texts aimed mainly at the Party and its members, Article 47 announced future changes: "Lastly, we will give a revolutionary political training to our intellectuals, both young and old, in order to meet the vast needs of our revolutionary work, and our work of national construction."

The first National Writers' and Artists' Conference had already been held in July 1949, three months before the new government was formed. Its 750 delegates had organized a National Writers' and Artists' Federation, with Kuo Mo-jo as chairman and Mao Tun and Chou Yang as vice-chairmen.

Several explanations can be found for the desire to win over the intellectuals in spite of the fact that the vast majority of them were bourgeois both in origin and mentality. Some arise from ancient attitudes toward learning: respect for the scholar, and the love of teaching and persuasion (as Mencius said, "The trouble is that one wants to teach others"). Other explanations lie in the bourgeois background of most of the Party's leaders. The chief reason is to be found in the limited number of intellectuals, and particularly of "superior" intellectuals, compared with the needs of the country. In 1956, China had more than 600 million inhabitants, only 100,000 of whom were first-class intellectuals—that is to say, products of universities and other institutions, whose value as scholars was still intact, and 3,840,000 of whom were "ordinary" intellectuals, products of secondary schools or technical colleges (see Chapter 12). Holding on to these intellectuals, putting them to work for the state, and rallying them willy-nilly to the Party and the regime constituted an objective necessity rather than a political choice.

The ideological reeducation of the intellectuals was undertaken as part of a general propaganda campaign whose intensity and forcible character are well known; it was also often carried out by courses lasting several months, held in regional "revolutionary universities" such as Peking in North China and Wuhsi in East China. Another method was to give noisy and nationwide publicity to a number of literary affairs which took on the artificial aspect of public examples. Those that caused the most stir were the Liang Shu-ming affair, the affair of the film *The Life of Wu Hsün,* and the Hu Shih affair. After this prelude, a campaign of a more political nature, the Campaign for Remolding of Intellectuals, was launched in November 1952. It lasted for a year, and the pattern of events repeated itself periodically—a literary starting point followed by ideological development. The Cultural Revolution was to begin in the same way.

The Liang Shu-ming affair

Liang Shu-ming, a noted philosopher and historian, was greatly influenced by Confucianism and Buddhism, both of which he had defended in several different works. A proponent of regional administrative autonomy and the rebuilding of the countryside, he was looked upon with favor by the Communists although he was a liberal. In 1949, he was one of the leaders of the Democratic League created in Hong Kong in 1941, and a member of the staff of the paper *Kuang-ming jih-pao (Daily Light).*[2]

In October 1951, Liang Shu-ming was asked to write a self-criticism dealing with his latest book, *The Meaning of Chinese Culture,* published in Chungking just before the arrival of the Communists. He was reproached mainly for having denied the existence of classes in Chinese society, claiming that the society was in a state of stagnation between feudalism, which had disappeared at the end of the old dynasties of Chou and Ch'in, and capitalism, which had never been fully established.[3] For a short time at least, Liang Shu-ming bravely confronted his attackers during a controversy which was to serve as a warning to liberals and "small parties," and to the *Kuang-ming jih-pao,* which acted as a cautious spokesman for them until the Hundred Flowers period. In 1953, Mao Tse-tung publicly insulted him during an unpleasant incident.[4] In 1955 he was criticized once more, and in the following year he again made apologies for past ideological mistakes.[5]

The Life of Wu Hsün affair

At the end of 1950, a film called *The Life of Wu Hsün* was shown in Shanghai. Wu Hsün was a noted historical figure of the middle of the nineteenth century. The seventh child of a poor peasant of Ihsien, Shantung province, he was born in 1838 and was orphaned at an early age. Because he had no money, he could not go to school and had to beg and join a troupe of jugglers to make a living. Later on, in memory of his difficulties, he tried to collect donations to found schools for poor children. Thanks to his tenacity, intelligence, and hard work, he managed to found several and was honored by the Emperor when he died in 1896.

The film about him was accepted by the Party without difficulty and was very well received from December 31 onward in all large towns. But in May and June 1951, the press began to publish sharp attacks on it. Far from being considered an exemplary individual devoted to the cause of educating the poor and serving the people, Wu Hsün was described as lacking in revolutionary spirit, for he had acted within the framework of the old society and had showed signs of personal ambition in his reformism and capitulationism. The *People's Daily* of January 10, 1951, wrote:

> Although they lived at the end of the Manchu Ch'ing dynasty, at a time when the Chinese people were engaged in violent struggles against aggressors from abroad and against feudal reactionaries within the country, people like Wu Hsün did not make the slightest attempt to shake the feudal economic base and its superstructure. They did the op-posite; they did their utmost to spread feudal culture, and to obtain a position that they did not have; in order to spread this culture, they did all they could slavishly to serve the feudal power.

The campaign was directed against cadres, Party members, and intel-lectual circles guilty of ideological blindness rather than against Wu

Hsün, a social outcast looking to the rich for support. The editorial in the *People's Daily* continued:

> For many authors, the development of history does not consist of re-placing the old with the new, but of making every effort to preserve the old and prevent it from perishing. It is not a question of using class struggle to overthrow the domination of the feudal reactionaries who must be overthrown but, like Wu Hsün, of disowning the class struggle of the oppressed, who have to capitulate in the face of this domina-tion. . . . Particular attention should be paid to the case of a certain number of Party members who are supposed to have grasped Marxism . . . but who lose all their critical faculties when they come across concrete historical facts, or concrete historical figures (like Wu Hsün). . . . The reactionary ideas of the bourgeoisie penetrate the ag-gressive Communist Party—is this not the truth? Whither has fled the Marxism that some members of the Party say they have learned?

This severe lesson which was aimed at all who had greeted *The Life of Wu Hsün* with a surprising lack of discernment and political maturity, came from the pen of Mao Tse-tung; its authorship was not known until fifteen years later.

The campaign continued and spread. On June 4, the minister of education recommended that discussions and criticisms be organized at all levels for a fortnight. They should relate to the film itself and to the "spirit of Wu Hsün," which was not to be confused with the true revolutionary spirit. Kuo Mo-jo, who had lavished considerable praise on Wu Hsün, and whose calligraphy graced the title of the pictorial version of the story, hurriedly made his self-criticism. He accused himself of having failed to place Wu Hsün in the context of his times, which were already revolutionary: "a typical mistake," he added, "arising from the petty bourgeois habit of speaking and writing without previously making a serious study of the subject."[6] As for the Party, it went so far in its denunciation of Wu Hsün as to create a travelling committee of inquiry to study his life and, with the help of various testimonies, to discredit him for good. He ceased to be an exemplary figure, becoming anonymous once more, one of the millions of vagabonds of his time.

The Inside Story of the Ch'ing Court **affair**

On April 1, 1967, a violent article by Ch'i Pen-yü, then still a member of the Cultural Revolution Group, appeared in the *People's Daily*. It was entitled "Patriotism or Treason" and dealt with the film *The Inside Story of the Ch'ing Court*, the showing of which Liu Shao-ch'i had allegedly approved in 1950. The film was based on several plays and showed the imperial court, the Boxers, and the foreign powers during the events of 1900. If the article and those that followed it are to be believed, Liu Shao-ch'i, contrary to the opinion of Mao Tse-tung and his wife Chiang Ch'ing, insisted on the distribution of the work, judged as defamatory of the Boxers, sympathetic toward the dynasty, and understanding toward the foreigners. The affair, if indeed it deserves the name, does not seem to have gone outside of a small circle; when considering alongside that of *The Life of Wu Hsün*, however, it reveals that in the cultural field, as in several others, Liu Shao-ch'i was in favor of more gradual change than Mao Tse-tung.

The denunciation of Hu Shih

In their determination to eliminate every rival cultural influence, the Communists made a vigorous and malicious attack on one of the greatest figures in the modern intellectual movement, the philosopher and historian Hu Shih. After the 1920s, and after the "Problems and Isms" controversy, Hu Shih, a former student of John Dewey, became less radical in his thinking.[7] Although he remained liberal in his ideas, he held diplomatic and cultural posts in the Nationalist government and then left for Taiwan, where he was president of the Academia Sinica.[8]

On December 2, 1951, a seminar on "the criticism of the thought of Hu Shih" was held in Shanghai. It was attended by eminent members of the university and journalism worlds, some of whom, like the historian Chou Ku-ch'eng, were, by a sort of ironic justice, abruptly purged during the Cultural Revolution in 1966. Hu Shih was attacked mercilessly both from a personal and a scientific point of view. His intellectual integrity and his methods of research came under attack. His roles in the anti-Confucian movement and in the movement for the use of spoken language in literature were questioned; he was compared to Wu Yu-ling, a violent enemy of Confucianism, and Ch'en Tu-hsiu, in spite of the political disgrace of the latter. Hu Shih himself was accused of ambition and careerism—he had been China's ambassador to Washington from 1942 to

1945—and generally of having "sold" himself to imperialist culture. Hu Shih's son, who stayed in Peking after 1949, was urged to denounce his father. Neither he nor the Party gained much credit from this particular baseness.

Campaign for the Remolding of Intellectuals

The great Campaign for the Remolding of Intellectuals began at the end of the autumn. Chou En-lai launched it in November 1951 when he called a meeting in Peking of several thousand intellectuals to urge them to reform themselves and join with the regime and the masses. Thereafter, one cultural official after another deplored and condemned the weakness and inadequacy of artistic and literary production. Hu Ch'iao-mu said yet again that many workers in the field of literature and art had forgotten that culture is only the superstructure of the basis economic edifice and that the masses wanted to look toward the future, not the past. In much more violent terms, Chou Yang proclaimed that the time had come when the confusion reigning in artistic and literary work could no longer be tolerated.[9] Ho Ch'i-fang, one of the few writers spared by the Cultural Revolution, recalled the Party's literary history and drew conclusions for the present.[10]

During the first months of 1952, the remolding campaign, which was linked to the Three-Anti Campaign and accompanied by a check of university operations, was at its height. Thousands of intellectuals, including Communists, were asking to carry out their own reeducation, by means of a program of appropriate reading, the examination of their lives and ideas, self-criticism, and public confessions. The most important among them had to hand over to the press an apologetic account of their past bourgeois errors. The case of Dr. Chou P'ei-yüan, dean of Tsinghua University and a physicist of international standing, is one example among several thousand.

Later events were soon to prove that, in the eyes of the Communists, the problem of the transformation of the intellectuals remained as acute as ever. The Yü P'ing-po or *Dream of the Red Chamber* affair and the Hu Feng affair were to produce further persecutions, until new methods, apparently more flexible than the old but equally authoritarian, were put into practice at the beginning of 1956.

Education and the training of cadres

While engaged in remolding intellectuals who had belonged to the former regime in order to win them over to the building of socialism, the Party was also undertaking a vast reform of education in the widest possible sense of the word: the education of youth in school and out of it, and the education of adults. In this field, the new regime had a relatively difficult point of departure. For centuries, an educational system based on the classics alone had frozen all knowledge, discouraged all impulse toward research, and guided all minds to the imitation of a supposedly golden age of the past. Although the system had changed, the old culture still exercised a powerful attraction. The educational system had not been reformed until 1906, and the reform, left to the discretion of the provinces, had taken many years, owing to the lack of teachers and also to the lack of a language adapted to modern times. Not until the law of 1929 on higher education and that of 1932 on primary and secondary education did China have a coherent, modern educational system.

Primary education, attended by children of six or more years, consisted of six years containing one cycle of four years and one of two years. Secondary education also lasted six years, comprising two cycles of three years each. University and specialized higher educational courses varied in length from three to five years.

According to the Communists, record enrollment figures before 1949 were as follows:[11]

Higher education	155,000
Secondary education, technical and professional	383,000
Secondary education	1,496,000
Primary education	23,683,000

Many students in higher education began to move toward scientific and technical subjects, as shown by figures for graduates during the best years before 1949:[12]

Industry	4,792
Agriculture	2,064
Economics	2,969
Medicine and pharmacology	1,236

Physics and chemistry	1,701
Teachers' training	3,250
Arts	2,736
Total	18,748

Although the Sino-Japanese War had completely disorganized education throughout the nation, each political regime developed its own education and the numbers increased twofold or threefold between 1932 and 1949.

On October 1, 1951, a "decision relating to the reform of the educational system" raised the age for primary school attendance to seven, reducing the duration of studies to one cycle of five years; maintained two cycles of three years for secondary schools (six or seven years in the case of technical schools); and fixed the length of courses in higher education at five years (three years for courses in technical subjects). Education was organized as shown in Figure 5.1.

The total number of enrollments in schools was to rise noticeably during the first three years of the regime (see Table 5.1).[13]

Table 5.1
School enrollments 1949-1952

Year	Higher education	Secondary (technical & professional)	Secondary	Primary
	(thousands of students and pupils)			
1949	117	229	1,039	24,391
1950	137	257	1,305	28,924
1951	153	383	1,568	43,155
1952	191	636	2,490	51,100

NB: At the end of 1953, the single five-year cycle in primary schools was replaced by two cycles, one of four years and one of two years, making a total of six years.

In higher education, the proportion of graduates in scientific and technical subjects increased steadily to fulfill the needs of future five-year plans. These results were particularly obvious from 1952, as shown by Table 5.2 on the number of graduates in various fields.[14] The decline of arts subjects as compared with scientific and technical subjects had begun in 1943; by now it had become a reality and this state of affairs was to remain.[15]

At the advanced research level, the Academy of Sciences was created in November 1949 to replace the Academia Sinica, which had moved to Taiwan and was continuing its work there. Kuo Mo-jo was president of the

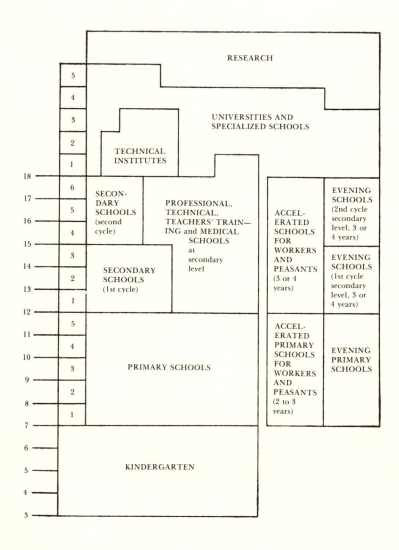

Figure 5.1   Organization of the educational system (1951)

Table 5.2
Graduates and their disciplines 1949-1952

Year	Industry	Agri-culture	Economics	Medicine and pharma-cology	Physics and chemis-try	Education	Arts
1949	4,752	1,718	3,137	1,314	1,584	1,890	2,521
1950	4,711	1,477	3,305	1,391	1,468	624	2,306
1951	4,416	1,538	3,638	2,366	1,488	1,206	2,169
1952	10,213	2,361	7,263	2,636	2,215	3,077	1,676

academy, which was divided into four sections: physics, chemistry, and mathematics; biology, geology, and geography; technical subjects; philosophy and social sciences. The tendency was toward applied research, and Soviet influence was noticeable. Progress was slow, however (see Chapter 13).

Working outside the education system in the strict sense of the term, the government began at an early stage to try to arouse interest in technical subjects, primarily by appealing to the younger generation. The effort was fully justified by the predominance of literary, artistic, and moral traditions in Chinese culture and by the mediocrity of the material environment in terms of modern standards. It was also preferable to turn public interest away from a political and cultural liberalism that was incompatible with Communism.

All possible forms of propaganda were used. Large numbers of popular technical magazines for all ages and all different levels appeared and flourished, in an effort to eliminate the little picture story books taken from traditional novels. Besides serving a political function, the press took on a strikingly educational function. Technical cadres, workers, and specialists constantly received praise; the smallest achievement or discovery was hailed as a remarkable advance that revealed the aptitude of the race for industrial invention. The newspapers of the past, which had been varied, full of all kinds of news, and often entertaining, now faithfully imitated the dreariness of Soviet publications. Not only did they print lengthy political texts but also technical articles and statistics; Marxist jargon competed with specialized vocabulary. Although the content, repetitiveness, uniformity, and austerity of the Chinese press make it seem tedious to the Western reader, it had a certain appeal for hundreds of millions of readers and listeners (papers are generally read aloud, with commentaries, for the illiterate). It often revealed the existence of a new or little-known world—that of science. The press was closely linked to great national ambitions, and the interest it aroused was comparable to that of science fiction in the West, particularly when it treated subjects that were about to become reality and would enable the country to equal the great powers in the fields of development and strength.

Because the Chinese have always loved titles of achievement, many technical diplomas were created, often corresponding to a very elementary standard of ability. But, at the same time, various measures were introduced to enable the cadre and the worker to enhance their professional value and prestige: evening classes, accelerated primary school courses reduced to two or three years, and secondary school courses compressed into three or four years. Campaigns for emulation and competition became more and more frequent. Rewards, in the form of titles—"work hero," "model worker"—decorations, and trips to Peking that included a meeting with Chairman Mao Tse-tung were generously distributed.

In brief, everything possible was done to glorify the role of workers and technicians in the new China. This economic consideration was backed by a lasting political consideration: that of confirming the primacy of the proletariat over the other classes, and enlarging it and improving its quality, since the Communist Party wanted to be its vanguard and its justification.

This educational policy, based on the training of numerous cadres and specialists of all kinds and on the upgrading of science and technology, was in tune with the needs of economic development, although the methods used were often rough and ready and politicization was carried to the extreme. The policy was continued successfully until the end of the first five-year plan in 1958. Later, when the leaders judged that they need no longer be dependent on the experience of more advanced countries, when politics had primacy over the rest and "red" took priority over "expert," there were drastic policy changes that were further accentuated by the failure of the Great Leap Forward and the disorders of the Cultural Revolution. For several years after 1966, educational policy was virtually sacrificed to the thought of Mao Tse-tung, which became the chief subject of all studies and the primary source of all knowledge.

Notes

[1] On the subject of the role of intellectuals in the development of the Communist movement, see Guillermaz, *A History of the Chinese Communist Party*, chapters 1, 18 (p. 227), and 27 (p. 368).

[2] Chief works: *Theories of Rural Reconstruction; Oriental and Western Culture and Their Philosophy.*

[3] See in particular the *Kuang-ming jih-pao* of October 5, 1951, and January 10, 1952.

[4] See the work by Chow Ching-wen, *Ten Years of Storm*, tr. Lai Ming (New York: Holt, 1959).

[5] At the Second Plenum of the Second National Committee of the People's Consultative Conference.

[6] See the *People's Daily* (June 7, 1951).

[7] See Guillermaz, *History of the Chinese Communist Party*, p. 53.

[8] Hu Shih was a prolific writer. Among other works, he produced *A History of Chinese Philosophy, A History of Literature in Spoken Language*, and *The Chinese Renaissance* (written in English). His articles and essays, in particular the article published by *Hsin Ch'ing-nien* (*New Youth*) on January 1, 1917, on the literary revolution, were to have the most influence on his times.

[9] Hu Ch'iao-mu and Chou Yang made their declarations on November 24 at a meeting of artistic and literary circles of Peking.

[10] Declaration of December 5, 1951.

[11] See *Ten Great Years*, p. 192.

[12] *Ibid.*, p. 196.

[13] *Ibid.*, p. 192. The statistics published between 1951 and 1953 are slightly different. The author has preferred to use those quoted in the above book, which are reliable until 1957.

[14] *Ibid.*, p. 196.

[15] In 1931, 74.5 percent of all students studied arts subjects, and 25.5 percent studied scientific and technical subjects. Owing to efforts on the part of the national government to promote its development, and thanks to the law of 1929, by 1934 the proportions were reversed: 30 percent and 70 percent. See *The China Yearbook*, 1936 (Shanghai: North-China *Daily News & Herald*, n.d.).

6 Foreign Relations: The Korean War

Foreign relations

The Soviet Union recognized the new regime twenty-four hours after it came into existence. The other socialist countries recognized it one by one during the same month. Strangely enough, the Albanians were the last to do so (November 23, 1949). In the free world, Great Britain recognized Peking as early as January 6, 1950, paving the way for several European states anxious to ensure good trade prospects (Holland, Denmark, Sweden, Switzerland, Finland) and several Asian states anxious to establish good neighborly relations (Burma, India, Indonesia, Pakistan).[1]

No Western influence could balance the current which, as the contemporary expression put it, inevitably led the new regime to "lean to one side." The Americans, and with them the countries of the Atlantic Pact, left their ambassadors in Nanking, waiting in vain for a gesture of good will that would justify, in domestic public opinion, a transfer of recognition to the new government after its formal inauguration. A climate of caution and mutual observation, which could be explained on the Communist side by the continuance of the civil war and by their lack of experience in foreign relations, was to develop into mistrust and indignation as a result of minor incidents. Peking's rough treatment of foreign firms, its refusal to apply certain customary international courtesies, the seizure of consular buildings, the persecution of numerous Protestant and Catholic missionaries, and U.S. sympathy for Marshal Chiang Kai-shek and his family, all prevented the establishment of diplomatic relations between Washington and Peking. On the other hand, realism on the part of Great Britain managed to safeguard Hong Kong and maintain old commercial ties. But London, like the Hague, had to be satisfied with an exchange of chargés d'affaires and "offices" instead of embassies.[2] As for France, its hesitation ended when China and North Vietnam established diplomatic relations (January 18, 1950). When the war in Algeria took the place of the war in Indochina and Peking recognized the Algerian provisional government in 1958, there was a further delay until January 27, 1964, when normal relations—normal insofar as Peking's unusual views on diplomatic practice allowed—were established between Paris and Peking. The importance and excellence of Sino-Soviet relations received striking confirmation on two occasions during 1950: once when Mao Tse-tung visited Moscow, followed by the signing of the treaty of February 14, 1950, and during the Korean War.

The treaty of February 14, 1950

On December 16, 1949, Mao Tse-tung, who had just left China for the first time in his life, arrived in Moscow accompanied by numerous experts who were later joined by still others. After visiting several regions of the Soviet Union, he returned to Moscow to sign the Treaty of Friendship, Alliance, and Mutual Assistance on February 14, 1950. With this instrument of diplomacy, Sino-Soviet relations were redefined in terms of a friendship of such strength that the preamble of the 1954 constitution deemed it necessary to stress its "indestructible" character.

From the Soviet point of view, it was essential both to preserve this vast new conquest for the revolution and to welcome into the socialist camp, both politically and militarily, an immense country whose position, size, population, and tradition destined it for complete independence. Instead of a "Chinese glacis," which would not doubt have satisfied Stalin, China had to be won and held by adequate international guarantees and by economic and financial aid carefully calculated and applied in areas useful to the Soviet economy. The Russians probably thought it would be unwise to remain the sole promoters of the revolution in Asia, especially as World War II had strengthened the American presence there considerably. Owing to a certain degree of solidarity between races, to the splendors of Chinese history and culture, to their thorough knowledge of the problems of the Asian continent, and to the numbers and influence of the Overseas Chinese everywhere, the Chinese could be useful as partners. The Russians were well enough informed to realize this and realistic enough to take advantage of it. The direction and the political and ideological frontiers of this cooperation were still to be determined. Future events were to give ample proof of the difficulties involved.

For their part, the Chinese Communists had to consolidate their regime in relation to the world outside, and above all to ensure their own safety with regard to the United States and Japan, seizing every chance to exclude the former from Korea and Southeast Asia. They also wanted, insofar as possible, to occupy an important position within the socialist camp, taking partial control at least of its Asiatic policy, and even of its policy toward underdeveloped countries in general. The image of the "twin stars" dates from this period.

Since 1917, the Chinese had also had occasion to observe that the replacement of the Tsarist regime by the Soviet regime had done little to lessen Russian pressure on their northern and western frontiers. Even if they had forgotten this, a number of events would have reminded them of it: the arrangements of Yalta (February 11, 1945), later confirmed by the Sino-Soviet Treaty of August 14, 1945 (the reoccupation of Port Arthur and Dairen by the Russians under the pretense of revenging their 1904 humiliation by the Japanese, the placing of the Chinese Eastern Railway under joint administration, and the final separation of Outer Mongolia from China); the plundering of Manchuria; and the maneuverings of the Russian ambassador in Nanking, General N. V. Roschin, to obtain an agreement on Sinkiang in 1948 during the death throes of the Nationalist government. An entente with Moscow was essential for ideological reasons, in view of the general international situation, and also for reasons of good neighborly relations. Although the time had not come to raise questions about the frontiers inherited from the past, it was time to straighten out existing relations and to prepare for the recovery of what had been lost at Yalta.

Manchuria and Sinkiang created the most delicate problems of all. In 1949, Manchuria contained half of China's total resources in energy and industry. Part of it thrust east of Lake Baikal into the Soviet Far Eastern Region, for which it might constitute a tempting and precious complement to a poor, sometimes difficult area. A satisfactory arrangement with the Russians might make it possible to increase the industrial strength of a region that was already advanced enough to serve as the nucleus of and model for the economic development of the whole country. Should tension mount between the two countries, there was the risk that a new Manchukuo might be created, though Communist this time. The Kao Kang affair at the end of 1953 was to show that the Chinese leaders paid special attention to the region to make sure that nobody among them gained too much influence there (see Chapter 9).

In Sinkiang, Sino-Soviet relations had long been complicated by questions of ethnic attraction: the Kazakhs, Kirghiz, and Tadjiks on the Chinese side of the border were less numerous than those on the Soviet side. Soviet influence in Sinkiang had grown temporarily during the Sino-Japanese War. The old Sino-Russian conflict over the valley of the Ili had never been resolved satisfactorily. The Tadjik frontier had still to be marked out in the difficult region of Pamir.

An analysis of Sino-Soviet relations in 1950 should also take into account the anxiousness of Mao Tse-tung to be recognized by the Kremlin and Stalin as head of state, head of the Party, and, above all, as a revolutionary theorist whose doctrine and experience had enriched Marxism-Leninism. An explicit acknowledgment of the value of the Chinese revolution for underdeveloped countries would have enhanced the historical stature of Mao Tse-tung and served Chinese ambitions. At Tsunyi in January 1935, Mao Tse-tung took over power within the Party in opposition to the faction of the "Twenty-eight Bolsheviks," who had the support of the Comintern. Circumstances (particularly the Sino-Japanese War and then World War II) had forced the Comintern to accept a fait accompli. The visit of Mao Tse-tung to Moscow was to efface past doubts and the disdain Stalin was suspected of harboring toward the head of the Chinese Communist Party.

In 1950, the Soviet Union offered all authentic Chinese Communists the sentimental attraction of an ideological capital and also, in its gigantic industrial combines and powerful industrial cities, a model of economic success and, since the victory of 1945, of military success as well. In 1949, Liu Shao-ch'i, addressing an audience made up of representatives of the two peoples, said:

> If we attach great importance and give particular appreciation to the friendship and cooperation between the Chinese and Soviet peoples, this is because the road travelled by the Soviet people is exactly that which the Chinese people must follow. The experience of the Soviet people in the construction of its country is one that deserves our attention.

He added confidently, and at the same time with an eye to the future:

> The Soviet people has been educated and trained by the great Lenin and by Stalin. It feels the same international love for the Chinese people

as for all other peoples. It is an unconditional love, and its help asks for no reward.[3]

The prestige of Soviet science, commonly portrayed by the daring image of a fertilizing wave which was to submerge China to its utmost advantage, was to oppose that of American science, which was well known to the intellectuals of the old society and obvious to the whole population once the bombs at Hiroshima and Nagasaki had abruptly ended the war with Japan.

The Chinese Communists looked on the Russia of 1950 as the China of the following generation; Sino-Soviet relations as a whole should perhaps be observed from this angle until 1957, at the end of the first five-year plan, which coincided roughly with Mao Tse-tung's second visit to Moscow.

The agreements signed on February 14, 1950, by Chou En-lai and Andrei Vishinsky consisted of three different documents: a Treaty of Friendship, Alliance, and Mutual Assistance; an agreement concerning the Chinese Changchun railway and the ports of Dairen and Port Arthur; and an agreement on financial aid. On March 27, they were completed by three further agreements on economic cooperation. Basically, the Treaty of Friendship, Alliance, and Mutual Assistance, valid for thirty years, promised mutual military aid if either party were attacked by Japan or any nation allied to Japan. Reciprocal consultations were to be held on all international problems of common interest. The second document stipulated that the Changchun railway should be returned to China once a peace treaty had been concluded with Japan and, at the latest, by the end of 1952. Soviet troops were to be withdrawn from Port Arthur within the same interval. The question of returning the port installations of Dairen was to be settled after the peace treaty with Japan. In the third document, the Soviet Union granted China a loan of $300 million,[4] repayable in ten years (1954 to 1963) at an interest of 1 percent. The agreements of March 27 created two mixed companies in Sinkiang for ten years (oil and nonferrous metals) and organized a Sino-Soviet civil aviation company for ten years, to run the Peking-Chita, Peking-Irkutsk, and Peking-Alma Ata lines.

Although the Treaty of Friendship, Alliance, and Mutual Assistance ensured China's military security as regards other countries and guaranteed China's early recovery of full sovereignty over Manchuria, the greater strength of the Soviet Union gave it permanent control over a large area of Chinese foreign policy; this was to be obvious during the Taiwan Strait crisis in 1958.

Economic cooperation was modest in relation to the size of the powers involved. It was, even so, essential to the Chinese, on account of their backwardness in scientific and technical matters; the Russians found it profitable insofar as it was carefully balanced by deliveries of commercial goods, brought in an interest of 1 percent, and also affected the neighboring region of Sinkiang.

The Korean War, which was to break out a few months later, altered the nature of Sino-Soviet economic cooperation from the outset because priority had to be given to military aspects. The return of the Changchun railway was not affected, but Soviet troops remained at Port Arthur for another year (agreement of September 15, 1952). Not until 1953—the year of Stalin's death, the end of the Korean War, and the launching of the first five-year plan—did Sino-Soviet economic relations take on a completely new dimension. Political relations also went through a period of harmony, until they began to sour in the aftermath of the Twentieth Congress of the Soviet Communist Party (February 14-15, 1956).

Because the Chinese leaders were anxious to create an atmosphere in which Sino-Soviet cooperation would prosper, a major propaganda campaign was launched within the Party and in the public at large aimed at fostering a better knowledge of the Soviet Union. On October 5, 1949, a Sino-Soviet Friendship Association was created in Peking, under the chairmanship of Liu Shao-ch'i. In 1952, it consisted of 1,260 principal and 44,778 secondary organizations and had 18 million members (more than the total membership of the Chinese Communist Party). Newspapers, periodicals, brochures, films, and books issued by the association were given wide circulation throughout Chinese society. The teaching of Russian was expanded and, when scientific, technical, and cultural cooperation began to develop in accordance with the first five-year plan, it seemed likely that China would soon adopt the Russian model, totally and permanently, in every sphere of modern life. This was a temporary and probably carefully calculated phenomenon, as future events made clear. "Mao Tse-tung certainly did not want to make China into an imitation of Russia; he only sent his country to school in Moscow so that at the end of its education it could become independent and master of its own house," as one analyst of Sino-Soviet relations puts it.[5] It would be hard to express it better.

The Chinese intervention in Korea[6]

For two thousand years, Korea had often been either partially or wholly the vassal of China and also looked to China as a source of cultural inspiration;

at the end of the nineteenth century, it became the stake in a three-sided struggle involving China, Japan, and Russia, the pretext for the Sino-Japanese War of 1894-1895 and, to a lesser extent, the pretext for the Russo-Japanese War of 1904-1905. The Treaty of Shimonoseki obliged China to acknowledge the independence of Korea (April 17, 1895); the Treaty of Portsmouth (September 5, 1905) obliged the Russians to acknowledge the existence of special Japanese rights in Korea. On November 15, 1905, Korea became a Japanese protectorate; on August 23, 1910, it was annexed by Japan. The Cairo Conference (December 1, 1943) made provisions for Korea to regain its liberty and independence, but the sudden ending of the war and Korea's strategic position led the Russians and the Americans to divide the country militarily at the 38th parallel, which in turn soon resulted in the establishment of opposing regimes in Seoul and Pyongyang.

The passing of the Chinese continent into Communist control, the departure of U.S. forces from South Korean territory, the weakness of the South Korean army, and several ill-considered American declarations allowed the North Koreans, Russians, and Chinese to think that Washington would not react strongly to a purely Korean show of force.[7] Perhaps those who initiated the conflict had in mind the precedent of the Japanese occupation of Manchuria in 1931, when the only international response had been the decision of the League of Nations to send the Lytton Commission. This false calculation did not take into account either the world political and military balance of power—which prevented the United States from giving in to direct pressure in an area extending from Europe to Asia—or the security of the Japanese archipelago.

The North Korean invasion of June 25, 1950, first led to the occupation of Seoul after only a few days; this was countered partly by the creation, in July, of an American bridgehead in the Pusan area, and partly by a powerful landing at Inchon (September 15-16) on the principal North Korean lines of communication. The armies of General Kim Chaek were thrown into disorder; they had to cross the 38th parallel again at the end of September, forced in their turn to give up almost all their territory. By the beginning of the autumn of 1950, the South Korean forces and the United Nations forces (almost entirely composed of Americans) under General MacArthur, were advancing rapidly toward the Chinese frontier, reaching it on the Yalu in the Chosan region.[8]

The defeat of North Korea caught the Chinese unprepared. At the beginning of the spring of 1950, they had made elaborate preparations for taking the Choushan archipelago, which the Nationalists evacuated of

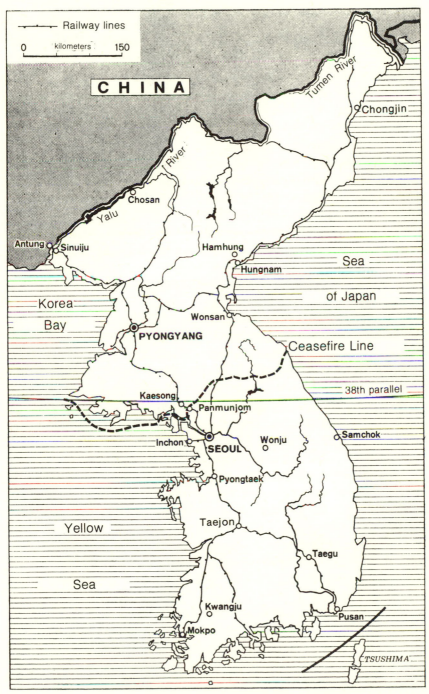

Map 3   Theater of operations in Korea

their own accord in May, and they also intended to seize the last islands along the coast—Kinmen, Matsu, and a few others. They had also begun to demobilize part of their armies, whose numbers were increased by the surrender of enemy troops. Although these arrangements were not enough to prevent them from intervening, they suggest that the intervention was not premeditated and that it was not considered until the middle of September.

The question was clearly one of great importance. First of all, the Chinese had reason to fear the spread of the war to their country; the destruction of their industrial potential in Manchuria, North China, and East China; coastal attacks from Taiwan; and perhaps a new outbreak of civil war, with direct support from American power. The least they could expect was that the newly begun restoration of their economy was likely to be slowed down, crippled, or even frustrated altogether. Much later, red guard newspapers were to accuse Ch'en Yün, the cautious economist, and P'eng Teh-huai, a soldier keenly aware of the technical cost of war, of being hostile to intervention.

On the other hand, if the Chinese did not intervene, they would allow the creation of a permanent danger—in the form of combined Japanese and American interests—on the frontiers of the Northeast. Failure to intervene might strengthen the recent military cooperation between Taiwan and the United States, which had followed President Truman's decision on June 27 to extend American military protection to the island under the guise of imposing neutrality. It would also clearly reveal the weakness of the new regime to the rest of the world. Lastly, in the likely event of a negotiated settlement of the question, the absence of the Chinese would allow a lasting expansion of Soviet influence, because the Russians would be the only people able to lead negotiations in that part of Asia. It is conceivable that the existence of strong Korean minorities in Manchuria (they numbered more than 1 million at that time), the close ties linking some Korean Communist leaders with the Chinese Communist Party since the days of Yenan, and the participation of Korean units in the Third Civil War in China may have served as moral and psychological arguments for intervention.

In fact, the decision lay more with the Soviet government than with the Chinese government, and apparently no alternative existed: the Chinese would intervene in return for Moscow's promise of diplomatic and military help should the war extend beyond Korea. It was hardly to be expected that the Russians could allow the disappearance of the North Korean regime—a regime which they had created and allowed to carry out the adventure of June 25—without jeopardizing the prestige and power of the entire Communist bloc. Yet, at the same time, a clash between the Soviet Union and the United States might lead to the localized use of nuclear weapons, possibly initiated by the Americans, who were less well placed than their adversaries for conventional warfare. Lastly, even discounting such fearsome possibilities, any Soviet military action in Korea would have to be fought against the U.N. forces, with inevitable consequences for the future of the organization, whereas the interests of Soviet world policy lay in preserving the United Nations.[9] In the last analysis, the Chinese solution was without doubt the most suitable. It tallied exactly with the idea underlying Stalin's policy since 1945: that China should stand between the zones dominated or influenced by the Soviet Union and the United States. Depending on the circumstances, it would allow either for a second attempt to carry out the unsuccessful coup of June 25, 1950, or for a gradual movement toward diplomatic negotiations, without endangering the integrity of the United Nations, of which China was not a member. It may be that the Chinese, once their security was assured, were not indifferent to the advantages of an operation that corresponded with their history since the Han dynasty. It fell in logically with anti-American propaganda, which had been particularly violent since 1947 and had recently been nourished by the guarantee of survival Washington had given to the regime of Chiang Kai-shek.

Because of the ties of ideology, the agreement of February 14, and great hopes of economic cooperation, China would have found it hard in the climate of 1950 to avoid suggestions or pressure from Moscow. This was the general opinion of the few foreign observers who were there in 1950. Nevertheless, as one study of the question points out, no important document has come to light to confirm or invalidate this hypothesis or any other.[10] During the Hundred Flowers movement, Marshal Lung Yün, a native of Yunnan, protested against the repayment of Russian military aid for the Korean campaign, an assertion lending itself to contrary interpretations. Nothing further came to light on this subject during the Cultural Revolution, which generally revealed little as regards foreign policy. The great Sino-Soviet controversies of the 1960s yielded countless secrets but kept this one intact.[11]

In any case, the Chinese did their utmost, before taking part in the war, to make the United States and the United Nations aware of their preference for an immediate return to the situation as it was before June 25. The declaration made by Chou En-lai on September 28, the communication to the Indian ambassador on October 2, and the declaration made by the

Chinese spokesman on October 10 all bear this out. Similarly, and to avoid involving their country in any legal consequence arising from their intervention, the Chinese were careful to create the fiction of an army of "volunteers" wearing none of the usual insignia. Thus, it was not China but this "volunteer" force that was fighting against the forces of the United Nations—also a deceptive term for essentially American troops.

On October 16, 1950, the first Chinese units crossed the Yalu by night and began a deployment which their adversaries had great difficulty in discovering. They met the South Koreans on October 26 and the Americans on November 2. Because of the great number of Chinese troops, who were sent in against a broken front and succeeded in encircling several poorly equipped South Korean units, the Chinese were able to gain the initiative and keep it for several months. Commanded by Marshal P'eng Teh-huai, they progressed along three main axes, forcing the Eighth Army under General Walker to retreat toward Pyongyang on November 27, while the right wing of the allied forces retreated to the ports of Hungnam and Wonsan on the east coast. Another Communist attack on January 1 forced the U.N. front to pull back south of Seoul by mid-January to a line running through Pyongtaek, Wonju, and Samchok. General Ridgway, who succeeded General Walker, undertook a series of methodical operations of limited scope with solid support from the air, enabling Seoul to be taken once more (March 14) while the front moved northward again to a line about 250 kilométers long on the 38th parallel. In April and May, the Chinese exhausted themselves in vain and costly attacks on an enemy who was well entrenched and had far better equipment; they eventually realized that their efforts were useless. On June 23, 1951, Jacob Malik, the Soviet delegate to the United Nations, called for armistice negotiations, which began on July 10 at Kaesong and, after several interruptions, resumed on October 25, 1951, at Panmunjom. Operations in Korea went on until the armistice was signed on July 27, 1953, but the mobile war was over and the last Chinese attacks of the summer of 1953 (June 14 and July 13) were inspired by political motives (see Chapter 16).

The domestic and foreign repercussions of the Korean War were of great importance to China, though it is not yet possible to say whether they were beneficial, particularly in the fields of economic development and international politics. Loss of life was enormous. If American sources are to be believed, there were about 900,000 killed, wounded, or missing. Deaths due to epidemics (plague and typhus) were also very numerous, and the Chinese had to disguise the deficiencies of their rudimentary health service by accusing the U.N. forces of practicing bacteriological warfare, a charge that was immediately taken up and enlarged upon by international Communist propaganda (March 1952). For a country whose annual increase in population exceeds 12 million, however, and whose manpower resources are almost inexhaustible, exceeding the demand for labor, these figures were low. The loss of many old Party cadres who had been spared by the civil wars was probably felt most keenly of all.[12]

The Chinese also had to take young cadres with a technical education away from jobs linked with production and have them service the modern weapons gradually supplied by the Russians: armored divisions, artillery, and aviation.[13] It is more or less certain that the Russians had to be paid for all or part of this equipment, though the price and conditions of payment are not known. The absence of basic information makes it hard to estimate with any degree of accuracy the cost of arming, equipping, maintaining, and transporting an expeditionary force of 700,000 or 800,000 men.[14] It should be mentioned that, on the Chinese side, the Korean war was based on infantry and mortars. The infantryman, sober and rustic in his habits, was not too costly. The arms and ammunition used by small units (including regiments) were generally of American or Japanese origin, having been captured from the Nanking Central Government, and were in plentiful supply. In the last analysis, it seems likely that the postponement of industrial development was the most damaging effect of the war on China's economy and finances. Only after the armistice of July 27, 1953, did Chinese leaders begin to mention the first five-year plan. It should be noted that the death of Stalin had also affected Sino-Russian relations, making them more favorable for Peking.

Politically speaking, the Korean War was to serve the new regime and help establish it more firmly. Patriotism, national solidarity, and vigilance in the face of possible enemies were the focus of great mass campaigns, the most important of which were the "Aid Korea! Resist America!" Campaign, launched in November 1950, the Campaign for the Elimination of Counterrevolutionaries, and the Three- and Five-Anti campaigns (see Chapter 2). With the war in Korea, loyalty to the Party and national instinct were intermingled. Lukewarm sentiments toward the former became nascent treachery toward the latter. The dispossessed classes made a point of showing their enthusiasm and offering all the financial support that they could still command in the form of gifts.

To a varying degree, all Chinese were aware of the astonishing demonstration that their country had just given to the outside world. China had crossed its frontiers for the first time since the nineteenth century and the Unequal Treaties. It had held in check the greatest military power in the world, and, thanks to the fiction maintained by the United Nations, the world as a whole. After a century of powerlessness and humiliation, it was a brilliant revenge. The West had to revise its judgments on the fighting value of the Chinese soldier and on the determination and energy of the regime. Chinese revolutionary propaganda in the under-developed countries was reinforced, particularly because the Chinese held up their success as an example:

> It is a lesson whose international meaning is of supreme importance. It proves beyond all doubt that the time when a Western aggressor could occupy a country by placing a few guns along the shore—and that time lasted for several countries—has gone for ever. . . . It proves that a nation, once aroused, which dares to rise and fight for its glory, its independence, and the safety of the fatherland, is invincible.[15]

In this respect at least, China could justifiably claim to be called new.

Now that some perspective has been gained on the affair, however, it sometimes seems that it had the worst possible consequences for China. The attack of June 27, which provoked the Americans to react on the Korean question and in Taiwan, interrupted a process of evolution which would almost inevitably have led to a rapid political and military conquest of Taiwan, to the disappearance of the Nationalist regime, to the establishment of normal diplomatic relations with other countries, and to the admission of China to the United Nations. Several questions directly affecting China's national interest would have been settled in this way, and the aggressiveness of China, being confined to theoretical problems or problems that were further away geographically, would have had less to feed on, and less justification.

The Korean War, however, facilitated and hastened the creation of an international security system in the Western Pacific, beginning with the conclusion of a peace treaty and a security pact between the United States and Japan (September 8, 1951), postponed the entry of China into the United Nations until 1971, maintained China's old attitudes of isolation and mistrust, and encouraged its doctrinal intransigence. Insofar as China had sooner or later to accept the modern doctrine of the need for international cooperation, the Korean War appears as an unfortunate mistake in itself and for the world community as a whole.

Notes

[1] Recognition by Yugoslavia was ignored, and recognition by Israel was not followed up. A distinction should be drawn here between recognition and the exchanging of diplomatic missions.

[2] Until March 13, 1972, the British mission in Peking was known as the "Office of the British Chargé d'Affaires." The two countries then decided to raise the status of their chargés d'affaires to that of ambassadors, thus putting their relations on a regular footing.

[3] Speech delivered to the Sino-Soviet Friendship Association.

[4] At the rate of $35 per ounce of pure gold.

[5] François Feijtö, *Chine-URSS, la fin d'une hégémonie (1950-1957)* (Paris: Plon, 1964).

[6] See Map 3.

[7] In particular the declaration made by Secretary of State Dean Acheson, on January 12, 1950.

[8] On the military aspects of the Korean War, see Robert Leckie, *Conflict: The History of the Korean War* (New York: Putnam, 1962), with its large bibliography.

[9] The Soviet Union withdrew from the Security Council in 1950, before the North Korean aggression. They did not return until August 1 of the same year.

[10] Allen S. Whiting, *China Crosses the Yalu* (New York: Macmillan, 1960).

[11] According to Khrushchev's memoirs (Paris: Laffont, 1971), p. 349-53, Mao Tse-tung, when consulted by Stalin on the advisability of the invasion of South Korea by North Korea, had been in favor of it, because he thought it unlikely that the Americans would reply with a military reaction. Chou En-lai is said to have gone to Sotchi later to see Stalin to discuss the possibility of a Chinese intervention, which was at first considered useless and then decided upon, after some hesitation.

[12] Mao Tse-tung was directly affected by the loss of his eldest son, Mao An-ying, killed in a bombing raid in November 1950.

[13] The development of Chinese national defense in general, including the effects of the Korean War on the appearance and doctrines of the People's Liberation Army, is dealt with in Chapter 14.

[14] See John Gittings, *The Role of the Chinese Army* (London: Oxford University Press, 1967), p. 75.

[15] P'eng Teh-huai, "Report to the twenty-fourth session of the Central Government Council" (September 12, 1953).

Part 2

The First Five-Year Plan
1953 – 1957

But the Communist Party of the Soviet Union emerged victorious
and, under the leadership of Lenin and Stalin, it learned not
only how to make the revolution but also how to carry on construction. It has built a great and splendid socialist state.
The Communist Party of the Soviet Union is our best teacher
and we must learn from it.

> *Mao Tse-tung,* "On the People's Democratic Dictatorship"

Lenin often said, "There is only one real, unique basis on which
a socialist society may be established. It is large-scale
industry."

> *Li Fu-ch'un,* Report on the first five-year plan to the
> Second Session of the First National People's Congress

Can we say that our Party already has economic theorists worthy
of the name? Certainly not.

> *Mao Tse-tung,* "Rectify the Party's Style of Work"

7 The Targets of the First Five-Year Plan and Soviet Economic Aid

Although the period from 1953 to 1957 took its name from the first five-year plan, one of the main features of these years was also a far-reaching transformation of social structures: collective farming replaced farming on a family scale and private ownership in trade and industry disappeared; at the same time, political institutions were strengthened by the 1954 Constitution, the Party defined itself anew at the Eighth Congress in 1956, and limited—though ultimately ill-fated—overtures were made to the intellectuals during the Hundred Flowers period. Abroad, both at Geneva in 1954 and at Bandung in 1955, the regime gave proof of moderation and experience and made its entry on the international scene. Generally speaking, it chose to build up China first of all and, possibly going against some currents of opinion in this respect, to put this imperative above that of the world revolution. When praising Stalin, seen as the builder of the Soviet Union, Ch'en Yun confirmed this choice.[1]

Seen in perspective, and compared with the disturbances that were to follow, the years from 1953 to 1957 appear ordered and productive, even though mistakes in planning and the speed of the changes created tension and mortgaged the future. Economic success and political wisdom gave China a prestige abroad which stretched far beyond the frontiers of the Third World. The style of the regime was beginning to resemble the Soviet model that emerged from the Twentieth Congress. This evolution, and the cost and limitations of Russian aid, prepared the way for a return to revolutionary self-determination, inspired and led by Mao Tse-tung. The first five-year plan was in fact to be the last. Thereafter, the Chinese revolution followed its own course; its meanderings were to baffle observers utterly, as indeed they still do.

The targets of the plan

The final version of the first five-year plan was not decided on until February 1955, two years after it had begun; its aim was to double industrial production between 1953 and 1957.[2] The reasons for this delay, according to Li Fu-ch'un, chairman of the State Planning Commission, were the lack of statistical information, an incomplete estimation of resources, the existence of several forms of economy, and, at a more general level, the inadequate experience of those in charge. Industrial production was supposed to increase by 98.3 percent, entailing an average annual increase of 14.7 percent as opposed to an increase of 23.3 percent in agriculture, with an average annual increase of 4.3 percent.[3] Priority was to be given to the construction of basic industry (despite some doubts about this, as Li Fu-ch'un said), which alone would be able to ensure the improvement of agriculture. The distribution of investment in the construction process is revealing: 58.2 percent in industry, 19.2 percent in transport and telecommunications, and only 7.6 percent in agriculture.

The total expenditure was considerable for a poor country. It amounted to 76,640 million yuan, or about $32,500 million for five years (at a rate of 2.35 yuan to the dollar), or 26,000 tons of gold. Only 55.8 percent of this total, about 42,740 million yuan, was devoted to basic construction, i.e., the creation and development of productive enterprises; the rest represented normal expenditure for an annual budget.

The first plan was financed by reinvesting an extremely high proportion of the national income: 22 percent, as Li Fu-ch'un said in June 1956. Domestic sources included normal taxation, the compulsory sale of part of the harvest to the state, bonds—issued in 1954—for the development of the national economy (about 6,000 million yuan, or $2,500 million, at a rate of interest of 4 percent), confiscations during the great campaigns, and profits from state-owned enterprises. Foreign sources were mainly Soviet loans and foreign currency sent by Overseas Chinese.

In practice, all enterprises to be developed or created during this plan and the following one were classified as "projects," either "above norm" projects (1,600 altogether, 694 of which were industrial) or "below norm" projects (6,000 altogether, 2,300 of which were industrial). "Norm" referred to an investment figure, which varied according to the type of enterprise.[4]

The budget allocation of 42,740 yuan for capital construction is shown in Table 7.1.

Table 7.1
Budget for capital construction in the first five-year plan

Sector	Millions of yuan	% of total
Industry	24,850	58.2
Agriculture, water, and forestry	3,260	7.6
Transport and telecommunications	8,210	19.2
Trade, banks, and deposits	1,280	3.0
Culture, education, and public health	3,080	7.2
Work carried out by town councils	1,600	3.7
Miscellaneous	460	1.1

It was assumed from the start that the first plan would be followed by a second one (1958-1962), and then by a third, so that by the end of 1967 the construction of China's basic industry would be completed, giving full independence in all scientific, technical, and technological fields.[5]

Table 7.2
Industry

Type	Unit	1952 Result	1957 Target	1957 Result
Coal	Millions of tons	63.5	113	
Steel	Millions of tons	1.4	4.1	5.24
Oil	Millions of tons	0.4	2.0	
Electricity	Millions of kWh	7,260	15,900	
Chemical fertilizer	Millions of tons	0.194	0.578	
Concrete	Millions of tons	2.9	6.0	
Aluminum (ingots)	Millions of tons	0	0.020	
Trucks	Units	0	4,000	
Cotton yarn	Millions of tons	0.7	0.9	
Cotton fabric	Millions of meters	3,829	5,583	

Tables 7.2, 7.3, 7.4, and 7.5 give the results for 1952, the year that marked the end of the period of economic rehabilitation, and the targets for the 1957 plan, as published in July 1955 after several adjustments.

Table 7.3
Agriculture

Type	Unit	1952 Result	1957 Target	1957 Result
Cereals	Millions of tons	154.4	181.59	185
Soybeans	Millions of tons	9.52	11.22	
Cotton	Millions of tons	1.3	1.64	
Cattle	Millions of head	56.6	73.6	
Horses, mules, and donkeys	Millions of head	6.1	8.3	
Sheep	Millions of head	61.8	113.0	
Pigs	Millions of head	89.8	138.3	

Table 7.4
Transport

Type	Targets for 1957	1957 Result
Railways	121 million ton/km	twice 1952 figure
	32 million passenger/km	59.5% more than 1952
Inland waterways	15,300 million ton/km	
	3,400 million passenger/km	
Coastal traffic	5,750 million ton/sea mile	
	240 million passenger/sea mile	
Road transport	3,200 million ton/km	
	5,700 million passenger/km	
Air transport	8,050,000 million ton/km	

Table 7.5
Trade and employment

Retail sales	1957 target	49,800 million yuan	80% more than 1952

Employment: a total of 4.2 million new jobs to be
created in state enterprises

From a geographical point of view, Northeast and East China remained privileged areas of industrial development. The second plan would then create new bases further inland, particularly in the Northwest (Paotow, Lanchow, Sian, Loyang) and Central China (Wuhan), with the aim of introducing more regions to modern life and meeting the needs of national defense more fully.

Those responsible for the first plan, particularly Li Fu-ch'un, seem to have come up against several criticisms, which they did their best to parry: overambitious targets, too much emphasis on and too many facilities granted to producer goods as compared with consumer goods (88.8 percent as opposed to 11.2 percent[6]), inadequate capital, China's backwardness in the technical field, and so on. The future was to bear out the truth of these criticisms, but in defense of the chairman of the Planning Commission may it be said that, whereas agriculture did not seem ready to absorb extensive investment, light industry lacked modern equipment which heavy industry was not able immediately to supply.[7] The remaining solutions would have relied on the self-interest of peasants and craftsmen, maintaining the situation resulting from the 1950 land law, in which the family's cultivation of its own land was the general rule. These solutions were rejected categorically on doctrinal grounds: "Socialism cannot be built up on the basis of a small peasant economy," as Li Fu-ch'un said, "It can only be built up on the basis of large collective industrial or agricultural undertakings."[8]

Li Fu-ch'un seems to have acknowledged, as did most of the Party at the time, that the disappearance of the small peasant economy would be a gradual process lasting for some time. He also seems to have believed that an increase of 23.3 percent in agricultural output (17.6 percent of which was foodstuffs) and 25.4 percent in raw cotton was already a high target.

The enlargement of the area under cultivation through the creation of state farms or through colonizatin by the peasants—2,587,000 hectares could be put into use during the plan—was to be added to the development of rural hydraulic engineering, soil transformation and the improvement of equipment and seed already forming part of the less original and widespread methods practiced by Chinese peasants to increase agricultural output. This output had more or less reached its highest possible level, given existing techniques, as the future was to show. The importance of chemical fertilizers appears to have been completely ignored.

Soviet aid

The first five-year plan was clearly inspired by Soviet precedents, as far as the distribution of effort and methods of construction and management were concerned. It was carried out with the financial and technical cooperation of the Soviet Union in the case of specific "large projects": factories, laboratories, roads, railways, canals, and the like. Although it is fairly easy to determine the general scope of the aid and the main ways in which it was applied, it is hard to estimate its financial value, and still more difficult to judge whether the advice given by the Russians, who were remote from Chinese realities, may not have contributed to the economic troubles and failures following the first plan, in spite of apparent initial success.

If arrangements concerning the delivery of military equipment, trade agreements in the strict sense of the term, and various conventions dealing with specific or local questions are ignored, and only long-term loans and Soviet participation in China's basic construction are taken into consideration, the aid from Moscow was as follows:

1. The granting of long-term credit: $300 million on February 14, 1950; 520 million rubles (equivalent to $130 million) on October 12, 1954.
2. Participation in the building of 258 "large projects":
   (a) 141 in May 1953 (50 old projects and 91 new);
   (b) 15 on October 12, 1954 (estimated at 400 million rubles);
   (c) 55 on April 7, 1956 (estimated at 2,500 million rubles);
   (d) 47 on August 8, 1958 (these 47 projects were probably not fully completed, owing to lack of time).
3. As a reminder, an agreement signed on February 7, 1959, concerning 78 projects valued at 5,000 million rubles, to be finished within eight years, which the withdrawal of Soviet advisers in the summer of 1960 left uncompleted.

The credits and the deliveries of equipment for the Soviet "projects" were repaid through the channels of trade exchanges (agricultural products, rare minerals); the conditions surrounding the price, transport costs, and exchange rates (the latter varied according to the type of operation) are not well enough known to enable specialists in economics and foreign trade to reach identical and definite conclusions as to the financial value of Soviet aid.[9] The amount assigned to military supplies is equally uncertain: some specialists estimate it as more than half the total help granted.

Figures quoted by both sides are useful because they throw some light on the subject, but they do not provide a complete answer. Li Hsien-nien, minister of finance, said in July 1957 that Soviet aid (long-term credit, industrial equipment, and sale of military supplies should all be included here) totalled 5,294 million yuan ($2,100 million), 2,174 million yuan of which (about $820 million) had already been used before 1953. Khrushchev, addressing the Twentieth Congress of the Communist Party of the Soviet Union in February 1956, gave the value of the Soviet contribution as 5,600 million rubles, to which should be added a further 2,500 million rubles for the fifty-five projects dating from April 7, 1956, if the comparison is to be exact. This gives a total figure of 8,100 million rubles, equivalent to $2,025 million at the rate of 4 rubles to the dollar. The Soviet periodical *Kommunist*, No. 12 (August 1968), states that socialist countries supplied China with equipment worth 2,500 million rubles and contributed to the carrying out of 350 large projects. Military aid does not seem to be included in this calculation. These figures are worth bearing in mind insofar as they give an indication of the size of the sum involved.

Above and beyond its monetary value, Soviet aid was important to China because it affected the most modern sectors of the country's economy—steel, oil, the electrical and machine industries, engine building, and electronics. Most of these sectors did not exist in 1949 and the Russians created them from scratch, sometimes starting with geological prospecting. Russian advisers—teachers, engineers and technicians—sometimes numbered more than 10,000 and were to be found in all areas of construction and institutions for technical education. Russian factories took in thousands of trainees, and Russian universities took in thousands of students. In 1958, for example, there were 7,000 Russian experts in China, and 7,000 Chinese students and 6,200 Chinese trainees in the Soviet Union, not to mention a smaller number of experts from Eastern European countries (particularly Rumanian specialists in the oil industry).

Several agreements for scientific and technical cooperation, accompanied by deliveries of laboratory equipment,[10] gave the Chinese practical and theoretical training, which they seriously lacked, in spite of the high quality of a few intellectuals with Western education. The Russians consequently made an enormous contribution to the training of senior and middle-grade technical cadres, a category that is usually a source of great difficulty in underdeveloped countries.

From an economic if not from a political point of view, Sino-Soviet cooperation was in some respects inconvenient for the Soviet Union. Although it gave the Russians close knowledge and indirect control of part of the Chinese economy and resources, it deprived them of industrial products that they themselves needed, whereas, apart from a few rare minerals, all they received in exchange were agricultural products of secondary importance, with the possible exception of tea.

For the Chinese, Sino-Soviet economic relations also had drawbacks. The cost of Soviet aid proved too high in relation to the rate of capital accumulation and available exports, and above all, in relation to Chinese industrial ambitions. The practice of concentrating heavy industry in combines or huge factories, like the ones at Loyang (tractors) or Changchun (trucks), seemed too large in scale, for medium-sized enterprises were more suited to administrative and technical conditions in China, and some material was too modern for the resources of the time in terms of qualified personnel. These conclusions made the Chinese reduce their imports as far as possible, taking their economic destiny into their own hands and "relying on their own efforts." This departure from the Russian economic model inevitably affected ideological and political relations as well; they began to deteriorate toward the end of the first plan.

Notes

[1] Declaration made on March 5, 1954, on the first anniversary of Stalin's death. Ch'en Yün was then deputy premier, chairman of the Committee of Finance and Economic Affairs, and minister of heavy industry.

[2] Report made by Li Fu-ch'un to the Second Session of the First National People's Congress, July 5 and 6, 1953.

[3] The increase over five years was 17.6 percent for food crops. Industrial crops and the development of rural handicrafts were in fact included in the 25 percent stated in the plan.

[4] For the steel industry, for example, this amounted to 10 million yuan ($4.2 million) for each enterprise, and to 4 million yuan ($1.7 million) for paper and rubber.

[5] The figures for this budget are from the report by Li Fu-ch'un mentioned earlier. The government invested 55,000 million yuan, 49,300 million of which went to economy and culture, an increase of 15.3 percent compared with the original figures. Private investment and investment by newly created cooperatives was low.

[6] Li Fu-ch'un admitted that this was higher than the figure for the first Soviet plan (85.9 percent and 14.1 percent).

[7] The share granted to agriculture (forests and irrigation work included) amounted to 8.2 percent of the budget, instead of 7.6 percent as planned.

[8] Report to the Second Session of the First National People's Congress.

[9] On the question of the total amount of Soviet aid, and particularly the many and varied exchange rates, see Feng-hwa Mah, "Foreign Trade," in A. Eckstein, W. Galenson, and Ta'chung Liu, eds., *Economic Trends in Communist China*, p. 693. See also Sydney Klein, *Politics Versus Economics*, p. 21.

[10] This included a 10-million-volt accelerator.

8 The Transformation of Economic Structures

The nationalization of industry and commerce

The accumulation of private capital and Soviet aid given in the form of long-term loans and industrial equipment were not enough, in the eyes of the Chinese leaders, to ensure the financing of so colossal an undertaking as the five-year plan. The prolonged existence of a liberal economy, even under strict control, also seemed incompatible with the doctrine underlying the regime. In this domain, as in others, the Soviet precedent was highly influential. In 1954, before the main targets of the plan were known, Tung Pi-wu, then chairman of the Party's Political and Legal Affairs Committee and a veteran of all the Chinese revolutions wrote as follows:

> As we know, the building of industry, particularly heavy industry, needs huge capital. According to the teaching of Lenin and Stalin, and according to the experience of the Soviet Union, this may only be obtained by practicing economy and by socialist accumulation.[1]

How to accumulate capital by socialist means, at the expense of an enormous and increasing mass of consumers whose shares were already meager, without unduly compromising the stability of the regime, which was determined to exercise every form of compulsion, was the question that arose at this point for the Chinese leaders and precipitated structural transformations. The disappearance of the private or semiprivate industrial and commercial sector—from which the state stood to benefit—was inevitable in spite of the promises in the Common Program, which was approved by the delegates at the Political Consultative Conference in September 1949.

Article 3 of the program clearly said that the state would confiscate "bureaucratic capital" but would protect the economic interests and private property of the bourgeoisie and "national capitalists," while Article 26 promised to "take public and private interests into account, as well as those of employers and employees." Moreover, this policy of tolerance was in line with the intentions expressed by Mao Tse-tung in December 1940, in "On New Democracy." At that time, the thought was to allow capitalist production to subsist or develop as long as it showed no signs of "dominating the economic life of the people." Within two or three years, however, industry was to be nationalized and agriculture was to undergo collectivization. The first serious dissensions within the Party must be attributed to these radical changes (see below).

In fact, the nationalization of industry was already well under way as a result of actions taken by preceding governments. The recovery of foreign enterprises, particularly the railways, since the beginning of the century, the return of Japanese enterprises in Manchuria and occupied China in 1945, and the concentration of powerful capital in the hands of financiers and businessmen who were related to some of the Kuomintang leaders had put half or more than half of the industrial capital in government hands before 1949, according to some authors.[2] The figure quoted by the Communists and compared with the value of production was only 34.7 percent, but it refers to 1949, a year with a high degree of uncertainty owing to political and military events.[3]

Official statistics give the following breakdown of industrial output in 1952:[4]

Socialist industry	56.0%
Mixed enterprises	5.0%
Private enterprises carrying out state orders	21.9%
Capitalist industry (selling its own goods)	17.1%

Between 1955 and the end of 1956, the private sector disappeared very quickly. Considerable pressure was brought to bear on the heads of concerns, who were persuaded to transform their private companies into mixed concerns and later into state enterprises. They were supposed to do so "enthusiastically," in the conviction that the socialist system was superior to the capitalist system.

It is indeed possible that some of them, tired of interference from the government, and at its mercy for both raw materials and sales, were more or less resigned to relinquishing their concerns. In this way, they partly escaped the climate of class hatred, which the Three- and Five-Anti campaigns had fanned to a white heat. To all appearances at least, the necessary transitions were treated with care. For several years, the owners received 5 percent of the profits of their old concerns. Many of them stayed on in their factories as salaried directors or technicians. The state could not do without their experience until politically reliable and professionally qualified personnel had been trained.[5]

In practice, the owners who had received these indemnities had to reinvest the proceeds in state bonds. Like all other citizens, former capitalists had to justify the withdrawal of any sizable sum from their bank accounts. The idealistic and reassuring picture of former capitalists who had been "relieved of their burdens" and discovered happiness was carefully created and maintained by the authorities and spread abroad by the credulity of some foreign visitors.

At the end of 1956, the process of nationalization was virtually complete: state or mixed enterprises amounted to 95.73 percent of the total, employed 98.73 percent of the working population, and accounted for 99.62 percent of production. The remaining 4.2 percent of the enterprises retained a purely illusory independence.[6] Eighty-five percent of trade also came under state control. All artisans, right down to the humblest ones—a total of 7,850,000 people—were grouped in hundreds of thousands of little cooperatives. By 1956, a year before the end of the first five-year plan, the "national bourgeoisie," the first of the revolutionary classes to be eliminated, had ceased to exist. It had lasted for just over half a century.

The collectivization of agriculture

The collectivization of the land was far more destructive of old Chinese traditions and institutions than all preceding policies. It had an immediate, direct effect on 80 percent of the population and an indirect effect on almost all Chinese through their families. The cadres and party leaders were no exception, as almost all of them came from country districts. At first, it seemed that the land reform of June 1950 would be followed by a long pause before the inevitable collectivization. The desire to respond to popular feeling, the need to increase output by careful handling of the best producers (i.e., the rich peasants), Mao's own writings, and the experience of the Communist bases, all lent weight to this assumption. No sooner had land redistribution been completed, however, than the regime began to adopt a collectivization policy, which gathered speed and grew steadily more radical.

The reasons for collectivization

In the eyes of those who supported immediate collectivization, haste was amply justified. First and foremost, it was essential not to jeopardize the work of the revolution, which was threatened by the fundamental conservatism of a society thousands of years old. "Capitalist" tendencies on the part of the new small landowners were already appearing in many places. Peasants sometimes sold their land, either because they were afraid of the coming collectivization, or simply because they were attracted by town life.[7] Tenant farming reappeared. The rich peasants, who for a time had been kept out of peasant associations, entered them and regained yet more influence.

"Now, in the new phase of the revolution, the struggle involved is above all that of the peasant masses against the rich peasants and other capitalist elements," said the resolution of the Sixth Plenum of the Seventh Central Committee on October 11, 1955. Former landlords still sometimes maintained industrial or commercial activities and, in a largely illiterate society, retained at least the prestige attached to education. The Chinese temperament, with its propensity to compromise, and the resignation characteristic of the peasantry did the rest. After the event, Mao Tse-tung used this situation to justify the development of cooperatives:

> As everyone has seen over the last few years, the influence of forces tending spontaneously toward capitalism is developing day by day in the countryside. New rich peasants are appearing everywhere and many prosperous middle peasants are trying to become rich peasants.[8]

The same arguments were used by Liao Lu-yen, minister of agriculture. Many of them reappeared in the attacks on Liu Shao-ch'i during and after the Cultural Revolution.

Collectivization would remove all danger of a return to the former society and prevent the peasants from getting mired in the bourgeois democratic phase of the revolution. It would help the Party by removing from the social scene the landlords and rich peasants who were fundamentally hostile to Communism. Based on an artificially created production group, it would allow the regime to control peasant loyalties and to dispense propaganda much more easily than at the family level.

In the view of its supporters, the economic advantages of collectivization would be just as great. In 1943, taking the Shen-Kan-Ning experience as an example, Mao Tse-tung had thought it possible to affirm that two production-team workers were worth three individual peasants. Ch'en Po-ta, speaking several years later, estimated that the creation of cooperatives could double production in the space of four or five years? He quoted the conclusions of several studies of Heilungkiang province, which stated that labor output in cooperatives was 15 to 20 percent greater than that of mutual aid teams.

Collectivization would allow agricultural efforts to be directed more successfully; it would also allow for closer control of production and consumption and a stricter policy in buying harvests. These considerations were particularly important because agriculture (primary and secondary products) accounted for 75 percent of the country's exports, 50 percent of its income, and a large proportion of the raw materials for light industry (cotton). If the entire agricultural economy came under state control, it would be possible to raise its value by putting surplus manpower and funds to a suitable use. Large-scale work of interest to the locality could be undertaken, and secondary agricultural activities (afforestation, fishing, rural handicrafts) encouraged. In practice, these theoretical views proved correct only to a certain degree.

The development of mutual aid teams and cooperatives

The first government measures were cautious and persuasive. At first, they aimed to encourage the creation and extension of mutual aid teams which were to be seasonal to start with, and later permanent. A "Project for a Decision on Mutual Aid and Cooperation" was drawn up on December 15, 1951, by the Central Committee. It was not made public, however, until February 25, 1953, by which time it had been amended, the movement had spread, and 14,000 cooperatives were already in existence. This reticence may have been due to the Party's prudent desire to appear to sanction peasant initiatives and avoid possible damage to its prestige in the case of obvious failure, or it may have arisen from disagreements among the leaders.

The peasants seem to have been receptive at first. According to official figures, the percentage of farms practicing mutual aid on a short- or a long-term basis grew steadily: 10 percent in 1950, 25 percent in 1951, 36 percent in 1952, 43 percent in 1953, and 60 percent in 1955. Initially, four or five families would pool their work, their tools, and their animals; then the group would grow to twenty or thirty, or in other words, the level of the hamlet; gradually, as land was put into common use, small cooperatives would appear here and there.

On December 16, 1953, the Central Committee adopted a "Resolution on the Development of Agricultural Producers' Cooperatives."[10] This marked the official launching of the movement. Its goals were still distant, however, and progress in 1954 and at the beginning of 1955 was slow. At the end of 1954, 400,000 cooperatives existed, but they only accounted for 7 percent of all families and 8 percent of the land. In the following year, the figure had not risen beyond 15 percent of the total rural population: 650,000 cooperatives grouping 16.9 million families, with an average figure of twenty-six families to a cooperative.[11] Furthermore, the movement seemed to be limited to the former Communist provinces of Shansi, Hopei, and to a lesser degree, the Northeast. In many places, newly created cooperatives were dissolved—15,000 out of 53,000 in Chekiang Province, for example. The land collectivization movement as a whole was in danger. Mao Tse-tung, who had been silent since 1949, intervened personally and forcefully. By speeding up the rate of formation of cooperatives, he removed any possibility of a return to the family economy.

At a meeting of regional and provincial Party secretaries, Mao pretended to think that the masses wanted collectivization and were ahead of the cadres and of "certain comrades who, like women with bound feet, totter forward, complaining to their neighbors that they are going too fast." The cadres must find the right way, he said, which was to lead the movement firmly without imposing it arbitrarily. The cadres should act unhesitatingly, "fearing neither the dragon in front of them, nor the tiger behind them."

The immediate tasks were to consolidate or reorganize existing cooperatives; prove their superiority by raising their output above that of family farms; create new cooperatives; encourage the peasants to embark on the road to socialism, looking to the poorest and most numerous for support and excluding rich and "upper middle" peasants for the time being; and make plans for collectivization, with careful preparation of the details. Half the farms in 1958, and all in 1960, should have reached the stage of semisocialist cooperatives. By 1967, at the end of the third five-year plan and after eighteen years of Communist rule, the socialist phase should have been reached everywhere, as had been the case in the Soviet Union.

The following passage is important for its content and its statistics. In retrospect, both the confidence it shows in the Russian model and some of its views on the importance and conditions of the development of agriculture in the economy are of supreme interest:

If, in the space of three five-year plans, we are unable to solve the problem of the cooperativization of agriculture, that is, progressing from small farms using animals to mechanized farms on a large scale, including large schemes organized by the state to bring land under cultivation with the help of machines (during three five-year plans, it is intended to bring 400 or 500 million *mou* under cultivation), then we will be unable to solve the present contradiction between the growing annual demand for grain and raw materials and the present low level of production in our chief harvests, our socialist industrialization will come up against grave difficulties, and we will not be able to accomplish it. The Soviet Union met this problem during the construction of socialism and solved it by planned leadership and the development of agricultural cooperatives. We too can solve it by the same methods.

A comparison of the targets given in this passage with the agricultural situation today—whether in terms of methods or production figures—condemns, if not collectivization, at least the way it has been carried out.

Mao Tse-tung made the speech on July 31, 1955, but it was not made public until October 17, along with a "Resolution on the Problem of Agricultural Cooperation" which took up its main points.[12] At about the same time, Mao Tse-tung wrote once again, forcefully and confidently, in favor of rapid, far-reaching collectivization. He did so in the preface to a three-volume collection of articles entitled *The High Tide of Socialism in China's Countryside.*[13] Although he estimated that all elementary cooperatives would have been formed by the end of 1956, he thought that completion of the transition to advanced cooperatives would have to wait until 1959 or 1960. Once that stage was reached, nothing would be impossible, and he predicted that agricultural output in 1967 would be 100 to 200 percent higher than the maximum production before 1949.

These documents had a decisive effect. At the end of 1955, 70 million peasant families were distributed among 1.9 million cooperatives. The number of families in cooperatives rose to 93 million at the beginning of 1956, and to 110 million in June. It is probable that, by the end of 1956, ten years ahead of the original schedule, all of China's 120 million rural families had been organized into cooperatives. Willingly or unwillingly, the Chinese peasants were drafted to march—if not to run—down the socialist road.[14]

Semisocialist and socialist cooperatives

The cooperatives for agricultural production fell into two types. The first—elementary or semisocialist cooperatives—were transitory and contained twenty to fifty families each. The members—all individuals of sixteen years and over—retained ownership of their land, tools, and animals and were paid according to a system of work points which took into account the different contributions of each one (including the initial financial contribution to the production fund and reserve fund), and the number of days worked. This was a complicated system to apply, since daily reckonings had to be made, and there were constant disagreements between cadres and peasants and among the peasants as to the value of each person's contribution (land, tools, and animals) and as to the quantity and quality of work supplied by each family. At least, contrary to what later happened in the people's communes, the evaluations were made in full view and with the full knowledge of the whole village, giving a personal quality to the efforts and the rewards.

The second type of cooperative—known as advanced or socialist cooperatives—contained between 100 and 250 families, depending on the density of the population. This type no longer took the peasants' contributions into account; it considered only the work supplied. Theoretically at least, members still owned their land, and title deeds and family registers were not destroyed. They also retained their houses and a small plot of land for a garden and poultry yard; the total area of all these plots amounted to between 2 and 5 percent of the arable land in the village. Members were paid in grain and in money, after various deductions: state taxes (roughly 19 percent of the total income), management expenses, social benefits, and capital for the development of the cooperative, all of which amounted to nearly 30 percent of the income. Between 60 and 70 percent of the harvest, or its equivalent in money, was eventually divided among the members. This percentage, however, included compulsory sales to the state; the quota was decided on for a three-year period on the basis of an average year, varying according to whether a region was rich or poor. Without going into the statistical details, it seems accurate to say that the state received about a quarter of the agricultural output in the form of either taxes or purchases at the rate fixed by the state. Once the rations had been decided on in 1953, the peasants received an average of 560 pounds of grain in the husk per person annually, at least in a period of normal harvests. This amount more or less meets the minimum needs of a peasant used to a monotonous diet of rice and vegetables, although it is almost entirely lacking in animal products.

The formation of agricultural cooperatives naturally entailed numerous regulations, which, at least in matters of management, granted a certain degree of autonomy to the cooperatives. The authoritative documents here are the previously cited "Resolution of the Sixth Session of the Seventh Central Committee" (October 17, 1955), which contains a great many details (payment, individual plots, secondary production, financial contribution, and reserve funds), and the "Model Ruling for a Production Cooperative," submitted at the same session, published on November 10, 1955, by the State Council, and adopted on March 17, 1956, by the Standing Committee of the National People's Congress.[15] The reader should look beyond their somewhat dry contents to try to imagine the extraordinary transformation of living and working habits involved in the reorganization of society, and the organization of new production relations in a rural world that had remained archaic. Thousands of obstacles existed, born of opposing interests (private interests, the interests of the various elements constituting the cooperative) or tenacious customs; to these must be added the lack of understanding of fundamental ideas that were indispensable for life in a collective organization—mass participation and planning, for example. Even if no conscious opposition existed, the task of organizing a suitable division of labor and properly managing a total of 700,000 superior cooperatives is an undertaking of such difficulty and scope that it is hard to imagine it. Real resistance did arise, though it was often disguised, taking an indirect and dilatory form that was in line with the oldest Chinese traditions.

Resistance to collectivization

Resistance to collectivization was to be found both at the peasant level and at the level of senior Party members. As was the case with the reform of 1950, the movement took on an unmistakably revolutionary character. A revival of the class struggle—which united poor peasants and former poor peasants who had become middle peasants against rich peasants who naturally were not much in favor of collectivization—was encouraged. In many places, however, the new middle peasants, now small landowners, showed little enthusiasm and seemed unwilling to go beyond the minor, undemanding stage of mutual aid. Livestock, of which there was little in any case, were often slaughtered, and food reserves that could no longer be hidden were eaten. Sometimes cadres who were too exacting or clumsy were assassinated. Several times—at the end of 1953, in the spring of 1955, and above all in the spring of 1957—movements of retreat from the cooperatives developed on quite a large scale. During the last one, 200,000 cooperatives that had been formed too hastily or were badly managed had to be dissolved. The government issued more and still more instructions.[16] On August 8, 1957, a Party directive instructed cadres to "proceed to widespread education of the masses in the countryside." Once and for all, the peasants had to be made to cast their lot with socialism and, at the same time, a permanent class struggle had to be maintained in the countryside.

These state demands came in addition to the already limited attractions of collective production. The system of planned purchases and supplies, introduced in November 1953 and redefined by the ruling of October 7, 1956, and the rationing system in force since the autumn of 1953, but revised on August 25, 1955, were applied increasingly strictly. In March and in August 1955, the policy known as "three fixed things" (*san ting*) became more clearly defined; the state fixed the quantity to be produced, the quantity to be delivered, and the quantities that could be bought from the state in time of need. The state also frequently ordered the cultivation of certain crops (mainly industrial ones, particularly cotton and products for export), sometimes in opposition to local preferences or needs. It also adjusted purchase prices at will, favoring rice and wheat at the expense of secondary products. Lacking competent administrative staff and technical facilities, and often hampered by political obligations, those in charge of agriculture sometimes made serious mistakes in collecting grain and, above all, in transporting and stockpiling it.

Collectivization suddenly transferred the daily economic activities of the family to the production group, going against a sentiment that was particularly deeply rooted in China. The ancient tradition acknowledging the state as owner of the earth and drawing a distinction between private and public lands, with periodic redistribution of public lands, had in fact been dead for several centuries. In spite of peasant discontent, however, collectivization seems to have been less badly received than in the other socialist countries. The reasons for this lie in certain characteristics of Chinese society, in the shortage of arable land, and in the skill shown by the Party with its previous agrarian experience.

The village in China has always been a powerful social unit, highly aware of its own identity, permeated by a deep sense of solidarity, and strengthened by the links of family and clan. This situation gave rise to certain economic relationships: the exchange of labor, loans of money or grain, mutual agreements, and the prolonged maintenance of family property in its entirety. Villages sometimes owned communal land. In a sense, the cooperatives had considerably enlarged the scope of ancient practices and developed the already strong personality of the village.

Chinese peasants also realized that division of the land created too many small plots; this aspect had been underlined by the reform of 1950. Thus, the cooperative amounted to a sort of reassembling of the land, which was acknowledged as useful, if not accepted with ease. Memories of the former state of affairs and its excesses were also still fresh. The peasants had not yet learned what it meant not to work for someone else. Although farming for the state sometimes seemed as hard as working for the former masters, it was at least done on a basis of equality, in the name of the public interest, and with the promise of a rapid increase in output.

Both state and Party affirmed that collectivization would allow an immediate increase in production. They assured the public that, by as early as 1962, the income of all members of cooperatives would exceed that of former middle peasants; 70 percent of the rural population would benefit. In all events, the cooperative appeared to be a kind of mutual insurance policy, guaranteed by the state that had enforced it. In a country under the constant threat of famine, where fulfilling one's duty toward the members of the family no longer able to work was a real burden, this idea carried considerable weight and balanced the loss of newly acquired independence and property. In any case, the high proportion of the population employed in agriculture (80-85 percent) and the lack of industrial, commercial, or tertiary jobs allowed no choice of attitude beyond that of resignation.

The Chinese peasant's acceptance of collectivization is perhaps best explained by the patience that had enabled him for centuries to submit to the authority of the moment. "If the wind is strong, give in to the wind, if the rain is strong, give in to the rain," as the old proverb goes. The Chinese peasant, still mindful of the wave of terror of 1950 and 1951, gave in to the wind and rain of revolution.

Opposition to collectivization within the Party

Contemporary writings, and particularly those of Mao Tse-tung, are perfectly clear about the existence of strong opposition to collectivization within the Party. Certain members, underestimating the enthusiasm of the peasants or the ability of the cadres, or thinking that collectivization might stir up rural hostility toward the towns, considered it "dangerous," as Mao Tse-tung said. Ch'en Po-ta, his expounder, devoted his entire speech at the Sixth Plenum of the Seventh Central Committee (October 4, 1955) to a justification of the policy of agricultural cooperation based on Mao's earlier writings, and to repeated condemnations of the illusions of comrades "who are perfectly satisfied with the present state of affairs in the countryside, and with small peasant farms." The resolution of the Sixth Plenum said of the opponents: "They launched the rightist policy of 'severe reduction' and in some places they dissolved large numbers of cooperatives by force and authoritarianism."

One question seems to have been at the center of the debate: whether or not mechanization of agriculture should precede collectivization. Mao Tse-tung mentioned it in his speech of July 31, 1955: "In agriculture, given the existing conditions in our country, we must create the cooperatives before being able to have many machines at our disposal."

The Sixth Plenum said much the same: "The aim of the cooperative movement is to bring 110 million peasant families from the method of individual farming to that of collective farming, and then to proceed to the technical transformation of agriculture." The experience of the Soviet Union was carefully studied by supporters and opponents of rapid collectivization. The following passage on the question particularly reveals Mao's ability to continue on his way while paying due respect to ideological formalities and political necessities:

> The great historic experience of the Soviet Union in the construction of socialism encourages our people and fills it with confidence as regards the construction of socialism in our country. But different points of view exist on the subject of this international experience.
>
> Some comrades do not agree with the Central Committee, whose policy is to adapt the cooperativization of agriculture and socialist industrialization to each other, although this policy was proved right in the Soviet Union. They consider that for industrialization the rhythm at present decided upon can be adopted, but as regards the cooperativization of agriculture, it is not necessary to adapt it to measures taken for industry, but on the contrary, to adopt a particularly slow rhythm. . . .
>
> Some comrades have taken the history of the Communist Party of the Soviet Union as a basis for the criticism of what they call precipitation and adventurism in our work of cooperativization of agriculture. . . .

We ought to oppose all idea of precipitation and adventurism which does not take into account the need for preparation, or the level of consciousness of the peasant masses. But we must not allow certain comrades to use this Soviet experience as a cover for their ideas of slowness.[17]

The account of the "struggle between two lines" brought to light by the Cultural Revolution suggests that Liu Shao-ch'i, Teng Tzu-hui, P'eng Teh-huai, and perhaps Kao Kang then represented the principal moderate elements among the leading figures. Liu Shao-ch'i, who currently bears the blame for this position, is said to have insisted that cooperatives should not be created until there were important quantities of collectively owned mechanized equipment. In his desire to protect and encourage the rich peasant economy (both old and new), he is supposed to have coined the slogan "Three Horses and One Cart," an ideal of prosperity which can be explained by the lack of draft animals, their small size, and the way they were harnessed one behind the other.[18] He is said to have led Teng Tzu-hui to dissolve 200,000 cooperatives in the spring of 1955, rather than reorganize them. He is also supposed to have incited Po I-po to write an article on June 29, 1951, that was completely hostile toward collectivization, backed by a reinterpretation of the 1950 land law.[19] During the mid-1970s, every remark attributed to old peasants condemned the blighting effects at the village level of the theories of Liu Shao-ch'i, "the renegade, enemy agent, and traitor to the working class."

In view of Liu's positions before and after 1953, it appears almost certain that the former president of the People's Republic felt inclined to protect production first and foremost, and particularly that of the rich peasants, who were carefully differentiated from speculators, and to proceed toward collectivization at a more cautious pace. In spite of his powerful personality and immense influence, Mao Tse-tung, who admits he disagreed with the Central Committee, had to take into account the feelings of Liu Shao-ch'i and his supporters. Mao's first remarks about extending collectivization over ten years could be explained by this.

Several documents of the Cultural Revolution also attacked P'eng Teh-huai for his hostility toward the collectivization of agriculture. Even Kao Kang, despite the fact that his suicide in 1954 occurred well before the "high tide" of the cooperatives, was placed among the violent enemies of collectivization. The Chinese Communist Party's extraordinary passion for secrecy and its desire to preserve its unity in the eyes of the outside world, which lasted until the Lushan Plenum, prevented its disagreements from becoming known, in spite of the importance of their subject matter and the rank of the people involved.

Notes

[1] New Year's article for *Pravda*.

[2] 46 percent, according to C. M. Wu, quoted by Yuan-li Wu, and between 30 and 55 percent according to Yuan-li Wu in *An Economic Survey of Communist China*, p. 201.

[3] *Ten Great Years*, p. 38.

[4] *Ibid.*

[5] The provisional ruling on mixed enterprises was published on September 6, 1954. See *Survey of China Mainland Press*, No. 884.

[6] In 1956, state industries (socialist industries) accounted for 67.5 percent of the total value of production, and mixed enterprises for 32.5 percent. The latter were not very different from socialist enterprises, except that the capitalists still earned a fixed interest from them. See *Ten Great Years*, p. 38.

[7] According to Ch'en Po-ta, in eleven *hsien* in Hopei, transactions rose from 43,830 in 1949 to 54,494 in 1950, and to 115,188 in 1951 (speech at the Second Plenary Session of the National Committee of the People's Political Consultative Conference).

[8] "On the Cooperativization of Agriculture" (July 31, 1955), in *Mao Tse-tung chu-tso hsüan-tu [Mao Tse-tung, Selected Readings]* (Peking, 1966), p. 313.

[9] Speech by Ch'en Po-ta at the Second Session of the Chinese People's Political Council.

[10] Published on January 8, 1954.

[11] 670,000 cooperatives containing 17 million families during the first half of 1955, as stated by Liu Shao-ch'i at the Eighth Party Congress on September 15, 1956.

[12] Resolution of the Sixth Plenum of the Seventh Central Committee (October 4-11, 1955), and explanations by Ch'en Po-ta on the problem of agricultural cooperation.

[13] The first preface, written in September 1955, was revised on December 27, 1955. A condensed edition of the three volumes appeared afterward, followed by commentaries on Mao's preface by Tang Hsien-chih (English translation in *Current Background*, No. 388, June 5, 1956).

[14] The figures of 110 and 120 million peasant families appear simultaneously in official texts. In about 1958 Chou En-lai mentioned 123 million families.

[15] Reference should also be made to Ch'en Yün's speech to the National People's Congress (July 21, 1955) on planned buying and selling of grain, which followed the directives of April 28, 1955, on the same subject, and the explanations given by Liao Lu-yen on the project for "Model Ruling for a Cooperative of Production" to the National People's Congress on June 15, 1956.

[16] The three directives of September 16, 1957, had significant titles: "Readjust the Work of the Agricultural Cooperatives," "Improve the Administration of Agricultural Production," "Revise the Method for Applying the Mutual Profits Policy Among Members of Cooperatives."

[17] *Mao Tse-tung chu-tso hsüan-tu*, p. 307.

[18] See "Struggle Between the Two Roads in China's Countryside," *Red Flag*, No. 16 (1967). English version in *Peking Review*, No. 49 (December 1, 1967).

[19] See *Peking Review*, No. 7 (February 13, 1970). The article of June 20, 1961, which it mentions, is cautious and reserved in its treatment of collectivization.

9 The First Open Rifts: The Kao Kang – Jao Shu-shih Affair, the Hu Feng Affair, the *Dream of the Red Chamber* Affair

Kao Kang

On March 31, 1955, a National Conference of the Chinese Communist Party—a highly exceptional authority composed of sixty-two members of the Central Committee and 257 provincial representatives—approved the measures taken by the Political Bureau since the Fourth Plenum of the Seventh Central Committee (February 6-10, 1954) on the subject of the "Kao Kang-Jao Shu-shih anti-Party alliance" and published a resolution on it.

Both these high-ranking figures whose experience and temperaments were completely dissimilar, had been missing from political life for more than a year. Their disappearance, considered alongside a "Resolution on the Unity of the Party" adopted by the Fourth Plenum and remarks made by Chou En-lai on the need to reinforce state security,[1] suggested that the Party was going through its first major internal crisis since coming to power. The resolution of March 31 confirmed these suppositions.

Kao Kang, born about 1902 at Hengshan, near the Great Wall in northern Shensi, was one of the few leaders who did not belong to the groups formed in the Central China bases. He came of peasant stock and was educated at the Yülin Teachers' Training College. Being a man of action more than an intellectual, he joined the Party in 1926 and, with his compatriot Liu Chih-tan, led several uprisings in the country districts of his native province.[2] After the arrival of Mao Tse-tung in Shensi and the death of Liu Chih-tan, Kao became the head of the Northwestern Bureau of the Party and, in 1945, chairman of the local government of

Shen-Kan-Ning, which contained some twenty districts, among them Yenan, in the provinces of Shensi, Kansu, and Ningsia. Meanwhile he became a member of the Political Bureau (1943); at the time of his disgrace, he ranked ninth.

In 1945, Kao Kang went to Manchuria with Lin Piao. At the end of 1948, he became first secretary of the Political Bureau of the Northeast; after Lin's departure, Kao in fact controlled the whole region. On August 27, 1949, he was elected chairman of the People's Government of the Northeast which was formed at Mukden (Shenyang). A month earlier, Kao had gone to Moscow to sign an important agreement on regional trade with the Soviet Union.

When the new regime was founded, Kao Kang was appointed a vice-chairman of the government (the sixth and last of the vice-chairmen) and on November 15, 1952, he was given the extremely important post of chairman of the State Planning Commission. He was called to Peking in 1953 and fell into disgrace less than a year later. In December 1953, the Political Bureau, at the prompting of Mao Tse-tung, drew up a draft "Resolution on Strengthening Party Unity." Two months later, in February 1954, this draft resolution was adopted by the Fourth Plenum of the Seventh Central Committee.

Curiously enough, Mao Tse-tung did not attend the session. The resolution was presented by Liu Shao-ch'i. He made an indirect attack on certain senior cadres, denouncing their individualism and condemning anti-Party factions within the Party. These attacks certainly seemed to be aimed at Kao Kang, but the fact that he and his group had been purged was not made public until March 1955.

The text of the indictment, presented by Teng Hsiao-p'ing to the National Conference of the Chinese Communist Party, is not available. The resolution does not offer any documentary proof or any established facts by way of support but is nevertheless categorical. After creating an "independent kingdom" in the provinces of the Northeast, Kao is reported to have tried to seize power in the state and the Party on the basis of "a pseudo-historical" distinction between the "Party of the revolutionary bases and the army" and the "Party of the white zones":

> In Northeast China and other places, he created and spread many rumors slandering the Central Committee of the Party and lauding himself, to sow discord and dissension among comrades and stir up dissatisfaction with the leading comrades of the Central Committee of the Party, engaged in activities to split the Party and in these activities

formed his own anti-Party faction. . . . He even tried to instigate Party members in the army to support his conspiracy against the Central Committee of the Party. . . . He claimed that he himself as the representative of the so-called "Party of the revolutionary bases and the army" should hold the major authority, that the Central Committee of the Party and the government should therefore be reorganized in accordance with his plan, and that he himself should for the time being be General Secretary of the Party and Premier of the State Council.

The report of Teng Hsiao-p'ing revealed that, instead of acknowledging his errors, Kao Kang committed suicide "in a final betrayal of the Party." Teng repeated more or less the same accusations the following year at the Eighth Congress. Liu Shao-ch'i merely mentioned the quashing of the "anti-Party bloc of Kao Kang and Jao Shu-shih who had plotted to seize the leadership of the Party and the state."

Jao Shu-shih

The conspiracy of Jao Shu-shih was linked with that of Kao Kang and judged at the same time. The motives, if not the aims, were different, however, and Jao was accused chiefly of rightist deviation. He was born in Linchuan in northeastern Kiangsi about 1901. Said to have joined the Communist Party in 1925, he studied at the University of Shanghai and then lived abroad for about ten years, apparently in the United States, where he was in charge of the New York newspaper *China Salvation Times* (*Chiu-kuo jih-pao*).[3]

On his return to China during the Sino-Japanese War, Jao served in the New Fourth Army and then joined Ch'en Yi in northern Kiangsu after the New Fourth Army incident in southern Anhwei in January 1941. In 1945, he was political commissar of the New Fourth Army and a member of the Central Committee. In 1949, because of his previous activities, it was quite natural for him to become one of the foremost cadres of the Shanghai region, remaining there until 1953 as chairman of the Administrative Committee of East China, a post in which he succeeded Ch'en Yi. In 1953 Jao took on the heavy responsibilities of the Organization Department of the Central Committee.

The resolution of March 31 gave no more details of the charges against Jao Shu-shih than it had in the case of Kao Kang; Jao was accused, somewhat vaguely, of personal ambition and "moderatism":

During his tenure of office in East China, he did his utmost to adopt a rightist policy of surrender to the capitalists, landlords, and rich peasants in the cities and the countryside. At the same time he did everything possible to protect counterrevolutionaries in defiance of the Central Committee's policy of suppressing them. After his transfer to the Central Committee in 1953, he thought that Kao Kang was on the point of seizing power in the Central Committee. Therefore he formed an anti-Party alliance with Kao Kang and used his office as director of the Organization Department of the Central Committee to start a struggle aimed at opposing leading members of the Central Committee and actively carried out activities to split the Party.

The resolution added that Jao Shu-shih had shown no signs of repentance and had persisted in his attacks on the Party. According to some rumors, Jao denied all complicity with Kao Kang right to the end and merely indicated that he was disheartened by the lowering of standards in the Party.

Twelve of their chief collaborators were condemned publicly alongside Kao and Jao and, if not dropped from the Party, were at least dismissed from their posts.[4] Everything suggests that this first purge of the regime was lengthy and widespread, at least as far as Northeast China, East China, and the various departments controlled by the two men were concerned.

The Kao Kang-Jao Shu-shih affair is scarcely better known now than it was in 1955, in spite of a few details that emerged during the Cultural Revolution. In the case of Kao Kang, personal ambition was certainly one of the causes. His blunt character and taste for action, his influence within the Party—he had been among the founders and leaders of the Party in the Northwest before Mao Tse-tung arrived there in 1935—the rapidity of his rise to become head of Shen-Kan-Ning and then of Manchuria, the most highly industrialized region of the whole country, and finally his promotion to the leadership of the greatest enterprise of the state, that of the plan on which the entire economic life of China was to depend, may have made him wish for a rank worthy of his capacities and responsibilities.

These great ambitions were revealed early according to a document published during the Cultural Revolution. From October 1942 until January 1943, while the Party was revising its history and trying to consolidate its unity, Kao Kang is reported to have convened a meeting of senior cadres of Shen-Kan-Ning. This meeting provided the opportunity for him to make a veiled attack on Mao Tse-tung and the Central Committee.[5] Kao Kang, belittling the line followed by Mao Tse-tung, praised his own, which opposed both rightist and leftist tendencies, trying in this way to attack "the great Tsunyi decision."[6] In 1943, at his instigation, a *Brief History of the Shen-Kan-Ning Border Region* was published for use in schools, though in fact it was issued to serve his aims and to raise the Shensi bases to the level of those of Kiangsi.

> The Northwest is a center, too.
> In the South is Canton, in the North Sian.
> In the South, the Ching Kang Shan,
> In the North, the Shao Chin Shan.

At the Seventh Congress in 1945, Kao Kang and his group opposed the line of the Congress. In 1954, if the resolution of March 31, 1955, is to be believed, Kao Kang had his sights on the second ranking position in the Party (that of Liu Shao-ch'i) and the state (that of Chou En-lai). The resolution of March 31 also indicated that Kao and Jao represented "bourgeois" reactionary forces, in objective alliance with "imperialism" against the changes either already under way or about to begin. It stated that the conspirators had no detailed plan, which suggests that their opposition was of a conservative kind, favoring the temporary maintenance of the private agricultural economy and mixed industrial economy.

This hypothesis finds support in the attacks made during the Cultural Revolution on P'eng Teh-huai, minister of defense, who was dismissed from his post in September 1959. He is said to have represented the group in the army whom Kao Kang tried to win over and—though no proof or details are furnished in support of this—to have been the guiding spirit of the 1953 conspiracy.[7]

Other interpretations are based on an internal conflict over planning. As chairman of the State Planning Commission, Kao could have used his influence to pay special attention to Manchuria, "his independent kingdom," on the grounds that the region is the heart of the modern Chinese economy. In this, he would doubtless have been able to count on the support of the Soviet Union, which was ready to help with the development of the Northeast so as to benefit the economy of Siberia. This was precisely the moment when Peking managed to withdraw from its agreements with the Soviet Union on the subject of mixed enterprises. The remarks made by Khrushchev, and the Chinese reply accusing the Russians of having given support to "anti-Party" groups, give some grounds for this view.

Whatever their nature may have been, the existence of internal disagreements over the economy seems to be confirmed by Teng Hsiao-p'ing in a passage of his report introducing the Party constitution at the Eighth Congress:

> At the National Conference on Financial and Economic Work in the summer of 1953, and again at the National Conference on Organizational Work in September and October of the same year, the Central Committee especially called upon all Party members to strengthen Party solidarity and oppose any acts that might endanger it. But these conspirators, bent on carrying out their intrigues to split the Party and seize power, turned a deaf ear to all these warnings.

The silence of Mao Tse-tung, who was absent from the capital from December 24, 1953, to March 24, 1954, while the Fourth Plenum was being held, adds yet another puzzling element. His attitude of reserve might have been due to reasons of health, which could have allowed personal rivalries to develop or could have precipitated them. It might also have been due to a desire to remain above quarrels among his inferiors that involved contact with the outside, or perhaps to a nascent antipathy to Liu Shao-ch'i. The choice of Ch'en Yün, a moderate who favored the methodical building up of the economy and the avoidance of all adventures in foreign policy, as successor to Kao Kang at the head of the State Planning Commission does not throw any further light on the matter. The most likely explanations for this complicated episode in Party history are to be found in personal ambition and lack of discipline on one side, and, on the other, fear and jealousy of those in high positions who came from "white zones" (Liu Shao-ch'i and Chou En-lai)—to quote the differentiation attributed to Kao Kang himself.

The case of Jao Shu-shih seems clearer than that of Kao Kang. Unlike Kao, Jao was probably a moderate man of tenacious and independent character, similar in this to his former chief Ch'en Yi, and perhaps tinged with liberalism acquired during his long stays in the West. It is conceivable that the excesses of that time, and particularly those of the Three- and Five-Anti campaigns, which ruined the economy of the large coastal cities, aroused his disapproval and led him to protect members of the bourgeoisie, as he was reproached for doing. Jao may later have drawn closer to Kao Kang, not because they shared the same ideas (Kao Kang was the originator of the Three- and Five-Anti campaigns), but because they had common interests. In all events, Jao's functions as head of the Organization

Department gave him considerable power, making it important for the head of the Planning Commission to be on good terms with him. Lastly it should be noted that in 1953 personal rivalries or opposition to a general line at the national level could find support both from a real following and from the regional structure inherited from the last civil war. The obvious conclusions were soon drawn from this state of affairs.

The conference of March 31 adopted a resolution creating control committees at the local, *hsien*, and province levels in order to purge the Party and prevent the resumption of factional activities. These various committees assumed a look of permanence, setting up offices and seeking the support of all possible mass organizations. This structure replaced the former disciplinary councils of the Party and helped to reinforce the central leadership and the action of public security bodies.[8]

The Kao Kang-Jao Shu-shih affair hastened the disappearance of the five great administrative regions that had succeeded the military and administrative committees in 1952, operating over the same area. After the decision of June 19, 1954, the provinces and special municipalities were directly dependent on Peking. This measure was inconvenient in that it eliminated regional coordination, which was useful from a political and economic point of view, and led to excessive centralization; efforts to remedy this in the economic field began in 1956.

The Hu Feng affair

The Hu Feng affair developed on a parallel with the Kao Kang-Jao Shu-shih affair; it was put to extensive political use and was above all a dramatic episode in the desperate struggle waged by the Communist intellectuals to try to retain some freedom of thought and expression within the limits of their commitment.

Hu Feng (whose real name was Chang Ku-fei) was an old supporter of the Communist Party, one of the closest disciples of the writer Lu Hsün, a member of the editorial staff of the periodical *Jen-min wen-hsüeh* (*People's Literature*), and a member of the National People's Congress. In December 1954, he strongly attacked the authoritarian policy of the Party and its sectarianism in literary matters during a meeting of the All-China Federation of Literary and Art Circles and the Chinese Writers' Union related to the Yü P'ing-po affair, which will be described later. He chiefly attacked Chou Yang, vice-minister of cultural affairs, who after Mao Tse-tung was the Party's leader in the literary field. Nearly twenty years earlier, during the summer of 1936, at the time of the League of Leftist Writers, the two men had taken opposing positions. This time Hu Feng also turned against Ho Ch'i-fang, literary editor of the *People's Daily*, and against Feng Hsüeh-feng, editor of the periodical *Wen i pao* (*Art and Literature*).[9]

In a letter addressed to the Central Committee in July 1954, in the foolish hope of raising doubts about the credibility of his adversaries, Hu Feng had attacked the "five daggers," plunged, as he put it, into the brains of revolutionary writers: compulsory Communist ideology; the life of the workers, peasants, and soldiers as the sole source of inspiration; ideological reeducation and reform; literary forms imposed by the Party; and subjects defined by the Party.[10] Hu Feng was attacked violently in his turn and was forced to make several self-criticisms between January and May 1955. On three different occasions (May 13 and 24, June 10), the *People's Daily* published collections of evidence against him, with anonymous prefaces by Mao Tse-tung.[11] These prefaces condemned the theories of Hu Feng in the name of the permanent class struggle and the dictatorship of the people and provided justification for what Hu Feng had called the "uniformity of opinion." As Mao added ironically, however, this opinion is "uniform and yet not uniform" at the same time, because the most advanced and least advanced elements give expression to contradictions whose resolution ensures the uninterruped progress of society. Hu Feng did not know how to differentiate between the contradictions among the poeple and those between the people and their enemies. To suppress the first type is a crime; to suppress the second is a duty.

Hu Feng was also denounced before the National People's Congress on July 23, 1955, by Shen Yen-ping, the minister of cultural affairs—or, to give him his other name, the writer Mao Tun—who applied to Hu the Party's five points on literature: the study of Marxism; the study of the condition of workers, peasants, and soldiers; ideological reform; criticism of national traditions to be used with discernment; and the serving of politics.

Other writers, like the dramatist Ts'ao Yü or the critic and scholar Yü P'ing-po, whom Hu Feng had defended a few months earlier, made despicable speeches against their fellow writer, or like Shu Wu, an old personal friend, handed over Hu's private correspondence. Hu was expelled from the All-China Federation of Literary and Art Circles and the Chinese Writers' Union and put into prison; according to some rumors, he went mad. He soon disappeared completely from public life.

The condemnation of Hu Feng gave rise to renewed persecution of a large group of intellectuals supposed to make up the "Hu Feng clique": the poet Lu Yüan, the novelist Lu Tien, the critic Ah Lung, the teacher Chi

Chi-feng, whom Ts'ao Yü had described as a "destroyer of the soul," and others, totalling 130 people.[12] Lo Jui-ch'ing, then minister of public security, attacked Hu Feng along with P'an Han-nien, one of the assistant mayors of Shanghai, accusing them both of infiltrating the Party with the intention of conducting counterrevolutionary scheming. Lo Jui-ch'ing fell into disgrace, accused of the same thing, ten years later when he was army chief of staff.[13]

At a general level, the Hu Feng affair was to serve as a warning to all educational and cultural circles. In the universities, the campaigns against Hu Feng delayed the holidays; debates and purges continued for a long time in all cultural organizations.

The Yü P'ing-po affair

The Yü P'ing-po affair, known as the *Dream of the Red Chamber* affair, was not entirely comparable with the Hu Feng affair, in that its chief victim, Professor Yü P'ing-po, was not a Marxist, had nothing to do with politics, and devoted himself to his research in classical literature. On the other hand, the book at the center of the affair was so popular that it caused a great stir, revealing the Party's attitude toward its cultural heritage. In this it was similar to the affair of the film *The Life of Wu Hsün*, the campaign against Liang Shu-ming, and particularly the one against Hu Shih, which it helped to revive (see Chapter 5).

At the end of 1953, *The Dream of the Red Chamber*, the famous late eighteenth century novel, came out in a new edition. Written by the scholar Ts'ao Hsüeh-ch'in (1724-1763), and completed by another, Kao O, it was published for the first time in 1791. The story of the unhappy love of Pao Yü (Precious Jade) for his cousin Tai Yü (Black Jade) had as its setting a rich though decaying family, the Chia, the portrayal of whose mentality, habits, and activities gave the novel so much value as a social document that several schools of though sought to interpret it; in this sense, Ts'ao Hsüeh-ch'in could be compared to Balzac. Moreover the book was written in the "spoken language" and was therefore accessible to everyone. Its appeal lay in its disillusioned elegance and melancholy, to which the author added a touch of his own mystery.

> Frivolous pages,
> Bitter tears.
> All speak of the author's madness,
> But who has understood him?

The book began like this, and the last chapter ended in desolation:

> It was a story of unhappy love,
> Of still sadder vanity.
> We pass like a dream,
> Let us not laugh at men's folly.

Professor Yü P'ing-po (his pen name was Ch'u Chai) was born in Chekiang in 1899. A poet, essayist and literary critic, and a pupil of Hu Shih, he had worked for thirty years on the book by Ts'ao Hsüeh-ch'in. He had won acknowledgment as an authority on the subject with the publication of *A Study on "The Dream of the Red Chamber"* in September 1952, a new version of an earlier thesis.

Both before and after republication of the work, Professor Yü P'ing-po, either because he was asked to or on his own initiative, set out his views in several articles, particularly in *Hsin chien-she (New Construction)* in March 1954, and in *Kuang-ming jih-pao* on March 1, 1954. He was relatively cautious—he denounced the "feudalism" of the book, taking shelter behind several appropriate Marxist quotations, but the spirit of his work was still that of the old literary school and was far removed from interpretations inspired by historical materialism; he failed to heed the warnings of Hu Ch'iao-mu, deputy minister of propaganda and one of the official Party historians.[14]

These inadequacies were noticed by two young research students at Shantung University, Li Hsi-fan and Lan Ling. Their articles were refused at first by *Wen i pao (Art and Literature)*, the periodical published by Feng Hsüeh-feng, but were accepted by the *Literary, Historical, and Philosophical Review* of Tsingtao University, Shantung, and by the *Kuang-ming jih-pao*. On October 23, the *People's Daily* gave its support, which was the signal for the start of a nationwide campaign. If later documents are to be believed, Mao Tse-tung apparently took a direct part in the proceedings:

> On 16 October 1954 Chairman Mao wrote a letter to the comrades of the Political Bureau of the Central Committee and other comrades concerned. He voiced warm support for the "nobodies" who "opened fire" on the bourgeois authorities, and sternly criticized and repudiated the bourgeois "big shots" within the Party who "are willing captives of the bourgeoisie." . . . Following this, he initiated a mass movement for

carrying out all-around and systematic criticism and repudiation against the reactionary thought of Hu Shih.[15]

On October 24, the Chinese Writers' Union opened a debate, with Yü P'ing-po and Lan Ling both present; Chou Yang took part.[16]

The main themes of the meeting were the struggles against "bourgeois idealism" in general, against the excessive importance accorded to artistic criteria in comparison with political and social criteria, and against the pernicious influence of Hu Shih. But apart from *The Dream of the Red Chamber,* one basic question was the relationship between the realism of the classics and socialist realism, and another was the whole issue of literary studies. Both problems were approached in a spirit of militant Marxism-Leninism. Chou Yang, as others were to do in later years, commented on "the deplorably backward state of ideological work in literary circles."

The debate of the Writers' Union was taken up during the autumn and winter of 1954 by many journalistic and cultural circles. In December, Kuo Mo-jo, president of the Academy of Sciences, launched another liquidation campaign against Hu Shih, which included all the most distinguished Chinese scholars in the field of social sciences: historians like Hou Wai-lu, Fen Wen-lan, Chien Po-tsan, Ho Kan-chih, Hu Hua, Lo Erh-kang; philosophers like Feng Yu-lan, literary figures like Mao Tun, Ting Ling, Ho Ch'i-fang, Feng Ting, Ai Ch'ing; political thinkers like Li Ta, Ch'en Po-ta, Ai Szu-ch'i; and Chou Yang himself.[17] Twelve years later, nearly all these great names had been swept away by the progress of history.

The trial of Professor Yü P'ing-po, who finally gave in to his assailants, was left far behind. Whether coincidentally or as part of the battle that had begun in 1936 between Chou Yang and Hu Feng, it had provided the first opportunity to raise the question—theoretically at least—of the role of traditional literature under the new regime. In 1954, such literature was not entirely censured nor its publication banned. Although many classical works and collections had been withdrawn from circulation in 1949, the leaders still approved of some, and many works published before 1949 or reprinted afterward were still available. The great novels in the "spoken language," *The Romance of the Three Kingdoms, The Water Margin, The Scholars, A Journey to the West (Monkey), The Palace of Eternal Youth;* the works of the great poets Tu Fu, Li Po, and Pai Chü-yi; and plays dating from the Yüan dynasty were reprinted. At the beginning of 1954, the Hsinhua publishing house brought out rare works from the imperial collections "so that the people may get to know classical art and literature."[18] This relatively tolerant attitude was to last for about ten more years.

Notes

[1] Report on government activity at the National People's Congress (September 23, 1954).

[2] See Guillermaz, *A History of the Chinese Communist Party*, Chapter 22.

[3] Some information mentions a stay in France, but this probably refers to his wife Lu Ts'ui.

[4] The resolution of March 31, 1955, mentioned Hsiang Ming, ex-vice-chairman of the Shantung Provincial Council, Chang Hsin-shan, ex-member of the regional government of the Northeast, Chang Ming-yüan, ex-vice-chairman of the Heilungkiang Provincial Council, Ma Hung, ex-member of the Liaotung provincial government and member of the Planning Commission, and several less known men.

[5] The Kao Kang report dating from this time attacked a document entitled "A Criticism of a Few Questions in the History of the Border Area."

[6] See Guillermaz, *History of the Chinese Communist Party*, pp. 253 ff.

[7] See the *People's Daily* (August 17, 1967).

[8] The Fifth Plenum of the Seventh Central Committee (April 4, 1955) adopted the resolution passed by the National Conference of the Party (March 31). It elected Lin Piao and Teng Hsiao-p'ing to the Political Bureau; the choice of the latter may be considered as a reward for his action against the "anti-Party" group.

[9] See the biography of Chou Yang in Chapter 29. For further details on the Hu Feng affair, see Merle Goldman, "Hu Feng Conflict with the Literary Authorities," *The China Quarterly*, No. 12, (October-December 1962).

[10] See the *Wen-hui pao* (May 30, 1955).

[11] May 13 and 24 and June 10. See *Current Background*, No. 891 (October 8, 1969), for two extracts in English from Mao Tse-tung's introduction, *Mao Tse-tung ssu-hsiang wan-sui*. See also Jerome Ch'en, *Mao Papers: Anthology and Bibliography* (London: Oxford University Press, 1970), pp. 52-56.

[12] See especially Chow Ching-wen, *Ten Years of Storm* trans. Lai Ming (New York: Holt, 1960).

[13] Speech by Lo Jui-ch'ing before the National People's Congress (July 17, 1955).

[14] On the origins of these articles see Wang Chang-ling, *Chung-kung ti wen-i chen fa feng (The Movement of Artistic and Literary Rectification of the Chinese Communists)* (Hong Kong, 1967). See also the text of the letter from Mao Tse-tung to the Political Bureau in Jerome Ch'en, *Mao Papers*, pp. 80-81.

[15] Pamphlet of the *Chieh-fang jih-pao (Liberation Daily)* of Shanghai. English version from *Current Background*, No. 884 (July 18, 1969).

[16] The debates were published in the literary supplement of the *Kuang-ming jih-pao* (November 14, 1954). English translation in *Current Background*, No. 315 (March 4, 1955).

[17] Communiqué issued by the Hsinhua Agency (December 9, 1955).

[18] Hsinhua Agency, Peking (January 6, 1954).

10 The 1954 State Constitution and Internal Administration: The New Party Statutes (1956) and Relations Between Party and State

The constitution of September 20, 1954

Five years after its formation, the People's Republic of China created a state structure,[1] which was intended to be permanent but lasted until the Cultural Revolution and the formation of the "revolutionary committees" in 1967 and 1968. The harmonious governmental and administrative edifice built by the constitution of September 20, 1954, cannot hide the totalitarian and partisan character of the regime. The new statutes gave the Communist Party a legal position and a leading role at every level in the hierarchy, while Party members held all the most important posts in the institutions of state.

The constitution was preceded by a long introductory report by Liu Shao-ch'i[2] and accompanied by texts giving the exact functions of each government institution; it consisted of a preamble and 106 articles intended to be in line with the Common Program and the organic law of 1949. It was in fact a constitution for a regime in the process of transition toward socialism. The principles had little more than a fictitious or temporary value, and the chief reality was the general organization of the state.

The National People's Congress, the supreme vehicle of state power and the only legislative body, was elected for a term of four years by provincial congresses, themselves elected by congresses at the *hsien* (district) and *hsiang* (administrative area of several villages) levels. The armed forces, the Overseas Chinese, and the national minority races had a certain number of seats reserved for them.[3]

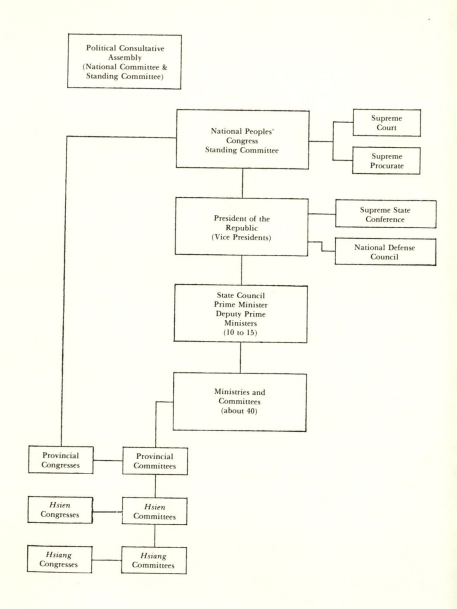

Figure 10.1   Organization of the People's Government (1954 constitution)

In practice, only one list of candidates approved by the Party existed.[4] The electorate could only exert moral pressure, brought to bear on individuals and excluding opinions. The electoral law of March 1, 1953, provided for one member for each 100,000 people in towns of more than 500,000 inhabitants, and one member for 800,000 inhabitants in the provinces (Article 23). These arrangements may be explained by ideological considerations and the low rate of urbanization (12-15 percent).

The National People's Congress amended the constitution, exercised legislative power, appointed the president and the vice-president of the republic, and voted the budget and the plans for economic development. It was to meet once a year for a short session of about two weeks to hear the premier's report and usually the reports of those in charge of the economy and the plan. There was no debate in the Parliamentary sense of the word, but a series of declarations were made, almost always of approval.

Between sessions the Congress was represented by its Standing Committee, which was to meet twice a month when convened by its chairman. Theoretically, this committee—which in 1954 consisted of a chairman, thirteen vice-chairmen and thirty-five members—was all-powerful, because it controlled the premier's activities and gave an opinion on everything falling within the domain of the Congress (except for the election of the president and vice-presidents of the Republic). Its authority was in fact weak, weaker than that of the Supreme Soviet, which it resembled in some respects.[5]

The president of the Republic, who was elected for four years and eligible for reelection, had to be at least thirty-five years of age. He presided over the National Defense Council, commanded the army, appointed and dismissed the premier, and represented China in all external affairs. He had the power, should he wish to exercise it, to convene an assembly peculiar to the Chinese constitution—the Supreme State Conference, over which he presided. This consultative assembly was made up of a few *ex-officio* members and various people appointed according to the president's wishes; its opinions were handed on to the National People's Congress and the government (State Council). It appears to have been created for Mao Tse-tung, who wanted a national audience for his views under certain circumstances so that he could go beyond the limitations of his role as head of the Party. He has availed himself of it about twenty times; at the Eleventh Supreme State Conference on February 27, 1957, he made his great speech on contradictions.

The State Council (Articles 47 to 52) consisted of about forty ministries or commissions under the authority of the premier and ten to fifteen deputy premiers.[6] It came under the control of the Party and, theoretically, of the National People's Congress Standing Committee and was, above all, an executive and administrative body in which the ministers and the vice-ministers supporting them often appeared as heads of departments. It had the right, however, to lay bills before the Congress and its Standing Committee (Article 49). The weakening of the Party during the troubled period of the Cultural Revolution from 1966 to 1969, and above all the exceptional personality of the late Chou En-lai, who was premier from 1949 to 1976, meant that the State Council took on more responsibilities and importance than the constitutional texts accorded to it.

Several specialized bodies were not controlled by the State Council, such as the National Defense Council, presided over by the president of the Republic.[7] The Supreme People's Court, the court of appeal and the court controlling all judicial activities, and the Supreme People's Procuratorate, the office responsible for the security of the state and the application of sentences, were directly responsible to the National People's Congress and its Standing Committee.[8]

The Political Consultative Conference was kept in existence, maintaining the pseudo-democratic facade of the regime. It had a thousand members ("small parties" and representatives of all sections of society) but no powers of decision. It met at the same time as the National People's Congress. A National Committee of about 300 members and a Standing Committee met between sessions.[9]

The regional institutions

People's congresses were elected locally at each of the three regular administrative levels: provinces (*sheng*), districts (*hsien*), and administrative villages (*hsiang*). Everyone aged eighteen years and older in possession of full civil rights had a vote.[10] The *hsiang* congresses, elected for two years, elected those of the *hsien*. These were also in office for two years and in their turn elected the provincial congresses for a term of four years. As a rule, a *hsiang* had between seven and thirty delegates, a *hsien* between thirty and forty, and a province between fifty and 600. The system naturally was also applied to territorial divisions inhabited by minority races: autonomous regions, subregions or *chou*, and autonomous *hsien*.[11]

These various congresses, which met for a few days each year, supervised the observance of laws and decrees and approved local budgets. At their respective levels, they were the vehicles of state power. In practice, their chief duty was to elect people's councils representing them to ensure that laws were executed; to this end they took the measures precribed by law and particularly by the organic law on local people's congresses and councils of September 21, 1954. The councils were under the constant control of their congresses, the councils at higher levels, and ultimately the State Council.

Presided over by their respective chairmen (heads of provinces, *hsien* or *hsiang*), these councils consisted of between twenty-five and fifty-five members for the provinces, between nine and thirty-one for the *hsien* and between three and thirteen for the *hsiang*. They met once or twice a month. They had at their disposal administrative and technical units and cadres of local origin or provided by the state.

The new Party constitution

Two years after the adoption of the 1954 constitution the Communist Party drew up new statutes, and the chief Chinese political organs acquired their final form.[12] The new constitution was presented to the Eighth Party Congress on September 26, 1956, by Teng Hsiao-p'ing, then general secretary of the Central Committee; it replaced the one passed by the Seventh Congress eleven years earlier[13] and lasted until new statutes were adopted at the Ninth Party Congress in 1969 (see Chapter 38). Those statutes were revised somewhat at the Tenth Party Congress in August 1973 (see Chapter 39).

The chief central organizations established in the 1956 constitution were: the National Congress, the Central Committee, the Political Bureau and its Standing Committee, a Secretariat, and various specialized departments. The National Congress, the highest organization in the Party, was elected for a term of five years and theoretically meets for one session each year. In fact, the 1,026 delegates of the Eighth Congress met only twice, in 1956 and 1958. Thirteen years passed before the Ninth Congress was held in 1969, but there was only a four-year interval until the Tenth was held in 1973. The Congress sits for a few days, hears reports from the various central bodies, and is supposed to determine the political line of the Party and revise its constitution. Under the 1956 constitution, its main responsibility was the election of the Central Committee (Articles 31 and 32).

The Central Committee was not only the organ directing the Party; it also had—and exercised—the right to direct the government: "The Central Committee guides the work of the central state organs and people's

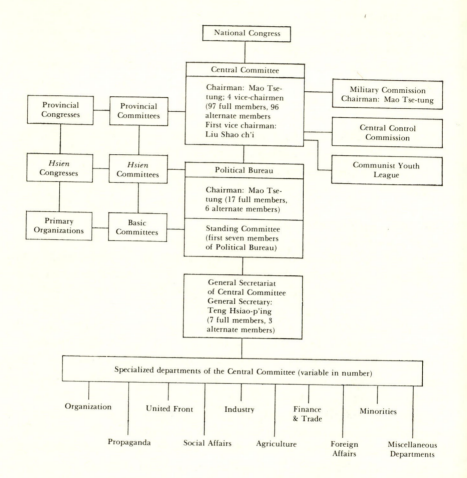

Figure 10.2   Organization of the Chinese Communist Party after the
Eighth Congress (September 1956)

organizations of a national character through leading Party members'
groups within them" (Article 34).

The Party's hold on the government was affirmed first of all at the level
of the Central Committee; the Central Committee also directed and
supervised the action of all provincial and local Party organizations or the
corresponding state organs. It was elected for a five-year term and
theoretically held two sessions a year. At the Eighth Congress it had ninety-
seven full members and ninety-six alternate members who attended

meetings but did not have the right to vote.[14] Its chairman (Mao Tse-tung) was also automatically head of the Party; the order of precedence of the four vice-chairmen in 1956 seemed to indicate the order of succession, at least for the first two: Liu Shao-ch'i, Chou En-lai, Chu Teh, Ch'en Yün. The members of the Central Committee generally hold important posts in the central, provincial, and local Party structures, as well as the government. The Central Committee elects the central bodies executing its policy: the Political Bureau and the Secretariat of the Central Committee. The chairman and vice-chairmen of the Central Committee also hold the same offices in the Political Bureau.

The Political Bureau, far from being merely the agent executing the resolutions of the Central Committee, regulates the life of the Party by its initiatives and decisions, and, by extension, the life of the whole nation. In 1956, at the end of the first session of the Eighth Congress, it had seventeen full members and six alternate members.[15] Its originality lies in the fact that the Bureau includes a Standing Committee made up formerly of its six, later seven, most important members. This small group is behind all the activities of the Political Bureau and meets constantly.

Under the provisions of the 1956 constitution, the Political Bureau had a Secretariat (belonging to the Central Committee and not to the Party). In 1956, it had seven members and three alternate members; Teng Hsiao-p'ing was the general secretary. A number of specialized departments and committees were controlled by the Central Committee through the Political Bureau and its Secretariat: Organization (An Tzu-wen), United Front (Li Wei-han), Propaganda (Lu Ting-yi), Social Affairs (Li K'o-nung), Agriculture (Teng Tzu-hui), Finance and Trade (Ma Ming-fang), Foreign Affairs (Wang Chia-hsiang), to mention a few of them. They constituted the upper framework of the Party structure, and those in charge were generally members of the Central Committee. One of these departments, the Military Affairs Committee, presided over by Mao Tse-tung himself, was particularly important (see Chapter 14).

The local and regional Party institutions reproduced the central organs to a certain extent. At the level of the province and the *hsien*, provincial and *hsien* congresses elect provincial and *hsien* committees for a three-year term (in the case of the province) or a two-year term (in the case of the *hsien*). The committees were to meet three times a year at the provincial level and four times a year at the *hsien* level, electing a standing committee and secretaries to take over the work from day to day. As Teng Hsiao-p'ing put it, the system of congresses and committees avoids having to resort to conferences that are not fully representative or have little authority. The secretaries have considerable power, for they often belong at the same time to one of the central institutions in the hierarchy.[16]

Underlying all the rest were the primary organizations. They were formed either within the enterprise (factory, administrative bodies, schools, production units, cooperatives, and the like) or in a residential context (village, street, quarter), wherever there were at least three titular members of the Party. When a primary organization had more than a hundred members, it could elect a primary committee as its executive unit. If local conditions made it necessary, subcommittees could exist for groups of more than fifty members. Every organization of less than ten members elected a leader.

The primary organizations are naturally of immense importance. They are points of contact between the Party and the masses. In this respect, they are responsible for propaganda (including that of personal example) and, to a large extent, for recruitment. They also must "pay constant heed to the sentiments and demands of the masses and report them to higher Party organizations . . ." (Article 50) and "guide and supervise the administrative bodies and mass organizations in their respective units . . ." (Article 51).

In this way, the basic primary organizations exercise legal guidance and supervision over all the activities of the administrative organs, collective bodies of every kind, and even, through the masses, over individuals, just as the Central Committee does at the top. Control commissions exist at all levels in the hierarchy. The late Tung Pi-wu presided over the Central Control Commission at the highest level until his death in 1975, but there is no mention of the Central Control Commission in the 1973 constitution.

The Communist Youth League and the Young Pioneers

The Communist Youth League was reestablished in 1949 as the Democratic Youth League, but resumed its former name in 1956. It is the Party at work among the younger generation, acting as an auxiliary (Article 56) or antechamber. It has the same structure as the Party and is subordinated to it at every level, with 920,000 organizations covering the country and including about 20 million adolescents and young people between fourteen and twenty-five years of age. The Young Pioneers, which will one day include almost all children, are between the ages of nine and fourteen years.

The Party exercises direct authority over all mass organizations and especially over the trade unions, which are called upon to serve production first, and then to promote the education and well-being of workers.[17]

The internal life of the Party

As in all other Communist parties in the world, life within the Party is based on "democratic centralism," the fundamental conditions of which are described in Article 19 of the Party constitution. The Chinese Communist Party is original in that it uses exceptionally far-reaching methods of mobilization and persuasion: large campaigns and "rectification movements" on a national scale, study (*hsüeh hsi*), periodic "downward transfer" of the cadres (*hsia fang*), and participation by intellectuals and cadres in manual work. These various activities create a permanent state of tension, not only in the Party but in Chinese society as a whole. Their immediate aim is to eliminate all lukewarm, incapable, or dangerous individuals and to prevent and root out all sorts of recurring heresies: "bureaucracy," "commandism," "regionalism," "sectarianism," "mountain stronghold mentality" (*shan-t'ou chu-i*), born during the years of civil and foreign war and perpetuated or developed by the exercise of power. But beyond maintaining doctrinal purity and revolutionary zeal, the moral values, habits, and attitudes of a society that had remained completely set in its ways for three or four thousand years had to be changed, and each one of its members be given "a revolutionary concept of life" (Ch'en Yün). The almost exclusively bourgeois origins of the intellectuals and cadres, the vast numbers and inveterate conservatism of the peasant mass, the passive, relatively anarchic temperament of the Chinese, their fundamental materialism, and the strength and persistence of the old family egoism can justify the anxiety of the leaders, who have learned from the failures of their predecessors.

A tendency toward moralizing and persuasion is part of the traditional heritage of this ancient country where people have always been ready to revere knowledge and education, identify moral with political ideas, and acknowledge the need for a single system of thought. The Communist lack of tolerance, combined with the Confucian lack of tolerance in the past, excludes all other forms of ideology and demands at least a formal adherence to the new doctrine. These old attitudes have been reinforced during the Party's struggle for power. The Chinese Communists had to find their base support in the vast peasant masses, who had to be aroused and persuaded into action before they could be mobilized effectively into the social struggle against the government and the national struggle against the Japanese. This imperative, present for more than twenty years, created a style and habits that persist today; the regime no doubt thinks them just as necessary now as in the past, considering the huge scale of the country and its population, and the strength of particularist feelings.

Relations between the Party and the state

A number of texts are available of laws, statutes, and rules concerning each of the various hierarchies—the Party, the state, the army, control organizations, economic organizations, and the like—but materials that would permit a complete study of their relations, the way in which decisions are made at each level, and the problem of centralization and decentralization, are rare and reveal little. In any case, relations at the top and at the different administrative levels (province, *hsien, hsiang,* and later people's communes) have varied greatly with the changes in the "general line" and the modifications in socio-economic structures.[18]

At the top, the Party, represented by the Political Bureau, is of course responsible for national policy and takes initiatives and makes decisions on the basis of information and studies supplied by specialized departments. The Political Bureau meets at irregular intervals, in Peking or in the provinces, sometimes with the participation of different heads of departments, depending on where the session takes place, or on the subjects discussed (enlarged meetings). Sometimes members who are not wholly in favor of the general line, or have been deliberately excluded, do not attend: Ch'en Yün and P'eng Teh-huai are good examples of this.

The Standing Committee of the Political Bureau seems to be constantly on call and responsible for making immediate decisions and for the day-to-day organization of the Party in general. Because it is a small group (seven in 1956, and nine—of whom six are living—in 1976), its composition places it above the Political Bureau. In the splitting up of this latter institution, it is tempting to see an effort to narrow the choice of future successors and a desire to prepare them to assume the supreme responsibilities. This idea recalls certain obscure remarks attributed to Mao Tse-tung on the division of his responsibilities between a first and second line: "I also wanted their prestige to be established before my death."[19]

The Secretariat was created in 1953 and gradually grew in size until it consisted of about ten secretaries and several deputy secretaries. The growth in numbers and the quality of the secretaries—they were all senior office-bearers—gave it great importance, both as an administrative office and because it had considerable powers of decision. Teng Hsiao-p'ing, who had held the post of general secretary from the beginning, was sent into disgrace in 1966, and the statutes of 1969 and 1973 do not mention a secretariat.[20]

Until 1966 at least, the Central Committee appears to have had the duty of approving, upholding, and giving legal form to the decisions of the Political Bureau, though at times after some delay. Work meetings, extraordinary meetings, meetings of provincial secretaries, enlarged meetings held alongside regular sessions, national conferences, and ad hoc committees all bear witness to the intense activity of the Central Committee, whose members were still numerous enough and of sufficient caliber to allow for independent currents of opinion, if not real opposition. The Eighth Central Committee, like its predecessors, was rather like a Party roster, for it still contained the great names of the Party's history, including the secretaries of the 1930s: Li Li-san, Wang Ming, and Chang Wen-t'ien, all of whom had been rivals of Mao Tse-tung. Since December 1958, the Central Committee appears to have assumed increasing influence over current events, but adjustments in the general line and the lengthening gaps between official sessions (none were held between September 1962 and August 1966) suggest the existence of deep-seated disagreements, a supposition that was fully confirmed by the Eleventh Plenum (August 1-12, 1966) and the Cultural Revolution.

In 1956, however, Mao Tse-tung—chairman of the Party, president of the People's Republic, the incarnation of the Chinese revolution and its triumphs—still carried more weight than any system. Although the discrediting of the personality cult in the Soviet Union affected him indirectly, leading to the omission of all references to his thought in the 1956 constitution (such references were in the 1945 statutes), he was still the leader, raised by destiny and genius above his original companions. Few of them dared venture into open opposition to him. Just before the Cultural Revolution, when some began to be worried by his initiative, Mao Tse-tung translated the veiled, passive resistance to him into vigorous, short formulas: "The directives of Mao Tse-tung are either applied or ignored," "The Khrushchevs in our midst." Elsewhere he complained, and here he must have exaggerated, that General Secretary Teng Hsiao-p'ing had, although continuing to respect him, ceased to keep him informed since 1959.[21] As will be seen later, the Cultural Revolution smashed every possibility of resistance and opposition based on the central institutions, which after the Ninth Congress (April 1969) became mere instruments of the ideological and political absolutism of Mao Tse-tung. On the other hand, owing to events, Mao became most sensitive to the opinions of those around him.

The Party's hold on the government, the administration, and all organizations from the summit to the roots was confirmed without ambiguity in the 1956 Party statutes:

> The Central Committee guides the work of the central state organs and people's organizations of a national character through leading Party members' groups within them. (Article 34)
>
> Primary Party organizations in the enterprises, villages, schools, and army units should guide and supervise the administrative bodies and mass organizations in their respective units so that they may energetically fulfill the decisions of higher Party organizations and higher state organs and ceaselessly improve their work. (Article 51)

The Central Committee or the Political Bureau normally addressed their directives to the State Council, which would transform them into instructions to the various ministries. Exceptions occurred to this rule. Furthermore, resolutions of the Central Committee, slogans coined and publicly promoted by Mao Tse-tung, editorials in the press, which is entirely official and regularly annotated for the cadres, constituted commands that were to be enforced immediately. This phenomenon naturally became even more pronounced when the normal hierarchy collapsed under the blows of the Cultural Revolution.

From April 27, 1959, until January 1975 (when the new constitution dropped the office of president), the offices of president of the People's Republic and chairman of the Party were no longer filled by the same person. Starting in 1959, the importance and style of work of the holders of the two offices began to vary a little. Liu Shao-ch'i was inclined to use the duties of president of the People's Republic to increase his stature in the international field, making frequent visits to Asia and Africa, whereas Mao Tse-tung had never been further than Moscow (in 1950 and 1957). Mao Tse-tung retained preeminence and precedence; divergencies between the two leaders were to develop within the Party rather than the state.

At the national level, as at the different territorial levels, relations between Party and state were considerably facilitated by the fact that the same men were present in both structures. In the executive branch in 1957 more than 70 percent were Party members—86.1 percent of the ministers, vice-ministers, and others of the same rank, and 130 out of 192 provincial governors and assistant governors.[22] On the legislative side, more than

50 percent of the members of the People's Congresses at all levels were Communist Party members.

At the provincial level, the relations between Party and state organs were more complicated than in the capital and naturally varied enormously depending on each case. The province is not an ancient institution, for the existing provincial divisions only date from the Ch'ing dynasty, but there are historical, economic, and sometimes linguistic reasons for their existence and they are of great importance to the Chinese. The province evokes local particularism, which is better represented in the provincial congresses and committees than in the administrative and technical hierarchies under the ministries in Peking, which are staffed by officials from other regions. The local Party secretaries, often natives or long-time residents in the provinces in their charge, but also often full or alternate members of the Central Committee and thus obliged to think of national interests, act as mediators who are responsible for maintaining a delicate balance. The Cultural Revolution revealed that they have strong local support; it also revealed the existence of a powerful regional current of opinion, which caused difficulties in the renewal of Party and state structures.

As under the Empire and the Nationalist government, the state institutions go no further than the *hsien* level. An extraordinary mingling of Party and state staff occurs here; the state furnishes ten times as many personnel as the Party.[23] This is a fairly natural proportion, for the *hsien* is the level at which administrative and economic measures are normally applied, while the *hsiang* (later the people's commune) remains the responsibility of the local collectivities. A constant effort is made to see that the *hsien* cadres are as varied as possible in their origins.[24] The Party seems to gain more power as it gets nearer to the primary level of society; Party cadres are in fact held more responsible than the rest for the results obtained in economic as well as political and cultural fields. Although it is a traditional division, the *hsien* has undergone more changes in its territorial boundaries than the province.

The *hsiang* has probably been changed more than any other of the administrative divisions since the old regime. Then, the population was left in the care of traditional leaders—heads of clans and families or village headmen, generally chosen from among the most influential clan heads. Now, the Party, no longer restrained and guided by the morality and prejudices of past generations, educates and organizes the people. Through its direct contact with and action among the masses, the Party is no longer merely a hierarchy, but is also a horizontal organization that keeps the masses in a state of perpetual mobilization. In country districts where educated people have been rare or nonexistent since the disappearance of the gentry in 1950, where new ideas and values have to be introduced and made to take root, where a new way of behavior has to be enforced, and modernization and socialism must be implanted, the Party's task is vast and endless. Its members barely amount to 1.7 percent of a poor yet conservative population. Party cadres, subject to responsibilities that are both permanent and constantly changing, are further taxed by the doctrine that the masses can never be wrong. The cadres are invariably at fault in every incident, every complication at the primary level, along with the "bad elements" who generally come from what were the most privileged classes of the old society and have been carefully set apart from the community. To accept the criticism of the masses in all sincerity and humility and to make periodic self-criticisms are elementary duties for cadres; the press also makes frequent mention of this.

The infallibility of the Party and the consequent disavowal of cadres derive from well-known ideological principles, but they also possibly owe something to traditional institutions. The severity of the emperor toward the scholar-officials—particularly in times of disorder and revolt—is related to that of the Party, like the authority and support granted to the hierarchies as a whole.

The cadre at the primary level is not alone, however. Activists, leaders of peasant associations, and particularly cadres from higher grades, helped him during the land reform, with local difficulties, and before the collectivization of 1955-1956. Thereafter, the authority of the cadres was no longer directed at families, but at production units, and it increased. Theoretically at least, their authority became absolute with the introduction of the people's communes in 1958; their management apparatus was to merge with the former administrative apparatus.

On the whole, the solution to the question of centralization and decentralization has roughly followed the same fluctuations as the general situation and the general line.[25] The completion of military operations, the need for a rapid rehabilitation of the economy, and the lack of reliable, qualified personnel at first justified some decentralization at the level of the six great administrative and military regions and at local levels, with the dangers inherent in this procedure. As Teng Hsiao-p'ing explained in his report introducing the 1956 constitution: "Not only during the anti-Japanese War and the War of Liberation but also in the first few years after the founding of the People's Republic of China, the Central Committee gave local organizations extensive powers to deal with problems independently, and facts have proved that it was perfectly correct to do so."

The Kao Kang-Jao Shu-shih affair and the consequent reinforcing of the control systems led, from the Fourth Plenum of the Seventh Central Committee (February 1954) onward, to a return to centralization, also required by the first five-year plan, and a need for uniformity in the new economic structures and new relations in production.

The people's communes and the Great Leap Forward involved an enormous effort in production in every direction with no real planning and also required the mobilization of all human, financial, and material resources at medium and lower levels and the freeing of every form of initiative. The result of this effort was inevitably further decentralization, starting in the autumn of 1956, preceded by excesses in the opposite direction: "Undue emphasis on centralization manifests itself not only in the economic, cultural and other administrative work of the state, but also in Party work."[26]

Starting in 1959, modifications in the people's communes and the halt of the Great Leap Forward brought an agonizing revision of targets and priorities, necessitating a return to rigorous control and centralization, particularly in industry. Three or four years of Cultural Revolution put the issue in the background, but the resulting exhaustion of the economy, polycentric tendencies, and weakening of the Party led to a renewed pragmatism chiefly inspired by local conditions.

In 1956, to come back to that year, the Party was more powerful than ever before: it not only guided the nation, it owned it, as Ch'u An-p'ing, editor of the *Kuang-ming jih-pao,* said in substance during the Hundred Flowers movement.

Notes

[1] See Figure 2.

[2] Report of September 15. Liu Shao-ch'i was chairman of the committee responsible for preparing the electoral law, and Mao Tse-tung was chairman of the committee in charge of preparing the draft constitution. The draft had moreover been drawn up by the Party.

[3] The first National People's Congress, which met in 1954, consisted of 1,226 deputies, 150 of whom represented the national minorities, 60 the army, and 30 the Overseas Chinese.

[4] Drawn up by an electoral committee (Article 47 of the electoral law of March 1, 1953).

[5] Its chairman was not head of the government, however, as in the Soviet Union. The Chinese arrangement had the merit of isolating the president of the Republic in his supreme functions, thus increasing the aura surrounding his role and his personal prestige.

[6] In 1954, it was made up of thirty ministries and five commissions: Planning, State Capital Construction, Nationalities Affairs, Overseas Chinese Affairs, and Physical Culture and Athletics. These figures have varied constantly since then.

[7] See the organization of national defense, Chapter 14.

[8] The late Tung Pi-wu, until 1975 vice-president of the Republic, was chairman of the Supreme People's Court in 1954.

[9] Chou En-lai presided over the Standing Committee in 1954.

[10] The number of voters on the electoral rolls in 1954 was 323,809,684; 85.88 percent of these voted in 214,798 basic units.

[11] On January 1, 1954, there existed over 200,000 *hsiang*, 2,023 districts and 150 units at the same level, 30 provinces and 14 municipalities direc.'y under the control of the government.

[12] An English version of the entire constitution was published in 1965. Only essential points are given here.

[13] See Guillermaz, *A History of the Chinese Communist Party*, pp. 369-70.

[14] The number on the Central Committee has increased steadily: in 1943, there were forty-three full and twenty-nine alternate members, and in 1969 170 full and 109 alternate members.

[15] Provision was made for a post of honorary chairman, which at the time seemed to be because of Mao's health rather than his age (sixty-three). The order of precedence was: Mao Tse-tung, Liu Shao-ch'i, Chou En-lai, Chu Teh, Ch'en Yün, Lin Piao, Teng Hsiao-p'ing, Lin Po-ch'ü, Tung Pi-wu, P'eng Chen, Lo Jung-huan, Ch'en Yi, Li Fu-ch'un, P'eng Teh-huai, Liu Po-ch'eng, Ho Lung, Li Hsien-nien. Alternate members: Ulanfu, Chang Wen-t'ien, Lu Ting-yi, Ch'en Po-ta, K'ang Sheng, Po I-po.

[16] The organization is similar in the minorities' autonomous zones.

[17] The trade unions are based on a law dating from 1950. In 1957 they had more than 16 million members.

[18] The best Western works on the subject are: Franz Schurmann, *Ideology and Organization in Communist China* (Berkeley and Los Angeles: University of California Press, 1966), and A. Doak Barnett, *Cadres, Bureaucracy and Political Power in Communist China* (New York and London: Columbia University Press, 1967). Both have large bibliographies.

[19] See the speech delivered on October 24, 1966, in the series entitled "Long Live the Thought of Mao Tse-tung." English version is in *Current Background*, No. 891 (October 8, 1969).

[20] Out of about fifteen secretaries or former secretaries during the 1960s, more than half fell victim to the Cultural Revolution: Teng Hsiao-p'ing, P'eng Chen, T'an Chen-lin, Lu Ting-yi, Lo Jui-ch'ing, Hu Ch'iao-mu, Liu Lan-t'ao, and Yang Shang-k'un are the best known of them. Several returned to favor after 1971—some temporarily like Teng Hsiao-p'ing, others remaining in relative obscurity like T'an Chen-lin, Lo Jui-ch'ing, Hu Ch'iao-mu, and Liu Lan-t'ao—but their vicissitudes may not be over.

[21] Speech of October 24, 1966. See *Current Background*, No. 892 (October 21, 1969), and Jerome Ch'en, *Mao Papers*, p. 40.

[22] Cf. *People's Daily* (September 13, 1957).

[23] A. Doak Barnett, *Cadres, Bureaucracy, and Political Power*, p. 205.

[24] *Ibid.*, p. 133. Of twenty-nine members of a *hsien* committee, fifteen came from other provinces (North China), seven from other districts in the province, and only seven were of local origin.

[25] Franz Schurmann, *Ideology and Organization*, is a useful work on the subject, at least from 1949 to 1966, particularly chapters 4 and 5, as regards taking decisions, decentralization, and control.

[26] Teng Hsiao-p'ing, "Report on the Modifications to the Party Statutes" (September 16, 1956).

11 The Eighth Party Congress and China in 1956

The Eighth Congress of the Chinese Communist Party, held from September 15 to 19, 1956 (1,016 delegates), was important from several points of view. It provided the opportunity for the leaders, in their reports and declarations, to give a general picture of China and its problems: collectivization of agriculture, nationalization of industry, initial results of the first five-year plan and targets for the second, attitude of the intellectuals. The most important documents—those that were to have lasting reference value—were the political report of the Central Committee, presented by Liu Shao-ch'i, and the Congress resolution resuming and approving it (Setember 27, 1956), Chou En-lai's report on the second five-year plan (1958-62), and Tung Pi-wu's report on judicial work. More than a hundred delegates spoke on problems within their sphere; about a hundred foreign delegates also spoke.[1]

Certain features of the Hundred Flowers movement, which was to come to a head several months later, and the first effects of the Twentieth Congress of the Communist Party of the Soviet Union (February 14-25, 1956) instilled a note of moderation in these documents that was to be reversed by the great events of 1958: the people's communes and the Great Leap Forward.

The Eighth Congress also gave a good idea of the structure, composition, and internal trends of the Party, which had risen from opposition to power since its last Congress.[2] Both structures and leaders were to remain in place from the Eighth Congress until the Cultural Revolution in 1966; this length of time explains, at least partly, why the intra-Party struggle became so bitter.

The Chinese economy in the autumn of 1956

The economy inspired the general line during the transition period. The Central Committee defined it this way: "to complete, step by step, the socialist transformation of agriculture, handicrafts, capitalist industry, and commerce and bring about, step by step, the industrialization of the country."

Liu Shao-ch'i devoted most of his report to praising the results of the first five-year plan and expressing his confidence in the success of the second. The main target of the regime was to build up Chinese economic power as quickly as possible by unifying all forces within the country with the help of socialist countries, chiefly the Soviet Union. Everything else followed from this: priority for heavy industry, slowing down of class struggle, gradual and peaceful transformation of the national bourgeoisie, a moderate foreign policy, and national defense organized on Russian lines. It could be said that everything that was later to cause opposition between Mao Tse-tung and Liu Shao-ch'i—attitude, doctrine, and practical measures—was already implicit in the documents of the Eighth Congress.

Liu Shao-ch'i announced that socialist transformation should be completed after five or ten years. The industrialization of the country was to take fifteen years (or slightly longer). Heavy industry, essential for the manufacture of the machines and equipment needed for production, naturally had priority over the light industry it stimulated. It was to be based on a geographical balance arising from the creation or development of new industrial complexes in inland areas (steelworks at Paotow and Wuhan) and was to result from a suitable balance between personal responsibility and collective leadership organized around the Party. With improved living conditions arousing the enthusiasm of workers and cadres, the system of salary differentials and bonuses was to be maintained and developed, and the principle "to each according to his work" was to be respected.

Nearer the first plan, it was already obvious that the targets for industry (a growth of 98.3 percent) would be achieved or overtaken and that China would at last be able to have the first elements of advanced industry (motors, machines, precision tools, aviation) at its disposal. The delays were insignificant, chiefly affecting the petroleum industry, various consumer goods, and edible vegetable oils.[3] The second plan also focused on heavy industry, technical development, and scientific training. Steel production was meant to increase from 4.2 million tons (the target for 1957) to 10.5 or 12 million tons, coal output from 113 to 190-210 million tons and electricity from 15,900 million kwh to 40,000 or 43,000 million kwh.[4] A similar effort was planned for railway transport: 4,000 kilometers during the first plan, and between 8,000 and 9,000 during the second. Light industry was intended to progress more slowly: the production of yarn would rise from 5 million to 8 or 9 million bales, edible vegetable oils from 1.79 million to 3.1 or 3.2 million tons, sugar from 1.1 million to 2.4 or 2.5 million tons, machine-made paper from 650,000 tons to 1.6 million tons.

Agriculture was less important in the report of the Central Committee (the Liu Shao-ch'i report) than might have been expected. The progress of collectivization was recorded without extravagant praise. Although Mao Tse-tung's criticism of rightist conservative tendencies was referred to, the general impression was one of cautiousness. Inadequate ideological preparation of the peasants, neglect of their individual interests, excessive constraints, and state mistakes are all mentioned.

Compared with the progress registered in industry, progress in agriculture was slow and the target of the first plan (a 23.3 percent increase in production) was barely reached.[5] The second plan forecast a figure of 250 million tons for cereal production, but the report underlined at the same time China's great agricultural handicaps: limited amounts of arable land compared with the size of the population, not enough chemical fertilizers (22 kilograms per hectare in 1962), and an extremely low level of mechanization, with little hope for its improvement. The immediate future of Chinese agriculture depended on irrigation, the improvement of seed, and the use of insecticides.

The more distant future was sketched in a twelve-year development plan (1956-1967), directly inspired by Mao Tse-tung, which was examined on January 25, 1956, during a session of the Supreme State Conference and altered on August 4, 1958 (see Chapter 19). With an optimism that nothing was to justify, Ch'en Po-ta affirmed on February 2, 1956, that the twelve-year plan for agriculture would allow 600 million more Chinese to be fed. "There are no signs of overpopulation in China," he added, at the very moment when the Party was embarking on a policy of resolutely lowering the birthrate.

The Liu Shao-ch'i report did not share this optimism. On the contrary, it is easy to pick out several reservations with regard to current policy and to collectivization without agricultural machinery, all of which could be said to be an acknowledgement of the facts rather than an expression of approval. It is clear that the issue of financing industry by agriculture, as raised by Mao Tse-tung in 1955, remained a cause for concern; perhaps this concern was also extended to the problem of food shortages in certain areas.

Optimism reappeared with the chapter on domestic and foreign trade. The home market was almost entirely socialized in the wholesale trade, and the network of specialized corporations had increased, while figures for retail trade had risen by 66.3 percent between 1952 and 1956, and a further increase of 50 percent was forecast for the period between 1957 and 1962.[6] Foreign trade rose by 65 percent in 1956 as compared with 1952, but no figures were given for forecasts beyond that year. Lastly, prices were stabilized and sometimes readjusted, in spite of mistakes and difficulties.

Other economic problems were raised—sometimes with considerable honesty and wisdom—during the Eighth Congress. Li Fu-ch'un, chairman of the State Planning Commission, stressed China's lack of experience in the field of planning and statistics, underlining the need to train personnel (after the Soviet pattern) and to render the systems more flexible, particularly at a local level, which is exactly what happened later on. Ch'en Yün defended the technical and administrative capacities of the "national capitalists," and was in favor of a degree of diversity and autonomy in small industrial and commercial enterprises, and a certain mobility in the price of some goods; he even defended the right of members of cooperatives to undertake subsidiary activities and to put their products on the market, under supervision. These wishes expressed an inclination that was soon to earn disgrace for their author.

Po I-po and Li Hsien-nien spoke on the national income, its sources and financing, and on prices and their stability. Po I-po indicated that the national income had increased by 9.5 percent between 1953 and 1956, while the rate of accumulation had risen by 19.5 percent per year, and the rate of consumption by 6.7 percent. He also pointed out that income from the budget had risen from 27.6 percent of the national income in 1952 to 31.5 percent in 1956. Of this, 29.9 percent in 1952 and 46.7 percent in 1956 were turned over to the building up of capital. He promised that, if the rate of accumulation remained at about 20 percent, with income from the budget at 30 percent or more of the national income, and expenses of building the country at 40 percent of state expenditure, rapid industrial development could be assured, although, of course, nothing could be achieved without tough struggles, privations, and thrift. On the whole, the Party seemed to look on the question of its economic development with courage, clear-sightedness, and confidence, although the backward state of its agriculture was beginning to cause anxiety.

The Party in 1956 and its characteristics

The other chief subject at the Eighth Congress, besides the economy, was the Party—its composition, evolution, and tendencies. The revised statutes, mentioned in Chapter 10, give an account of the Party's organization and general rules of operation, but the characteristics revealed in the documents of the Eighth Congress suggest numerous points of contrast with earlier congresses.[7] Party membership increased ninefold between 1945 (1,210,000 members) and 1956 (10,734,384 members), amounting to 1.74 percent of the population. Nine-tenths of the members had joined after 1945, and more than half after the Party's rise to power in 1949.[8] This development made no fundamental change in the composition of the Party from the point of view of the social origins of its members.

Table 11.1
Social origins of Party membership in 1956

Social origin	Number	% of Party
Workers	1,502,814	14
Peasants	7,414,459	69.1
Intellectuals	1,255,923	11.7
Miscellaneous	558,188	5.2

These proportions reflect the composition of the population as a whole. Although the position of the army was much weaker after the end of the civil wars, it may seem surprising that the proletariat, a privileged class easy to arouse and control, had not progressed further. Its numerical weakness, the Party's stiff criteria for admission after 1949, and the fact that the towns were slow to come under Communist control explain this anomaly, which was relative, however, for peasants were five times as numerous as workers in the Party but were thirty times as numerous in the nation as a whole.

The intellectuals, who supplied the vast majority of cadres and almost all the senior cadres, retained a prominent position, and their numbers grew further in 1957. The proportion of them within the Party was then 14.7 percent as against 13.7 percent for workers and 66.8 percent for peasants. Basically, the Party was young: 67 percent of its members were between the ages of twenty-five and forty-five, 25 percent were under twenty-five and only 8 percent were over forty-five. Women constituted only 10 percent of the total membership, but most of them were of a higher caliber than the average militant. Almost all of them had cadres' responsibilities. The ethnic minorities (35 million inhabitants) began to be represented in the Party, which badly needed cadres drawn from them in order to exercise political control over them. They provided 294,933 members, or only 0.84 percent of the total number.

In 1956, admission to the Party was controlled more effectively than during the civil wars or the early years of the regime, when fear or ambition inspired many to rally to it. The prospective member had to be eighteen years of age and be proposed by two current members. With certain exceptions, candidates had to pass a trial period of one year. The recruitment of the basic stratum of the Party does not seem to have been a source of any particular worry for the leaders. It was made up of young newcomers, mainly of peasant origins, who were docile and happy to have an allegiance setting them apart from the rest and giving them a chance to rise. This was not the case for the cadres, who, in the words of Stalin, quoted by Mao Tse-tung, "are a decisive factor, once the political line is determined."[9] In 1956, the Party required a great deal of its 300,000 cadres at the *hsien* level or above. The Party lacked cadres everywhere, as Teng Hsiao-p'ing said. Seniority carried weight when it came to selection. He added that the training of cadres who were specialists in production techniques or had a thorough knowledge of any of the various branches of learning was essential for the construction of socialism. Such insistence was not surprising at a time when industrialization dominated the political line.

Mao Tse-tung, like Liu Shao-ch'i, also stressed the importance of Marxist-Leninist training as the only way to oppose a subjectivism that seemed to bear a close resemblance to the overbearing, often paternalistic attitude shared by all Chinese officials throughout history. The higher ranks of cadres above all were urged to be on their guard against mistakes liable to isolate the Party from the masses, and to approach their new tasks in a spirit of objectivity and realism.

The success of the Communist movement can largely be explained by the high quality and lack of self-interest of the Communist Party cadres compared with those of its adversary, the Kuomintang. The Communists were all trained, both morally and physically, during the long, tough struggles of war. A clearly defined tradition had formed during the years in Kiangsi, on the Long March, and in Yenan. The most admirable aspects of this were energy, self-confidence, uprightness, sense of mission, and devotion to the people, but these were too often offset by fanaticism, ignorance, narrow views, suspicion, arrogance, and excessive harshness toward individuals. This tradition began to weaken after 1949. The cadre was no longer a leader of rebels, but a civil servant. In a society that excludes all possibility of personal gain, all success was seen in terms of the Party hierarchy, and a certain careerism was the result. The problems were no longer the same, so the criteria for selection were also changed. Once economic tasks had acquired more importance than military ones, the cadre, who up till then had been a soldier, propagandist, and administrator, came into contact with scientists and technicians in the factories and with intellectuals in the administrative organs, universities, and schools, and naturally had to come closer to them. The Eighth Congress tried to redesign the ideal cadre, who would be protected from political errors by a sound Marxist-Leninist ideological education but would also be capable of working in all the most modern sectors of the economy. This effort was shortly to be threatened by the steps Mao Tse-tung took to restore absolute priority to politics.

The leadership of the Communist Party aged as time went on, for few new leaders emerged, as had been the case with the Kuomintang. Between 1921 and 1945, the average age of a member of the Political Bureau rose from twenty-nine to forty-nine. In 1956, it was about sixty. The Central Committee was slightly more youthful after its enlargement to nearly 200 regular and alternate members, but it did not include a single representative of the younger generation. This question of increasing age seems to have been ignored by the leaders, and it does not seem to have created a state of tension with the basic stratum, for the aging group at the top retained all its authority and prestige.

Because of the recent Kao Kang-Jao Shu-shih affair, the subject of the need for unity could not fail to be introduced. Several historical events were recalled as a result. One after the other, Mao Tse-tung, Liu Shao-ch'i, and Lin Po-ch'ü underlined previous deviations. In the same vein, Li Li-san made a self-criticism of astonishing humility.[10] Although homage was rendered—in slightly muted tones—to Mao Tse-tung's unwavering leadership of the revolutionary movement since the Tsunyi Conference in January 1935, the principle of collective leadership and the development of internal democracy within the Party were discussed at length and firmly supported by Mao Tse-tung, as Liu Shao-ch'i said, with a tinge of perfidy. Lastly, whereas the general program of the 1945 constitution had referred to the thought of Mao Tse-tung:

The Chinese Communist Party takes the theories of Marxism-Leninism and the combined principles derived from the practical experience of the Chinese revolution—the ideas of Mao Tse-tung—as the guiding principles of all its work,[11]

The 1956 constitution made no mention of it:

The Communist Party of China takes Marxism-Leninism as its guide to action. Only Marxism-Leninism sets forth the laws of the development of society and correctly charts the path leading to the achievement of socialism and communism. . . . Consequently, the Party in its activities upholds the principle of integrating the universal truths of Marxism-Leninism with the actual practice of China's revolutionary struggle, and combats all doctrinaire or empiricist deviations.

Observers could not fail to notice the change at the time, though without drawing pointed conclusions. The movement throughout the socialist camp toward collective leadership after the death of Stalin, the position of the Chinese toward the personality cult, and the lack of violent conflict within the Party, which was engrossed in the five-year plan, seemed to lessen the importance and meaning of the change. Although the press of the Cultural Revolution held P'eng Teh-huai responsible for it, it is hardly possible to go any further today. In any event, it seems that cirumstances did not allow Mao Tse-tung to react publicly, and, given his considerable authority within the Party, he probably did not deem it necessary.

Thus, in the autumn of 1956, China seemed absorbed in emerging from its backward state and engrossed in internal problems; the nascent Soviet policy of peaceful coexistence and the solidarity between socialist countries freed China from serious worries abroad. The Eighth Congress paid relatively little attention to questions of foreign policy and national defense. Speaking of foreign policy, Liu Shao-ch'i echoed the spokesmen from Moscow: "Under these circumstances, the world situation is tending toward a relaxation of tension, and now lasting world peace has started to become a possibility." And Mao Tse-tung, in his opening declaration, said: "Owing to ceaseless efforts on the part of peace-loving countries and peoples, the international situation already shows a tendency toward *détente.*"

In spite of the customary violent language, China was to pursue the moderate foreign policy it had practiced since 1954, in line with the official view of the international situation (see Chapters 15 and 16).

The budget for national defense was cut, and national defense was scarcely mentioned in the texts of the Eighth Congress. The second five-year plan placed it fifth and last in its provisions, in the vaguest possible terms: ". . . to reinforce national defense and raise the level of the people's material and cultural life on the basis of increased industrial and agricultural production."[12]

Less than a year later, this harmonious picture of a serene China, full of confidence in itself and its destiny, was wiped out. A terrible storm swept the garden of a Hundred Flowers. With it, the history of the regime was to enter a zone of alternating turbulence and calm, from which it has not emerged.

Notes

[1] The reports and speeches were published as a whole in Peking by the Central Committee Services. The Foreign Languages Press published the most important of them.

[2] The Seventh Party Congress met in April 1945 and held a second session in March 1949. See Guillermaz, *A History of the Chinese Communist Party*, p. 369.

[3] Po I-po gave the annual increase over the first four years of the plan as 23.9 percent for heavy industry, 14.8 percent for light industry, 12.6 percent for handicrafts, and 14 percent for productivity. The Chinese national income was reported to have increased by 9.5 percent each year, and the rate of accumulation by 19.9 percent.

[4] See targets and results of first and second plans, Chapters 7 and 20.

[5] 185 million tons were produced eventually instead of 181.59 million, but the accuracy of agricultural forecasts is dependent on the effects of the monsoon climate on the harvests; figures only acquire full meaning when treated as averages over three to five years.

[6] A report on trade was also submitted to the Eighth Congress by Tseng Shan, minister of trade.

[7] See Guillermaz, *A History of the Chinese Communist Party*, pp. 445-48.

[8] The combining of various sources gives the following figures: 1937, 40,000; 1940, 800,000; 1945, 1,214,128 (Seventh Congress); 1949, 4,448,000; 1951, 5,800,000; 1956, 10,734,384; 1957, 12,700,000; 1959, 13,960,000; 1961, 17,000,000. The upheavals of the Cultural Revolution were to change the composition, characteristics, and function of the Party considerably; membership was set at 28 million at the Tenth Congress in 1973.

[9] Mao Tse-tung, "The Role of the Chinese Communist Party in the National War," in *Selected Works*, 2:202.

[10] Guillermaz, *A History of the Chinese Communist Party*, p. 205.

[11] Conrad Brandt, Benjamin Schwartz, and John K. Fairbank, *A Documentary History of Chinese Communism* (Cambridge, Mass.: Harvard University Press, 1958), p. 422.

[12] Political report of the Central Committee (given by Liu Shao-ch'i).

12 The Hundred Flowers and Antirightist Movements of 1956 – 1957

On May 2, 1956, Mao Tse-tung, in a speech to the Supreme State Conference, developed various themes with liberal overtones, illustrating them with an old image from the Warring States period: "May a hundred flowers bloom, and a hundred schools of thought contend." The complete, authentic text of the speech will never be known, but the expressive, poetic phrase he used was taken up several days later by Lu Ting-yi, head of information and propaganda in the Party.[1] The essential part of what Lu Ting-yi said, at a conference of writers, was that the differences between the various schools in literature, the arts, and science should be allowed to flourish. As far as ideology was concerned, idealism and materialism were to be allowed to confront each other; the latter would slowly but surely triumph over the former:

> We cannot fail to notice that although art, literature, and scientific research are closely linked to class struggle, they are not, after all, the same thing as politics. Politics are a *direct* form of class struggle. Art, literature, and social science give expression to class struggle, sometimes directly, sometimes indirectly.

"Art for art's sake" is a rightist error, as Lu Ting-yi says elsewhere, but to assimilate art, literature, and science to politics is a leftist error. Serving the peasant, worker, and soldier does not mean that one cannot write on other subjects. In fact, the choice of subjects in art and literature is vast. It is not limited to what exists today but extends to what has existed, what will exist, and even to what will never exist "and to the spirits of the heavens and to animals and birds that speak." The acceptance—with discernment and modification—of the national cultural heritage, and with it the contributions from the Soviet Union and other socialist or nonsocialist countries, will help the development of the China of today. Lastly—and this is one of the most important points of the speech of the head of propaganda—it was time to deal with the sectarianism of certain Party members who tended to monopolize academic studies in philosophy and the social sciences, and with the hostility of certain intellectuals who kept the Party at a distance.

Although Lu Ting-yi was careful to provide justification for the criticism of Hu Shih, Liang Shu-ming, and Yü P'ing-po, to refer to Mao Tse-tung occasionally, and to urge his audience to further study of Marxism-Leninism, the content and the tone of his speech could imply that a great breath of liberalism was about to sweep over the regime and that the spirit of the Twentieth Congress of the Communist Party of the Soviet Union and de-Stalinization were about to reach China. A little later, on June 19, the writer Mao Tun in his turn praised the Chinese cultural heritage in the face of influences from abroad: "Must we beg with the golden bowl we hold in our hands!"—an old popular image that must have struck a chord in many of his listeners.

In fact, the statements made by the minister of propaganda followed and enlarged upon those of Chou En-lai, who had spoken a few months earlier at a conference called by the Central Committee to study the question of the intellectuals (January 14-20, 1956). Talking to the 1,249 people present at the conference, the premier stated that China did not have enough intellectuals, particularly higher intellectuals, to meet the needs of its general development. Thus, it was necessary simultaneously to bring intellectuals closer to the Party leadership, to help them reform their ideology, to mobilize them, and to raise their professional value so as to put them to better use. On this last point the premier admitted that the Party and the government had made mistakes and announced that important initiatives would soon be taken.

Kuo Mo-jo, chairman of the Academy of Sciences and vice-chairman of the People's Political Consultative Conference, developed the same subject on January 31, 1957, at the second session of the Second National Committee of the People's Political Consultative Conference. Referring to the figures mentioned by Chou En-lai, he said that China had only 100,000 "higher" intellectuals, only 35 percent of whom had been trained after the liberation, and 3,840,000 ordinary intellectuals.[2] Of the first category, 10 percent were hostile to the regime, 10 percent were simply "retrograde," 40 percent were indifferent or politically backward, and only 40 percent really upheld socialism.

To improve the situation, a twelve-year plan (1956-1967) was announced to educate a million higher intellectuals. An office responsible for ensuring that Chinese specialists were used correctly was to be created by the State Council. Intellectuals were to work on their own specialty for five-sixths of their working time. In exchange, the Party urged them to draw nearer to the masses and to socialism, and to cooperate sincerely in the work of national construction.

The speeches by Chou En-lai and Kuo Mo-jo had been prepared or accompanied by various Party conferences at the provincial level. The "small parties," which included a high proportion of intellectuals, had broached the question by holding a conference on the unity and reform of their parties (December 2-14, 1955); everything showed that the speeches of Lu Ting-yi and Mao Tse-tung arose, initially at least, from more general domestic considerations.

At the beginning of 1956, the collectivization of agriculture and the nationalization of industry were nearly complete, the first five-year plan was in full operation, and the second was in preparation. The issue now was not merely one of liberalizing the condition of intellectuals but of fully using them and transforming them, like the workers and peasants, into "active workers for socialism." The policy practiced until then had failed, in terms of participation—figures quoted by the premier prove this—and in terms of the quality of studies and original work produced. In the scientific and technical field, all scholars of any value were usually torn between the Western liberal tradition, which had educated them, and their patriotic feelings. The oldest among them had difficulty in adapting themselves to Soviet norms and methods. Because of their origins, they all met with suspicion or at least a lack of understanding on the part of cadres who were intellectually their inferiors. Social scientists, deeply inhibited by an ideology with which they were ill acquainted, and which they feared, had ceased to produce important or original works. Historians were content to publish collections of materials; the great writers and playwrights remained silent or took refuge in worthless or futile works, leaving the way open to young amateurs who lacked both professional knowledge and talent. The Chinese intelligentsia seemed to have lost its genius. Only a few old painters such as Hsü Pei-hung (Ju Peon), Ch'i Pai-shih, and Fu Pao-shih, or actors such as Mei Lan-fang or Chou Hsin-fang, who were protected by their lack of political sympathies in the past and upheld by the prestige of Chinese painting and theater, rather than by personal reputation, still produced work of high quality.[3]

Because the need to build the economy was more pressing than all other needs, it was possible, in the name of the collective effort, to allow some tolerance as to literary and artistic content and form, which would naturally be contained within the limits prescribed in 1942 in the "Talks at the Yenan Forum on Literature and Art." At the same time young authors would be trained and reach maturity under the twelve-year plan.[4]

It is impossible to judge the extent to which the Twentieth Congress of the Communist Party of the Soviet Union, held a few weeks after the declarations of Chou En-lai and Kuo Mo-jo, may have reinforced this current in China, but, with the declaration of Lu Ting-yi on May 26, it took on a precise doctrinal form that was probably similar to the terms used by Mao Tse-tung on May 2. The Eighth Congress made only one brief reference to the Hundred Flowers. Liu Shao-ch'i went no further than one general remark: "To enable our science and art to flourish and serve the cause of socialist construction, the Central Committee of the Party has put forward the policy of 'Let a hundred flowers blossom, let a hundred schools of thought contend!' "

The evolution of the socialist bloc, the events of October in Poland, and the Hungarian uprising, were probably the immediate causes precipitating the movement, extending it from the field of culture to that of general policy.

On February 27, 1957, at the Eleventh Supreme State Conference, Mao Tse-tung delivered a speech of the greatest importance, "On the Correct Handling of Contradictions among the People." This text, which remained secret at first and was published in a revised version on June 19, 1957, in a totally different political climate, deserves analysis; it is essential to an understanding of the thought of Mao Tse-tung and can be said to clarify several aspects of the Cultural Revolution.[5]

Society, said Mao Tse-tung, offers two types of contradictions. "Antagonistic" contradictions exist between the new society and its irreconcilable enemies (reactionaries and counterrevolutionaries), who must be eliminated ruthlessly. "Nonantagonistic" contradictions exist among the people and are more numerous. They begin between the individual and the group and are to be found everywhere, even between the masses and their leaders. These temporary contradictions, constantly reborn in one form or another, must be eliminated by the 1942 formula of "unity, criticism, unity," so that the initial harmony can temporarily be restored.

This general observation leads to the reexamination or redefinition of several notions: the variable nature and dimensions of the people, the changing content of contradictions, the transformation of "antagonistic" and "nonantagonistic" contradictions, the meaning of the term "dictatorship of the people," and the interplay of centralism and democracy.

In the case of China, Mao Tse-tung affirmed that "It will take a fairly long period of time to decide the issue in the ideological struggle between socialism and capitalism in our country."

The mistaken ideas of the bourgeoisie must be criticized and the "poisonous weeds" they produce must be rooted out. On the other hand, all other ideas or literary and artistic work will be encouraged and accepted, insofar as they fulfill the following six criteria for setting the "fragrant flowers" apart from the "poisonous weeds":

1. Words and actions should help to unite, and not divide, the people of our various nationalities.
2. They should be beneficial, and not harmful, to socialist transformation and socialist construction.
3. They should help to consolidate, and not undermine or weaken, the people's democratic dictatorship.
4. They should help to consolidate, and not undermine or weaken, democratic centralism.
5. They should help to strengthen, and not weaken or encourage people to deviate from, the leadership of the Communist Party.
6. They should be beneficial, and not harmful, to international socialist unity and the unity of the peace-loving peoples of the world.

These criteria, added Mao without a trace of irony, are the basis for the principle of "long-term coexistence and mutual supervision" governing the relations between the Communist Party and the "small parties."

Mao Tse-tung made several references to the events in Hungary of December 1956; he saw in them an excellent example of "antagonistic" acts resulting from contradictions among the people and encouraged by counterrevolutionaries from within and without. These events were followed by "some unrest among a section of our intellectuals, but no serious storms," and by a few strikes among Chinese students and workers in 1956. Mao took these as a warning and as justification for the process of sorting out contradictions, the existence of which many did not dare to acknowledge openly. These events also justified "a comprehensive review of the work of suppressing counterrevolutionaries."

By June 18, however, when the revised version of the text was made public, the Hundred Flowers were fading, and this fact took away much of the meaning of Mao's remarks, for his attitude at the outset seems to have bordered on semi-liberalism. This at least is the impression gained from reading the supposedly authentic version of the speech, as it was delivered and recorded on February 27, 1957. The six criteria just mentioned do not appear there, but Mao Tse-tung apparently agreed to reinforce the position of the "small parties" in government and administrative bodies and to abolish Party committees in the educational system. He is said to have gone so far as to recommend the publication in China of the works of Chiang Kai-shek and the broadcasts of the Voice of America.[6] Although the abolition of Party committees is extremely doubtful (the assertion was vigorously disputed by Mme Shih Liang, then minister of justice), the last proposal, which may have been no more than a joke, is, although surprising, consistent with Mao's style; he did not hesitate to publish Khrushchev's propositions in the Chinese press at the height of the Sino-Soviet quarrel.[7]

The speech that Mao Tse-tung delivered on March 12, 1957, to the National Conference of the Party on Propaganda Work probably revealed more about his intentions, if not his fundamental thinking, than the speech "On the Correct Handling of Contradictions among the People."[8] He took up the question of the intellectuals once more, in the context of the inevitable socialist construction in which they had to be integrated. Out of about 5 million higher and ordinary intellectuals, a small minority (between 1 and 3 percent) was frankly hostile to Marxism, he said, while another minority (10 percent) included Communists and sympathizers relatively well educated in Marxism. The rest, the large majority, were patriots who supported the regime to varying degrees but needed political education. The education of the educators—and all intellectuals are educators—was a permanent necessity, especially in times of great change in the social system. The problem was to remold, reclaim, and integrate the intellectuals by bringing them closer to the workers and peasants and getting them to change their bourgeois view for a proletarian view of the world. The solution did not exclude the blooming of a hundred flowers and the contending of a hundred schools.

Besides this old theme, which was handled forcefully and often taken up by militants during the Cultural Revolution, the speech of March 12 contained the announcement, in much clearer terms than had been the case in the speech on contradictions, of a rectification movement in the Party with the possible participation of outside elements. It was no longer simply a question of winning over the intellectuals and of increasing the expression of scientific, artistic, and literary thought within the framework of Marxist thought, but of criticizing three major errors in ideology and working style—subjectivism, bureaucratism, and sectarianism—which Mao had already denounced during the Eighth Congress. Instead of being weakened by criticism, the Party would find its prestige enhanced and its cadres strengthened, while non-Marxists would confirm their confidence in the Party. The Party's policy must be to open itself up, not to turn in on itself, for it has nothing to fear: "Marxism is a scientific truth; it does not fear criticism and criticism will not triumph over it."

On April 27, the Party launched a rectification movement in the spirit of the Hundred Flowers and the speech of March 12.[9] All positive forces had to be mobilized in order to develop unity, and through it, socialist construction. All sections of society were invited to join freely in the movement, which was to be led with determination but without violence, "as gently as a breeze or a mild rain." After an interval of surprise and hesitation, the results were unexpected and startling. A wave of hostility, growing more and more powerful, daring, and vociferous, swept against the Communists. It was extremely violent on the part of the universities, the administration, and the representatives of the "small parties." The official press, particularly the *People's Daily* and the Shanghai *Wen-hui pao*, and the democratic press, the *Kuang-ming jih-pao*, published extremely abusive and threatening articles; the whole constituted an astonishing anthology of the weaknesses of the regime and the resulting discontent.

Chang Po-chün and Lo Lung-chi, ministers and vice-chairmen of the Democratic League, Chang Nai-ch'i, another minister and vice-chairman of the Association for Democratic Construction, Lung Yün, ex-governor of Yunnan, and many other leading figures of the "United Front," made appeals for increased independence, more authority, more participation, and greater freedom of opinion and expression for their parties. They protested against the exclusive power of the Communists and often against the existence and leadership role of Communist Party committees within state institutions. They demanded an end to arbitrary judgments and the publication of civil and criminal codes. Lung Yün attacked the exploitation of China by the Soviet Union and, since he was of Lolo origin, defended the minority races. Ch'u An-p'ing (editor of *Kuang-ming jih-pao*) pointed out that all twelve deputy premiers were members of the Communist Party.

The illusion of democracy was also frequently denounced. "The National People's Congress and the People's Political Consultative Conference are two paper flowers decorating the democratic facade," wrote the *Shenyang jih-pao* on June 10. Various prominent people, like Chang Hsi-jo, said that the Communist Party thought that it had conquered the Empire; others said that its members were building moats and walls between themselves and the masses and were losing their prestige; still others said that Party members enjoyed large privileges and were gradually forming a new class. Shao Li-tzu, a former Communist who had rallied to the regime, pointed out that Party men alone controlled all the services of the state and the collectives from the *hsien* downward. Teng T'o, who will be mentioned again at the beginning of the Cultural Revolution, deplored the monotony of the press. The economist Ma Yin-ch'u and the historian Chien Po-tsan complained that the regime did not change quickly enough. Ch'en Ming-shu, one of those who had taken part in the Fukien rebellion in 1933, attacked Mao Tse-tung himself, denouncing his rages, his impulsiveness, and his pride. Many of these attacks took place at a discussion meeting of the "small parties" from May 8 to June 2.

University teachers and students reacted strongly; Professor Ko P'ei-ch'i came straight to the point, saying that the masses wanted to "overthrow the regime and kill all Communists," while a girl student, Lin Hsi-ling, was considered a heroine for the appeals she made to take up arms and rebel. Serious troubles occurred in several universities, particularly Wuhan, where big-character wall-newspapers appeared in great profusion, like those of the Cultural Revolution, and with them "democratic walls" and "gardens of liberty."

Criticisms were levelled by various sections of society against the management of the economy, the excesses of the "mass campaigns," and the absence of civil and criminal legislation. It need hardly be said that few Communists allowed themselves to be caught up in this dangerous game.

The Communist leaders, astonished and worried by this wave of accusation and hostility, reacted quickly and harshly; a counterattack was organized simultaneously through the press and political, administrative, and educational organizations, in which elements of the proletariat were made to take part as far as possible. "Why This?"—the first editorial in the *People's Daily* on June 8—was presented as a warning; it accused rightist elements of wanting to isolate the Party and eliminate it from the political scene, and of seeking to reject socialism and return to "bourgeois dictatorship." Others followed, until the editorial of July 1, the most violent of all, attacked the "small parties" (chiefly the Democratic League) and several newspapers (*Wen-hui pao*). Then an attempt was made to gain credit for a cynical version of events, according to which the policy of liberalization was intended merely to bring "antagonistic contradictions" out into the open and to force enemies of the regime and rightists to give themselves away. The poisonous weeds had to be allowed to grow so that they might be pulled up. But the altered version of the speech of February 27 was published on June 18, and a campaign running counter to the first had already been launched.

The non-Communist ministers belonging to "small parties," whose supporters were made to disown them, were eventually dismissed from office at the beginning of 1958, after being forced to humiliate themselves, recant, and ask for punishment. Chang Nai-ch'i, minister of food, Chang Po-chün, minister of communications, and Lo Lung-chi, minister of timber industry, all had the same treatment. Many other prominent people also had to repent. Three office-holders at the University of Wuhan, the site of troubles described as a "small Hungary," were shot.

The Antirightist Movement of 1957 made itself felt in the administration, the press, and the Party. It also affected distinguished members of the literary world: the authoress Ting Ling, already half in disgrace, the poet Ai Ch'ing, who has since died, the director of the People's Literature Publishing House, Feng Hsüeh-feng, and the head of the Art School, Chiang Feng. Authors found that their royalty rights had been cut by half to combat their bourgeois tendencies.[10] Chou Yang drew up the balance sheet of the purge in these circles when he spoke to the Chinese Writers' Union on September 16, 1957:

> A mortal blow was struck at the reactionary ideas of the bourgeoisie, the potential strength of our writers and artists and of the new forces in these fields was liberated, the fetters the old society put on them were removed. . . . A completely new army is now being formed of proletarian literature and art.

His speech, entitled "A Great Debate on the Literary Front," is one of the key documents in the cultural history of the regime.

It is impossible to give an accurate estimate of the purge that followed the Antirightist Movement of the summer and autumn of 1957. The figures are lost among the statistics published by Lo Jui-ch'ing, then minister of public security, for the period from June 1955 to October 1957: 100,000 counterrevolutionaries and "bad elements" (the former numbered 65,000). Out of this total, 5,000 were Party members, 3,000 were members of the

Communist Youth League, and 220 belonged to state organizations. 1,770,000 people had been the object of an inquiry, and 130,000 "serious cases" had been discovered. Several million people were sent down to the country.[11]

Shortly after the beginning of the antirightist counteroffensive, Mao Tse-tung went to Shanghai, Tsingtao, and various other provincial towns, as though he wanted to leave the responsibility for his failure to others (Liu Shao-ch'i and Teng Hsiao-p'ing). Although it was never formally abandoned—it has not been abandoned, even today—the theme of the Hundred Flowers gave way to that of "democracy under centralized direction."[12] The advances made to United Front elements were forgotten.

In September, at the Third Plenum of the Eighth Central Committee (September 20, to October 9, 1957), Teng Hsiao-p'ing mentioned the Antirightist Movement, which had assumed a national scale. He justified it by noting that on the whole the Party remained healthy, and he drew a moral from this: "In the great debate of the Hundred Flowers, we lit a brazier to consume our enemies and our own weaknesses at the same time."

A little later, on October 13, 1957, Mao Tse-tung convened the Supreme State Conference once more. It may be that this was the last time a debate was held on the Hundred Flowers and the Antirightist Movement, for on November 2, 1957, he left for Moscow. This journey was to have immense consequences for the situation within China, as well as for the situation within the socialist bloc.

Notes

1 See *The People's Daily* (June 13, 1956).

2 According to Kuo Mo-jo, these 100,000 intellectuals included: 31,000 teachers, 25,000 medical specialists, 3,000 scientific research workers (above the rank of assistant lecturer), 31,000 engineers, 6,000 artists, men of letters, and writers, and 5,000 other experts. To compare these statistics with those given by Mao Tse-tung several months later, see below in this chapter.

3 Hsü Pei-hung, who was well known in France, where he spent several years, died in October 1953.

4 On this subject see the report by Chou Yang to the second session of the Council of the Chinese Writers' Union (February 27, 1956).

5 Not to be confused with "On Contradiction," a philosophical text written at Yenan in 1937 to oppose dogmatism.

6 See the parallel Roderick MacFarquar draws between the two speeches in MacFarquar, ed., *The Hundred Flowers* (New York: Praeger, 1960).

[7] The Russians did not accept the idea that contradictions could exist in Russia between the leaders and the rest.

[8] This document was not published until June 1964.

[9] The text of the Central Committee directive on this movement was published on April 30.

[10] *People's Daily* (October 5, 1957).

[11] See Hsüeh-hsi, No. 1 (1958). The results of the struggle against the rightists and of the Antirightist Movement also figured in the documents of the Second Plenum of the Eighth Party Congress (May 5-23, 1958), and names of victims were given for about ten provinces.

[12] See also the directive of September 12, 1957, on the continuing of the Antirightist Movement and of a movement for socialist education in enterprises, and that of August 8 on the organization of a socialist education movement in country districts.

13 Cultural Policies During the First Five-Year Plan

Education

The spirit and ambitions of the first five-year plan left their imprint in various fields, which had to be adapted and oriented to serve the building of the economy.

Education is probably the most important of these. The reforms of 1951 had appreciably modified the educational system and its purposes (see Chapter 5). The training and specialization of cadres naturally had to be adjusted to present and future plans. Higher education and technical and professional education at the secondary level were the branches to undergo most development. A particular effort was made in the field of scientific research, so that China could be freed of foreign experts.

The numbers of enrollments and of diplomas awarded follow a roughly parallel progression in education as a whole; they are shown in Tables 13.1 and 13.2 [1]

Detailed statistics reveal that engineering schools at the higher-education level increased most of all (34-40 percent of the students). Official figures show that, in comparison with the best years before 1949, there were four times as many enrollments at the higher education level, 2.8 times as many in technical and professional education at the secondary level, 4.7 times as many at the secondary level, and 2.6 times as many at the primary level. In ten years, the number of diplomas awarded in higher education increased by 430,000, of which 130,000 belonged to the technical branch (which developed twice as fast as the whole of higher education), while those in technical and professional education at the secondary level rose 1.3 million.

Table 13.1
Educational enrollments during the first five-year plan (thousands of students)

Year	Higher Education	Secondary-level Technical and Professional Training	Secondary Education	Primary Education
(1952)	(191)	(636)	(2,490)	(51,100)
1953	212	668	2,933	51,664
1954	253	608	3,587	51,218
1955	288	537	3,900	53,126
1956	403	812	5,165	63,464
1957	441	778	6,281	64,279
(1958)	(660)	(1,470)	(8,520)	(86,400)

Table 13.2
Diplomas awarded during the first five-year plan (thousands of diplomas awarded at the end of the cycle)

Year	Higher Education	Secondary-level Technical and Professional Training	Secondary Education	Primary Education
(1952)	(32)	(68)	(221)	(5,942)
1953	48	118	454	9,945
1954	47	169	649	10,136
1955	55	235	969	10,254
1956	63	174	939	12,287
1957	56	146	1,299	12,307
(1958)	(72)	(191)	(1,313)	(16,225)

This progress should be accepted with many reservations, considering the lenient criteria for selection, hasty training of teachers, lack of facilities and equipment (buildings, laboratories, textbooks), short courses in some subjects, and too large a place given to politics in the curricula, as the critics said during the Hundred Flowers. A great effort was made to increase the quantity of students, however, and the authoritarianism determining their choice of specialization made it possible to move toward meeting economic needs.

At the primary school level, collective enterprises began to create and run schools for the children of their families; this helped to raise the school attendance rate and guide pupils toward a branch of practical education. The illiteracy rate among adults remained high. The estimates current before 1949 (70-80 percent among the peasants, 60 percent among the workers) did not change much for people over thirty years of age. Almost 100 percent of the women in country districts were illiterate.

In 1957, scientific research was carried out in 580 establishments employing more than 28,000 research students and technicians, amounting to three times as many students and technicians as in 1952.[2] The Academy of Sciences, of which Kuo Mo-jo was chairman, consisted of forty-one institutes with 2,063 research students.[3] Scientific research still seemed to be weak, badly organized, and backward, however, when considered in relation to the needs of the economy. In June 1955, the research plan of the Academy of Sciences (a five-year plan) was still being revised, while a fifteen-year plan was no more than a vague proposal. This may be why scientific planning was first handed over on March 14, 1956, to a special committee of the Planning Commission with Marshal Ch'en Yi as its chairman, and then in May 1957 to a permanent committee of the State Council. Meanwhile the former committee, with the help of Soviet experts, drew up a twelve-year plan for scientific development (1956-1967) which, as Liu Shao-ch'i said at the Eighth Congress, aimed at reaching the same level as the rest of the world in the fields of science and technology. In other words, China was to be made independent in these fields, as well as in industry, by the end of the third five-year plan, 1962-1967.

Reform of the written language

The question of the reform of the written language was linked with the education question and with the more general question of knowledge and how to transmit it. It had already arisen in a different, even more important form at the beginning of the century with the explosion of Western ideas and science, and had received a solution in principle, thanks to Hu Shih, Ch'en Tu-hsiu, and several others. The question then was whether the use of the literary language (*wen-yen*) was compatible with the modernization of China. The reply could only be in the negative. The literary language was accessible to an extremely small number of scholars (perhaps 1 percent of the population). It could not suitably express Western scientific concepts. It was both imprecise and subtle, lending itself to poetry, ethics, and metaphysics, but was little suited to logical reasoning. "But our written language is too difficult. It is poetic. It imprisons ideas. . . . All the power contained by intelligence remains in the hands of scholars, and an immovable order is founded on difficulty and wit," as the Chinese interlocutor of Paul Valéry said.[4] The spoken language (*pai-hua*) was written as it was spoken, using the same characters as *wen-yen*, but its structure was much closer to that of Western languages. It gradually replaced the written language, which was dropped in everyday use, disappearing gradually as Latin did in Europe at the end of the Middle Ages.[5]

In October 1949, two completely different problems appeared, arising from similar considerations. One was concerned with the simplification of characters. The great number of characters could be reduced by eliminating all those that duplicated others or by giving another meaning to characters written and pronounced in the same way. Complicated characters could also be simplified by cutting down the number of strokes—some needed as many as twenty. The second problem concerned the use of an alphabet and would have involved abandoning the characters. Because these two questions are at the heart of the Chinese cultural heritage and involve China's adaptation to the modern world as well as individual intellectual capacities, a brief account of the decisions taken, how they were taken, and to what end is in order here.

The reform of the written language as a whole was first entrusted to an association, created in October 1949, then to a study committee, constituted on February 5, 1952, and eventually to a reform committee, set up on December 23, 1954; the leading figure in charge of it was Wu Yü-chang.[6] The reform took final shape in the autumn of 1955, during a national conference (October 15-23), followed by a scientific conference (October 25-31) whose decisions were ratified by the State Council (January 28, 1956).

As far as the simplification of characters was concerned, 1,055 characters with several different forms were eliminated; 515 characters in current use and 56 roots were abbreviated, in groups, to make it easier to learn them gradually. Later on, 96 and then 100 more simplified characters were added to the list. This resulted in a considerable saving of time in the use of the 4,000 or 5,000 characters that are indispensable to every literate person. Archaic or useless words were later to be listed apart from the rest; the great Chinese dictionaries contain as many as 40,000 to 60,000 characters.[7] Lastly, it was decided to write from left to right, a small measure given the fact that each character represents one syllable, but it would help the

Chinese get used to reading Western or phonetic texts.[8] The committee had the sense not to reduce words or expressions of several syllables to a single character.[9] Simplified characters, which could be more numerous, are now in general use. The younger generation is increasingly cut off from old books, which have been extensively removed from circulation by the regime or destroyed by the million during the Cultural Revolution. Chinese from Taiwan or elsewhere have some difficulty in reading mainland news papers, in addition to the difficulties that arise from differences in style, political vocabulary, and content.

A project was published on February 12, 1956, on the question of giving the language an alphabet. The Jesuits had come up against this problem in the seventeenth century; it had been under discussion for fifty years and had been followed closely by the Communists from the earliest days of the Party.[10] The Latin alphabet was eventually selected after the consideration of several alphabets, including the Cyrillic and other, entirely original ones. The first formula proposed, based on thirty letters (twenty-five Latin letters with the omission of V, two adapted from Latin, one Cyrillic, and two international symbols), was quickly changed and the twenty-six Latin letters were retained, with a sign added to the syllables to indicate the four tones of the Peking dialect. The State Council finally adopted this transcription on November 1, 1957, and its decision was approved by the National People's Congress on February 11, 1958.

In 1956, as is still the case now, the use of the alphabet was above all a phonetic means of unifying local dialects and accents on the basis of the pronunciation of Peking, which was described as the "common spoken language" (*p'u-t'ung hua*), rather than a replacement for the characters. On January 6, 1956, instructions were issued by the State Council consisting of practical measures to achieve this, ranging from classes to the compulsory use of *p'u-t'ung hua* in the state services, the army, and schools. All children from the third year in primary school upward had to be able to speak it from 1960 on.[11] A national committee for the propagation of *p'u-t'ung hua* was created. Curiously enough, it was presided over by Ch'en Yi, who was well known for his strong Szechwan accent. It should perhaps be added that when the Chinese adopted a latinized transcription for the characters, they were not really concerned about making it easier for foreigners to transcribe Chinese names, much less study the Chinese language. Publications in foreign languages still use various systems of transcription for this, adapted more or less to the language in question.

Without trying to make a forecast on the basis of past events, it is clear that simplified characters have been adopted easily because they remain within the Chinese historical tradition and are true to the Chinese genius, but the use of the Latin alphabet has spread little. The press is virtually unaware of it, and schools use it only in the early stages of learning to read. The Cultural Revolution dealt it a blow that may prove fatal.[12] It seems that Mao Tse-tung and his supporters, like the traditionalists, (which is less of a paradox than it may appear), accepted alphabetization with resignation rather than enthusiasm. The question of abandoning characters in its favor will apparently not have to be decided by the present generation. The example of Japan has proved beyond question that traditional ideographic writing is not incompatible with scientific and technical progress.

The press, publications, and the cinema

Periodicals, books, radio, and cinema are considered first of all as instruments of class struggle and secondarily as means of information or distraction. They are controlled, through various ministries, by the Party's Propaganda Department, of which Lu Ting-yi was in charge until June 1966. According to official figures, the number of periodicals rose considerably between 1952 and 1957. During this time, the combined circulation of Peking newspapers and the great regional papers grew from 1,609 million to 2,224.4 million copies, with periodicals growing from 204.2 million to 315 million copies, and books from 785.7 million to 1,278 million.[13]

The *People's Daily,* which printed 550,000 copies a day in 1954 (plus several supplements) is the great national newspaper. It is the organ of the Central Committee of the Party, combining the propagation of doctrine with news, education, and official information. It sets the tone for the press as a whole, and its editorials are often reprinted elsewhere. The Antirightist Movement of 1957 gave it increased authority over other papers for particular categories of readers: *Kuang-ming jih-pao*, the former paper of the Democratic League, for cultural circles; *Kung-jen jih-pao* (*The Worker's Daily*), the organ of the trade unions; *Chung-kuo ch'ing-nien* (*Chinese Youth*), representing the Communist Youth League; *Ta Kung pao* (*Impartial Daily*), read by economic circles. Provincial papers reproduced the *People's Daily* at a local level. The *Chieh-fang-chün pao* (*Liberation Army Daily*) and perhaps the Shanghai *Wen-hui pao* were the only ones that apparently maintained a little independence. In 1955, according to fragmentary statistics, there were 265 newspapers, 17 of which circulated on a national scale, and 305 periodicals (190 million copies). Other statistics in 1956 give a total of 347 national or provincial newspapers, and 484 periodicals.

Periodicals improved over time in quality and variety. *Hsüeh-hsi* (*Study*), later replaced by *Hung-ch'i* (*Red Flag*), was the doctrinal review for cadres, *Shih-chieh chih-shih* (*World Knowledge*) dealt with foreign policy, and *Hsin kuan-ch'a* (*New Observer*) with political, economic, and social questions. Although they were totally lacking in objectivity, they did at least give accurate information on the position of the government and the Party. A few research periodicals, within the limits imposed by ideology and the secrecy inherent in the regime, were of real scientific interest, though they were of a much lower standard than corresponding Western publications.

The need to keep the cadres, the public, and all those in responsible jobs properly informed, the serious approach to the first five-year plan, the importance of the economy compared with politics, the influence of Soviet experts—albeit indirect—probably explain this improvement in periodicals. It ceased with the disorders, and later the disappointments, of the Great Leap Forward, giving way to verbose and inconsistent writing about politics and ideology in 1966.

Despite some progress, the number of books published remained low in relation to the population: 20,000 titles and 900 million volumes in 1954.[14] About 2,000 works were translated from foreign languages (mainly scientific books for educational use). Several novels were extremely successful. *Defend Yenan,* which was later condemned on the pretext that it had helped to glorify P'eng Teh-huai, sold 500,000 copies in 1954. Soviet novels were also published and printed in quantity (*How Steel was Tempered* by Ostrovski ran to 850,000 copies). A few old popular novels were reprinted.[15]

The cinema made little progress; the number of films released each year (dubbed or made in China) increased from 43 to 119 between 1952 and 1957,[16] while the number of projection teams rose from 1,110 to 6,692. Film distribution posed various technical and material problems, and the cinema has for a long time been superseded by the theater, which continued to develop (2,017 troupes in 1952, 2,808 in 1957), and retained pride of place over a tradition that was still novel.

Religious policy

Although on their guard, and theoretically hostile toward all religions, whatever their nature—in spite of the religious freedom guaranteed by Article 88 of the 1954 constitution—the Chinese Communists showed some tolerance, organizing religions in the name of patriotism and the building of socialism, and using them for international contacts, which the Bandung conference extended to many Islamic and Buddhist nations (see Chapter 15).

Muslims generally belonged to the institutional framework of the minority races and were consequently better equipped than some to resist pressure, both by the ethnic origins of the largest of their groups and by the virile quality of their faith. As regards their religious and cultural practices, they were better treated than members of other faiths.[17] On the other hand, because they were more readily suspected of nationalism and were quick to rebel, as they did in certain parts of the Northeast in 1952 and 1953 during the land reform, they came under strict political supervision. On May 11, 1953, they were grouped into a Chinese Islamic Association, inaugurated in Peking. Named as their chairman was the Tartar Burhan, a returned student from Germany and Russia who had rallied to the regime in 1949. The association asserted itself politically by adopting as its own the great aims of the regime: the building of socialism within the country and the movement for peace abroad. During the period of the first five-year plan, two national congresses were held (November 1955 and December 1956).

The Buddhists benefited from China's improved relations with Burma, Cambodia, and Ceylon, from visits to Peking of several political figures of the Buddhist faith, and from the 2,500th anniversary of the Buddha's birth. The restoration of temples and of great sculptural monuments famous throughout the world, the sending of Buddhist missions abroad, and the publication of periodicals like *Modern Buddhism (Hsien-tai Fo-hsüeh)* helped disguise the fact that the Buddhist Association, which was founded in 1953 and extended to several provinces in 1957, had become entirely political and was an auxiliary of the Communist Party, while the clergy received severe treatment, being considerably cut down in numbers and status and increasingly obliged to enter agricultural or handicraft production.[18]

In 1957, the regime created a Taoist Association under the patronage of several second-rank public figures. This action did not improve the difficult situation of the priests and members of this old, authentically and exclusively Chinese religion. Taoism was considered more dangerous than the other religions because it had more support among the people, was closer to popular superstitions, and provided a more fertile field for the development of secret societies.

The Party's policy toward Christians, always suspected of serving foreign interest—American-British in the case of the Protestants and Roman in that of the Catholics—was one of organized nationalization. The Chinese Protestants held their first national congress on August 6, 1954. The 232 members, representing 400,000 Protestants of various denominations, elected a national committee of 150 who declared their support for the government and their mistrust of American imperialism. The Catholics were less inclined than the Protestants to allow themselves to be drawn into politics. Their unity, their sense of hierarchy, and the discipline of Rome gave them a better defense against ideology. The arrest of numerous Catholics in Shanghai at the time of the Legion of Mary affair, the imprisonment of an important segment of the clergy, including Msgr. Ignatius Kiung, bishop of Shanghai, the expulsion of all foreign missionaries and of Msgr. Riberi, the papal nuncio, and the confiscation of religious establishments (schools, hospitals) combined to create a serious situation.[19] Chinese Catholics found it doubly hard to stand up to patriotic arguments, for historically they had always been suspect. They had to submit to the "Three Autonomies" Movement—administrative, financial, and apostolic autonomy—which broke their temporal allegiance to the Pope. On the other hand, the Communists did not try to intrude in matters of dogma and allowed services to continue on a reduced scale in certain churches. This apparent toleration did not prevent them from trying to divide Chinese Catholics by provoking and supporting individual movements like the Council of Nanking, in which the leading figure was Vicar-General Li Wei-kuang.

1957 was a difficult year. The promises of the Hundred Flowers were not kept. On July 15, 1957, in the middle of the Antirightist Movement, the 3 million Chinese Catholics held a conference in Peking, at which they acknowedged the moral and doctrinal authority of the Pope but made many reservations as to his leadership. Shortly afterward, a Patriotic Association of Chinese Catholics was formed. Bishops were appointed and consecrated without authority from Rome; in 1957, they numbered nearly fifty. The Chinese Catholic church survived, but it was on the verge of schism.

The minority races

The 1954 constitution stated that all the races in China were equal (apart from the Han, there are fifty-four ethnic minorities, numbering more than 35 million people in all), but it confirmed the loss of their right to self-determination. In this, it was much less liberal than the constitution of the Chinese Soviet Republic of 1931, which had acknowledged that right. The 1954 constitution went still further, forbidding any action that might "hamper the unity of nationalities"—in other words, any expression of local nationalism. To balance this, it guaranteed some regional administrative autonomy, which did develop during the first five-year plan. The Sinkiang Uighur Autonomous Region was inaugurated in October 1955. In July 1957, the Kwangsi Chuang Autonomous Region and the Ninghsia Hui Autonomous Region were created. In the case of Tibet, difficulties arising from local resistance and the Khampa rebellion (1956) delayed the creation of an autonomous region until 1965.[20]

Little by little, established practices were extended to create autonomous *chou* and *hsien,* as provided in Article 53 of the 1954 constitution. The autonomous regions were responsible to Peking in the same way as the provinces; the Nationalities Committee of the Council of State, presided over from 1954 on by the Mongol Ulanfu, was given the task of adjusting laws and regulations to suit each different ethnic group. The Central Committee of the Party, with the support of its Nationalities Department, decided on policy toward the minority races. Li Wei-han, head of this department and of the United Front Department, was the most prominent figure in this policy.

From 1953 to 1957 the whole regime made a great effort to train more cadres from minority races in the specialized institutes, the most important of which were those in Peking and Kunming (Yunnan), to bring more members of minority races into the Party, not to hinder the cultural life of the autonomous territories, and to open them more to modern life. On a parallel with the reform of the Chinese written language, ways of writing minority languages were studied. The Latin alphabet was generally adopted for this purpose, although the Cyrillic alphabet was sometimes used at least temporarily, as in the case of Mongol, Kazakh, and Tadjik. Books, periodicals, and radio became increasingly important. In 1957, about thirty newspapers and periodicals existed, with print runs of 24,440,000 copies of papers and 2,440,000 of periodicals. In the same year, 14,620,000 books were published.[21] Numerous ethnographic and linguistic studies were conducted by the Academy of Sciences, which published the results; a less scientific periodical—*Unity of the Minorities (Min-tsu t'uan-chieh)*—was produced for the public at large.

School attendance rose little, perhaps because of the lack of teachers. The figures quoted by Chou En-lai for 1953 [22] (2,546,000 pupils at primary level, 163,000 at secondary level, and 5,500 in higher education) show no great change until 1958, a year in which statistics were unreliable in any case.

Minority policy, backed up by an effort at colonization that was sometimes considerable, particularly in the frontier regions of Sinkiang and Inner Mongolia, went hand in hand with extensive Han and socialist penetration, preparing the ground for the Party's eventual goal of assimilation. The dazzling parades of the minority races resplendent in their national dress, in sharp contrast with the sober Chinese garb and a delight for the foreign visitor, could not hide the reality. The minority races were probably not taken in by the role they played. The attacks on local nationalism, skillfully mingled with rightist tendencies, during the Antirightist Movement in 1957 gave proof of this; further proof was afforded by the Cultural Revolution ten years later.[23]

Population and demographic policy

The unified political organization of the regime and its broad reach enabled it to carry out a general census of the population, impossible until then because of the inadequate administrative structures under the Empire and the troubles of the Republican era. The Chinese, amazed and anxious at the discovery, were told that they numbered more than 600 million—to be precise, 601,938,035 on June 30, 1953 at midnight.[24] The population as a whole was composed of 547,283,057 (93.94 percent) Han and 35,320,360 (6.06 percent) ethnic minorities.[25] The figures included Overseas Chinese (11,743,320) and Taiwan Chinese (7,591,298), though a direct census had not been made of the last two categories. Of those living on the mainland, 13.20 percent were town dwellers, (77,257,282) and 86.74 percent lived in country districts (505,346,135). Men slightly outnumbered women at 51.82 percent. Just as important as these total figures was the revelation that the annual rate of increase, obtained through partial statistics based on 30 million people, was about 2 percent (birthrate 3.7 percent, deathrate 1.7 percent). These figures and the conclusions to be drawn from them, in spite of official optimism and the well-known hostility of Marxism to Malthusian theories, were to result in a birth control policy, at least during the years covered by the plan. It was carried out under various pretexts: public health, immediate needs of production.

Shao Li-tzu seems to have been the first to raise the question of contraception at the National People's Congress of September 1954; he distinguished between Malthusian theories and the right of every couple to have access to scientific information on contraception. The question was raised by different leaders during the years that followed, and legislation was gradually drawn up covering contraception, abortion, sterilization, and the suitable age for marriage. In 1957 and 1958, contraceptive propaganda was issued throughout the country, though the essential material means were not available.

The principle of birth control was helped by the declining authority of the older generation, the tendency toward equality between the sexes, and the development of hygiene. But love of children, the moral obligation to ensure male descent, and all kinds of prejudices were still extremely strong. The efficacy of the propaganda is doubtful, and no enquiry or partial census has given any details. With the spring of 1958 and the studied optimism of the Great Leap Forward and the people's communes, birth control campaigns were officially abandoned. The rector of Peking University, Ma Yin-ch'u, who had for a long time stubbornly supported the campaigns on economic grounds (low rate of productivity and saving in China, the handicap of a large population in a society destined for automation), was severely criticized and had to resign from his post. [26] Demographic questions were rarely raised thereafter and then received brief treatment. The last figure quoted by an official document gave the Chinese population (including 10 million inhabitants of Taiwan, but excluding Overseas Chinese) as 656,630,000 at the end of 1957.[27] Since 1958, no general or partial statistics have been given on birth, mortality, or marriage rates.[28] It looks as though the Chinese leaders no longer dare to face the agonizing problem of multitude.

Notes

[1] *Ten Great Years*, p. 192. Figures quoted before this reference work was published often do not tally exactly with those it gives, particularly in the case of technical and professional education.

[2] See *Ten Great Years*, p. 194.

[3] New China News Agency (June 2, 1955). Kuo Mo-jo added that 600 institutes, with 3,000 research students, were in the charge of about thirty ministries. It appears that these figures only covered qualified research students, excluding technicians and other employees.

[4] Paul Valéry, *Regards sur le monde actuel* (Paris: Gallimard, 1945).

[5] This is a simplified summary of the question. Hu Shih examines it in his work *Chung-kuo hsin-wen-hsüeh yün-tung hsiao-shih* (*A Short History of the New Literature Movement*) (Taipei, 1957).

[6] Wu Yü-chang (1878-1966) was one of the oldest members of the Chinese Communist Party. He was a student at the University of Lyons after World War I.

[7] For a general view of the question of Chinese writing, see C. Milsky, *Preparation of the Script Reform in the People's Republic of China* (The Hague: Mouton, 1974).

[8] Newspapers are sometimes still written vertically, as is the case of most periodicals and newspapers in Taiwan or for Overseas Chinese.

[9] Wu Yü-chang summarized the work and proposals of his committee and the national conference in an article in the *Kuang-ming jih-pao* (January 18, 1956).

[10] Particularly by Ch'ü Ch'iu-pai, the former Party secretary. A transcription had been used experimentally in 1928 in the Chinese colony in Vladivostok. The Communists issued a newspaper in the Latin alphabet during the anti-Japanese war (see Guillermaz, *A History of the Chinese Communist Party*, p. 343).

[11] This measure was made public by the Hsinhua Agency on February 10, 1956.

[12] In August 1966 the transcription vanished from street names and names of railway stations. A little earlier the *People's Daily*, *Hung Ch'i* (*Red Flag*) and the *Kuang-ming jih-pao* had eliminated their subtitles in transcription. Since 1972 the subtitles have reappeared in the *Kuang-ming jih-pao* and a few periodicals.

[13] See *Ten Great Years*, p. 207.

[14] Best prewar figures, as quoted by the Communists: 9,000 titles and 178 million copies (in 1936); these figures probably do not include Manchuria.

[15] The general evolution of trends in literature and art is discussed in Chapter 21.

[16] *Ten Great Years*, p. 206.

[17] The largest and most compact group is that of the Uighurs in Sinkiang, with 3,640,350 members, to which should be added the Kazakhs, the Kirghiz, and the Tadjiks. Other Muslim groups of Chinese race are much more scattered and amount to about the same number of believers: 3,559,350.

[18] The treatment given to the Buddhists in Tibet and Mongolia falls within the context of policy toward minority races. That mentioned above applies above all to Buddhists in China itself.

[19] The Vatican issued the following figures on the situation of Catholics in China: 17 bishops and apostolic envoys were in prison; 6 bishops and archbishops had died in prison; 2,645 priests and missionaries had been expelled; 98 foreign priests had been imprisoned; and 200 Chinese priests and members of religious orders had died as a result of persecution. Radio Vatican (December 22, 1954), quoted by *Le Monde* (December 24, 1954).

[20] The Tibetan question will be dealt with in Chapter 21 with regard to the 1959 rising; the situation between 1953 and 1957 will be mentioned at the same time.

[21] *Ten Great Years*, p. 210. The paper printed slightly fewer copies in 1957 than in 1952, then increased to 39.8 million in 1958.

[22] Report of September 23, 1954, to the First National People's Congress.

[23] See the report of October 19, 1957.

[24] These figures were published on November 1, 1954, under the headings of provinces and minority races. The choice of 1953 as the year for the general census was determined by the election of the First National People's Congress.

[25] These were divided into (in millions): Chuang (Kwangsi), 6.6; Uighurs, 3.6; Hui, 3.6; Yi, 3.2; Tibetans, 2.7; Miao, 2.5; Manchu, 2.4, Mongols, 1.4, Pu-yi, 1.3; Koreans, 1.1; miscellaneous, 6.7.

[26] See his "New Theory of Population," in an appendix to Leo A. Orleans, "Birth Control, Reversal or Postponement," *The China Quarterly*, No. 3 (July-September 1960).

[27] *Ten Great Years,* p. 11. Much later, several leaders spoke in terms of 700 or 720 million Chinese, and now of about 800 million, but this should be considered as a rough indication.

[28] In 1973, however, Chou En-lai said that the Chinese population was increasing at an annual rate of about 2 percent.

14 The New Military Institutions

Chinese military institutions underwent far-reaching changes during the first five-year plan for several reasons: the impact of the Korean War on organization, armament, and military technique; the influence of the Soviet model; the priority given to the building up of the economy; a national foreign policy based to a large extent on ideological propaganda; and the fact that security from external attack was ensured by the Sino-Soviet treaty of February 14, 1950. Changes in structure, form, and recruitment in keeping with the 1954 constitution, and a change in attitude above all, meant that for several years the Chinese armed forces followed the Soviet pattern until the worsening of ideological and political relations between Moscow and Peking led them back toward their former tradition.

In 1952, Hsiao Hua, assistant director of the army's Political Department, announced coming changes in "The People's Liberation Army On the Road to Modernization."[1] This vigorous speech contained all the ideas suggested by its title: the importance of a good general education for soldiers, the need for a large national defense industry, the unification of the People's Liberation Army and the former Nationalist forces, the valuable example of Soviet military science, the usefulness of the Korean battlefields for the logistical and technical training of the armed forces, particularly the air force, and the proposal to adopt compulsory military service. As Hsiao Hua said in summary, "the People's Liberation Army must attain a perfect command of modern military techniques." Surprisingly enough—particularly because the speaker held a senior post in the Party—less importance than usual was attached to political education and the revolutionary tradition.

Three years later the government, reorganized on the basis of the 1954 constitution, adopted modern military legislation and organization of the Soviet type, enacting the important laws or regulations of 1955: the regulation of February 8 on the status of officers; the regulation of February 12 on decorations and medals; and the law of July 30 on compulsory military service. The appointment of ten marshals on September 27, 1955, was the final symbol of this spectacular evolution.

With the conscription of 1955, the old people's army, born of the patriotism and enthusiasm of the masses, came to an end. The new law, mainly inspired by the Russian system, required that in theory every citizen aged eighteen was to serve three years in the army or public security forces, four years in the air force or the land-based navy, or five years in the fleet; he then belonged to the reserve until the age of forty (first reserve up till the age of thirty, second reserve from thirty to forty).? In fact, because 5 to 6 million men reached eighteen each year, whereas the armed forces numbered 3 million, the real yearly intake was around 700,000. A variety of criteria—physical and intellectual capacities, social origin, political loyalty—were brought into play and permitted a remarkable selection to be made. The selection was further enhanced by the high prestige the new regime had bestowed on the soldier's profession by going against deep-seated pacifist currents and abolishing ancient prejudices. When a man was called up, his departure was accompanied by demonstrations of patriotism and solidarity. When he came back, the village gained a future cadre, who had been trained politically and intellectually during his national service.

Conscription made numerous reservists available to the state; they also formed the backbone of the militia, gave premilitary training to young people, and, above all, formed an element whose loyalty to the Party had been tested. P'eng Teh-huai gave the introductory report to the National People's Congress on the new law on compulsory national service. He stressed the need to build up a powerful modern force, justified, with supporting figures, a policy of demobilization, had little to say about the masses, and, as the tendency then was, placed his speech in the context of international détente, as did Yeh Chien-ying and Liu Po-ch'eng.

Because the army was a regular army by origin, a classic structure had to be provided, leading to a certain degree of professionalism and specialization. For the first time in its history, the army was given ranks distinct from the duties to be carried out, and a wide range of salaries. The new hierarchy was differentiated by insignia imitating those of the Soviet army: epaulettes with golden stripes and stars, embroidered collars, and colors, which varied from one branch of the armed forces to another. Cadres were given dress uniforms; previously, only their equipment had distinguished them from men in the ranks. Several decorations were created: Order of August 1, Order of Independence and Liberty, Order of Liberation, all marking different periods in the military history of the regime (1927-1935, 1937-1945, 1946-1950); and each order was divided into classes.

On the National Day, October 1, 1955, the ten new marshals—Chu Teh, P'eng Teh-huai, Lin Piao, Liu Po-ch'eng, Ho Lung, Ch'en Yi, Lo Jung-huan, Hsü Hsiang-ch'ien, Nieh Jung-chen and Yeh Chien-ying—appeared in full array, complete with their field-marshal's batons, at the traditional military parade. The men in the ranks also had new uniforms—forage caps or flat caps, wide trousers, short jackets, and boots in Russian style. The navy and air force uniforms resembled the international type. Nothing recalled the humble uniforms of past wars.

The military organization was—theoretically at least—an integral part of the state system once the constitution of 1954 was in force. Thus, the president of the Republic commanded the armed forces and was chairman of the National Defense Council (Article 42). The Council, which was supposed to replace the Revolutionary Military Council, originally had ninety-two members, including about thirty generals of the former regime. Its functions were largely honorary and resembled those of the former Strategic Council of the Nationalist government.

The Ministry of National Defense had under its authority the General Staff, the General Logistics Department, and the General Political Department; these in turn were at the head of various commands and service arms.[3] Although the Ministry of National Defense was responsible to the State Council, the real authority lay with the Party and more specifically with its Military Affairs Committee, chaired by Mao Tse-tung. This committee's composition is not known in detail, though it appears to have had less than twelve members. It seems to have had seven small specialized departments to carry out its work and sometimes to have called large conferences.[4]

The Political Department was the Party within the army.[5] From the top down to the company level, it consisted of a hierarchy of Party committees and political commissars or instructors running parallel to the different ranks in the army hierarchy. Its chief functions were to countersign, except in case of emergency, orders given by commanders of units, to propagate Party ideology and policy, and to organize and direct the educational and cultural life of the army. Frictions inevitably developed as the functions of the command became more complex and further removed from political functions. A strong proportion of Party members among the officers, 90

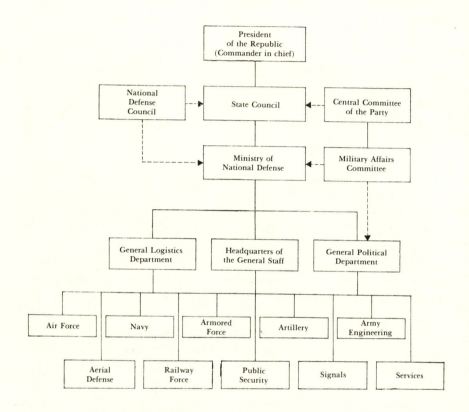

Figure 14.1   Organization of the military (1954)

percent among the older and 30 percent among the younger, and 10 percent among the noncommissioned officers, according to reliable estimates, helped to maintain satisfactory cohesion.

In June 1954, China was divided into thirteen large military regions (see Table 14.1), each known by the name of its chief town, which directed one or several provinces (military districts).[6] The military districts (provinces) were themselves subdivided into subdistricts (generally into the *chuan ch'ü* divisions of civil administration) and garrisons corresponding to important towns.

Table 14.1
Military regions, 1954

Military regions	Corresponding districts	Military regions	Corresponding districts
Peking	Hopei, Shansi	Kunming	Kweichow, Yunnan
Shenyang	Liaoning, Kirin, Heilungkiang	Chengtu	Szechwan
Wuhan	Hupei, Honan	Lanchow	Shensi, Kansu, Ninghsia, Tsinghai
Tsinan	Shantung	Sinkiang	These three autonomous regions were not divided into military districts
Foochow	Fukien, Kiangsi	Inner Mongolia	
Nanking	Kiangsu, Anhwei, Chekiang	Tibet	
Canton (Kwangchow)	Kwangtung, Kwangsi, Hunan		

The order of battle of the Chinese army in 1955 and the years following comprised thirty to forty armies with three divisions each (between 50,000 and 60,000 men to an army and from 15,000 to 20,000 to a division on a war footing), about fifty specialized independent divisions (cavalry, artillery, armored, railway, airborne, antitank, antiaircraft, public security), about fifty independent regiments, and miscellaneous services. The total number of men in the various arms and services of the army probably amounted to 2.6 million.

The firepower of the units, particularly in the case of the artillery, remained well below Western standards, and strategic mobility was low; arms of Russian origin began to be copied in China, under new names.

The patience and endurance of the Chinese soldier and his intelligence and docility generally make him a good infantryman. His capacity to move rapidly and remain on the move for a long time, to live in all climates under conditions of minimum supplies and comfort, and to undergo severe hardship made him particularly useful in operations over theatres of war with poor communication channels, or in other words roughly anywhere in Central and East Asia. On the other hand, the technical branches were less well manned, though this weakness became less pronounced owing to the length of national service and to economic development.

The air force and the navy were part of the People's Liberation Army. In 1955, they were almost entirely dependent on the Russians for their equipment and technology. The air force (between 200,000 and 250,000 men) had between 2,300 and 3,000 aircraft: between 1,600 and 1,900 fighters (MIG 15, MIG 17, later MIG 19 and a few MIG 21), from 300 to 400 IL 18 bombers, and out-of-date transport or training aircraft (TU 4). It was organized into airborne divisions: eighteen to twenty fighter divisions, five bomber divisions, one transport division, and special regiments. The navy (150,000 men) had 200,000 tons of small craft, a few submarines (about twenty ocean-going submarines of the W class and one or two of the G class equipped for launching missiles about 1960), a landing force (30,000 men), and a small naval air force (500 aircraft). It was divided into three fleets: Northern, Central and Southern. Its capabilities were limited to coastal defense.

The general characteristics of the conventional armed forces changed little until 1966. Technical levels and the quality of equipment declined (particularly in the air force) as a result of the combined effect of the misfortunes of the Great Leap Forward and the end of Sino-Soviet military and technical cooperation after 1960.[7]

The militia, a legacy of the civil and foreign wars, was provided for by Article 23 of the Common Program of 1949 and was constituted on the basis of the administration of territories and sometimes of enterprises. It was not properly and systematically organized until the appearance of the people's communes in 1958 or even four or five years after that, when people's war came back into favor. Theoretically, the militia came under *hsiang* and *hsien* civil authorities, reverting to army command at the administrative level above that of the *hsien*. Its numbers were impossible to assess with accuracy and corresponded to available resources of arms; traditional or makeshift weapons (pikes, sabers, rough and ready firearms) could equip part of it. Above all, it was an inexhaustible reserve of men for the regular army and in the case of invasion was the basis of a widespread land defense.

Toward the end of the first five-year plan, the Chinese began to consider the acquisition of nuclear weapons. The Atomic Energy Institute was created in May 1957, and on October 15 of the same year a technical aid agreement for the production of nuclear weapons was signed with the Soviet Union.[8]

The financing of economic development gradually reduced the size of the military budget, and it is difficult to analyze it. It is probably about $2,500 million, on an average, representing 22 percent of the national budget; this proportion dropped below 20 percent in 1956 and 1957.

The great changes undergone by the military institutions in 1954 and above all in 1955 had predictable political consequences a few years later. They appreciably weakened the influence of the Party (and particularly its General Political Department) at the various levels of the army hierarchy, developed a form of professionalism in many officers (mostly among young officers trained in military academies), lessened the participation of the army in production, reduced the importance given to political work in the units, and consequently affected the revolutionary spirit of both cadres and men. These changes also considerably diminished the army's participation in the work of economic reconstruction. Although large semimilitary agricultural units still worked on land reclamation and development in Sinkiang and other frontier regions, the number of working days supplied by the army to the civilian sector fell to 4 million in 1956. Lastly, to a certain extent, these changes meant that the army no longer loaned cadres to carry out administrative duties in time of difficulty (land reform, collectivization) or sent them to help regions that were underprivileged or in the grip of public calamities.

The temporary triumph of this line was acknowledged by Ho Lung in his great speech of October 1, 1956, on "The Democratic Tradition of the Chinese People's Liberation Army":[9]

> For a time a few persons who stuck to bourgeois views on military affairs came to the fore again and created trouble in the new historical period following the founding of the Chinese People's Republic. In the name of building a modern regular army, they advocated the abolition of the Party committee system in the army, which in reality meant abolishing the leadership of the army by the Party, weakening political work, and negating the democratic tradition and mass line of our army.

It seems possible that the decline in political work was highly perceptible, for in 1956 at the time of the Eighth Congress, itself moderate in inspiration, a few signs warned of a reversal of the trend.[10] The reversal came with the Antirightist Movement, which was carried out in the army, as in the country as a whole, after the failure of the Hundred Flowers. It gained momentum in 1958 and became irresistible in 1959 when Marshal Lin Piao replaced Marshal P'eng Teh-huai as minister of national defense.

Notes

[1] Speech of July 31, 1952, on the twenty-fifth anniversary of the army before the National Committee of the Political Consultative Conference.

[2] These periods were later changed to four years in the army, five years in the air force, and five in the navy. Age limits are naturally different for cadres on the active or the reserve list. Students of universities and higher educational establishments receive preparatory training to become officers or noncommissioned officer cadres.

[3] See Figure 14.1. Some departments—Instruction, Cadres, Inspection, Finance—were sometimes considered autonomous.

[4] See Ralph L. Powell, "The Military Affairs Committee and Party Control of the Military in China," *Asian Survey* (July 1963).

[5] See Article 35 of the Party statutes.

[6] The territorial divisions took on great political importance from 1967 on, when the Cultural Revolution dismantled the regular political and administrative structures.

[7] For information on the characteristics, numbers, and organization of the Chinese armed forces, see the specialized works listed in the bibliography. The aim of this chapter is to give a general idea, because of the later role of the military in the internal political life of the country.

[8] The Russians refused to honor this agreement in 1959. See Chapter 25.

[9] *People's Daily* (August 2, 1965).

[10] T'an Cheng, then assistant director of the army's General Political Department, reported that the cadres showed authoritarianism, neglected ideological work, and cut themselves off from the masses (September 23, 1956).

15 Foreign Policy 1953 – 1957 (1): The Geneva and Bandung Conferences

With the Korean War China made a sudden, spectacular return to the international scene. During the period of the first five-year plan, Chinese foreign policy became more pacific and gained in breadth and confidence. China's vocation as an Asian country was revealed by three international conferences: the two Geneva conferences (on Korea and Indochina) in 1954, and the conference of Bandung in 1955. In the following year, Chou En-lai made a long trip during which he visited eleven capitals in Asia and Eastern Europe, giving proof of his country's mounting prestige and of the importance of Peking as regards problems within the socialist bloc.

Even so, relations with the Soviet Union dominated Chinese foreign policy. The death of Stalin early in March 1953 made great developments possible in the economic field, but ideological relations began to worsen after the Twentieth Congress of the Communist Party of the Soviet Union in February 1956. The visit of Mao Tse-tung to Moscow in the autumn of 1957 for the fortieth anniversary of the October Revolution seems to have played a large part in the great internal changes in China in 1958.

The Geneva conferences

Two conferences were held in Geneva, one after another, in the spring of 1954. The first, devoted to Korea, was the result of the provisions of Article 4 (Point 60) of the armistice agreement signed at Panmunjom on July 27, 1953:

In order to insure the peaceful settlement of the Korean question, the military Commanders of both sides hereby recommend to the governments of the countries concerned on both sides that, within three months after the Armistice Agreement is signed and becomes effective, a political conference of a higher level of both sides be held by representatives appointed respectively to settle through negotiation the questions of the withdrawal of all foreign forces from Korea, the peaceful settlement of the Korean question, etc.[1]

The three-month interval was not observed, in spite of the insistence of the socialist bloc, in whose interest it was to obtain the departure of the United Nations troops. On September 28, 1953, V. M. Molotov, then foreign minister of the Soviet Union, proposed a conference of five powers: United States, Soviet Union, France, Great Britain, and China. The Chinese made similar proposals on November 30, 1953, and Chou En-lai stated them once more on January 9, 1954.

Eventually the conference held in Berlin from January 25 to February 18, 1954, attended by four ministers of foreign affairs (United States, Soviet Union, France, and Great Britain) decided to call a conference—or rather two conferences—in Geneva on April 26, 1954, to settle the Korean and Indochinese questions. The participants were to be invited either by the Soviet Union or by the Western allies.[2]

The Geneva conference on Korea ended on June 15, having achieved nothing, neither the withdrawal of foreign armed forces nor the reunification of the country. The intransigence of Syngman Rhee and Foster Dulles—represented by General Bedell Smith—was due to the importance of South Korea for the security of Japan. That of Chou En-lai and Nam Il was due to the refusal to accept free elections under international control.

Chou En-lai tried in vain to save the conference at the last moment with a suggestion that meetings be limited to seven members and a proposal that members state their intention to resume work with a view to achieving a "united, independent and democratic" Korea, by peaceful means. This maneuver, which had a mere propaganda value in the circumstances, failed.[3] But for the first time, with the exception of the intervention of Wu Hsiu-ch'uan at the United Nations Security Council on November 28, 1950, the Chinese regime took a real share in international discussions and its premier distinguished himself by his talent, his flexibility, and his skill in rapidly making the best of the most unexpected situations.

The conference on Indochina opened almost immediately, with the same representatives of the great powers. Its vicissitudes and results obviously fall outside the scope of this book, but it is worth commenting on the positions and general attitude of the Chinese delegation, led by Chou En-lai, then premier and minister of foreign affairs, assisted by two vice-ministers, Chang Wen-t'ien and Li K'o-nung, together with Wang Ping-nan, secretary-general of the Chinese delegation.[4] From the beginning of the conference, the Chinese showed great moderation, stating often and openly that theirs was a totally disinterested attitude. At no time did they betray any national covetousness or appear to set conditions; they went no further than to remind the conference that they had a right to sit at the United Nations and to repeat that their one ambition was to see peace reestablished in Indochina.

This skillful policy appeared to confront American "warmongering" and great concern about pacts and military aid with Chinese goodwill, focused on peace, coexistence, and negotiated solutions. Seen against the background of the timely declaration made by Chou En-lai, Nehru, and U Nu on June 27 and 28 on the value of the "Five Principles of Coexistence,"[5] it could not fail to reassure most Asian states and encourage their neutralism. Chou En-lai, with his courtesy and charm, won over the representatives of states at Geneva, or other diplomats passing through, particularly Cambodians and Laotians.

There can no longer be any doubt that the true desire of the Chinese, for both internal and external reasons, was to see the negotiations end in an armistice in Indochina. Several times, when the fate of the conference seemed to be endangered, they were quick to make the necessary gesture—sometimes openly and sometimes off-stage—to set the wheels in motion once more, and everything suggests that from time to time they brought all available pressure to bear on North Vietnam. The drawn expression on Chou En-lai's face on the day the Korean conference failed, and the carefully controlled but genuine pleasure he showed on July 20 and 21 were sufficient evidence of his satisfaction about an armistice that was destined to serve the interests and reputation of his country to perfection.

Peking's attitude is adequately explained by the fear that the Indochinese conflict might become international. This would have upset all Chinese plans for the building of the economy, then in full development, and engaged Chinese armed forces in Southeast Asia, as had already happened in Korea, ultimately threatening the existence of the regime. Peking's attitude also formed part of a new Asiatic policy, illustrated a year later by the Bandung conference.

Until then, the Asian countries had been invited to follow China's example in throwing off "feudalism" and "colonial or semicolonial exploitation"; now, regardless of their regime or social system, their nationalist feelings were encouraged and inflamed and they were urged to eliminate American influence and practice real neutrality. The reassuring image of China was there to help them and the American military presence in the Far East was to lose all apparent justification. As long as China, busy building up its country, remained a second-class military power, and the young Asian nations, lacking sufficient revolutionary maturity, were not ready to carry out a new democratic, followed by a socialist, revolution, the prime object was to keep the Americans out of the continent.

Quite apart from ideological antagonism, the policy of Washington rivaled that of Peking in that it sought to consolidate the nationalism of the new states (sometimes to the detriment of the former colonial powers), hasten the training of qualified technical and administrative cadres, help with economic development, do away with the mistrust of the West, and lead to bilateral alliances or regional security pacts. Briefly, the Americans had to be prevented from building up an anti-Communist system on the eastern and southern flanks of China, which would not be a military threat but would be a considerable obstacle to future revolutionary expansion and to immediate national interests. Thus, there were certain similarities in 1954 between the Soviet policy of hostility toward European unification and the Chinese policy of hostility toward greater solidarity, if not unity among non-Communist nations.

A glance at the messages sent and the declarations made by Chou En-lai after the success of the Geneva conference on Indochina shows the extent to which the theme of peace, peaceful coexistence, and the usefulness of periodical consultations between Asiatic states had temporarily replaced the theme of China acting as the guide and example for future revolutions. Everything possible was done to isolate the Americans morally and politically in the eyes of public opinion, excluding them from the general movement for peace.

On the Indochinese peninsula, the Geneva conference had strengthened the political and economic position of Peking. The control of Tonkin by the Vietminh enhanced China's security and offered economic advantages, particularly because the valley of the Red River was the natural outlet of three or four of China's southwestern provinces and was already equipped. At the same time, the boundary of the seventeenth parallel tended to make

Hanoi more receptive to Peking's suggestions. In this respect, for reasons of both general policy and regional interest, Chinese views on the immediate future seemed to be entirely different from those of the Vietminh, as is shown by a comparison of the speeches given by Chou En-lai and Pham Van Dong when the latter was in Peking on August 2 and 3, 1954.

The tone of the remarks made by Pham Van Dong was violent; he drew attention to the Pathet Lao and the Khmers-Issaraks as well as the Vietminh. The Geneva agreements were treated as an initial, not a final, victory. As he said on August 3, 1954:

> The Geneva conference is for us a victory but is only the first phase of the victory. We still have to consolidate and develop this victory. The Geneva conference has opened up a new vista for the peoples of Vietnam, Khmer, and Pathet Lao who are struggling for peace, unification, independence, and democracy. The Vietnamese people and the Vietnam Lao Dong Party will go on working for new victories in line with President Ho Chi Minh's report on the new situation and new tasks. . . . They must continue to strengthen the close unity with the peoples of Khmer and Pathet Lao for the full realization and the respective national rights of the three Indochinese states.

Chou En-lai rendered only meager homage to the Vietminh: "The Vietminh delegation has played an important part in obtaining peace at Geneva." He carefully omitted mention of the Pathet Lao and the Khmers-Issaraks. On the same day, he declared at the Vietnamese embassy:

> The agreement on the restoration of peace in Indochina concluded at the Geneva conference is a momentous contribution toward consolidating world peace and security, particularly peace and security in Asia. It testifies to the fact that peace has again conquered war. It facilitates further relaxation of world tension and opens the way for settling other major international issues through negotiation. More and more people are now coming out for the peaceful coexistence of states with different social systems. People are getting increasingly disgusted with those who insist on the so-called policy of strength which seeks arms expansion and war preparation.

The Chinese were particularly interested in Laos and Cambodia, as well as in Vietnam. Chou En-lai treated the representatives of both countries with the utmost consideration and cordiality and gave only slight support to the rebel movements. This attitude derived from local political conditions that differed greatly from those in Vietnam, but it was also in line with Chinese interests: the present and future influence of Vietnam had to be curtailed in these two countries of different race, language, and culture, both destined to return to the vassalage of Peking some day in a modern guise. With the same end in view, Chou En-lai often stated that China favored the maintenance of a French presence in Indochina. These were not merely conventional phrases intended to soften the bitterness of France's renunciation of Indochina; the aim was to prevent Laos, Cambodia, and South Vietnam from turning toward other powers, particularly the United States, and to raise further obstacles to Vietnam's appropriation of the heritage of the French Union.

The Geneva conference on Indochina stabilized the situation in Southeast Asia for a few years, showed the importance of China on the international scene, and revealed that Peking's attitude was one of conciliation up to a point; in all this, it was an event of great importance in the history of the Chinese Communist Party. Within a few years, circumstances of the Indochinese problem had changed. The worsening relations between China and the Soviet Union, the evolution of Russia and the United States toward a détente foreshadowing a sharing of influences, and the American military presence in Vietnam placed the problem in a completely different world context and changed the whole of Chinese policy toward the peninsula.

The Bandung conference

The conference that brought together twenty-nine African and Asian nations at Bandung in Indonesia from April 18 to 24, 1955, was like a collective awakening of economically backward countries, most of which were emerging from the wreckage of former colonial empires and wanted to escape the pressures of attractions of the different power blocs. In the event, the presence and influence of a massive and densely populated China, which though Asian was the second power in the Communist bloc and was fired by a revolutionary and expansionist policy, was to falsify the spirit of the conference in spite of China's cautiousness, and to condemn its undertakings to failure in the long run.

Officially, the Bandung conference was due to the initiative of the five countries of the Colombo pact: Burma, Ceylon, India, Indonesia, and Pakistan, who met at Colombo from April 5 to May 2, 1954. A preparatory conference was held at Bogor on December 28 and 29, 1954, at which the five prime ministers drew up a list of the twenty-nine members[6] and defined the general aims of the projected conference under four heads:

1. Develop goodwill among the nations of Asia and Africa and search for and promote their common interests.
2. Study the social, economic, and cultural problems of the states involved and their relations with each other as regards these problems.
3. Examine questions of particular interest affecting national sovereignty, racism, and colonialism.
4. Consider the position of Asia and Africa in the modern world and study their contribution to the development of international peace and cooperation.

The authors of the communiqué were careful to point out that because the chief aim of the meeting was to establish contact between the nations invited, leading to an exchange of information, no changes were implied in existing diplomatic relations. The intention was not to create a regional bloc either.

Chou En-lai set to work against this background. He entered into the spirit of apolitical neutrality but still turned the delegates' attention to China. His two speeches on April 19 recalled first the historical reasons for solidarity among Asian countries: colonialism, racial discrimination: "The population of Asia will never forget that the first atom bomb exploded on Asian soil." The defense of peace and the respect for the Five Principles of Peaceful Coexistence were to lead toward a "united front," which he did not mention by name but which recalled China's domestic experience in some of the terms used. Chou En-lai emphasized China's confidence in Communism but was careful to avoid creating any ideological confrontation. Maintaining the policy declared at Geneva, he reassured China's smaller neighbors, making gestures of friendship toward the Philippines and Thailand, the two most deeply involved with Western countries, and denouncing the "subversion" that had come from Taipei.[7] It was a skillful, ingratiating speech that could only wound those absent, although no direct reference was made to a Western power or to the Southeast Asia Treaty Organization, to which three of the nations present (Pakistan, the Philippines, and Thailand) belonged. On April 23, speaking to the heads of eight delegations, he said that the Chinese government was prepared to open negotiations with the United States with a view to obtaining a détente in the Far East and particularly in the Taiwan Strait.

Chou En-lai and Nehru were the two most prominent figures at the conference; Chou En-lai emerged as the more striking of the two, because of his greater personal energy and also probably because his country seemed already to be meeting the problems of underdevelopment with courageous, efficient, and perhaps exemplary solutions. The Five Principles, which became the Ten Principles of Coexistence, soon appeared as a formula that was more representative of Chinese than Indian foreign policy; the parallel between the two men and the two states at the meeting of the Third World grew into open rivalry a few years later, mainly because of events in Tibet.

Sino-Indian relations

After the exchange of diplomatic missions between the two states on April 1, 1950, Sino-Indian relations became progressively clearer and better. Delhi, whose first ambassador, K. M. Panikkar, was an energetic man who was friendly to the new regime, several times served as a go-between for the combatants in the Korean War. The agreement for the "peaceful liberation" of Tibet, concluded on May 23, 1951, between Peking and the local Tibetan government, left the latter in a position of regional auton- omy, as the Indians wanted (see Chapter 21). On April 29, 1954, India decided to sign, in Peking, a treaty of commerce and communications concerning Tibet, a treaty that did away with the last remaining facilities inherited from Great Britain. A month later, during a pause in the Geneva conference, the Chinese premier stayed in Delhi from June 24 to 27, on his way back to Peking. Chou En-lai and Nehru, each anxious to enlarge the role of his country and the Third World countries in international affairs, published a joint communiqué on June 26 restating more formally the Five Principles for Peaceful Coexistence, which had already been included in the preamble to the previous agreement. The immediate aim was to influence the powers gathered at Geneva in the direction of peace. In the more distant future, the Five Principles were to mark, as Nehru put it, "a certain historic change in the relations of the forces in Asia."

On October 19, 1954, Pandit Nehru visited Peking, returning the visit of Chou En-lai to India, and a few days earlier, on October 14, an important commercial agreement was signed in Delhi between the two countries.

After Bandung, a series of official visits made no appreciable changes in Sino-Indian relations, which had begun to develop in a climate of mistrust, as though a competition between the men and the systems was virtually under way. Chinese policy toward Tibet was hardening and, to avoid a major crisis, Pandit Nehru appears to have advised the Dalai Lama and the Panchen Lama, when they came to India on an official visit in November 1956 for the 2,500th anniversary of the death of the Buddha, to return to their country of their own free will. Chou En-lai went to India twice (November 29, 1956 and January 2, 1957); his visits maintained appearances for a time.

Sino-Indonesian relations

Indonesia was to occupy a particularly important position in the new Chinese policy of rapprochement with the Third World. A good understanding with a country of 80 million inhabitants, rich resources, and a strong Communist Party, which had fully recovered from the disasters of 1948, would make it possible to sweep out the remaining Western influence in Southeast Asia and to prepare for a Pyongyang-Peking-Hanoi-Djakarta axis, which was almost achieved a few years later.

These ambitions made it advisable to obtain a proper status for the numerous and often rich Chinese colonies of almost 3 million people who were scattered over all the large islands of the Indonesian Republic.[8] Their economic role, the difficulties they experienced in trying to be assimilated by a mainly Muslim society, and their allegiance to a powerful country aroused mistrust and jealousy on the part of their hosts. A clearly defined status would remove one of the obstacles to Sino-Indonesian cooperation and could act as a precedent and model for other countries with large numbers of Chinese inhabitants.

The negotiations, in preparation since December 1954, ended in the important treaty of April 22, 1955, whose principal provision forced all Chinese residents to choose between Indonesian and Chinese nationality within the following two years. Because of opposition within the country, chiefly from Masjumi, the great Muslim party, the treaty was not ratified until 1960 and was never properly enforced, but the moral effect at which it aimed was temporarily and partially achieved.

The Indonesian Prime Minister, Ali Sastroamidjojo, went to Peking right after the Bandung conference. The usual demonstrations of courtesy and friendship did not prevent him from openly dissociating himself from Communism and proclaiming his religious faith. In September and October 1956, President Sukarno made a two-week visit to Peking, during which both states expressed their support for each other on various international questions (West Irian, Taiwan, the entry of China to the United Nations).

Sino-Burmese relations

Bandung also brought closer relations between China and Burma, the first Asian country to recognize China. The visit of Chou En-lai to Rangoon on June 28, 1954, during the Geneva conference, resulted in a joint communiqué, which was similar to the one published the day before by Chou En-lai and Nehru in New Delhi and based on the acknowledgement of the Five Principles. U Nu made a return visit to Peking in December 1954. Beneath his humility and his manifest gratitude for the tolerance of the Chinese toward Chinese Nationalist army remnants commanded by Li Mi, who were operating on the frontier of China and the Shan States, or for the acquisition of 150,000 tons of rice, appeared a determination not to allow Peking to play any part in Burmese internal affairs.[9] Eventually road, air, and telegraphic communications between the two countries were improved but the frontier dispute, which was further complicated by local incidents and the existence of rival Communist movements which did not acknowledge the authority of Rangoon, remained unsolved in spite of a joint declaration made on November 9, 1956.[10]

Relations with Cambodia, Laos and Nepal

Owing to its vocation for neutrality, which it proclaimed at Geneva, and probably also because it harbored a large Chinese colony, Cambodia was still the object of flattering attentions from Peking. Prince Sihanouk made the first of his many state visits to the Chinese capital on February 14, 1956, and a little later (June 21) received economic aid amounting to $22 million for the development of the textile industry and the construction of a cement plant.

In August, 1956, the Prime Minister of Laos, Prince Souvanna Phouma, was entertained by the Chinese leaders.

Nepal, the stake in an old Sino-Indian rivalry, gradually began to return to the Chinese sphere of influence. After normal diplomatic relations had been established between the two countries on August 1, 1955, Nepal signed a trade agreement on its exchanges with Tibet (September 20, 1956), and then an economic aid agreement for a credit of 60 million rupees (October 7, 1956). These good relations did not prevent Chinese infiltration, and Nepalese Communist leader K. I. Singh was received in Peking in 1954.

The emergence of China in the Middle East

The image of the People's Republic of China, mainly created at Geneva and Bandung, also enabled China to gain an opening in the Middle East. Until then, Taipei, where several highly influential Chinese Muslims had taken refuge (General Pai Ch'ung-hsi, General Ma Pu-fang and General Ma Hung-k'uei), had been fortunate enough to keep its rival out of that part of the world and thus retain numerous Arab votes at the United Nations. But between 1955 and 1957, the Nationalists finally lost the support of Egypt, the Sudan, Syria, and the Yemen.

Peking presented China as a Muslim power, a trading partner, and the defender of countries of the Third World against "imperialism." From these three points of view, the revolutionary Egypt of Colonel Nasser was particularly fertile ground. Before 1949, cultural links already existed between the two countries, and particularly between the University of Al Azhar and the Muslims in Sinkiang. The Chinese textile industry could easily use Egyptian cotton, in spite of its high quality, and then the Five Principles of Coexistence and neutralism appeared as an attractive middle way for the new Egypt. Sino-Egyptian relations began with a cultural agreement signed on May 31, 1955. Minister of Religious Affairs Hassan El Bakhouri signed it for Cairo, and the Muslim Burhan, chairman of the Chinese Islamic Association, signed for Peking. Surprisingly enough, considering who the negotiators were, strictly religious questions had no place in it. On the other hand, the agreement explicitly recalled the spirit of Bandung.[11] A little later, on August 22 of the same year, the first Sino-Egyptian trade agreement was signed, valid for three years, for the sum of £20 million sterling. Formal diplomatic relations were established between the two states on May 16, 1956.

The crisis of the autumn of 1956 earned the full support of the Chinese for their new friends. The Chinese could only approve the nationalization of the canal, though they were careful to maintain the principle of freedom of navigation resulting from the Constantinople Convention of 1888, and express support for Egypt during the military intervention of the British, the French, and the Israelis. Noisy demonstrations were organized in

Peking against the British and the French, and on November 3 Chou En-lai addressed an offensive protest to London and Paris. Sino-Egyptian relations grew distinctly cooler over the following few years, however, and went through a serious crisis in 1959.

In the rest of the Arab world, the Chinese won the recognition of the Sudan on January 4, 1956, Syria on July 2, 1956, and the Yemen on August 21 of the same year. Several trade and cultural missions were exchanged.[12]

China and Afghanistan

On January 22, 1955, the Chinese opened diplomatic relations with Afghanistan, which borders on Pamir for nearly 100 kilometers and has historical links with China and all of Asia. René Grousset describes it as the "turntable of Asian destinies." Relations between the two countries developed appreciably over the years that followed.

China and the rest of the world

Various arrangements, mainly of a commercial nature, were signed with several countries of the free world. They produced only minor political repercussions, as in the case of Pakistan, committed to SEATO and the Baghdad Pact (CENTO), Japan, which was almost a part of the American economy, or France, which was prevented from recognizing Peking first by the war in Indochina and then by the events in Algeria.[13]

Oddly enough, the Geneva conference on Indochina gave birth to a new type of diplomatic meetings parallel to the conference. These took place regularly after August 1, 1955, between the Chinese ambassador in Warsaw (Wang Ping-nan) and the American ambassador in Prague (Alexis Johnson). The origin of these meetings lay in the fate of eighty Americans still held in China and about 5,000 Chinese students resident in the United States. Although they were suspended from time to time, these meetings continued until 1970.[14] Behind the limited aims of these meetings it was possible to discern the immense shadows of real problems: the question raised by U.S. supremacy in the Pacific and the Chinese desire for hegemony in East Asia. Several times, in 1955 and 1956, Peking suggested a meeting between Chinese and American foreign ministers and proposed that a collective security pact be established in the Pacific. A temporary adjustment was not inconceivable at that point, but the question of

Taiwan was at the heart of every arrangement, and here the opposition in principle was doubtless more insurmountable than that created by political and strategic circumstances.

After the Geneva conference, the Peking leaders publicly stated their right to Taiwan, appealing to the patriotism of the inhabitants of the island, often through the offices of senior civil servants under the old regime who had rallied to the new: Dr. Wong Wen-hao, former chairman of the Executive Yuan, a distinguished geologist educated in France, was the most eminent among them. This campaign seemed to have several purposes: to call international attention to the Taiwan problem in the course of settling the Indochinese conflict, to incite the Soviet Union to pay more attention to it, and to open a dialogue with the Americans, which, though sterile, would nevertheless reinforce Peking's position and serve propaganda purposes. Chou En-lai stated his desires clearly in a speech at the National Committee of the People's Political Consultative Conference on January 30, 1956: "Over the past year, our government has repeatedly indicated that, apart from a liberation by war, it is also possible to liberate Taiwan by peaceful means."

Like the consummate actor that he was, he recalled that the Chinese Communist Party and the Kuomintang had twice fought alongside each other. At Phnom Penh, in an ironic retort to Western journalists, he said that Chiang Kai-shek would find a warm welcome in Peking and a post worthy of his rank.

Nevertheless, the Chinese never agreed, as the Americans requested, to abandon the right to resort to force in return for the withdrawal of the guarantee that the Seventh Fleet would defend the Nationalist government on Taiwan against attack. Because Taiwan was an integral part of China, regardless of the political regime in power, the right to military occupation was one of the attributes of Chinese sovereignty. In other words, the withdrawal of the Seventh Fleet was an external affair to be settled by an agreement between China and the United States, whereas the return of Taiwan was an internal problem to be settled directly between the two Chinese parties. The position of Peking remains the same today.[15]

The failure of the attempts at rapprochement between China and the United States, a rapprochement that was virtually unimaginable while Foster Dulles was alive, and the deterioration of Sino-Soviet relations, were behind the serious crisis that arose in 1958 in the Taiwan Strait. The result helped greatly to guide Chinese foreign policy toward its present independence.

Notes

[1] Quoted by Robert Leckie, *Conflict: The History of the Korean War* (New York: Putnam, 1962).

[2] Certain states were anxious to avoid any gesture liable to be interpreted as an open or tacit recognition of certain other states, while the question of membership or non-membership of the United Nations also raised problems of procedure.

[3] The proposals of Nam Il (six-point proposal) and Molotov were equally unsuccessful, but Chou En-lai made his with greater skill and was unquestionably the dominating figure at the closing session.

[4] The negotiations opened on May 8. On the vicissitudes of the conference see Philippe Devillers and Jean Lacouture, *End of a War: Indochina 1954* (New York: Praeger, 1969).

[5] Mutual respect for the territorial integrity and sovereignty of the states, nonaggression, noninterference, mutual equality and advantages, peaceful coexistence.

[6] Afghanistan, Cambodia, Republic of Central Africa, China, Egypt, Ethiopia, Gold Coast, Iran, Iraq, Japan, Jordan, Laos, Lebanon, Liberia, Libya, Nepal, Philippines, Saudi Arabia, Sudan, Syria, Thailand, Turkey, Democratic Republic of Vietnam, Yemen, and the five nations behind the conference.

[7] An airplane carrying members of the Chinese delegation to Bandung was sabotaged in Hong Kong on April 11 and was lost off Borneo.

[8] The Chinese population was generally estimated at between 2 and 3 million, 30 percent of whom were born on the mainland, and 70 percent in Indonesia. Nine-hundred Chinese schools contained 300,000 pupils. At the census of 1971 the Indonesian population was reckoned at 120 million inhabitants.

[9] See his speech of December 10, 1954, in Peking. U Nu declared that the Burmese were too proud to be the playthings of anyone, and made an astonishingly outspoken plea for Sino-American reconciliation. Chou En-lai gave a curt reply, asking U Nu to get a "certain state" to withdraw its forces from the territories of other states.

[10] During this period, two important Burmese delegations visited Peking, one led by the commander in chief of the armed forces, General Ne Win (September 28, 1955) and the other, concerned with the economy, led by deputy Prime Minister U Kyan Nygin (December 4, 1957); Chou En-lai visited Rangoon on December 20, 1956.

[11] A second agreement was signed on April 15, 1956.

[12] Lebanese and Iraqi trade missions went to China in 1955 without provoking any modification in the political relations between the two states and Peking.

[13] On September 1, 1956, an important French trade mission led by Henri Rochereau, chairman of the government Economic Affairs Committee, went to Peking and signed trade agreements. This was Rochereau's second visit to Peking. A French parliamentary delegation also went there in October 1955.

[14] Seventy-three were held between August 1, 1955, and December 31, 1957. The last meeting was the 135th, held on January 20, 1970.

[15] See the declaration of the Chinese foreign minister (June 13, 1956).

16 Foreign Policy 1953 – 1957 (2): Sino-Soviet Relations

The sudden death of Stalin on March 5, 1953, gave a new impetus to Sino-Soviet relations that was favorable to Peking. The man whom Mao Tse-tung called "the central figure of the revolution since Lenin"[1] never gave full trust or unreserved support to the Chinese Communist Party, and particularly not to the man whom the Party chose as its leader at the Tsunyi conference in January 1935.[2] There is no need to go into the unkind remarks Stalin is said to have made about the Chinese Communists, which may have arisen from a desire to mislead American or Yugoslav interlocutors, for the facts are convincing enough. Stalin's decisions during the 1927 crisis could have been due to inadequate knowledge of the internal situation in China, but Soviet pressure on Yenan to free Chiang Kai-shek at the time of the Sian incident in December 1936, Russian military aid to the Nationalist government alone during the Sino-Japanese War, the terms of the treaty of August 14, 1945, the fact that the Chinese Communists were advised to act cautiously and slowly between 1945 and 1949, and the reestablishment of Russian privileges and interests in Manchuria under the treaty of February 14, 1950, show clearly that, in Stalin's mind, state relations were far more important than ideological solidarity. Mao Tse-tung spoke on the subject on September 24, 1962, at the Tenth Plenum of the Eighth Central Committee. He pointed out that Stalin, fearing that China would go the same way as Yugoslavia and that Mao would go the same way as Tito, had created difficulties over the signing of the treaty of February 14, 1950, and had not placed his trust in the Chinese until the winter of 1950, during the Resist America and Aid Korea Campaign.[3] These remarks were not known outside the country until

1967, but in 1963 the Chinese Communist Party stated publicly and with some bitterness:

> Long ago the Chinese Communists had first-hand experience of some of his [Stalin's] mistakes. . . . In the late 1920s, the 1930s, and the early and middle 1940s the Chinese Marxist-Leninists represented by Comrades Mao Tse-tung and Liu Shao-ch'i resisted the influence of Stalin's mistakes.
>
> For instance, Stalin gave some mistaken advice on the subject of the Chinese revolution, but after its victory, he admitted his mistake.[4]

The vagueness of this text is obvious. In fact, circumstances never allowed the Chinese to say freely all they might have said about the Soviet dictator. While they were winning power and right up to the time of the Twentieth Congress of the Communist Party of the Soviet Union, they were in many respects beholden to the Russians, while the cold war made it essential to preserve the unity of the socialist bloc. Even so, they were on the verge of a break in relations just before Stalin's death, if a remark made by Khrushchev in Warsaw in 1956 is to be believed. After 1956 and the beginning of their differences, the name of Stalin became a symbol both of an uncompromising attitude in international affairs that was more and more in line with Chinese wishes, and of determined opposition to the revisionist tendencies of his successors, who were regarded as mediocre and lacking in unity. Stalin and Mao Tse-tung shared so many characteristics—first and foremost their authoritarian style—that any criticism of the former was bound to affect the latter.

The visit of Chou En-lai to Moscow for Stalin's funeral showed, even down to minor details in etiquette, that for internal reasons having to do with the Soviet Union and the socialist bloc, the new Soviet leaders set a high value on collaboration with the Chinese. The years from 1953 to 1956 were a sort of honeymoon in the relations between the two countries and the two parties.

On March 30, 1953, the Chinese, who had more freedom of initiative and felt that an increase in Soviet economic aid might be forthcoming, began a diplomatic maneuver with a view to a cease-fire in Korea in which they agreed that prisoners refusing to return to their own country should be entrusted to a neutral state. The removal of this obstacle, which had been hampering the Panmunjom negotiations since May 1952, was to make it easier to conclude the armistice. The talks opened again on April 27, 1953, and ended on July 27 in spite of incidents and maneuvers on the part of the indomitable Syngman Rhee. China was able to devote all its attention to the construction of the economy.

Two months after the death of Stalin, Soviet aid, which had been the subject of laborious negotiations since Chou En-lai's visit to Moscow in August 1952, took on new dimensions and grew from year to year. As already stated, the agreements of May 1953 provided for Russian participation in 91 new projects, making a total of 141, a figure that increased to 156 on October 12, 1954, 211 on April 7, 1956, 258 on August 8, 1958, and, theoretically at least, 336 on February 7, 1959 (see Chapter 7). Numerous arrangements completed the details of Sino-Soviet collaboration in scientific, technical, financial, and commercial fields. V. V. Kuznetsov, an economist, engineer, and assistant minister of foreign affairs, was appointed Soviet ambassador to Peking on March 11, 1953.

Political relations also seemed to be developing satisfactorily. The Chinese, without taking a clearly defined position in the quarrels between Stalin's inheritors, applauded the elimination of Beria and his execution.[5] The accession of Khrushchev to the post of first secretary of the Communist Party of the Soviet Union did not give rise to any particular comment.

On September 29, 1954, an impressive Soviet mission including Khrushchev, Bulganin (first vice-chairman of the Cabinet), Mikoyan, and other Soviet government officials of high rank was welcomed with great pomp in Peking. They were invited to attend the Chinese National Day and prolonged their visit until October 11.

This visit marked China's final emancipation, for the last treaties limiting its territorial and economic sovereignty disappeared. Complete Chinese control over the naval base of Port Arthur, which had been in foreign hands since 1898, was restored and came into force on May 14, 1955. Russian shares in the mixed Sino-Soviet companies created in 1951 were transferred, in return for an indemnity from which the Chinese stood to gain.[6] Furthermore, a loan of 520 million rubles was granted in addition to earlier loans and an agreement on railways provided for the completion of a direct line from Aktogay to Urumchi, between Russian and Chinese Turkestan. A joint communiqué was issued by the Chinese, the Russians, and the Mongols on the construction of a further section between Ulan Bator in Outer Mongolia and Chining on the Suiyuan Chinese railway, to be finished by January 1956, a project dating from 1952. Communication links between China and the Soviet Union were greatly improved in consequence. A scientific and technical agreement was also signed.[7]

As regards foreign policy, China and the Soviet Union confirmed the similarity of their views on all main world issues, particularly those specifically concerning China: Taiwan, Korea, Japan, and Peking's seat at the United Nations. Although the statement was couched in moderate terms, there were many indications that the Chinese urged their allies to press for a settlement of these questions, particularly that of Taiwan, which had been discussed at length in the press in August before the arrival of the Soviet delegation and taken up again in December when the security treaty was signed between the Nationalist government on Taiwan and the Americans. Their growing prestige, and the easing of tension brought by the end of the Indochinese war and the armistice in Korea, may have made the Chinese feel that the time was ripe. If the Taiwan question were settled in principle, that of the entry of China to the United Nations would naturally follow, preparing the way for coexistence which at this point was compatible with China's domestic needs.

Chou En-lai made a forceful, if repetitive, statement on this subject to the First National People's Congress on September 23, 1954:

> Everyone can see that all our efforts are directed toward the construction of our country, to make it into an industrial, socialist, prosperous, and happy country. We work peacefully and we hope for a peaceful atmosphere and a peaceful world: this fundamental fact determines the peaceful policy of our country as regards foreign policy.[8]

However, the future quickly revealed that the questions that interested the Soviet Union most of all were not those concerned with Asia. In spite of the image of Mme Sun Yat-sen, who saw "the great Soviet Union and our China like two giants, hand in hand and shoulder to shoulder, marching to victory,"[9] Peking retained a secondary position in the leadership of the socialist bloc.

Sino-Soviet solidarity remained apparent rather than real and foundered when the Soviet policy of détente got under way, before even the beginnings of a solution had been found for China's own problems.[10]

During 1955 the climate of relations between Moscow and Peking was friendly. The main event was the signing of an important agreement on the peaceful use of atomic energy (April 29). The beginnings of a reconciliation between Moscow and Belgrade did not produce any hostile reaction on the part of the Chinese, who had already opened normal diplomatic relations with Yugoslavia on January 10, 1955. On the other hand, a long visit by Khrushchev to India, Afghanistan, and Burma (November 18 to December 21) probably displeased them.

The Twentieth Congress of the Communist Party of the Soviet Union (February 14-25, 1956) revealed the first crack—barely apparent—in Sino-Soviet relations. Its chief points—criticism of Stalin, criticism of the personality cult, peaceful coexistence, and different roads to socialism—could not fail to arouse the attention of the Chinese, owing to their repercussions in China and to their effects on the world revolutionary movement, which the Chinese claimed to inspire, at least partially. Because their diplomatic policy had started on a moderate phase, however, and because the question of the transition to socialism mainly concerned Western countries with parliamentary institutions, the Chinese reacted most strongly to the first two points.

The condemnations of Stalin and the personality cult cut Mao Tse-tung and the Party he had led for more than twenty years to the quick. These events came a few months after the Eighth Congress, which was to revise the Party constitution and thereby affect the organization and inner workings of the Party, as well as the role of its leaders. But although the Chinese were probably deeply displeased, they could only express themselves within certain limits. The delicacy of the subject, the importance of Soviet economic aid, and the attitude of the Chinese representative at the Twentieth Congress (Marshal Chu Teh, already an old man, was caught unawares like all the delegates and apparently applauded de-Stalinization without giving it much thought) all had a moderating effect. Chinese reactions eventually came out into the open in the shape of an important text, "On the Historical Experience of the Dictatorship of the Proletariat," an article published by the *People's Daily*, based on discussions that had occurred during an enlarged meeting of the Political Bureau![11] As was to be expected, the role of Stalin and the personality cult were the most important subjects and the judgments on these two parallel topics are well balanced. Stalin's work as the defender of Lenin's heritages and as the builder of a powerful socialist economy was magnified. His mistakes—the personality cult, excessive suppression of counterrevolutionaries, lack of vigilance on the eve of the war with Germany—are acknowledged without indignation. The final judgment was expressed with the utmost simplicity: "Stalin was a great Marxist-Leninist, yet at the same time a Marxist-Leninist who committed several gross errors without recognizing them for what they were."

The writers of this important text, in which Mao Tse-tung had a hand, as some passages show, exonerate their Party of all suspicion as regards the cult of personality. Scrupulous practice of democratic centralism and collective leadership, observance of the principle of the "mass line," and thorough acquaintance with the law of contradictions had banished subjectivism and contributed to the correction of several well-known deviations, a list of which was given yet again. The whole article, however, was an attempt to justify, at least indirectly, the preeminence of Mao Tse-tung, whose thought is implicitly assumed to inspire the Party.

> Marxism-Leninism acknowledges that leaders play an important role in history. The people and their Party need outstanding personalities who can represent the interests and the will of the people and stand in the forefront of the historical struggles to lead them. To deny the role of the individual, the role of the vanguard and leaders, is completely wrong.

The questions of Stalin and of the cult of personality were played down in 1956, only to come out into the open seven years later, when the Chinese threw off all mental reserves and restraints of language and went so far as to say that Khrushchev's repudiation of Stalin in the name of the struggle against the cult of personality was totally mistaken and had been carried out "with hidden intentions" at the cost of innumerable lies. They also stated that Sino-Soviet differences arose in 1956 with the Twentieth Congress of the Communist Party of the Soviet Union, "the first step on the revisionist road."[12]

Shortly after the publication of "On the Historical Experience of the Dictatorship of the Proletariat," Mikoyan arrived in China, bringing with him renewed proof of Russian interest in the first Chinese five-year plan. Under the terms of the agreement of April 7, 1956, fifty-five new projects were added to the 156 projects already under way.

If the Chinese are to be believed, the new agreement did not prevent Mao Tse-tung from giving Mikoyan the opinion of the Chinese Communist Party on the question of Stalin, or from coming back to it again on October 23 and November 30, 1956, with Soviet Ambassador P. F. Yudin.[13] Whatever the case may be, in public the Chinese Communists showed discretion and patience. They did not react to the dissolution of the Cominform (April 18), were apparently indifferent to the disgrace of Molotov when he was dismissed from the Foreign Ministry (June 1), and, through Liu Shao-ch'i, approved the reconciliation between Tito and Khrushchev, which they saw primarily as a first step toward the autonomy and equality of all Communist parties (June 20). They sent a distinguished ambassador, Wu Hsiu-ch'üan, to Belgrade.

The Eighth Congress provided the opportunity, through the presence and statements of Mikoyan, for a further demonstration of Sino-Soviet solidarity, soon to be put to the test by events in Poland and Hungary. The Russian delegate conceded to the Chinese the right to apply Marxism-Leninism in an original way, defended the Twentieth Congress, and condemned the cult of personality in general, which probably displeased Mao Tse-tung. He laid almost suspicious emphasis on solidarity, and on the permanence of Sino-Soviet friendship:

> The enemy would really like to create a split in our relations and make a breach, however small, in our friendship. But only imperialist thinkers whom history condemns to failure can dream this dream. They see our friendship in the light of their bourgeois relationships. Their speciality is to get on well today, to separate tomorrow, and inflict mutual injury. Never has there been a friendship in the world comparable with that between our two great peoples and our two great parties.[14]

The Chinese also spoke of the eternal and indestructible nature of the unity and friendship between the two countries, though in less extravagant terms.

The first effects of de-Stalinization in the Eastern European socialist countries were barely mentioned in the Chinese press, though the coming to power of Gomulka in Warsaw during the events in Poland in October met with approval.[15]

On November 1, a few days before the crushing of the Hungarian insurrection (November 4), an official communiqué was issued by the Chinese government in support of the Soviet declaration of October 30 on the principles of developing and reinforcing the friendship between the Soviet Union and the socialist countries. It also stressed the need to put relations between Communist nations on a basis of equality and mutual respect for each other's sovereignty and territorial integrity:

> Some socialist countries have neglected the principles of equality between nations in their relations with each other. An error of this sort whose nature is bourgeois and chauvinist in essence can, when it is committed by a great power, severely wrong the cause and solidarity of socialist countries. Errors like this have given rise to tense situations which would not otherwise have arisen, such as that in Yugoslavia in the past, and in Poland and Hungary now.

During the Budapest uprising, however, the Chinese were so closely involved with the Russians that, once it was over, they claimed that the military suppression of the uprising had succeeded as a result of their advice.[16]

Peking's attitude seems to have been moderate in the Poland affair where the Russians wanted to use force, and radical during the Hungarian affair, where the Russians were ready to capitulate "and abandon socialist Hungary to the counterrevolution," as the Chinese later said. This apparently contradictory approach can probably be explained by the difference in the situations and also by the fact that the Chinese wanted to find a balance between the cohesion of the socialist bloc "led by the Soviet Union" and the autonomy of Communist parties, or rather states.

On December 29, 1956, a second important text, "More on the Historical Experience of the Dictatorship of the Proletariat," threw more light on Chinese feelings about the Hungarian uprising and particularly on the conclusions to be drawn from it. The first cause of the uprising was "imperialist" action, which had played a fundamental and decisive part; Chinese reserves about peaceful coexistence were already apparent. Then followed a study of the road taken by the revolution and the building of socialism in the Soviet Union, of the merits and errors of Stalin, of the struggle against dogmatism and revisionism, and of international proletarian solidarity.

The article defended the Soviet Union and acknowledged its position as the center of the international Communist movement; Soviet experience had, however, included some errors that should serve as lessons to be studied and remembered. Stalin, although a staunch Communist, made mistakes that in themselves do not condemn the socialist system. Dogmatism that loses sight of national realities is dangerous, but in the struggle against this revisionism is not to be tolerated. Proletarian internationalism must be combined with patriotism and equal rights, on pain of arousing deep animosity between parties and countries of different sizes.

In fact, under the guise of calling for proper equality and greater autonomy for individual parties, the text sought to use events to bolster China's ideological and political role. Although "too heavy for a satellite," as Ch'en Yi said at Geneva in 1962—and militarily and economically still too weak to lead the Communist world, it is tempting to add—China was still the first nation to benefit from an evolution enabling socialist states to obtain a better hearing in Moscow.

The year 1957 began well. A joint communiqué stressing the unity of Sino-Soviet views on the Hungarian affair was published on January 11. Chou En-lai arrived in Moscow on January 7 from Peking and was there again on January 17 and 18 after visits to Warsaw (January 11-16) and Budapest (January 17) which won him the reputation—largely assumed—of being the fortunate mediator between Communist parties in power. Still, for the first time in history, China had made its influence felt in European affairs, which was an astonishing reversal of the situation a mere thirteen years after the end of the Unequal Treaties.

As seen from the outside, no events of note occurred during the next few months. In October 1957 an agreement on new techniques in national defense was signed in Moscow. Its nature and contents were not revealed. Later on, it became known that it provided for the supply of sample atomic bombs to China, together with technical data on manufacturing them. It was an agreement of the utmost importance, and when the Soviet Union denounced it in June 1959, a severe deterioration in relations between the two countries resulted.[17]

November 1957 was to be a crucial month for the future of Sino-Soviet relations and for the future of the socialist world as a whole. The fortieth anniversary of the October Revolution (November 7 by our calendar) was celebrated with great ceremony, as was to be expected. The outstanding event was the launching of the first earth satellite (Sputnik) on October 4 and a second on November 3, a considerable technical and military achievement. Above all, the occasion was marked by a Conference of the Twelve Communist and Workers' Parties in power (November 14-16), followed by a meeting attended by sixty-four Communist and workers' parties (November 16-19).

Mao Tse-tung stayed in Moscow from November 2 to 20 and led the Chinese delegation at the twelve-party conference. The statement it issued, "Declaration of the Communist and Workers' Parties of the Socialist Countries," owed much to his views. On four main points (leadership of the socialist bloc and relations between brother parties, the question of war and peace, the question of the transition to socialism, and dogmatism and revisionism) the Chinese flattered themselves that they had obtained the rectification of proposals of the Twentieth Congress, which they considered mistaken.

The Soviet Union was "at the head" of the "invincible bloc of socialist states." It was the "first and strongest socialist power." Even so, "socialist countries base their mutual relations on the principle of complete equality, respect for territorial integrity, political independence and sovereignty, and nonintervention in internal affairs." A brotherly understanding existed among them and they aimed at developing and improving their economic and cultural collaboration.

The homage to the preeminence of the Soviet Union was important in that it implicitly condemned polycentralism and all the centrifugal tendencies of the system. On the other hand, it increased the obligations owed by the Soviet Union (particularly in economic aid), and, in the name of complete equality between parties, excluded all pressure on other countries. If carried to its logical conclusion, it instituted an unavowed right of veto through the unwritten law of unanimity. When the Chinese supported a centralizing principle, while momentarily preventing it from taking effect, they were perhaps thinking of the day when, according to Lenin's promise, the center of the world revolution would move eastward once again.[18]

On the question of war or peaceful coexistence, "the essential problem of world politics," the Chinese had to admit that the union of socialist forces "could prevent an outbreak of war." This adherence to the spirit of the Twentieth Congress was also consistent with the spirit of Bandung and the foreign policy line previously followed by the Chinese. Subsequent events, however, and revelations made by the Russians in 1963, showed that this line no longer represented the true feelings of Mao Tse-tung. The implications of his famous expression, "The East Wind prevails over the West Wind," certainly extended beyond the mere literary image, and when compared with remarks he made to the Soviet leaders and to other foreign statesmen, shows that his thought was undergoing a profound change. The following year brought startling proof of the change in the order of things both at home and abroad![19]

According to the Chinese, the question of transition to socialism aroused the sharpest discussions of all with the Communist Party of the Soviet Union. The Chinese set up "determined" opposition to two Russian proposals and put forward one of their own. Eventually, a compromise between alternative ways of handling the transition from capitalism to socialism was adopted: the acquisition of power without civil war, and a transition to socialism with recourse to nonpeaceful methods. The principles enunciated by the Twentieth Congress of the Communist Party of the Soviet Union were both acknowledged and limited.

The Chinese also managed to obtain the condemnation of revisionism, "the chief danger under present conditions," but they acknowledged, with the other parties, that "dogmatism and sectarianism can both represent the chief danger at particular stages in the development of a Party." In fact, revisionism and antirevisionism were to dominate the Sino-Soviet controversy in 1960 and above all in 1963; the seeds of this were already present during the 1957 conference.

The visit of Mao Tse-tung to Moscow in the autumn of 1957 was probably one of the summits in the history of the international Communist movement. The head of the Chinese Communist Party had to face and accept some hard facts. Moscow intended to remain the center of the world revolutionary movement and, in spite of polite treatment and several formal concessions, Mao's personal influence was bound to remain limited. On a more general plane, equality between Communist and workers' parties was merely a demonstration of international courtesy and no exception was made for the Chinese Communist Party.

The advent of nuclear weapons, a dominant factor in international politics, prevailed over doctrines that were themselves subordinated more than ever before to considerations of state. It inevitably led to a lessening of tension between East and West and from there to a state of Russian and American coexistence.

China was the victim of the new situation. The settling of its international claims was given second place, after détente and the settling of questions directly affecting the Soviet Union (particularly that of Germany). Moscow was probably not in a position to induce Washington to give way over Japan and Taiwan and was only mildly concerned with strengthening Peking's hold in Southeast Asia. As to China's economic development, the Russians were engaged in peaceful competition with the United States and their aid was based not on unlimited fraternal generosity inspired by international proletarianism, but on clearly understood mutual advantage. In this respect, China was in a much better position than the Eastern European countries. The policies adopted by Stalin's successors were in direct opposition to Chinese interests, whether in domestic or foreign policy or in ideology.

China had to prepare to "rely on its own strength" in every field, and in that of economic construction first of all. It also had to establish ideological ascendancy and political influence in all the countries of the world, and particularly in Asia, Africa, and Latin America, by moving farther and farther away from Moscow and embodying more and more the true revolutionary ideal. In 1950, Mao went to Moscow as a pilgrim visiting the holy city of socialism and asking for favors. In 1957, he attained an international stature almost comparable with that of Stalin, whose memory he defended; his audience consisted of the leaders of all the Communist parties in the world. A new Mao Tse-tung had been born.

Notes

[1] See "The Greatest Friendship," *Pravda* (March 9, 1953).

[2] See Guillermaz, *A History of the Chinese Communist Party*, p. 253.

[3] See an English text of this speech in "Chinese Law and Government," *IASP Journal of Translations* 1, No. 4 (1969).

[4] "On the Question of Stalin," *People's Daily* (September 13, 1963). Mao Tse-tung's and particularly Ch'en Po-ta's various texts on Stalin, written for special occasions and published earlier, mainly praise him. Even so, Mao admits that the works of Stalin were virtually unknown to him until the war with Japan. This ignorance was presumably intentional, and Mao had to put an end to it to consolidate his position within the Chinese Communist Party and the international Communist movement.

[5] See *People's Daily* (December 27, 1953).

[6] See Chapter 6. This policy of transfer was practiced simultaneously by the Soviet Union in several European and Eastern countries.

[7] During this visit, the number of shared projects rose from 141 to 156; the 15 new projects represented a total of 400 million rubles. See Chapter 7.

[8] The rest of the speech is in the same vein and addresses each Asian country in turn.

[9] Speech of November 6, 1954, on the anniversary of the October Revolution. Ambassador Yudin showed more restraint: "The Chinese People's Republic has become a powerful nation and a great force."

[10] If the *Memoirs* of Khrushchev are to be believed, the Chinese raised the question of Outer Mongolia unsuccessfully during Khrushchev's visit to Peking in 1954. The antipathy of Khrushchev for Mao Tse-tung also seems to date from the same time.

[11] *People's Daily* (April 5, 1956).

[12] See "On the Question of Stalin," *People's Daily* (September 13, 1963).

[13] See "The Origin and Development of the Differences between the Leadership of the CPSU and Ourselves," *People's Daily* (September 6, 1963).

[14] "Collected texts of the Eighth Congress" (Chinese edition), p. 884.

[15] At the time, the Western press reported the existence of rumors to the effect that Mr. Ochab, first secretary of the Polish Workers' Party, was encouraged to adopt a more independent attitude toward Moscow when visiting Peking for the Eighth Congress of the Chinese Communist Party.

[16] Nikita Sergeevich Khrushchev, *Khrushchev Remembers* (Boston: Little Brown, 1971), pp. 397-99, mentions great variations in the attitude of Peking, represented by Liu Shao-ch'i who had been invited to come to Moscow for consultations during the Hungarian affair.

[17] See "The Origin and Development of the Differences between the Leadership of the CPSU and Ourselves," *People's Daily* (September 6, 1963).

[18] See François Fejtö, *Chine-URSS: la fin d'une hégémonie (1950-1957)* (Paris: Plon, 1964).

[19] On the question of peace and war, see Chapter 25.

Part 3

The Chinese Road to Socialism
1958 – 1962

Is it conceivable that a socialist state which has set up the
dictatorship of the proletariat for the first time should make
no mistakes of any kind whatsoever?

> *Lenin,* quoted by Mao Tse-tung, "On the
> Historical Experience of the Dictatorship
> of the Proletariat" (April 5, 1956)

A person does not know how to apply in Fuhsien what he has
learned in Yenan.

> *Mao Tse-tung,* "Reform Our Study" (May 1941)

17 The Search for a Chinese Road to Socialism

In perspective, and in contrast with the tumultuous years that followed, the China of the first five-year plan (in spite of periodic upheavals like the mass campaigns and the Hundred Flowers and Antirightist movements) appears as a centralized, well-ordered, balanced country with a realistic attitude, aware of the extent and gravity of its difficulties but moving confidently toward the future. Whether true or false, this is the image accepted by the outside world. For many young nations, China was a model of conscientiousness, courage, and success. The old industrial nations also found much to admire in the regime, although at times they disapproved of its harshness and its tendency toward isolation, as well as its ideology, revolutionary passion, and efforts to proselytize. They were worried by the possible addition of China's huge economic and human potential to the already considerable power of socialist Eastern Europe in the "not too near and not too distant" future.

A few months after the end of the first five-year plan, when the second plan had only just begun, China rushed headlong of its own free will into the unknown, which resulted firstly in economic chaos and then, from 1966 on, in unparalleled political confusion. Social and economic structures became totally unrealistic, while the rhythm of production and pace of work became insane. Extensive readjustments were clearly necessary at the end of 1958, and their scope increased in 1959. In 1960, as a result of obvious difficulties in food supply, priority was placed on agriculture and the industries best serving it. Resistance became apparent among the leadership: a "rightist" group was ousted along with National Defense Minister P'eng Teh-huai at the Lushan Plenum in August 1959. A real though disorganized line, opposed to the policy if not the thought of Mao Tse-tung and the man himself, gradually emerged; for a while it was neutralized by a return to more moderate choices, but it reappeared just before the Cultural Revolution, which eliminated its chief representatives.

Foreign policy hardened, for it reflected internal tendencies. China quarrelled, disagreed, or even had military confrontations with all its powerful neighbors—the Soviet Union, Japan, and India; its relations with the United States grew more tense. Relations with some of the states in the Middle East and with North Korea and Cuba went through periods of crisis. The new African governments that had opened relations with China began to have their doubts. Albania was the only remaining faithful and unconditionally loyal ally.

The first cause of all these astonishing changes was unmistakably the will of Mao Tse-tung. He imposed the turning point of 1958—the Great Leap Forward and the people's communes—just as he had imposed accelerated collectivization in 1955, and as he imposed the Cultural Revolution eight years later. It may well be asked what this will was based on, and what were the realities behind it and its ultimate ambitions. All these questions need to be examined in order to determine whether and to what extent the change was the result of a system with grandiose goals or whether it simply arose from the sequence of events.

Because the most obvious changes concerned the organization and forms of production, it seems logical to treat economic affairs first of all, and then to discuss social affairs.

The results of the first five-year plan

The first five-year plan apparently yielded the expected results in the field of economic production. Compared with the index figure of 100 in 1949, the national income rose to 170 in 1950 and 260 in 1957.[1] Over the same period, the index of agricultural and industrial production combined rose from 177.5 to 297.6—or, in plain figures, from 82,720 million yuan in 1952 to 138,740 million yuan in 1957.

In quantity, industry got off to an impressive start from a low point of departure. Between 1952 and 1957, the total value of industrial production grew from 34,330 million yuan to 78,390 million yuan, which was an increase of 128 percent (an annual average of 18 percent) over a period of five years, while the modern sector of industry alone was valued at 55,600 million yuan. This progress was also apparent in the increase in the numbers of engineers and technicians, and in the numbers of workers employed in industry between 1952 and 1957: the former grew from 164,000 to 496,000, and the latter from 4,939,000 to 9,008,000.[2]

Quality progressed as well. Thanks to Soviet aid, advanced sectors of industry appeared: engines, electronics, precision tools, and oil. Geographically speaking, the balance improved as well, as large industrial centers were implanted or existing ones were enlarged in Central China (Wuhan), the Northwest (Paotow, Lanchow), and the West (Szechwan).

Rail transport gained a further 6,652 kilometers of line (making a total of 29,862 kilometers in 1957). Goods transported rose from 60,160 million ton/kilometers in 1952 to 134,590 million ton/kilometers in 1957. Transport by road, waterway, or sea improved much more slowly, owing to the high cost of material and fuel. In spite of this, the road network was doubled, increasing from 127,000 to 255,000 kilometers between 1952 and 1957, with a traffic of 3,940 million ton/kilometers in 1957. Although airlines were still at a rudimentary stage, they reached a figure of 79,870,000 passenger/kilometers in 1957 as against 24 million passenger/kilometers in 1952.

Economic progress as a whole was confirmed by successful foreign trade, which according to official figures rose from 6,460 million yuan in 1952 to 10,450 million in 1957, including both exports and imports.[3]

The relative stagnation of agriculture alongside the progress of industry is striking. In terms of percentage, agricultural production—including industrial and subsidiary crops—grew from an index figure of 100 in 1949 to 148.5 in 1952 and 185.1 in 1957.[4] In plain figures, food crops reached 185 million tons, an increase of 20 percent over 1952. Cotton reached 1,640,000 tons, 26 percent more than in 1952.[5] To put it briefly, whereas industry showed an annual increase of 18 to 20 percent, agriculture, which had to guarantee the financing of industry, because it contributed 75 percent of the exports and represented 55 percent of the budgetary resources of the state, only grew by 4.5 percent per year (4 percent in the case of food crops).

This lack of balance was aggravated by several factors. The rate of increase of the population, generally reckoned at an annual 2.3 percent, added between 12 and 15 million consumers each year and should be deducted from the rate of increase in agricultural production.[6]

In 1957, the government had still not succeeded in lessening, by large-scale hydraulic engineering work, the effects of the monsoon climate, which was particularly violent, impossible to forecast, and often resulted in considerable variations with a direct impact on planning.

Agricultural production, even under a collective system, is certainly much harder to estimate than industrial production. The size and diversity of the country; difficulties in storage, transport, and distribution (between 30 and 40 million tons were involved each year); the concern among cadres as among the basic strata about local or regional interests or about tendencies among the peasants to whom it was wiser to give in, all make for highly unreliable statistics, as does the lack of experience, freely admitted, on the part of the statisticians themselves.

Toward the end of the first five-year plan, the Chinese economists found that agriculture could not meet the cost of the growth of industry (which included refunding debts to the Soviet Union) until industry was able to finance its own growth. In this situation, the politicians saw two possible solutions. The first was an agonizing reappraisal, from which agriculture stood to gain, of the second five-year plan. Its targets had been defined at the Eighth Party Congress (1956), and it had been drawn up on the basis of Soviet aid and advice. This solution was contrary to the firmly established idea that a close and direct link existed between socialism and heavy industry and departed from a tested model, which in 1957 was still accepted by all the leaders in every field of development. It also appeared difficult to apply. Chinese agriculture was of a traditional and intensive type; tools and equipment were largely individual; the cultivated area was small compared with the population; there were not enough technical cadres; and chemical fertilizers were not used. All these factors weighed against large-scale investment in the form of state farms, for instance. Bringing new land under cultivation was scarcely practicable except in the cold regions of Manchuria, Mongolia, and Turkestan and would need excessively costly mechanization.[7]

The second solution—the one that was chosen—was to rely on a general heightening of the ideological awareness and working power of the masses in all the chief sectors of national activity, and particularly in industry and agriculture. A huge effort was to be asked of the workers and craftsmen in the towns so that the maximum amount of work could be completed in the minimum amount of time. The peasants were to be offered intensified collective action, inspired technically by the twelve-year plan for agriculture, and increasingly turned toward large communal projects (irrigation, soil improvement, afforestation, local roadbuilding) and light industry under the direction of the advanced cooperatives.

The mobilization of the entire rural and urban population was to be achieved on the physical, moral, and ideological planes. It was to upset ways of life and attitudes, as well as centuries-old working habits of diligent but excessive patience. At the same time it was to bring about a long-awaited technical revolution at all levels.

At the beginning of 1958, this mobilization gave birth to the mystique of the Great Leap Forward, which was to force China almost overnight out of its backward state and launch it into an era of rapid and regular development following the example of the great modern states. In the towns, industry provided the framework for the mobilization; in the countryside, the solution was soon found in the unexpected formula of the people's communes, since the cooperatives were considered too narrow in scope and agricultural vocation to be able to absorb a large labor surplus.

Apart from its economic goals, however, the Great Leap Forward was also a means of propelling society toward the future, with no possibility of return to the still powerful traditional ties of family and villages. To the Communists, Chinese society was still too close to the sleepy rhythm of its history and consequently too ready to feel nostalgia for certain things, not the least of which were liberty and private interest. By stepping up collectivization and extending it from the economic plane to the administrative, social, cultural, and educational planes, it would be possible to change habits of mind and facilitate the ideological education of individuals. It is impossible not to take the thought of Mao Tse-tung into account at this point.

In this, Mao Tse-tung stayed close to the Chinese tradition, while still wanting to remain a Marxist; he thought nothing could be done that was not based on man himself. This aspect of his thought is often pointed out in military matters and wrongly taken for a rationalization of China's technical backwardness; it is, however, a fundamental attitude and applies to all the rest of his ideology. The man in question, however, has to be a Communist. Like the "superior man" of Confucius in his search for knowledge ("Our attitude toward ourselves should be 'to be insatiable in learning' and toward others 'to be tireless in teaching,' " Mao Tse-tung said,[8] "When does the sage cease to learn? When the lid of his coffin is nailed down," Confucius said), Mao is, however, fundamentally different from him because the striving for perfection does not occur among an elite whose example gradually spreads through the masses, but among the masses themselves, organized and guided by the Party. The people's commune of the future was to be the setting and the chief agent in this transformation.

The Great Leap Forward and its lack of proportion can also be explained by the fact that Mao Tse-tung was ill prepared to understand the complexity of the difficulties involved in the development of a modern industrial society. The effects of his ignorance of doctrine and lack of direct experience were magnified by the charismatic quality of his authority and the lack of outstanding economists in the Party. Of the three best known ones, Ch'en Yün was thoroughly reserved but silent, while Po I-po was mildly enthusiastic but cooperative. The third, Li Fu-ch'un, agreed to be the engineer of the Great Leap Forward in his capacity as chairman of the National Planning Commission.[9]

The Great Leap Forward and the people's communes may be explained—apart from the actual circumstances—by ignorance, voluntarism, and revolutionary impatience on the part of Mao Tse-tung. They also revealed a desire to acquire doctrinal freedom, which was intensified by the disappointments that had accumulated over ten years. Since 1949, the Chinese had constantly declared, sometimes using slogans of great impact, that the history of their Party had opened a new road to emancipation for "colonial and semicolonial" peoples. On November 16, 1949, Liu Shao-ch'i said to an international audience:

> The road chosen by the Chinese people is that which the various colonial and semicolonial countries struggling for their independence must follow.

On June 23, 1951, shortly before the thirtieth anniversary of the founding of the Party, Lu Ting-yi, the usual Party spokesman, head of the Propaganda Department of the Central Committee, stated a law:

> The classic type of revolution in imperialist countries is the October Revolution. The classic type of revolution in colonial and semi-colonial countries is the Chinese Revolution.

In 1953, Ch'en Po-ta, the accepted proponent of the thought of Mao Tse-tung, pointed out that Mao had acquired a special position in the line of Marxist thinkers:

> Mao Tse-tung has put himself on a level with the great Marxist theorists by giving a deeper, more concrete development to the theory of Stalin and Lenin on the revolution in colonial and semicolonial countries.[10]

How these statements were left behind as Chinese pretensions grew will be seen later.

Although the Russians often praised the intrinsic value of the Chinese revolution for the countries of the Third World, they never took up the theme of "the Chinese road" to revolution or admitted that the ideological vocation of Mao Tse-tung or the Chinese Communist Party was great enough to guarantee or justify the delegation of political power. The terms of the communiqué of the Conference of Eighty-One Communist and Workers' Parties in 1960, which ventured furthest in this direction, were carefully weighed and were confined to events, to the exclusion of doctrine:

> The people's revolution in China struck a crippling blow to the positions of imperialism in Asia and made a considerable contribution toward changing the relationship of world forces in favor of socialism. By giving a new and powerful development to movements for national liberation, it has had an enormous influence, particularly on the peoples of Asia, Africa, and Latin America.[11]

In Moscow in 1957, in spite of several formal concessions aimed at preserving the appearances of ideological unity, the Russians had managed to get the socialist bloc as a whole to share their views. The result was that the Chinese rationalized this blow to their pride by deciding to go their own way as far as internal problems were concerned. At the least, on the subject of people's communes in particular, they could make light of the sort of orthodoxy about which Khrushchev reminded them at the Twenty-first Congress of the Communist Party of the Soviet Union:

> It would be a grave mistake to decree Communism when all the necessary conditions are not yet ripe for it. We should simply have discredited the idea of Communism, compromised the initiative of the workers, and delayed the movement toward Communism.[12]

At most, they could dream of setting themselves up as an example for underdeveloped countries in the phase of constructing socialism, just as they had already set themselves up as an example in the phase of winning revolutionary power.

A text of the greatest interest on the genesis of the people's communes and the Great Leap Forward came to light during the Cultural Revolution: a speech delivered by Mao Tse-tung on January 28, 1958, to the Supreme State Conference.[13] Mao Tse-tung is filled with admiration at the awareness and zeal of the masses, but saddened by the poverty of China in spite of the richness of its long history, culture, and resources. China, he believes, could and should catch up with England within fifteen years. The country, sure of its ardor and possibilities, should not only advance but explode: "Our nation is like an atom . . . and after the fission of the atomic nucleus of our nation, thermal energy will be released which becomes so formidable that we will be able to do what was beyond our ability before."[14]

Although the text consists of extracts or a summary and has not yet been proved historically authentic, its familiar style, its mingling of events with doctrine, the China of yesterday with that of today, with no real transition between them, resemble the style of Mao Tse-tung so closely that its authorship can scarcely be doubted.

According to another text of equal importance, which was published by the Shanghai newspaper *Chieh-fang jih-pao* (*Liberation Daily*) at an uncertain date and dealt with the struggle between the two lines within the Party, Mao Tse-tung also declared at Chengtu in Szechwan in March 1958, at a routine meeting of the Central Committee, that all possible forces ought to be released, both objective and subjective.[15]

The Great Leap Forward was given official sanction at the Second Session of the Eighth Party Congress, held in Peking from May 5 to 23, 1958. In the report by Liu Shao-ch'i, the movement is described as a "great revolutionary leap toward the building of socialism." Several slogans in the report were attributed—perhaps intentionally—to Mao Tse-tung: "Work hard for three years for the radical transformation of the face of most regions in our country," and again, "Catch up with England in fifteen years." The suggestion of a triumph over the earliest of the "imperialist" powers was enough to fire everyone with enthusiasm.

Turning to facts, Liu Shao-ch'i announced that the spring had marked the start of "a Great Leap Forward on every front of socialist construction," but he stressed first and foremost the progress of industry; the effort in agriculture was to take the form of the improvement of irrigation and plowing implements and a higher rate of participation in collective work. No mention was made of rural people's communes, which were, however, already being created, particularly in Honan where the "Sputnik" commune appeared in April.[16]

Although Liu Shao-ch'i rejected the criticisms of those who feared that the Great Leap Forward would result in a tense, unbalanced situation, he did so without much conviction, and the overriding impression of his speech is one of lack of warmth and inspiration. References to a "Great Leap Forward" in 1956 also helped to diminish the full significance of his statements. No mention was made of the second five-year plan, which, although nothing explicit was said, appeared to have been abandoned completely and to have no further use other than as a reference for statistics.

Unfortunately, the text of Mao's speeches at the Second Session of the Eighth Party Congress is not available. On the other hand, he is known to have visited several rural areas of Hopei, Shantung, and Honan in August 1958. This trip convinced him that in the countryside, the Great Leap Forward should be based on a broader organization than that of the socialist cooperatives. The people's communes had been born. Not until the enlarged meeting of the Political Bureau was held at Peitaiho (the Deauville of pre-Communist China) on August 29, 1958, did they make their true entrance on the historical scene. The resolution adopted stated that people's communes had multiplied rapidly in several regions in the spirit of the Great Leap Forward, thanks to the ideological progress of the population, that they had arisen as a response to the needs of basic construction in the countryside, and that they would ensure the industrial development of the countryside:[17]

> Large-scale agricultural capital construction and advanced agri-cultural technical measures demand the employment of more man-power. The development of industry in rural areas also demands the transfer of a portion of manpower from the agricultural front. Thus, the demand is more and more urgent for the mechanization and elec-trification of our countryside.

Consequently, agricultural cooperatives could no longer meet the needs of accelerated socialist construction.

The resolution of Peitaiho laid down the size of communes: from 2,000 to 20,000 families in extreme cases. It stated that elementary cooperatives must become production teams, which reduced their role to that of organizing their work; it tolerated unequal wealth among advanced cooperatives which had become large production teams or brigades; and it advised, unwillingly, a gradual approach in absorbing what little private property remained and flexibility in the problem of compensation.

Lastly, the Peitaiho resolution was careful to say that the property system of the commune was still a collective one; property did not belong to the whole people. It added that the distribution system was to be based on the formula "to each according to his work" and not "to each according to his needs." It also pointed out that the commune was the best organization for the building of socialism and the gradual transition toward the

Communist society, for which it would be the basic unit. The conclusion was a rash one:

> It appears now that the realization of Communism in our country is no longer a thing of the distant future. We should actively employ the form of the people's commune to produce a concrete path for transition to Communism.

Many of those in leading posts and many cadres wanted their communes to be the first to enter the new society.

Notes

[1] The usual estimates quoted it as $30,000 million in 1952, and $45,000 or 50,000 million in 1957.

[2] *Ten Great Years*, p. 180. The numbers of workers and other employees in industry rose from 15,804,000 to 24,506,000 during the first plan.

[3] *Ten Great Years*, p. 175.

[4] *Ibid.*, p. 118.

[5] For agriculture as a whole, including industrial and subsidiary crops, the average increase between 1952 and 1957 was 4.5 percent per year.

[6] According to *Ten Great Years*, p. 8, the population grew from 595,550,000 in 1953 to 656,630,000 in 1957, but the rate of increase probably slowed down thereafter.

[7] In 1957 the 710 state farms only cultivated a little more than 1 million hectares out of 110 million and had available to them 10,177 tractors of only 15 horsepower (communiqué issued by the Statistical Bureau, April 13, 1959).

[8] "The Role of the Chinese Communist Party in the National War," *Selected Works*, 2:210.

[9] See the next chapter for an account of Mao's individual responsibility for planning, or, to put it more accurately, for the absence of planning.

[10] Ch'en Po-ta, *Mao Tse-tung on the Chinese Revolution* (Peking: Foreign Language Press, 1953).

[11] Official text reproduced by the *Nouvelle Revue Internationale* (December 6, 1960).

[12] Some documents dating from the Cultural Revolution suggest that Mao was badly informed, if not as to the advisability of achieving Communism in a state of abundance, at least on the unfortunate Russian experience with communes during the early years of their regime.

[13] "Chinese Law and Government," *ISAP Journal of Translations* 1, No. 4 (1969).

[14] *Ibid.*, p. 12.

[15] *Current Background*, No. 884 (July 18, 1969). On the same subject, see also a note of February 19, 1958: "Sixty Methods of Work," *Current Background*, No. 892 (October 21, 1969), and Jerome Ch'en, *Mao Papers*, p. 57.

[16] The name "people's communes" had possibly not been chosen at this point.

[17] The Peitaiho resolution was published in the *People's Daily* on September 19.

18 The Great Leap Forward

The Great Leap Forward was in the dimension of time what the rural people's communes—a direct result of it—were in space. Haste, its chief characteristic, spread to every sector: industry, agriculture, trade, and, at least as a consequence, to science, culture, and education, all of which are also related to production—or, to put it briefly, to the whole life of the nation.

The Great Leap Forward was mainly a mental attitude. The frenzy that took hold of the entire people was expressed in both words and deeds. In the communes, people went to work with banners flying and, if possible, led by a band. Many-colored banners, decorated with slogans, were planted in the fields. Like the flags and standards, pennants and ensigns of the battlefields of old, they served as rallying points, raising morale; such military symbols were perfectly suited to the circumstances. Great battles had to be won in the field of production. They were conducted on the different fronts with "work armies." Machines and tools had become weapons, the worker or peasant producer became a soldier who was expected to embody the usual martial virtues: discipline, devotion, sacrifice, and team spirit. "A factory is a military camp. In front of his machines, the worker is as disciplined as a soldier," as the Wuhan resolution said in December 1958. Consequently, the changes of this period occurred in a wartime kind of atmosphere made up of a mixture of excitement and constraint; although this atmosphere can be explained by the totalitarian, ruthless nature of the regime, it was also due to China's critical situation at the time. The pressing need for economic construction had the urgency of a drive for national salvation. To a varying degree, all were conscious of this.

In industry—the main subject of this chapter—the Great Leap Forward was to result in the defining of priorities, the fixing of new targets in terms of figures, rapidity of work, the combining of new and archaic methods, decentralization of many enterprises (an attempt to increase the numbers of small, rudimentary concerns, considered inexpensive), and an astonishing increase in manpower, as the numbers of industrial and clerical workers increased in the space of one year (1957-1958) from 24,506,000 to 45,323,000.[1]

The general meaning of the Great Leap Forward and its priorities was given in the communiqué issued by the Sixth Session of the Eighth Central Committee, held at Wuhan from November 28 to December 10, 1958:

> The development of our national economy by leaps and bounds this year has proved the correctness of the whole group of policies laid down by the Party: the policy of simultaneous development of industry and agriculture on the basis of giving priority to heavy industry; the policy of simultaneous development of heavy and light industries; the policy of effecting an overall leap forward on the industrial front with steel as the key link; the policy of simultaneous development of national and local industries; the policy of simultaneous development of large enterprises and medium-sized and small enterprises; the policy of simultaneously employing modern and indigenous methods of production, and the policy of combining centralized leadership with a full-scale mass movement in industry—in a word, the policy of walking on two legs and not on one or one-and-a-half legs. The Great Leap Forward in our industrial and agricultural production in 1958 is a great practice. Through this practice we have not only found a broad way to build socialism, but also gained rich experience in marching along this broad way. This will make it possible for us not only to continue the Leap Forward in 1959 but to do much better.[2]

In short, everything had to be produced immediately and in large quantities, for the only clearly defined priorities concerned heavy industry, and particularly steel. The official formula put it as "more, quicker, better, and cheaper." These ambitions quickly became apparent in the targets for industry for 1959, which were calculated on the basis of the "unprecedented" results supposedly achieved in 1958.[3] The following table gives these results and, anticipating events slightly, also gives the revised figures after the Lushan Plenum in August 1959.

Table 18.1
Results of the Great Leap Forward (1958 figures and
1959 revisions)

Targets and results	Steel	Coal	Energy	Fertilizer	Cereals	Cotton
1958 results announced (millions of tons)	11.08	270			375	3.31
1958 revised results (millions of tons)	8				250	
1959 original targets (millions of tons or million kWh)	18	380	40,000 million kWh	1.3	525	5
1959 revised targets (millions of tons)	12	335			275	2.3
1959 final results (millions of tons)	13.3	347.8			270.05	2.41
1960 targets (millions of tons)	18.4	425			297 (approx.)	2.6 (approx.)

Taken as a whole, the total value of agricultural and industrial production was said to have increased by 70 percent between 1957 and 1958, a greater increase than that for the years between 1952 and 1957 (68 percent). This fantastic amount was corrected with the revision of statistics and came to no more than 31 percent (39.3 percent for industry and 16.7 percent for agriculture, with a total value of production of 241.3 thousand million yuan).[4]

Both the value of the statistics given for the years 1958 and 1959 and the industrial repercussions of the failure of agriculture will be discussed later (see Chapter 20). The atmosphere and conditions of industrial production are more important here. The lack of planning, or to put it more accurately, the reduction of planning to the fixing of general numerical targets, was the dominant feature. This was acknowledged by Mao Tse-tung at Lushan; he blamed himself for it but placed the true responsibility on the National Planning Commission and local ministries and departments.

The Planning Commission and the ministries have been in existence for ten years. Suddenly, at Peitaiho, they ceased to concern themselves [with planning]. The directive on planning consisted in having no plan; what was called no concern for planning meant ignoring overall balance; the necessary amounts of coal, or iron, or the means of transport, were no longer calculated, but coal and iron cannot move alone, they need trucks. I did not foresee this. I did not look into this, nor did XX, and nor did the premier. I knew nothing of this—not that I want to shift the blame from myself, but this does shift the blame from me all the same because I am not chairman of the Planning Commission. Before August last year, I concentrated mainly on the revolution. I know nothing about construction, and I understand nothing about industrial planning.[5]

The lack of rational, detailed planning, aggravated by the preeminence of the Party and ideology, together with the acceleration of the pace of production, plunged China's industrial economy into a state of chaos from which it was not disentangled until the restoration of order in 1960 and 1961. Men no longer had command over events. The technical cadres, inhibited by the primacy of political instructions, and overtaken by events, carried out their work and kept silent for fear of being accused of rightist conservatism, of lack of faith in the masses, or—worse still—of sabotage.[6] The Soviet advisers were paralyzed and no longer played any effective role. The lack of any scientific and technological tradition on the part of those in authority and the masses did the rest. The machines were overtaxed and almost worn out; raw materials and finished products, manufactured with no thought given to their usefulness or to real transport capacity, were largely wasted.

Lastly, in this atmosphere of disorder, excessive decentralization added still more disastrous effects to the existing situation. The encouragement of local initiative and local investment by the relaxation of the sometimes paralyzing hold of central power was no doubt justified. The first five-year plan had shown the inconvenience of overcentralization, particularly in the varied domain of light industry and consumer goods, and suitable measures had been carried out in 1956. These were taken still further in 1958, and a great many concerns (80 percent, according to some experts) were transferred to the provinces, where some of them, at least, created smaller branches in the hsien. Vast sectors of industry were consequently further removed from any eventual state plan, and their fate was placed, with little or no control, in the hands of local authorities of doubtful competence.

The campaign to produce steel in "backyard furnaces" is probably the most striking illustration of the absurdity of the Great Leap Forward. It highlighted the ignorance and voluntarism of the cadres, the docility and credulity of the masses, and the puerility of the theory known as "walking on two legs." The responsibility for the initiative lay with Mao Tse-tung himself, who was probably encouraged by K'o Ch'ing-shih, later mayor of Shanghai, and faithfully followed by the Political Bureau?

> Did the initiative for the great campaign for producing iron and steel come from K'o Ch'ing-shih or from me? From me. I spoke of it to K'o Ch'ing-shih, saying it would produce 6 million tons. Later I spoke to everyone about it. XX thought it was possible. In June I spoke of 10.7 million tons. It was carried out and put in the communiqué of Peitaiho. . . . A great disorder was created by 90 million people moving into action[8]

During the second half of 1958 a large part of the Chinese population—country people and townspeople, intellectuals and manual workers, and occasionally specialists in iron smelting and refining—were removed from their normal jobs and put to work collecting and melting down scrap metal, even down to humble kitchen utensils. Three million tons of poor steel, which could be counted in the statistics and was used for little more than individual agricultural tools, was produced in this way. No more need be said here, for enough eyewitness accounts already exist of this vast collective aberration. Even so, it should be borne in mind as an example of the all-powerfulness of Mao Tse-tung and of the backwardness of a society that was ready to accept the most extravagant commands without discernment or comment.

The result of the small blast furnace campaign was not, however, entirely negative. Although it took the peasants away from their work, contributing in this way to the failure of agriculture, it gave them—though this was little more than a caricature—a few rudiments of technical knowledge and launched provinces, districts, and communes on a sort of treasure hunt as they explored and inventoried local resources (mainly iron and coal), which sometimes turned out to be workable. A few small enterprises, later taken over and standardized by experts, thus made their own contribution to the large mining or industrial centers, and met some local needs. National needs were further served when the big steel mills at Wuhan and Paotow came into service in 1959.

The steel-producing campaign was not the only one. Experiments in the production of fertilizer were strongly encouraged. Newspapers were full of advice or designs for small workshops with an uncertain or ludicrously small output. More serious campaigns for the improvement of agricultural tools were also launched, sometimes in highly pretentious terms.

The Great Leap Forward in education and culture

The hopes engendered by the Great Leap Forward resulted in a large inflation in the numbers of students and technicians, who later found themselves at a loss, with no future, when the readjustments of the 1960s came about. Sending them back to the land or to outlying provinces (Sinkiang, the Northwest and the Northeast) was a source of disappointment or discontent. A comparison of the years 1957 and 1958, especially in higher and technical education, is particularly revealing as to the initial optimism of the leaders (see Table 18.2)?

Table 18.2
Student enrollment, 1957 and 1958 (thousands of students)

Years	Higher education	Secondary education & technical training	Secondary education	Primary education
1957	441	778	6,281	64,279
1958	660	1,470	8,520	86,400

Another "leap forward" was scheduled to take place in higher education and specialized secondary education in 1959 and 1960. According to a speech by Li Fu-ch'un to the Second National People's Congress, 280,000 new students were to be absorbed into higher education.[10] These figures do not appear to have been retained. After 1960 official statistics only mention the number of diplomas obtained upon completing a course of study and their categories; scientific and technical diplomas were well ahead of the rest. In 1961, nearly 160,000 diplomas were granted in the universities and other higher educational establishments, with another 170,000 given in 1962; 60 percent of the recipients were members of the Communist Party or of the Communist Youth League.

During the Great Leap Forward in education in 1958, the principal efforts were naturally concentrated on industrial and agricultural domains, on the creation of technical schools and institutions both for and by industrial firms, on increasing the number of secondary agricultural schools, and on combining study with productive labor. On the latter point, economic and ideological considerations met. Lu Ting-yi wrote an important article on the subject—"Education Must be Combined with Productive Labor" (August 16, 1958)—after a conference convened by the Central Committee in April and June 1958. The text contains many ideas which were taken up again by the Cultural Revolution, along with a vocabulary that was to become very familiar. Teaching must not remain above the class struggle, but must at the same time contribute to it and to raising the level of production. Chou En-lai's speech on April 18, 1959, to the National People's Congress (First Session of the Second Congress) made this perfectly clear in terms that also foreshadowed the Cultural Revolution:

> Facts show that a suitable combination of education and productive labor can contribute to strengthening the links between school and society, allying theory and practice and bringing about step-by-step the fusion of intellectual and manual work, and allow our educational establishments to be transformed from day to day into a new sort of schools capable of training new men with a Communist outlook.

The premier added that Chinese experience in this radical revolution in education was still preliminary and therefore inadequate.

The year 1960 gave rise to several projects for total reform of the educational system by shortening primary and secondary schooling from twelve years to ten years, according to various methods then being tested![11]

The failure of the Great Leap Forward, of the Socialist Education Movement, and of the Cultural Revolution added new elements to the question. The closing down of the universities between 1966 and 1970 cancelled out the progress achieved in training cadres during the Great Leap Forward. It might be said that the surplus of technical cadres, trained hastily with varying degrees of success during that period, met the needs of industry without too much difficulty, though industry had ceased to progress. Both the Great Leap Forward and the Cultural Revolution show the application of the two supreme and ever-present guiding principles in education in modern China: total subordination to politics, and strict subordination to the needs of the state, to the exclusion of individual preferences.

Notes

[1] *Ten Great Years*, p. 180.

[2] *People's Daily* (December 17, 1958). English text in a special number of *China Reconstructs* (February 1959).

[3] The results for 1958 and the targets for 1959 are given in the communiqué of the Sixth Plenum of the Eighth Party Congress (December 10, 1958), published by the Hsinhua Agency on December 17, 1958.

[4] Report by Li Fu'ch'un to the National People's Congress (March 30, 1960).

[5] See Ting Wang, *Chung-kung wen-hua ta ke-ming tzu-liao hui-pien (Selection of Documents on the Great Cultural Revolution of the Chinese Communists)*, Vol. 3, p. 24. Extracts from Mao's declaration at Lushan on July 23, 1959. The text of the declaration has been published by various Chinese and Western periodicals.

[6] See in particular "Refute Those who Doubt the Mass Line on the Industrial Front," *Hung Ch'i*, No. 12 (November 16, 1958).

[7] K'o Ch'ing-shih, first Party secretary in Shanghai from 1955, became mayor in November 1958.

[8] Speech of July 23, 1959, at the Lushan Plenum, quoted above.

[9] Source: *Ten Great Years*, p. 192. An article in the *Peking Review* (December 2, 1958) gives slightly higher figures for 1958.

[10] Compared with 152,000 in 1958-1959 and between 70,000 and 90,000 during the years before that. Candidates were given permission to take a competitive examination and the selection was made thereafter.

[11] Report by Lu Ting-yi to the National People's Congress (April 9, 1960).

19 Rural People's Communes and Urban Communes 1958

In size, organization, and functions, the people's communes differed considerably from the cooperatives in which they had originated.

Structure

The production team (*sheng-ch'an tui*) was the basis of the structure. It was frequently the former elementary or semisocialist cooperative. In terms of land, it encompassed a hamlet (*chuang*) or small village (*ts'un*) of houses huddled together in the northern provinces, a wheat growing region where water is scarcer than in the rice growing region of the central, western or southern provinces, where the houses are scattered in small groups. It generally consisted of between twenty and fifty families (100 to 250 people) and had between 200 and 600 *mou*—that is, between fifteen and forty (or sometimes fifty) hectares of cultivable land.[1] The carrying out of daily tasks was entrusted to groups varying in composition and size; the members tended nevertheless to remain together. Small groups also existed (*hsiao tsu*) for the purposes of education and political discussions.

Above the team came the large production team (*sheng-ch'an ta-tui*), often known as production brigade in the West. It was roughly the equivalent of the former advanced or socialist cooperative. Depending on the region and on local conditions, it took in between 150 and 200 families, or between 800 and 1,000 people—usually about ten teams—and worked 2,000 *mou* (150 hectares) on the average.

Then came the people's commune itself (*jen-min kung-she*). In its first version—that of 1958—it consisted of approximately 5,000 families and 60,000 *mou* (4,500 hectares) of land.[2] In practice, it varied greatly, according to population density and mobility; it had between ten and twenty brigades. As far as the territory was concerned, the commune was made to correspond to the administrative village (*hsiang*) as far as possible, by adjusting one or the other or both at once. Theoretically, the *hsien* (district) was intended to be the final stage in the evolution, giving a total of about 2,000 communes for the whole of China. In fact, several communes corresponding to *hsien* were created in small and lightly populated districts. Sometimes several *hsiang* communes joined together to form associated communes (*lien-she*).

The arrangement of the different elements making up the commune, and in particular the number of teams to a brigade and the number of brigades to a commune, varied according to time, place, situation, and local circumstances. By noting the number of peasant families,[3] the highly variable but usually known number of *hsiang* and communes, the stability of the production team—linked to the land by their homes—the number of hectares under cultivation,[4] and detailed information on specific cases published in the press or observed on the spot, it is generally possible to trace the history of broad changes in commune organization, at least in China proper. It is difficult to take minority populations into account because of the vast disparity between their numbers and the huge territories they occupy (6 percent of the total population of China, and between 50 and 60 percent of the area of the country), and also because of their generally pastoral or semisedentary type of economy.

The functions of the commune

Theoretically at least, the rural people's commune was a perfect example of an organization with multiple functions: economic, administrative, social, educational, and military.

Economic function

The economic function of the commune was obviously the most important. For a start, by means of the commune, it was possible to mobilize all masculine labor in the rural districts and much female labor as well. Because agricultural work as such did not occupy more than 120 or 130 working days, it was theoretically feasible to create "work armies" to be used according to the possibilities, needs, and development plans of the commune, while the disappearance of family plots of land made the peasants concentrate all their efforts on collectively owned land. Vast work projects were carried out on the land, all using purely human labor (digging thousands of irrigation trenches, or deep plowing, for example), while some new techniques (close planting, careful hoeing and weeding, spreading of mud from ponds and rivers, and so on) that were considered more profitable were easier to enforce. Both large-scale work and new techniques were sometimes executed or applied without preparation or discernment, defeating their own ends and sometimes destroying the delicate balance that had existed for generations.

It was thought that the commune would also provide a large enough geographical setting for additional activities, particularly the exploitation and use of different resources on commune territory: small mines, quarries, and watercourses. The enlargement and regrouping of existing handicrafts would allow light industry of local interest to be developed (fertilizers, chemicals, cement, textiles, tools, pottery, and the like). These products could be sold to neighboring communes. Secondary agricultural activities (the cultivation of trees, fish ponds, and medicinal plants) could be undertaken. In this way, the initiative and capital of the commune would compensate for the disappearance—regrettable from an economic point of view—of private initiative and private capital. It was thought that the peasants would be more willing to invest what little savings they had in local projects than they would be to buy state bonds.

The setting up of large communal services (refectories, sewing workshops, laundries, nurseries) would also free a great many women for production, avoid waste, and permit greater control of consumption.

The promoters of the commune also thought that the new organization, by encouraging the peasants to go beyond their agricultural activities and by creating a few embryonic light industries, would make the backward masses aware of technical methods, stimulate their creativity, and, generally speaking, awaken the countryside to a new, modern life.

Social function

From a social point of view, the people's commune was to be the basic unit of socialist society, closely associating workers, peasants, soldiers, and

bureaucrats, gradually erasing the differences between social and professional categories, between intellectuals and manual workers, and
between town and countryside in attitudes and customs. By lessening the
importance of the family, it would stress communal living to an
unprecedented degree—in the fields of work, food, leisure activities and
housing—and would eradicate once and for all the notion of property
(which was quickly restricted to clothes, furniture, a few miscellaneous
objects, and a little money), personal interest, and individualistic
tendencies. By providing a transition between the property of the
cooperative and that of the whole people, the commune would prepare for
the final form of the future society and, in the terms of the resolution of
August 29, 1958 (resolution of Peitaiho), would serve as a "short cut" to
Communism.

The resolution of December 10, 1958 (Wuhan resolution), although
more restrained than that of Peitaiho, still strongly expressed the hopes
placed in the people's communes:

> The development of the system of rural people's communes . . has
> shown the people of our country the way to the gradual industrializa-
> tion of rural areas, the way to the gradual transition from collective
> ownership to ownership by the whole people in agriculture, the way to
> the gradual transition from the socialist principle of "to each according
> to his work" to the Communist principle of "to each according to his
> needs," the way gradually to lessen and finally to eliminate the dif-
> ferences between town and country, between worker and peasant, and
> between mental and manual labor, and the way gradually to lessen and
> finally to eliminate the internal function of the state.

Educational function

The communes also had an educational function. They were responsible
for primary education, part of secondary education, and adult education.
This duty relieved the state of the responsibility for schooling, lightening
its financial burden, and was consistent with tradition, for many villages
and temples had always had their own schools. Education in China had
never been completely centralized, and all centralization was recent. In the
spirit of the communes, education was also to be included in a broad
movement to link manual labor and study. Many exaggerations and
misconceptions arose from this aim, which in fact corresponded to

practices that were widespread in the Chinese countryside. The life of Mao Tse-tung gives a good example of this.

Lastly, the question of education in people's communes was directly tied to the need to train qualified personnel to manage them, for the vast majority of rural people were illiterate.

The military function

The military function of the people's communes was important in peacetime and could assume vast importance in wartime. In peacetime, the commune was a center for preparation for military duties, for instructing and mobilizing the reserve force, and for providing support for the families of those called up. It had a militia, more or less adequately armed, which was generally made up of former soldiers and activists of tested loyalty. The militia answered to civil authority up to and at the level of the *hsien;* it was rarely used beyond that level. In times of stress, it helped maintain order and oppose banditry, acted as the auxiliary of the public security forces and, if need be, of the army itself. Commune rules wisely stipulated that the posts of leader of the commune and commander of the militia could not be held by the same man.

In time of war—particularly thermonuclear war—the self-contained nature of the commune would enable it to emerge as a true survival unit, capable of outlasting the destruction of the great urban centers and the higher administrative and military institutions. Better yet, the communes as a whole were like a cellular tissue; if some sections were destroyed by nuclear warfare, the others would unite to re-form the structure and heal the social chaos.

Administrative function

The people's commune was also an administrative mechanism, for its organization formed part of the structure of the state. The commune and the *hsiang* were a single unit for administrative purposes, with the same leaders; the word *hsiang* quickly fell into disuse in official contexts. This illustrated a fundamental difference between the commune and the cooperatives, which were nevertheless the partial embodiment of individual interests and constituted—theoretically at least—an autonomous collectivity confronting the state. In a country with truly democratic institutions, the creation of communes would have given the masses an advantage over the central power. Decentralization, spreading from the economic sphere to other spheres, would have given the basic stratum of the population important means of exerting pressure on the government. The opposite occurred in China: the mingling of the functions of the *hsiang* with those of the commune reinforced, if this were necessary, the authority of the Communist Party, which thus took over the management of economic affairs through its directing committees in all administrative institutions. By tightening the bonds between existing groups of people, not only in their productive activities but even in their living arrangements, the people's communes greatly increased the Party's propaganda facilities as well as its political control over the people.

President Liu Shao-ch'i gave what was perhaps the best summarized account of the meaning of the people's communes, which he rightly believed had been set up too soon, when he said: "The people's commune is not merely a cell for the organization of production, but for the organization of the life of the people itself.'⁵

Management

The management structure of the commune reproduced to a certain extent that of the *hsiang* which it replaced. At the top was a congress of representatives of the commune, elected for two years, as laid down by the constitution of 1954 and the electoral law of 1953. Although it was widely representative, its powers were still as theoretical as those of the *hsien* and provincial congresses. The congress of representatives elected a management committee, which was the executive body of the commune. It had between twenty and thirty members, was presided over by a director (*she chang*), who had several assistants, and had a number of specialized offices: administration, agriculture, livestock, industry, finance, trade, education, and miscellaneous services (refectories, nurseries, old people's homes, and so on). Ad hoc committees were often created to study and find solutions for temporary or particular problems. A control committee, elected by the congress of representatives and responsible to the control committee of the *hsien* in which the commune was located, supervised its activities and probably those of the state, province, or *hsien* services, enterprises, and organizations that were within its territory.

Diagrams of the organization of a commune are available in a few cases, and these reveal considerable variations in the situation, size, and activities of each one. The diagram in Figure 19.1 represents an average commune and is based on several actual examples. Beneath this appearance of democracy, the Party—whose members filled many of the posts in the structure just described—had the real control over the destiny of the commune, as was laid down by Articles 59 and 60 of the Party constitution. The secretary of the Party primary committee (or branch committee), who was elected for one year (see Chapter 7 of the constitution), was in fact the most important person in the commune.

Beneath the commune, a local congress of the production brigade appointed its representatives to the commune congress and also elected its brigade leader, theoretically for a year, and provided him with assistants and a small management committee. A small control committee was also appointed. The production team also elected a team leader who, with his assistants, formed a small committee to run the organization and oversee the execution of the work of the team.

In 1958, according to the statutes of the Sputnik commune, which served as an example for all the others, it seems that the management was highly centralized at the level of the commune.[6] Following the instructions issued by the state planning authorities, the commune drew up its plan for production and economic development without much consultation with the production brigades. Once the higher level had given its approval, the plan for the commune was divided among the brigades, which apportioned the work among the teams.[7] Financing, accounting, and financial control also appear to have been highly centralized at the commune level. As a result, the commune virtually owned the most important means of production, just as it owned the resources on its land except when these were too abundant or too valuable, in which case they were exploited by the state, the province, or the *hsien*.

The question of the level at which production tools were owned was naturally a fundamental one, because of its practical effects and psychological element. The ownership level was changed several times later on, but the provisions of Article 4 of the statutes of the Sputnik commune were probably followed everywhere initially. According to Article 4, when cooperatives merged to form a commune, they had to hand over all their means of production to the commune. Article 5 stated that members of cooperatives or isolated families should also transfer to the commune their ownership of land, houses, livestock, and trees.

The system of payment, which ultimately determined whether the members of the commune were satisfied or not, also appears to have been decided at the commune level, with an arbitrary equalization between

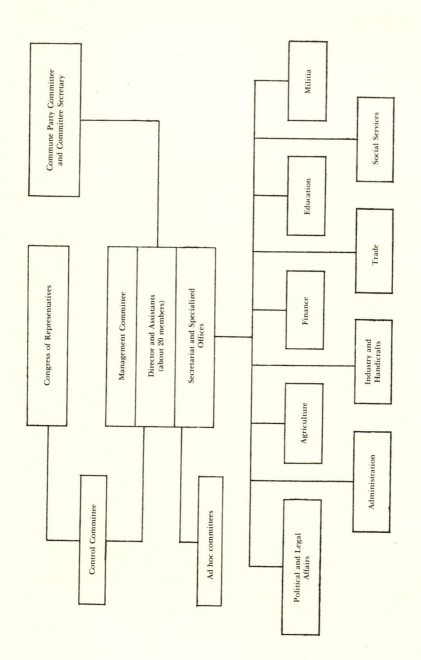

Figure 19.1   Organization of a rural people's commune

brigades and infinite variations in local cadres' interpretations of the spirit of the commune. In 1958, the greatest variations seem to have occurred in the system of payment at the primary level. Some communes went very far indeed in distributing foodstuffs with no control at all. Others, on the contrary, applied strict rationing. Most of them adopted a sort of halfway system known as "half food supply, half salary." Li Hsien-nien, then minister of finance, pointed out that the distribution of food-stuffs or services was inspired by the formula "to each according to his needs" and corresponded to a system of five, six, or seven necessities being guaranteed by the state: food, clothing, medical treatment, maternity care, education, housing, and marriage and funeral expenses. The salary, when adjusted to individual work, varied between 4 and 15 yuan ($1.63 to $6.10) per month, half of which was paid in cash and the rest in foodstuffs.[8] Even so, the Sputnik commune appears to have taken more careful account of the nature and quantity of work contributed by each individual and to have emphasized bonuses (at most, a quarter of the total salaries). The result was a strange contradiction, for having eliminated ownership of the most humble possessions, the system then paid a salary in cash according to the work contributed.[9]

The commune of 1958 represented a new leap forward in collective living. Its two most extreme examples were the disappearance of private dwellings—materials, bricks, tiles, and wood could be delivered to the commune for the construction of new houses, which could be rented out to cover the cost of upkeep and repairs[10]—and the creation of communal dining rooms, whose use the authorities did not always dare to enforce; even so, 3.4 million of them existed in country areas by the end of 1958. These two obligations, along with the system of payment and compulsory participation in political life, were to bring about the failure of the original version of the people's communes, sometimes even before they were put into practice; almost all the other characteristics were already part of the system of advanced cooperatives.

It seemed at first that the extraordinary formula for the people's communes was going to succeed. There were several reasons for this optimism. The harvest of 1958 was an exceptionally good one, totalling 250 million tons according to the revised statistics of 1959, as against 185 million in 1957. It was due to good weather conditions and also perhaps partially to the progress of the cooperatives which, after their three or four years of existence, were beginning to work efficiently. In all events, the fact helped to reduce peasant discontent appreciably.

Because the commune experiment occurred within the context of the Great Leap Forward, it was accompanied by firm promises of prosperity. Filled with hope, the peasants were all the more ready to accept the principle of a total, intensive mobilization. By carefully attributing the initiative for the communes to the peasants themselves, the regime had started a movement in which each person had to go along, even if he was not taken in by it.

Urban communes

Parallel to the rural people's communes, urban communes were launched during the summer of 1958 in Peking and certain other towns. The movement lost considerable ground during the next year owing to insufficient preparation and the unpopularity of the new communes. The movement for rural people's communes had had a convenient point of departure in the production cooperatives, but the point of departure for urban communes was merely the small groups (*hsiao tsu*) of each quarter. Furthermore, city people were opposed to the urban communes because they feared that they would have to give up their private property and homes, as had been the case in country districts, and suspected that further efforts would be asked of them.

The urban commune movement was revived, with more precautions in the spring of 1960, and linked closely to light industry. According to official figures, it involved in some way 52 million townspeople. There were then 1,027 urban communes grouping 60,000 small workshops, 180,000 dining halls, and 120,000 nurseries.[11] These figures should not create any illusions. The contribution made by the urban communes to production as a whole was of little monetary value (in 1959, it amounted to 2,000 million yuan out of a total of 102,000 million), but it was useful, for it provided for the manufacture of many small consumer goods and services. The texts distinguish broadly between: (a) ordinary urban communes undertaking small-scale manufacture in their neighborhood; (b) urban communes created alongside large industrial centers; (c) urban communes working alongside administrative institutions and schools. The last two types played an auxiliary role and made life a little easier for the labor force and regular personnel by setting up dining halls, nurseries, laundries, sewing workshops, and various repair shops.

Urban communes also often constituted the basic framework for political activities and further education and accustomed the inhabitants of towns to collective living, just as they did in the countryside. Unlike the rural communes, they had no true administrative functions. They do not appear to have had any serious effects on property (except on individual freedom), but their low salaries and the disturbances they caused in family life did not make their development particularly easy. They appear to have lost vitality little by little, until the press virtually ceased to mention them.

Notes

[1] The *mou* (or *mu*) amounts to roughly one-fifteenth of a hectare.

[2] According to *Ten Great years*, at the end of December 1958, a total of 26,578 communes existed, containing 123,250,000 peasant families, giving an average of 4,637 families per commune. In April 1960, T'an Chen-lin, in charge of agriculture, mentioned 24,000 communes working about 64,000 *mou* (4,226 hectares). Some communes were very large, however, as in the case of the model commune Sputnik, with 9,300 families and 43,000 inhabitants. It had taken in twenty-seven superior cooperatives and had four *hsiang*.

[3] 123,250,000 in December 1958, a figure which probably increases by about 2 million each year.

[4] The statistics vary slightly here. The figure of 107 million hectares is generally accepted, but does not take into account the fact that some places yielded two or three annual harvests.

[5] Liu Shao-ch'i defended people's communes in *The Triumph of Marxism-Leninism in China* but this text was written for the tenth anniversary of the People's Republic of China and was published in *The New International Review* on September 14, 1959.

[6] On this subject see "How to Administer Communes, Using the Statutes of the Sputnik Commune," *People's Daily* (September 4, 1957), and the draft statutes.

[7] In fact, agricultural production was subject to double planning at each different level (province, *hsien*, and commune): first, targets of the plan, then the highest possible targets above preceding ones, which, once achieved, became the official targets. The system gave rise to what the economist Choh-ming Li aptly describes as a "self-acceleration of output targets," leading to a sort of "great leap in statistics."

[8] See "What I have seen in the communes," *People's Daily* (October 17, 1958).

[9] Article 14 of the statutes. Article 15 provides for a system of free food supply depending on degree of need.

[10] Article 20 of the statutes.

[11] Li Fu-ch'un in *Hung ch'i*, No. 16 (August 16, 1960).

20 The Modification of the People's Communes: The Failure of the Great Leap Forward

The first signs of anxiety as to whether the people's communes were functioning properly appeared four or five months after the resolution of Peitaiho. The Eighth Central Committee held its Sixth Plenum at Wuchang (one of the three towns that had combined to form Wuhan) from November 28 to December 10 to examine the results of the year 1958, fix the targets for the year 1959 in the economic field, and reconsider the whole problem of people's communes. Its deliberations resulted in two extremely important statements: the communique of the Sixth Plenum and the "Resolution on Certain Problems Concerning the People's Communes."[1] Although the details are not known in full, the Sixth Plenum had been prepared by a working session held at Chengchow in Honan, from November 2 to 10, which was chaired by Mao Tse-tung and attended by certain members of the Central Committee, various provincial secretaries, and other cadres.

After the customary optimistic introduction, the resolution, which was about twenty pages long, continued with a section containing criticisms and constructive proposals on the general theme of the need for reforms and their extent. It acknowledged that because of the newness of the communes, the urgency of work in the fields in the autumn, and the campaign to produce steel (a veiled criticism aimed at its promoters) the rural people's communes had not had time to "consolidate their organizations, perfect their working systems, or systematically settle the new questions concerning production, distribution, livelihood and welfare, management and administration".

The resolution also stated that different opinions existed on some questions, and that it was essential to achieve unity in points of view within the Party and the public and to correct the organization and operation of the communes. It then went on to provide a much more accurate and prudent definition of the general mission of the communes than that of the resolution of Peitaiho, and it raised various specific questions.

Individual efforts and interests were to be treated with more consideration. Under normal conditions, the system of eight hours work and two hours study was to be respected. When large-scale work was under way, provision was to be made to ensure at least eight hours sleep and four hours for rest and breaks. Social benefits were to be developed and improved. The right to private property was confirmed and enlarged:

> Some people think that the switch to communes will call for a redistribution of existing property for personal use. This is a misconception. It should be made known among the masses that the means of livelihood owned by members (including houses, clothing, bedding, and furniture) and their deposits in banks and credit cooperatives will remain their own property after they join the commune and will always belong to them.

Individual secondary activities were allowed, and debts incurred before the establishment of the communes were not abolished.

The payment system was to be revised, and the cash payment was to be made larger than the payment in kind. The rule "to each according to his work" remained in effect, because its retraction would "tend to dampen the working enthusiasm of the people." It was pointed out, with justification, that the Communist system of distribution "to each according to his needs" was only possible under conditions of plenty. A vast information campaign on this subject was to be carried out among the population "from a Marxist-Leninist point of view." In all this, the aim was to counteract the effect of the unwise resolution of Peitaiho. Similarly, the communes were encouraged to develop the manufacture of salable products and to trade with each other and with the state.

> Some people, attempting to "enter Communism" prematurely, have tried to abolish the production and exchange of commodities too early, and to negate at too early a stage the positive roles of commodities, value, money, and prices.

Lastly—and this was without doubt the most important point and the one best conveying an idea of the extent of the necessary adjustment—all Party committees at the levels of the provinces, autonomous regions, and special municipalities were instructed to restore orderly operations in the communes between December 1958 and April 1959, after a thorough examination of the situation and the elimination of doubtful or incompetent elements. Inspection groups consisting of "a thousand, several thousand, or ten thousand people" would be set up by the Party secretaries, while exhibitions, criticism sessions, meetings, and exchanges of experiences would be organized to raise the level of all the people's communes in China.[2]

In spite of the modifications of the spring of 1959, the general situation worsened during the year, until gradually and almost imperceptibly, by a process lasting until 1962, the communes went through radical changes which nearly destroyed their distinctive character and brought the real level of collectivization down once more to that of the production team.

From August 2-16, 1959, the Eighth Central Committee held its Eighth Plenum in Lushan, Kiangsi. Seven or eight years later, the rest of the world learned bit by bit how, and in what context, rightist opposition arose there. The chief figures in that opposition were P'eng Teh-huai, minister of national defense, Chang Wen-t'ien, one of the early Communist leaders, and Chou Hsiao-chou (see Chapter 21).

At the time, the publication of new statistics correcting those of 1958 and reducing the targets for 1959 astounded outside observers, who were cut off from the real situation in China and often too ready to believe in and sympathize with the efforts of the Party.[3] The elimination of moderate elements, whose criticisms were borne out by the correction of targets, seemed to indicate that the regime had admitted its mistakes and was determined to forge ahead, rallying to the slogan of the Great Leap Forward and with the people's communes as its best illustration.

Official optimism was maintained during the Second Session of the Second National People's Congress (March 30 to April 10, 1960). According to the March 30, 1960, report by Li Fu-ch'un, chairman of the State Planning Commission, the grain harvest in 1960 was expected to be 10 percent above than that of 1959, which had officially exceeded 270 million tons.[4] Heavy industry was expected to increase its output by 32 percent as compared with the preceding year, and light industry by 24 percent. The chief stress was already on agriculture, however. It was the "basis" of the economy, while industry remained the "dominating factor." The building of socialism was to be based on the production of grain and steel. Great efforts were to be made to sustain agriculture; financial aid to rural people's communes was increased by 50 percent. The need to speed up technical change and the modernization of agriculture, particularly mechanization, was to find its expression in a vigorous campaign based on the forty points of the twelve-year agricultural program (1956-1967), revised for the last time and presented to the National People's Congress by T'an Chen-lin, director of the state Office of Agriculture (April 6).

The *People's Daily* of March 31 quoted Mao Tse-tung: "With grain and steel everything becomes possible." This brief sentence shows both the trend of evolution and the hope that heavy industry would not be sacrificed to the development of agriculture, which was essential.

After the National People's Congress, anxiety began to be apparent in the press, first in the form of allusions to widespread bad weather, lack of balance in the development of the towns and the countryside, and the birth of a mass movement of industrial support for agriculture and urban support for the countryside.[5]

In August, a noteworthy article by Li Fu-ch'un, head of the State Planning Commission, recalled past struggles against "rightist" deviations and the way in which the principle of the Great Leap Forward and the system of the people's communes, both eminently suited to the development of the national economy, had been preserved. He added that, although industry and agriculture ought to be developed at the same time, agriculture should take priority and that the production of grain should have priority over all the rest.[6]

The core of the general line is to mobilize, under the leadership of the working class, all available forces, first of all the great strength of the over 500 million peasants, to bring about a continued leap forward in the national economy through the adoption of various forms and methods suited to China's specific conditions.

The theme of the prime importance of agriculture was widely taken up by the press, and gradually a vast "agricultural front" was formed. Workers from the towns, no longer needed in industry once the pace had slowed down, arrived by the million to reinforce this front; they numbered 20 million in all, according to Minister of Agriculture Liao Lu-yen, speaking in 1961. Hundreds of thousands of cadres and students went to strengthen the structures of the people's communes. It was no longer a case of simultaneous development of agriculture and industry, for all sectors of the national economy had to work for the benefit of agriculture.[7] The space devoted to agriculture in the daily press, under the most eloquent titles, rapidly became quite astounding. Some of the instructions—how to gather berries and wild plants, how to make the best of the poorest soils—were as worrying as they were revealing. There was no evidence to prove that several inland regions were not already suffering from famine.[8] In the towns, rationing became more and more strict and the allowance fell from between 40 and 60 pounds to between 25 and 35 pounds a month; there was a shortage of vegetables. Overseas Chinese sent in five times as many food parcels as usual. The Chinese government began importing grain from Australia and Canada; 6 million tons were bought in 1961 (worth $350 million at the 1961 rate of exchange), amounting to a third of all imports, and this in terms of a strong currency. Later, in May 1962, tens of thousands of Cantonese peasants, tired of hunger, whom the cadres could no longer hold back, reached Hong Kong. The British authorities were not able to take them all in.

At first bad weather conditions alone were responsible for the difficulties. More than 60 million hectares out of 106 million were affected, 26 million of these seriously. It was admitted, without entering into details, that the targets for agriculture and for light industry, which depended on agriculture for its raw materials, could not be reached.[9] During the last months of 1960, however, articles began to make direct references to the working of the communes. A particular effort was made to define more accurately the respective prerogatives and responsibilities of the commune, production brigade, and production team, to the advantage of the levels below them. The fundamental problems—accumulation and distribution, method of payment, and participation by the cadres in manual work—were all raised from a practical and an ideological viewpoint.[10]

The Ninth Plenum of the Central Committee, held in Peking from January 14 to 18, 1961, revealed the full gravity of the situation in language that was perfectly intelligible even to those least familiar with Marxist style:

> In view of the serious natural calamities that affected agricultural pro-
> duction for two successive years, the whole nation in 1961 must con-
> centrate on strengthening the agricultural front, must carry on the
> policy of taking agriculture as the foundation of the national economy
> and of developing agriculture and grain production in a big way by the
> whole Party and the whole people, must step up support for agriculture
> by all sectors and occupations and must exert the utmost effort to win
> a better harvest in agricultural production. In the rural areas efforts must

be made to consolidate further the people's communes, carry out the various policies concerning the people's communes and the rural economy, adopt effective measures to take good care of the livelihood of the people's commune members. . . .

After encouraging the cultivation of secondary food products, and advocating the development of "primary rural markets," the Plenum's communiqué strongly denounced the opposition by "bad elements" of the government and the Party (10 percent), sabotage by "insufficiently reformed bourgeois remnants," and the errors of certain cadres whose ideological level was inadequate.

> They lack sufficient understanding of the distinction between socialism and Communism, of the distinction between socialist owner-ship by the collective and socialist ownership by the people as a whole, of the three-level ownership of the people's communes with the pro-duction brigade as the basic level, and of the socialist society's prin-ciples of exchange of equal values and of remuneration according to work.

This condemnation, which was followed by a rectification movement and purge and by instructions on the "sixty points concerning work in the countryside," seemed to be addressed mainly to the leaders who, because of illusions, incompetence, or impotence, had neglected their communes and had not made a proper attempt to control production and consumption. But in many other cases, on the contrary, excessive and severe economic control by the cadres was responsible for the food shortage that the government could no longer disguise. At about this time, Mao Tse-tung told François Mitterand that calamities that had been "unknown for a century" had struck the country; he denied the existence of famine, but admitted to a "scarcity.[11] A few months later, speaking to Field Marshal Montgomery, he stated that the grain harvest for 1960 had been 150 million tons.[12]

Although the principle of the people's commune was never criticized (on the contrary, its existence was said to have saved the country from still worse disasters), the actuality gradually assumed a new look, which it has kept until now, through the vicissitudes of the Socialist Education Movement and the Cultural Revolution.

The reformed communes

Although the commune, like the Great Leap Forward and the general line, was still one of the three "red flags" that was to guide the masses, the emphasis was now on decentralization. The commune level no longer appeared to be the level at which all-powerful commands were given but was now the one for controlling, coordinating and readjusting. To the extent that a commune ownership level still existed, it was concerned only with nonagricultural enterprises (small factories, workshops and mines), enterprises whose products were of interest to the commune as a whole (fertilizer, small tools, services), or those in which the state had a share.

The production brigade became henceforth the normal level of ownership (land, animals, and tools) and management. It regulated production, through application of the formula "three promises and a reward" (san pao i chiang), meaning that the brigade must produce the quantities fixed by the plan, at the agreed price, in the stipulated time, but it was entitled to keep any surplus in production. The brigade became the true accountancy unit. Later on this task was handed over to the production team, while the brigade retained all financial responsibility.[13]

In the last analysis, however, the true production level was that of the team, because it was there that the individual faced reality. Its yield could not be jeopardized by arbitrary decisions. Members' willingness and interest in their work were to be encouraged at all times. On this basis, the production team—or, in other words, the old natural village, sometimes regrouped—was granted a sort of charter of its customary rights: the "four fixed things" (szu ku-ting). This expression meant that the team was to be guaranteed the use of fixed quantities of manpower (at least 80 percent of the total manpower), draft animals, land, and tools. Thus, the commune could not longer make sudden and inopportune requisitions, removing the peasant from his normal activities and putting him to work on various collective projects. In theory, the unfortunate mistake of the "backyard furnaces" could not happen again. Furthermore, small tools obtainable from the makers and secondary products were by rights the property of the team. The team also had the right to participate in the drawing up of production plans. The peasants were thus able to guard against overzealous planning and, thanks to their knowledge of local conditions, avoid certain blunders, either in the choice of crops or in the use of supposedly miraculous techniques.

Great efforts were also made to win the allegiance of the individual peasant, who was granted several "small liberties." These included the rights to maintain a home of his own, to raise poultry, to rear one or two pigs, and above all to keep a plot of land (5 percent of the arable land). He was allowed to sell the produce of this plot, on the primary market at fixed prices, on condition that it included no grain, cotton, or oil—all goods that could be sold to the state alone. Thenceforth, this private production of secondary foodstuffs (vegetables, pork, poultry, and the like) was an "objective necessity" and "helped the socialist economy."[14] Like individuals, the collectives had the right to sell their surplus on the free market.

The individual's share in the proceeds was also increased. Peasants were no longer paid on the basis of a more or less fixed salary, but on the known and tried system of "work points" corresponding to the effort contributed and the type of work done. A large proportion of the salaries (about 70 percent) were to be paid in cash and not in kind. All this was a long way from the commune of 1958, which fed everyone as much as they wanted, or at least tried to do so.[15]

The size of communes underwent a fundamental change; the average size was a third of the former area. As a result, the number of communes rose from 24,000 to 70,000 at the beginning of 1962. Instead of evolving toward a *hsien* framework of 2,000 communes, commune structure tended to revert to that of the old cooperatives, which were a mere tenth of the size of the commune of 1962.

The essential point here is that the Party never dared—following the example of several socialist countries—to abandon the principle of the collectivization of agriculture. Nor did it dare to ask each family to make its contribution to the production quota, for this would have been tantamount to granting the family the use if not the ownership of a piece of land. But the question did arise in principle and—in certain provinces at least—in practice. It was a major cause of the Cultural Revolution. From 1961, although the collectivization of agriculture persisted, it had fallen back to the lowest level, that of the production team. The situation was clearly summed up in a widely read Chinese magazine:

> At the present stage, the superiority of collective agricultural economy must be shown above all by means of production teams placed under the leadership of communes and brigades.[16]

The reasons for the failure of the communes

The failure of the communes of 1958 can be explained first by the fact that they were too large and aspired to too high a degree of centralization. The commune covered an area of nearly 200 square kilometers, with little or no means of transport; it had forty or more villages under its leadership and authority over between 20,000 and 40,000 people, 10,000 or more of whom were laborers whose extremely varied activities had to be determined every day, taking into account rather·unpredictable weather conditions. All this called for a competent, versatile, and energetic administrative staff and technical personnel who could work unhindered by ideological do's or don'ts. The inadequacy of the cadres quickly became apparent, in spite of the help of cadres sent by the towns and the army. Although the commune was too big for the proper organization and supervision of agricultural activities, most of which were of a scattered, almost entirely traditional nature, with an almost total lack of machinery, the commune was also too small for industrial activities, for raw materials, technical cadres, and workers with a professional training were also lacking, except in a few cases.

The supervision by cadres seems to have been too close. Many of them could not help wanting to attract attention to themselves by starting collective projects that needed extensive resources and manpower, to the detriment of agricultural production in the strictest sense. Such supervision was reinforced by the administrative fusion of the commune and the *hsiang,* and by the ideological authority of those commune leaders who were also Party members. Because any disobedience or suggestion on the part of members of the basic strata ran the risk of being interpreted as hostility to the regime or sabotage, and of being punished as such, there was no adequate counterbalance to their arbitrary will, and often to their ignorance of problems of cultivation.

The readjustments of the years between 1959 and 1961 give clear proof of the unsatisfactory distribution of functions among each of the three levels of the commune. The allocation of tasks, which had been in the hands of the production brigade, did not make sufficient allowances for differences in situation from one production team to another, "which made enthusiasm wane," as Tao Chu (first secretary of the Central-South China Bureau) put it. He added that the question could be resolved by making the production team the basic budgetary unit.[17] What he meant was that since the work was done in full view of each team member, only the team could distribute the product in accordance with the effort. In other words, the team should have a real share in the material benefits involved.

Moreover, the peasants lacked ideological and political education. They were not adequately prepared for complete equalitarianism and, after a point, found collective life unbearable because of their profound attachment to a powerful family tradition that was still close. The forcible movement of villages or regrouping of hamlets not only shocked them but aroused superstitious fears, for it was thought that such changes could not be acceptable to the spirits of the ancestors and the gods of the earth. The abuse of the contribution of the peasants need not be pressed here, for it had already provoked a reaction in the shape of the Wuhan resolution of December 1958.

Peasant discontent did not result in mass uprisings, which would have been almost inconceivable in a country that was firmly ruled by a strong administration, although there were disturbances and assassinations of local leaders. These resulted in general apathy and false obedience, which were more in tune with the national temperament than open violence. This state of mind affected the army, despite its careful selection and privileged treatment. The peasant origins and solidarity of its members eventually transcended its discipline and morale, as is shown by a series of important documents that reached the West by way of Tibetan rebels.[18] One factor alone appears to have prevented the discontent from degenerating into an irreparable situation—the preservation or restoration of the "private plots," which, as the Japanese economist Shigeru Ishikawa points out, reassured the peasants a little and helped them retain their psychological equilibrium, for they earned between 20 and 30 percent of their income from private plots.[19]

The failure of the rural people's communes also resulted from mistakes in leadership concerning economic questions as a whole. These errors were caused by a certain inability of the leaders of the Party and the state to grasp the full complexity of the needs of development or to understand fully China's special characteristics. These questions will be mentioned again later on in connection with the economy as a whole. In the present context, it is enough to point out that the overly hasty creation of communes was quite damaging (in most cases they were formed simply by merging or regrouping existing advanced cooperatives); the diversity of their functions, and above all their size would have justified preliminary studies and careful experiments. This haste was entirely out of character with the Party's previous caution in all agrarian policy and is one of the mysteries of this vitally important period. No complete explanation for it has yet come to light.

The failure of industry

In a country where agriculture provided half the resources of the state and supplied two-thirds of foreign trade commodities, it is hardly surprising that industry would rapidly feel the repercussions of the failure of agricultural production.

The good harvests of 1958 and the first illusions of the Great Leap Forward resulted at first in a rapid increase in industrial production, so much so that, according to official sources at least, the essential targets of the second five-year plan (1958-1962) had been reached two or three years ahead of time. Li Fu-ch'un's report to the National People's Congress on March 30, 1961, gives the last firm figures published before 1970. Table 20.1 gives these figures, along with some statistics quoted by the Hsinhua Agency (January 23, 1960), and compares them with the 1962 targets of the second five-year plan.

Table 20.1
Production figures of 1959 and targets for 1962

Table 20.1

Products	1959	1960 targets	1962 targets	Units
Steel	13.30	18.40	10.5-12.0	Millions of tons (excludes steel from backyard furnaces)
Coal	347.80	425	190-210	Millions of tons
Electricity	41.50	55.50[a]	40-43	Millions of kWh
Crude oil	3.70	5.20	5-6	Millions of tons
Cement	12.23		12.5-14.5	
Wood	41.20			Millions of cubic meters
Chemical fertilizers	1.33		3.0-3.2	Millions of tons
Cotton yarn	8.25		1.5-1.6	
	(millions of bales)		(millions of tons)	
Grain	270		250	Millions of tons
Cotton	2.41		2.41	Millions of tons
Sugar	1.13			Millions of tons
Salt	11.04			Millions of tons

[a]Between 55 and 58 million kWh according to other sources.

In the Li Fu-ch'un report, industrial production in 1959 is estimated at 163,000 million yuan (an increase of 35 percent compared with 1958) and agricultural production at 78,300 million yuan (16.7 percent more than in 1958). The national income rose by 21.6 percent compared with 1958. Investment in capital construction rose by 24.5 percent.

Li Hsien-nien read the state budget for 1959 (income 54,160 million yuan, expenditures 52,700 million yuan) and the proposals for the 1960 budget: expenditure 70,020 million yuan.[20] This optimism, which was not shared by leaders, collapsed during the year 1960. The funds set aside for heavy industry were mainly turned over to agriculture and supporting light industries.[21] Foreign trade, deprived of most of its agricultural exports, reduced its imports of equipment and motor fuel. Such foreign currency as was available had to be reserved mainly for buying Australian and Canadian wheat. The yuan fell to a quarter of its value on the Hong Kong free market.[22] Table 20.2 shows the sharp drop in foreign trade; imports fell by 50 percent between 1960 and 1962.[23]

Table 20.2
Foreign trade 1960-1962 (millions of US dollars)

Year	Exports	Imports	Total
1960	2,075	1,931	4,006
1961	1,620	1,368	2,988
1962	1,597	1,082	2,679

Soviet statistics give similar figures: 3,606 million rubles (exports 1,868 million, imports 1,738 million) for 1960, and 2,411 million rubles for 1962 (exports 1,437 million, imports 974 million).[24]

Industrial problems were further complicated by the withdrawal of Soviet advisers in July 1960. The *People's Daily* of December 4, 1963, stated that Moscow's decision brought about the departure of 1,390 experts, the annulment of 340 contracts for the sending of experts, and the abandonment of 257 projects involving scientific and technical cooperation, not to mention reductions in the supplies of equipment.

With the failure of 1960 no more reference was made to the Great Leap Forward, except in purely formal terms. It was supposed to have been achieved. To avoid publishing figures that would have revealed not only that the projects for 1960 had been unsuccessful, but also that in every field the results had fallen behind those of the second five-year plan in 1959, statistics were no longer quoted.[25] From then on, the Chinese economy was to inspire speculation and controversy among the few Western experts in the Chinese economy. Nearly all of them agree that the situation slowly began to get better from 1962 on. An easing up on rationing, the resumption of work in some industries (fertilizer, oil, light industry), and the improvement in foreign trade seemed to show a movement away from the "three black years" (1959-1961). It also appears that the practical side of industrial production had been appreciably improved: a rational coordination existed once more between the different sectors, management was improved by a better definition of responsibilities, accountancy was healthier, distribution circuits were shortened, a struggle against waste was instituted, and some of the material benefits allowed to former heads of capitalist firms were renewed.

Chou En-lai's report to the Third Session of the Second National People's Congress (March 27 to April 16, 1962), of which only an analysis was made public,[26] confirmed with great caution and many omissions the correction of the situation, which did not imply any changes in priorities among economic tasks. The main recommendations of the ten-point program of readjustment for 1962 included an emphasis on agriculture (particularly grain, cotton, and edible oils), a reduction of the urban population, a cutback in construction, strict economy, improved planning, and balance among the various production sectors.[27] The results of the program were never officially announced. Table 20.3 consists of averages compiled from the most reliable estimates. These approximations are impossible to check, and there may have been some subsequent reductions in the quantities produced.

Table 20.3
Estimated production in 1962

Products	Units	Estimated quantities	Remarks
Electric power	Million kWh	40,000–43,000	
Coal	Million tons	270	
Crude oil	Million tons	5-6	
Steel	Million tons	10-12	(7 million according to some sources)
Cement	Million tons	6	
Chemical fertilizer	Million tons	2	
Cereals	Million tons	182-185	(probably 185 million tons in 1960)

Notes

[1] The communiqué appeared in the Hsinhua Agency bulletin on December 17. The resolution appeared in the Chinese press on December 19.

[2] See also "Large-Scale Mass Movement to set the People's Communes to Rights," *Hung Ch'i*, No. 2 (January 16, 1959).

[3] See Table 18.1. The revision of targets was published on August 26, 1959. It seems to have been suggested for the first time at the Seventh Plenum of the Eighth Central Committee, held in Shanghai in March and April 1959.

[4] In fact the 1959 harvest must have been about 175 million tons.

[5] See in particular the *People's Daily* (July 17, 1960).

[6] *Hung Ch'i* (August 16, 1960).

[7] *People's Daily* (August 25, 1960).

[8] In spite of affirmations to the contrary given by several foreign visitors whose (largely superficial) experience of the country was perforce limited to a few large towns.

[9] Editorials of December 29, 1960, and January 1, 1961, *People's Daily*, and many other articles.

[10] See in particular the *People's Daily* (November 20, 1960). In July 1960 the Academy of Sciences had held a congress in Tientsin of teams doing research into people's communes. The reports given show that directives tending toward decentralization dated from as early as the spring of 1959.

[11] *L'Express* (January 23, 1961).

[12] *Sunday Times* (Magazine Section), London (October 15, 1961). Among the many reconstructed statistics for the period 1958-1965, see Kang Chao, *Agricultural Production in Communist China, 1949-1965* (Madison: University of Wisconsin Press, 1970) Chapter 10. The author gives the following figures from 1958 up to and including 1965 for grain (in millions of tons): 205, 170, 150, 160, 170, 182, 195, 200.

[13] See "Reinforce the Organization of the Production Brigades," *Hung Ch'i*, No. 2 (1961). The decision of May 20, 1963 (known as "The First Ten Points") underlined the beneficial effects of the 1961 measure.

[14] See the *People's Daily* (April 22, 1961).

[15] A good example of the system is to be found in *Shih-shih shou-ts'e* (Current Events), No. 6 (March 21, 1959); English translation in *Extracts from China Mainland Magazines*, No. 175.

[16] *Shih-shih shou-ts'e*, No. 7 (April 6, 1962).

[17] See T'ao Chu, "The People's Communes Go Forward," *Hung Ch'i*, No. 4 (1964). An English version was published by the Foreign Languages Press.

[18] *K'ung-tso t'ung-hsün* (Work Bulletin), translated into English by Chester J. Cheng. *The Politics of the Chinese Red Army: A Translation of the Bulletin of Activities of the People's Liberation Army* (Stanford, Calif.: The Hoover Institution, 1966).

[19] See his article in the *Far Eastern Economic Review* (September 29, 1960).

[20] 42,910 million yuan of which were devoted to the construction of the economy, 8,620 million to state expenditure, 5,800 million to national defense, and 500 million to aid to foreign countries.

[21] Yuan-li Wu estimates the fall in industrial investment as 6 percent in 1960-1961. See *The Economy of Communist China: An Introduction* (New York: Praeger, 1965), p. 103.

[22] Stuart Kirby in *Current Scene* (Hong Kong, July 20, 1962).

[23] Source: Jan Deleyne, *The Chinese Economy* (London: Deutsch, 1973). Figures quoted in the *Far Eastern Economic Review* or by Sidney Klein, *Politics Versus Economics*, p. 5, are largely the same.

[24] *Kommunist*, No. 12 (August 1968).

[25] On statistics in general see Choh-ming Li, *The Statistical System of Modern China* (Berkeley and Los Angeles: University of California Press, 1962).

[26] Hsinhua Agency (April 16, 1962).

[27] The editorial of the *People's Daily* (January 1, 1962) and the communiqué published by the Tenth Plenum of the Eighth Central Committee are also in the same vein, though the second is slightly more confident in tone than the first.

21 Evolution of Internal Affairs 1958 – 1962

The central events of the five years between the end of the first five-year plan in 1957 and the Tenth Plenum of the Eighth Central Committee in September 1962 were naturally the immense efforts required by the Great Leap Forward and the misfortunes of the people's communes. In both cases, politics and ideology were closely linked to the economy, both in the decisions taken at the summit and in the daily life of the masses. Certain key events deserve to be mentioned because of their impact on the life of the Party and the state or in the field of cultural affairs, which was also soon to be thrown into confusion.

The Party: the crisis of Lushan

Between 1958 and 1962, the Party called five plenary sessions of its Central Committee, [1] and the Eighth Party Congress held its Second Session from May 5 to 23, 1958. At the time at least, only very limited accounts were given of the discussions and tensions that arose. The Lushan Plenum was the only partial exception.

Generally speaking, compared with the Eighth Party Congress, the Party leadership remained stable and the composition of its membership changed little. In the spring of 1958, purges at the summit involved a few "rightists," alternate members of the Central Committee, and a few senior provincial cadres, who were accused of regionalist errors, or nationalist errors in the case of minorities. These were scarcely more than sequels of the Antirightist Movement that had followed the Hundred

Flowers. The documents of the Second Session of the Eighth Congress mention about twelve who were excluded and criticize seven or eight others, among whom were Ku Ta-ts'un, formerly a member of the East River soviets in Kwangtung, Feng Pai-chü, important historically for his action in Hainan before 1949, and P'an Fu-sheng, former first Party secretary in Honan; all three were partially reinstated a few years later. When Marshal P'eng Teh-huai, Chang Wen-t'ien, and Chou Hsiao-chou were dismissed at the Lushan Plenum in August 1959, the Party went through its most serious crisis since the Kao Kang-Jao Shu-shih affair in 1954.

Insofar as the most reliable texts make it possible to sort out the events, it appears that on July 14, 1959, Marshal P'eng Teh-huai, minister of national defense, former second in command of the Red Army throughout the Second Civil War and the War of Resistance against Japan, former commander of the "volunteers" in Korea, and fourteenth on the list of members of the Political Bureau, addressed a personal letter to Mao Tse-tung entitled "Points of View," using oblique and subtle terms to convey his impressions of and anxiety about the Great Leap Forward and the people's communes. P'eng Teh-huai had just been on a trip to gather information and had visited Hunan—his and Mao Tse-tung's native province (he went as far as Shaoshan, where Mao was born)—Central China, and the Northwest. He came back convinced that the disadvantages brought by the Great Leap Forward outnumbered the advantages, resulting in particular in a serious disturbance of the balance between the different sectors of production. P'eng also pointed out that the statistics were indecisive and sometimes misleading, that unsupervised refectories were wasteful, and that the communes were premature. In spite of his veiled style, he went so far as to write: "If the Chinese workers and peasants were not as good as they are, a Hungarian incident would have occurred in China a long time ago."

Mao Tse-tung reacted hotly to this letter. On July 23, probably speaking to the Political Bureau, he is reported to have accused P'eng Teh-huai of being ambitious, a "false 'superior man' " (wei chün-tzu), even referring in violent terms to the possibility of a new resort to guerrilla warfare: "I will lead the peasants to overthrow the government. If your Liberation Army will not follow me, I will raise a Red Army, but I think the Liberation Army will follow me."[2]

With a verbal energy that was sometimes trivial in its expression, Mao Tse-tung rejected the criticisms of the minister of national defense, though he denied neither the existence of occasional discontent among the peasantry nor difficulties in rationing. He admitted that 30 percent of the population actively upheld the regime, 30 percent were unfavorable toward it, with the remaining 40 percent following in the wake of those in favor of it. Few declarations have shed as much light as this on the personality and deepest feelings of the head of the Chinese Communist Party, and in particular on his faith in will power and his relative indifference toward economic problems and the social and ideological changes they required.

The members of the Political Bureau apparently dispersed after this bout, and Mao Tse-tung decided to convene the Eighth Plenum of the Central Committee on August 2, 1959.

According to the version made public during the Cultural Revolution, the Eighth Plenum witnessed a direct confrontation of the "two lines," the first upheld by Mao Tse-tung and the majority of the Committee, and the second by P'eng Teh-huai; his chief of staff, Huang K'o-ch'eng, a native of Hunan and early companion of Mao in the Autumn Harvest Uprising; Chang Wen-t'ien, a former Party secretary and one of the "Twenty-Eight Bolsheviks" of Pavel Mif; and Chou Hsiao-chou, another Hunanese, first secretary of the Party for Hunan, and reportedly former private secretary to Mao Tse-tung. The second group was supported by Liu Shao-ch'i, who later abandoned it.

The resolution passed on August 16, 1958, by the Eighth Plenum was extremely harsh toward P'eng Teh-huai and his supporters and at the same time revealed the nature and extent of the criticisms levelled at current policy:

> In essence he [P'eng Teh-huai] negates the victory of the general line and the achievements of the Great Leap Forward, and is opposed to the high speed development of the national economy, to the movement for high yields on the agricultural front, to the mass movement to make iron and steel, to the people's commune movement. . . . The mass of facts brought to light . . . prove that the activities of the anti-Party clique headed by P'eng Teh-huai prior to and during the Lushan meeting were purposive, prepared, planned, and organized.

The opponents, described as "the right opportunist anti-Party clique," were also accused of having wanted to prolong the Kao Kang-Joa Shu-shih conspiracy. Urged on by his personal ambition, P'eng Teh-huai had for some time been "making vicious attacks and spreading slanders" against Mao Tse-tung and other leaders and had used the Lushan Plenum as an opportunity to launch an offensive against the Party. P'eng's position at the top of the military hierarchy and "his tactics of feigning candor and simplicity" made him particularly dangerous. His errors were interpreted in the light of his "bourgeois" origins and explained by his taste for leadership. The true nature of his attacks on the Party was that he represented "the interests of the bourgeoisie" against the dictatorship of the proletariat and the socialist revolution.[3]

In spite of all this, and probably because many members of the Central Committee could appreciate the fact that the criticisms were justified, and also because of the personal popularity and high rank of Marshal P'eng Teh-huai, the opponents of Lushan were merely dismissed from their posts and in theory retained their "membership or alternate membership on the Central Committee or Political Bureau." The resolution of the Eighth Plenum was not made public until August 16, 1967, eight years later and in the middle of the Cultural Revolution.

Once the Lushan crisis was over, currents of opinion disapproving of the Great Leap Forward and the people's communes still persisted. They were expressed with caution, however. The elimination of the P'eng Teh-huai group, the restoring of order in the communes, and the halt of the Great Leap Forward helped to disarm the critics. They came to life again, gaining new strength, when the question of returning to the radical policy of 1958 arose once more.[4]

In January 1962, Liu Shao-ch'i, who until then had been inclined toward compromise, is reported to have openly attacked the current policy during a work meeting of the Central Committee. He thought that the people's communes were badly managed, with 30 percent of their difficulties arising from natural calamities and 70 percent from human errors. The Great Leap Forward seemed to him to have neglected all criteria of profitability. He is also said to have tried to reinstate P'eng Teh-huai and his supporters. When replying, Mao Tse-tung apparently had the solid support of Lin Piao, for whom the supreme revolutionary leadership was a delegated form of collegiate leadership. Lin Piao later said on October 1, 1966: "We owe all our achievements, all our victories, to the far-sighted thought of Mao Tse-tung."

The January episode was repeated at Peitaiho in August 1962. The remarks attributed to Mao Tse-tung at that time—on the continued existence of the political and ideological struggle and on the rebirth of the bourgeoisie in the socialist regime—are in tune with classic Maoist thought and were brought up again at the Tenth Plenum of the Eighth Central Committee. Judging by other precedents, it is likely that Mao was insulting toward Liu Shao-ch'i, though admittedly his remarks may have been intensified later to match the tone and vocabulary reserved by the red guards for the former president of the Republic, as for all their enemies.[5]

In spite of these internal disputes, the changes affecting the leaders— after those resulting from the Lushan Plenum—were not truly significant and are no easier to interpret today than they were at the time. At the Fifth Plenum of the Central Committee (May 25, 1958) Lin Piao became fifth vice-chairman of the Party and seventh and last member of the Standing Committee of the Political Bureau. This move, which was merely an enlargement of the group and took place before the Great Leap Forward and the people's communes had received official sanction, was not directed against anyone. An explanation can be found in the eclipse of Ch'en Yün, fifth member of the Political Bureau and already in silent disagreement with the new line advocated by Li Fu-ch'un, the other economist and thirteenth member of the Political Bureau.

Until the Cultural Revolution, nothing was said against Ch'en Yün; his portrait was still to be seen in public buildings alongside those of the other members of the Standing Committee. He represented the spirit of the first five-year plan, whose chief architect he was. His condemnation would have reflected on a work that had given the regime a solid economic basis. As Ch'en Yün had probably ceased to take part in the work of the Standing Committee, the nomination of Lin Piao brought the committee back to its full membership quota. At the same time Lin Piao was then in a better position to succeed P'eng Teh-huai, which he did in the following year, and later on to move up to the second place in the Party.

The Political Bureau appointed by the Eighth Party Congress was enlarged by the nomination of K'o Ch'ing-shih, Li Ching-ch'üan, and T'an Chen-lin during the Fifth Plenum of the Eighth Central Committee; it had twenty members, reduced to eighteen by the deaths of Lin Po-ch'ü (1960) and Lo Jung-huan (1963). K'o Ch'ing-shih died in 1965.

The Secretariat grew larger and seems to have assumed greater importance under the direction of Teng Hsiao-p'ing. Two new members joined it, Li Fu-ch'un and Li Hsien-nien, probably appointed because of their economic and financial responsibilities in the management of the Great Leap Forward.

At the Ninth Plenum (January 1961), when economic difficulties were at their worst, the Central Committee decided to strengthen its hold on the Party provincial committees (and above all on their secretaries) by installing permanent delegations or bureaus in the six great regions formed during the period from 1949 to 1954. The continued absence of planning and the wide variations in the application of the formula of the people's commune made it necessary to take the country in hand once more. The prime necessity was probably to combat regionalist tendencies that had developed out of this situation and the spirit of decentralization fostered by the Great Leap Forward. As the Great Leap Forward, now replaced by the modestly termed "consolidation," no longer existed in fact and was only occasionally mentioned in the vocabulary, the Central Committee tended to reinforce its control in every domain. Judging by the positions taken by the six regional bureaus during the Cultural Revolution, it seems likely that the bureaus were staffed by men who favored a moderate line closer to that of Liu Shao-ch'i than to that of Mao Tse-tung.

The conversion of the remnants of the bourgeoisie

In the wake of the rectification movement of 1957, several campaigns were developed to win over circles that had so far kept their distance from socialism—the national bourgeoisie and the intellectuals. At the beginning of 1958, the Offer Your Heart to the Party Campaign bore a strange resemblance to a liturgy, with banners, cardboard hearts, and canticle-like slogans lending a comic side to it. Later on, beginning in the summer of 1960, "Meetings of the Immortals" (shen-hsien hui) appeared. The tone of these was set in a speech by Li Wei-han, who was in charge of the united front.[6] A system of self-education and mutual education, the meetings brought together small groups of members of the former bourgeoisie belonging to the "small parties." In order to draw closer to socialism, they would sit around a table, discuss points of doctrine, and comment on current events, led by a qualified member of the Communist Party. This method, at once compelling and persuasive, was not entirely foreign to Chinese ways of thought and traditions. If the press is to be believed, the campaign had reached a million people in May 1961.[7]

At the end of 1958, the Party admitted to membership 317 well-known members of the bourgeoisie, who were also outstanding intellectuals. The new recruits included Kuo Mo-jo; Li Szu-kuang, a geologist of international repute; Ch'ien Hsüeh-shen, the nuclear physicist; Madame Li Teh-ch'üan (widow of "Christian General" Feng Yü-hsiang); the great actor Mei Lan-fang; and others. Entrance to the Party was for the first time an honorary distinction representing a promotion on the social scale. At approximately the same time, many well-known Communists and non-Communists who had suffered in 1957 as a result of the Hundred Flowers returned to favor. This was so for the former ministers Chang Po-chün and Lo Lung-chi, and for Ch'u An-p'ing, Fei Hsiao-t'ung, and General Lung Yün.

Campaigns for individual and collective study developed within the Communist Party itself, where they found justification in the youth of the rank and file. Out of 17 million members, 80 percent had entered the Party after 1949, 70 percent after 1953, and 40 percent after the Eighth Party Congress in 1956; many of the newcomers found criticism and self-criticism hard to accept, or, on the contrary, having been more or less obliged to enroll, they showed too much indifference or tolerance. Here again the methods were intended, theoretically at least, to be educational and adapted to each individual case, as the slogan "a key for each lock" put it.[8] The essay by Liu Shao-ch'i, "How To Be a Good Communist," which had first appeared in 1939, was revised and published in *Hung ch'i* on August 1, 1962, possibly with an eye to this reeducation. It had in fact been widely used during the 1942 rectification movement (Cheng Feng Movement). After 1966, the reprinting was considered an attempt to substitute Liu's "revisionist" thought for that of Mao Tse-tung. A little earlier, to celebrate the tenth anniversary of the regime, Liu Shao-ch'i had published *The Triumph of Marxism-Leninism in China*, a text for a special occasion, intended for foreign readers. Although he defended and explained the Great Leap Forward in this publication, he showed moderation, stressing the objective and inviolable nature of economic laws.[9] Mao Tse-tung, however, had the fourth volume of his works published at this time (1960), an event that was accompanied by a movement for the study of his thought. The contemporary commentaries underlined the "correctness," tactical ability, and flexible realism of Mao's leadership, while the "Yenan working style," suited to difficult moments, returned to favor.

As regard state institutions, the period from 1958 to 1962 saw few big changes, except that Liu Shao-ch'i was elected president of the Republic at the first session of the Second National People's Congress.[10] Tung Pi-wu and Mme Sun Yat-sen were elected vice-presidents at the same time, while Marshal Chu Teh became chariman of the Standing Committee of the National People's Congress.

A few months earlier, during its Sixth Plenum at Wuhan, the Central Committee had approved Mao Tse-tung's own proposal not to renew his candidacy.

The plenary session of the Central Committee deems this to be a completely positive proposal, because, relinquishing his duties as chairman of the State and working solely as chairman of the Central Committee of the Party, Comrade Mao Tse-tung will be enabled all the better to concentrate his energies on dealing with questions of the direction, policy, and line of the Party and the state; he may also be enabled to set aside more time for Marxist-Leninist theoretical works, without affecting his continued leading role in the work of the state. . . . If some special situation arises in the future which should require him to take up this work again, he can still be nominated again to assume the duties of the chairman of the state in compliance with the opinion of the people and the decision of the Party.

Coming as it did after the first adjustments to the people's communes, this news gave rise to extremely varied interpretations, ranging from the dismissal of Mao Tse-tung on the grounds that he was responsible for the early failures of the people's communes, to the wish to facilitate his succession, since Liu Shao-ch'i would be head of state and first of the five vice-chairmen of the Party at the same time. It is now known that in February 1958 Mao Tse-tung had expressed the wish to be relieved of the presidency of the People's Republic, both for reasons of health and because of the need for time for reflection.[11] In all events, it was a turning point in his intellectual career. It implied that his ideological interests were increasingly reaching beyond national limits. His trip to Moscow in 1957 and the direction taken by the Soviet leaders, as well as the desire to find new ways to develop China through the Great Leap Forward and the people's communes, had led Mao to construct and define his individual vision of Marxism-Leninism and to extend it to the world revolutionary movement as a whole.

On September 17, 1959, Lin Piao became minister of national defense, and General Lo Jui-ch'ing, until then head of public security, was appointed chief of the General Staff, replacing General Huang K'o-ch'eng. The Ministry of Public Security was put in the hands of Hsieh Fu-chih, who had been with the Party since the days of Chingkangshan and was then first secretary for the province of Yunnan. During the Cultural Revolution, he became chairman of the Peking Revolutionary Committee and he retained this office until his death at the beginning of 1972.

On October 1, 1959, less than two weeks after his nomination, Lin Piao published "Forward Under the Red Flag of the General Line and the Military Thought of Mao Tse-tung." This important work definitively guided the army back to its pre-1949 tradition and also toward the study of the thought of Mao Tse-tung in general, without altering the primacy of the Party over the army.

Cultural evolution[12]

Either because the Party first concentrated entirely on the immense economic effort, or because its failures led to a slight relaxation of its grip in return for a more cooperative spirit all around, its policy toward cultural figures became much more flexible. The principles remained the same, however, as Lu Ting-yi recalled: "The primary task in our literary and art work is to use the weapon of literature and art greatly to enhance the socialist and Communist consciousness of the people of the whole country and to raise the level of their Communist moral qualities."[13]

The most frequently recurring themes were those of proletarian culture fighting against the "bourgeois" influences tending to develop in socialist countries under the guise of "humanism." In this respect, the "bourgeois" theory of human nature too easily accepted by the revisionists (denunciation of the influence of Lukacs) ought to be opposed by proletarian solidarity and not by the misleading motto of "liberty, equality, fraternity." Culture should remain determinedly antirevisionist, for revisionism saps the revolutionary will of the masses, tending to eradicate the distinction between just and unjust wars and thereby creating pessimism and defeatism. The spirit of the Hundred Flowers was to remain guided by the six political criteria defined by Mao Tse-tung himself (see Chapter 12). Although the old was to continue to exist, it was to be of less importance than the new, as the slogan "The present must be thick, the old must be thin" (*hou chin pao ku*) put it.

The old still came to the surface from time to time. In November 1962, a great conference was held on Confucius in Tsinan, the capital of his native province. A hundred and fifty philologists, sociologists, historians, and philosophers took part and produced about a hundred studies.

Important papers acted as a point of reference for the cultural policy of the period. The Third Congress of Literary and Artistic Workers, held in Peking from July 22 to August 13, 1960, made them public. Many well-known people spoke, among them the writers Pa Chin and Mao Tun and the politicians Lu Ting-yi and Chou Yang, and their contributions often shed useful if not very objective light on contemporary Chinese literature as a whole. As may be expected, Chou Yang set the line to be followed in his speech "The Road of Socialist Art and Literature in China." Aside from the expected statements on the purpose of literature and art, the historical importance of Mao's "Talks at the Yenan Forum on Art and Literature" (1942), and the meaning of the Hundred Flowers, the reader is struck by the emphasis on national aspects of culture, both style and content, in the name of serving the masses:

> Our literature and art have a tradition dating back thousands of years; they have accumulated a rich fund of creative experience and have formed our own national forms and styles popular with the people throughout the ages. If revolutionary literature and art possess no national features, if they cannot create new national forms suited to the new content on the basis of our own national traditions, they will not easily take root and blossom among the broad masses of the people. The national character and mass character of literature and art are inter-connected and indivisible.

Chou Yang also spoke of the alliance between revolutionary realism and romanticism as Mao Tse-tung understood and practiced it. Personal initiative and revolutionary vision should accompany realism, so that the ideal of today may become a reality tomorrow. Revolutionary romanticism must lead to the creation of heroic images and figures, plenty of which exist in all the literatures of the world. It must lead everyone toward an ideal, all individual ideals being dominated by Communism, "the soul of all literary and artistic creation." Chou Yang ended his speech by recalling some of the great Chinese writers of old, such as Ch'ü Yüan, Szu-ma Ch'ien, Tu Fu, Kuan Han-ch'ing, and Tsao Hsüeh-ch'in, and more recent ones like Lu Hsün and inevitably Mao Tse-tung, exhorting all Chinese writers to show themselves worthy of their era.

The years from 1958 to 1962 did not produce any more great writers than had the preceding years, but in addition to a great number of occasional writings inspired by the Great Leap Forward, many novels, films, plays, and narratives appeared. The Cultural Revolution would later regard these as "poisonous weeds"; their destruction would also consume Chou Yang and others like him (see Chapter 27). Many classical works were reprinted, often in attractive editions, ranging from the complete works of the poet Tu Fu whose 1,250th anniversary fell at that time, to literature of the fantastic, a selection of which was published with a preface by Ho Ch'i-fang entitled "Don't Be Afraid of Ghosts."

The theater and the cinema developed steadily: 3,515 theatrical companies existed in 1959, as compared with 1,000 ten years earlier; they employed 260,000 professional actors, among whom were 180,000 young men and women trained in nine institutes of higher education and seventy schools (8,000 pupils). Old plays, adapted and modernized, had not disappeared from the repertoire and were preferred by the public to the new plays. The 400 different varieties of opera were catalogued and studied; national forms were kept alive. The prominent actor Mei Lan-fang, who unfortunately died in 1961, was put in charge of the development of the theater. The senior Communist leaders were the best connoisseurs and often the most ardent defenders of the classical theater; as Teng Hsiao-p'ing said—a remark that the red guards took up later on—"He who does not know the Szechwan opera knows nothing of civilization."[14]

In 1959, film attendance amounted to a meager total of 4.1 million, but this was a great advance for China. The producers were asked to extend the subject matter, often limited to questions relating to the construction of socialism, so as to include past revolutionary struggles and screen adaptations of classical and modern works. They did only too well and were soon to regret it. Between 1949 and 1962, more than 800 foreign films were dubbed in Chinese, among them Western films based on works of Tolstoy, Dostoyevsky, and Shakespeare.

The great Buddhist sculptural works were restored, and the museums were filled with archaeological finds; at the same time, the Peking government made an indignant protest when works of art were sent from Taiwan for an exhibition in the United States. Traditional painting was still held in honor, as were the last great painters. Classical China was still present, even in popular editions and school books. It seemed as though the people's communes and the Great Leap Forward had, by their failure, contributed to the slowing down of cultural development which would otherwise probably have been as radical and as rapid as the economic and social development.

Religious problems

A certain degree of religious tolerance persisted, although all faiths were strictly subordinated to politics. The Muslims, who were the least badly treated, still maintained some contact with the outside world, thanks to the Chinese Islamic Association, led by Burhan. The Buddhists held the third national conference of their association from February 13 to 27, 1962, and were allowed to continue theological research, but their foreign links were limited and severely controlled. The Catholics also held a national conference in January 1962. From 1957 on, their archbishops had consecrated a number of bishops without the consent of Rome. The new "patriotic" clergy, whose best-known representative was Msgr. P'i Shu-shih, made periodic attacks on U.S. "imperialism" and on its "instrument," the Vatican, both "mortal enemies" of new China. French kings and the Holy Roman Emperor, in their desire to be the sole masters of the temporal world and the ecclesiastical hierarchy, had often had still less respect for Rome in their time, although they shared the same faith. Whether or not it still retained its illusions, Rome showed both caution and understanding toward a church that the regime had both created and condemned to be short-lived.

In January 1961, the Protestants also held their national conference, again with antiimperialism as the motto. The Chinese Christian churches continued their sickly existence and appeared to have only a few more years ahead of them.

The minority races

The Tibetan revolt

The Chinese presence in Tibet, reestablished in 1910 after nearly a century of eclipse, disappeared once more in 1911 at the fall of the Empire. In 1950, the Tibetans tried to resist the advance of the Chinese Communist forces in the Chamdo (Changtu) region. Their pathetic attempt at resistance ended with the signing of an "agreement of peaceful liberation" on May 23, 1951, providing for regional autonomy, religious freedom, and the maintenance of the revenues of the Lamaist faith. In return, the Tibetan army was to be reorganized, foreign affairs were to be taken over by the central government, and a "political and military" committee was to be created.[15] After the entry of the Chinese troops into Lhasa, Peking tried to make use of the Dalai Lama and the Panchen Lama, after the reconciliation between the two, with a (traditional) preference for the latter. An effort was made to gain better control over Tibet and to integrate it into national life. An important network of military roads was built: Sining-Lhasa, Kangting-Chamdo-Lhasa, Lhasa-Gyangtse-Gartok, and a road from Lhasa toward Yatung on the frontier of Bhutan and Sikkim (see Map 4). Tibet was cut off from India, for a long time its natural outlet; this was finally achieved by the Sino-Indian agreement of April 29, 1954, on trade and communications, abolishing the last privileges the Indians had inherited from the British.

Tibetan liberties gradually disappeared. Some of the ministers of the Dalai Lama were dismissed; administrative divisions were created; propaganda activities were begun with a view to severing the monasteries from their roots among the people and drying up their resources; Chinese settlers were brought into a country that was already extremely poor in spite of its small population (1,270,000 inhabitants); and Tibetan Communist cadres were trained at nationalities' institutes. All these factors contributed to increased tension and discontent, which resulted in local rebellions from 1954 on, and particularly in 1956 and thereafter. The most important of these, that of the Khampas in eastern Tibet, spread southward, gathering momentum in 1958 and 1959 until Chinese communications with Szechwan were threatened.[16]

On March 9, 1955, the Chinese government decided to set up a preparatory committee for the establishment of a Tibetan Autonomous Region. The fifty-five-member committee was inaugurated on April 22, 1956, by Marshal Ch'en Yi, who had come from Peking for the occasion. Its chairman was the Dalai Lama, assisted by the Panchen Lama, and it was mainly run by Generals Chang Ching-wu and Chang Kuo-hua, both of whom had been in charge of the region since 1951. In December 1955, however, the Chinese, aware of opposition among the Tibetans and possibly also sensitive to the efforts made by Pandit Nehru, suddenly decided to postpone the application of the "democratic reforms" until the completion of the second five-year plan (1958-1962), though the training of new cadres, patriotic and socialist education, and efforts toward development all continued. Interference by the Chinese in the economic, social, and cultural life of a population who for centuries had been hostile toward them and the increasingly urgent pressure Tibetans brought to bear on the Dalai Lama eventually forced the local Tibetan government into open rebellion. After some vicissitudes, the details of which are obscure, the Dalai Lama denounced the agreements of May 23, 1951, and March 17, 1959. Like one of his predecessors who in 1910 had been in a similar situation, he left Lhasa to take refuge in India. The town rebelled during the night, two days after his departure.

The rebellion was quelled in a few days. The Chinese then decided to dissolve the Tibetan government immediately and transferred its powers to a Preparatory Committee for the Autonomous Region of Tibet. The committee was set up on April 22, with the Panchen Lama as its chairman *ad interim;* it was directed by Ngapo Ngawang Jigme, vice-chairman and secretary general, and its aim was to bring about the democratization and socialization of Tibet by means of a series of gradual measures. The first of these was summarized in the formula "Three Antis and Two Reductions"; the targets of the three antis were rebellion, serfdom, and forced labor, while the two reductions concerned land rent and interest rates. Landlords, both religious orders and laymen, were weakened by this and condemned to disappearance sooner or later. Religious beliefs were theoretically given careful treatment. New Tibetan cadres were trained, and new administrative structures were set up in the seventy-two Tibetan *hsien.*[17] A land reform, often carried out on the basis of the buying back of land, was put into effect among the sedentary section of the population (870,000 as opposed to 260,000 nomad herdsmen), the numbers of schools and dispensaries were increased, and Tibet began to emerge from centuries of feudal and theocratic rule and to enter the modern age.[18] This official image could not conceal the difficulties of the real situation. In April 1961, the advance toward socialism was suspended for five years. Changes on the land got no further than the stage of mutual aid teams. Initially, before causing upheavals in the social and political system, the Chinese seem to have wanted to act as beneficient colonists by raising agricultural output and developing the economy.

This moderate line was quickly reversed, partly owing to the deterioration in Sino-Indian relations, which led in the autumn of 1962 to a brief but disastrous war for India. Meanwhile, the rebellion of March 19, 1959, had raised the question of Tibet at an international level. A resolution revealed the embarrassment of the United Nations; it asked China and the Chinese, though without naming them, to respect the principles of the charter and the Declaration of Human Rights. India did not vote and later received the just reward for its abstention.

The development of Sinkiang and the flight of the Kazakhs

Worsening Sino-Soviet relations, as much as the Great Leap Forward, encouraged the Chinese to make a great effort toward colonization in Sinkiang. Local nationalist tendencies were consequently intensified. They found further nourishment in the fact that Chinese held posts of responsibility in all sectors, including teaching, while Peking's land policy was not approved of by the Muslim population. In 1961, groups of rebels tried to create a Republic of East Turkestan. In July 1962, part of the population of the Ining (Kuldja) region, and of Tach'eng, possibly threatened with deportation to the interior, emigrated en masse to Soviet Kazakhstan. The Chinese held the Russians responsible for this (see Chapter 25).

The movement for the romanization of Chinese resulted in the adoption of an alphabet of twenty-six Latin letters and eight special letters for transcribing the Uighur and Kazakh languages, a measure that came into force on February 10, 1960. Arabic and Cyrillic scripts disappeared. Another link with sister nationalities in the Soviet Union was broken.

Whatever the friction between the Han and the minorities, economic progress was rapid. The army production corps and the new settlers carried out extensive agricultural development. The Karamai oil wells gained in importance and produced about 3 million tons in 1970. On the other hand, the political situation and the lack of steel brought work to a halt on the last stretch of the railway line intended to link the Russian railways (Turk-Sib) to the Chinese railways. The stretch from Urumchi to the Soviet frontier remains unfinished today.

Inner Mongolia

As in Sinkiang, and for the same reasons, a great effort toward colonization and development was made in Inner Mongolia. It was made easier by the vast superiority in numbers of the Han compared with the Mongols of the various "leagues." With the building of the steel mills at Paotow in 1959, an already powerful modern industrial center, based on 17.3 percent of the reserves of iron for China as a whole, was added to the light industry born of stock breeding—wool, leather and meat.

The fiction of regional autonomy, the selfless devotion of the Mongol Ulanfu, and a rapprochement at the diplomatic level between Peking and Ulan Bator helped for a time to contain nationalist tendencies that were never far below the surface, as was proved by the uprisings early in 1962 against the program for imposing permanent settlements on the seminomadic members of the banners.

Other minority problems

In other regions inhabited by minorities, the Han met resistance efforts that were doomed to failure. This was the case in the Hui zone in

Ninghsia created on October 25, 1958, and among the Chuang in Kwangsi.

On the whole, the problem of the attitude toward minorities tended to evolve toward firmer control from the capital. This trend may be explained by several factors: the migration of several million Chinese from the coastal provinces to the Northwest and the Northeast, economic efforts, the extension of communications, the adoption of the Latin alphabet for minority languages, and political and ideological tension between China and the Soviet Union, the rival multinational state. Neither the readjustment that followed the Great Leap Forward nor greater tolerance in the field of culture were to reverse the trend. The vast economic importance of the minority regions, their geographical size, the location of the largest of them on the Soviet frontier, their small population, and a long colonial tradition all explain the authoritarian policy of Peking. Unlike the Russians, the Chinese Communists never considered adopting a federal solution nor allowing the creation of Communist Parties within each of the different nationalities of the People's Republic. The revolutionary spirit of the Tenth Plenum and the Cultural Revolution increased Han domination of the minority races and ensured a better preparation for their complete sinification.

Notes

[1] The Fifth Plenum was held on May 25, 1958, in Peking, the Sixth from November 28 to December 10, 1958, in Wuhan, the Seventh from April 2 to 5, in Shanghai, the Eighth from Augut 2 to 16, 1959, at Lushan, and the Ninth from January 14 to 18, 1961, in Peking.

[2] The letter of P'eng Teh-huai and the verbal reactions of Mao Tse-tung have inspired various publications in English and Chinese. See particularly the bilingual collection of documents entitled *The Case of P'eng Teh-huai, 1959-1968* (Hong Kong: Union Research Institute, 1969).

[3] *People's Daily* (August 16, 1967); English text in *Peking Review*, No. 34 (August 18, 1967). The attack on the "bourgeois" origins of P'eng Teh-huai is in contradiction to the extremely difficult conditions he experienced during his childhood and youth. Many episodes in his life bear witness to his merit and determination. He was, however, a colonel in the Nationalist Army when he joined the Communist movement in 1928 at the age of twenty-six.

[4] The old economist Ma Yin-ch'u, who in 1958 had openly stated his opinions in the fields of economy, politics, and philosophy, was dismissed from his post of president of Peking University in May 1960.

[5] On the incidents of January and August 1962, see the English translation of the Chinese entitled "Outline of the Struggle Between the Two Lines from the Eve of the Founding of the People's Republic of China through the Eleventh Plenum of the Eighth C.C.P. Central Committee," *Current Background* No. 884 (July 16, 1969).

[6] Speech of August 14, 1960. The gist of what Li Wei-han said was that socialism and the elimination of classes could not be achieved without an ideological transformation of man himself.

[7] *People's Daily* (May 16, 1961).

[8] Among other articles in the *People's Daily,* see those of October 12, 1961, and January 13, 1962.

[9] "Problems of Peace and Socialism" (September 14, 1959).

[10] The National People's Congress held the following sessions between 1958 and 1962: February 1-11, 1958, Fifth Session of the First Congress; April 18-22, 1959, First Session of the Second Congress; March 30-April 10, 1960, Second Session of the Second Congress; March 27-April 16, 1962, Third Session of the Second Congress. The Third Congress met for the first and only time from December 27, 1964, to January 4, 1965.

[11] See *Sixty Work Methods* (draft) in the English translation in *Current Background,* No. 892 (October 21, 1969), or in Jerome Ch'en, *Mao Papers,* p. 75.

[12] Social development from 1958 to 1962 will be treated in Chapter 26 with the launching of the Socialist Education Movement, for which it gives at least a partial explanation.

[13] Declaration of July 22, 1960, at the Third Congress of Literary and Artistic Workers.

[14] On Chinese theater before the Cultural Revolution, see Andre Travert, "The Attitude of the Communist Party towards China's Cultural Legacy," in E. F. Szczepanik, ed., *Economic and Social Problems of the Far East* (Hong Kong: University of Hong Kong Press, 1961).

[15] See Guillermaz, *A History of the Chinese Communist Party,* p. 425.

[16] The census of 1953 gives 2,776,000 Tibetans, 1,500,000 of whom lived outside Tibet proper, chiefly in Szechwan and Tsinghai.

[17] Tibet includes one municipality, seven special regions, and seventy-two districts. By 1962, the Party had 6,000 cadres (including 300 *hsien* and district cadres). 1,000 Tibetans are Party members and 2,000 belong to the Communist Youth League. See the article by Chang Ching-wu in *People's Daily,* March 25, 1962.

[18] See the report of the Panchen Lama to the thirty-third session of the Standing Committee of the Second National People's Congress (December 14, 1960) for an authorized version of the situation in Tibet. On the other hand, the Dalai Lama, who had taken refuge in India, stated that 70,000 Tibetans had fled their country and that 17,000 others had died between March 1959 and September 1960.

22 Foreign Policy 1958 – 1966 (1): General Development, Indian Subcontinent, Black Africa, Near East and Arab States, Latin America

The hardening of the line within the country during the Great Leap Forward was quickly extended abroad. From 1958 on, China went through a series of tense situations and crises with the great foreign powers; at the same time Peking tried to take advantage of the changes in the Third World, especially in the countries formerly under colonial rule in Africa. Sometimes this hard, uncompromising, and dogmatic line suddenly gave way to a flexible, understanding, and pragmatic approach that took account of the situation rather than the principles involved. Occasionally, the two lines met on the subject of a single country (Cuba, Japan, Egypt), causing much perplexity among outside observers trying to understand the motives and aims of Chinese diplomacy. These variations, the steady deterioration in relations with the Soviet Union, the reversal in Chinese policy toward the Indian subcontinent where Pakistan, a member of SEATO, took the place of India, and Peking's continued intrusion into the Near East did not make China abandon its policy of caution, rendered necessary both by military weakness and by a complicated system of security pacts and agreements based on the power of the United States.

Although the Tenth Plenum of September 1962 heralding the Socialist Education Movement and, after that, the Cultural Revolution, corresponded to a change in emphasis in internal policies, the same was not true of foreign policy. Four years were still to pass before events at home took complete priority over foreign policy, justifying the sacrifice of important diplomatic and ideological positions. After 1966, China was too engrossed in its own affairs, too engrossed in setting itself up as an example, to give way to calculations. Any calculations made were long-term ones, whose success depended on that of the second revolution Peking had embarked on.

For this reason, the chapters on foreign policy carry on into 1966, instead of stopping, as does the rest of Part 3, in 1962. Moreover, 1964, the year China entered the nuclear powers club, is not a crucial one, for the results of this spectacular achievement were negligible at an international level. As events are somewhat lacking in coherence and logical progression, it seems preferable to describe Chinese foreign policy over the period in question by regions rather than in chronological order. Because each region involves different problems, separate chapters will deal with the following subjects: the Indian subcontinent, Africa, the Arab states, and Latin America; Japan, Korea, and Southeast Asia; the West, international organizations, and disarmament; and the Soviet Union and the socialist bloc. These problems, the events to which they give rise, and the results constitute the material for the following chapters.

The Indian subcontinent

India

The development of domestic affairs, the Tibetan revolt in 1959, the observance by Pandit Nehru and his country of the African and Asian policy of neutrality, and the rapprochement between India and the Soviet Union and between India and the United States all help to explain the behavior of China as regards the Indian subcontinent. A few minor frontier incidents occurred as early as the autumn of 1958, revealing certain weak points, but the Tibetan revolt was the start of a true deterioration in Sino-Indian relations. The fact that the Dalai Lama settled at Tezpur, in Indian territory, in a sense brought India back into Tibetan affairs, or, as Peking saw it, into Chinese internal affairs. Chinese suspicion grew stronger when the Dalai Lama appealed to the United Nations. Just when the military repression in Tibet was arousing feeling in India owing to the cultural and historical links between the two countries, when the Chinese presence was making itself felt on the frontiers of India and in the Himalayan states, and when the Peking press had begun to make personal attacks on Nehru,[1] a badly calculated move on the part of New Delhi provided the Chinese with an opportunity to shed light on and dramatize the frontier question. Pandit Nehru and Chou En-lai had already raised the question several times during their meetings, but for different reasons both sides had tacitly post-poned finding a solution to it.

On December 18, 1958, Pandit Nehru brought the question into the open. He had for some time been alarmed by the publication of Chinese maps showing as Chinese territory regions at either end of the Sino-Indian frontier, which India either claimed or had occupied as heir to the British colonial empire. Nehru was also worried by the existence of a Chinese strategic road in Ladakh (the Aksai Chin area) in the western sector. Chou En-lai replied on January 23, 1959, proposing that the status quo be maintained. On March 22, in the middle of the Tibetan crisis, Nehru categorically refused to accept the Chinese suggestion and asked for explanations.

The Chinese premier delayed his reply until September 8; it left the Indians with no illusions as to Peking's continuing interest in the question. The Chinese claims involved 90,000 square kilometers of territory lying south of the McMahon Line, which the Tibetans had accepted on March 24, 1914, without the acknowledgment of the Peking government of the time, 2,000 square kilometers in the central sector of the frontier, and 33,000 square kilometers in the uninhabited area of Ladakh, on which subject the treaty of 1842 seemed extremely vague (see Map 4).

Letters, notes, and statements were exchanged throughout the autumn and winter, while the situation remained the same in the areas concerned.[2] The Sino-Indian idyll, which had lasted since 1951, ended in the Himalayas, leaving the Indians with the feeling that they had been tricked and exploited.

From April 19 to 25, 1960, Chou En-lai visited New Delhi at the invitation of Nehru, but the frontier question came no nearer to a solution, except that committees of experts were set up. The Chinese attributed the failure of the talks to "imperialism" and "Indian reactionary forces," and, true to their usual habits, they insinuated themselves between the Indian government and the people: "The Common Wish of a Thousand Million People," the titles in the People's Daily put it on April 27.

There were only minor incidents in 1961 and the beginning of 1962, but on April 13, 1962, the Chinese spokesman raised the question again, reviewed all the negotiations,[3] and accused the Indians of making dangerous unilateral modifications in the military status quo by patrolling the frontier and planting new posts. This fit of temper seems to have been related to the Dalai Lama's visit to New Delhi and various remarks made by Nehru on Chinese colonial action in Tibet.

The Chinese made more protests in May. When India refused a proposal to renew the Sino-Indian trade agreement of April 29, 1954, upon its expiration on June 3, 1962, the Chinese set up customs posts on the Tibetan frontier. Above all, they struck a hard and unexpected blow at India when they announced their intention of opening negotiations with Karachi with a view to determining the frontier between Sinkiang (Chinese Turkestan) and the part of Kashmir controlled by Pakistan but claimed by India like the rest of Kashmir. At the beginning of August, it looked as though talks were about to reopen, based on the reports of the experts.[4] But new incidents occurred in August and September. A violent campaign was carried out against the "duplicity" of Nehru, who was given an extremely severe warning on September 21, which was renewed on October 14: "Mr. Nehru, hold your horse back from the edge of the precipice."[5] China proposed that troops on either side be withdrawn 20 kilometers from the frontier, while India demanded that China evacuate all occupied territory and only agreed to discussions about Ladakh. The Chinese attributed belligerent remarks to Nehru, trying to prove that they were premeditated and that aggressive intentions lay behind them.

On October 20, at 4:00 A.M., the Indian chargé d'affaires in Peking, P. K. Bannerjee, was summoned to the Ministry of Foreign Affairs. In blatant bad faith, the Chinese accused the Indians of having launched full-scale attacks against the western and eastern areas of the frontier: the Chinese, their patience sorely tired and afraid that their retreat would be cut off, had been forced to defend themselves. A diplomatic protest followed, with an indictment accusing Nehru of having refused three offers to negotiate.

From October 20 to November 22, a tough and powerful Chinese offensive, which was both rapid and accurate, developed along the two contested stretches of the frontier. The Indian units were inadequately equipped and ill prepared for fighting in mountainous areas; they fought rarely and badly and were easily outmaneuvered by their adversaries. In the area of Ladakh, the Chinese extended their occupation to include the Chushul region, near Lake Spangur, and took several posts (Demchok, Jara La). But their progress was most spectacular and worrisome south of the McMahon Line. Near the eastern frontier of Bhutan, they took Tawang and the Se Pass, advancing as far as Bondi La and almost reaching Assam, which they seemed about to cut off and occupy by driving down to the middle Brahmaputra Valley. Near the Burmese frontier, they got as far as Walong on the Luhit River, 100 kilometers from Sadiya and the oil wells at Digpoi, and also near the Naga tribes who periodically revolted against Delhi. The Indian forces lost more than 3,000 men and were thrown into

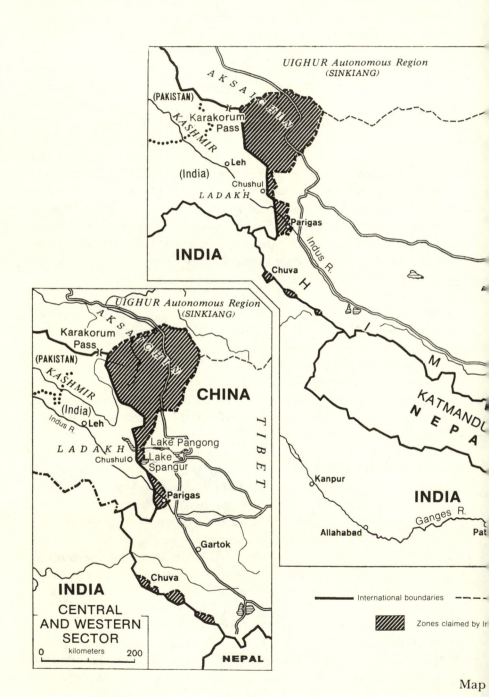

UIGHUR *Autonomous Region*
(SINKIANG)

(PAKISTAN)

A K S A I C H I N

Karakorum
Pass

K A S H M I R

Leh

(India)

Chushul

L A D A K H

Parigas

Indus R.

INDIA

Chuva

H I M

UIGHUR *Autonomous Region*
(SINKIANG)

A K S A I C H I N

Karakorum
Pass

(PAKISTAN)

K A S H M I R

(India)

Indus R.

Leh

CHINA

T I B E T

Lake Pangong

Chushul

Lake
Spangur

L A D A K H

Parigas

Gartok

Chuva

INDIA
CENTRAL
AND WESTERN
SECTOR

0   kilometers   200

NEPAL

KATMANDU

N E P A

Kanpur

INDIA

Ganges R.

Allahabad

Pat

International boundaries ――――

Zones claimed by Ir

Map

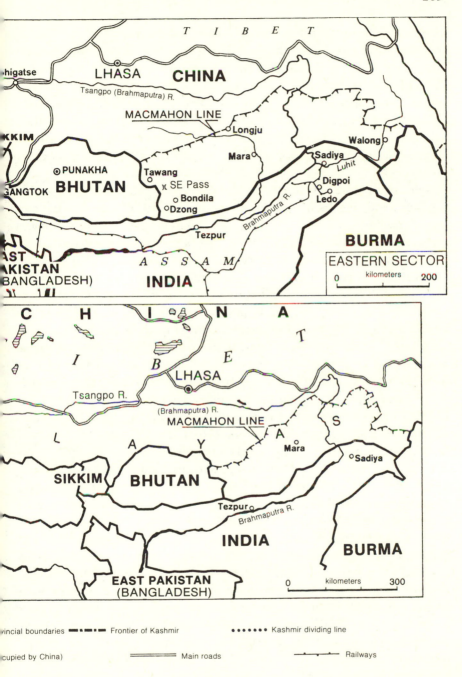

no-Indian frontiers

disorder.[6] The rest of the world looked on in astonishment, which increased when the Chinese troops called a cease fire all along the front on November 22. The previous day, the Chinese government had announced the unilateral withdrawal of all its units, not only to the old frontier as it was on November 7, 1959, but 20 kilometers further back, leaving only police on the border itself. At the same time, the Chinese government called once more for negotiations, as it had done on October 24 and November 4 during the operations, with detailed proposals for military disengagement.[7]

A double political maneuver backed the Chinese military offensive. On the one hand, the Indian government was accused of having long ago joined the "imperialist camp" on the grounds that it had helped the Americans by sending 6,000 soldiers to the Congo under cover of the United Nations in Belgrade, and, more recently, accepted American military help. On the other hand, several times, and in particular on November 15, Peking asked the neutral Afro-Asian countries to help find peace through negotiation, as though Nehru, forgetful of the spirit of Bandung and the Five Principles of Peaceful Coexistence and led astray by "nationalist" and "capitalist" Indian elements against the will of the people, had to be brought back to the fold. These invitations did not prevent Peking from turning down an offer of mediation from Colonel Nasser on November 2. As the future was to show, the Chinese refused to be satisfied with anything less than direct negotiations which would give them the upper hand under all circumstances; this seems to prove that in their eyes the question involved far more than a mere quarrel over frontiers.

From the Chinese point of view, several converging explanations can be found for the Sino-Indian crisis of 1962. For Peking, the understanding attitude adopted by the Indians at the beginning of the Chinese takeover in Tibet had paid off in full. In 1951 and 1954, Pandit Nehru had not deigned to use the advantages he still possessed. When he acknowledged that Tibet was an integral part of the People's Republic of China, he relinquished in advance all political or juridical basis for negotiation. The Chinese position on this point was the stronger because they had at first respected a de facto situation on the frontier (at least in the eastern sector) but had not given it de jure confirmation. In 1959, when the Tibetan government disappeared for good, placing Tibet once more under the direct authority of Peking by means of the fiction of the Preparatory Committee for the Autonomous Region of Tibet, special consideration for India was rendered superfluous. On the contrary, the presence of the Dalai Lama in Indian territory, not far from the Tibetan frontier, and the persisting dissidence of the Khampas and other Tibetan elements would incline Peking to adopt a policy of intimidation toward New Delhi, for reasons of national security.

After ten years of maintaining the status quo the Chinese had to reopen the frontier question again without much delay to prevent existing boundaries from being sanctioned purely by use. The issue of the frontier between the two countries was also linked with the principle of questioning the boundaries imposed on China by the Unequal Treaties. The legacy of history could only be accepted with reservations. The Chinese made their gesture as regards India and entered into an agreement with Burma in 1960, with an eye to future settlements that were still excluded by the existing balance of power and political and ideological considerations.

The development of Indian policy after 1959 also worried the Chinese. Indian neutrality, although its motives were mainly economic, implied good relations with the United States, Great Britain, and the Soviet Union, at the risk of attracting part of the Afro-Asian world toward a closer cooperation with the great powers, to the detriment of Chinese influence. To counteract this misguided neutralism, which rivaled that recommended—though not practiced—by the Chinese, China had to lower Nehru's personal prestige, presenting him as a class enemy; it also had to humiliate India and discredit the rival political system New Delhi represented.

Soviet interest in India from 1955 on, the Russians' generous economic aid,[8] their military aid, their policy of maintaining Peking and New Delhi at an equal distance, and the clumsiness of Khrushchev's suggestion, made during the Lebanon crisis of 1958, that India should take the place of China at the summit conference inevitably excited Chinese jealousy, spite, and irritation. China's reproaches were not groundless when it accused the Soviet Union of dropping all Marxist-Leninist criteria in the analysis of the Sino-Indian question and of completely abandoning proletarian internationalism.[9] Possibly the Chinese wanted to provoke a major crisis so as to embarrass the Soviet Union and make Moscow revoke the declaration made by the Tass Agency on September 9, 1959, forcing the Russians to take the part of the Chinese and in any case cut off military aid to India. If what the Chinese said is true, the first Russian reactions probably encouraged them in their illusions.[10] The calculation turned out to be a bad one, however, for the Russians were obliged to counterbalance American influence in India, and above all to keep the leadership over the socialist bloc. They could not allow one member of it to force their hand.

Lastly it is worth noting that armed conflict with India, a country which was not protected by any security agreement, was easy to keep within reasonable bounds and would allow a release of nationalist feelings to compensate for the helplessness of the Chinese Communists when faced with Taiwan or other regions of East Asia. In their choice of season—just before the winter, which quickly paralyzes communications—the Chinese showed that they had set a limit on their military action. To have gone any further would have seriously altered the image of China among neutralists, aroused suspicions that a spirit of conquest lay beneath the pretext of the frontier question, and created a dangerous international situation that would in any case have been highly favorable to the influence of the great powers on the Indian subcontinent. The withdrawal of the Chinese forces was both a cautious gesture and a stroke of genius. China recovered its reassuring aspect of a generous, peace-loving power, quick to make itself respected. The way was left open for the resumption of negotiations. Chinese moderation contrasted with the adventurism shown by the Soviet Union over Cuba at the same moment, and the Chinese leaders were not the last to draw a parallel between the two events.

Even so, a settlement was not negotiated and the world is still waiting for it today. Six nations of the Colombo Plan met from December 10 to 12, 1962, and submitted a proposal which, though apparently accepted by both sides, was never put into effect.[1] In 1963, the situation seemed to be without any possible resolution. Relative calm prevailed, however, in spite of minor frontier incidents and the internment of 2,300 Chinese in India; on March 3, China and Pakistan signed a treaty on the Kashmir frontier question. The year 1964 brought many subjects for mutual accusations. After the death of Pandit Nehru (May 27) Chinese attacks were shifted to President Shastri, who followed the same line as his predecessor. Denunciations of poverty in India, protests against the arrest of pro-Chinese Indian Communists, and controversies over the Himalayan states (particularly at the time of the assassination of Prime Minister Jigme Dorji of Bhutan on April 5, 1954) followed one after another.

In 1965, a new military and political crisis arose as a result of armed conflict in the autumn between India and Pakistan. On September 16, ten days after the fighting broke out between India and Pakistan, the Chinese government issued what amounted to an ultimatum to the Indian government, giving it three days to dismantle fifty or so small military installations on the Sikkim frontier; the time limit was soon deferred. The pretext and the relative proximity of Sikkim to the East Pakistan frontier suggested that Chinese troops were about to resume large-scale operations, as in 1962, and cut off Assam and Bhutan from India. This was not so, however, and the Chinese quickly pretended to be satisfied. Their intervention nevertheless made Indian army headquarters take account of their threat and of the particularly careful choice of the point at which it would be enforced. Needless to say, on the subject of the India-Pakistan conflict, Peking loudly supported Pakistan, condemning the "criminal Indian agression" several times; the success of the Soviet mediation at Tashkent (January 4-10, 1966) met with scant approval.

The rapprochement between India and the Soviet Union, already commented on by Peking when President Shastri visited Moscow in May 1965, helped to poison Sino-Indian relations still further; things were at a standstill between the two countries when the Cultural Revolution began.

Pakistan

The difficulties between India and China inevitably brought Pakistan and China closer to each other, in spite of great differences in their systems of government, their ideologies, and their commitments toward the rest of the world. Pakistan was a Muslim republic first and foremost, with close ethnic and cultural affinities with the West; from October 1958 on, its leader was Marshal Ayub Khan, an outstanding military figure strongly influenced by Britain in his attitudes and education. Theoretically, the country had little in common with Communist regimes. However, because Pakistan bordered on China over a distance of 500 kilometers, in a region that was important because of the Mintaka and Gilgit passes, and because it was constantly in difficulty with its neighbors India and Afghanistan, it decided to recognize China in January 1950, following the example of London.[12] A few trade agreements ensued.

The Bandung conference does not seem to have brought the two states much closer, possibly owing to the part played by Pandit Nehru. Mme Sun Yat-sen and Chou En-lai went to Karachi in December 1956, but it was apparently only a courtesy visit.

Pakistan joined the Manila Pact (SEATO) when it was formed on September 8, 1954. Militarily, this alliance seemed mainly to provide a way to obtain equipment; politically, it appeared to be a way to obtain indirect protection against aggression from the Soviet Union or pressure from India.

This concern was shown once more in Pakistan's membership in the Bagdad Pact (CENTO), alongside Iraq, Iran, Turkey, the United States, and Great Britain, and in its military agreement with the United States of March 1959, in which Pakistan gave permission to install missile launching pads on its territory.

The general development of Indian-Pakistani and Sino-Indian relations, combined with the cooling off of Sino-Soviet relations and the increased interest shown by the Soviet Union in India, led Pakistan to an important turning point. In 1961, it apparently took the initiative in Sino-Pakistani discussions, which ended on March 2, 1963, with the settling of the Kashmir-Sinkiang-Tibet frontier question. Similarly, starting with the General Assembly of 1961, Pakistan voted in favor of Peking's representation in the United Nations. This new political orientation, even if dictated mainly by circumstance, led Pakistan to cut down its military participation in SEATO and align itself with the increasingly tepid attitude of France.

The treaty of March 2, 1963, was the culmination of several years of development. The territorial consequences were slight, although Pakistan gave up nearly 30,000 square kilometers already occupied by the Chinese, in return for about 2,000 square kilometers, but the treaty ratified a significant change at the international level. From then on, China had a hand in affairs in the Indian subcontinent and obtained the support of Pakistan in exchange for that of India, on whom it could exert pressure, to the advantage of Pakistan, as happened during the Indian-Pakistani conflict in the autumn of 1965. On the other hand, although Pakistan was a Muslim state, its support could not counterbalance that of India in the Middle East and in the neutral world in general.

Sino-Pakistani friendship was demonstrated by frequent state visits. When Ayub Khan was in Peking from March 2 to 9, 1965, he showed, however, that Pakistan did not intend to extend the collaboration beyond the Indian subcontinent.[13] The visit of President Liu Shao-ch'i to Karachi from March 26 to 31, 1966, gave rise to completely unexpected, though serious, domestic consequences. Economic exchanges were inevitably small, in spite of a Chinese loan of $60 million (February 1965). Even so, Pakistan was the first non-Communist country to open a regular airline route to China (April 29, 1966).

Nepal

Diplomatic relations between Nepal and China have developed steadily; they were established on August 1, 1955, and expanded in September and October 1956 through an agreement on the maintenance of friendly relations between the two countries (September 20, 1956) and by the grant of a Chinese loan of 60 million rupees to Nepal (October 7, 1956). In March 1960, Nepalese Prime Minister B. P. Koirala paid a visit to Peking, where he signed a frontier agreement and an economic agreement (March 21). The former provided for the demarcation of the existing frontier, which was more than 1,000 kilometers long. Once the question of Mount Everest had been settled—China got its northern face and Nepal got its southern face, with the line running right across the summit—no particular difficulties were involved. The economic agreement granted Nepal a further loan of 100 million rupees for three years, in addition to 40 million rupees still outstanding from the previous loan. A month later, Chou En-lai and Marshal Ch'en Yi stopped in Katmandu in their turn, on their way back from Delhi, and signed a treaty of peace and friendship on April 28, 1960. Since then, despite a few frontier incidents, economic and cultural relations have developed steadily, much to the displeasure of the Indians.

In September and October 1961, King Mahendra of Nepal, who had resumed his full powers the year before and whose personal feelings toward India were not the most cordial, paid a visit to Peking, which provided the occasion for elaborate entertainments and showed how far Nepal had already turned away from the Indian sphere of influence to that of China. On October 5, 1961, a frontier treaty was signed, replacing the agreement of March 21, 1960.[14] At the same time, the Chinese undertook to build a road from the Tibetan frontier to Katmandu. In September 1965, it was decided to extend it as far as Pokhara, in the heart of the country. Nepal still had links with India, in the shape of the 1950 agreements, but was running the risk of becoming a protectorate.

Ceylon

Relations between China and Ceylon were excellent, thanks to the political tendencies of the Ceylonese government after the death of Sir John Kotelawala in 1956. Chou En-lai and Mme Sun Yat-sen paid an official visit to Colombo from February 26 to 29, 1964. Trade relations, based on China's need for rubber and Ceylon's need for rice, were brisk until 1960 but were affected by the failure of the Great Leap Forward; they began to get going again in 1963 and the agreement of February 28, 1964, confirmed their importance.

Africa

The decolonization of one African country after another, beginning in 1958, could not fail to attract the attention of China and the Chinese Communist Party. The ideological pretensions of the latter, always ready to inspire revolutions in the Third World, combined with the political aims of the former, wherever possible, to bring about the downfall of the power of America, which was regarded as the highest and most formidable expression of "Western imperialism," and to win as many voters as possible at the United Nations in order to take the place of Taipei and thwart "the two-China plot." These two central themes recurred in all letters, diplomatic speeches, and messages, no matter to whom they were addressed or on what occasion. They were accompanied by a discourse that usually sounded artificial on the existence of historical relations between China and the African country and the similarity of their situations as regards "imperialism and colonialism," which were considered responsible for poverty and cultural and economic backwardness. All ended with phrases that opposed the Chinese people, "the most faithful ally," to American imperialism, "the cruelest enemy of all the peoples in the world," as in Chinese parallel maxims![5]

Although China and the Chinese Communist Party had as yet little experience of Africa, they had learned to wield the weapon of ideology far beyond their frontiers. At Bandung, which furnished the first opportunity for lengthy contacts with Africa, China made every effort to appear the first among the underdeveloped nations rather than a Communist state. The fact that China was a nonwhite nation sheltered it from a certain amount of suspicion, excessive sensitivity, or radical reservations. In the eyes of countries formerly under colonial rule, China was the epitome of a nation that had shaken off both foreign ascendancy and traditional structures, freeing itself both from "imperialism" and from "feudalism," to use the terms adopted by all revolutionaries, whether nationalist or Communist. China's experience was impressive for several reasons: its history, the personality of Mao Tse-tung, the vast scale involved, its early successes, and its efforts to find short cuts to economic fulfillment and social progress.

The Chinese government did its best to maintain this image in compensation for other disadvantages such as remoteness, a limited capacity for supplying aid, and absence from the United Nations, thus winning the hearts of political leaders and forging closer links with the masses. African visitors were given unforgettable receptions. Dazzling, grandiose, and highly colored shows sometimes massed as many as 500,000 people along lengthy itineraries. These were accompanied by vast public rallies, tours, and sumptuous banquets, all of which far outdid what the West or the Soviet Union had to offer in the same line. The policy of welcome was not limited to foreign heads of state and ministers but was extended to persons in the cultural fields and to representatives of political parties, trade unions, and bodies of all kinds, who visited Peking by the hundreds and were duly photographed alongside Chairman Mao Tse-tung. The slightest event or incident in Africa immediately gave rise in Peking and throughout China to demonstrations of solidarity or protest, and to "weeks" generally organized by the Sino-African Friendship Association.

The presence of foreign students in Peking was encouraged. Just as their elders went to be educated in the West at the beginning of the century, so almost 200 African students attended Peking University in the early 1960s. This was, however, the weak point in Chinese propaganda. There, confronted with the harshness and inadequacies of the regime and shocked by occasional outbreaks of xenophobia, most of the African students left before the appointed time; many preferred to be revolutionists in Paris rather than in Peking.

In spite of its poverty, China granted large loans to African countries; the most reliable estimates set the figure at nearly $300 million between 1956 and 1964.

Guinea, the first to rebel against the French Community, whose "sinister designs" and fragility, it made be added, were constantly denounced by Peking, was also the first African state to establish diplomatic relations with China, on October 4, 1959![16] Sekou Touré was the first African head of state to visit Peking; on September 13, 1960, he signed the first treaty of friendship between China and an African power. A loan of 100 million rubles, without interest and repayable in ten years, was granted to prop up Guinea's economy, which "French colonialism wanted to stifle," and the way was opened to Chinese technical aid experts.

Several African states attained independence in 1960, a particularly good year. Ghana established diplomatic relations with Peking in September and Mali in October. China was recognized by Dahomey, Niger, and Upper Volta, but Madagascar did not respond to Peking's advances. The Second Afro-Asian People's Solidarity Conference held in Conakry (April 1960), the Second Conference of Independent African States (June 1960), and the African Foreign Ministers' Conference (August 25, 1960) all helped to spread Chinese ideas. But the difficulties in the former Belgian Congo, which attained independence on June 30, 1960, provided the best opportunity of all for this. The murder of Patrice Lumumba in February

1961 and the constitution of a unified government at Leopoldville interrupted Sino-Congolese diplomatic relations; the violent and troubled times that followed enabled China to attack both the United States and its "instruments," the United Nations, and the old and new "colonialisms" and their "rapacity."[17]

The year 1961 was marked by recognition by Tanganyika (December 8), whose President, Julius Nyerere, paid several visits to China. Later on, Tanganyika and Zanzibar, which had meanwhile become Tanzania, served as important bases for Chinese penetration into Central Africa. On July 1, Rwanda and Burundi recognized China.

Somalia, which was known to Chinese sailors of the T'ang and Sung dynasties, had recognized China on December 15, 1960, and established diplomatic relations on July 2, 1962; Uganda did likewise on October 8 of the same year. China and Ghana signed a treaty of friendship and cooperation when President Kwame Nkrumah visited Peking (August 18, 1961);[18] the turn of Mali came on November 3, 1964. "The antiimperialist and anticolonialist torch lights up the whole of Africa," said the headlines of the *People's Daily* on December 1, 1962, and in the following month the Chinese press was able to hail the arrival of the first Chinese ship to land at a port on the west coast of Africa.

At the Third Afro-Asian People's Solidarity Conference in Moshi, Tanganyika (February 4-10, 1963), the Chinese delegation, led as the previous one had been by Liu Ning-yi, distinguished itself by presenting a six-point program that was full of propaganda but lacked real content, while a recommendation urged India and China (above all the latter) to accept the proposals of the Colombo powers.

At the end of 1963, Premier Chou En-lai and Foreign Minister Ch'en Yi embarked on a tour of black and white African countries, which caused an enormous stir. The aim was of course to show, by visits to ten or so different capitals, that China had, in the space of a few years, come to occupy a position of great importance in the African continent, and also to deal a blow to the influence of Moscow. Sino-Soviet relations had never been worse, as the great controversy of the summer and autumn had just shown. On two vital points—the emancipation of colonized people and the complete political and economic liberation of new states—the Chinese were, from an ideological point of view, in a position of strength that they were determined to put to good use. Their opposition to the Russians had found expression two months earlier in a vicious attack: "Apologists of Neocolonialism" (October 22, 1963). The Russians, abandoning the struggle in the "chief storm zone of the world revolution," thereafter deemed it necessary to help the economy of developing countries through efforts parallel to, if not associated with, those of the United States. Soviet ideas and policy as regards Africa led them to commit disastrous mistakes during the Congo affair. During the Algerian war, this line brought the Soviet Union to the side of "French imperialism": "The attitude toward this problem, which is the most serious in present world politics, constitutes the dividing line between Marxist-Leninists and modern revisionists."

Chou En-lai's visit occurred in a political and revolutionary context. With his usual skill, the premier managed to maintain a delicate balance between generally uncommitted African governments, which were basically traditionalist or bourgeois, and the idea of revolution. In this he was helped by deceptive and apparently identical terms of vocabulary; his famous remark, "Revolutionary prospects are excellent throughout the African continent," made during his speech at Mogadishu, can be interpreted in many different ways. This speech, delivered like a challenge just as he was leaving Africa (February 1964), offers an excellent summary of Chinese ideas and ambitions in this part of the world.

Hostility toward "imperialism," "colonialism," and "neocolonialism," all "rotten to the core," was expressed with an energy that was enhanced by images borrowed from old Chinese poems:

> A thousand sails pass alongside a wrecked ship;
> Beyond the dead tree stands a forest
> In the prime of spring.

Chou En-lai commented:

> The ranks of the revolutionary peoples of the world are like a thousand sails floating majestically in the sea wind. The revolutionary cause of the peoples of the world is like a forest growing in the prime of spring.

The list of the "eight Chinese principles for supplying economic aid" was closer to reality than these triumphant visions and outlined a Chinese strategy for economic penetration in Africa that will be discussed below. All eight— unlike aid given by more advanced countries—are devoid of any ulterior motives. Everything is said with a view to giving African and Asian countries—the latter represented by China—a feeling of fraternal solidarity arising from common problems:

At present mutual aid and economic cooperation between our African and Asian countries are still on a modest scale. However, the fact that we share the same experience and are in similar positions enables us to have a better understanding of our reciprocal needs; our mutual aid and our economic cooperation are sure, they can be adapted to real needs, they are fair and equally beneficial to each side, and useful for the independent development of the various countries. This mutual aid and economic cooperation will continue to increase in scope and in quantity in proportion to the developing of the building up of the nations in the Afro-Asian countries.

Chou En-lai's itinerary embraced past successes and hopes for the future: Egypt (December 14-20), Algeria (December 21-27), Morocco (Decembr 27-30), Tunisia (January 9-10), Ghana (January 11-16), Mali (January 16-21), Guinea (January 21-26), Sudan (January 27-30), Ethiopia (January 30-February 1), Somalia (February 1-4).[19] At Mogadishu, Chou En-lai decided not to visit Tanganyika, Kenya, and Uganda owing to the troubled situation in some of the countries, and left for China, setting off almost immediately on another trip covering Asian countries and hardly setting foot in Peking.

Chou En-lai's "safari," as it came to be called,[20] brought a steady stream of African guests to Peking, particularly in 1964 and 1965: Masemba-Debat, president of the Congo (Brazzaville) (September 28-October 3, 1964), Modibo Keita, president of Mali (November 1-7, 1964), Julius Nyerere, president of the Republic of Tanzania (February 18-23, 1965), Aden Osman, president of the Democratic Republic of Somalia (July 21-28, 1965), to name only the chief visitors. Ch'en Yi, for his part, went back to Mali and Guinea and to Algeria in September 1965. Liao Ch'eng-chih represented China at the Afro-Asian People's Solidarity Conference at Winneba (Ghana) from May 9 to 16, 1965. The visits were backed up by treaties of friendship and a series of similar economic and cultural agreements.[21] The Central African Republic, Mauritania (July 26, 1965), and Gambia all recognized China.

In 1965, however, it seemed that the Chinese had exhausted the possibilities of new friendships. Various factors put a stop to Chinese expansion—anxiety aroused here and there by their presence, and sometimes by certain of their activities, serious competition from experts sent by Taiwan, a better knowledge of internal difficulties in Peking, whose help eventually appeared minimal compared with that of the Soviet Union and the West, and lastly several coups d'état in various African capitals. Burundi, whose Queen Thérèse Kanyongau had visited Peking in March 1963, expelled all Chinese diplomats in January 1965. Dahomey and the Central African Republic broke off relations with China (January 3 and 6, 1966). Then the rich country of Ghana broke off relations on the day that Nkrumah arrived in Peking for his second visit (February 24, 1966).

In 1966, relations between China and the black African states went into cold storage, although ten states still had to be won over or rewon.

The Near and Middle East and North Africa

The revolution in Iraq on July 14, 1958, affected both Chinese policy in the Middle East and the system of regional alliances. The geographical foundations of the Bagdad Pact crumbled, and the Chinese won new allies for the revolution. Mutual recognition at a diplomatic level (July 16) was followed by a trade agreement (January 3, 1959).

The influence of the Chinese over the radicals of Bagdad quickly irritated Egypt, who after welcoming Syria into the United Arab Republic turned toward Iraq. The reception given to the Syrian Communist Khalid Bakdash in Peking, where he made a public attack on Colonel Nasser and Nasser's severe treatment of Egyptian Communists created an awkward situation between Peking and Cairo, which lasted several years.

> Certain people in power in the United Arab Republic have launched attacks against the Republic of Iraq and then against the Soviet Union, the great friend of all Arab peoples. It is clear that such actions are not in the interest of the cause of Arab national independence, so that it is impossible for the peoples of Arab countries to give them their sympathy.

These open reproaches came from Chou En-lai, speaking to the National People's Congress on April 18, 1959.

This situation was kept in existence by certain steps taken by Egypt concerning the conference of Nonaligned Nations held in Belgrade in 1961, by Egypt's sympathies for India during the Sino-Indian crisis of October-November 1962, and by its acceptance of considerable American and Soviet aid. The fact that Sino-Egyptian relations were cool did not prevent the conclusion of several economic and cultural agreements, nor visits from political and military delegations, one of which was that led by Ali Sabri in April 1963; but the Chinese tended to transfer their efforts toward the Maghreb, and especially toward Algeria, which was a better starting point for activities in black Africa.

Both because Algeria had adopted the Chinese method of armed insurrection based on a "united front," and because it was an important element in China's policy toward Arab countries, China immediately gave moral and financial support to the Algerian rebellion against France. The most prominent leaders of the National Liberation Front (NLF)—Ferhat Abbas, Krim Belkacem, Youssef Ben Kedda, Ahmed Francis—and trade unionists and combatants were entertained in Peking; Algerian "weeks" and "days" were held there; and a mission representing the NLF and later the provisional government of the Republic of Algeria (October 5, 1960) were also set up in Peking. This superior position enabled the Chinese to attack the reserved attitude of the Soviet Union and the treason of the French Communist Party, which was accused of following the "French monopolist bourgeoisie."[22]

After the Evian agreements (March 18, 1962), China offered an Algeria "left covered in wounds" aid in the form of gifts and direct services. These were the best suited to appeal to the imagination of the people: 9,000 tons of wheat, 3,000 tons of rolled steel, 21 tons of medicines, as well as several doctors who were sent to work in the countryside, and later on the dispatch of a cargo ship of 13,000 tons and military equipment for the Militia. With that modest gift, China intended to eclipse the work of the French in Algeria. Between 1962 and 1966, ten agreements of various kinds were signed—economic, technical and cultural. One (October 28, 1963) included a loan of $50 million. The two countries exchanged a growing number of missions until the summer of 1965; the fact that their national days fell close together (October 1 and November 1) gave them an added importance.

From February 22 to 27, 1965, an Afro-Asian economic seminar was held in Algiers, the chief interest of which lay in the speeches made by the Chinese delegate, Nan Han-ch'en, who outlined China's current economic strategy:

> Consequently, our highly important and successful experience dic-
> tates that we stress the development of agriculture and light industry in
> order to develop heavy industry progressively and accelerate the rhythm
> of industrialization.

Nan Han-ch'en made no mention of the disappointments of the period from 1958 to 1962 and unashamedly set up the experience of his own country as an example:

In fact the Chinese experience has proved that it is perfectly possible to transform a backward national economy over a relatively short space of time, on condition that the orientation chosen is the correct one, that the policy followed is right, and that the people work hard.

The economic seminar in Algiers also provided an opportunity to recall the "eight Chinese principles for supplying economic aid," formulated by Chou En-lai the preceding year on his African tour; mutual equality and advantage, respect for the sovereignty of states, loans without interest or at a low rate of interest, stress on helping develop independent economic systems, investment at minimum expense in the projects likely to show the most rapid results, supplying of the best Chinese equipment at world prices, technical training of the personnel of aided countries, equality in the salaries paid to Chinese experts and to experts from the countries concerned. [23] The speech by the Chinese delegate, who a year later was to be put to death or made to commit suicide by the red guards, ended in the customary way, with an appeal to struggle against "imperialism" and "colonialism."

China's great hopes for Algeria were bitterly disappointed several months later. Algiers was chosen as the meeting place for the second Afro-Asian conference, ten years after Bandung, and the date decided upon was June 29, 1965. China would have played the leading role, as the greatest power present, particularly after having exposed India's weakness. The progess of emancipation of African states, the war in Vietnam, and the exclusion of the Soviet Union would have been profitable propaganda themes. The coup d'état of Colonel Boumedienne and the elimination of Ben Bella took place ten days before the conference was due to begin. In spite of Chinese insistence to the contrary, the conference was postponed to November 5. Meanwhile, the international situation changed considerably. In Indonesia, President Sukarno was divested of power after the unsuccessful pro-Communist coup d'état on September 30, 1965; the Soviet Union regained some influence in Africa and Asia; and a military conflict broke out between India and Pakistan. As a result, the second conference was abandoned, this time on the advice of the Chinese, whose opinion ran counter to that of the Algerians. The "second Bandung" never took place.

Sino-Moroccan relations were established on November 1, 1958; they were courteous though not cordial and were nourished mainly by economic arrangements that benefited both parties, such as the exchange of Moroccan phosphates for Chinese tea, which experts from Peking tried to introduce.

Tunisia stayed aloof for a long time but eventually recognized China after Chou En-lai's quite unexpected visit to Tunis (January 9-10, 1964). It had cause to regret the action when China made vicious attacks on Bourguiba and his doctrine "born of a rainfall of dollars." [24]

Yemen and other Arab countries

On January 12, 1958, the Yemen signed a treaty of friendship and economic, technical, and cultural agreements with China, providing among other things for the building of a road 500 kilometers long between Sana and Hodeidah, the creation of a textile factory at Sana, and financial aid amounting to $17 million. This agreement was replaced by another signed on June 9, 1964, when Yemeni President Abdulla Al Sallal went to Peking. Since then China has kept a watchful eye on developments in the Arab peninsula and supplied generous moral and material support to the rebels of Dhofar. With the exception of Iraq, China made little progress in the Persian Gulf. Contact with Kuwait (a goodwill mission led by Nan Han-ch'en visited there on June 10, 1965) had no immediate results.

Political and economic relations with Syria were resumed in 1963, and several missions were exchanged.[25] Relations with Lebanon and other Arab states remained nonexistent or at least unsatisfactory until 1966.

Afghanistan

China's difficulties with the Soviet Union and its quarrel with India led Peking to turn its attention toward Afghanistan, thought without endangering relations with Pakistan. The Chinese have apparently never taken a stand on the differences between Kabul and Rawalpindi, particularly on the problem of Pushtunistan. The treaty of friendship and nonaggression signed at Kabul on August 26, 1960, by Marshal Ch'en Yi was completed by an agreement determining the frontier (November 22, 1963) and a trade agreement. The frontier agreement was important because the Afghan corridor, which is about 80 kilometers wide, lies within nondemarcated regions of Pamir. This is still true of the Sino-Russian frontier from the Afghan frontier as far as the Kizil Jik Darman pass.

The Afghan king and queen visited China from October 30 to November 13, 1964, and President Liu Shao-ch'i returned their visit from April 4 to 8, 1966. In the interval, a protocol on the frontier question and an agreement for economic and technical cooperation were concluded on March 24, 1965. Sino-Afghan relations remained on a strictly bilateral level, avoiding all references to ideological questions, the Soviet Union, or the United States, and merely praised Afro-Asian solidarity. The history of Afghanistan and its location among so many powerful neighbors made this reserved attitude entirely necessary; the Chinese had little hope of changing it.

Latin America

Although the Chinese Communist Party had had contact with various South American Communist Parties from 1956 on, the Chinese took no real interest in Latin America before 1960.[26] Generally speaking, the aim was to carry their ideological and political hostility toward the United States to the Western Hemisphere, to find, if possible, new fields for the application of Chinese revolutionary doctrines and methods, and particularly, in the immediate future, to attract all parties and movements, whether Communist or of Communist inspiration, toward themselves. In spite of the great distance involved, the Chinese found themselves in a relatively familiar world in this respect, thanks to the similarity of certain social problems and the existence of large and long-established colonies of Chinese workers and merchants, particularly in Cuba, Peru, and Mexico.[27]

The rise to power of a socialist regime in Cuba naturally caught Chinese attention and, with the help of the events of 1962, gave them a better reason for action. The rivalry between China and the Soviet Union was also more apparent in relation to Cuba than it was in relation to the small Communist Parties of Latin America.

On March 16, 1960, a China-Latin American Friendship Association was founded in Peking, presided over by Ch'u T'u-nan. In September, Fidel Castro transferred the Cuban diplomatic mission from Taipei to Peking. Latin American visitors to Peking were already numerous but quickly became even more so. The most famous of them all, Che Guevara, signed an agreement to exchange representatives of ambassadorial rank, as well as important economic arrangements. China granted a five-year loan of 240 million rubles to Cuba, without interest, and trained various categories of Cuban technicans. A little earlier, it had undertaken to buy 500,000 tons of sugar from Cuba annually over a period of five years, in return for rice, soybeans, and pork.

In December, President Dorticos made a state visit to Peking, preceded and followed by numerous missions. Further trade, technical, and cultural cooperation agreements were to follow. Che Guevara returned to Peking in February 1965, a few months before he disappeared. Some people attributed his disappearance to the fact that he was influenced by the Chinese revolutionary model.

Havana was, for the Chinese, an admirable observation post and an excellent base for propaganda and activities directed toward the Caribbean and Central and South America, all of which were going through a critical period: the Dominican Republic (November 1961), Panama (January 1964), and above all Cuba itself (October 1962).[28] The consequences of the Cuban crisis were considerable. The whole affair seemed to justify Chinese accusations of adventurism and capitulationism levelled at Khrushchev; at the same time, it revealed Cuba's vulnerability and total dependence on the Soviet Union in economic and military matters. In this respect, it set a distance between Havana and Peking. The visits of Fidel Castro to Moscow in April-May 1963, and particularly in January 1964, the conference attended by seven pro-Russian Communist Parties in Havana in November 1964, and Cuba's participation in the "schismatic" conference of 1965 (see Chapter 25) emerged as landmarks in an unexpected evolution.

Just before and after the "Tricontinental Conference" in Havana (January 1966), an apparently commercial conflict arising from the delivery of Chinese rice grew into a major political crisis. The *People's Daily* of February 22, 1966, accused the Cuban premier of having "mingled his voice in the anti-Chinese choir" and slandered China in two declarations dated February 2 and 6, which were later published by the Chinese press. This was the situation at the start of the Cultural Revolution.

In the rest of the Latin American continent, the Chinese inevitably had to limit their activities to propaganda, such as invitations issued to prominent members of various political, trade union, and cultural circles. But as soon as the ideological break with the Soviet Union allowed them to do so, from the summer of 1963 on, they made open efforts to split the Communist Parties of the various countries by encouraging the creation or development of pro-Chinese groups, mainly in Brazil, Colombia, and Peru. Compared with orthodox Communists and Castroists, from whom they differed appreciably on various points of doctrine, the number and influence of these groups still seemed weak in 1966. At all events, their progress, as was the case with all revolutionary movements throughout the continent, appeared to be doomed by the backwardness of the rural areas, the scant success of guerrillas, and the frequent military coups d'état, which put power into the hands of men who were intolerant of all political ideas differing from their own.

Notes

1 See in particular the editorial entitled "The Tibetan Revolution and the philosophy of Nehru," *People's Daily* (May 6, 1959).

2 In particular the letter from Nehru to Chou En-lai dated September 28, the reply of October 6, and the letter from Peking dated December 26, 1959 (all published on January 3, 1960).

3 Twenty-two notes had been exchanged. They were circulated among the members of the Chinese National People's Congress, along with the reports of Indian and Chinese experts in December 1960.

4 A Chinese note dated August 4 accepted the Indian proposals.

5 Editorial of the *People's Daily* (October 14).

6 The Chinese stated that, as of December 26, they had taken 33 officers and 2,156 noncommissioned officers and men prisoner, releasing 609 who were sick or wounded.

7 On this question as a whole, and particularly on the war of 1962, see Neville Maxwell, *India's China War* (London: Cape, 1970).

8 5,000 million rupees were promised or granted between 1955 and April 1963, according to the Chinese. See "The Truth on the Alliance of the Leadership of the Communist Party of the Soviet Union with India against China," *People's Daily* (April 2, 1963).

9 *Ibid.*

10 *Ibid.*, for the declarations made on October 13 and 14, 1962, by the Chinese ambassador. See also "Serious Area of Tension in Asia," *Pravda* (September 19, 1963).

11 The Chinese acceptance, accompanied by a few reservations, was dated January 19, 1963. India gave its acceptance on January 25 of the following year.

12 Diplomatic relations were not established in fact until May 1951.

13 Marshal Ayub Khan showed considerable independence on the Vietnam question, going so far as to try to bring about a rapprochement between the Chinese and American viewpoints.

14 A protocol was added on January 23, 1963.

15 On this, see *Hung ch'i* (March 16, 1960).

16 Peking was quick to recognize Guinea on October 7, 1958, just after it attained independence.

17 See in particular the Chinese declaration on February 14, 1961.

18 It resulted in a loan to Ghana of 7 million Ghana pounds.

19 Chou En-lai made a rapid trip to Albania from December 30, 1963, to January 9, 1964.

20 See W. A. C. Addie, "Chou En-lai on Safari," *The China Quarterly*, No. 18 (April-June 1964).

21 In particular, friendship treaties with Mali (November 3, 1964) and Tanzania (February 20, 1965). Several economic aid programs were launched and resulted in limited trade exchanges.

22 See "On the Defenders of Neocolonialism," *People's Daily* (October 22, 1963).

23 This text is a summary of the original.

24 See "Whom does Bourguiba Serve?", *People's Daily* (November 20, 1965).

25 A Chinese loan of 35 million Swiss francs was increased to 70 million by the agreement of February 12, 1963.

26 On the revolutionary situation in Latin America and on the relations between Peking and the Latin American Communist Parties, see Ernst Halperin, "Peking and the Latin American Communists," *The China Quarterly*, No. 29 (January-March 1967). See also Cecil Johnson, *Communist China and Latin America 1959-1967* (New York: Columbia University Press, 1970).

[27] These amounted to about 31,000 Chinese in Cuba, 30,000 in Peru, 6,700 in Brazil, 4,200 in Ecuador. See *The Geographical Review* (January 1968) for a fuller account.

[28] Mao Tse-tung made a personal declaration on the subject of Panama on January 12, 1964. As to Cuba, the Chinese made a declaration on October 25 in support of one made by Krushchev on October 23, but their real point of view and their criticisms of the Soviet premier were chiefly developed in the *People's Daily* of November 15, 1962.

23 Foreign Policy 1958 – 1966 (2): Japan, Korea, Southeast Asia

Japan

Sino-Japanese relations were mediocre for several reasons: the privileged relations between America and Japan, the existence of normal diplomatic links and well-developed trade exchanges between Tokyo and Taipei, and the fact that, legally, Peking and Tokyo were still at war with each other. In 1958, they were subjected to sudden, sharp tension.

On March 5, 1958, an important trade agreement, signed by an unofficial Japanese group, provided for exchanges valued at £35 million sterling and for the establishment of trade missions in both countries. Its terms gave the Chinese representatives, who were to work in a liberal country without restrictions, certain advantages that were reciprocal only in theory, for the Japanese representatives would be working in a closed, totalitarian society. The Kishi government had approved the agreement in spite of this when, on May 2, the flag of the People's Republic of China was torn up at the Nagasaki fair. The incident led to a rapid hardening of attitude on the Chinese side and was used as a pretext to suspend the March 5 agreement.

There were several forewarnings of this behavior; it was a reflection of the climate within China at the time. It can also be explained by the Chinese desire to exert pressure on Japanese political life in one or several ways: by affecting the coming elections, which in any case renewed the Kishi majority in the government; by winning over some members of the Liberal-Democratic Party; by seeking the support of the socialist opposition, which was more powerful than the insignificant Japanese

Communist Party;[1] or simply by encouraging any kind of neutralist opinion.

Soon, motivated by national interest and a policy of rapprochement, China made a sharp attack on the mutual security treaty signed by Tokyo and Washington on January 19, 1960, forgetting that the Sino-Soviet treaty of February 14, 1950, was itself directed against Japan and Japan's eventual allies. The themes of the attacks were economic expansion, the renaissance of Japanese militarism, and the "aggressive" character of the new treaty, which made Japan into an American "nuclear base." Kuo Mo-jo, who had old and close family ties with Japan, was asked to translate these in a message addressed to the Japanese people, over the head of the government.

This campaign and the suspension of trade relations did not prevent numerous visits from taking place on each side, particularly after the coming to power of the Ikeda cabinet (July 19, 1960). These moves were mainly useful in that they made prominent figures in Japan come out against the policy of their government toward Peking and maintained a dialogue that was taken up again seriously in the autumn of 1962, resulting in the memorandum of November 9. This provided for annual exchanges amounting to £ 36 million sterling (about $100 million) between 1963 and 1967. On December 27, another trade agreement was signed with an independent Japanese group. Semiofficial relations and private relations, in addition to the trade agreements, enabled Japanese visitors to make political declarations. The Chinese had no great illusions as to their sincerity, but they helped Chinese propaganda and provided justification in Chinese eyes for a slightly shameful compromise with a country that was not only a former enemy but an integral part of the American political, economic, and military system in Asia.

The arrangements of 1962, and the restoration of the economy after the abandoning of the Great Leap Forward, brought a rapid increase in Sino-Japanese trade, as shown by the figures in Table 23.1.[2] After reaching figures as low as $22.5 and $23.3 million in 1959 and 1960, Sino-Japanese exchanges in 1963 regained about the level attained in 1957 ($141 million).[3] In the same year, industrial and trade exhibitions were held in both countries, while trade representatives and journalists of each country also took up residence in the other country.[4]

The Chinese also redoubled their propaganda toward Japan. Mao Tse-tung made his own contribution by continuing to receive Japanese delegations of all kinds, to whom he sometimes made highly meaningful remarks. This was the case when a mission of Japanese socialist members of the Parliament visited Peking; Mao attacked the Russian presence in

Table 23.1
Sino-Japanese trade 1963-1965

	1963	1964	1965
Japanese exports to China (thousands of dollars)	62,417	157,739	245,036
Japanese imports from China (thousands of dollars)	74,600	157,750	224,705
Total	137,017	315,489	469,741

Siberia in their hearing (July 10, 1964). This slight improvement in Sino-Japanese relations by way of private groups stopped in November 1964 when the Sato cabinet came to power, for it leaned further toward the United States than had the previous one. Japanese expansion in Southeast Asia, the "basic treaty" signed by Japan and South Korea on June 22, 1965, and the development of the war in Vietnam, which was favorable to the Japanese economy, were all unlikely to encourage a rapprochement.

The Chinese tried to exploit all social conflicts in Japan: the question of the return of Okinawa to Japan; the arrival of American nuclear submarines in Japanese waters, which provoked a blistering declaration by Mao Tse-tung (January 27, 1964); the "Three Arrows Operation" affair;[5] and the intentions of certain Japanese circles regarding Taiwan. Particular efforts were made to attract Japanese youth; China also asked for the reestablishment of regular sea and air links, though with no success. Trade relations, however, benefited from the poor political relations between China and the Soviet Union and continued at a high level.

The Chinese Communist Party also had the satisfaction at first of seeing the Japanese Communist Party leaning toward its side. The expulsion of two Communist members of the Diet who had voted to have Japan sign the Moscow Treaty on the Nonproliferation of Nuclear Weapons and the refusal of the Japanese Communist Party to approve the calling of a new conference of Communist Parties suggested by Krushchev were signs of a certain solidarity, which continued until the eve of the Cultural Revolution.[6]

In February 1966, the secretary of the Japanese Communist Party, Kenji Miyamoto, met a Chinese delegation, led by P'eng Chen, in Shanghai. This was the last official function of the Mayor of Peking before his disgrace two or three months later. It was also the last pro-Chinese action of the Japanese Communist Party, which, after holding its Tenth Congress in the following October, moved rapidly toward Moscow's point of view.

Korea

After the failure of the Geneva conference on Korea in 1954, no real efforts were made to break the diplomatic deadlock or to reunite the two halves of the country. On February 5, 1958, North Korea, supported by the whole socialist bloc including China, took the initiative and proposed the withdrawal of all foreign troops from South and North Korea. Chou En-lai went to Pyongyang on February 14 and on February 19 a joint Sino-Korean communiqué announced that all Chinese troops would gradually leave North Korean territory before the end of the year. This was achieved by October 26, but the gesture met with no response from the South Koreans or the Americans. The disturbances accompanying the fall of Syngman Rhee in April 1960 did not affect the problem of reunification either. The treaty signed by Japan and Korea on June 22, 1965, which provoked a vehement protest from the Chinese on June 26, made reunification seem further away than ever. The importance of Korea for the security of Japan removed all hope of the peninsula regaining its unity, except in the case of a collapse of the South Korean regime or the departure of the Americans from Japan.

Economic relations between China and North Korea, based on a five-year trade treaty of September 27, 1958, and on frontier agreements particularly concerning shared sources of energy, appear to have been satisfactory and to have had considerable effect locally. They were further encouraged by large Chinese loans (420 million rubles in February 1960).

Political relations were based on the treaty of friendship, cooperation and mutual aid of July 11, 1961, a real military defense alliance, which no doubt had secret clauses and was similar to the Russo-Korean treaty signed two days earlier in Moscow. Relations seem to have remained satisfactory up to the visit to Peking of Choi Yong Kun, vice-chairman of the Korean Workers' Party (June 5-23, 1963). The joint communiqué published on this occasion took shelter behind the two Moscow declarations of 1957 and 1960 and endorsed several Chinese dogmas concerning modern revisionism and peaceful coexistence. On these two points, the existence of two Koreas, and the American presence in South Korea, Pyongyang and Peking could not fail to be drawn closer together.

Between 1958 and 1960, the North Koreans were tempted to follow the example of the Chinese and the Great Leap Forward (the movement known as the Flying Horse); several times they also appeared to uphold Peking's views in the ideological quarrel of the 1960s. This support, which was in all events circumspect, ceased in 1965. Anxiety as to its security and the needs arising from economic development made North Korea handle its two great neighbors with the utmost care. It approached them by turns rather than simultaneously, depending on the circumstances and the balance of influence within its own leadership, which was usually closer to the Soviet Union than to China, for past experience had shown that Chinese interference was to be feared more than that from other sources.[7] In spite of exchanges of several distinguished visitors, relations were poor in 1966 and worsened during the Cultural Revolution; the North Koreans disapproved of its excesses and possibly feared it might be contagious. Pyongyang was thrown back on Peking once more by the brisk recovery in Japanese foreign policy which began in 1969-1970.

Burma

Burma, like Cambodia, afforded excellent proof of the Chinese desire to establish good understanding between their country and those neighbors who professed neutrality. Consequently, they were fairly discreet in their support for the Burmese Communists—at least for those known as the "white flag"—but gave considerable publicity to the chief event of the time, the signing of a treaty of nonaggression and a draft frontier agreement on January 28, 1960, by General Ne Win and Chou En-lai. The treaty engaged each country not to enter into an alliance directed against the other. The Burmese undertook not to join SEATO against the wishes of the Chinese and limited their national sovereignty to a certain extent, whereas the guarantee they received in return was illusory considering the disproportionate strength of the two countries. The final version of the frontier agreement was signed on October 1, 1960. It was of little importance in itself, because the Chinese gave back about 200 square kilometers and received about 300,[8] but it took on an exemplary value as an element in Peking's propaganda. Its good effects lasted for some time: these included exchanges of visits (U Nu and General Ne Win visited Peking, and Liu Shao-ch'i, Chou En-lai, and Ch'en Yi went to Rangoon) and various economic arrangements, particularly the granting of a £30 million loan repayable between 1971 and 1981 (the agreement of January 9, 1961).

The final removal of U Nu by General Ne Win and the emergence of a Revolutionary Council with socialist tendencies on March 2, 1962, did not impair Peking's good relations with Rangoon; on the contrary, it strengthened them. The Chinese Communist Party nevertheless still maintained real links with the Burmese Communists, as was apparent when the Chinese government turned against General Ne Win several years later.

Indonesia

Difficulties over the settlement of the problem of Chinese residents in Indonesia did not stop the strengthening of links between the two countries. Progress in this respect was so rapid that some people saw the formation of a vertical axis running through Pyongyang, Peking, Hanoi, and Djakarta, even going as far as to imagine that an Asian United Nations could grow up around it.[9] The Chinese never seem to have taken these possibilities seriously, beyond a few suggestions put forward by Chou En-lai; they were reduced to nothing by the consequences of the unsuccessful coup d'état of September 30, 1965.

Until then relations between the two regimes had been founded on a common interest in Afro-Asian solidarity, which had originated in Indonesia, parallel situations as regards Wester Irian and Taiwan, a common rejection of the "colonialist trap" of a "Greater Malaysia," and the personal evolution of Sukarno. From 1960 on, Sukarno, on the basis of NASAKOM (an acronym for the combination of nationalist, Muslim and Communist ideologies), had taken Communist ministers into his government, while his temperament—flexible, yet authoritarian—inclined him toward "guided democracy," possibly inspired by his first visit to China in 1956.[10]

President and Mme Liu Shao-ch'i and Marshal and Mme Ch'en Yi visited Indonesia from April 10 to 12, 1963, in honor of the "new rising forces" who professed to be violently anti-Western; the "pomp" of their visit was frequently and unjustly criticized. In the summer of 1964, relations grew temporarily cooler as a result of proposals for a federation uniting Malaysia, the Philippines, and Indonesia (MAPHILINDO), but they soon improved once more. In 1965, Indonesian Foreign Minister Subandrio visited Peking from January 23 to 28, and Chou En-lai and Marshal Ch'en Yi went to Djakarta from April 16 to 26 to celebrate the tenth anniversary of Bandung and prepare for the "second Bandung" scheduled to take place in Algiers during the summer.

Increasingly intimate relations between the Indonesian Communist Party (PKI) and the Chinese Communist Party did not offend the government of Sukarno. Important PKI delegations went to China in 1963.[11] In May 1965, P'eng Chen represented his Party at the forty-second anniversary of the PKI, repeating in his speech an image that the Chinese liked to spread:

> As comrade Aidit has said, "On a world scale, Asia, Africa, and Latin America are the village of the world, while Europe and North America are the town of the world. If the world revolution is to be victorious, there is no other way than for the world proletariat to give prominence to the revolutions in Asia, Africa, and Latin America—that is to say, the revolutions in the village of the world.[12]

P'eng Chen held that the contradiction between "oppressed nations" and "imperialism" was the chief contradiction in the modern world, and the attitude adopted on this point was the best criterion by which to distinguish Marxist-Leninists from revisionists. His remarks included a merciless denunciation of revisionists in the style of Khrushchev, accusing them of racism, of disrupting the revolutionary national liberation movements, and pursuing a policy of cooperation between the Soviet Union and the United States which could decide the fate of the whole world. No other anti-Soviet document matched the violence and insults of the speech by the mayor of Peking. Even so, he fell from grace a year later, accused of the revisionism he had condemned with such energy.

The sudden collapse of Sukarno and the destruction of the Indonesian Communist Party after September 30, 1965, came as a terrible blow to Chinese policy in Asia. The hope of outflanking the Americans in Southeast Asia and setting up a regional unit capable of resisting Japanese economic expansion disappeared so suddenly that several Indonesian missions (among them a military mission) were surprised by the event in the middle of friendly visits to China. The Chinese press was so mortified that the news was not published for three weeks.

In Indonesia the reversal of the situation led to a resurgence of endemic sinophobia, and numerous incidents took place against which Peking was powerless. On February 3, 1966, the Chinese embassy at Djakarta was burned and the diplomats were handled roughly, as the office of the British chargé d'affaires and the British diplomats would be eighteen months later in Peking. The PKI, a faithful ally of the Chinese Communist Party, lost its dynamic secretary general and, after having attained a membership of 2 million and reigned over the most powerful trade union (SOBSI), went back to the situation of its worst period in 1948. In spite of all this, and although economic aid from China to Indonesia was suspended, diplomatic relations continued between Djakarta and Peking, even after the Indonesian ambassador lapsed into dissidence. This is a further example of an attitude of political realism on the part of the Chinese leaders; not until the aberrations of the Cultural Revolution did they abandon it, and then only for a short time.

Vietnam, Laos and Cambodia

Although the Chinese adopted a sterner line in their foreign policy in 1958, they were still in no hurry to modify the situation created by the Geneva agreements of 1954. For some time, they took no initiative and made no important diplomatic gesture. It was only after the action of the North Vietnamese in South Vietnam that the Chinese became more and more involved politically. At the same time, the elements of the problem gradually grew beyond a purely local context. It was no longer solely a question of maintaining Chinese influence and interests in Vietnam, but of opposing the extension of the American presence on the Asian continent, of blocking the rapprochement that had been developing since 1956 between Moscow and Washington, and of justifying Chinese doctrines on the revolutionary emancipation of the people in the eyes of the socialist bloc and the Third World. Because the Chinese were reluctant to embark on or allow themselves to be drawn into direct military action, however, they adopted a policy of caution, under a highly aggressive verbal disguise.

Vietnam

In Vietnam, where the main problem was reunification, the Chinese had no choice but to support Pham Van Dong's proposals on March 7, 1958, in

Saigon. This they did by making an appropriate declaration referring to the Geneva agreement and denouncing American military aid to South Vietnam. It naturally met with no response.

Two years later, on May 14, 1960, when Chou En-lai visited Hanoi on his way back from a journey to Cambodia, a Sino-Vietnamese communiqué was issued that showed less anxiety about Vietnam than about Laos, for it requested that the International Control Commission return there. In fact, the question of Laos concerned Peking the most from 1960 until the second Geneva conference (May 16, 1961-July 23, 1962). Relations with Vietnam consisted in the main of economic and commercial negotiations. On January 31, 1961, the two countries signed an agreement under which China granted North Vietnam a new loan of 141,750,000 rubles, repayable in seven years. This loan was the basis of a Chinese technical aid program, which was applied to twenty-eight projects in industry and transport. It was the extension of financial aid totaling $500 million between 1954 and 1960.[13]

Washington's support for the Ngo Dinh Diem government in the fight against Communist subversion and SEATO's tendency to associate with South Vietnamese observers and prepare for possible future action in Laos and Vietnam (both zones were covered by the treaty, at least as far as latitude 21° 30′ north) provoked a protest from Hanoi, which Peking upheld in a declaration on April 13, 1961.

The propaganda duel in which the two capitals engaged over the heads of the delegates of fourteen powers gathered in Geneva to achieve the neutrality of Laos was an indication of the inextricable situations to come. For the Americans, the aim was to maintain an intact and independent South Vietnam in the face of attacks from Hanoi under cover of the National Liberation Front, formed in December 1960 and backed up by North Vietnamese regular troops coming in by way of Laos. The Chinese were less concerned with supporting the patriotic struggle of the South Vietnamese rebels than with opposing the transformation of South Vietnam into "a colony and an American military base," a "jumping-off point" in the direction of Laos and the rest of the peninsula.[14] The visit of the military mission led by Marshal Yeh Chien-ying to Hanoi in January 1962 appeared as a reply to the visit of General Maxwell Taylor, a specialist in "limited war," to Saigon in October 1961 and occurred just before the setting up in Saigon of a "military aid command," which, as the Chinese foreign minister said on February 24, was already an operational command affecting peace and Chinese security in Asia. Here again the object was mainly to give support to a North Vietnamese protest of February 18.

The years 1962 and 1963 were focused on Laotian affairs; no really important events took place in Vietnam. Delegations were exchanged, followed by detailed economic arrangements, in the approved fashion among socialist countries. The assassination of Ngo Dinh Diem was acknowledged, though without any particular emphasis, and his successors—possible interlocutors—were treated with care, at any rate at first. The Chinese studied with great care, however, the development and methods of supplying American military aid to South Vietnam.[15]

The year 1964 saw the beginning of a new chapter during which Peking's policy toward Vietnam came to life again. President Johnson's tendency to internationalize the war in Vietnam and to interest the United Nations in Indochinese affairs provoked violent reactions in the Chinese press.[16] On the tenth anniversary of the first Geneva conference, the Chinese government delivered a warning to the American government, asking it once more to return to the 1954 agreements. In August, the naval incidents in the Gulf of Tonkin and the first bombing raids of the American air force in North Vietnam triggered enormous demonstrations throughout China. In a declaration published on August 6, which was accompanied by a letter from Marshal Ch'en Yi, the foreign minister, to his North Vietnamese colleague Xuan Thuy, the Chinese government formally rejected any U.N. intervention and called for the convocation of the Geneva conference. Once again this was a gesture in support of a Vietnamese declaration of August 9, rather than a real initiative on the part of the Chinese. The war had by now reached the doorstep of South China; it raised the problem of a possible Chinese intervention, the form this should take, and the limits to be set to it, and was accompanied by grave internal differences insofar as intervention entailed a reexamination of Sino-Soviet relations. Another important sign of the times that was hard to interpret clearly was the establishment in Peking of a permanent delegation of the South Vietnamese National Liberation Front (September 18).

In the spring of 1965, while military escalation was becoming more apparent owing to the increase in the number of American soldiers in South Vietnam and the extension of the bombing in Tonkin, China took up the four points that the North Vietnamese had just drawn up on April 8, as a condition to all solutions of the Vietnam problem, in answer to the American formula of "negotiation without preliminaries."[17] It seems unlikely that the four points, to which should be added the "five points" put forward by the NLF on March 22, 1965, had been decided upon without consultations between Hanoi and Peking. The stress laid on the withdrawal of foreign military forces suggests that the Chinese had a large share in their conception.

The intransigence of the Chinese, entrenched behind their demand for the maintenance of Vietnamese sovereignty, appeared just as intense in the autumn of 1965 when the Chinese foreign minister held his celebrated press conference (September 29); the possibility of an invasion of China, rather than the subject of Vietnam, made the explosive Ch'en Yi momentarily throw calmness to the winds and challenge the world at large. All things considered, he showed more caution than daring in his remarks on Vietnam (see Chapter 24).

China revealed its weakness by not reacting to serious air or sea incidents.[18] It went no further than to support, in a declaration of July 3, 1966, the North Vietnamese declaration of June 30, when the bombing raids reached the suburbs of Hanoi. However, this passivity in action was compensated for by an even sterner line in diplomacy; China rejected the possibility of a new Geneva conference, seeing it as an attempted maneuver by the United States, the Soviet Union, and India, and claiming that in erasing the demarcation line between North and South Vietnam by their actions from the air, the Americans had torn up the Geneva agreements and "reduced them to ashes in the flames of their aggression."[19]

When the *People's Daily* published these lines, Chief of Staff Lo Jui-ch'ing had been absent from public life for seven months. At first rumor had it that he had been instructed to install a headquarters in the Southwestern provinces to prepare for a possible military intervention in Vietnam. Several signs suggested that he and some of his collaborators[20] favored intervention in the form of a joint action of the socialist bloc. These views were unlikely to be approved by Mao Tse-tung and Lin Piao, who could not have embarked on this line without renouncing at the same time the political and ideological independence they had sought and practiced since 1960, interrupting the Cultural Revolution, which had just begun, and dangerously strengthening the opposition, which they wanted to overcome.

The Soviet Union, given the state of its power relations with the United States, could not run the risk of generalized war over a region that was of secondary importance from a national point of view and where a positive result would benefit China first of all. Lo Jui-ch'ing was too devoted to the international vision of Communism and too convinced of the solidarity of the socialist bloc; he later paid a heavy price for his errors and illusions.

Laos

Laos was weak from every point of view, but its position along the Mekong river made it an ideal channel of penetration into the heart of the Indochinese world. For this reason, after the Geneva conference of 1954, the Chinese were particularly careful to prevent their neighbor from coming under American influence by having a government hostile to Communism, or from placing itself under the de jure or de facto protection of SEATO. For the moment, the Chinese preferred a neutral, friendly Laos to a country ill prepared for the rigors of totalitarianism, since the Pathet Lao, their territories, and their army would survive and remain an essential instrument of pressure and penetration. Prince Souvanna Phouma was popular, easy to approach, and committed to France; the Chinese ultimately preferred its distant and discreet influence to any other. For a long time, he was a head of government after their own hearts, though under the nominal authority of the king. They skillfully managed to get him to visit Peking, where he signed a communiqué with Chou En-lai on August 25, 1956, strengthening the neutrality of Laos without any countereffect on national unity.

Two years later, however, the Laotian right wing won the day when Phoui Sanaikone came to power on August 18, 1958. This reaction was sparked by the difficulties involved in the integration of the Pathet Lao, as laid down by the 1954 Geneva conference, and by the persistent North Vietnamese incursions into the northeastern part of the country. It can also be explained by the importance of American financial and military aid, which was essential to a state with serious economic difficulties that could no longer look to France for support.[21]

On February 11, 1959, the royal Laotian government judged that it had complied with the requirements of the Geneva military agreements, declared that it was free of all obligations to them, and asked for the recall of the International Control Commission, whose usefulness was in any case lessened by systematic obstruction on the part of the Polish representative. This decision, endorsed by Washington the next day, again raised the question of Laos in Peking and Hanoi.

The Chinese government protested on February 18, urging the co-chairmen of the Geneva conference to restore the former situation rapidly. It protested again on May 18 when, after the defection of two battalions of Pathet Lao which had not been properly integrated into the royal troops, Prince Souphannouvong, head of the Pathet Lao, was placed under guard in Vientiane and threatened with trial. There was another Chinese protest in September when the Laotian government asked for the dispatch of a committee of inquiry. A Soviet proposal for the convocation of a new Geneva conference was not followed up (September 14). In November, Secretary-General Dag Hammärskjold of the United Nations visited Vientiane, much to the displeasure of Hanoi and Peking.

The internal situation in Laos grew more complicated in 1960. In January, a pro-American extreme right-wing group provoked an insurrection (General Phoumi Nosavan and Prince Tiao Somsanith), to which neutralist elements replied with a coup d'état on August 9 led by Captain Kong Le, bringing Prince Souvanna Phouma back to power; they were opposed by the government of Savannakhet in southern Laos (Prince Boun Oum and General Phoumi Nosavan), which had the support of Thailand. The State Department tried to win back Prince Souvanna Phouma, whose neutralist tendencies seemed to be leading in the direction of Peking, which he was proposing to visit on December 12. The internal situation grew considerably worse, however. Laos seemed to be in the grip of a civil war; at this, the Soviet Union and North Vietnam, supported by China, called for the convocation of the Geneva conference and the return of the International Control Commission.[22] This suggestion, which was taken up in another form by Prince Sihanouk on January 1, 1961, was pursued by Prince Souvanna Phouma, who visited Peking with his half-brother, Prince Souphannouvong, from April 22 to 25, 1961. A less important Laotian delegation visited the province of Yunnan at the same time.

The Geneva conference on Laos was preceded by a cease fire (May 3) and helped by a meeting of the three princes (Souvanna Phouma, Souphannouvong, Boun Oum) in Zurich; it was attended by fourteen powers and lasted from May 16, 1961, to July 23, 1962. The conference was long and difficult, but eventually the powers were made to recognize the declaration of neutrality of the royal Laotian government published on July 9, 1962; theoretically, Laos was placed out of reach of foreign interference.[23] Furthermore, although a government of national union was constituted on June 23, it was impossible to form a truly neutralist regime. The three factions, left (Souphannouvong and Phoumi Vongvichit), right (General Phoumi Nosavan) and neutralist (Souvanna Phouma and Kong Le), remained and still had the support of different political and military elements. This situation arose partly from a traditional lack of cohesion in a country that had for a long time been made up of a conglomeration of principalities; it was also the result of a tacit agreement between the two superpowers, the United States and the Soviet Union, each of whom wanted to maintain within the country, through the group of Phoumi

Nosavan on one side and the Pathet Lao on the other, a minimum of guarantees and the means of action should the need arise. Neither would take the risk, as the French wanted them to, of placing their trust in the unknown in the shape of a truly neutralist government led by Prince Souvanna Phouma.

The Chinese, who adopted an extremely harsh tone throughout the conference with regard to the United States and its closest allies (Thailand and South Vietnam), but who at each meeting fell into line with the Soviet position and stressed the need for a peaceful settlement and for neutrality without outside control, had grounds for satisfaction. Laos appeared temporarily out of reach of an American intervention, whether direct or under cover of SEATO, and removed from Soviet influence, which had been manifested at one point by considerable logistical support in the military field. Lastly, the North Vietnamese also had to be more cautious and restrained in their military activities, which were limited to covering the Laotian section of the Ho Chi Minh Trail.

For a year, Chinese influence in Vientiane seemed to be growing. Regular diplomatic relations were established on September 7, 1962. General Phoumi Nosavan went to Peking on December 2, 1962, in his capacity of deputy prime minister and minister of finance and, while praising the friendship between Laos and China, obtained a long-term loan and the extension of the Mengla-Phong Saly road as far as Nam Tha near Ban Houei Sai.[24] The visit of King Savang Vatthana to Peking from March 6 to 10, 1963, confirmed the development. Even the April 1 assassination of Vientiane Foreign Minister Quinim Pholsena, who was neutralist but whose attitude towards the Communists was one of understanding, did not seem to trouble Sino-Laotian relations very much.[25]

But on April 19, 1964, when Prince Souvanna Phouma had just returned from a visit to Peking (April 4 to 7), elements of the Laotian right wing (Kouprasith, Siho) seized power in Vientiane and forced a reshuffling of the government. It was the beginning of a new crisis, which lasted until the spring of 1974. Soon afterward, Prince Souvanna Phouma, thought to be dominated by the "Savannakhet group," lost favor in Peking and was attacked on several occasions. The Chinese tried to appeal to the authority of the Geneva co-chairmen and called for a further conference [26], but eventually made the best of the situation, which was in many respects similar to that at the beginning of 1961. Laotian neutrality, violated by the presence of North Vietnamese along the eastern frontier and by the activities of the American air force based on Thailand, existed in name only and reflected the military balance of power. Unity within the country seemed further away than ever. The attempts to form a coalition government integrating the different military forces resembled the periodic efforts of the Nationalist government in Nanking and the Chinese Communist Party during the Third Civil War from 1945 to 1949. At present, the indigenous Communist leadership has taken over. To what extent it is influenced or dominated by the Chinese is not yet clear.

Cambodia

Alongside the vicissitudes of Sino-Laotian relations, Sino-Cambodian relations seem remarkably serene and, in spite of the versatility of Prince Sihanouk, characterized by an even progression toward China. The first move toward a rapprochement was made in 1956, when Prince Sihanouk went to Peking for the first time. There he signed the communiqué, which was customary at that time, on the "five principles of coexistence" (February 18) and received substantial economic aid (see Chapter 15). The establishment of formal diplomatic relations (July 24, 1958) was a further occasion for Prince Sihanouk to visit his new friends (August 15, 1958).

Closer political links were created in 1960. Chou En-lai, who had unobtrusively visited Cambodia in November 1956, paid another, official visit with Marshal Ch'en Yi (May 5 to 9). The joint communiqué stressed peaceful coexistence, neutrality, and Afro-Asian solidarity, without going far beyond the usual generalities. But the third visit of Prince Sihanouk to Peking of December 15-20, 1960, was of greater importance, for on December 19 a treaty of friendship and nonaggression was signed, along with several economic agreements. These inaugurated a period of active political, economic, and technical collaboration. The deterioration of relations between Cambodia and its neighbors South Vietnam and Thailand, and the consideration shown by the Chinese to Prince Sihanouk during both the preparations for the second Geneva conference and the conference itself, brought him still closer to Peking. From 1963 on, the prince went to Peking almost every year.[27] His aim was to obtain China's help in convening an international conference that would guarantee Cambodian frontiers and neutrality, and to find a replacement for American economic aid, which he finally rejected completely on November 19, 1963. He failed in his first aim, despite Chinese support, for reasons external to Sino-Cambodian relations.[28] As far as his second aim was concerned, he had to be satisfied with a relatively modest gesture increasing the aid already granted to start light industry.[29] On the other hand, the military mission led by General Lon Nol (leader of the coup d'état of 1970) in March 1963 and the fifth visit of Prince Sihanouk to Peking in the autumn of 1964 brought Cambodia light arms and equipment for 22,000 men.

Prince Sihanouk paid for China's generosity and its promises of help in the event of foreign complications with some outrageous remarks on the subject of the United Nations, his neighbors, and the Americans, the "sole and unmistakable heirs of Nazism," forgetting the help he had asked for and received, just as he also forgot his past condemnation of Communism and the People's Republic of China. The total picture was one of political instability, which the future later confirmed.

The Chinese themselves became more and more reserved in their remarks, as the Indochinese situation appeared increasingly dangerous. The inconsistencies of the Cultural Revolution gave rise to a serious crisis in Sino-Cambodian relations, bringing them to the verge of a breakdown.[30]

Notes

[1] It held only three seats in the Diet of 1960 (2.93 percent of the total votes cast).

[2] Sidney Klein, "A Survey of Sino-Japanese Trade 1950-1966," *The China Mainland Review* (Hong Kong, December 1966); the source is the Customs Department of the Japanese Ministry of Finance.

[3] Similar to the figures for exchanges between Japan and Taiwan: $153 million in 1962.

[4] Japanese industrial exhibition of October 1963 in Peking and Shanghai. Chinese exhibition in Tokyo in April 1964.

[5] This was a hypothetical operation based on a study by Japan's Self-Defense Agency; it would have been used in a conflict in North Asia. It was revealed to the Diet by a Japanese member on February 10, 1965.

[6] It was strengthened by difficulties in relations between the Communist Party of the Soviet Union and the Japanese Communist Party, beginning in 1961 and particularly in 1964.

[7] The independent spirit of the Koreans is sometimes summarized by the formula "juche," meaning roughly "self-reliance," which Kim Il Sung had put forward in December 1955.

[8] The Chinese gave back a stretch of land in the Shweli Valley in the Nam-Wan region, and received two others, one near Hpimaw, and the other in the area inhabited by the Pan Hung and Pang Lao tribes.

[9] Indonesia, irritated by the attitude of the United Nations over the West Irian question, withdrew from the organization on January 7, 1965.

[10] The second took place in June 1961, a few weeks after the visit of Marshal Ch'en Yi, minister of foreign affairs, to Djakarta (March 28 to April 2).

[11] Missions led by Sutardi, Imron, and Aidit himself on his return from Moscow in August 1963.

[12] Lecture at the Aliarcham Indonesian Academy of Social Science, May 25, 1965. English text published by the Foreign Languages Press, Peking.

[13] Soviet aid to North Vietnam over the same period amounted to $125 million. See Kurt London, *Unity and Contradiction* (New York: Praeger, 1962), p. 239.

[14] See the editorial of the *People's Daily* (October 19, 1961).

[15] According to Peking, the number of American advisers in Vietnam increased from 200 in 1954 to 8,500 in May 1962.

[16] See the editorial of the *People's Daily* (May 18, 1964).

[17] They may be summarized as follows: (1) acknowledgement of the independent sovereignty and territorial integrity of Vietnam; (2) respect for the military clauses in the Geneva agreements of 1954, removal of foreign military bases and withdrawal of foreign troops; (3) liberty for the South Vietnamese population to decide its own affairs in agreement with the program of the NLF and without foreign intervention; (4) peaceful reunification without foreign intervention.

[18] On April 12, 1966, an American A-3B bomber went astray over Kwangtung and was shot down. On May 12 five American fighters destroyed a Chinese plane over Yunnan. Small Chinese boats were shot at by machine guns on several occasions in the Gulf of Tonkin.

[19] *People's Daily* (July 18, 1966).

[20] One of them was General Hsiao Hsiang-jung, head of the army's General Administrative Department.

[21] $190 million between January 1, 1955, and June 30, 1959, according to the American White Paper on Laos (November 14, 1959).

[22] Chinese declarations of December 14 and 19, 1960, and another by Ch'en Yi on February 22, 1961.

[23] The documents of the conference include a declaration and a separate protocol dealing mainly with the withdrawal of foreign troops and the working of the International Control Commission, which was in fact deprived of all independence of action and consequently of any real efficacity.

[24] See the joint communiqué of December 4, 1962.

[25] The incident was made use of under the guise of a Chinese governmental declaration (April 16, 1963).

[26] Declaration of June 9, 1964, proposals of May 26, 1964, and the declaration of July 3, 1966, which no longer mentioned a new conference.

[27] From February 8 to 28, 1963, from September 26 to October 7, 1964, from September 22 to October 4, 1965.

[28] On this subject, see the letter from Chou En-lai to Prince Sihanouk of August 27, 1962, and the Sino-Cambodian declaration published on May 5 when President Liu Shao-ch'i visited Phnom Penh.

[29] The rebuilding of an airport was included. An agreement for an airline between Phnom Penh and Canton was signed on November 15, 1963.

[30] Relations between the People's Republic of China and Thailand, Malaysia, Singapore, and the Philippines are described in Chapter 45.

24 Foreign Policy 1958– 1966 (3): United States, Western Europe, International Organizations, Disarmament

United States

The hatred nourished by the Chinese government for that of the United States has few parallels in contemporary history. Chinese policy as a whole between 1958 and 1966 took its inspiration from the desire to get every people to share that hatred, to arouse it or to feed it on every possible occasion, and to isolate the Americans, particularly their leaders. A sort of "united front" spread against America, finding expression in insulting and violent slogans. The classic divisions among the Western world, the socialist world, and the Third World became more complicated, so as to shrink the circle around the enemy more thoroughly. The intermediary zone formed by the Third World was joined by another constituted by advanced capitalist countries tyrannized or exploited by the Americans: Japan, Western Europe, Canada. At the same time, Peking tried to carry the struggle to the Latin American continent and to the very heart of the United States by lending the black problem such importance that Mao Tse-tung himself made several impassioned declarations on the subject.

From 1963 on, however, part of the Chinese hatred, concentrated until then on the United States, was transferred to the leaders of the Soviet Union, who were guilty of drawing closer to the Americans, to the Indians, who refused to give way on the frontier question, and to the Japanese, whose economic expansion was causing anxiety. Soon it was accompanied by a feeling of encirclement, superbly described by Ch'en Yi in his press conference of September 29, 1965:

If the U.S. imperialists are determined to launch a war of aggression against us, they are welcome to come sooner, to come as early as tomorrow. Let the Indian reactionaries, the British imperialists, and the Japanese militarists come along with them! Let the modern revisionists act in coordination with them from the north! We will still win in the end. . . . For sixteen years we have been waiting for the U.S. imperialists to come in and attack us. My hair has turned grey in waiting.[1]

Faced with these unbridled attacks, the Americans used the tactics best calculated to irritate the Chinese—silence and patience. They professed to see in these outbursts the result of Chinese inexperience in international relations, the incorrigible reflection of an extremist ideology, and a need for compensation born of China's military weakness.

In reality, the Chinese resentment was deeply sincere, arising both from ideology and politics, with politics supplying the concrete justification for ideology. America was the symbol of much-hated capitalism and liberalism; its presence in the East thwarted the restoration in East Asia of a Chinese hegemony that was thousands of years old. It protected the remains of the Nationalist government and deprived Peking of that unparalleled instrument of politics and propaganda, a permanent seat—including the right of veto—on the Security Council of the United Nations. America also furnished daily proof of the weakness of a China that stood alone.

Such was the psychological climate underlying the history of Sino-American relations between 1958 and 1966, for relations did exist after a fashion, both at the somewhat singular level of meetings between ambassadors, and at the less obvious level of tacit behavior toward one another. The Taiwan Strait crisis of the summer of 1958 is probably a good illustration of the subtle links binding these two categories of relations, in spite of the fact that it was equally tied up with Sino-Soviet relations.

The Sino-American conversations in Warsaw went through a crisis in April 1958, when each side accused the other of rendering them useless, while at the same time making it clear that it wanted to maintain them.[2] Although based on limited grounds for dispute (repatriation of Chinese residents in the United States and liberation of Americans detained in China), or on practical proposals (partial suspension of the embargo, exchange of journalists), all the meetings also touched on the question of Taiwan, which was the obvious preliminary to any adjustment in the situation. When Washington asked the Chinese Communists to enter into an engagement not to resort to arms to liberate Taiwan, they asked that the two states enter into a mutual engagement not to use force to settle differences between them, a skillful suggestion from the point of view of their propaganda, but one that was totally unacceptable to the Americans, in view of their agreements with Generalissimo Chiang Kai-shek since 1954 and their military superiority (see Chapter 15).

During August 1958, after several weeks of tension punctuated by various military incidents and by active propaganda on the part of Peking with a view to the reconquest of Taiwan, the Communist artillery and air force began a heavy bombardment of the islands of Quemoy (Kinmen) and Matsu, which ensure the strategic defense of the Taiwan Strait. In answer to this feeler, aimed at determining Washington's intentions, the Americans deployed air force and naval troops in the region, while President Eisenhower made a vague declaration intended to leave Peking uncertain as to his intentions concerning the defense of the islands. Tension mounted over the next few days, and it seemed likely that it would lead rapidly to fighting on the spot, which would be liable to develop into generalized hostilities.

A declaration by Foster Dulles, then secretary of state (September 4), dispelled the last doubts as to American determination to protect the threatened offshore islands. The Soviet Union kept a careful eye on the situation. A tough letter from Khrushchev to President Eisenhower (September 7) enabled the Chinese not to lose face; on September 6, convinced that they were isolated, they beat a retreat. Chou En-lai made a solemn reaffirmation of China's right to continue its military action but declared that he was ready, in the interests of peace, to resume the Warsaw talks between ambassadors. The storm abated. On October 6, Minister of Defense P'eng Teh-huai decided to suspend the bombardment of the islands for seven days. This measure was prolonged by two weeks on October 13, and the situation soon returned to the status quo ante. On October 31, Mao Tse-tung, in compensation for his retreat, published a collection of statements that he had made between 1940 and 1958: *Comrade Mao Tse-tung on "Imperialism and all Reactionaries are Paper Tigers."* This confident, disdainful title was ill suited to the circumstances, and Mao Tse-tung himself seemed to admit it in one of his last sentences: "Yet imperialism is still alive, still running amuck in Asia, Africa, and Latin America."[3]

Two years after the Taiwan Strait affair, the security treaty signed by Japan and the United States on January 19, 1960, gave rise to a new and violent anti-American campaign. The Chinese commentators tried to prove that, under the guise of maintaining peace and security in Asia, the treaty prepared for a return of Japanese militarism, the supply of nuclear power to the Japanese armed forces, military collusion between Japan, South Korea, and Taiwan, and a collaboration between SEATO and a future "Northeast Asia Organization." The "heroic" struggle of the Japanese people against the country's rearmament and the analogies between American policy in Western Germany and that in Japan were not forgotten. It was easy for the Chinese to find in the American press, even in the Senate itself, false proofs of U.S. "war-mongering," and in the European press proof of growing lack of unity in the Western camp (see also Chapter 23).

American advances aimed at creating a better atmosphere between the two countries were constantly denounced as maneuvers intended to lead world opinion astray. This was the case with the statement of February 19, 1960, by Parsons, then in charge of Far Eastern affairs, in which he acknowledged the existence of China, and admitted the lack of adequate solutions for reopening exchanges between the two states. The Chinese replied with a long commentary in the *People's Daily*, "Parsons in a Dilemma" (March 4), which listed all their complaints. The text had no ideological content, but was full of impassioned declarations, making it of great importance for a psychological evaluation of the problem of Sino-American relations.[4]

The ratification of the Japanese-American Security Pact and the affair of the U2 shot down in the Soviet Union in May 1960 at the time of the interview between Eisenhower and Khrushchev, and the four-power summit meeting in Paris provoked a huge new wave of demonstrations against the United States and in support of the Soviet Union. The Americans were accused of having consciously tried to make the summit conference a failure,[5] and this explanation, like the importance and scale of the demonstrations, was aimed primarily at discouraging Khrushchev's policy of détente and at influencing the Conference of Eighty-one Communist and Workers' Parties due to be held in Moscow in the autumn of the same year.

The visit of President Eisenhower to Asia, and in particular to Taiwan (June 20-27), did nothing to alleviate the situation. The Chinese press launched constant attacks against the president of the United States, jeering at the cancellation of the visit to Japan. An anti-American propaganda week (meetings, parades, exhibitions) spread the agitation to all the large towns in China from June 21 to 27.

The years that followed were less tense. Problems calling for a bilateral solution—Taiwan, the Chinese proposal for a nuclear-free zone in Asia and the Pacific, and exchanges of journalists—made no progress. A very indirect suggestion from Ch'en Yi with a view to a foreign ministers' conference was not taken up.[6] On the other hand, at every opportunity raised by events abroad or within the United States, the Chinese press launched into violent and often insulting attacks. Disarmament, nuclear tests, "the two Chinas plot," voting on the entry of China to the United Nations, the Berlin question, journeys undertaken by the president or the vice-president of the United States, economic difficulties, messages on the state of the Union, elections, as well as American policy in Asia and the Third World gave rise to systematic accusations. The height of absurdity was reached in a declaration by schismatic archbishop P'i Shu-shih: "Kennedy, a Great Insult to the Catholic Faith."[7] Later on the assassination of the president was greeted with cruel and shocking caricatures. All this literature was employed in a systematic effort to make America, both within and without, hideous to look at, just as the Chinese theater gave hideous faces to evil-doers. The "ugly American," who was both ferocious and cowardly, made frequent appearances on the stage; this has not happened so far, apparently, in the case of the Russians.

The actual behavior of both sides was cautious, however; violations of the Chinese maritime frontier, twelve miles from the shore, on September 4, 1958, or rarer still, of Chinese air space, only gave rise to "serious warnings," a formula whose paternalistic tone and frequent repetition would have been worrying if it had not been quite obviously in line with the imperial tradition. The number of them now amounts to nearly five hundred. Whether out of fear of complications or unwillingness to reveal its weaknesses, the Chinese defense never reacted except when really forced to do so.[8]

In 1963, China made full use of the racial conflicts in the United States. Mao Tse-tung himself entered the lists when he sent a public message to the black leader Robert Williams, denouncing the "treachery of the double dealing" of the Kennedy administration, which repressed the black population while pretending to protect it. The chairman of the Chinese Communist Party went on to speak to the world at large: "I call upon workers, peasants, revolutionary intellectuals, enlightened personages of all colors in the world, white, black, yellow, brown, etc., to reunite against the racial discrimination practiced by U.S. imperialism and to support the American Negroes in their struggle against racial discrimination."[9] Anti-American demonstrations began again when Robert Williams visited Peking (October 1963).[10]

In 1964, Mao Tse-tung once more intervened, because of incidents in the Panama Canal zone (January 12), and took the opportunity to enumerate the crimes of American imperialism, now more than ever the "worst enemy of all peoples in the world." In 1965, Mao Tse-tung for the third time made an appeal to all countries against America (May 12) on the subject of the Dominican Republic and, according to established custom, campaigns in the press and street demonstrations again took up the theme of American tyranny, often in the form of caricatures. "The Johnson Doctrine of Neo-Hitlerism" was the title given to an editorial in the *People's Daily*, linking the doctrine to the line of capitulation pursued by modern revisionists under the inspiration of Daladier and Chamberlain (March 14). In 1966, the Chinese were aroused by aerial incidents of April 12 and May 13: "Bear Deepest Hatred Toward the Enemy"[11] summarized a climate that no peace-making gesture from Washington could restore to serenity.[12]

Sino-American relations could be described as worse in 1966 than early in 1958, if that were possible; nothing, not even the evolution of Sino-Soviet relations, appeared likely to change this situation. China delighted in surrounding itself with potential adversaries, creating the conditions for an encirclement for which it had an inner need—a modern version of its isolation of old.

Western Europe

The Chinese attitude toward the West, principally Great Britain, France, and West Germany, was guided by two series of considerations pointing in different directions. On one hand, all three states had to be discredited politically and ideologically—by attacks on their system of government, their allegiance to the United States, the colonial past and the neocolonial present of the first two, and the Hitlerian past and the present "vengeful" attitude of the third—in order to weaken the Atlantic Pact and the United Nations, while facilitating Chinese action in the Third World at the same time. On the other hand, while the United States had to be isolated and inner contradictions had to be developed within the capitalist world, care also had to be taken not to arouse the suspicion of new states that had retained political, economic, cultural, and sentimental links with the former tutelary power. At the same time, all political and economic benefits of bilateral relations with any of the former colonial powers had to be put to good use. Given these limits, Chinese policy was of necessity fluctuating; in contrast with the systematic harshness toward the United States, it often showed realism and flexibility.

Great Britain

Diplomatic relations with Great Britain remained technically incomplete, though adequate, with occasional moments of real or artificially contrived tension. One of these occurred in July 1958 when Jordan was occupied by British troops. Anti-British demonstrations swelled the anti-American demonstrations inspired by the landing of elements of the Sixth Fleet in Lebanon. Among the numerous pretexts for Chinese indignation were the transformation of Malaya and Singapore into Malaysia, which was supposedly won over to SEATO and the free world (September 13, 1963); the British intervention in Kuwait, a "provocation against the Arab peoples" (January 1961); British support for India; the vote on the U.N. resolution on Tibet; the situation in Laos; many international events; and, naturally, various incidents in Hong Kong.[13] The Chinese also attracted a few prominent Englishmen, who were either useful to them or simply friendly to Peking (Malcolm MacDonald, Field Marshal Montgomery) and who supplemented the normal diplomatic activities.

No fundamental changes took place in the basic situation. The Hong Kong emporium still fulfilled its essential commercial and financial role, benefiting both Peking and London, and remained a vital and reassuring link between China and the financial assets of the Overseas Chinese.

France

The war in Indochina until 1954 and the Algerian war that followed it gave Peking the chance to recognize the governments rejecting French authority, thereby preventing the establishment of diplomatic relations between France and China for some time. The solution of these conflicts, the contacts between the two countries in Geneva in 1954 and above all in 1961-1962, and visits by various prominent Frenchmen to Peking helped to prepare the way. The orientation General de Gaulle gave to French foreign policy as a whole from 1962 on and the decisive development of Sino-Soviet relations in 1963 logically led to the restoration of a French presence in Peking. On January 27, 1964, a joint communiqué published in Paris and Peking announced that the French and Chinese governments had decided to establish diplomatic relations. The communiqué had been preceded by an exploratory mission by Edgar Faure to Peking, and a courtesy visit to Taipei by General Pechkoff, the personal envoy of General de Gaulle.

The French decision was a source of great satisfaction to the Chinese. It helped restore their prestige abroad, which had been considerably undermined by the failure of the Great Leap Forward and the people's communes. It also brought them the sanction of France, as it were, in the eyes of the many new French-speaking states in Africa. French culture, by contributing to the diffusion of an ideology that had acquired respectability, would also contribute to its own gradual disappearance. In the Atlantic camp, French recognition without the justification provided by the vulnerable position of a nearby colony, as in the case of England, was yet another potential cause of discord, as the Chinese emphasized on the first day: "It goes without saying that the establishment of diplomatic relations between China and France is an event which is highly displeasing to American imperialism, which tries constantly to isolate China, and to its followers."[14] This theme was taken up again publicly with particular violence, a rare breach of diplomatic usage, on July 14, 1964, at the French Embassy itself by Marshal Ch'en Yi, minister of foreign affairs.

As time went on Franco-Chinese relations were characterized by similarities between their respective situations in several fields. General de Gaulle and Chairman Mao, both among the last survivors of a remarkable era, had great esteem for each other, as was borne out by a last, splendid gesture—Mao Tse-tung sent a wreath to be laid on the tomb of General de Gaulle. De Gaulle had long since ceased to be "the representative of the bourgeoisie closely associated with large financial capital," and no further mention was made of the "bayonets of the fascist rebels," which had carried him to power.

Although the first French atomic explosion in the Sahara on February 13, 1960, was described by Peking as a "criminal act," later detonations in the same place or in the Pacific were passed over without comment. The refusal of both countries to sign the Moscow Treaty on the Nonproliferation of Nuclear Weapons on July 25, 1963, and the boycotting by France of the Geneva talks on the limiting of nuclear armaments created a real complicity between Paris and Peking, while the Chinese were quick to give wide publicity to de Gaulle's declaration on the subject on July 30, 1963. Similarly, when France maintained its distance from the United Nations or suggested modifications in the Charter, it appeared to justify Chinese criticisms of the international organization. China's consistent hostility toward the idea of Europe—in this it was close to the Soviet Union—found support and certain arguments in the reservations of the French. The Chinese Communists became all the more willing to uphold the government of General de Gaulle as their relations worsened with the

French Communists from 1963 on. But France and China discovered that their views converged more than anywhere else in their common mistrust of the power-sharing between the Soviet Union and the United States, which they repudiated in the name of national independence.

In the last analysis, however, no real cooperation could be built up, though some no doubt thought it could. At the two Geneva conferences, France and China, both anxious to bring peace to Indochina and prevent foreign intervention, had identical interests that could lead to similar attitudes. In 1965, the harder line adopted by the Chinese on Vietnam was to render useless all French efforts to open a serious dialogue. Equally, the Chinese exclusion from the United Nations made all cooperation impossible at that level. Disarmament, accepted in principle on certain conditions that were not the same for both parties, was in fact rejected; it could never become the subject of a dialogue so long as neither government had completed its program of nuclear armament.

During the years following the recognition of January 27, 1964, France and its diplomatic mission in Peking were awarded no special privileges. French "colonialism" was in fact denounced with regard to Somalia and the West Indies. The cultural exchanges were useful mainly to the Chinese, both because they were backward in scientific and technical fields and because they refused to provide suitable conditions for qualified research students. A glance at the statistics of France, West Germany, and Great Britain shows that commercial benefits do not correspond to the intimacy of diplomatic relations.

The storms of the Cultural Revolution severely shook the illusions of Franco-Chinese friendship and further reduced the limited cooperation between the two states.

West Germany

During the first years of the regime, the Chinese often used the specter of German rearmament to evoke that of Japanese rearmament, both of which were encouraged by the United States. Equally, the Chinese denounced the political consequences of West Germany's and Japan's rapid recovery of economic power, particularly as far as the Third World was concerned. Later, because of the existence of two Germanies, the German question became an increasingly important element in the relations between China and the socialist bloc. Although Peking attacked the rapprochement between Bonn and Moscow, so as to add to Pankow's anxiety, it treated West

Germany with care, for it wanted to encourage all desires of independence from Washington.

As Nationalist China had done earlier, Communist China held German scientific and technical achievements in great respect, and the lack of diplomatic ties was no obstacle to a rapid growth in trade, which quickly outstripped the trade between France and China.[15]

The government of the German Federal Republic, faithful to the traditions of its predecessors, whom the Treaty of Versailles had deprived of exterritorial privileges and concessions, and restrained by the desire to avoid hurting Washington's feelings, abstained from all political initiatives and merely exchanged press correspondents.

International organizations

As a result of the Korean War and the continued existence of the Nationalist government in Taiwan, and in spite of certain proofs of moderation and its stress on the Five Principles of Peaceful Coexistence, the People's Republic of China had not been able to enter the United Nations between 1949 and 1956. It was no more successful between 1958 and 1966, when it had the support of many new African friends. Admittedly, Peking made no great effort in this direction. The spirit of the Great Leap Forward, when transposed to the field of foreign relations, created new reasons for tension and for adopting a defiant attitude toward the outside world.

On December 15, 1961, the Sixteenth Session of the General Assembly struck a serious blow at Peking's hopes by deciding for the first time that the question of Chinese representation was an "important question" requiring a two-thirds vote as stipulated by Article 18, Paragraph 2, of the Charter. On December 20, the Assembly adopted a resolution on the Tibetan question. Although the resolution was a moderate one, nothing could alter the fact that in the eyes of the Chinese the United Nations was interfering in Chinese internal affairs, thereby violating its Charter.

The Chinese made an energetic protest, attacking the organization as a "voting machine" in the hands of the United States. Later on, when Indonesia withdrew from the United Nations on January 7, 1965, Chou En-lai launched a series of terrible accusations against it and appeared to be on the point of setting up a rival "Revolutionary United Nations Organization," based on a Peking-Djakarta axis. Few observers let themselves be taken in by this comedy. The Chinese could not be unaware that the new nations of Asia and Africa prized and intended to retain a forum that enabled them to express their views in front of all the rest and to play a real role in international life. Nor could they be insensitive to the great advantages of a permanent seat on the Security Council, including the veto when the time came. In 1960, Foreign Minister Ch'en Yi had given a balanced summary of the Chinese position:

> We are convinced that U.S. imperialism's manipulations of the United Nations will sooner or later break down and that the Chiang Kai-shek gang will sooner or later be ousted from it. The lawful seat of the People's Republic of China in the United Nations will sooner or later be restored. This, of course, takes time. We are not in a hurry; we can wait. Under no circumstances will we barter away principles and sovereignty; any attempt to make a restoration of China's seat in the United Nations a bait for our acceptance of the "two Chinas" scheme is doomed to failure.[16]

China's aim was to enter the United Nations proudly, with the intention of becoming the spokesman of the Third World countries saved from the grip of both "imperialism" and "neo-revisionism," and from the power-sharing of the United States and the Soviet Union. All the rest was merely a disguise or a temporary tactic. In 1966, the Chinese Communists were convinced that the Taiwan question was the only obstacle remaining in the way of their entry to the United Nations. Once the United Nations stripped Taiwan of its rights to represent China and did not recognize it as the state of Taiwan, the question would virtually be solved. This certainty produced an attitude of ironic and hostile intransigence in Peking, which was justified by events five years later.

Disarmament

For a long time, China supported Soviet initiatives and theories on disarmament, suggesting occasionally the addition of a nuclear-free zone in the Pacific, which would then be rid of American bases. Kuo Mo-jo voiced these opinions in April 1958 and Chou En-lai made a resounding declaration on the subject at the Swiss Embassy on August 1, 1960.[17] The People's Republic of China supported the Geneva conference on disarmament (March 15, 1960) without actually taking part and on the understanding that only its signature could commit it. At the same time many of China's leaders were careful to point out in advance that they had no illusions, as long as "imperialism" continued to exist.[18] Propaganda and doctrine were thus reconciled.

The signing of the Moscow Treaty on the partial suspension of nuclear tests (July 25, 1963) gave the Chinese the opportunity to say what they really thought. This they did with extreme bluntness in three declarations, on July 31, August 15, and September 1. They attacked the about-face of the Soviet government, which after rejecting the draft treaty proposed by the United States and Great Britain on August 27, 1962, finally accepted it. This "treason" was at the same time a "trick" creating an "illusion of peace" and sanctioning an unacceptable monopoly of nuclear power. It was further proof that the Soviet leaders intended to ally themselves with the American leaders to impose their laws on the peoples of the world.

The Chinese government added its own proposals to this censure; these have until now constituted the official doctrine on disarmament: (1) Proclamation by all countries in the world on the prohibition and destruction of nuclear weapons; (2) removal of all foreign military bases; (3) creation of nuclear-free zones; (4) discontinuance of all tests and suppression of laboratories; and (5) convocation of a conference of the heads of government of all the countries in the world to carry out the above measures.[19]

The Chinese proposals were repeated in substance upon the announcement of the explosion of the first Chinese atom bomb on October 16, 1964. China recalled that it had always advocated the total destruction of nuclear weapons. The obduracy of American imperialism had forced it to make them in order to break Washington's monopoly. The announcement added: "The Chinese government solemnly declares that at no time and in no circumstances will China be the first to use nuclear weapons."

After stressing that the Chinese atomic bomb constituted both a great encouragement to all revolutionary peoples engaged in struggle and a considerable contribution to world peace, the Chinese government renewed its proposal that a summit conference of all countries in the world be called to discuss the prohibition and destruction of nuclear weapons. The aim was to disarm the critics among the nations that had signed the Moscow agreements and all those who might one day be disturbed by China's power.

The detonation of the second Chinese atomic bomb (May 14, 1965) was greeted by a more sober communiqué; the bomb's success was attributed to the Party's general line and to the thought of Mao Tse-tung. Chinese tests then became matters of routine and no longer gave rise to declarations of principle and intent. The Chinese have continued to refuse to take part in the lengthy negotiations of the Geneva conference on disarmament in spite of their progress and in spite of detailed suggestions. They have also refused to join the "nuclear club" of the five. This attitude is inspired by the need to preserve freedom of action, while also appearing to safeguard that of small countries without nuclear weapons. It is unlikely to be changed before China has, if not parity with the superpowers, at least adequate means to respond to any attack.

Notes

[1] English version published by the Foreign Languages Press (Peking, 1966). The official text of these declarations is said to be less strong than the original.

[2] See the Chinese declarations of April 12 and June 30 and the American declaration of April 14, 1958.

[3] Only those aspects of the events of the summer of 1958 that related strictly to the Chinese and the Americans have been summarized here. The Taiwan Strait crisis was an important moment in Sino-Soviet relations; Khrushchev's refusal to allow the Chinese to force his hand made a large contribution to their retreat from the crisis.

[4] See the *People's Daily* (May 20, 1960).

[5] In May 1960 the Foreign Languages Press published a selection with a significant title: *Two Tactics, One Aim.*

[6] Interview granted on October 11, 1961, to M. W. A. Cole, director of the Reuter Agency.

[7] Hsinhua Agency, January 23, 1962.

[8] The Cultural Revolution brought an interesting article to light on this subject, in which the caution of Lin Piao is opposed to a certain willingness to accept risks on the part of Lo Jui-ch'ing.

[9] Hsinhua Agency Supplement, No. 26 (August 9, 1963).

[10] At the same time, a text dated March 8, 1963, entitled "On the Declaration of the Communist Party of the United States of America," brought together a collection of attacks against American policy and is worth noting. It also constitutes a violent denunciation of the "revisionist" nature of the American Communist Party and its tendency to "prettify imperialism" and support presidents Eisenhower and Kennedy.

[11] *People's Daily* (May 13, 1966).

[12] See the article entitled "Old Airs, New Conspiracies," *People's Daily* (March 29, 1966).

[13] See, for example, "Look at Your Face in the Mirror!" *People's Daily* (November 12, 1962).

[14] Editorial of January 29, 1964, in the *People's Daily.* The text deserves to be quoted in full.

[15] To take 1966 as an example, West German exports amounted to $129.4 million and French exports reached $92.2 million. This difference became still larger during the years which followed, when West German exports were two or three times as important as French exports.

[16] *Peking Review* (June 1964); Ch'en Yi was replying to questions from a Japanese journalist.

[17] See interview with Kuo Mo-jo in *Shih-chieh chih-shih,* reprinted in *Peking Review* (April 15, 1958), and the declaration by Chou En-lai in *Peking Review* (August 9, 1960).

[18] Declaration by Teng Hsiao-p'ing on May 20, 1960, and declaration by Liu Ch'ang-sheng at the meeting of the General Council of the World Federation of Trade Unions, June 8, 1960.

[19] The above is a summary of the Chinese proposals, which figure in the declaration of July 31, 1963. The proposals were addressed to all heads of government in the form of a letter signed by Chou En-lai and dated August 2, 1963.

25 Foreign Policy 1958 – 1966 (4): The Socialist Bloc

All the waters of the Volga cannot wash
away the shame you have brought upon the
Communist Party of the Soviet Union and
upon the Soviet Union herself.

Statement by the Chinese, September 6, 1963

General development

The eight years that followed Mao Tse-tung's last visit to Moscow and the adherence of the People's Republic of China to the Common Program of the twelve Communist and Workers' Parties in power (November 1957) witnessed the consummation of a gradual but final ideological break between China and the Soviet Union and the growing weakness of the political, economic, and cultural links between the two countries. Several times a break in diplomatic relations appeared imminent. Sometimes, on the other hand, particularly after the Conference of Eighty-One Communist and Workers' Parties in October and November 1960 and at the departure of Khrushchev in October 1964, it seemed that everything could still be patched up once more.

This was not so, however. The Maoist version of Marxism-Leninism asserted itself more strongly and became more clearly defined. Conflicts between national interests accumulated, intensified during the Cultural Revolution, and resulted in military confrontations, which, though localized, still awakened old, forgotten fears among the Russians and earned China its political emancipation from the socialist bloc.

Yugoslav revisionism

The ideological debate resumed in the spring and early summer of 1958, in a roundabout way, by means of Yugoslav affairs. Several extremely violent articles in the *People's Daily* were quickly followed by two major texts contributed by the two most experienced theorists of the Party, Ch'en Po-ta ("Yugoslav Revisionism is the Product of Imperialist Policy," June 1) and K'ang Sheng ("Yugoslav Revisionism Replies Exactly to the Needs of the U.S. Imperialism," June 14). These attacks, apparently motivated by the tension that was beginning to mount once more between Moscow and Belgrade, were handled by the Chinese in such a way as to constitute a warning to the Soviet leaders.[1]

The crises in the Near East and the Taiwan Strait

A few weeks later, Mao and Khrushchev found themselves face to face, as a result of the crisis between Lebanon and Jordan. Khrushchev, who paid an unexpected visit to Peking (July 31 to August 3), wanted it to be settled by the United Nations. Because China was not a member, India was to take its place on the Security Council. The suggestion was doubly repellent to the Chinese, and they turned it down bluntly. Khrushchev had to reverse gears, but he made things worse by suggesting the creation of a joint naval command in the Far East, a proposal that Mao interpreted as an attempt to control Chinese initiatives in that part of the world and as a breach of Chinese sovereignty.[2]

The Chinese, perhaps encouraged by Khrushchev's rash proposals, or more probably wanting to show that they too could act independently, forcing the Russians to take their part, decided to act alone to test American intentions by pretending to want to seize the coastal islands of Quemoy and Matsu, which served as advance posts for Taiwan. The reactions of Washington and pressure from Moscow combined to make Peking renounce the project. Although Russo-Chinese solidarity was ostensibly reaffirmed by Khrushchev's letter of September 7 to President Eisenhower, the fact remained that the Russians had let China down and it had suffered first an affront and then a diplomatic defeat. The granting of further Soviet economic aid in the form of forty-seven new "projects" (making a total of 258) and the signing of several scientific, technical, and commercial agreements could not make up for these secret wounds to China's national pride.[3]

The Twenty-First Congress of the CPSU and the Camp David spirit

The year 1959 began with the Twenty-First Congress of the CPSU, which was mainly devoted to the seven-year plan of the Soviet Union. Chou En-lai led the Chinese delegation. He spoke in terms of unity, in spite of sabotage, as he put it, by American imperialists and Yugoslav revisionists, and gave a modest justification of the people's communes (January 28). Additional Soviet aid, covering seventy-eight projects and accompanied by a loan of 500 million rubles (February 7) was added to the economic collaboration between the two countries and was particularly valuable to the Chinese in the light of their hopes for the Great Leap Forward.

Until Khrushchev's visit to the United States (September 15 to 28) and his meeting with President Eisenhower at Camp David, Sino-Soviet relations were ostensibly good. Subjects for mutual discontent were taking shape, however. Khrushchev's hostile remarks on the people's communes at Warsaw in July, the elimination of P'eng Teh-huai just after he had led a military mission to the Soviet Union from April to June 1959 (the influence of his hosts was apparent a month or two later at Lushan), and Soviet neutrality on the Sino-Indian frontier question (Tass statement of September 9, 1959) helped to prepare the way for another confrontation.

That confrontation took place on September 30 and October 4 when Khrushchev, fresh from his trip to the United States, paid his third visit to Peking for the tenth anniversary of the regime. He was still full of the Camp David spirit and advised the Chinese against "testing by force the stability of the capitalist system."[4] He tried to soothe their impatience over Taiwan by reminding them of the precedent of the Far Eastern Republic at the end of World War I. The Chinese refused to be associated with his statements, and various foreign witnesses reported on the extremely cold relations between the two men, which persisted until the first secretary of the Communist Party of the Soviet Union departed. Appearances were still maintained, however, and Khrushchev's success in the United States was praised as an important contribution to world peace, on the understanding that it was primarily a result of pressure from the masses on the American leaders. On December 21, the *People's Daily* took the opportunity offered by the eightieth anniversary of the birth of Stalin, who was "the implacable enemy of imperialism" and, in spite of his errors, "the artisan of the great successes won by the Soviet Union over the last forty-two years," to publish an article calculated to irritate the Soviet Union, which was passed over without comment.

The skirmishes of 1960; withdrawal of Russian advisers

The year 1960 brought the Chinese great satisfaction on the two closely linked questions of war and détente. K'ang Sheng, the Chinese observer at the conference of the Political Consultative Committee of the Warsaw Treaty Organization, made a violent attack on the leaders of the United States, their feigned pacificism, their dream of "peaceful evolution" of the socialist countries, and their repeated sabotage of disarmament. Several aggressive articles had already appeared to revive mistrust of imperialism and to show the need to support "just wars"; Lenin, whose ninetieth anniversary it was, was called to the rescue in a long and important article by the editorial committee of *Red Flag* entitled "Long Live Leninism!"[5] A few days later, the U2 affair (May 1), which aborted the Paris conference, came at precisely the right moment to justify the Chinese in advising caution and mistrust. Although they tactfully supported Khrushchev, now the wiser for his experience, against Eisenhower, they could not resist the chance to teach him a lesson: "We have always supported talks, but never have we nourished the slightest illusion as to the possibility of achieving a lasting peace through negotiations alone," said Teng Hsiao-p'ing. In June, the conference of the World Federation of Trade Unions in Peking (June 5-9) witnessed a fencing match between the Russian delegate and the Chinese delegate, Liu Ch'ang-sheng, who warned his listeners against the error of thinking that war could be eliminated as long as imperialism contined to exist, for only the triumph of socialism in the world could lead to general and complete disarmament.

The disagreement at the Third Congress of the Rumanian Workers' Party in Bucharest from June 24 to 26 was much more serious. Khrushchev, who was determined to pursue his policy of coexistence, launched a "surprise attack," backed by eighty pages of documents, against the Chinese Communist Party, denouncing in insulting terms its bellicosity, leftism, nationalism, and "Trotsky-like" methods of action with regard to the CPSU. P'eng Chen, the Chinese delegate, replied with a protest against the abusive use to which the CPSU put its credit when imposing its will on the other parties and disagreed with several opinions expressed by Khrushchev (June 26); but he signed the communiqué of the meeting, "out of consideration for the general situation."

Although the controversy seemed to be dying down, Russian technicians began to leave China in July 1960. The exodus involved 1,390 specialists, scattered among 250 enterprises. A roughly equivalent number of Chinese students and trainees in the Soviet Union also returned home. All the agreements for scientific and technical cooperation (343 contracts and 257 projects) were suspended. Two newspapers, one published in China by the Russians, the other in Russia by the Chinese, were suppressed. As the Chinese put it, the ideological quarrel had moved into the realm of state relations.

The Conference of Eighty-One Communist and Workers' Parties

The Conference of Eighty-One Communist and Workers' Parties, held in Moscow from November 11 to 25, 1960, brought a new brief rapprochement. The CPSU admitted that coexistence ought not to exclude armed revolutionary action and that wars of aggression remained a possibility as long as imperialism persisted. The Chinese delegation, led by Liu Shaoch'i and Teng Hsiao-p'ing, acknowledged that war between states was not inevitable and that some forms of the passage from capitalism to socialism could be peaceful. Dogmatism and revisionism received similar condemnation, the second slightly more than the first.[6] For the Chinese public, a great victory of unity in the Communist world, of Sino-Soviet friendship, had been won. It was now merely a question of defending world peace, which was threatened by the contradictions and difficulties among the imperialists.[7]

The year 1961 was dominated by the pacifying effects of the conference and the disasters that had dealt a serious blow to Chinese exports—in other words, commercial compensation for Soviet aid. It was a year full of practical activities with virtually no political and ideological controversies. In April, the Russians agreed to defer repayment of the sums owed by the Chinese, spreading them over five years. The Chinese, who still owed $320 million to the Soviet Union and were spending $340 million more to buy grain abroad, were in a difficult situation.

The Twenty-Second Congress of the CPSU

The Twenty-Second Congress of the Communist Party of the Soviet Union met in Moscow from October 17 to 31, 1961, and gave rise to some unexpected incidents. On October 17, the Chinese delegates, Chou En-lai, P'eng Chen, T'ao Chu, and K'ang Sheng, left their seats to avoid shaking hands with Khrushchev, whose report on the activities of the Central Committee had just criticized Stalin and sharply attacked the Albanians.[8]

Two days later, Chou En-lai attacked the way in which the first secretary of the CPSU had handled relations with the Albanian Workers' Party. He reproached Khrushchev for making these statements at the congress of one party alone, not during a debate in which all fraternal parties were involved. Then, on October 23, after having ostentatiously placed a wreath on Stalin's tomb two days earlier, Chou En-lai left P'eng Chen in charge of the delegation and went back to Peking. This gesture resulted in the removal (which had been under consideration) of Stalin's body from the Lenin mausoleum in Red Square. The Albanian affair gave China an ally in the West, but it set the ideological and political quarrel going once more; the point of no return was reached in 1962 and 1963.

Serious frontier incidents, unknown to the rest of the world at the time, took place in the spring of 1962. Tens of thousands of Kazakhs in the Ili region of China crossed the frontier into the neighboring Soviet state of Kazakhstan at the instigation of the Russians, who, the Chinese claimed, refused to send them back.[9] Chinese persecutions of local nationalists and the effects of collectivization, which the local population accepted less willingly there than in China proper, were behind these migrations, which were made relatively easy by the geographical setting.

A Sino-Soviet commercial agreement was signed on August 28, but it was mainly concerned with suspended accounts; China soon made it a point of honor to pay all its Soviet debts before they were due.

The Cuban crisis

The Cuban crisis in the autumn was a godsend to the Chinese, for two reasons. It enabled them to condemn "American imperialism," the blockade, and the armed provocations aimed at revolutionary Cuba (statement of October 23) and later to denounce the errors, pusillanimity, and then the "capitulationism" of the "revisionists"; Khrushchev received special blame for his capriciousness and adventurism.[10]

The controversies of winter 1962-1963

At the congresses of the Bulgarian Communist Party (November 5-14), the Hungarian Socialist Workers' Party (November 20-24) and the Czechoslovak Communist Party (December 4-8), the Chinese put up a vigorous defense against accusations of sectarianism and nationalism and, while still making passes at the Yugoslav shadow, came to grips with Russian substance; they attacked both Soviet policy and Soviet doctrine.

Then, between December 15, 1962, and March 8, 1963, a first series of seven explicit articles appeared in the *People's Daily* and *Hung ch'i:* "Proletarians of All Countries Unite Against the Common Enemy" (December 15, 1962); "The Differences Between Comrade Togliatti and Us" (December 31, 1962); "Leninism and Modern Revisionism" (January 5, 1963); "Let Us Unite Under the Banner of the Moscow Declaration and Statement" (January 27, 1963); "Where the Differences Come From: A Reply to Maurice Thorez" (February 27, 1963); "More on the Differences Between Comrade Togliatti and Us" (March 4, 1963); "Comments on the Statement of the Communist Party of the United States" (March 8, 1963).

A little later two articles appeared that were particularly concerned with the attitude of the socialist camp to the Indian question: "A Mirror for Revisionists" (March 9, 1963); "The Truth about How the Leaders of the CPSU have Allied Themselves with India Against China" (November 2, 1963).

All these documents define Peking's fundamental position on many questions, contributing many revelations or confirmations of the real state of Sino-Soviet relations. In the name of the unity that ought to be maintained against the enemies of Communism, the Chinese had reproached the Soviet Union at the Twenty-Second Congress with bringing their differences with Albania into the open. In their turn, they gave unrestrained vent to their feelings. Their bitterness and grievances went far beyond ideology and were no doubt exacerbated by the scandal that took place during the Sixth Congress of the East German United Socialist Party (January 15-21, 1963). While the Chinese delegate Wu Hsiu-ch'üan was denouncing the Yugoslavs, he was suddenly interrupted by "a din of booing, whistling and stamping."[11] Within the socialist camp, the Chinese appeared not only isolated but increasingly unpopular.

The crisis of summer 1963; the Chinese letter in twenty-five points

Another attempt at reconciliation was made during the summer of 1963. Although the Chinese continued to publish the texts just mentioned, while also publishing many of the theses and attacks of their enemies and raining insults on Khrushchev, Mao Tse-tung received the Soviet ambassador, Tchervonenko, on February 23. The ambassador delivered a letter from the CPSU (dated February 21) proposing a meeting between representatives of the two parties.[12] The Chinese Central Committee accepted on March 9.[13] On March 30, the Russians suggested that the meeting be held on July 5, in Moscow. Peking agreed.

On June 14, the Chinese took a step carefully calculated to lead either to a Russian capitulation or to an open ideological break; this took the form of a letter in twenty-five points, which was intended as a reply to the opinions stated in the Russian letter dated March 30. The Chinese letter, entitled "A Proposal Concerning the General Line of the International Communist Movement," summarized Peking's positions on a series of fundamental questions, making frequent references to the declaration of 1957 and the statement of 1960, but above all it attacked, albeit indirectly, Soviet positions on numerous points of doctrine (peaceful coexistence, peaceful competition) or practical questions (the Albanian affair, relations of equality and reciprocity between "fraternal parties").

The refusal of the Russians and other members of the socialist camp to allow the circulation of the letter of June 14 on their territory, and the incidents engendered by Chinese attempts to circulate it in Moscow and Berlin, ensured that the conference would take place in an unfavorable atmosphere.[14]

Nevertheless, the meeting began on the appointed day. Teng Hsiao-p'ing, P'eng Chen, K'ang Sheng, Yang Shang-k'un, Liu Ning-yi, Wu Hsiu-ch'üan and P'an Tzu-li made up the Chinese delegation. On July 14, the Russians in their turn replied to the letter of June 14 with "unbridled" attacks, in the words of the Chinese. On July 20, the talks were adjourned. The Chinese delegation returned home almost immediately.

The basic reason for the failure of the meeting was clearly the irreducible gap between the real positions of the two parties, with their different interpretations of doctrinal formulas common to both (those of the declaration of 1957 and the statement of 1960) or at least similar. The immediate cause was the prospect of the treaty shortly to be signed by the British, the Americans, and the Russians on the partial suspension of nuclear tests (treaty of July 25), which Peking tried in vain to oppose. It would have been extremely humiliating for the Chinese to be in Moscow at the same time as the Western parties to the agreement. Their resentment and their point of view were fully expressed in the statement published on July 31 (see Chapter 24).

After the failure of the meeting, the controversy continued at a slower rate, though it remained just as vigorous in form and content, revealing conflicts between the two states as well as the two parties. A Chinese declaration (August 15) asserted that the Russians were contradicting themselves and denounced the Soviet wish to monopolize nuclear weapons in the socialist camp. On this subject, the statement revealed an astonishing secret—the refusal of the Soviet Union to honor its military commitments to China.

> As far back as June 20, 1959, when there was not yet the slightest sign of a treaty on stopping nuclear tests, the Soviet government unilaterally tore up the agreement on new technology for national defense concluded between China and the Soviet Union on October 15, 1957, and refused to provide China with a sample of an atomic bomb and technical data concerning its manufacture. This was done as a presentation gift at the time the Soviet leader went to the United States for talks with Eisenhower in September.[15]

The motives behind Soviet caution were probably many, such as the possibility of a future international agreement against the dissemination of nuclear weapons, anxiety about the Chinese initiative in the Taiwan Strait in 1958, and the conviction that the Chinese were becoming more hostile toward the Soviet Union. In any case, the Chinese were left with the feeling that they had been betrayed both as allies and as Communists: "The Soviet leaders' betrayal of the Soviet people, of the countries in the socialist camp, and of the people in the whole world cannot be denied."[16]

The statement of August 15 was a mere beginning. It was followed over the next year by a series of nine documents, all in reply to the Russian letter of July 14, 1963, which shed further light on the chief points in the controversy, sometimes very crudely indeed. They were titled: "The Origin and Development of the Differences Between the Leadership of the CPSU and Ourselves" (September 6, 1963); "On the Question of Stalin" (September 13, 1963); "Is Yugoslavia a Socialist Country?" (September 26, 1963); "Apologists of Neo-colonialism" (October 22, 1963); "Two Different Lines on the Question of War and Peace" (November 19, 1963); "Peaceful Coexistence—Two Diametrically Opposed Policies" (December 12, 1963); "The Leaders of the CPSU are the Greatest Splitters of Our Time" (February 4, 1964); "The Proletarian Revolution and Khrushchev's Revisionism" (March 31, 1964); and "On Khrushchev's Phony Communism and Its Historical Lessons for the World" (July 14, 1964). These materials are of course equally valuable for the history of the socialist movement and for Chinese history.

In vain the Soviet Union suggested, on November 29, 1963, that the polemics be brought to an end, that various frontier questions be settled by friendly discussions, and even that its specialists return to China. The Chinese insolently rejected these suggestions (letter of February 23, 1964), spurned a further appeal in March, and did not hesitate to reopen the quarrel with the publication of several volumes of extracts hostile to China from the Soviet press. Then in May 1964, the Chinese published the text of seven letters exchanged with the Russians from November 1963 on. The style of the four letters written by the Chinese Communist Party stands out as particularly tough, sarcastic, and insulting.

From the autumn of 1963 to the summer of 1964, Sino-Soviet relations were dominated by the question of the calling of a conference of Communist and Workers' Parties, proposed by Khrushchev, who was more determined than ever to have the Chinese doctrines and leaders condemned, so as to restore obedience and unity within the socialist camp. This plan failed because of the centrifugal tendencies of the Italians, the reluctance of the Rumanians, and the embarrassment it caused to the Asian parties (the Japanese and the Vietnamese). After a number of dilatory maneuvers, the Chinese refused categorically to be associated with a general meeting, going so far as to abstain from attending a meeting of delegates of the twenty-six Communist and Workers' Parties belonging to the drafting committee of the 1960 conference. The Conference of the Twenty-Six was eventually held from March 1 to 15, 1965, under the title of a consultative conference; nineteen parties were represented there, but it broke up without setting a date for the general conference and without producing any important texts. The *People's Daily* condemned it as illegal and schismatic and announced that it intended to continue the relentless public denunciation of modern revisionism and its agents.[17] Meanwhile, the prospect of further confrontations within the international Communist movement had led the Russians to launch a vigorous ideological and political counteroffensive against the Chinese, summarized in the Suslov Report of February 14, 1964.[18] Along with the testimony of Palmiro Togliatti, published on September 4, 1964, the Suslov Report was one of the two authoritative documents of the period as regards the Communist movement in general and all aspects of Sino-Soviet relations in particular.

A violent confrontation between the Chinese and the Russians at the March 1964 Afro-Asian People's Solidarity Conference at Algiers, a quarrel as to whether or not the Russians should join in the second Bandung conference, planned for the summer of 1965, Khrushchev's cruel taunts about China's poverty and pretensions, and several articles in *Pravda* helped to make the atmosphere heavier still.[19] Quarrels between individuals, ideologies, and states became intermingled. Mao Tse-tung, in a remark already mentioned, brought up the Siberian frontier question when speaking privately to a delegation of Japanese Diet members (July 10). The Chinese reprinted all of Khrushchev's pro-Stalin speeches and opportunistic speeches in August 1964; in the same month, they also published the last pamphlet attacking him in the series already mentioned, "On Khrushchev's Phony Communism and Its Historical Lessons for the World."

The successors of Khrushchev

A few weeks later the Chinese had the immense pleasure of seeing their constant enemy fall from grace; the first Chinese atomic explosion, which followed two days afterward seemed to celebrate their victory like a gigantic fireworks display. As a political figure, Khrushchev, "that inveterate conspirator who usurped the leadership of Party and state in the Soviet Union," was quickly trampled underfoot, and the moral of all this was drawn to serve as a warning to his successors. The pamphlet "Why Khrushchev Fell" was a long catalogue of reproaches: "his hostility toward socialist China, which he wanted to overturn" and "his hatred of the Communist Party and Comrade Mao Tse-tung" figured large among them.[20]

After a calm period lasting several months, probably intended to put the new CPSU leadership to the test, and a meeting between Kosygin and Mao in Peking (February 10, 1965), the Chinese attacks began again. Almost everything there was to be said on the substance of the quarrel had come out in 1963 and 1964. The Chinese merely threw discredit on Khrushchev's successors, who practiced his policies after his fall: "The Triumph of Leninism" (April 22, 1965); "Carry the Struggle against Khrushchev Revisionism Through to the End" (June 14, 1965); "On Unity of Action in the New Leadership of the CPSU" (November 11, 1965); "The Leaders of the CPSU are Traitors to the Two Moscow Declarations" (December 30, 1965).

The last important gesture that the Chinese made before the Cultural Revolution was to refuse an invitation to attend the Twenty-Third Congress of the Communist Party of the Soviet Union, although they took the opportunity to denounce the plot hatching between Washington and Moscow to dominate the world (March 1966).

The substance of the controversies

Between 1958 and 1966, as in the preceding period, the ideological controversies between Moscow and Peking and their respective standpoints concealed national aims. The same political problems are always to be found underlying the words, whose style was sober in the case of the Russians and impassioned in that of the Chinese, a difference that may be explained by the difference in maturity of the two parties, as well as by the Chinese sense of the dramatic. First came the question of détente, which was disguised by other names—coexistence, peaceful competition, peaceful transition to socialism. Then came that of the leadership of the socialist camp, involving the independence or equality of the parties. Last came the questions arising from the Third World. Behind them loomed others that sometimes stood out clearly and were more specific and easier to name— Taiwan, Japan, Southeast Asia, the United Nations, disarmament, economic and military relations. Above all these hovered the redoubtable personality of Mao Tse-tung, both compliant and inflexible, head of state and also already the equal of Lenin, through his contribution to doctrine and his influence on the international revolutionary movement.

The presentation and analysis of the divergencies are further complicated by the projection of concrete problems on an ideological plane. The observer, however, unlike the principals, does not have to follow blindly the conventions of language. For this reason, it is best to try to translate Chinese doctrines and positions into political terms first, setting aside the Russian counterpropositions, since to expose and comment on the latter is beyond the scope of this book. Looking at things from the broadest viewpoint possible, the gradual movement of the Soviet Union toward ending the cold war and establishing a state of détente and collaboration with the West amply explains the deterioration in its relations with China. A détente, combined with the balance created by the fear of nuclear weapons, was leading the world toward a Soviet-American sharing of power, which China, a superpower in terms of area, population, resources, and history, could not accept. Even if this sharing of power was imaginary or confined to the future, détente weakened the Chinese position in the socialist camp and in the world as a whole. It sacrificed Chinese aims to those of the Russians. It reduced their role as allies, either in an eventual military conflict or in terms of revolutionary expansion. Under the guise of economic competition, détente helped reclassify all nations according to their productive capacity and standard of living; in some cases, it even brought about closer ties between states having a common need for trade; it also took into consideration historical, cultural, and moral traditions held in common by some nations. It meant that China would have a harder time obtaining benefits from "proletarian solidarity" in the form of financial aid and technical assistance.

Basically, détente involved the United States, with which China was in direct confrontation over Taiwan, Southeast Asia, Japan, and the United Nations. The risk was that most of these questions would be frozen for a long time and that others would move toward a point of no return. Détente was also bound to diminish China's political and ideological influence in the developing countries. Peking felt it had a mission to these countries to provide inspiration, drawn from its own experience and codified by Mao Tse-tung, and could not hope to rival the great industrialized countries in terms of economics.

China also feared, as the West hoped, that détente would gradually lead to a progressive liberalization within the socialist camp as a whole, presumably beginning with the European satellite states and ending with China. China, however, had entered a hard period, a phase of great internal tension needed to ensure the convergence and control of its efforts toward construction. No relaxation was acceptable; the resounding failure of the Hundred Flowers had provided ample proof.

The refusal of the Chinese to accept détente was expressed by the particular meaning they gave to peaceful coexistence and its other side, the problem of peace and war. Peaceful coexistence implied the recognition of the existence of other states with whom the absence of war justified the establishment of political, economic, commercial, and sometimes cultural relations. These relations should never be allowed to obscure ideology and revolutionary targets. The necessary compromises had one aim only, that of helping the construction of socialism at home and of unmasking and isolating the aggressive and war-mongering forces of imperialism abroad. Peaceful coexistence should be clearsighted and intransigent, never sacrificing the interests of peoples to those of governments, never slowing down the class struggle in the capitalist countries. Lastly, peaceful coexistence should never be extended to include relations between oppressed peoples and their oppressors.

To help put such a rigid theory into practice, the Chinese took it on themselves to draw up numerous and subtle distinctions between socialist and capitalist countries, between nationalist and "imperialist" countries, beween "imperialist" countries and capitalist countries in general, and also between different "imperialist" countries.[21]

The problem of peace and war was treated in a similar way. War was not to be sought after, but its possibility was not to be denied so long as "imperialism" lasted. Above all, blackmail with a view to war was not to be given in to, but was to be resisted by uniting all possible forces for common action—socialist forces, democratic forces, and liberation forces—for in the long run, when faced with the masses of the whole world, "imperialism" was nothing but a "paper tiger." This doctrine was in complete opposition to the cooperation between the two great nuclear powers, the United States and the Soviet Union, which aimed at settling world problems and preventing war.

The Chinese attitude toward a possible nuclear war was optimistic, contrary to the pessimistic view of Togliatti, for whom the atom bomb transcended ideologies. They thought that "the appearance of nuclear weapons has not and cannot modify the fundamental principles of Marxism-Leninism concerning war and peace";[22] they believed that another world war would inevitably bring the end of imperialism and the victory of socialism. In their estimation of war, the Chinese gave priority to "just wars"—wars of national liberation and revolutionary civil wars that strengthen the masses and the socialist camp; for these, greater risks must be taken. In fact, as they put it, to oppose mobilizing the masses against the nuclear blackmail of "American imperialism" and to oppose revolutionary wars means to oppose the revolution itself. Experience has proved that such wars do not lead to generalized war.

In reality, the Chinese based their behavior not on doctrine, but on relative strength; in this, they differed little from other states in the world. Their daring vis-à-vis India and their caution everywhere else are proof enough. It is to be hoped that this will always be so.[23]

The most important question after that of détente was that of the leadership of the socialist camp; the crisis of 1963 gave abundant proof that the Conference of Twelve Communist and Workers' Parties in power held in 1957 had not provided a satisfactory answer to it (see Chapter 16). The statement of 1960 merely underlined the avant-garde nature of the Communist Party of the Soviet Union, but the Albanian affair at the Twenty-Second Congress of the CPSU, like the letter in twenty-five points of June 14, 1963, showed that in the eyes of the Chinese this did not call for subordination. The Chinese Communist Party made it clear that a national Party could be bound only be resolutions that it had signed following free discussions held during an international meeting. Resolutions passed by the congress of this or that Party could not be considered binding by the other Parties, even if they had sent a delegation to attend the congress.

The Chinese pointed out that the acknowledgment of a majority and a minority would bring with it the legalization of splinter group activities, which would be capable both of breaking the unity of the international Communist movement and of disrupting the unity of each party. They also thought that a national congress should not be allowed to provide the opportunity for attacks on another Party and that differences should not be made public. They also asked, obviously with the withdrawal of the Russian specialists in mind, that ideological disagreements should not affect relations between states.

On the whole, the Chinese position appeared to arise from a wish for complete independence, but it can also be explained by the fact that the Chinese Communist Party was in the minority within the international movement. The Communist Party of the Soviet Union, traditionally the object of respect, saw itself as being given only moral or material responsibilities for the solidarity of the proletariat but no corresponding rights. Its political, military, and economic strength gave it special weight, however, which could do without formal acknowledgment.

The premature optimism of the parties who signed the statement of 1960 as regards relations between socialist states is worth noting: "One of the greatest achievements of the world socialist system is the practical confirmation of the Marxist-Leninist thesis that national antagonisms diminish with the decline of class antagonisms."

For the Chinese, the first and most urgent task of the developing countries was still to continue the struggle against "imperialism, colonialism, and neo-colonialism." It took priority over the economic problem, in spite of the latter's importance. The Chinese Communist Party accused the Soviet Party of having given priority to peaceful coexistence and peaceful competition, substituting them for revolutionary struggle, or practicing a dubious and often selfish and chauvinistic policy of economic aid, of cooperating with the Americans in helping backward countries, and of relying on the United Nations for the elimination of colonial regimes.

The official Chinese viewpoint was naturally in line with the history of the Chinese Communist movement. Unlike the revolution in the Soviet Union, which was essentially an internal phenomenon, the Chinese revolution, which brought together Nationalists and Communists, turned first of all against foreign domination. The Chinese Communist Party, reduced to nothing after the Long March, resumed its growth during the eight years of struggle against the Japanese invasion. The viewpoint also corresponded to the doctrine that the Chinese had developed out of their own experience and for which they sought recognition. The abandonment of revolutionary struggles deprived them of a powerful historical, moral, and ideological argument in their political action. Because of its low level of economic development, China could not successfully enter into the economic relations—including aid—that existed between the great powers and the Third World. China's frustration was increased by the fact that the Asian part of the Third World to which the Soviet Union, the United States and the former colonial powers all paid equal attention, directly affected Chinese interests. Khrushchev's visit to Indonesia and India in February 1960 and the sizable Soviet aid granted to India and Burma could only displease Peking.

Racial antagonism, which placed China on the same side as the developing countries (although in this respect the Chinese were inclined to have an attitude of superiority because of their history), helped to intensify the rivalry between China and the Soviet Union in the Third World.

China also wished for military independence, while retaining the cover of security agreements with the Soviet Union, whose nuclear protection was to remain indispensable for some time to come. The Chinese refused to be integrated within the Russian defense system; at the same time, they accused the Russians of having broken their promise to contribute to the creation of a Chinese atomic weapons industry. Peking could be forgiven for its lack of logic in view of the sacred nature of national interest, but the same latitude could not be allowed to Moscow, where the ideological solidarity of the socialist camp was soon to find its political expression of the theory of "limited sovereignty."

The Chinese opposition to disarmament as understood by the Russians and the Americans was also aimed at obtaining complete freedom of action in their foreign policy, hence their refusal to sign the Moscow Treaty on the Nonproliferation of Nuclear Weapons of July 25, 1963, which came into force on August 5. Their aim was naturally camouflaged beneath the doctrinal affirmation of the unchangeably "ferocious" nature of imperialism. As a result, Chinese nuclear development could be presented not as a national necessity, but as an indispensable contribution to the revolutionary movement in general and to world peace.

The claim of independence for each state in its way of building socialism and the negation of the principle of "international division of labor" (which should not, even so, exclude disinterested aid given in a spirit of proletarian internationalism) were also the ideological translation of an obvious Chinese interest. It found expression in the refusal to join

Comecon, in the unorthodox formula of the people's communes, and the slogan of "self-reliance," to cite a few examples.

Chinese opposition to de-Stalinization and to the Russian tendency to "place the leader and the masses in opposition to one another" can be explained by the personality of Mao Tse-tung. The letter in twenty-five points (June 14, 1963) made an allusion that was very far-reaching in this respect:

> What is more serious is that, under the pretext of "combating the cult of the individual," certain persons are crudely interfering in the internal affairs of other fraternal parties and fraternal countries and forcing other fraternal parties to change their leadership in order to impose their own wrong line on these parties.

Could the Chinese really have been thinking only of Enver Hoxha?

Toward the middle of 1966, Sino-Soviet relations underwent a great change. The alliance of February 14, 1950, placing China under Soviet military protection was still in existence, but during the ideological controversy its limits became more sharply defined and the whole became more precarious. The Chinese were aware of this. They avoided initiatives that involved a risk, and let their foreign interventions go no further than verbal assurances, maintaining illusions by their forceful style. At the same time they continued to direct their national defense, placed in the hands of the masses and the artisans of a modern striking force, along increasingly defensive lines.

In compensation for this political restraint, the Chinese conducted antirevisionist ideological action in all countries and in all Communist Parties throughout the world. Dissident factions had already been created here and there; they were described as Marxist-Leninist to show where their orthodoxy lay. Some Asian and European parties, without necessarily sharing the Chinese views, were sympathetic toward the idea of independence and unwilling to contribute to a break in the international Communist movement. This was so in the case of the Rumanian Workers' Party, and in that of Communist Parties in Asia. The latter, depending on the margin for maneuver inherent in their geographical and economic situations, equivocated and hesitated between the two currents. In the West, the Italian Communist Party, led by Togliatti and his successors, actively defended the decentralization and diversification of the international Communist movement in order to preserve its fundamental unity.

The Chinese ruined the earliest results by attacking their own Party and giving an image of their situation and their aims that was often incomprehensible and always misleading. One thing alone seemed certain during the troubled years that followed—a greater hostility than ever on the part of the Chinese leaders toward those of the Soviet Union, an ideological hatred later transformed by the military confrontations on the Ussuri into a national hatred.

Notes

[1] See the editorials of May 5 against Yugoslavia and those of June 4 and 25 against revisionism and neutralism.

[2] The article "The Origin and Development of the Differences Between the Leadership of the CPSU and Ourselves," *People's Daily* (September 6, 1963) merely said: "In 1958, the leadership of the CPSU put forward unreasonable demands designed to bring China under Soviet military control. These unreasonable demands were rightly and firmly rejected by the Chinese government." But at the Tenth Plenum (September 24, 1962) Mao Tse-tung stated: "From the second half of 1958, he [Khrushchev] has attempted to block the China seacoast, to launch a joint fleet in China to dominate the coastal area, and to blockade us. Khrushchev came to China because of this problem." See the English version in "Chinese Law and Government," *IASP Journal of Translations* 1, No. 4 (1969). Khrushchev, in his *Khrushchev Remembers* (Boston: Little Brown, 1971), p. 447, only mentions the building, on Chinese territory, of a radio station for the purpose of liaison with the Soviet submarine fleet.

[3] These were chiefly an agreement on technological questions (January 18), an agreement on scientific and technical cooperation (April 25), and a trade and navigation treaty (April 23).

[4] See "The Origin and Development of the Differences Between the Leadership of the CPSU and Ourselves" (September 6, 1963).

[5] *Hung ch'i* No. 8 (April 16, 1960).

[6] The list of mistaken theses, which were left out of the draft declaration, is especially interesting for the study of the evolution of the Communist revolutionary movement. See "The Origin and Development of the Differences Between the Leadership of the CPSU and Ourselves."

[7] See particularly *People's Daily*, editorials on December 7 and 12, 1960.

[8] The tension between Tirana and Moscow since 1961 worsened after the Fourth Congress of the Albanian Party in February. Like the tension between Moscow and Peking, it was followed by total suspension of Soviet aid, which was replaced by Chinese aid, while Soviet submarines left the base at Valona.

[9] Nearly 60,000 people between April and August 1962, according to George Moseley, "A Sino-Soviet Cultural Frontier, the Ili Kazakh Autonomous *Chou*," *Harvard East Asian Monographs* (Cambridge, Mass., 1966).

[10] For a doctrinal anti-revisionist view, see "Defend the Purity of Marxism," *Hung ch'i* (November 16, 1962).

[11] See "Let Us Unite Under the Banner of the Moscow Declaration and Statement," *People's Daily* (January 27, 1963).

[12] Published in the *People's Daily* on April 4.

[13] Hsinhua Agency, March 14.

[14] Three members of the Chinese embassy in Moscow and two Chinese students in the Soviet Union were expelled by the Russians for their part in the circulation.

[15] English Text in *Peking Review* (August 1963).

[16] English text in *Peking Review* (August 1963).

[17] "A Comment on the March Moscow Meeting," *People's Daily* (March 23, 1965).

[18] The report, presented to the Central Committee of the CPSU, was not published in the Soviet press until April 3.

[19] In particular the speech by Khrushchev on April 15, 1964, when Gomulka visited Moscow.

[20] *Hung ch'i*, No. 21-22 (November 1964).

[21] See in particular "Peaceful Coexistence: Two Diametrically Opposed Policies" (December 12, 1963).

[22] "The Differences Between Comrade Togliatti and Us," *People's Daily* (December 31, 1962).

[23] To the Chinese views on the possibilities of nuclear war, the Russians replied that if the nature of imperialism is like that of the tiger, and unchanging, the socialist elephant, a peaceful animal that does not attack others, is so powerful that even the tiger has respect for its strength.

Part 4

The Socialist Education Movement and the Cultural Revolution and Its Aftermath 1962 – 1976

Life within our Party is struggle, not peace
or compromise; this is one of its chief characteristics. Our Party ought to engage in struggle
within itself so as to become a firm, powerful,
progressive Party, full of vigor for the fight.

Lin Piao

It is not easy to accept the thought of Chairman
Mao. Many comrades who took part in the Long March
have not managed to go right through with it. Some
want to risk their necks and shed their blood for
the revolution, and yet they have been unable to
follow the thought of Chairman Mao. This provides
food for thought.

Ch'i Pen-yü (October 12, 1966)

A sweet potato, even if it has a spot on it,
is still a sweet potato. But if it is not given
immediate attention, it will end up by rotting
completely.

The poor peasants of the brigade of
Kiangshan in Chekiang

26 The Tenth Plenum of the Eighth Central Committee and the Reappearance of Class Struggle

The Tenth Plenum of the Eighth Central Committee, held in Peking from September 24 to 27, 1962, apparently brought no modifications to the policy of readjustment followed between the Sixth Plenum (Wuhan, December 1958) and the Ninth Plenum (Peking, January 1961). In the countryside, the collective spirit persisted at the basic level, that of production teams, and the "small liberties" remained. Industry reflected the same prudent line: heavy industry was reduced to the essential minimum while light industry, aid to the agricultural front, and efforts to improve the quality and increase the variety of products were stressed. Theoretically, industry recovered by 15 percent between 1963 and 1964, and by 11 percent between 1964 and 1965. In view of the fact that many factories had slowed down or ceased production altogether, these comparisons are not very meaningful. The Tenth Plenum, however, revealed an astonishing change in both the spirit of the regime and the way in which it was developing; the convulsions of the Cultural Revolution may be said to have originated there.

The Tenth Plenum gave new life to the half-forgotten theme of the permanence of class struggle. The vigorous resolution adopted by the Central Committee was aimed at the Party rather than at society as a whole:[1]

This class struggle is complicated, tortuous, with ups and downs, and sometimes it is very sharp. This class struggle inevitably finds expression within the Party. Pressure from foreign imperialism and the existence of bourgeois influences at home constitute the social source of revisionist ideas in the Party. While waging a struggle against foreign and domestic class enemies, we must remain vigilant and resolutely oppose in good time various opportunist ideological tendencies in the Party.

This passage was followed by a reference to the Lushan Plenum, which had crushed rightist opportunism, "that is to say, revisionism," and an appeal for vigilance against dogmatism and revisionism. In the imagery of popular propaganda, this long tirade was compressed into a terse, severe warning from Mao Tse-tung to the nation: "Comrades, we must not forget class struggle."[2]

After the relative easing of tension during the preceding years, this change of course probably took place at the behest of Mao Tse-tung, who was always ready to make one revolutionary wave follow on another. Also, 1962 was a suitable year, for China was beginning its economic convalescence. It was also, without any doubt, a defensive reaction of opposition to trends emerging with increasing clarity within society, the administration, and the Party: declining revolutionary ardor, increasing irresponsibility, and above all a tendency to pursue tried and true methods of recovery.

In the large towns, a privileged proletariat was growing used to its material advantages, bonuses, and the eight-hour day. The hour of great revolutionary fervor had passed, and political activities often became simply a ritual based on events and themes handed out by the Party.

In the countryside the recession of 1959-1962 had encouraged the peasants' innate leanings toward ownership. Premier Chou En-lai acknowledged this development and the form it took in his report of December 21 and 22, 1964, to the Third National People's Congress:

For quite a long period, the landlord class, the bourgeoisie and other exploiting classes which have been overthrown will remain strong and powerful in our socialist society; we must under no circumstances take them lightly. At the same time, new bourgeois elements, new bourgeois intellectuals, and other new exploiters will be ceaselessly generated in society, in Party and government organs, in economic organizations, and in cultural and educational departments. These new bourgeois elements and other exploiters will invariably join hands in opposing socialism and developing capitalism.[3]

Switching from generalities to the particular case of the years between 1959 and 1962, the premier dwelled on the fact that violent attacks had been launched from within and were aiming at further decollectivization:

> In the domestic field, quite a few people actively advocated the extension of plots for private use and of free markets, the increase of small enterprises with sole responsibility for their own profits or losses, the fixing of output quotas based on the household, "going it alone" (i.e., the restoration of individual economy), "liberalization," "reversing previous correct decisions," and capitulationism in united front work; in the international field they advocated the liquidation of struggle in our relations with imperialism, reactionaries, and modern revisionism, and reduction of assistance and support to the revolutionary struggle of other peoples. They used their bourgeois and revisionist viewpoints to oppose our general line of socialist construction and the general line of our foreign policy.

The struggle between upholders and opponents of the general line went on well beyond 1962 and developed in the highest ranks of the Party. Among many others, Ch'i Pen-yü, an ardent partisan and later a prominent victim of the Cultural Revolution, bears witness to this:

> When the *"san tzu i pao"* formula was proposed in 1962 and also during the period of difficulties, the struggle was extremely violent.[4] At that time, if our great helmsman had not kept a firm hold on the tiller, our country would have found itself in a precarious situation. At the time, those calling for quotas to be fixed on a basis of the household were not comrades belonging to the lower strata or primary level cadres. This line was constantly put forward from 1962 to 1966. Some of the questions were of the kind concerning the Party alone and could not be discussed publicly.[5]

Many indications in the supervised press or published by the red guards in narratives and anecdotes, or in direct quotations, bore out the existence of a strong liberal current in the countryside. The fixing of a production quota based on a family plot of land seems to have been tried out in several regions at least, and particularly in Anhwei and Honan. In some districts of Honan people's communes rented up to 20 percent of their land to the peasants, who were reported to have said as a result, "The private plot is like a son to us, the rented field like an adopted son, and the field belonging to the commune is an orphan." It was later revealed that a third of the land belonging to a commune in the Lankao area of Honan had been divided anew and distributed to the families before 1962.[6] The decision of May 20, 1963, gave a lengthy account of sabotage, murders, bribery, usury, speculation, buying and selling of land, the return to influence of former landowners, and the appearance of counterrevolutionary organizations, sometimes acting under cover of religious sects (see Chapter 27).

According to Liu Shao-ch'i, only 15 percent of the total number of people's communes were working in accordance with the rules and were managed correctly. It is now established that President Liu Shao-ch'i, Teng Hsiao-p'ing, Chu Teh, Ho Lung, Teng Tzu-hui, Ch'en Yün, and also T'an Chen-lin, in charge of agriculture, were the most highly placed upholders of a flexible line, though they sometimes disguised their opposition to the general line by supporting readjustments, or else by "ultra-leftist" arguments, or occasionally by theories on the relationship between methods of cultivation and collectivization. Chu Teh was flatly accused of having urged the Party to follow rural trends toward farming on a family basis. The economist Ch'en Yün went still further and is said to have stated in 1962 that the division of the production quota on a family basis was a halfway measure, "nothing but an application of Mercurochrome to a wound," and that land should be redistributed to each individual. Teng Hsiao-p'ing is said to have pointed out that it does not matter whether a cat is black or white so long as it catches mice. On December 5, 1964, T'ao Chu was supposed to have written a "black letter" to Liu Shao-ch'i on restoring capitalism in the countryside; he was also said to have introduced a system of responsibility made up of bonuses, fines, and loans of land in some *hsien* in Kwangtung. Under the protection of Liu Shao-ch'i, Chang Wen-t'ien, one of the most senior of those expelled at Lushan, was sent to the Institute of Economic Studies in October 1960; there, in collaboration with its director, Sun Yeh-fang, he wrote fourteen notes or studies and put forward capitalist ideas in several documents, such as "Views on Various Questions Relating to Trade in Towns and Markets in the Countryside" and "Personal Notes on Socialist Economy," both of which encouraged a return to farming on a family basis.[7] These and many other similar accusations show that the question of the efficiency and productivity of the peasantry arose at the highest levels of the Party organizations. Although the general line in agriculture was not officially modified, the debate at least halted the possibility of a return to the extremist solutions of the summer of 1958, and it was feared that the pragmatists would eventually win the day.

In literature and art, although the wind did not blow from the right as it had at the time of the Hundred Flowers, the tolerance shown during the readjustment period had enabled revolutionary authors, both non-Party and Party members, to maintain some personal attitudes (see Chapter 21). These authors came from well-to-do urban families, particularly in Shanghai; they kept alive a literature appealing to a limited, educated public, which was in fact in opposition to the literature for the masses recommended by Mao Tse-tung at Yenan in 1942. They had by now virtually ceased to write, but their past works were sometimes revived on stage and frequently on screen, thanks to the development of the film industry.

Spring in February, adapted from a novel by Jou Shih, describes the melancholy perplexities of a primary school teacher who is governed by his feelings rather than by revolutionary zeal. *The Peach Flower Fan,* from a famous historical opera whose action took place during the transition from the Ming to the Ch'ing dynasty, had rival scholars as its chief characters and raised, at least indirectly, the dangerous question of political allegiance. The *Lin Family Shop*—based on a short story by Mao Tun and adapted by Hsia Yen—*The Song of Youth, Town Without Night,* and *Beleaguered City* were films of great artistic value, like those based on the preceding novels. Their truthfulness and poetry put them into an international class; however, their revolutionary content was extremely low, it must be admitted, for anyone with a Communist conscience.

In the theater the traditional opera went through a similar period of popularity, with a similar repertory of old plays peopled by characters belonging to the old society. This period of relative freedom also produced works whose later condemnation signaled the beginning of the Cultural Revolution, such as *Hai Jui Dismissed from Office,* and the subtle, biting satires *Evening Chats at Yenshan* and *Three Family Village* (see Chapters 28 and 29). The old culture persisted, and in December 1963 Mao Tse-tung described the world of art and literature as "still governed by the dead."

Minor though genuine signs of development were apparent in Chinese society as a whole. The great mass campaigns had more or less disappeared with the Antirightist Movement following the Hundred Flowers and with the abandoning of the Great Leap Forward. The rising generation of tens of millions of young people had come of age politically, "knowing nothing of the bitterness of the past, but only the sweetness of the present"; Mao Tse-tung openly expressed anxiety at this. The empty promises of the Great Leap Forward, summed up in the slogan "Three Years of Labor, an Eternity of Happiness" had caused enthusiasm to wane. The tension that had previously been considerable and permanent seemed less severe; zeal for work appeared to be falling off slightly; and even civic discipline seemed to diminish and to be accepted less readily in the fields of road traffic and hygiene, for instance. Here and there, a tendency toward bureaucracy, an outstanding characteristic of the old Chinese imperial regime, was showing signs of revival.

The stress on light industry had increased both the quality and variety of consumer goods. The population dared to show interest in goods such as pens, watches, bicycles, colored fabrics, and toys, considered as great luxuries in a country as poor as China. The stock, which was often copied from foreign models, was displayed with greater care. Would-be buyers crowded around the novelty counters and into tailors', hairdressers', and photographic shops, and bazaars became more numerous.

Family life was still important. Children received as much loving attention as ever. Although traditional feast days and customs had vanished from the towns, they were often still observed in the countryside, funeral rites included.

It should be emphasized, however, that these were slight changes, perceptible only by comparison with former years. They revealed a return to a more human way of life, rather than a serious deterioration of authority and morality.

The foreigner visiting China between 1962 and 1966, whether as a tourist, an official guest, or a diplomat, was always struck by the appearance of the towns, kept astonishingly clean by collective efforts undertaken by each district or street.[8] Public services were adequately carried out. The population of the towns was modestly and uniformly, though decently, dressed, showed no obvious signs of serious under-nourishment, and included no beggars or vagabonds, both of which were unthinkable in a totally organized society. Crimes and thefts, noticeably absent from the press, were apparently rare; anyone guilty of either had little hope of escaping the watchfulness of the masses.

In the countryside, houses and agricultural implements still looked much the same. The little fields were merged into large tracts of land, with more irrigation canals than before in the rice-growing regions; teams of men and women were scattered over them, but their members wielded the hoe or the plow just as the peasant couple, man and wife, had done before. The same dominant impressions prevailed everywhere: an extremely low standard of living, ensuring a basic minimum corresponding to local conditions and apparently shared equally; docility and tractability on the part of the population, which was firmly though unobtrusively held in hand; and stupefaction and often friendly curiosity on the part of Chinese who came face to face with a foreigner before being turned hurriedly away by officials or sometimes by private individuals. To this picture must be added the conditioned reflexes or attitudes developed day by day by the cadres and kept up by the fear of committing a sin against the ideology or opposing the official line, albeit unwittingly. A traditional respect for conventions and rites made it easier for the Chinese to comply with these requirements. Truly spontaneous enthusiasm was not to be found, and little spirit of initiative existed except among the ambitious. It is not difficult to imagine how hard a task the leaders have to reshape the institutions and transform the mentality of a society which is still remote from the modern world and living in carefully maintained ignorance of it.

The Socialist Education Movement was conceived in 1957 by Mao Tse-tung, but later circumstances prevented it from being put into practice; after the Tenth Plenum, it became an instrument in this transformation. More than the mere defensive reaction of a developing society against the foreign contagion of neo-revisionism, it was intended to be dynamic and forward-looking. Its chief aim became to bring about an irreversible revolution in man himself, while at the same time revolutionizing the organization, relations, and techniques of production.

Apart from the resolution, the Tenth Plenum also produced a speech by Mao Tse-tung, which was interesting both for its tone and for its revelation of certain details (September 24), a report by Ch'en Po-ta on the agricultural situation, a report by Li Hsien-nien on trade, and another by Li Fu-ch'un on industrial questions.[9] No important change was made in personnel. P'eng Teh-huai and still less Ch'en Yün do not seem to have been replaced in the Political Bureau, where they probably no longer occupied their seats. On the other hand, Lu Ting-yi, K'ang Shang, and Lo Jui-ch'ing were taken into the Secretariat and the control apparatus of the Party was strengthened at all levels, as was to be expected in view of Mao's appeal for vigilance. No clear opposition seems to have been expressed by those present at the Plenum, who numbered eighty-three full members out of a total of ninety-six, and eighty-seven alternate members out of ninety-four. The Tenth Plenum was probably the last one held in a spirit of agreement and unity.

Notes

[1] The Tenth Plenum was preceded by a working session of the Central Committee, held at Peitaiho a month earlier, during which the need for a "socialist education movement" was accepted.

[2] The persistence of class struggle under a socialist regime was stressed by Mao Tse-tung in his speech of September 24, 1962, at the Tenth Plenum. See "Chinese Law and Government," *IASP Journal of Translations* 1, No. 4 (1969), p. 85. See also Lin Piao, "Report to the Ninth Congress of the Chinese Communist Party."

[3] English version published in *Peking Review*, No. 1 (January 1, 1965).

[4] The phrase *san tzu i pao* means enlarging of individual plots, development of free markets, increase in small-enterprise responsibility for gain and loss, and the fixing of the production quota on the basis of the family.

[5] Ch'i Pen-yü, declaration of October 12, 1966, in a speech to detachments of the militia of the Aeronautical Institute in Peking and red guards of the College of Geology.

[6] Hsinhua Agency, June 9, 1968; Lankao is the *hsien* of the "good" Party secretary, Chiao Yü-lu. He may be imagined struggling against these same tendencies; see Chapter 27. An exhibition centered around him was held in Peking in July 1966.

[7] *The Red Flag of Finance and Trade* (February 15, 1967).

[8] The author can bear witness to this himself. Between the autumn of 1964 and that of 1966 he visited almost every province in China, from Manchuria to Szechwan and from Shantung to Shensi. Earlier, he spent many long periods there, from 1937 on.

[9] The only one of these speeches available today is that by Mao Tse-tung; an English version exists in "Chinese Law and Government" *IASP Journal of Translations*, 1, No. 4 (1969). Ch'en Po-ta gave the agricultural report.

27 The Socialist Education Movement

The Socialist Education Movement appeared partly as a real psychological campaign aimed at the entire population, supplementing the usual, already intense propaganda, and partly as a series of special measures directed at the most vulnerable social categories: political, administrative, and technical cadres; students (i.e., future cadres) and peasants; and lastly intellectuals, writers, and artists.

The main effort was concentrated on ideology and revolutionary morality for the Chinese population as a whole, and for each category of it. Ideology was essentially, if not entirely, based on the works of Mao Tse-tung and in particular on the texts most suited to provide each person with a basic system of morals made up of altruism, courage, perseverance, confidence in the face of difficulties, and a spirit of self-sacrifice toward the national community and socialist construction.

For the masses, Mao's works were usually limited to three texts, later known as the "Three Good Old Texts" or the "Three Constantly Read Articles": "In Memory of Norman Bethune," "Serve the People" and "The Foolish Old Man Who Moved the Mountains." All three dated from Yenan days, and the titles speak for themselves.[1] Their contents, and a few extracts from lesser known texts, quickly became the source of all reflection and the guide in all action. The thought of Mao Tse-tung invaded every aspect of daily life. A real cult was centered around it, including ritual and ceremony, and in the press, radio, cinema, and political meetings, it took on an indescribable obsessional quality.

The Socialist Education Movement, in its broadest terms, was based on the study of Mao's thought and on the imitation of the army. Directions for the latter were given in an important editorial in the *People's Daily* of February 1, 1964, entitled "The Whole Country must Learn from the People's Liberation Army." Since 1959, the army had returned to its people's army tradition (see Chapters 14 and 41); its methods of indoctrination were fully developed, it was wholeheartedly loyal to the spirit of its head and creator and was to become a model of civic virtue, moral perfection, and ideological rigor for the entire nation. Everyone was expected to imitate the army's strength of character and optimism in the face of difficulty (the nation would triumph here just as the army had triumphed over its enemies), its total lack of self-interest (the soldier had no personal belongings), its acceptance of collective living, and its zeal in spreading ideology. In order to give this exemplary behavior concrete form, the army presented individual heroes or groups of heroes to the masses for their admiration. The individuals, like Lei Feng, Sun Lo-yi, and Wang Chieh, were plain soldiers and workaday heroes. They all came to a tragic though banal and inglorious end, like Chang Szu-teh, the hero of "Serve the People," but the notebooks they left, which are published in facsimile, testify to their total devotion to Chairman Mao and the masses. Their ideal is summarized in a sentence from the notebooks of Lei Feng: "To be a screw which does not grow rusty. A screw does not attract attention, but no machine can work without screws." The groups of heroes remained revolutionary and pure under all circumstances, like the "Good Eighth Company of Nanking Road," who resisted all the temptations of the great city of Shanghai, as described in the film about them, *Sentinels Under the Neon Lights.*

Support the Army, Love the People

As had been the case during the founding of the people's communes and the Great Leap Forward, the military vocabulary was present throughout everyday life. Popular military literature developed, the best example of which was the novel *Song of Ou-yang Hai.* Exhibitions, campaigns, and slogans praised the union and mutual love of the people and the army: "Support the Army, Love the People," "United, the Army and the People will Go Forward Together." The teams of soldiers propagating the thought of Mao Tse-tung grew more and more numerous and magnified the tutelary role of the army in relation to the masses.

The army's organization and methods were also copied. Many administrative and particularly economic bodies followed its example by creating political departments to stimulate, coordinate, and control not only their political activities, but also a large proportion of their administrative and technical activities. To help them, the army sent teams imbued with its spirit, experience, and working habits. Later, the directive of May 7, 1966, urged the army to become a great school for political and cultural as well as military training, and to extend its interests to agriculture and production in general.[2] These decisions and methods made it considerably easier to replace the tottering state structures with military structures when the Cultural Revolution was at its height.

The cadres and manual labor

The cadres were a prime source of anxiety. The age-old cleavage between the scholar/civil servant and the common man had once more to be avoided at all costs in the new society. Cadres' regular participation in the physical labor of the workers and peasants at the primary level met this need. The principle of participation was not unknown. It had been the rule at certain moments in the Party's history, and particularly during the anti-Japanese war. At that time, it had both a symbolic character and a propaganda function in spurring production. The leaders had to be brought closer to the masses by carrying out humble work identical to theirs. It had the additional role, at a time of economic difficulty, of emphasizing the fact that everyone should assure all or part of his own livelihood. Many contemporary pictures show Mao Tse-tung and the chief Party leaders digging vegetable patches near the cave dwellings in Yenan which provided them with a home and shelter.

Later, the practice of getting cadres to perform physical labor continued in a more spasmodic way. The instructions of the Central Committee, published on April 27, 1957, devoted a long paragraph to the question, which was taken up again in detail by precise directions (May 10 and 13, 1958). At the time, the press published quantities of photographs of Mao Tse-tung, Chou En-lai, and other Party dignitaries pushing wheelbarrows or conveying baskets of earth on carrying poles during the building of the dam to form the artificial lake at the Ming Tombs. The Antirightist Movement after the Hundred Flowers also witnessed the sending of many cadres and intellectuals back to the countryside. This movement was partly mingled with the reversion of cadres to the lower ranks, known as the Hsia Fang Movement. After the Tenth Plenum of the Eighth Central Committee (September 1962), the reasons behind manual work for the cadres were more complex.[3] Several years of shortages had naturally focused attention on land problems and the reactions of rural society and reduced the need for administrative and technical cadres in the factories. The Party and the chief power structures were burdened by excessive bureaucracy while the supply system for the towns was still unsatisfactory. Sending civil servants to the countryside helped relieve the towns and seemed to demonstrate the leaders' solicitude for agriculture. It is clear, however, both from the press and private conversations, that the prime considerations were ideological and moral. People in leading positions, ministers and vice-ministers, disappeared for several months at a time. Even the president of the Republic found his "field for experience" at Taoyuan, a village in the district of Founing in Hopei. He also apparently discovered subjects for reflection there that may have determined his attitude toward the Socialist Education Movement in the countryside.

The physical work of the cadres was carried out according to rules excluding the unexpected, summarized by the slogan "Three Fixed things and a Substitution" (*san ting yi ting*). The three fixed things were the place, the time, and the task. The cadre was meant to be made capable of standing in for an ordinary worker should the need arise. The expression *tun t'ien* (standing on a certain point), which occurred frequently, suggests concentration on a limited field. Sometimes prominent people had to carry out the most repulsive tasks; this humility was thought to raise them above the level of ordinary people. Administrative and technical cadres belonging to production enterprises usually worked in their own factories alongside the workers.

No overall figure for the number of days of manual labor contributed was made public. Practices may have varied so that it was impossible to compile statistics. Theoretically at least, cadres in enterprises seem to have spent two half-days a week in the workshops. In the countryside, the periods often lasted several months.

Two categories of cadres seem to have been given particular encouragement to participate in manual work: the administrative staff of provinces, districts, and people's communes, and senior officers in the army. The former, who were periodically urged to take a front row position among the peasants, particularly when work on the land was at its height (sowing and harvesting) and in time of public disasters, had an exemplary hero in the person of Chiao Yü-lu, the "good Party secretary" of the district of Lankao in Honan, who died at his work. Senior army officers, despite their rank, had to spend a month every year at the company level, as plain soldiers. This practice, begun early in 1958, was naturally intensified.[4] The abolition of rank after June 1, 1965, strengthened it still further. The army also frequently sent teams to the villages, though this was not so much for physical work as for mobilizing the population for political or administrative tasks and for spreading Maoist thought.

Teachers and students in the countryside

Teachers and students sent into the countryside in the same spirit as the cadres were urged to share in manual work. This found added justification in the eyes of the Communists because a large proportion, if not the majority, of the students at the higher education level were still of bourgeois origin. No set rule on the national scale makes it possible to reconstruct even approximate statistics, but even the figures we have are significant. In the autumn of 1964, 270,000 students and middle school pupils from Peking and Shanghai went to help with the harvest. At roughly the same time, the Academy of Sciences, known to consist of about 20,000 research students, sent a thousand of them for a two to three months' stay in country areas.

As with the cadres, living conditions were the object of precise instructions expressed in slogans easily understood by everyone. As one of them said, the "three withs" (*san t'ung*) had to be practiced, which was to eat, lodge, and work with the peasants. In practice, the students were often assigned administrative and accounting duties or sometimes cultural functions, such as writing the history of the village or the commune for the peasants.[5]

The "half-work, half-study" system

Under another name, "education combined with productive work," the "half-work, half-study" system (*pan-kung pan-hsüeh*) dates from 1958. In February of that year Mao Tse-tung spoke on the subject, and a little later Lu Ting-yi summarized in an official text the conclusions of a conference held in June on educational work.[6] He recalled all the antecedents of the question and spoke of the difficulty involved in applying it and the controversies it had aroused. He used the expression "cultural revolution," attacked "authorities" and experts, and recalled that all social sciences—including education—ought to follow the path of politics. Nothing in this rigorous text hinted that the spokesman of both government and Party would be one of the first and most illustrious victims of the changes he was advocating.

The disorganization after the failure of the Great Leap Forward thwarted the plans drawn up in 1958. They reappeared in 1964, and above all in 1965 in the context of the Socialist Education Movement. Premier Chou En-lai, who attributed them to Liu Shao-ch'i, spoke of the plans in cautious terms, emphasizing that they were an experimental step in a long-term policy of adjustment of socialist and Communist education.[7]

The "half-work, half-study" system was inspired by ideological considerations which had been well known since the creation of the people's communes, those of eliminating little by little the difference between physical and intellectual work and of giving an all-around education to the young, to make "new men" out of them. Other, more practical reasons were behind it as well: the need to make local institutions particularly industrial concerns and people's communes, responsible for part of primary, secondary, and vocational education; to intensify the schooling of young peasants without taking them away from the land; and to spread and develop notions of and a taste for technical skill and physical effort in university and school circles, the members of which still bore the imprint of the literary tradition and were unwilling to indulge in physical exertion. The half-work, half-study schools were set up hastily, with inadequate resources, and resulted in serious troubles in the normal educational system. The after-effects would have become apparent in the universities and higher technical institutes if the Cultural Revolution had not disrupted education and called for its complete reappraisal.

No overall figures exist on the extent of the half-work, half-study system; it was chiefly left to the initiative of the localities that bore its expenses. The adaptations of it seem to have been extremely varied. Sometimes pupils were sent temporarily to a neighboring industrial enterprise where they were put into separate workshops; sometimes rudimentary workshops were set up in schools.[8] In country towns, many secondary schools were simply transformed into agricultural training schools. The closing of all educational establishments between the summer of 1966 and the summer of 1967 interrupted the experiment, though it now seems to have been left behind by the general direction of the educational system (see Chapter 40).

The Socialist Education Movement in the countryside

The failure of the Great Leap Forward naturally had a greater effect on the morale and revolutionary spirit of the population in the countryside than elsewhere. Serious discontent and probably major social disorders were avoided at the cost of the reorganization and adjustments already mentioned. The process of decollectivization had to be stopped; confidence in the Party had to be renewed; and primary level cadres had to be purified and full authority restored to them. During the "black" years, many of them had been trapped between the demands or inertia of the masses and the requirements of the hierarchy. A certain equilibrium had eventually been attained, an indirect result of which was that institutions and methods became frozen to some extent, causing revolutionary dynamism to wane, and encouraging the bureaucratic tendencies of the Party and of the organs of production and control. Management had replaced revolution.

In the spirit of the Tenth Plenum, and within the general context of the Socialist Education Movement, an effort was made to launch the revolutionary movement once more at the lowest level, to give new impetus to production, and a new start to collectivization when the time came. Former poor and lower middle peasants of the 1950 land reform were approached once more, and their revolutionary role was restored to them, a role that had lost its economic and social justification when they were integrated into the cooperatives between 1954 and 1956 under the same conditions as the rich and upper middle peasants. They were again grouped in associations, for they were considered to be united by past bitterness, and were required to behave as activists, helping and enlarging the action of the Party and of the administration. They supported and if necessary stimulated and controlled the cadres, opposed individualistic tendencies or leanings toward farming on a family basis, took the initiative at times in work for the public good, which was carried out by the population mobilized for the occasion, and saw to it that contracts with the state were respected.

The action of the poor and middle peasant associations received generous support from propaganda praising their devotion to the Party and their unselfishness. Numerous examples were quoted as proof: communes supplying more than the agreed quota, peasants spontaneously handing over their private plots, and a less individual reckoning of work points, for a growing preference existed for replacing them with a monthly salary corresponding to a "standard" worker's output. In this spirit, the Tachai brigade in northeastern Shansi became the model for all the rest. Without help from the state—this doubtful point is always emphasized— its members made the best of mediocre, badly sited land through prodigious terracing work, refusing to be discouraged by setbacks. A national exhibition centered on Tachai was held in Peking, while a vast movement known as "imitate Tachai" was launched, to be followed by about a hundred communes in different provinces.

More than ever before cadres in country districts were both encouraged and punished by the Party. The best among them were praised throughout the whole country, sometimes becoming heroes of films, though they were also constantly urged "not to look at flowers from horseback," but to be present wherever work was going on and to share in the peasants' labors while still carrying out their normal tasks. Purges were carried out each year and some complained of this: "In springtime we are thought to be useful, in the summer we are sent into the fields, in the winter we are good for nothing," as some of them said.

Many important texts, for a long time unknown, were devoted to the Socialist Education Movement in the countryside; they contained a mixture of ideology, politics, economics, and practical measures. Though little is known about their effects, a careful reading sheds considerable light on the true situation in the villages and on the nature and complexity of the problems of a rural society still bearing the imprint of conservatism and peasant individualism, in spite of ten years of changes.

On May 20, 1963, the Central Committee issued a ten-article "Decision of the Central Committee of the Chinese Communist Party on Questions Relating to Present Work in the Countryside (Project)," which became known as "The First Ten Points." Twenty individual reports from provincial and district committees accompanied it, serving as a justification. The aim, in the spirit of the Socialist Education Movement, was to arouse the peasant masses, who were mobilized around the poor and middle peasant associations, and at the same time to carry out the necessary inquiries and put things in order. In this respect, Article 8 laid special stress on cleaning up both the accounting system and the system of work points, which was of particular interest to the peasants and had never been used correctly by many communes, brigades, and teams since the start of collectivization. An exact inventory of existing stocks and an audit of the management of public funds were carried out with the help of the mobilized masses. Local leaders had to share conscientiously in manual work and unite with the masses. About 95 percent of them were considered in advance as "good" or capable of reform once they had recognized their errors or their mistakes. The clean-up movements were intended to become a permanent phenomenon, but two or three years were enough to regain control of the countryside without disturbing production and to prevent a degeneration into revisionism that would lead ultimately to a counter-revolutionary restoration.

"The First Ten Points" were followed in September 1963 by another ten-point instruction also described as a project and known as "The Later Ten Points." It was supposedly the work of a prominent member of the Party "always acting in connivance with Liu Shao-ch'i." It tended to give the Party greater control over the purging and mobilization of country-dwellers, primary organizations, and to reduce class struggle. Furthermore, it allowed full importance to material encouragements. A year later, in September 1964, these "Later Ten Points" were revised under the influence of Liu Shao-ch'i and also, according to his enemies, of his wife (Wang Kuang-mei) because of her "nauseous" experience gained at Taoyuan.[9]

Afterward, President Liu was accused of having tried to obscure the problem of purges and reform by upholding the theory of "the crossing of contradictions within the Party and outside it," adopting a line "apparently leftist, but rightist in fact," to confuse all the cadres, and of thus effacing the differences between cadres who were truly revolutionary and faithful to the thought of Mao Tse-tung, and those who were "engaged on the capitalist road."[10]

On January 14, 1965, a national work conference convened by the Political Bureau of the Party issued a fourth document, entitled "Present Problems Arising from the Socialist Education Movement in the Countryside." This text took up "The First Ten Points" at greater length, laying particular stress on the gravity and sharpness of the class struggle developing in the countryside and within the Party itself. It made violent attacks on the "authorities" in the Party "taking the capitalist road," "authorities" who were often "highly placed" and were "at the front of the stage or behind it." The need to pursue the Four Clean-ups (*szu ch'ing*) Movement and the Socialist Education Movement, with the help of 95 percent of the cadres and the masses, was vigorously stated once more. The document, known as "The Twenty-Three Articles," stated that:

> A serious, sharp class struggle exists in our towns and in the country-side. After the basic socialist transformation of property, class enemies hostile to socialism want to use "peaceful evolution" to establish capitalism again. This class struggle has inevitably been reflected in the Party. The leadership of a number of communes, teams, and units has become corrupt or has been infiltrated, and our work is coming up against many difficulties.

The real state of affairs proves that it is enough for the Party to continue to apply all the decisions of the Central Committee relating to the Socialist Education Movement more thoroughly and strictly, to maintain firmly the principle of class struggle, to look for support to the working class, the poor and middle peasants and revolutionary cadres, for many problems still persisting in the towns and the countryside are easy to discover and to solve. The Socialist Education Movement in existence for two years must be pursued and carried through to the end without flinching.

"The Twenty-Three Articles" gave a new name to the Socialist Education Movement, the Four Clean-ups Movement (politics, economics, organization, ideology) and encouraged the creation of a triple alliance between cadres, masses, and work groups, leading at a practical level to the creation of "leading cells" (Article 5) and sometimes to "seizure of power" (Articles 9 and 10), an expression which the Cultural Revolution brought out into the open. The Four Clean-ups Movement was to be carried out in six months in the case of a production team, a year or more in that of a district, in three years in a third of China, and in six or seven years in the country as a whole.

"The Twenty-Three Articles" led to renewal of control over the Chinese countryside, with 80 percent of the population once more thoroughly in hand. Beneath its conventional vocabulary and its careful language, the obstacles confronting the supporters of a renewal of the class struggle are easy to perceive, considering the real situation of the peasantry after the failure of the Great Leap Forward and of the people's communes on the 1958 model. Today it seems likely that resistance of this nature made Mao Tse-tung transfer the conflict to a more general political plane and approach it by the more convenient angle of culture. The Cultural Revolution was born of this double choice.

The Socialist Education Movement in cultural circles

The renewed control over intellectuals and the transformation of culture, both in content and means of expression, before its chief figures changed, were apparent as early as 1963 and quickly spread to every field of art, literature, and the social sciences.

The theater

From both a social and traditional point of view, the most important cultural sector was the classical theater, still widely popular in spite of various corrections and adjustments arising from the new ideology (see Chapter 21). Everything changed from 1963 on, and particularly after the summer of 1964 when the Festival of Peking Opera based on contemporary themes was held, and when the influence of Chiang Ch'ing (Mme Mao Tse-tung), hardly suspected until then, began to make itself felt against that of Chou Yang, Li Mo-han, the great actor Chou Hsin-fang, and a few less well known actors; she was careful to look over both old and new plays personally.

From then on the theater no longer set out to appeal to initiated audiences, members of the former bourgeoisie, or the people; its function was to spread the ideology, and to "serve the worker, the peasant, and the soldier." The great subjects from history, novels, and legends disappeared and with them the emperors, generals, and ministers, who were replaced by peasants, workers, and soldiers, as well as Chinese, Vietnamese, African, and Latin American guerrilla fighters. The decor lost its symbolic nakedness and became more concrete and accessible to all. New plays merely took events from banal examples of everyday life and transposed them to the stage, enlivened by politics and revolutionary moralizing. The least mediocre of them, such as the *Red Lantern*, referred to episodes during the anti-Japanese resistance, or, like *Raid on the White Tiger Regiment*, to an incident in the Korean War. The form remained unchanged, however: dialogues alternated with passages of falsetto singing; the insipid naive words were often impossible for the audience to follow without the projection of the characters of the text on the screens at either side of the stage. Each province retained its special form of expression; the operas from Hunan, Chekiang, Kiangsu, and Szechwan competed with Peking operas for equal renown.

The academies of dramatic art, particularly those at Changchun, Tientsin, and Shanghai, taught and propagated the new opera, which quickly became known as the "socialist drama." Classical works were only performed on feast days and rapidly disappeared altogether.[11] The public, after a period of reserve toward the new opera, either because of conformity or the inborn taste of the Chinese for the theater, which also had the advantage of being cheap, resolved to accept it.

Modern spoken plays, whose existence as a genre in China went back no further than the beginning of the century, also went through a radical development. Class struggle, the struggle for production, contradictions between the old and the new society, and the education of the younger generation in the ways of revolution were the chief sources of inspiration, as in the case of opera. Both the subject matter and the style appeared so completely lacking in interest that in spite of their goodwill, none of the playwrights of the old school, not even Ts'ao Yü, could bring themselves to conform with them completely. *Lei Feng, Li Shuang-shuang, After the Harvest, Never Forget, Red at Every Generation,* and *Fury Over the Andes* are the most representative of the new plays. Sometimes a hint of poetry persisted in titles such as *The Snow Greets the Spring* and *The Countryside is Studded with Flowers,* as though to make up in advance for the boredom and colorless character of the themes. A violent campaign of criticism was launched in February and March 1965 against the play *Li Huei-niang,* drawn from a story of the Ming dynasty. It was the work of an old Communist playwright, Meng Ch'ao, and gave a foretaste of the Wu Han affair with which the Cultural Revolution opened.

The folk plays of the minority races were unfortunately not spared. A festival held in Peking on November 27, 1964, allowed the extent of damage to these cultures to be judged; until then their freshness and originality had been respected.

The cinema

All the foregoing remarks on the theater are true of the cinema as well. Many plays in the new style were adapted for the screen; the outstanding films mentioned in the previous chapter disappeared. Several of them were nevertheless shown for a time so that they could be criticized; artificial controversies developed in the press around films or plays later described as "poisonous weeds." The most frequent reproaches directed against the authors, whether Party members or not, were those of humanism, pessimism, pacificism, and the idealization of the foreign adversary or the class enemy. Most of these authors were hard hit later when the Cultural Revolution took to the streets, and several of the best known of them committed suicide.

Foreign productions did not escape criticism either; the first to suffer were the films by the Russian producer Grigori Tchoukrai, *The Forty-First, Ballad of a Soldier,* and *The Clear Sky.* From 1964 on, no foreign works appeared on Chinese screens.[12]

Literature

Literature, like the theater and the cinema, also suffered the effects of the Socialist Education Movement. The orientation of literature came under discussion once more in relation to various old and modern works and, once again, violent attacks were launched in the name of revolutionary radicalism. One of the chief of these touched Shao Ch'uan-lin, vice-chairman of the Chinese Writers' Union and the defender of the "intermediate character" theory of ordinary, everyday people, who were sometimes ill at ease or hesitant, as opposed to "heroic characters." The critics made it clear that, in the eyes of the Party, only heroes with "red faces" and "hard bones," chosen from the workers, peasants, and soldiers, had an educative value for the masses.[13]

Many other authors were denounced by the press—Hao Jan for *A Great Sun in the Sky*, Han Shui for *Go Forward Courageously*, Ou-yang Shan for *Bitter Struggle*, *Three Family Street*, and *A Distinguished Generation* (a trilogy tracing the history of the revolutionary movement in detail from 1919), and Lo Pin-chi for *Before the Wedding*—to quote only the most prominent of them. Jou Shih, author of *February*, (well known through its adaptation for the screen), was not spared even though he had been shot by the Kuomintang in 1931. Two or three of his novels, among them *The Death of the Old Times* and *The Three Sisters*, received their share of criticism.[14]

Social sciences

The new current could not spare the social sciences, particularly philosophy and history. Paradoxically, Chou Yang, the first great victim of the Cultural Revolution, was the one to set it in motion in his speech on October 26, 1963, at the Chinese Academy of Sciences. He thought that the first task of workers in philosophy and social sciences was to reject modern revisionism, to study Marxism-Leninism anew, and to spread it. Humanism, the result of a mistaken understanding of the theory of contradictions, was to be condemned for this reason. The scientific character of socialism should be maintained and founded on the study of the legacy of history from the point of view of proletarian ideology. Workers in philosophy and social sciences were thus urged to switch gradually and consciously to Marxism.

Official criticism was then directed at the great historians of bourgeois origin whose ideological development was considered inadequate. Chien Po-tsan and Hou Wai-lu were spared temporarily, but Chou Ku-ch'eng received different treatment. Although widely esteemed for his *General History of the World,* he came under attack because of his views on the economic development of contemporary China and his general conception of the progress of history. He was justly rewarded for his attacks on the great Hu Shih.

The Spirit of Chinese Philosophy was strongly criticized because of the importance it gives to the expression "knowledge," to the detriment of the needs of the proletariat.[15] Some political philosophers received worse treatment still. Feng Ting, author of *Banal Truth, The Communist Conception of Life,* and *The Historical Responsibilities of the Proletariat* was reproached with having altered the nature of historical materialism and with propagating the ideology of the bourgeoisie.

Yang Hsien-chen, one of the great theorists of the Party, who advocated more or less openly the revisionist theory "two combine into one," was accused of marrying dialectical materialism and subjective idealism and was subjected to repeated denunciations outlasting the Cultural Revolution.

Performing and visual arts

The same supposedly proletarian current began to be apparent in the field of the arts, music, and dancing, to the detriment of traditional or Western influence. New musical works were introduced in Shanghai during a big festival (May 12, 1965); *Ode to the Red Banner* by Wu Chi-ming won the prize. Ballets of military inspiration became increasingly numerous. The model for these, afterward perfected still further, was *The Red Detachment of Women,* which is still shown to distinguished visitors.

Chinese sculpture, which has been mediocre since the Han and T'ang dynasties, with the exception of Buddhist statuary, declined to its lowest point, producing allegorical groups barely worthy of a waxworks museum. A classic example of this is the collection of recent figures, "The Rent-Collector's Courtyard," made in Szechwan. Painting came to an end with the last great painters of the preceding generation, Hsü Pei-hung (Ju Péon) and Fu Pao-shih,[16] outdoing the most mediocre socialist realism and choosing ordinary, base and insignificant subjects, with an attempt at traditional style.

Personnel changes

This new departure in cultural affairs was accompanied by significant changes in the people involved. Mao Tun, a powerful personality in the realm of the novel and the short story, an old revolutionary, but above all a man of letters, was dismissed from the Ministry of Cultural Affairs, where he was replaced by Lu Ting-yi, minister of propaganda and official Party spokesman (December 1964). The distinguished playwright Hsia Yen was dismissed from his post as one of the vice-ministers of culture a few months later.

This thrusting aside of the Communist writers of the 1930s to make way for holders of political posts, who were shortly dismissed in their turn with Lu Ting-yi and most of his subordinates and nearly all the old Communist writers, was highly meaningful. It obviously heralded the end of the "united front" policy in force since 1942 in the cultural field. The Party had to get rid of intellectuals who were incapable of being remodeled and entering into the new spirit. They had become useless and cumbersome, and their survival constituted a source of danger; their presence alone was enough to oppose the strictly "proletarian" development of culture. The relative liberalism of the Hundred Flowers, which practiced a fairly generous tolerance of the national heritage and certain foreign influences, and which by a strange paradox had been defended by Lu Ting-yi, himself inspired by Mao Tse-tung in Lu's speech of May 26, 1956,[17] was about to perish.

Notes

[1] See the Mao Tse-tung, *Selected Works*, 2: 337, and 3: 227 and 321, respectively.

[2] This directive provided inspiration for the schools for cadres, known as the May 7 cadres' schools, created during the Cultural Revolution (see Chapter 41). A Chinese text of the May 7 directive of 1966 was published by the Hong Kong magazine *Ming pao*, No. 46; it is particularly revealing of Mao's tendency to return constantly to the spirit of Yenan.

[3] See *Hung ch'i*, No. 13-14 (July 1963), for a justification of the participation of cadres in productive labor.

[4] See here John Gittings, *The Role of the Chinese Army*, pp. 193ff.

[5] A movement developed at the time to write the "four histories" of the family, the village, the people's commune, and the factory. See the *People's Daily* (December 28, 1964) for an example of this.

[6] *Education Must be Combined with Productive Labor* (Peking: Foreign Languages Press, 1958).

[7] See the report to the First Session of the Third National People's Congress (December 1964).

[8] These different solutions were noticed by the author in Szechwan, Shantung, and Kiangsi.

[9] See "Struggle Between the Two Roads in China's Countryside," *Peking Review*, No. 49 (December 1, 1967). The article is a translation of one in *Hung ch'i*, No. 16.

[10] See, among other texts, "Defend the Great Achievements of the Four Clean-ups Movement," *Hung ch'i*, No. 4 (February 1967).

[11] The following operas were put on for National Day in 1964: *The Reconciliation of the Constable and the Chancellor, The White Serpent, The Boar's Forest, The Third Meeting, The Goddess of the Waters Loves a Young Scholar, The Amazon Yang Pai-feng.*

[12] On the criticism of the cinema in general, see the *Kuang-ming jih-pao* of March 9 and 10, 1965.

[13] Yao Wen-yüan, who rose rapidly on the political scene during the Cultural Revolution, wrote an article against "intermediate characters" in the *People's Daily* (December 20, 1964).

[14] See the article by Ho Ch'i-fang, *People's Daily* (November 8, 1964).

[15] Feng Yu-lan, *The Spirit of Chinese Philosophy*, trans. E. R. Hughes (London: Kegan Paul, 1947).

[16] Fu Pao-shih died shortly before the beginning of the Cultural Revolution, which also closed down the Hsü Pei-hung museum.

[17] "May a hundred flowers bloom, and a hundred schools of thought contend" (see Chapter 12).

28 "The Tocsin Sounds the Cultural Revolution"

We have constantly fought back against the attacks
launched by the bourgeoisie from 1959 onward.
Especially since last November, when Comrade Yao
Wen-yüan published his article "On the New Historical
Drama *Hai Jui Dismissed from Office*" and sounded the
tocsin of the great proletarian cultural revolution,
a mass counteroffensive against the bourgeoisie's
attacks has opened up.

"Long Live the Great Proletarian Cultural
Revolution," *Hung ch'i*, No. 8 (1966)

The Wu Han affair

The beginnings of the Cultural Revolution, as it was to become six months later, went unnoticed by all foreign observers, by the Chinese population, and by those who were to be its chief actors. The Wu Han affair, today considered as the starting point, allowed its true nature and its range to become apparent only gradually, for it seemed to form part of the movement of reaction against liberal tendencies in intellectual circles. The existence of similar political tension within the Party was suspected, but nothing emerged to confirm the rumors and suppositions. The important working session held by the Central Committee in September and October 1965 was long kept secret; so were the "February Outline Report" proposed by P'eng Chen and the "May 16 Circular" issued by Mao Tse-tung, which condemned it.

Two dramas were in fact being played out. One, acted on the stage, appeared to be a controversy like many others and was reminiscent of the affair of the *Life of Wu Hsun* in 1951, while the other, behind the scenes, questioned the general trends of Chinese domestic and foreign policy.

These two will be dealt with separately, partly for the sake of clarity and partly to preserve the viewpoint of those who saw it happening.

On November 10, 1965, Yao Wen-yuan, editor of a Shanghai newspaper, the *Wen-hui pao*, wrote a signed article making a violent attack on a well-known and esteemed university professor, historian, and occasional playwright, member of the Democratic League, and since 1949 (an important point) one of the assistant mayors of Peking: Wu Han. A specialist in the history of the Ming dynasty and the author of a biography of its first emperor, Wu Han had in 1961 written a play entitled *Hai Jui Dismissed from office.* In 1569, under the reign of Ming Emperor Chia Ching, Hai Jui, then fifty-four, a scholar-official from Hainan known for his integrity and his desire to alleviate the misery of the people, was inspector of several districts in Kiangnan, which was roughly equivalent to the present Nanking-Shanghai-Soochow area. His position led him to pronounce sentence on the son of a scholar belonging to a powerful local family for the murder of a peasant and the seduction of his daughter. Although he knew he had been disowned by the court and was about to be dismissed from his post, Hai Jui still had the guilty man and his accomplices executed, and then after handing over his official seal and mandate to his successor, he retired with dignity to his family estate.

Wu Han had taken the precaution of pointing out in the preface to the play that Hai Jui first placed his great human qualities at the service of his class, that he fought against the excesses that the mandarins committed in order to perpetuate feudalism, and that he retained full respect for the emperor who had almost had him executed, later mourning his death. This caution could not disarm the critics. Hai Jui in fact proved by his conduct that good mandarins had existed, upright men who served the people. Worse yet, the Hai Jui of the play, like the historical Hai Jui, made every effort to restore to the peasants land seized from them by the rich landowners with the support of the scholar-officials, and to lower the rent paid by tenants. His steadfastness in the face of imperial authority was approved and held up as an example: "Hai Jui lost his office, but he neither bowed down nor tried to escape. As what he did was right, the people of that time upheld him and praised him. Hai Jui must be given a place in history; his virtues are such that they deserve to be imitated today."[1]

When it first appeared in January 1961 in Peking *Wen i pao,* and later in a separate volume, Wu Han's play did not produce any reaction, but when the time came his enemies tried to present it as a disguised attack on the "general line" and on Mao Tse-tung. The play was in fact written just over a year after the Eighth Plenum of the Eighth Central Committee at Lushan. As has already been described, this session witnessed a clash between those who supported the maintenance of the commune system in its entirety, and those who favored a more liberal agricultural policy, tending toward a return to a limited degree of private property. It was also at Lushan that the intransigent Marshal P'eng Teh-huai, head of the "rightists," lost his office. In both cases, there were grounds for some comparisons with the conduct and personality of Hai Jui.

The character of Hai Jui had first appeared in various forms in the spring of 1959, before the Lushan Plenum. The famous actor Chou Hsin-fang, at the suggestion of Chou Yang, as red guard papers later said, had put on a play in Shanghai centered around Hai Jui, *Hai Jui Addresses the Emperor*. A little later, in June, Wu Han published a short story called *Hai Jui Condemns the Emperor,* and for this reason, if remarks attributed to Hu Ch'iao-mu (the author of *Thirty Years in the History of the Chinese Communist Party*), are to be believed, the name of Hai Jui had come up at Lushan. According to some people, Hu Ch'iao-mu also encouraged Wu Han to publish another article on Hai Jui on September 21, 1959, in the *People's Daily*. Lastly, in December of that year, a volume of four texts was published under the name of the first of them, *The Story of Hai Jui*. These various writings did not give rise to any more polemics than did the publication of *Hai Jui Dismissed from Office*, but it is possible that the subjects and dates aroused suspicion.

For a long time Yao Wen-yüan was thought to be the prime mover of the attacks on Wu Han; then official insinuations suggested that Mao Tse-tung was determined to lead the action against the supporters of P'eng Teh-huai personally. "The unpleasant word in the play is 'dismissed,' " as he is reported to have said, meaning that he believed in the intentions of Wu Han. In opposition to this interpretation, Chiang Ch'ing (Mme Mao), in a meeting of red guards on April 12, 1967, revealed the real origins of the Wu Han affair? It seems that one day in 1965 Chiang Ch'ing, in the presence of the chairman, expressed certain doubts as to the meaning of *Hai Jui Dismissed from Office* and suggested writing them down. For seven or eight months, Chiang Ch'ing, with the help of Yao Wen-yüan and Chang Ch'un-ch'iao, a political commissar of the Nanking military region and head of propaganda in the Shanghai Party Committee, wrote and rewrote an article, which remained secret until the day it appeared in *Wen-hui pao,* signed by Yao Wen-yüan.

According to Chiang Ch'ing, Mao Tse-tung, under the influence of P'eng Chen, was at first indulgent toward Wu Han and the historians in general. Although this indulgence was not apparent in official texts, it is possible that Mao may have been won over gradually to the views of his wife, who had been hostile to Wu Han since 1962. In any case, by September 1965 this conversion was complete, as was borne out by the "May 16 Circular."[3] Chiang Ch'ing certainly had a large share in the responsibility for the Cultural Revolution, at least as regards its immediate causes and the conditions under which it began.

The article by Yao Wen-yüan, supported by solid historical references, accused Wu Han of giving a false interpretation and exaggerating the qualities of Hai Jui, whose true motive was to perpetuate the oppression exercised by the mandarinate, and of portraying the peasants as resigned and lacking all class consciousness. Yao Wen-yüan also transferred the question of returning land to the peasants to the present day, seeing Wu Han as one of those who slandered the people's communes and as an ally of the exploiters belonging to the old society and of the "rightists" within the Party. His article was published again by Chieh-fang-chün pao (Liberation Army Daily) on November 29 and on the following day by the People's Daily.

On December 30, Wu Han attempted to make a self-criticism in the People's Daily, but this gave rise to a new campaign which found material both in the inadequate explanations in the self-criticism and in the moderate and clumsy remarks of some of his friends, among them the historians Chou Ku-ch'eng, Chou Mao-t'ung, Yang K'uan, and Liu Ta-chieh. A second self-criticism (January 12, 1966) quickly isolated him, and Wu Han then had almost all the press against him, including the newspaper Kuang-ming jih-pao, the former organ of the Democratic League. It was recalled that Hu Shih, the greatest and most constant enemy of the Communist movement in the realm of culture, had considerably influenced Wu Han's education. Questions were also asked as to what Wu's attitude had been when the poet Wen Yi-to was murdered at Kunming in 1946; doubts were expressed as to Wu's physical and moral courage.[4] Afterward, criticisms of Wu Han reappeared periodically in the press, and particularly in April when Teng T'o and other members of the "black band" to which Wu Han also belonged were accused in their turn (see Chapter 29).

No important Party member raised his voice either to condemn or defend Wu Han. Supporters or future victims of the Cultural Revolution held their peace. There was general surprise at the silence of leading figures in the Ministry of Cultural Affairs, which was directly concerned. The silence of P'eng Chen, mayor of Peking, whose assistant Wu Han was, aroused equal surprise. It is easier to explain now that the part played by Mao Tse-tung and Chiang Ch'ing in the disgrace of the author of *Hai Jui* has become known. The "May 16 Circular" (see Chapter 29) showed that Wu Han was defended by some of his friends from the accusation of wanting to support those ousted at Lushan. It seems probable that P'eng Chen tried to eliminate politics from the criticisms affecting him indirectly and to place the controversy on a purely academic and cultural plane.

Criticisms of prominent intellectuals

In January and February 1966, the editorials and articles in the press stressing the priority of politics and the role of the masses in the field of culture were more numerous and their tone was harsher. On January 16, the *People's Daily* urged the "philosophy workers" to go among the workers, peasants, and soldiers. On January 20, the same paper carried an article entitled "The Working Class Can Maintain Science and Culture." On January 24, another appeared under the heading "Give Priority to Politics to Reach the Summit in Science." It may now be assumed that this was done to give the masses a better preparation for the active role which was shortly to be entrusted to them during the Great Proletarian Cultural Revolution. At the time, the texts seemed perfectly in line with the Socialist Education Movement and this was enough to give them meaning.

At the beginning of 1966, Wu Han was not the only one to be criticized, for three other powerful figures in the intellectual world, the historian Chien Po-tsan and the writers Hsia Yen and T'ien Han, all extremely close to the Party, underwent severe attacks before being completely thrust aside by the Cultural Revolution.

From 1952 on, Chien Po-tsan, head of the Department of History at Peking University, had published many articles on historical research and the teaching of history. Faults were found in almost all of them; the doctrinal journal of the Party, *Hung ch'i,* and the newspaper *Kuang-ming jih-pao* were the most persevering in their denunciations. Chien Po-tsan was shown up as a "bourgeois" who was opposed to class struggle and unaware of its role in his interpretations of history and as an upholder of "historicism." In many respects, and particularly on the subject of the role of important people and that of peasants, his case resembled that of Wu Han. The Party had a duty to unmask this false Marxist and to fight against his "poisonous theories."[5] The attacks continued throughout the Cultural Revolution.

An entire conception of history came under attack through Chien Po-tsan. This was the traditional conception, which neglected the aspect of class and mass movements and placed great importance on individual people and accidental events, in direct contradiction to the Marxist-Leninist conception, which claimed to be scientific.

Hsia Yen, whose real name was Shen Tuan-hsien, was one of the early revolutionary authors. As a journalist, essayist, novelist, playwright, and translator he had been linked to the political and literary life of China for forty years. He took part in the Northern Expedition in 1927 and described the difficult life of the intellectual circles in Shanghai in *Memories of the Town of Sadness.* His play *Sai Chin-hua*[6] was drawn from an episode in the Boxer Uprising and included among its characters the German General Waldersee and a singer devoted to her country; it was popular throughout China. His past, the fact that he was a former vice-minister of culture (October 1964 to April 1965), his career as a prominent literary figure, and his collaboration and friendship with Kuo Mo-jo were not enough to prevent him from being accused of spreading bourgeois, individualist, and humanitarian ideology.[7] *Sai Chin-hua* in particular was singled out for a full-scale attack for its lack of class spirit, its false patriotism, and, perhaps above all, for giving an unflattering picture of the Boxers.[8]

T'ien Han, whose real name was T'ien Shou-ch'ang, chairman of the All-China Dramatic Association, film producer, playwright, translator, teacher, and author of the words of the national anthem, was at that time attacked for only one of his plays, *Hsieh Yao-huan,* an episode from a peasant revolt under the reign of the Empress Wu Tse-t'ien in the seventh century.[9] As in the case of Wu Han, the criticisms were brought to bear on an over-flattering portrait of sovereigns who were by definition incapable of serving the interests of the people, and on passages whose allusions were considered hostile to the Party and to socialism. They were slight compared with the accusations awaiting him at the end of the year: collusion with the Kuomintang, rebellion against the Party, and so on. The official press and the red guard papers would then insult him in the most offensive way, calling him a "chameleon" and "father of theatrical monsters."[10]

On April 14, 1966, Kuo Mo-jo, chairman of the Academy of Sciences, a brilliant intellectual, man of letters, and archaeologist, but also the bard of the new regime, who had recently rallied to Communism, made his self-criticism at a meeting of the Standing Committee of the National People's Congress:

In the past decades, a pen has always been in my hand, writing and translating works amounting to many millions of words. However, in the light of present standards, what I have written, strictly speaking, should all be burned. It has no value, none whatsoever.[11]

Kuo Mo-jo placed the thought of Mao Tse-tung above all else, accusing himself of not having studied it thoroughly enough, and shouldered his share of responsibility in the errors committed in the realm of literature and the arts. By this ostentatious and prudent gesture, he cut himself off openly from the accused men, his former friends and collaborators, and made a final, irrevocable sacrifice to the thought of Mao Tse-tung of a reputation for moral uprightness and strong character that had, in fact, been damaged for some time.

Notes

[1] Wu Han, preface to *Hai Jui Dismissed from Office.*

[2] *Hung-se wen-i (Red Art and Literature)* (May 20, 1966).

[3] The circular said that Mao Tse-tung had "given instructions" as to the criticism of Wu Han at a meeting of the Standing Committee of the Political Bureau during the work session of the Central Committee in September and October 1965.

[4] *People's Daily* (June 3, 1966).

[5] See "The Bankruptcy of Bourgeois Historicism," *Kuang-ming jih-pao* (April 23, 1966).

[6] Henry McAleavy translated the play into English with the title *That Chinese Woman: The Life of Sai Chin-hua* (London: Allen & Unwin, 1959).

[7] See particularly "Bourgeois Ideology in the Works of Hsia Yen (Ho Ch'i-fang)," *People's Daily* (April 1, 1966).

[8] See *Kuang-ming jih-pao* (March 12, 1966 and July 29, 1971).

[9] See *People's Daily* (February 1 and 24 and March 8, 1966).

[10] See particularly the chief newspapers of December 6, 1966.

[11] See *People's Daily* (May 5, 1966). This English translation occurs in the *BBC Summary of World Broadcasts*, FE/2136, and was quoted in *The China Quarterly*, No. 27 (July-September 1966), p. 192.

29 "Open Fire at the Black Line": From Wu Han to Teng T'o and The Fall of P'eng Chen

From Wu Han to Teng T'o

On May 8, 1966, the Teng T'o affair began to be publicly known; its political significance was clearly apparent immediately, unlike the Wu Han affair, to which it gave renewed life. *Chieh-fang-chun pao* printed an editorial with a resounding title, "Open Fire at the Black Anti-Party and Anti-Socialist Line," signed by Kao Chu. On the same day, *Kuang-ming jih-pao* contained a similar article, signed by Ho Ming: "Heighten our Vigilance and Distinguish the True from the False." Both papers also included a long explanatory text, "Teng T'o *Evening Chats at Yenshan* is Anti-Party and Anti-Socialist Double-Talk."

Hung ch'i (No. 7) attacked the "bourgeois" position of the *Peking Daily* and the periodical *Frontline* with an article by Ch'i Pen-yü, a name shortly to become more widely known. In Shanghai, articles by Yao Wen-yuan, the first critic of Wu Han, appeared on May 10 in *Wen-hui pao* and *Chieh-fang jih-pao*, denouncing the *Notes from Three Family Village*, a series of chronicles already several years old, written by three authors, Teng T'o, Wu Han, and Liao Mo-sha, under the collective signature of Wu Nan-hsing.[1] All newspapers reprinted his article the next day. About a dozen similar attacks followed in the *People's Daily* in May and in the press as a whole.

For those acquainted with the facts, the Teng T'o affair had begun on April 16, when the *Peking Daily* and *Frontline* printed a voluminous though somewhat empty criticism of the *Notes from Three Family Village* and *Evening Chats at Yenshan*. It was accompanied by a self-criticism by the editors, who accused themselves of having lacked vigilance and given in to bourgeois influences, instead of taking inspiration from the spirit of the proletariat. The sincerity of this self-criticism was questioned in most of the articles just mentioned.

Teng T'o

Teng T'o, a native of Shantung, was a man of about fifty, and an important figure in the world of the press. After working on the *New Century* and several periodicals in Shanghai before 1937, he was a member of the team in charge of the Communist newspaper *New China*, published in Chungking with the permission of the Nationalist government during the Sino-Japanese War. He later took charge of the newspaper of the liberated zones in North China (*Chin-Ch'a-Chi Jih-pao*) before becoming editor of the *People's Daily* between 1954 and 1960. Although his star began to wane after this period, since 1959 he had been a member of the Peking Party Committee and editor of the committee's quarterly review, *Frontline*. He was an essayist and occasional historian, a man deeply imbued with classical culture and a member of the Academy of Sciences (philosophy and social science), and without any doubt a polemical writer of great talent.

From March 1961 on, Teng T'o began to publish *Evening Chats at Yenshan* in the *Peking Evening News*, of which he was in charge, followed by the *Notes from Three Family Village*, with the collaboration of Wu Han and Liao Mo-sha, in *Frontline*.

Liao Mo-sha

Before the Sino-Japanese War, Liao Mo-sha, a journalist like Teng T'o, had belonged to the League of Leftist Writers in Shanghai and made an ironical attack on Lu Hsün for his "lacework literature"; he later published several novels that did not receive much attention: *Trip to Hsien-yang, Leaving the Court of Yin*. In 1961, under the name Fan Hsing, he produced several works encouraging the literature of the fantastic and pointing out that it was inoffensive, giving examples such as *There Is No Harm in Ghosts, Refined Jokes on the Subject of Ghosts*, and taking classical literature as a basis. After working on the *Notes from Three Family Villages*, he wrote no more, except to retract his theory on ghosts (March 1965). In 1961, Liao Mo-sha was put in charge of the "United

Front" Committee of the municipality of Peking and in addition presided over several local committees (education, the fight against illiteracy).

In the eyes of his critics, particularly Yao Wen-yüan, Teng T'o, while apparently drawing on old authors for new lessons, was in fact attacking the leadership and certain cadres of the Party. Indirectly, by "pointing at the mulberry tree and insulting the acacia," in a language rich in hints and fables and in the name of moderation and common sense, he denounced the tyranny, vainglory, boasting, fanaticism, the lack of a sense of reality, the wordiness, and the clichés of the Party. In a typically Chinese way, by allusions, he made ironical comments on the Great Leap Forward, the people's communes, and the thought of Mao Tse-tung; here his criticisms were joined by those of the Soviet revisionists.

On the other hand, Teng T'o and his friends praised some of the virtues of traditional education, such as self-control, the refusal to humble oneself, the dignity of forging one's own way. They hailed "highly educated people." They recalled with sympathy upright mandarins who were friends of the people, such as Li San-tsai or the members of the Tung Lin faction, thus repeating the mistake made by Wu Han and by other supposedly Marxist historians.

Teng T'o, in his succinct, incisive, and varied style, in the richness and poetical quality of his imagery, and in the aptness of his quotations, had affinities with Lu Hsün; like Lu Hsün, he was prevented from expressing himself freely. At times, a line of classical poetry was enough to call up the melancholy charm of the past:

> Sounds of wind, rain and reading of books all fill my ears;
> Family, state and world affairs, I show concern for them all.

At other times through folklore and tales (*The Family Wealth Consisting of a Single Egg, Special Treatment for Amnesia*), he linked himself with the most easily accessible and sometimes the crudest of popular tradition.

It is hard to say whether and to what extent the readers of Teng T'o, Liao Mo-sha, and Wu Han related their stories and fables to current events. The *Peking Daily,* and particularly its evening edition, was immensely popular in a country where the press, given over to political exhortation, is infinitely bleak and unappealing. It should be pointed out, however, that in 1961-1962 (the chronicles appeared until the autumn of 1962), the Chinese could still read legends and tales of former days. Until the middle of 1966, these could be found in extremely varied forms, from the old illustrated editions to the little picture story books similar to our own comic books. The great popular novels, *The Water Margin* (translated by Pearl Buck as *All Men are Brothers*), the *Romance of the Three Kingdoms*, and many others were still available, as were the classics, many of which had been brought out in impressive new editions (see Chapter 21). Consequently, even if he had not attacked the doctrine and the Party, Teng T'o was intolerable insofar as his choice of subject and his personal form of talent helped to keep alive the memory of and a taste for the past.

With a total lack of appropriateness and humor, the critics took the *Evening Chats at Yenshan* and the *Notes from Three Family Village* and singled out the most successful passages from the point of view of irony or the aptness of the remarks. With the help of a plentiful supply of quotations and dates, they tried to prove the existence of a deliberate plot, carefully organized from 1961 on and becoming more and more elaborate owing to economic difficulties. Wu Han, with *Hai Jui*, had been the advance guard of the force; Liao Mo-sha had followed with his articles on ghosts; Teng T'o, with his *Evening Chats at Yenshan*, was the "commander-in-chief" who had to be saved at the price of sacrificing the other two. Sometimes the critics dropped their war imagery and described the group of the *Notes from Three Family Village* as keeping a "sinister inn" where an anti-Party, antisocialist, and rightist line was developed. Only when the watchword of class struggle was brought back by the Tenth Plenum of the Eighth Central Committee did the conspirators fall silent and scatter, covering up their retreat by false mutual criticisms. "Out of thirty-six stratagems, the best is to take flight," as the last number of the *Evening Chats at Yenshan* said on September 2, 1962.

The criticisms of Teng T'o, Liao Mo-sha, and Wu Han came from all circles, and repeated themselves over the months, reappearing throughout the Cultural Revolution and becoming more and more insulting, as was only to be expected.

The targets aimed at by means of Teng T'o and his friends were naturally the press and various cultural circles in the capital, and beyond them the mayor of Peking, first Party secretary of the municipality, and number five in the Political Bureau: P'eng Chen.

The papers and periodicals the *Peking Daily*, the *Peking Evening News*, *Frontline*, and Peking *Wen i pao*, carried on for a few weeks longer, after having seen their editorial staff reshuffled and been obliged to make their self-criticism. They were eventually suppressed one after another during the months of July and August.

Meanwhile, purely political events speeded up, particularly at the end of May, when P'eng Chen and Lu Ting-yi were eliminated in complete silence and Chou Yang publicly disgraced, while Lin Piao moved up, and at Peking University the first salvo was fired, beginning the Cultural Revolution. These events, which at the time were ignored or inadequately understood, were accompanied by a series of editorials and articles intended to fix the general direction of the Cultural Revolution, and to give its partisans powerful psychological and political support.

The fall of P'eng Chen

P'eng Chen, born in Shansi at the beginning of the century,[2] belonged to the first generation of Chinese Communists. Like Liu Shao-ch'i, he gained his experience in action among the workers in North China until the eve of the Sino-Japanese War. He was arrested several times, imprisoned for six years, and apparently was not present in Kiangsi or during the Long March. Once war broke out, he took part first of all in partisan operations behind Japanese lines on the Hopei, Shansi, and Chahar borders, then became assistant director of the Party School at Yenan, member of the Central Committee at the Eighth Congress (1945), and then, from 1945 to 1946, Party Secretary for Manchuria.

In 1966 P'eng Chen was the tenth ranking member of the Political Bureau, second secretary of the Central Committee and, most important, secretary of the Peking Party Committee. His offices in state institutions were vice-chairman and secretary of the Standing Committee of the National People's Congress and mayor of Peking from 1951 on. He was a statesman of international standing and had often been a member or leader of delegations abroad, in particular at the Congress of the Rumanian Workers' Party in Bucharest in June 1960 and at the Twenty-Second Congress of the Communist Party of the Soviet Union in October 1961; his chief responsibility seemed to be relations with the Japanese and Indonesian Communist parties.

He was a tall, strong, open-faced man, and he was always good-tempered; his vigor and his baldness made him slightly reminiscent of Mao Tse-tung as a younger man. The overall impression he conveyed was one of flexibility and goodwill, which was contradicted by his role during the mass trials in Peking in 1951, and by the known toughness of his ideological standpoint.

P'eng Chen was considered an ambitious man and was one of the three or four possible successors of Mao Tse-tung. His power—although considerable—was confined to the capital, whereas among his likely rivals

Chou En-lai controlled the administration, Liu Shao-ch'i and Teng Hsiao-p'ing the apparatus of the Party, and Lin Piao the army. During the winter of 1965-1966, it was rumored briefly in Peking that P'eng Chen and T'ao Chu were rivals; the fact that the rapid though ephemeral rise of the latter coincided with the fall of P'eng Chen seemed to justify this in retrospect. Until early in 1966, P'eng Chen still appeared to be well thought of by Mao Tse-tung and to have access to him. He was apparently asked, or took it upon himself, to draw up the charter of the future Cultural Revolution, either at the working session of the Central Committee held in September and October 1965, or perhaps earlier still, if it is true that a "Committee of Five" formed for the purpose already existed in July 1965.

According to various detailed accounts, given by red guards,[3] P'eng Chen called a meeting of the "Enlarged Committee of Five" on February 5, 1966; it was a drafting committee or study group, which seems to have been split into two rival factions. P'eng Chen, Lu Ting-yi, minister of propaganda and culture, Hsü Li-ch'ün, and Yao Ch'in, assistant director of propaganda for the Central Committee, were on one side; on the other were K'ang Sheng, who had long held office in the Party and was an alternate member of the Political Bureau, and Kuan Feng, a lesser-known figure. During the meeting, P'eng Chen is reported to have supported a declaration by Hsü Li-ch'ün, defended seventeen "black documents" of which nothing more is known, and refuted the criticism associating *Hai Jui Dismissed from Office* with the meeting of the Central Committee at Lushan in August 1959. K'ang Sheng is said to have denounced the errors of P'eng Chen, criticized Wu Han, and defended Kuan Feng and the "leftist groups" which he had apparently organized to criticize incorrect tendencies.

After the meeting, Hsü and Yao wrote a report for the Central Committee. The text was approved on February 5 by Liu Shao-ch'i and then, modified and given a more general form, was presented to Mao Tse-tung, then at Wuchang. After Mao in his turn had added a few remarks, the authors of the report corrected it before submitting it once more to Liu Shao-ch'i and Teng Hsiao-p'ing. With the help of a maneuver by these two, the final text, considered as having been approved by Mao Tse-tung, was distributed to Party members, bearing the stamp of the Central Committee, on February 12. On February 18, Hsü Li-ch'ün presented it to the leaders of the press, literature, and the arts; they formed four committees to discuss it.[4] The "February Outline Report," distributed to the Party in this way, provoked various reactions and was sharply attacked by the supporters of K'ang Sheng and Ch'en Po-ta.

At some moment—the precise date is not known today, but it seems to have been before March 30—Mao, who at first was hesitant or was perhaps prevented from doing so because of bad health, suddenly moved toward the left. The Secretariat of the Central Committee (April 9-12), the Standing Committee of the Political Bureau (April 16), and the Political Bureau (May 4) met one after the other. P'eng Chen, Lu Ting-yi and Yang Shang-k'un were attacked and isolated. The "May 16 Circular," addressed to the higher levels of the Party—provinces, districts, and army regiments—was the outcome of the meetings. It was a sudden, vigorous attack on P'eng Chen and his supporters. The Cultural Revolution had, beyond all doubt, moved onto a political plane.

The "May 16 Circular" of 1966, made public a year later, annulled the "Outline Report," dissolved the "Group of Five," and decided to place a new group in charge of the Cultural Revolution and to make it directly responsible to the Standing Committee of the Political Bureau. P'eng Chen, accused of "forging" the "February Outline Report" "according to his own ideas" in an arbitrary fashion and of usurping the name of the Central Committee, and of acting "without the approval of comrade Mao Tse-tung," came in for severe attacks.

A doctrinal refutation in ten points picked out the chief errors of the "February Outline Report": (1) Attempts to turn the Great Proletarian Cultural Revolution toward the right and toward academicism; (2) refusal to criticize Wu Han and the rightist opportunists of 1959; (3) encouragement of freedom of expression, which was taken to mean bourgeois liberalization and not the meaning that Mao gave it in March 1957, speaking at the National Party Conference on Propaganda Work; (4) refusal to admit the "class nature of truth" and the dictatorship of the proletariat over the bourgeoisie; (5) indirect glorification of "academic authorities" belonging to the bourgeoisie; (6) rejection of Mao Tse-tung's formula "No construction without destruction"; (7) putting "scholar-tyrants" belonging to the bourgeoisie on the same footing as hypothetical "scholar tyrants" of the proletariat; (8) support for a "movement for the rectification of the left"; (9) recommendations of "caution" and "circum-spection" in the directing of the Cultural Revolution, whereas the great majority of Party committees were still far from understanding their role as leaders and from playing it competently and conscientiously; and (10) resistance to the true thought of Mao Tse-tung as formulated long ago, and distortion of his thought to give it a revisionist meaning.

On the whole, as the writers said in their summary, the proposals opposed the carrying through of the socialist revolution right to the end;

they opposed the line drawn up for the Cultural Revolution by the Central Committee with comrade Mao Tse-tung at its head; they attacked the proletarian left, defended the bourgeois right, and prepared public opinion for the return of the latter. The conclusion of the "May 16 Circular" of 1966 was even more striking than these doctrinal refutations. It was a real cry of alarm, a call for a purge, and was infinitely disturbing because the future victims of the Cultural Revolution still remained anonymous:

> Those representatives of the bourgeoisie who have sneaked into the Party, the government, the army, and various cultural circles are a bunch of counterrevolutionary revisionists. Once conditions are ripe, they will seize political power and turn the dictatorship of the proletariat into a dictatorship of the bourgeoisie. Some of them we have already seen through, others we have not. Some are still trusted by us and are being trained as our successors, persons like Khrushchev, for example, who are still nestling beside us. Party committee at all levels must pay full attention to this matter.[5]

The style and imagery, which gave the "February Outline Report" the appearance of a vast conspiracy, must have caused a considerable stir within the Party organization. None of this was visible to the outside world, however. The events which must presumably have taken place at the highest levels during the three months between the circulation of the "February Outline Report" and its condemnation were also unknown to the rest of the world. Today it is still impossible to say with certainty how and when P'eng Chen was eliminated; he was apparently forbidden to enter his own offices.

The first point coincided with a temporary eclipse of Mao Tse-tung, who was almost entirely absent from public life until May 10; many persistent rumors attributed this to a serious operation. As to the second point, various indications suggest that the ousting of P'eng Chen and Liu Jen, first and second secretaries of the Peking Party Committee, announced on June 3, coincided more or less with the publication of the "May 16 Circular." It was presented as a "great victory of the thought of Mao Tse-tung" and accompanied by extremely noisy demonstrations; according to some people, it was backed up by precautionary measures on the part of the army in the region of Peking. None of this was apparent at the time, and as many units were stationed permanently near the capital, it may be that the need to call in further troops did not arise.[6]

The appointment of Li Hsüeh-feng to the post of P'eng Chen looked like a compromise. Li Hsüeh-feng had been first Party secretary for North China since 1953, and Peking was—geographically at least—in the area for which he was responsible. He seemed to owe his rise to a large extent to Teng Hsiao-p'ing and Lin Piao; later events showed that he greeted some of the new tendencies with a certain reserve.[7] Liu Jen was replaced by Wu Teh, first secretary for the province of Kirin, a man whose origin and experience made him eminently suitable for transfer to Peking.[8]

Shortly after their arrest by red guards in December 1966, P'eng Chen and Liu Jen, who had been purged without being mentioned by name at first, reappeared in public with notices hanging around their necks, subjected to extreme humiliation. At that stage the Cultural Revolution had for some time provoked repeated acts of violence; this was to continue for several more years.

The conquest of the Ministry of Culture

The chief office-bearers in the Ministry of Propaganda and Culture, and first of all Minister Lu Ting-yi and the most important vice-minister, Chou Yang, disappeared at the same time as P'eng Chen.

Lu Ting-yi, who had constantly been in the front line of events, owing to his post as Party and government spokesman since 1949, vanished in complete silence. He was born in Wuhsi in Kiangsu in 1904, joined the Party in 1925, studied at the Communications University in Shanghai and at the Sun Yat-sen University in Moscow, and had a long career as activist in the Communist Youth League and as propagandist in Kiangsi and at Yenan. In 1960, he went to the Soviet Union with Liu Shao-ch'i and Teng Hsiao-p'ing to try to lessen the gap between the ideological viewpoints of Moscow and Peking.

Lu Ting-yi opened the Hundred Flowers Campaign with his famous speech of May 26, 1956: "May a hundred flowers bloom and a hundred schools of thought contend." In line with the policy of the moment, he spoke against sectarianism in the scientific, artistic, and literary domains, recalled the value of the national heritage properly understood, and stressed once more the usefulness of studying foreign cultures (see Chapter 12). As the spokesman for Mao Tse-tung and the Central Committee, he did not come under immediate attack but was simply forgotten. No successor was appointed officially until August, when T'ao Chu replaced him for a short time.[9]

Chou Yang became the center of attention and indignation for the press; his past life and position in the world of culture made him more important than his minister. A native of Hunan like Mao Tse-tung, but about fifteen years younger, Chou Yang (Chou Ch'i-ying), formerly a student in Japan, had been the most important figure in the Communist or pro-Communist literary movement since the creation of the League of Leftist Writers in 1930. After acting as assistant to P'eng Chen in North China after the beginning of the Sino-Japanese War, in 1939 he was appointed director of the Lu Hsün Academy at Yenan, where he was editor of the review *The Literary and Artistic Front.*

His various posts as vice-minister of culture, assistant director of propaganda, vice-chairman of the All-China Federation of Literary and Art Circles, editor of its periodical (*Wen i pao*), and alternate member of the Central Committee, as well as his experience and reputation, made him the real leader of literary circles in the widest possible sense. Through his writings he had become the chief exponent of Maoist thought on culture and, in this capacity, had led the fight against all forms of "deviationism" that had been a salient feature of the forty-year history of the Party and the regime.[10]

Chou Yang was subjected to open, relentless, and merciless attacks. His prewar career as a militant and intellectual came under fire. He was reproached with having raised the cry of a "national defense literature"—which had been, however, approved by the Party and the Comintern—in opposition to that of "mass literature for a national revolutionary war" then upheld by the great Lu Hsün and (so it is said today) by Mao Tse-tung. He was also accused of having followed the errors of Wang Ming during the Sino-Japanese War.

During the period after 1949 Chou Yang was accused of having allowed the publication of large numbers of reprehensible works, of interpreting too liberally the policy of the Hundred Flowers (he is reported to have said that "all that is not harmful is useful" and to have encouraged variety in subject-matter), and, generally speaking, of upholding the concept of "literature for the whole people" after 1959.

According to his critics, Chou Yang had constantly been guilty of hypocrisy in "selling black goods in colored wrappings," by needling Mao Tse-tung over the Hundred Flowers ("may one flower bloom, may one school of thought contend"), and by secret opposition to the reform of Peking Opera.[11]

Even so, none of the great texts for which Chou Yang was responsible were attacked. They contained the usual references to Mao Tse-tung and ideas and expressions that the Cultural Revolution would not have disowned. He showed unswerving loyalty to the proletarian concept of literature and to the principle of "serving the needs and interests of the masses," and he had unceasingly condemned both bourgeois and revisionist literature for their "individualism," their "humanitarianism," and their "pacificism." He, too, wanted to "uproot the poisonous plants" and make fertilizer of them. In his various references to tradition, he stated that it should be considered from an entirely new ideological viewpoint; when he allowed that bourgeois culture and art could continue for a time, it was because he thought that the working class was strong enough to "triumph by means of free competition and discussion."[12]

The main reasons for the violent campaign against Chou Yang no doubt lay in the desire of Ch'en Po-ta and K'ang Sheng to seize control in the fields of propaganda and culture, and also in Chiang Ch'ing's jealousy of and dislike for him; in any case he was probably closer in his ideas to the "February Outline Report" than to the radicalism of the supporters of the Cultural Revolution.

Notes

[1] Wu for Wu Han, Nan for Ma Nan-tun, pseydonym of Teng T'o, Hsing for Fang Hsing, pseudonym of Liao Mo-sha.

[2] In 1899 or in 1902, depending on the biography.

[3] In particular *Tung-fang ch'an-pao (Fighter of the East)* (May 25, 1967).

[4] English and Chinese texts in *CCP Documents of the Great Proletarian Cultural Revolution (1966-1967)* (Hong Kong: Union Research Institute, 1968). This English text also appears in *Survey of China Mainland Press*, No. 3952 (June 5, 1967).

[5] English version in *Peking Review*, No. 21 (May 19, 1967).

[6] A dramatic account of the affair was given by the Yugoslav agency Tanjug, who obtained it from Chinese confidants.

[7] Like P'eng Chen, Li Hsueh-feng came from Shansi. He was the right-hand man of Teng Hsiao-p'ing during the Sino-Japanese War, and later on of Lin Piao in the Central-South region 1949-1954. Li was appointed a full member of the Central Committee at the Eighth Congress, and then became fifth secretary of the same committee. From 1954 on, he was put in charge of the Department of Industry of the Central Committee.

[8] Wu Teh, a native of Hopei, was political commissar there of the column of Lu Cheng-ts'ao during the Sino-Japanese War. After that he successfully held several posts in the field of economy and finance.

[9] On the other hand, Lu Ting-yi appeared alongside P'eng Chen, Lo Jui-ch'ing, and other highly placed members of the regime during the public accusation meetings in December 1966.

[10] In particular: "A Great Debate on the Literary Front" (September 16, 1957), "The Path of Socialist Art and Literature in China" (July 22, 1960), "The Battle Tasks in Philosophy and Social Science Work" (October 22, 1963), already referred to. In 1963, however, during a conference at Dairen on the peasant short story, Chou Yang is reported to have attacked

the policy of the Great Leap Forward and the people's communes, thus giving grounds for his subsequent disgrace (*People's Daily,* October 27, 1966).

[11] Among the numerous articles in the official press and that of the red guards, see the one in *People's Daily* (August 30, 1966) and that in *Kuang-ming jih-pao* (November 23, 1966).

[12] See "A Great Debate on the Literary Front" (September 16, 1957). In his *Literature and the New Popular Art,* Chou Yang thought it feasible to continue to use traditional popular forms (songs, opera, stories) to which the masses were firmly attached (Peking, 1954).

30 "Sweep Away All Monsters!"

Taken as a whole, the five articles published by the *People's Daily* in the first week of June, each on a clearly defined theme, look like the first statement of the doctrine of the Cultural Revolution. Wu Leng-hsi, editor of the *People's Daily* and head of the Hsinhua Agency (New China News Agency), had just been purged with P'eng Chen and the chief office-holders in the Ministry of Culture. Ch'en Po-ta had replaced Wu, bringing with him a team from the *Chieh-fang-chün pao,* and Peking took over from Shanghai as the center for propaganda.

The article of June 1, "Sweep Away All Monsters," announced that a huge revolutionary, cultural, and proletarian wave was gathering force in socialist China, "which contains a quarter of the world's population."

For the last few months, in response to the militant call of the Central Committee of the Chinese Communist Party and Chairman Mao Tse-tung, hundreds of millions of workers, peasants and soldiers, and vast numbers of revolutionary cadres and intellectuals, all armed with Mao Tse-tung's thought, have been sweeping away a horde of monsters that have entrenched themselves in ideological and cultural positions. With the tremendous and impetuous force of a raging storm, they have smashed the shackles imposed on their minds by the exploiting classes for so long in the past, routing the bourgeois "specialists," "scholars," "authorities," and "venerable masters" and sweeping every bit of their prestige into the dust.[1]

The style and the imagery bear an astonishing resemblance to the *Report* on an *Investigation of the Peasant Movement in Hunan,* written in 1927, in which Mao Tse-tung announced that a vast revolutionary wave of peasants was about to break across the country. As the editorial said, the old thought, culture, customs, and habits had to be eradicated and new ones had to be created. Mao's thought, a real "spiritual atom bomb," would be the instrument of change, which was "without precedent in the history of humanity."

The writer of the article, however, made no attempt to minimize the coming difficulties. He foretold that in the long run a real struggle for power was involved which could call for the full mobilization of the masses, pass through many vicissitudes, and take a long time. This suggests that far more than a question of doctrine was at stake and that powerful people—the "persons like Khrushchev who are still nestling beside us" of the "May 16 Circular" of 1966—were implicitly under attack.

The next day, June 2, the *People's Daily* editorial was entitled "A Great Revolution that Touches the People to Their Very Souls." As the socialist revolution and the Socialist Education Movement spread further, the editorial pointed out, the question of a proletarian Cultural Revolution inevitably arises. This affects not only society, but man himself, whose conception of the world must be changed. No compromise is possible between the bourgeois conception and the proletarian conception; within each individual, the two concepts are "like two armies face to face in battle," one of which must perish. This interesting article also noted, quoting Mao Tse-tung, that although the material determines the spiritual, the spiritual in return reacts on the material, and the superstructure (ideology) reacts on the economic base. It stressed once more the eternal nature of the struggle, a result of the eternal nature of the contradictions: "It will always exist, in a thousand years, ten thousand years, or a hundred thousand years. Even if the earth were destroyed and the sun extinguished, elements of it would still remain in the universe."

The text also recalled the beautiful image of Han Yü which Mao Tse-tung has often quoted: "The tree longs for calm, but the wind never ceases."

On June 4, the *People's Daily* attacked the motto "Liberty, Equality, Fraternity."[2] Although progressive during the French Revolution, it was now merely bourgeois and reactionary. The Cultural Revolution had to condemn it because some people had "raised its black banner" so as to transform class struggle into mere intellectual discussions, and in any case it would take the edge off the pugnacity of the proletarian left. Lastly, the editorial pointed out once more that the ideology of the "reactionaries" could not be removed so easily as their possessions; because ideology concerned elements of the state and the Party, the danger of a restoration of capitalism remained a reality.

The article of June 7, taken from *Chieh-fang-chün pao,* "Mao Tse-tung's Thought Is the Telescope and Microscope of Our Revolutionary Cause," emerged as the most interesting of all. Although it recalled, without much originality, that the most powerful ideological weapon against the "monsters" was the thought of Mao Tse-tung, certain features of the monsters were becoming clearer. They were "loyal in appearance and traitors in secret," "smiling tigers," "demons with human faces," and brandished the red flag to combat the red flag, the thought of Mao Tse-tung to combat the thought of Mao Tse-tung. This was a "new feature of class struggle under the conditions of dictatorship by the proletariat." One criterion alone allowed these enemies within to be uncovered, the thought of Mao Tse-tung, "which enables minute things to be perceived, and through them great things to be understood," much as the sun of *Chantecler,* Edmond Rostand's play, revealed the outlines and the tiny details.

The question of loyalty to Mao Tse-tung had apparently already arisen by way of ideology:

> The attitude adopted toward the thought of Mao Tse-tung, acceptance or resistance, support or opposition, affection or hatred, is the dividing line, the touchstone by which to distinguish authentic revolution from pseudo-revolution, revolution from counterrevolution, Marxism-Leninism from revisionism.

On June 8, the last important editorial in the series, "We are the Critics of the Old World," exhorted the 700 million Chinese to destroy the old world in order to be able to build a new one. This incitement to criticism quickly became a veritable incitement to revolt. The origins of the red guards and revolutionary rebels, of their various excesses, and of the vast development of the wall newspapers are all to be found in the substance of this article.

Needless to say, many other aggressive texts appeared later in June. Some were devoted to particular questions,[3] others did little more than paraphrase what had gone before or repeat themes from the army press.[4] An editorial in *Hung ch'i* is worth mentioning because of its international import[5] Entitled "Long Live the Great Proletarian Cultural Revolution," it claimed that the Cultural Revolution was the only real way to eliminate completely the ideological sources of revisionism. The Soviet Union, where no proper cultural revolution had been carried out, was the prime example. In contrast, in spite of the difficulties provoked by representatives of the bourgeoisie "who had infiltrated the Party" throughout its history, China continued its triumphal advance, under the two red banners of the thought of Mao Tse-tung and of the Great Proletarian Cultural Revolution.

The "first shot" in the Cultural Revolution

Since early in May Peking University (known as Peita for short) had been in a state of confused agitation as regards the Cultural Revolution and the Teng T'o affair. On May 25, a teacher, Mme Nieh Yuan-tze, and six members of the department of philosophy put up a wall newspaper making an extremely violent attack on President Lu P'ing, who was also Party secretary for the university. Lu P'ing, Sung Yen, assistant head of the Department of Higher Education of the Peking Party Committee, and Mme P'eng P'ei-yun, assistant secretary of the Party for the university, were accused of having stifled the development of the Cultural Revolution at Peita by all kinds of maneuvers and artifices (refusal to allow big wall newspapers to be put up, refusal to allow general meetings to be held, and the like). The document ended with a dramatic call to arms:

> Revolutionary intellectuals, the hour to fight has come! Let us unite! Raise high the great red banner of the thought of Mao Tse-tung, unite around the Central Committee and Chairman Mao! Break all the controls and the evil plots of the revisionists resolutely, radically, totally, completely, destroy all monsters, and all revisionist elements like Khrushchev! Carry through the socialist revolution right to the end! Protect the Central Committee! Protect the thought of Mao Tse-tung! Protect the dictatorship of the proletariat!

Lu P'ing, a political cadre of long standing, with a lengthy record of activities in the trade unions and youth organizations, former assistant minister of the railways, member of the National People's Congress for Peking, reacted strongly in the name of the discipline of the university and of the Party. A state of turbulence approaching anarchy began to develop and clashes occurred between students; the effects were considerable and widespread.

Peking University, founded in 1898, had always played a big part in Chinese revolutions. The May Fourth Movement of 1919 started there; Ch'en Tu-hsiu and Li Ta-chao, the founders of the Chinese Communist Party, taught there; each important national event roused an echo there; and many students from Peita joined the Communist bases during the Sino-Japanese War. This important strategic position where liberal currents still ran deep—so much so that Mao Tse-tung himself was worried by it—had to be conquered for the Cultural Revolution.

On June 3, Wu Teh, new assistant Party secretary for the municipality of Peking (see Chapter 29), went to Peita. He announced the dismissal of Lu P'ing and P'eng P'ei-yün from their posts at the university and on the university's Party committee and set up a work group directed by a senior cadre, Chang Ch'eng-hsien, who was soon afterward criticized in his turn. The operation was backed up by an editorial in the *People's Daily*, which was calculated to cause a stir: "To Be Proletarian Revolutionaries or Bourgeois Royalists?" It was a regular indictment of Lu P'ing, accusing him of having been the instrument of the former Peking Party Committee led by P'eng Chen. On the afternoon of June 1, Mao Tse-tung learned of the wall newspaper written by Mme Nieh, gave his approval, said it should be published, and declared that the "first cannon shot of the Cultural Revolution" had just been fired.

The setting up of work groups, not only at Peking University but in all institutes and secondary schools in the capital, and sometimes in the provinces, did not make for a calmer situation. The work groups were composed of senior Party members and were sent out by the Political Bureau (theoretically the Central Committee) to try and calm the agitation and check the development of the new revolutionary spirit. They were later accused of having been directly influenced by Liu Shao-ch'i, and when he made his first self-criticism he acknowledged he had carried out moderating action, though he held the Central Committee as a whole responsible for it.

For about fifty days, Chinese political life seemed to be concentrated in the schools of Peking. The students were quickly plunged into extremist revolutionary activities, each vying with the rest; teachers and pupils suspected of being tepid or who had been singled out on the basis of their social origins were given rough, insulting treatment. On the basis of various criteria, people were divided into various categories for praise or humiliation: "five red species," "seven black species." Some "species" (*lei*) with the reputation of being bourgeois were forbidden to join in songs in praise of Mao Tse-tung; "The East is Red" and "Sailing the Seas

Depends on the Helmsman," were considered the most sacred. Sometimes students were no longer allowed to read or even to touch the books by Mao Tse-tung. These distinctions gave birth to the first red guards, whose name recalled a moment in what was already ancient history of the Communist Party.

The situation became clearer in the second half of July. The work groups were opposed by the chief representatives of the radical wing of the Cultural Revolution; Chiang Ch'ing, Ch'i Pen-yü, K'ang Sheng, and Kuan Feng in their turn paid visits to the universities and schools of Peking to destroy the recently begun work of restoring calm and to fan the revolutionary zeal of the students to the highest possible fire, flattering them, professing to be "their pupils," and sometimes intimidating them.[6] On July 24, the work groups were withdrawn. Ch'en Po-ta, inspired probably by a speech by Mao Tse-tung on July 22, suggested that Cultural Revolution organizations should be created to replace them,[7] a method which was enlarged and given a sort of official sanction by the Central Committee in its resolution of August 8.

The withdrawal of the work groups from the educational establishments was the first success achieved by the representatives of the extremist wing of the Cultural Revolution. They had emanated from the new Peking Party Committee and had been approved by the Central Committee led by Liu Shao-ch'i in the absence of Mao Tse-tung; Mao had explicitly condemned them, as K'ang Sheng confirmed on July 22.[8]

Eventually, under the pretext of gaining time to reform the educational systems and programs—in fact in order to extend the agitation of the Cultural Revolution beyond the schools—the Party decided, on July 26, to close the universities and secondary schools for six months, which became several years. July 26 marked the return of Mao Tse-tung to Peking; the convening of the Eleventh Plenum of the Central Committee gave the Cultural Revolution a charter and structures of its own.

Meanwhile the fortress of Peking University had been taken. The first red guards and "revolutionary rebels" quickly extended their sphere of action well beyond the capital, and the first wave of disorders engulfed the big Chinese cities.

Notes

[1] Hsinhua Agency (June 1, 1966).
[2] "Tear Aside the Bourgeois Mask of Liberty, Equality, and Fraternity!"

[3] This was so in the case of the editorial ("Capture the Positions in the Field of Historical Studies Seized by the Bourgeoisie," *People's Daily* (June 3, 1966).

[4] See in particular the editorials "Raise High the Great Red Banner of the Thought of Mao Tse-tung" and "Never Forget Class Struggle," *Chieh-fang-chün pao* (April 18 and May 4, 1966).

[5] *Hung ch'i*, No. 8 (1966).

[6] See in particular the speech given by Chiang Ch'ing on July 24 at the School of Broadcasting.

[7] Assembly, committee, and groups. See speech of July 26.

[8] "Chairman Mao never sent you a work group, it was sent you by the new Peking Committee" (declaration of July 22 at Peking University). The outstanding feature of the visit of Chiang Ch'ing to Peking University on July 22 was a violent criticism of the role of the work group led by Chang Ch'eng-hsien "who has done nothing to enlighten you or mobilize you." Mao's hostility to the work groups was expressed in declarations made on July 21 and 22 to senior Party members. An English version is to be found in Jerome Ch'en, *Mao Papers*, pp. 24-34, and in *Current Background*, No. 892 (October 21, 1969).

31 The Return of the Great Helmsman and the Eleventh Plenum Of the Eighth Central Committee

While these great events shook the Party and cultural circles, their ultimate cause remained a complete mystery. Officially at least, the Central Committee had not met since its Tenth Plenum in September 1962. The public knew nothing of the "February Outline Report" and the "May 16 Circular." Although it was obvious by now that a confrontation was going on between powerful groups, nobody could claim to be able to name them. The chief unknown quantity was the role of Mao Tse-tung, who since November 1965 had made no public appearances, had received no foreign guests, had ceased to comment on the current situation, and whose very whereabouts were unknown. Early in May, rumors were rife in the capital and among foreign circles. The chairman was said to have had a stroke, and eminent Western specialists (one Czech and another Italian, it was reported) had come to give him treatment or to operate on him. There was also talk of the progress of Parkinson's Disease, from which some people believed him to have been suffering for several years. At one time he was even said to have died.[1]

On May 10, the press published a photograph of him with an Albanian mission led by Mehmet Shehu. It was enough to banish rumors of his death or total physical disability but not enough to prove that he still had command of the Party, and through it of the state. Two further appearances in photographs, one when the Nepalese heir to the throne visited Peking and the other at the opening of the Conference of Afro-Asian Writers, seemed to confirm, better than the first had done, that he was in a satisfactory state of health. Then, on July 26, the whole press was covered with huge headlines, accompanied by photographs, announcing that on

July 16 Mao Tse-tung had swum in the Yangtze for an hour and five minutes, covering a distance of 15 kilometers; this was an astounding record, even allowing for the speed of the current and previous performances of the man himself.

Five thousand people, among them Wang Jen-chung, Party secretary for Hupei, had swum in the river at the same time, pushing rafts carrying images of him or covered with slogans and multicolored banners. Two hundred thousand others had witnessed the feat, which the rest of the country, the diplomatic representatives, and the foreign press heard about ten days later, giving a perfect illustration of the hermetic nature and the watertight divisions existing in Chinese society.[2]

The Wuhan episode, its orchestration, and the dithyrambic comments in the papers gave the Chinese population resounding proof that their glorious leader was physically and intellectually intact and that he was making a return as their leader and as leader of the Cultural Revolution. "Follow Chairman Mao and Advance in the Teeth of the Great Storms and Waves" was the headline of the *People's Daily;* at the same time, it reprinted a poem written by Mao Tse-tung in 1956 in similar though less dramatic circumstances, along with a translation into current Chinese:

> I have just drunk the water of Changsha
> And eaten the fish of Wuchang once more.
> I cross a ten thousand *li* river
> While my eyes rest on the sky of Chu.
> What does it matter if the wind blows and the waves buffet me?
> It is better than idling in my courtyard
> And today my cup is full.

> Near the River the master said:
> "All that flows by is like this water."
> The masts shake in the wind,
> The rocks of the Tortoise and the Snake are still,
> Great plans are taking shape.
> A bridge flies from South to North,
> The eternal barrier has become a pathway.

> Stone walls are thrown up to the West
> They halt the clouds and the rain of the mountains of Wu,
> The lofty gorge becomes a smooth lake,
> The changeless goddess wonders at this strange world.[3]

The Eleventh Plenum of the Eighth Central Committee

The Eleventh Plenum of the Eighth Central Committee, held from August 1 to 12, 1966, was not announced beforehand. After the publication of the decision of August 8 on the Cultural Revolution, suspicions were aroused, but they were not fully confirmed until August 12, when the final communiqué was published. Judging by information gathered afterward, it appears that the Central Committee was scheduled to meet in Peking in the second half of July (July 21 is the most likely date) in Mao's absence, at least for the first sessions. Teng Hsiao-p'ing, the general secretary of the Central Committee, who was first urged not to change the plans, seems to have allowed himself to be intimidated by injunctions from Mao Tse-tung himself. The purge of P'eng Chen several weeks earlier, the fact that the Peking Party Committee had been taken over by a group less favorable to the body of opinion represented by Liu Shao-ch'i, and possibly pressure from the army, meant that he could not maneuver in safety.

A similar mystery surrounds the numbers of those present, full members, alternate members, and delegates from various Party organizations, who did not have the right to vote but who influenced the full members. Unlike the preceding ones, the final communiqué was silent on this point and also said nothing of the changes within the Political Bureau and the Secretariat.

The Central Committee published two texts, the "Decision of the Central Committee of the Chinese Communist Party concerning the Great Proletarian Cultural Revolution," known as "The Sixteen Points," and the final communiqué entitled "Communiqué of the Eleventh Plenary Session of the Eighth Central Committee of the Communist Party of China," which revealed more of the tensions which must have been felt during sessions.[4]

The sixteen points of the decision of August 8 reflect a situation and convey a corresponding intention. Certain persons "taking the capitalist road" had made their way into the Party, where some held leading posts. They looked for support to cultural institutions "not in correspondence with the socialist economic base." These elements had to be struggled against and overthrown, the institutional framework had to be transformed, and the old customs inherited from the former society had to be changed. The elimination of the undesirable elements depended above all on the capacity of the Party to mobilize the masses and the ability of the masses to undertake suitable action to "liberate" themselves.

Within the Party the left had to be "discovered" and "strengthened," the middle had to be won over, and the right isolated, so as to "achieve the unity of more than 95 percent of the cadres and more than 95 percent of the masses." The majority of cadres were "good" or "comparatively good." Those who had made serious mistakes, were incompetent, or were imprisoned by routine but were ready to turn over a new leaf would find themselves in the camp of the Proletarian Cultural Revolution later on. The rest, the "anti-Party, antisocialist rightists must be fully exposed, refuted, overthrown and completely discredited, and their influence eliminated" (Article 8).

The masses were to educate themselves by "revolutionizing" themselves. Their initiative and their criticisms were to be respected, while disorders were not to be feared. "Fullest use" was to be made of denunciations and of "big-character posters and great debates to argue matters out." (Article 4).

"Cultural revolutionary groups and committees" were to be organized to direct the revolution alongside the Party. They were to be "the organs of power" and should be "permanent, standing mass organizations." Their members were to be elected by the masses, and the masses could replace or recall tham at any time (Article 9). It seems justifiable today to think that the creation of "cultural revolutionary groups and committees," whether as an expedient to intimidate the opposition or as a deliberate transfer of sovereignty from the Party to the masses, was a serious mistake. The creation of a parallel, rival hierarchy cut off the majority of cadres from the Cultural Revolution. It also divided authority, creating a situation of increasing anarchy.

A close reading of the texts, however, shows that caution and readiness to compromise were advocated as much as daring and stirring up disorders. "Any method of forcing a minority holding different views to submit" was "impermissible," for the minority had to be protected and won over by reasoning. Active counterrevolutionaries guilty of murder, sabotage, or theft of state secrets were to be treated in accordance with the law (Articles 6 and 7).

The masses were not to be aroused against the masses. Production was not to be disturbed (Article 14). Scientists, technicians, and those working with them were to be treated with care, as long as they were "patriotic" and were "not against the Party and socialism" (Article 12).

The dimensions of the Cultural Revolution were clearly delimited and defined. The main efforts were to be aimed at the "cultural and educational units and leading organs of the Party and government in the large and medium cities" (Article 13). The Socialist Education Movement was to be continued in the countryside and in industrial concerns in the cities. The army was to carry out its own Cultural Revolution, directed by the Party's

Military Affairs Committee and the army's General Political Department (Article 15).

An invocation of the thought of Mao Tse-tung and an exhortation to study it, which concluded "The Sixteen Points," (Article 16), placed Mao's authority entirely at the service of the Cultural Revolution, so that its enemies were totally paralyzed. All those accused, including the most senior members of the regime, invoked the great name and claimed to belong to the new movement. The result was bound to be utter confusion.

The final communiqué of the Eleventh Plenum, published on August 12, seemed much vaguer and more violent than "The Sixteen Points" of August 8, though it repeated some of the same themes. Dealing with the past, the communiqué approved a series of documents on which action had been taken after the Tenth Plenum and which had been kept secret; their titles show they were of the greatest interest.[5] As to the future, it laid exaggerated emphasis on the infallibility of Mao's thought, assimilating it to Marxism-Leninism and stating that it had become "the guiding principle for all the work of our Party and country." The thought of Mao Tse-tung, in conjunction with the "mass line," seemed to impose considerable restraint on the role of the Party:

> The mass movement in which workers, peasants, soldiers, revolutionary intellectuals, and cadres study and apply Comrade Mao Tsetung's works in a living way has ushered in a new era of direct mastery and application of Marxism-Leninism by the laboring people.

In contrast to this, the revisionism of the leaders of the Soviet Union was violently attacked and they were accused of having betrayed

> . . . Marxism-Leninism, betrayed the great Lenin, betrayed the road of the Great October Revolution, betrayed proletarian internationalism, betrayed the revolutionary cause of the international proletariat and of the oppressed peoples and oppressed nations, and betrayed the interests of the great Soviet people and the people of socialist countries.

In their rage the Chinese leaders went so far as to denounce the formation, by the Soviet Union and the United States of America, of a "new 'Holy Alliance' against Communism, the people, revolution, and China." The communiqué concluded, "We must be fired with great, lofty proletarian aspirations and dare to break paths unexplored by people before and scale heights yet unclimbed."

The end of the Eleventh Plenum gave rise to incredible scenes of mystic exaltation centered around the person of Mao Tse-tung. The hands that had shaken his were sanctified and touched others, which were then sanctified in their turn. Statues of Mao were produced by the thousand, to be carried through the streets by processions, or set up surrounded by flowers, like holy relics on an altar, becoming the centers of a regular cult. These astonishing demonstrations went on throughout the Cultural Revolution, sometimes reaching the intensity of real collective hysteria provoked by a mixture of politics and religion, and involving accidents in which people were killed or hurt.[6]

The gods of antiquity, and revolutionary rulers like Saint-Just, were laconic. When Mao Tse-tung appeared to the people on August 12, he merely declared: "Look after the affairs of the state, carry the Proletarian Cultural Revolution through to the end." This brief, simple sentence was propagated through the length and breadth of the country and seemed to confer a sacred mission on the rising generation.

August 18, 1966

Had the Cultural Revolution originated among the people, not among the leaders, August 18 could be described as the first great revolutionary day. The Party leaders appeared in a new order. In homage to the army, all the chief leaders were in uniform, the red guards made their appearance, and Mao Tse-tung, by accepting their armband, gave them official recognition and sanctioned their role.

True proof of the compromise arrived at by the Eleventh Plenum was to be seen on the Gate of Heavenly Peace (T'ien An Men). A new hierarchy in the Political Bureau and its Standing Committee replaced the former one. Lin Piao came immediately behind Mao Tse-tung, followed by Chou En-lai, T'ao Chu, Ch'en Po-ta, Teng Hsiao-p'ing, and K'ang Sheng. Liu Shao-ch'i, president of the Republic, had fallen from second to eighth place; the distinguished Marshal Chu Teh fell from fourth to ninth on the list.[7]

A careful examination of the press statements that followed the Eleventh Plenum shows that although it had reshuffled the Political Bureau, the Central Committee had refused to eliminate completely those representing one of the currents in the Party, whether because of inner tension or because it wanted to maintain its prestige in the eyes of the outside world. Consequently, the economists Ch'en Yün and Po I-po, Marshal Ho Lung, and T'an Chen-lin, who was in charge of agriculture, were still on the Political Bureau, which gained several new members soon to be catalogued as belonging to the opposition. This was the case of T'ao Chu and Wang Jen-chung; T'ao Chu came fourth on the list.[8]

Lin Piao, minister of national defense, to be known thereafter as "closest comrade in arms of Mao Tse-tung," and the theorists Ch'en Po-ta and K'ang Sheng had clearly reaped the fullest benefit from the Eleventh Plenum. Even so, and this is important, Liu Shao-ch'i and Teng Hsiao-p'ing and their supporters still retained some influence. The fact that they were there, face to face with the red guards, proved that the compromise was a real one; the same compromise was shortly to become apparent in the senior ranks of the Party, in the regional and provincial apparatus, before being extended to the levels of the district and the primary committees.

The deliberately military coloring given to the rally on August 18 is easy to explain. The martial nature of the Cultural Revolution had to be stressed, first of all by recreating for it the atmosphere of past struggles. It was a return to the tough, heroic period when the army went through terrible hardships to assure the victory of Mao Tse-tung and the Communist movement. To recall it was to infuse the masses with the courage and confidence they needed to win a second revolution. The army, in its purity and faithfulness to Mao, seemed from then on to move up to a position ahead of the Party, whose ranks contained "monsters" and "evil geniuses." The military hierarchy also had to be won over in its entirety and possible opponents intimidated at the same time; a few days earlier, on August 1, important political and economic tasks had already been entrusted to the army.

The intention was also probably to give further prestige to Lin Piao, adding his renown as former commander of the Fourth Field Army and minister of national defense to the prestige of the man himself. This was necessary, because his slight build, his sickly, hesitant appearance, his monotonous delivery as he stumbled through a speech that he found hard to read owing to poor eyesight, and his strong provincial accent, could not fail to diminish his stature in circumstances such as these. In all the aging group, Chou En-lai and T'ao Chu were the only ones to emerge as full of self-confidence and as properly rounded personalities. Mao Tse-tung, an unbending figure, heavy in face and in body, slow, inexpressive and almost statue-like, dominated the event in silent, sovereign majesty.

"Like a million sunflowers . . ."

On August 18, the demonstrators began their march at dawn and the whole town echoed with the song "The East is Red," like a hymn to the glory of their idol:

> The East is red,
> The sun is rising,
> Mao Tse-tung has appeared in China. . . .
>
> Chairman Mao
> Loves the people,
> He is our guide. . . .

A million of them marched, as they were to do seven times more, with their little red books in their hands, past the high crimson gate and the marble bridges of the Forbidden City, shouting and stopping to hail Mao Tse-tung. A group of them, students from Tsinghua University, was invited to join the leaders on the balcony of the Gate of Heavenly Peace and fastened an armband with the characters 'red guard' (*hung wei-ping*) around the arm of the "great helmsman," who became the foremost red guard of his empire.

The birth of the red guards, whose name was chosen from among those of several similar organizations, appears to have been spontaneous, and their revolutionary nature was contested, initially at least.[9] The first ones seem to have appeared at the Middle School attached to Tsinghua University, but they spread fairly rapidly to other schools and many universities. Their name recalled all that was most heroic in the history of the Party—the Canton commune, the Central China bases—and helped all the groups adopting it to take on a paramilitary style. Toward the end of August "commands" were created, and a "General Liaison Department" was set up.

Initially at least, red guards came from the universities and schools. They had to fulfill certain precise requirements as to their social origins, however, and be the son or daughter of a revolutionary cadre, of a revolutionary "martyr," of a poor or lower middle peasant, or of a worker. The idea was later extended, and the red guards included many government workers or employees of commercial enterprises or factories, until they were eventually lost in the vast mass of "revolutionary rebels."

The red guards were allowed the free run of the streets—"Don't be afraid of disorders"—and on August 20, two days after the great demonstration of August 18, Peking began to suffer an alarming week of violence, murder, and destruction, for which the red guards were wholly responsible. Their victims were the remnants of the former bourgeoisie, many of whom still lived on in the capital, cadres, often senior ones, in the Party and the administration, large numbers of teachers, and intellectuals in general. At the same time, these pseudo-revolutionaries also attacked many vestiges of the old folklore and culture.

Mobile groups went about either on foot or on bicycles, accompanied by drums and gongs, accosting passersby whose clothes, shoes, or hair styles were less uniform than those of the majority, chasing them, handling them roughly, or sometimes arresting them, while the police studiously kept out of the way. Groups of youth, often mere children, armed with the portrait of Mao Tse-tung, organized raids on houses on their own initiative; they seized and often destroyed anything reminiscent of the "feudal" past or of Western influence—books, phonograph records, works of art, family photographs and papers, and "black documents."[10] Some people, chiefly old people, were beaten for hours on end, punched, kicked, and thrashed with belts by adolescents, while girls had their heads shaven and pet animals were killed. In many cases, individuals or whole families were sent back to their native villages, with notices hung around their necks and packs on their backs. They were to be seen on the roads, or gathered at the stations, or chased through the streets. The red guards invaded the shops, forcing the managers to change traditional names for "revolutionary" ones. Restaurants, barber shops, tailors, photographers, secondhand book shops, and the rare antique shops still surviving were hunted out with special care and covered with posters in the form of an ultimatum. Decorated or carved facades and statues were disfigured with hammers; colored tiles were wrenched off, and the stone lions and dragons guarding old doorways were roped up and dragged off like captives to their destruction.

The last three churches in Peking were closed to worshippers and stripped of their ornaments and furnishings; Buddhist and Taoist temples near the capital were badly damaged; and stone statues of animals or people lost their heads, while stone tablets were smashed. In some places, particularly in front of the Convent of the Sacred Heart where a few foreign nuns still lived (they were publicly humiliated and whipped), the demonstrations became distinctly xenophobic. The tombs in the Western cemetery were damaged, their religious symbols were torn off, and the graves of Western soldiers were destroyed.

In the old quarters, the names of streets and lanes reminiscent of the past, whose origins nearly always recalled former customs or past events, were changed to fit in with the new vocabulary. Even cars had their model names changed, absurdly, to "antiimperialist" or "antirevisionist," depending on where they came from.

When night fell, groups of old women and children, armed with sticks, gathered before their houses or patrolled the *hutung*.[11] They were protecting themselves against "bad elements," though no one could say who these really were. In the still unchanged setting of the old city, the strange spectacle of these old people and children in the darkness, dressed in their traditional clothes, took the onlooker straight back to the nameless terrors of the Middle Ages.

Officially, the violence, childishness, murder, and destruction were brought to an end a week later, though in fact they continued for a few more days. On the morning of August 28, groups of students began preaching moderation before the majestic Front Gate (*Ch'ien Men*). The *People's Daily* editorial called for calm and asked for red guards to follow the example of the army, to be disciplined, to obey "The Sixteen Points," to persuade (*wen t'ou*), not strike (*wu t'ou*), whether it was a case of settling accounts with "those in authority taking the capitalist road" or one of "internal" differences. During the following days, the troubles were less obvious. Even so, individuals suspected of a lukewarm attitude toward the Cultural Revolution, members of the former bourgeoisie, and certain Party officials were still persecuted.

Soon afterward the town was covered with posters of all sizes, reporting the increasing numbers of incidents in the provinces between the red guards and the supporters of Party organizations. The red guards had just been let loose against the latter, with orders, in the words of "The Sixteen Points" of August 8, to eliminate the enemies of the Cultural Revolution.

Notes

[1] It seems certain today that Mao Tse-tung left Peking for Hangchow (Chekiang) after the difficult working session of the Central Committee in September-October 1965, remaining absent until the summer of 1966.

[2] The eleventh competition for crossing the Yangtze was taking place at the same time; it is not known whether Mao Tse-tung created the occasion for his reappearance or whether he merely made use of this sporting event.

[3] Translated from the author's translation into French.

[4] English version in *Peking Review*, Nos. 33 and 34 (August 12 and 19, 1966).

[5] Some of them were known later on, particularly the "decisions" of May 20, 1963, on present work in the countryside and of January 14, 1965, on some problems relating to the Socialist Education Movement in the countryside ("The First Ten Points" and "The Twenty-Three Articles"). See Chapter 27.

[6] On the evening of October 1, 1966, when Mao Tse-tung moved toward the crowd, protected by rows of soldiers, unconscious and bloodstained red guards were constantly being carried to the first-aid posts. Seen in perspective, the spectacle of frenzied crowds, dealing out death by accident, was more reminiscent of scenes of fanaticism in the Middle Ages than an orderly demonstration by a movement that was materialistic in inspiration.

[7] The hierarchy of the Political Bureau before the Eleventh Plenum was as follows: Mao Tse-tung, Liu Shao-ch'i, Chou En-lai, Chu Teh, Ch'en Yün, Teng Hsiao-p'ing, Lin Piao, Tung Pi-wu, P'eng Chen, Ch'en Yi, Li Fu-ch'un, P'eng Teh-huai, Liu Po-ch'eng, Ho Lung, Li Hsien-nien, Li Ching-ch'üan, T'an Chen-lin, plus six alternate members.

[8] It appears that the Political Bureau, whose composition was never made public officially, was as follows (regular and alternate members): Mao Tse-tung, Lin Piao, Chou En-lai, T'ao Chu, Li Fu-ch'un, Ch'en Yün, Tung Pi-wu, Ch'eng Yi, Ho Lung, Li Hsien-nien, T'an Chen-lin, Nieh Jung-chen, Yeh Chien-ying, Ulanfu, Po I-po, Li Hsüeh-feng, Hsieh Fu-chih.

[9] In a speech on August 2, Kuan Feng, then an important member of the Cultural Revolution Group, affirmed in the face of various criticisms that the red guards were revolutionary, Communist, and legal.

[10] The destruction of the red guards and the destruction wrought by owners of pre-1949 books by way of precaution probably did away with thousands of valuable books and family archives.

[11] The term for the narrow lanes that are typical of Peking.

32 The Red Guards Versus the Top Party Apparatus (August – November 1966)

From the end of August until the end of November 1966, life in Peking was ruled by the compromise decided by the Eleventh Plenum of the Central Committee. The Cultural Revolution Group headed by Ch'en Po-ta seemed to be growing more and more active, but its enemies, Liu Shao-ch'i, Teng Hsiao-p'ing, and Po I-po, to mention only the most important, were rarely attacked, and when they were it was by means of allusions. The hated names of P'eng Chen and Lo Jui-ch'ing were mentioned only by accident. Everything went on as though the first-mentioned group were still being converted and rallied to the revolution; the important working session of the Central Committee, held in October and presided over by Mao Tse-tung, seems to have been the occasion for a first, fairly moderate self-criticism on the part of the president of the Republic (October 23). The red guards' campaign against him, in which he was called the Chinese Khrushchev, did not begin until November 23, in the usual form of wall posters (see Chapter 33).

On the other hand, the promoters of the Cultural Revolution did their utmost, in accordance with "The Sixteen Points" of August 8, to extend the revolution to all large provincial towns, "seizing power" there in all Party organizations. The red guards were the instruments of this dissemination and seizure of power. To develop and maintain the red guard movement in the provinces, a perpetual exchange of enthusiasm and "experience," as the fashionable term put it, was created to move in both directions between the capital and the rest of the country and extended to include exchanges between the large towns. The procedure adopted to achieve this was the one used with more moderation during the "great campaigns" of the early years of the regime.

First of all, red guards from the universities in Peking, backed by elements from the Cultural Revolution Group and the army's General Political Department, went to the cities. They incited the formation of local red guards who, following the example of events in Peking after August 20, created disturbances in the schools, branches of the administration, and in the streets, arresting or molesting members of the former bourgeoisie, "those in authority," cadres, and other individuals suspected of having a lukewarm attitude toward the Cultural Revolution. A revolutionary climate was created, and revolutionary organizations proliferated, to be quickly turned against the Party committees. The latter, feeling that they were under a direct threat, resisted in the name of the maintenance of law and order. Violent clashes occurred. Schools, administrative departments and enterprises were divided into countless similar, rival, or opposing factions, leading rapidly to intense confusion.

Compared with the numbers of students, the movement of people from the capital toward the towns was considerable, amounting to several thousand.[1]

The red guards from the provinces in their turn went to Peking, spontaneously to start with and later in a more carefully controlled way, to receive the message directly from Mao Tse-tung himself and appear as the authentic bearers and executors of his thought. The journey to the capital and its wonders, hundreds or thousands of kilometers from their birthplaces, was to them both a pilgrimage, crowned by the march past the "great helmsman" who watched them from the gates of the imperial palace, the unforgettable source of further devotion, and a conditioning process, carried out by the fraternal reception teams they met there.

Thirteen million young people, all the students attending universities or institutes of higher education, at least one out of every ten pupils from secondary schools and technical colleges, and delegates from thousands of administrative units and production units went to Peking, where until November 25 nine huge rallies were held, as well as numerous meetings, mainly in the large circular stadium of the Workers' Club. Sometimes the journeys took the form of a "Long March" for several hundreds of kilometers across the North China countryside, where the winter cold had already begun.

The young people were lodged in rudimentary fashion in schools, public gardens, and unfinished buildings, or else camped in the open; they behaved like soldiers, walking in step and reading aloud in unison extracts from the "little red book" of quotations from the works of Mao Tse-tung as they visited the tourist attractions, had their photographs taken in front of the Forbidden City or the bronze lions at the Summer Palace, which were rapidly rehabilitated. They covered the walls of Peking with posters giving news of their provinces and showed curiosity rather than hostility when confronted with foreigners, whom most of them had never seen before. The overriding impression they gave was of a docile, naive mass in utter subordination to a totally exclusive ideology—youths who could be aroused to histrionic or hysterical behavior when those in command decided it for them. The inhabitants of Peking were quick to react to the huge additional burden the young people represented, for they caused disruptions in the food supply and in public transport. The red guards replied to these criticisms in their posters, protesting that they were extremely frugal and pointing out that the capital belonged to them, too, as it did to the whole of China.

For foreign observers, the presence in Peking of the red guards from the provinces meant the opening up of a country which for a long time had been sealed off in watertight divisions. Each group, anxious to inform the others, and to reach national opinion, put up its posters in several different districts. Under the title of "news from such-and-such a province," the Chinese reader (or the foreigner able to read Chinese) found indignant, highly colored accounts of clashes and bloodshed caused there by the Cultural Revolution, or denunciations of local officials or of the state of various institutions or their methods of work. Although these hasty and sometimes imprudent readings gave no information on the situation in the countryside or on the real feelings of the cadres and the population, at least they told readers of the behavior of the categories under attack and enabled them to classify senior officials according to tendency. For the first time, a semi-independent press appeared alongside the official press, which was still carefully controlled, and although it was impossible to go to the provinces, the provinces came to Peking.[2]

The provinces also visited each other. Horizontal contacts between the great cities, or between parent or rival universities, complemented the vertical contacts between the capital and the provinces. Later, mutual help was given in the form of propaganda "commandos"; local interests reacted more sharply than ever.

"Bombard the headquarters"

From the start the speeches made by Lin Piao and Chou En-lai at the mass rallies from the Gate of Heavenly Peace, the harangues of other leaders, and the editorials of the chief newspapers conveyed the anxiety to keep the Cultural Revolution within two limits. At the top, the moral authority of Mao Tse-tung, Lin Piao, and the Central Committee as a body had to be preserved. T'ao Chu stated that all other persons, including himself, could be censured. Criticisms in the streets helped in this way to overcome the obstinate, silent opposition persisting at the top of the hierarchy. At the bottom, resistance in the six regional bureaus of the Central Committee had to be dislodged and the Party committees in the twenty-one provinces, the five autonomous regions, and the two special municipalities had to be purged and reorganized.[3] The level of the 2,117 districts (*hsien*) had to be left untouched. Practical effects of the Cultural Revolution were to be confined to the highest levels of the Party apparatus; the base (primary committees) and the intermediate levels (district committees) were to be excluded. This is how "Bombard the headquarters," used by Mao Tse-tung in his poster of August 5, 1966, should be interpreted.

Two main trends emerged fairly quickly within this general line. One, a cautious, moderate current, was represented by Chou En-lai, Ch'en Yi, and Li Hsien-nien; the other, more radical current, aiming at the maximum extension of the revolution and intensification of its rhythm, was that of the Cultural Revolution Group headed by Ch'en Po-ta. Needless to say, further shades of difference, some of them considerable, existed within each of the two groups.

Chou En-lai, as premier, had direct and real responsibility for all sectors of national life; he was a specialist in the art of wielding power rather than a theorist, but he was too much of a realist to enter a head-on conflict with the new movements. He acted with great skill, looking for support when necessary to the authority of Mao Tse-tung and "The Sixteen Points." On September 17, speaking from the Gate of Heavenly Peace, he stated clearly that only committees above the district level should be criticized. Earlier, on September 10, he had urged a group of red guards not to believe that Mao's phrase "Bombard the headquarters" was an invitation to systematic criticism of all Party organs because all were bad. If you "bombard" everything, as he put it, Mao's leadership will be left to operate in a vacuum. A few units and a few leaders must be criticized for having committed errors of leadership at a specific moment, but they must not be assimilated to the "bad elements" of the "black line." He pointed out that the case of Peking, where P'eng Chen and his city committee had held power, was not necessarily repeated throughout the rest of China.

On many occasions, giving examples, he accused the red guards in no uncertain terms of going too far and of indulging in simplistic sectarianism. He tried to maintain their discipline by calling them "army reserves" and advising them to imitate the virtues of the army. A concern for a proper respect for production was apparent at an early date and reappeared many times in his statements; it may have inspired several significant editorials in the *People's Daily* on the subject.[4] On November 30, when many industrial enterprises were already a prey to disturbances, Chou and Ch'en Yi sharply reproached a delegation of workers who had come to Peking uninvited. Chou En-lai pointed out that the Central Committee was still in the process of studying how and under what conditions factories and mines could "join in the revolution and share in production"; the document resulting from its deliberations would then be discussed by the large and middle-sized concerns: "I regret to say I cannot go any further; we have said all there is to say on the Sixteen Points; as for concrete problems, we are examining them at the moment. What can we discuss?" At the same meeting, Ch'en Yi declared: "There are 300,000 workers who are the source of life of the economy and 500 million peasants; what would happen if everyone came [to Peking]? The students are not responsible for the nation; they can take a holiday to join in the revolution, whereas you cannot."

The moderation of Ch'en Yi, which became aggressive at times, was apparent throughout. Those hostile to the Cultural Revolution (former landlords and rich peasants, counterrevolutionaries, bad elements, and rightists) probably amounted to 20 million people, as he said one day. They could be destroyed, but that would not be in accordance with the thought of Mao Tse-tung; it would arouse reactions and would not serve the interests of the movement. On another occasion (September 14, 1966) he added that it is proper to engage in armed struggle with enemies abroad, but struggle by persuasion must be applied in the case of those within. He repeated, with Chou En-lai, that it was unnecessary to destroy existing hierarchies, "without which the masses cannot be stirred into movement," saying that, before leaders were criticized, their mistakes, if they had made any, should be sought out and analyzed. With Ch'ü Ch'iu-pai, Wang Ming, and Li Li-san, the Central Committee had made many mistakes, but it could not be accused of having been "counterrevolutionary" for all that. Li Fu-ch'un, Li Ning-yi, Li Hsien-nien, T'ao Chu, T'an Chen-lin, Yeh Chien-ying, and Hsieh Fu-chih seem to have supported Chou En-lai at this point; they were present beside him at the meetings organized to welcome red guards from the provinces.

The Cultural Revolution Group, which represented the radical school of thought despite some variations of opinion among its members, had a proper institutional status. During the winter it gained more and more influence and came out on top for a time. It originally consisted of between fifteen and twenty people: Ch'en Po-ta, chairman; Chiang Ch'ing, vice-chairman; their assistants Wang Jen-chung, Liu Chih-chien, and Chang Ch'un-ch'iao; and Wang Li, Kuan Feng, Yao Wen-yüan, Mu Hsin, Ch'i Pen-yü, Cheng Chi-ch'iao, and several other less well-known members. K'an Sheng had the title of group adviser.[5]

Later, disagreements or changes in views eliminated several members—moderates like Wang Jen-chung and Liu Chih-chien disappeared early in 1967, while radicals like Kuan Feng, Mu Hsin, and Ch'i Pen-yü left in the autumn of the same year. The radical members—Ch'en Po-ta, K'ang Sheng, and perhaps Chiang Ch'ing to a lesser degree—deliberately gave a dramatic, even anarchic turn to the Cultural Revolution. Several times, Ch'en Po-ta, alluding to Chou En-lai, denounced those wanting to create opposition between the Cultural Revolution and production, "those who think that the masses, once aroused, lack reason." "Those who are afraid of the masses are afraid of revolution," Ch'en said on October 24, and set himself up as an example, encouraging criticisms of himself in what was in fact a truly Confucian manner. "If I am right, criticism is of no importance, and if I am wrong, it is regrettable not to be criticized."

On October 29, Ch'en Po-ta and Wang Li, replying to questions from students from Fukien, told them to take the "exchange of experiences" to a level below that of the districts; exemption was to be granted only to people's communes busy with the harvest. On November 11, Chang Ch'un-ch'iao declared to students that plans existed for taking the Cultural Revolution into the factories at the right moment and that until then their duty was to prepare for this by getting into contact with the workers after hours. A little later (December 17), Ch'en Po-ta launched a violent call to struggle. "We are ready to sacrifice ourselves, many of our comrades have already sacrificed themselves, but we will continue to advance." Ch'en Po-ta's zeal halted, however, at the sacred precinct of the Ministry of National Defense: "Small reasons encourage us to enter, but much more important ones urge us not to."

The personal position of Lin Piao, who until the summer of 1971 had benefited the most from the Cultural Revolution, appeared at the outset as halfway between the two trends already mentioned. His vocabulary was restrained, and less impassioned than that of some, though he was in favor of setting the masses in motion and at first was apparently little concerned with the possible effects of disturbances on production. Some of his utterances served to interpret some of the most original elements of Mao's thought. When commenting on the "mass line," for instance, he pointed out that to allow the masses to educate and liberate themselves and to set themselves in motion corresponded to the role and the new development of the theory of the mass line linked with the thought of Mao Tse-tung. This line would result in the practice of a "great democracy" expressed in watchwords and slogans, as well as in posters, dialectic, and the examination and criticism of leading organisms and Party and government leaders, the purpose of which was to achieve one day a regime of popular democracy, following the example of the Paris Commune. The great Cultural Revolution would then have succeeded, revisionism would have been torn out by the roots, and the great revolution of souls accomplished.[6]

Developments in Peking

In Peking, thanks to the presence of Mao Tse-tung and the elimination of P'eng Chen and his group from the Peking Party Committee, the Cultural Revolution had an easy triumph at first. It took on more tangible forms there than elsewhere; these included another series of extravagant demonstrations of devotion to the leader and his thought and the criticizing of large numbers of the most senior government and Party officers in a way that was naïve and captious, unjust and cruel, all at once.

At the time the Western press gave full descriptions illustrating the first point. Portraits of Mao Tse-tung were to be found everywhere, even in hotel rooms reserved for foreigners. "Quotations" from his works appeared on the windshields of cars, on the handlebars or fenders of bicycles and pedicabs. They covered the walls, windows, and shutters of the shops, reproduced on strips of paper of different colors. Processions following "His" photograph trooped along the avenues. The much-revered name was pronounced a thousand, ten thousand times a day on the radio, preceded by repeated epithets: "Our great great leader, great great supreme commander, great great helmsman; our most respected and beloved great leader Chairman Mao!"

His spoken words or quotations from his published works were always printed in boldface type or in red (vermilion had customarily been reserved for imperial decrees in the past), while from time to time his photograph was spread over a half or a whole page. The bookshops contained nothing but his works, displayed on shelf after shelf, until the effect was hypnotic. There were few references to the other leaders, except possibly Lin Piao and Chou En-lai, possibly in order not to detract in the slightest degree from the attention due to Mao; even Lin Piao was rarely given his title of vice-chairman of the Party and was usually referred to as the "close comrade in arms of Mao Tse-tung."

The red guards made up for the silence surrounding these two by attacks on other leaders. Comfortable social origins, careless remarks or remarks interpreted in bad faith, doubt as to the degree of enthusiasm shown, gossip and slander were all grist to the mill for these young people, who, unaware of the import of their doings and totally inexperienced, were convinced that they represented the future of the country, as Mao Tse-tung had promised. They had not a word to say of the services rendered by their illustrious elders to the revolution, and no respect for heroic actions in the past. The most distinguished political and military leaders did not escape denunciation in the most vile and vehement terms possible. What was happening was no longer the calculated desanctification of former leaders; all actions were determined by the law of the species on the march, trampling underfoot the old, the weak, and the useless in its headlong advance.

In accordance with a process apparent throughout the Cultural Revolution, criticisms and attacks were graduated; they moved higher and higher up the scale, referring to their object anonymously at first, then under an insulting pseudonym, and lastly by name. The attacks would begin in pamphlets and tracts distributed by the red guards, appearing several months later in the ordinary press, which would give them official sanction.

Liu Shao-ch'i, Teng Hsiao-p'ing, T'ao Chu and marshals Chu Teh and Ho Lung were not directly attacked before November 23, but this was not so in the case of many other ministers and members of the Central Committee. Many great names on the long list had already been mentioned, such as Liu Lan-t'ao, first Party secretary for the Northwest; Li Pao-hua, first Party secretary for Anhwei and the son of the great Li Ta-chao, one of the two founders of the Party; Wang Feng, first Party secretary for Kansu; An Tzu-wen, head of the Organization Department of the Party; T'an Chen-lin, minister of agriculture; Po I-po, former minister of finance; Ho Ch'ang-kung, an old Hunanese comrade of Mao Tse-tung, a former student-worker in France, and vice-minister of geology. Alongside them were hundreds of senior civil servants, university teachers, and prominent members of cultural circles (highly suspect since the fall of Chou Yang and Lu Ting-yi), members of the Young Communist League, including their leader, Hu Yao-pang, and trade unionists, all of whom were survivors of the heroic days, men who were wholeheartedly devoted to their cause and had already proved it in the face of threats and persecution.

The authors of the attacks were apparently red guards from the same departments as their victims; the posters denouncing them were first put up outside the buildings housing the departments and also outside the building of the local Party Committee, opposite the former Peking Club in the old Legation Quarter, before being put up along the streets and avenues. Sometimes posters that were too daring or were premature were taken down as soon as they were put up. Anonymous elements were obviously on the watch, to inspire and control the Cultural Revolution. Sometimes the people under attack were summoned to answer accusations at meetings that could end in death, murder, or suicide. Minister of Coal Industry Chang Lin-chih, the great humorist and writer Lao She, who drowned himself in a pond, and Nan Han-ch'en, the well-known specialist in Chinese foreign trade and a former associate of the "Christian General" Feng Yü-hsiang, all perished in this way.[7]

The proliferation of red guards of all origins and the excessive zeal shown by those responsible for propaganda eventually resulted in incidents in Peking and the surrounding region. Some clashes appear to have occurred at night in front of the Gate of Heavenly Peace; others, confirmed by posters, involved groups of workers from several factories in the suburbs. The Peking population as a whole grew blasé, only taking an interest in the most recent posters, and a moderate interest at that; it reserved its enthusiasm for the official demonstrations.

The main interest of the period had shifted and was to be found in the provincial cities rather than in Peking. The question was whether the red guards would manage to "seize power"—in other words, take over the Party committees and bring about purges. The tone and the reticence of the official press, and above all the accounts in red guard pamphlets and newspapers, revealed how difficult an enterprise this was. At Tientsin, some trade unions resisted and the secretary of the pedicabs' union died of his injuries. At Sian, bloody clashes occurred between students from the Communications Institute and others from the Industrial Institute, who were described as "royalists." In Szechwan, incidents began on August 28 and were still going on on September 5 and 6. They involved the University of Chungking, the Foreign Languages School, the Agronomy Institute of the Southwest, and several other institutions. Disturbances occurred in Central China as well, where 1,300 teachers and students were brought under control by the local authorities in Nanking; others were reported in Pengpu in Anhwei, in Nanchang in Kiangsi, in Hunan, at Urumchi in Sinkiang, at Lanchow in Kansu, at Kweilin in Kwangsi, and in the Northeast at Shenyang, where twenty-four red guards were defenestrated on October 25.

The following two examples, picked out by the author from among the hundreds of reports by red guards on the posters all over the walls of Peking, seem to be fairly typical. The first tells of events in Laiwu, Shantung, on August 26 and covers seven printed sheets full of details. Students just back from Peking began to stir up the population of the town. The local Party committee intervened, calling for calm. The students refused the appeal, quoting Mao Tse-tung. "There is only one Mao Tse-tung," said the committee, "Bring him here if you can." On August 26, the committee mobilized the masses and a violent clash ensued. Out of 396 students, 253 were wounded, eighteen of them in the head and two in the stomach. The school's wounded amounted to 84 percent as the students proudly concluded. Perhaps because the wounds were not serious, or possibly owing to its political loyalties, the local hospital would have nothing to do with the victims.

In Kweiyang, five red guards from Peking arrived at Number 7 Middle School on September 5. They questioned the pupils on the study of Mao's works, the rejection of the "four old" and the adoption of the "four new." While being taken to the guest house, the young people, sons of workers and peasants, declared that the "headquarters" must be "destroyed" (the town and provincial committees of the Party). Others declared immediately that they were ready to die to protect these committees, "the representative of the thought of Mao Tse-tung." Two thousand people fought in front of the buildings of the two committees, members of which must have been extremely uncertain of their convictions or simply fainthearted, for, as the posters said, "They saw nothing, heard nothing, and said nothing."

Resistance to the red guards was organized almost everywhere to the rallying cry of "Protect the Party committees!"

As far as can be gathered from all the information available today, the first fortnight of September was a particularly turbulent period in the provinces. It coincided with the first wave of enthusiasm of the red guards, whose actions were quickly moderated as a result of their own blunders and following warnings from the top. Chou En-lai turned on students complaining to him of the hostile reception given them by workers, saying they had only themselves to blame. He said, in essence, that when you go to the workers, it is to learn and not to give them a lesson. He went further still, adding that the workers had enough experience to carry out their own revolution without help from the students.

At this stage, the Cultural Revolution does not seem to have affected life in the countryside, except perhaps in the immediate neighborhood of some of the large cities. The Party—including the group led by Ch'en Po-ta— acted with the utmost caution and renewed the annual order to halt all political conflicts, in particular the Four Clean-ups Movement, between the spring sowing and the autumn harvest.

Two or three months after "The Sixteen Points" of August 8, the Cultural Revolution had not succeeded in reaching the first and most important of its targets, "the seizure of power" in the "headquarters." Everywhere, or almost everywhere, leaders of the Party committees were still in place, defended by those whom they represented, helped by local loyalties, and encouraged by the fact that basically the situation was unchanged in that Liu Shao-ch'i, Teng Hsiao-p'ing, and their supporters were still members of the group of leaders, although their position was not what it had been.

Another important point was also becoming clear. In spite of the original intention of those who had launched it, the Cultural Revolution had begun to spread, automatically in a sense, to urban workers and employees, who were called upon to defend the regional, provincial, and municipal committees and consequently to oppose the new movement. It is hardly surprising that at the end of 1966 the revolution started to move in two new directions: maneuvers intended to intimidate Liu Shao-ch'i and the upholders of the moderate line, and participation by the workers who had to be won over or won back without endangering economic production.

Notes

[1] Speaking at the Foreign Languages Institute on September 14, Ch'en Yi stated that several thousand red guards were still going to be sent into the provinces from the Peking headquarters to "struggle, learn, and propagate"; 1,200 of the students listening to him were going to form four groups and go to several towns he listed.

[2] Several times the leaders asked the red guards to omit certain geographical, economic, or military details. They also put a rapid stop to publication of remarks attributed to Mao Tse-tung, other than the texts generally referred to. As Chou En-lai stated, the thought of Mao Tse-tung belongs to the whole world; its adulteration could entail extremely serious consequences for the international revolutionary movement (September 10, 1966).

[3] Taiwan is the twenty-second province. The city of Tientsin became a third special municipality soon after this.

[4] See in particular that of November 10, 1966.

[5] Wang Jen-chung, a survivor of Kiangsi days, took part in the Long March, and was second secretary of the Central-Southern Region and first secretary of Hupei province. Liu Chih-chien, a trade unionist, had been lieutenant-general and assistant director of the army's General Political Department.

[6] See *Hung ch'i,* No. 15 (1966) for the speech given by Lin Piao at the sixth red guard rally on November 3, 1966.

[7] Yang Hsiu-feng, the former minister of higher education, was reported to have survived an attempt to commit suicide. Li Ta, one of the twelve to take part in the First Party Congress in 1921, whom Mao Tse-tung admitted had died, is also said to have been a victim of the red guards.

33 The "Hidden Turning" of the Cultural Revolution: From the Slide Toward Anarchy to the "Triple Alliance" and the Revolutionary Committees (November 1966 – February 1967)

During the three months of the winter of 1966-1967, the Cultural Revolution narrowly escaped plunging the whole of China into anarchy; both national unity and the regime were probably endangered for a time.[1]

Within the Party, Liu Shao-ch'i, referred to in the official press by the long epithet, "Top Party person in authority taking the capitalist road," came under violent attack in red guard publications and posters and was threatened, if not physically assaulted, outside his residence at the Chungnanhai (Central and Southern Sea); the red guards published his first self-criticism. The great opponents, P'eng Chen, Lo Jui-ch'ing, and Lu Ting-yi, were at last mentioned by name, dragged into accusation meetings, and beaten up. Avowed upholders of the Cultural Revolution—T'ao Chu, Ho Lung, and T'an Chen-lin—were suddenly relegated to the ranks of its enemies. Chou En-lai, Ch'en Yi, and Li Hsien-nien were included in the attacks by extreme leftists or by "rightists" in disguise, or in purely formal criticisms, in the accepted context of the free expression of contradictions.

In the country as a whole, the Cultural Revolution was officially extended to the workers; some rural groups were also affected. Currents of "economism," "ultra-democracy," and anarchism became more pronounced and were roundly refuted on ideological grounds. Acting on orders from Mao Tse-tung, the army intervened in several large towns where it was willing to do so and where the situation was particularly bad, in order to halt the decay in the authority and machinery of government and to save the Cultural Revolution. The leaders began to look for new formulas. "The great alliance" and the "triple union" led to the formation of "revolutionary committees," which were intended to replace both the Party committees and those of the Cultural Revolution. Order was restored to some extent, varying from province to province. The state of tension and the problems did not disappear, however; by spring, the situation was calmer but basically just as serious.

The attacks on Liu Shao-ch'i, Teng Hsiao-p'ing, and their supporters

On November 23, posters twenty pages long against Liu Shao-ch'i, Teng Hsiao-p'ing, Po I-po, and Wang Kuang-mei (Mme Liu Shao-ch'i) appeared in the streets of Peking. Liu's first self-criticism was published briefly on December 26. Throughout the months that followed, the attacks on the president of the Republic and the general secretary of the Central Committee proliferated under many different forms—tracts, selected texts, and insulting caricatures.[2] These writings said that Liu Shao-ch'i was devoured by ambition, that he wanted to be the Karl Marx of China, that he nourished a deep hatred for Mao Tse-tung, and that he was trying to oppose his own reprinted works to those of Mao in a spirit of jealous rivalry. Like Khrushchev acting against Stalin, he was said to have collected material against Mao (an episode known as the Belvedere Pavilion Affair) and to have been trying to oust Mao since 1958.

The ideology of Liu Shao-ch'i, as apparent in his writings, was termed incorrect. The president of the Republic was said to have advocated the philosophy of "servile submission," which, by calling for blind obedience and discipline, killed all critical and revolutionary spirit and encouraged self-interest, recommending "small sacrifices" to obtain "large profits." In politics, Liu Shao-ch'i had allegedly committed a great many accidental or deliberate mistakes, sometimes "leftist," sometimes "rightist," and sometimes "apparently leftist but in reality rightist." He was charged with being more or less directly opposed to collectivization, hoping to place mechanization first, and it was said that he did not believe in the general line, the people's communes, or the Great Leap Forward. To his accusers, his mistakes were particularly obvious in the agricultural field, but they noted other, equally obvious ones, in other domains, such as industry, information, and national defense.

These criticisms, based on little more than scraps of quotations, were later supplemented by definite accusations of capitulationism, misuse of authority, and treachery. They resembled real hate campaigns and were combined with a few clearly defined ideological themes collected under the title of "six black theories" (see Chapter 38).

The excesses, insults, and trivialities of the red guard texts are not worth lingering over, but the fundamental criticisms and the anecdotes intended to illustrate them show Liu Shao-ch'i in quite a favorable light: he was moderate and realistic in his political judgments in the face of Mao's sudden, irrational initiative, and a classic Marxist-Leninist in his ideology, in spite of occasional anti-Soviet outbursts, all of which is quite understandable in view of his revolutionary career as a trade unionist.

The man himself was discreet and unassuming; it may be for these two qualities that he was chosen to take the second place in the Party after Mao Tse-tung, in the certainty that his sober personality could never overshadow that of the chairman. No convincing proof of his ambition exists. On the other hand, Liu probably could not accept with an easy conscience the cult of the thought of Mao Tse-tung, which was carried to a degree far exceeding national necessities and excluded all other efforts toward doctrinal knowledge. He would probably have subscribed to Teng Hsiao-p'ing's reply to students: "You say that Chairman Mao developed Marxism-Leninism, but how do you know this, since you never read anything but his works?"

General Secretary of the Central Committee Teng Hsiao-p'ing was an almost dwarfish figure, with his head sunk between his shoulders, though with a fearless gaze and quick intelligence. A native of Szechwan, and formerly a student in France and Russia, he had long worked as an associate of his compatriot, Marshal Liu Po-ch'eng. Teng was attacked with the same violence as Liu Shao-ch'i. At a purely personal level, he was reproached with his taste for good food, his passion for bridge and the theatre, and his taste for comfort. Politically, he was presented as having subtly detracted from Mao Tse-tung and as being always ready to put Marxism-Leninism and the Party above all else. Attempts were made to prove that he made light of principles in the name of a particularly deep-seated realism in agricultural policy.

The economist Ch'en Yün, who had long been in disgrace, was accused of counterrevolutionary revisionism, of plotting against Mao Tse-tung, and of economic defeatism. The red guard press called him the Chinese Mikoyan, attributing to him some extremely pessimistic judgments on the financial situation and on rural conditions.[3]

The distinguished Marshal Ho Lung, one of the leaders in the Nanchang military uprising on August 1, 1927, who had been in charge of the Shansi-Suiyüan zone during the war against Japan, was described as a "brigand"

and a "warlord," which in fact he had been, for a time. Various episodes in his prerevolutionary life were revealed—or invented—as were some of his leftist "deviations." His hostility toward Mao Tse-tung, his friendship with P'eng Chen and Teng Hsiao-p'ing, his support for Wu Han, and his recommendations in political affairs were all reproved.[4]

According to the red guard posters, P'eng Chen and other important figures were arrested on the morning of December 4, on the instigation of Chiang Ch'ing. Soon afterward, they were all taken to the Workers' Stadium where for six hours they were subjected to criticisms and insults. Photographs show P'eng Chen, Lu Ting-yi, Liu Jen, Yang Shang-k'un, and other "revisionists" with their hands tied behind their backs and their heads bowed, in the supremely humiliating postures the Chinese have always liked to inflict on their prisoners.

Lo Jui-ch'ing, the former chief of staff, who had been absent from political life for a year, was arrested on December 20 by "elements of twenty-seven units" from military institutes and schools. He also was shown to the masses, but he continued his opposition in defiance of Lin Piao, whom he asked to resign his office.[5] Several months earlier he had tried to commit suicide by throwing himself out of a window, and in photographs and caricatures he appears with his leg in a cast. The red guard papers devoted entire editions to these "victories" of the Cultural Revolution.

In Szechwan, red guards seized P'eng Teh-huai, the former minister of national defense, and the most prominent of those defeated at the Lushan Plenum in August 1959. He was accused of hostility toward the thought of Mao Tse-tung, opposition to the "three red flags" (the general line, people's communes, the Great Leap Forward) and of having contacts with the leaders of the Soviet Union. The passage condemning him in the Resolution of Lushan was not published in the official press until August 16, 1967, eight years after the event.

Many senior cadres in the Party and the administration also came in for verbal or written attacks or physical assaults. Yang Shang-k'un, head of the Staff (or General) Office of the Central Committee, was accused of having given information on the committee's work to the Soviet Union.[6] Sometimes the children of "revisionists" came under attack, in spite of being members of the red guards. This happened to the son of Liu Shao-ch'i, the daughter and son-in-law of Chou Yang, the daughter of Lo Jui-ch'ing, the daughter of Ho Lung, and the son of Wang Ping-nan, one of the deputy ministers of foreign affairs. On the other hand, the son and daughter of T'ao Chu were persuaded to criticize their father; the children of Liu Shao-ch'i were later forced to do the same thing.

Disturbances in the provinces

Disorder and confusion were growing in the provinces. Chiang Ch'ing herself told the supporters of the Cultural Revolution to guard against anarchism and ultra-democracy and spoke roughly to some of the youngest and most irresponsible among them: "You will become the little monkeys of the proletariat" (December 17). This did not prevent her from redoubling her attacks on Liu Shao-ch'i and particularly on Wang Kuang-mei. Chiang Ch'ing's jealousy of the President's wife took the most elementary forms, as was borne out by the "necklace affair," referring to a piece of jewelry Mme Liu Shao-ch'i wore during an official visit to Indonesia.

Some of the leaders were particularly worried, however, by the effects of the political situation on production; it was a question of the participation of the workers in the Cultural Revolution. To insist on their participation was to take the divisions and disturbances into the factories, whereas to reject it was to enlarge the steadily widening gulf between the red guards and the proletariat. As already mentioned, Chou En-lai on November 30 tried to restrain the workers from participating, announcing at the same time that the Central Committee was studying instructions on the subject.

The instructions were made known by an editorial in the *People's Daily* on December 26. Several vital points emerge from an analysis of this important text:

1. In spite of the results obtained by the working class over seventeen years, many enterprises had been subject to capitalist, revisionist, or even feudal influence as regards ideology and the direction of production.

2. "Bad elements" had made their way into the Party and put up obstinate resistance to the correct line of Mao Tse-tung, encouraging revisionism and, by extension, capitalism. To safeguard the socialist system, it was no longer possible not to carry the revolution into the factories.

3. The method of Mao Tse-tung consists of putting politics above all else. Production is not therefore based on material stimuli. So, once the political face of China had changed, the spiritual forces would become great material forces.

4. The workers were sad to see that the Cultural Revolution had not yet reached the factories. Henceforth, in accordance with the orders of Mao Tse-tung and the Central Committee, they would be able to participate "victoriously" in the revolution and remain at their posts in production.

5. Some minorities, however, had invoked the tasks of production against those of the revolution. "Authorities" claiming to be incarnations of the Party resisted and threatened and tempted people with practical advantages, even encouraging armed struggle. The Central Committee had therefore decided that no leader of an enterprise, if criticized, could take revenge by reducing salaries, dismissing workers, or questioning the validity of posts and work contracts.

6. The workers were authorized to create their own Cultural Revolution committees or groups, asked not to allow a slackening off in production, not to fight among themselves, and not to destroy things, but to follow the thought of Mao Tse-tung and continue the movement right to the end.[7]

The decision to take the Cultural Revolution into industrial enterprises and into country districts was confirmed by the editorial of the *People's Daily* on January 1, 1967. It was the first great task of the new year; it was to be conducted in the context of "The Sixteen Points" to complete the Four Clean-ups Movement.

The editorial attacked those who believed "revolution" and "production" were incompatible: "If the Great Proletarian Cultural Revolution develops in offices, schools, and cultural circles only, it will stop halfway." On the pretext of following historical precedents, particularly that of May 4, 1919, intellectuals, students, and teachers were encouraged to go into the factories and the countryside in an organized, planned way to mingle with the great masses of workers and peasants. This is the most interesting point in the editorial; it also recalled the historical origins of the Cultural Revolution, calling it "the great event of the first sixty years of the century," one "touching the destiny of states and the international revolutionary movement."

Experience rapidly proved how little enthusiasm the workers felt for joining and upholding a Cultural Revolution which they had not initiated and from which they had little to gain. The workers were aware of being the true justification for the Party, although they were not its principal base; they had their own organization, cells, and trade unions and were older than the student propaganda groups who arrived, claiming to instruct them, as in the early days when the workers knew nothing of the ways of revolution. All possibilities of jealousy set aside, the workers could hardly be expected to give the intellectuals a warm welcome. Generally speaking, they were also hostile to all outside intervention, whether from other regions or from other organizations. They sensed that the Cultural Revolution would call for a renewal of efforts and austerity and knew that one of the charges held against its enemies was the policy of self-interest and material rewards, which they could not fail to approve of, though more or less in secret. Their salaries, ranging from 40 to 150 yuan a month, and their substantial production bonuses were liable to be cut or suppressed with no real compensation. This was such a formidable obstacle to the spreading of the Cultural Revolution in the industrial world that on January 11, 1967, the Central Committee issued a circular to all levels in the Party, denouncing "economism."

The enemies of the Cultural Revolution, in their desire to sabotage it, were doing their best, the text said, to destroy the collective economy of the state and the people for the temporary benefit of a few. They incited the masses to call for raises in pay and encouraged the peasants to ask for individual ownership of property. Workers and peasants were urged to heighten their vigilance and defend collective production. Those in charge of agencies of the Central Bank and all state and collective enterprises should refuse to meet expenses not conforming to the normal administrative rulings. Even so, to avoid too direct a confrontation with the claims of the workers and the peasants, the Central Committee pointed out that certain unreasonable situations left over from the past could be amended after an inquiry among the masses. Other more detailed measures were aimed at limiting possible friction between the peasants and the intellectuals working in the countryside. The latter were told to participate efficiently and calmly in production, while any differences that arose should be settled at the local Party level. The Central Committee circular ended with an appropriate slogan, "Down with the bourgeois line, down with economism!" It was given the widest possible distribution.

The army's first intervention

In spite of all efforts, the actions of the red guards and the "leftist elements" alone—cadres, employees and workers—could not impose the Cultural Revolution on the rest of the country. The army had to be called upon in several large towns where the revolution was losing ground. This happened in Shanghai and Tsingtao and in the provincial capitals of Shansi, Kweichow, Heilungkiang, and Shantung before the method gradually spread to the entire country.

The order to the army to intervene in the Cultural Revolution was included in the instructions of January 23 and 28, 1967, of the Party's Military Affairs Committee.[8] It was preceded by a reorganization of the army's Cultural Revolution Group on January 11. Hsü Hsiang-ch'ien was chairman and Chiang Ch'ing became adviser, to the great displeasure of Chu Teh. The best-known of its other sixteen members were Hsiao Hua, Yang Ch'eng-wu, Hsü Li-ch'ing, Kuan Feng, and Wang Hsin-t'ing.

Now that the Cultural Revolution had reached a new phase in the class struggle, said the preamble to the instructions of January 28, the army should cease its attitude of nonintervention. Eight points followed, the most important of which was the first:

It is necessary to give resolute support to the true proletarian revolutionaries, win over and rally the great majority, resolutely oppose the rightists, and take resolute measures of dictatorship against conclusively proven counterrevolutionary organizations and counterrevolutionary elements.[9]

In fact, these instructions, general in nature, dated from January 28, whereas the order to intervene in Shanghai was unmistakably older. For several months, the situation in the immense city of Shanghai had been worsening steadily. By the autumn of 1966, the "revolutionary rebels" had made little progress there, for they numbered a few thousand out of a total of several million workers, as Chang Ch'un-ch'iao said, speaking of the month of October.[10] In November and December, different factions proliferated. Disturbances and strikes had brought with them a creeping paralysis of the railways, the port, the main public services, and the economy in general. This state of affairs was made all the more intolerable by the prospect of a victory by elements that did not wholeheartedly support the Cultural Revolution but upheld local First Party Secretary Ch'en P'ei-hsien and Mayor Ts'ao Ti-ch'iu. On January 4, possibly following a decision by Yao Wen-yüan and Chang Ch'un-ch'iao, eleven revolutionary mass organizations in Shanghai, followed on January 11 by thirty-two others, managed to "seize power" and hold on to it. They were congratulated in a message from Mao Tse-tung on January 9 and in another from the Central Committee on January 11. The first message gives the impression that the initiative behind the "seizure of power" came from within the staff of the two great papers of the Shanghai Party Committee, the *Wen-hui pao* on January 4 and the *Chieh-fang jih-pao* on January 6, both of which were supported from the start by the local garrison. Mao Tse-tung is reported to have approved the army's action in Shanghai by a special instruction issued on January 21, and, in fact, on January 25, the theme of army intervention was taken up by the *People's Daily*.

Senior local office-holders must have been affected by the coup, for the message of January 9 tried to make light of anxiety caused by their departure. "We will not eat badly plucked pork just because Chang the butcher is dead," it said, borrowing from the spoken language.

In Shansi, a local rebel command formed during the night of January 12, seized the local Party organizations and those of the provincial administration, and destroyed or scattered the enemy elements. It then hastened to call on workers, peasants, and cadres to "grasp the revolution and promote production," giving orders for the resumption of regular administrative and financial procedures. The terms of the proclamation prove beyond all doubt that fighting and disturbances occurred before and possibly after the "seizure of power." Work stoppages, encirclement of and attacks on the "revolutionary rebels" by about 10,000 workers, rather than political differences in the strictest sense, probably provoked the intervention of the army, which then took over as the representative of authority.

In Kweichow, one of the poorest provinces in China, where, according to their enemies, "revisionists" in control of the Party since January 1966 were trying to restore private enterprise, encouraging "economism" and causing a reign of "white terror," a "General Command of the Revolt of the Proletariat" seized power on January 25 in all the local organizations. As in Shansi and Shanghai, production tasks were put on the same footing as revolutionary tasks, but the army's iron hand was more apparent in Kweichow than in the other two places; all opponents were threatened with arrest and the punishment normally reserved for active counterrevolutionaries.

In Heilungkiang, the army is reported to have intervened at Harbin about January 23, 1967. In the autumn of 1966, troubles between various factions had apparently spread rapidly throughout the province; food stocks were reportedly divided among the people, and land, which was plentiful in this newly settled region, was distributed, while the peasants created a militia of their own free will. Sung Jen-ch'iung, a member of the Central Committee, political commissar in the army at Shenyang, and alternate member for Liaoning of the National People's Congress, had been sent to Harbin a few days earlier, though without managing to remedy the situation. By the end of January, however, the supporters of the Cultural Revolution had gained the upper hand once more, with the backing of the army, and under the leadership of P'an Fu-sheng, the first Party secretary. In Shantung, the "rebels" first seized power in the great port of Tsingtao (January 22); their example was followed in Tsinan almost immediately.

The official press gave generous coverage to the results obtained by the Cultural Revolution in certain provinces but said much less about the situation in the rest of the country. Information on the latter was given by red guard papers and posters. Their news was ephemeral and fragmentary but enough even so to reveal the gravity and extent of the disorders. Disturbances affected almost all the large towns and were both more widespread and more violent than the trouble caused by the red guards during the autumn of the previous year. They involved a large proportion of workers and employees in the towns and also peasants in the adjoining country districts. The leaders of the Cultural Revolution, judging by the number and tone of their warnings, were fully aware that a real danger existed of paralysis, anarchy, and civil war.

In January and February intervention by the army became a normal and legal procedure. Several accounts exist of the subject, often full of details, relating in particular to events in Sinkiang (the Shihhotze and the Ining affair), Inner Mongolia (Huhehot), Honan (Chengchow), Hunan (Changsha), Shantung (Hutou), Hopei (Fangshan and Paoting), Fukien, and so on.

The situation differed considerably from one town to another, with the army sometimes supporting the "rebels," sometimes acting against them, either deliberately, or through ignorance, or simply to maintain public order. It was often difficult to tell the real "rebels" and their enemies apart, for the latter were just as vociferous in their claims of allegiance to Mao Tse-tung and the Cultural Revolution, and everything suggests that, quite apart from questions of personal preference, the local military leaders were often highly perplexed. Some interventions were skillfully carried out, whereas others were apparently extremely brutal. An independent artillery regiment used heavy artillery and grenades on January 26 at Shihhotze; nearly 100 people died and 500 were reported missing. The "seizures of power" were also accompanied by the usual masquerades: Liu Tzu-hou, first Party secretary for Hopei province was paraded through the streets dressed in a hat with a pheasant's feather and a red robe embroidered with dragons (the imperial symbol). These incidents foreshadowed others, more serious and more numerous, of the following spring.

The first revolutionary committees

During the first months of the Cultural Revolution, those behind it were mainly concerned with taking over the Party apparatus, either by dismissing their enemies from important posts or by winning them over. The Cultural Revolution groups and committees created at each level helped maintain revolutionary impetus and provided the means for operating controls and purges. Through them, the masses were theoretically able to bring pressure to bear on the Party, which represented a mere 3 percent of the population, and assure its constant renewal. A sort of direct democracy would be established as a result; the Paris Commune was to serve as a reference, if not a model. It may well be that in anticipation of this far-off day, the intention was to confirm the "seizure of power" in Party committees as a whole by convening a new Congress, the Ninth, which would be entirely in favor of the new orientation of the Chinese revolution.[11]

The rapid deterioration of the internal situation forced the leaders of the Cultural Revolution to abandon these plans, to try and find a remedy for the anarchy, and to take power by other means. The "bombarding of the headquarters" by the red guards had not led to the purging of Party committees, and the reign of the masses, wielding sovereign power by means of "communes" like the Paris Commune, which were tentatively created in Shanghai (February 5) and Peking (January 31), was obviously premature. Therefore, another, more realistic and flexible formula was created—the "revolutionary committees."

These were more realistic in that they were based on the principle of a "triple alliance" of cadres who were "still good" (implying that these were the majority), representatives of the army, and representatives of the masses, who in fact embodied part of the real power, already organized or half organized. Their flexibility was apparent in that they provided the link between the old and the new order and allowed for a certain variety in these arrangements to take account of a situation that varied greatly from one province to another.

In practice, the creation of revolutionary committees came up against enormous difficulties of different kinds, arising from the Party, the army, and the masses themselves. Most elements of the Party apparatus were hostile to the Cultural Revolution, for many reasons. It was an unexpected, hasty development of the pattern of Marxist-Leninist organization, which retained the loyalty of the older cadres, and particularly those who had been active among the workers in the "white zones." It also tended to weaken the role of the Party among the masses and favored more self-effacing behavior on the part of those in office. After the unfortunate experiences of the Hundred Flowers, the people's communes, and the Great Leap Forward, all born of the initiative and insistence of Mao Tse-tung, the Cultural Revolution aroused only moderate enthusiasm. This was exacerbated by the fact that many cadres owed their promotion and their reputation to the supporters of the Liu Shao-ch'i current, who for ten years had held the most important posts in the leadership.

Last—and not least—seventeen years after coming to power the Party could no longer ask its senior cadres, now at the height of their career and ability, and made circumspect by their age and the hardships of the "black years," to feel once more the enthusiasm of the old heroic days. It is significant that the exhortations to study and self-criticism of 1965 and 1966 were addressed above all to senior cadres and to the higher ranks in the army's regimental commands.

Based in different areas and faced with very different situations, the cadres, whether those of the Party or of the state, rarely reacted in a unanimous and unambiguous way. Some were obliged by circumstances to join the revolution, which they did in all loyalty; others openly opposed local attempts to "seize power" and sometimes maintained their opposition for a long time. Most of them wanted to hold on to their office by joining the movement and trying to take over its leadership from the red guards and other "revolutionary rebels" who were inexperienced and at odds among themselves. In the spring of 1967, they met with considerable success and their action, by encouraging the appearance of the "February adverse current," halted the expansion of the revolutionary committees, added to the general confusion, and caused much embarrassment to Peking. Later, T'an Chen-lin was accused of having inspired the February adverse-current, which was justified in the eyes of some of the leaders by the existing state of anarchy.

The army, whose reactions and behavior assumed increasing significance as the scope of its mission was enlarged, was too close to the innermost life of the Party not to be affected by the Party's internal turmoil; this was particularly true in the case of the army's General Political Department, whose senior members often held office in the local civilian hierarchy. The political commissar of a military region or district was almost invariably one of the provincial Party secretaries.[12] This particular aspect and the concern to maintain its unity explain why the army at first remained outside the Cultural Revolution, going along with it and upholding it, but not becoming embroiled in it.[13]

The order of January 28 obliging the army to intervene to "support the elements of the left" was understood and applied in different ways. To begin with, the local military leaders (military regions and districts) seem to have been anxious to stop the disturbances from going beyond the limits set by "The Sixteen Points" of August 8, 1966, and to prevent the crushing and disappearance of active supporters of the Cultural Revolution. Their next step was to take over the preparations for setting up revolutionary committees. At this stage, they gradually took on the role of arbitrators between the numerous local currents and factions and also began to act as the intermediary between the provinces and the capital. At times, faced with the failure of the civil administration and with a stand-off between rival revolutionary groups, they simply had to assume power under cover of control commissions. This assumption of authority was especially rapid and obvious in frontier regions inhabited by ethnic minorities (Sinkiang, Tibet, Inner Mongolia), where national sovereignty and security were at stake.

The difficulties encountered in setting up the revolutionary committees came primarily from the masses themselves. In all enterprises, administrative and educational establishments, and in all parts of the towns groups of all sorts proliferated, using the term red guards or revolutionary rebels as a screen and adding unusual, repetitive, or picturesque names, such as "The Red Regiment of the New Army" (Heilungkiang), "Association of Old Comrades for Exchanging Experiences" (Kiangsu), "The Industrial Army" (Szechwan), "Glorious Veterans" (Heilungkiang), "Iron Horsemen" (Honan), "Bind the Grey Dragon," "Fire of Black Phantoms" (Hunan), and countless "Red Flags." The problems involved in determining the real orientation and importance of each one, in holding off those led by false revolutionaries, extremists, or anarchists, and in getting others to establish links, merge, and elect representatives in common were almost insurmountable. Once the questions were settled at a local level, the province, in many cases the military region, and Peking still had to agree to the solutions adopted and approve the choice of the people elected.

Some of these difficulties are illustrated by the case of a textile mill at Kweiyang, whose common sense was quoted by the official press as an example.[14] A dozen different units coexisted in the mill, with a membership of more than 1,000 revolutionary rebels. For a long time, they refused to combine to form a single organization, as each unit claimed the right to lead the rest, on grounds of seniority, numbers, or outstanding zeal. At last it was suggested that each rebel transfer his or her allegiance to a new organization based on the workshop. On the basis of individual workshops the representatives of the masses gradually emerged in the enterprise, but it is not hard to imagine the personal problems and difficulties of all kinds, not to mention the arbitration involved in the extension of this kind of process to all the administrative bodies and enterprises in the country.

Even when the supporters of the Cultural Revolution were in the majority, the revolutionary committees were slow to get organized. For example, take the procedure followed when the autonomous administrations of the minority areas were created. "Preparatory committees" were formed first of all, so as to test the loyalty of individuals and the stability of arrangements, while allowing the necessary time for negotiations with the capital. The latter were not always easy. Besides personal factors, local economic interests and often interprovincial rivalries had to be taken into account, all of which recalled certain aspects of the situation on the eve of the Sino-Japanese War.

One year after "The Sixteen Points," only four provincial revolutionary committees had been formed, plus those of the two special municipalities of Peking and Shanghai. The Heilungkiang Revolutionary Committee was formed on February 10, that of Kweichow on February 13, that of Shantung on March 1, and that of Shansi on March 18. The Shanghai and Peking committees were formed, respectively, on February 24 and April 20. A large proportion of army officers and political commissars were to be found among the leaders of all of them.

The situation in the countryside

The situation in the large towns is quite well known thanks to the red guard press, but the same is not true of the countryside. Whether through mistrust, ignorance, or a desire not to commit themselves, and because initially they had been kept outside of the movement by "The Sixteen Points," the peasants reacted little and late to the Cultural Revolution.[15] Their mentality, still typically "feudal," as the Communists would say, is fairly well reflected in the reply of an old peasant to Ch'en Po-ta, who was urging him to say what he thought on a doctrinal point: "You cadres are the father and mother of the people, how could we dare hold an opinion!"

The disturbances did not reach some of the country districts until after the autumn harvests, and particularly from December on. They appear to have been encouraged by instructions from the Central Committee, dated December 15, 1966, which were intended to be discussed and tried out before general application and contained many careful references to "The Sixteen Points," "The First Ten Points," and "The Twenty-Three Articles."[16] The participation called for was to happen on the spot. As Ch'en Po-ta said later, it is a crime to mobilize the peasants to go into the towns.[17]

Generally speaking, it appears that the peasants had in most cases seized the opportunity offered by the weakening of the central authority and the confusion of the local cadres to lighten their collective duties, returning to farming on a family basis, with full use if not ownership of implements and animals. The official press made frequent references to the disorders, though without providing geographical details, and gave renewed warnings.[18]

On February 20, 1967, the Central Committee issued a circular to the poor and lower middle peasants and to the cadres of rural people's communes, which was extremely revealing of the difficulties of the moment. It was an appeal for total cooperation, calling on them to back the Cultural Revolution, but above all to support production. These peasants, who were only a part of the rural population, represented the masses. With the cadres, "the overwhelming majority" of whom "are good or comparatively good," and the local army units (and in fact the militia), they were asked to eliminate sabotage and mobilize all forces for production, without sectarianism. Anxious to prescribe concrete measures, the Central Committee called for meetings of the cadres and also of the three levels of the commune, brigade, and production team to prepare the spring plowing.[19] Using the same pretext, the *People's Daily* urged the people's communes to stop "seizures of power."

Judging by appearances, by the end of February the Cultural Revolution was almost running out of breath, or at least was ready to pause for a time. There are indications of this in the conciliating methods adopted to create new organizations by the merger of existing ones, in measures to preserve, if not develop, production, in the more careful treatment of the major opponents, after the ignominious handling they had received in December and January, in the instructions for the correct treatment of cadres,[20] and in the slight abatement in the war of words with Moscow. This all meant nothing; disturbances grew steadily worse until the middle of the summer, when the whole country seemed about to topple into civil war.

[1]The uncertainties of this period led to the choice of a chapter title borrowed from the book by Victor Serge, *Le Tournant Obscur* (Paris, 1951) dealing with the years between 1923 and 1927 during the Russian Revolution.

[2]The documents on Liu Shao-ch'i were so numerous that individual reference cannot be made to them, and they have to be summarized. The strangest of all were a series of lantern slides, with a commentary, intended to be shown in public.

[3]See in particular the *Tung-fang hung* (*The East is Red*) (January 27, 1967) on the subject of economic difficulties in 1962.

[4]*Ibid.*

[5]Lo Jui-ch'ing had already been arrested once in March 1966 in Hangchow on orders from Lin Piao. See the paper *Hsin Peita* (January 20, 1967).

[6]Yang Shang-k'un, also from Szechwan, had studied at Sun Yat-sen University in Moscow and was a member of the group known as the "Twenty-eight Bolsheviks" of Pavel Mif and Wang Ming. See Guillermaz, *A History of the Chinese Communist Party.*

[7]The trade unions (16 million members), seriously weakened by the discrediting of their leaders, disappeared altogether. Their paper, the *Kung-jen jih-pao* (*Workers' Daily*), suspended publication from January to March 1967.

[8]Chinese and English texts of the instructions of January 23 and 28 appear in *CCP Documents of the Great Proletarian Cultural Revolution (1966-1967)* (Hong Kong: Union Research Institute, 1968). The order to intervene, given by Mao Tse-tung to Lin Piao, dates from January 23.

[9]*Ibid.*, p. 211.

[10]See the declaration of Chang Ch'un-ch'iao, reported by red guard papers, in *Survey of Mainland China Press*, No. 4145 (March 25, 1968).

[11]In the autumn of 1966, Mao Tse-tung spoke of calling the Ninth Congress in a year's time.

[12]Like T'ao Chu, Li Ching-ch'üan, and Wang Jen-chung, to mention only a few victims of the Cultural Revolution.

[13]Pupils from certain army schools or institutes joined in red guard activities, however.

[14]See the *People's Daily* of March 1 and 8, 1967. The Kweiyang method was mentioned again in the autumn of that year.

[15]For an overall view of the situation in the countryside and agricultural production during the Cultural Revolution and since then, see Chapter 40.

[16]See the Chinese and English texts of the instructions of December 15, 1966, in *CCP Documents of the Great Proletarian Cultural Revolution (1966-1967).*

[17]July 11, 1967. See *Survey of China Mainland Press*, No. 4023 (September 19, 1967).

[8]See in particular *People's Daily* (January 23 and 27, 1967).

[9]See English text in *Peking Review*, No. 9 (February 24, 1967).

[)]See *Hung Ch'i*, No. 4 (1967).

34 The Cultural Revolution in a Blind Alley (February –June 1967)

The optimism born of the formula of the "triple alliance" and its practical outcome, the "revolutionary committees," was not to last. The setting up of provincial revolutionary committees turned out to be so slow that none emerged between March 18 and August 12, when one appeared in Tsinghai, an outlying province peopled mainly by ethnic minority races. The only other committee created was that of Peking, on April 20.

Tendencies toward anarchism grew more pronounced from May on, as proved by a new spate of articles condemning it. In May particularly, violent clashes occurred in Szechwan. In the summer, military insurrections seriously endangered national unity; the most outstanding incident was the affair surrounding the arrest of Hsieh Fu-chih and Wang Li at Wuhan (July 20). It was doubtless this, as well as the outbreak of real local civil war in Canton, which led to the much less radical policy that followed and to a renewed attempt to restore the hierarchies.

At the summit Liu Shao-ch'i, Teng Hsiao-p'ing, T'ao Chu, and many others were subjected to violent, cruel attacks, some of which shed light on the entire history of the Party and the regime.

The Peking revolutionary committee

According to a remark by Ch'en Po-ta on January 24, the "seizure of power"should normally take three months when "revolutionary rebels" go about the "great alliance" correctly. Ch'en Po-ta also pointed out that no difficulties arose where the workers were given a proper share in events.

This was the case in Shanghai, an industrial city of long standing. In Peking, where the proletariat was not based on such ancient traditions, the process was slower and also more methodical, so that it was held up as an example.

Some groups, which are hard to identify, tried first of all to create a "people's commune of Peking" which the red guards of the schools and institutes chose to ignore (January 31).[1] Then, under the pretext that the enemies of the Cultural Revolution were getting organized and creating a "little alliance," the characteristics of the "great alliance" were more clearly defined. A "preparatory bureau" was created to precede the formation of a "liaison bureau." More than 1,000 units in the municipality joined it immediately. After that, two months of negotiations, punctuated by numerous incidents, were needed before the "seizure of power" and the setting up on April 20 of a revolutionary committee, presided over by Hsieh Fu-chih, one of the many deputy premiers and minister of public security. Meanwhile, to maintain order and speed up developments, the municipality of Peking had been placed under the control of the army on February 11 and a special organization had been set up, also presided over by Hsieh Fu-chih.

One after another, measures were introduced quickly to restore order and plan new institutions. On February 22, a meeting was held, attended by representatives of red guard organizations, the army, and the cadres. On March 3, most of the cadres who had been suspended or had lost power were restored to office. On the same day a congress of red guards from educational establishments was held. On March 19, the poor and lower middle peasants from the rural zones of Peking held their congress (2,500 delegates), which was followed by that of the organizations of the "revolutionary rebel workers" on March 22, and that of the secondary schools on March 26.

On April 20, the new Peking Revolutionary Committee was proclaimed with due solemnity. Its chairman was Hsieh Fu-chih; it had four vice-chairmen, among whom were Ch'i Pen-yü and Wu Teh, both thought to have shared in the semi-disgrace suffered by Li Hsüeh-feng, and ninety-seven members, including twenty-four workers, thirteen peasants, seventeen members from the army, thirteen militia cadres, and six members of the university. Chou En-lai, Ch'en Po-ta, K'ang Sheng, Li Fu-ch'un, Chiang Ch'ing, Hsiao Hua, and Yang Ch'eng-wu attended the ceremonies. The speeches by Hsieh Fu-chih, Chou En-lai, and Chiang Ch'ing and the message addressed by the new revolutionary committee to Mao Tse-tung made repeated and violent attacks on Liu Shao-ch'i (though without naming him, and—as only to be expected—on P'eng Chen and the old Peking Party Committee.

In April, the campaign of hostility toward the president of the Republic resumed with renewed intensity; at the same time, a campaign was carried out to win over hesitant cadres.

According to information from an unreliable source, a "committee for crushing the group of Liu Shao-ch'i," initiated by various red guard organizations, was created in Peking on March 21. Its founding coincided with the publication of several articles attracting particular attention, of which the first was by Ch'i Pen-yü on the film *The Inside Story of the Ch'ing Court* (see Chapter 5). Other articles immediately echoed his. They contained new and merciless analyses of the works of Liu Shao-ch'i, and particularly of *How To Be a Good Communist,* which voices the "docile tool" theory, placing a higher priority on obedience and organization than on politics, and suppressing the ideas of the dictatorship of the proletariat, democratic centralism, and class struggle.[2]

To make the cadres rally to the Cultural Revolution, every effort was made to prove that Liu Shao-ch'i had been their constant enemy, particularly during the Socialist Education Movement. Two important articles appeared in *Hung Ch'i* (No. 5) to this effect: "The Bourgeois Reactionary Line on the Question of Cadres must be Criticized and Repudiated" and "Hit Hard in Order to Protect a Handful is a Component Part of the Bourgeois Reactionary Line."

The "Chinese Khrushchev," as his official nickname was, was presented as the incarnation of capitalism and reaction, and the criticisms went far beyond his person: "We must, through criticism of the top Party person in authority taking the capitalist road, reply first of all to all the challenges launched by the bourgeoisie in the ideological domain."

Although the discredit ultimately fell on the nation and the Party, every effort was made to throw dishonor on the president of the Republic. It was reported that certain members of the Party who had been imprisoned by the Kuomintang in North China had been authorized by Liu Shao-ch'i to repudiate Communism and betray their comrades. Liu Shao-ch'i was said to have found loyal supporters later among these "renegades."[3]

He was made to appear ridiculous as well. Caricaturists were mobilized to portray the head of state in a thousand insulting ways, the most frequent being as a miserable insect being crushed by the works of Mao Tse-tung, or as a pupil of Khrushchev savoring, with his master, the liquids oozing from a rotten fish, the symbol of capitalism.

Written or verbal attacks and hostile mass demonstrations naturally spread to the provinces; each professional category held Liu Shao-ch'i responsible for the deviations, errors, or failures in its domain and linked its criticisms to the immediate necessities of the moment.

Condemning the top Party person in authority taking the capitalist road should be a stimulus and a help for cadres who have made mistakes; it should enable them to join the revolutionary line of Chairman Mao and hold high the "revolutionary great alliance and the revolutionary three-in-one combination,"

as the Shanghai radio said on April 17. Toward the end of April, there were fewer attacks on Liu Shao-ch'i in the official press, but they were intensified in July, when Liu made another self-criticism (July 9). "Beat the dog, even when it falls in the water," said some newspapers, quoting a text by Lu Hsün. Attacks by the revolutionary rebels persisted and named their victim directly, as was also the case in harangues by the chief leaders of the movement.

Teng Hsiao-p'ing, T'ao Chu, Po I-po, and An Tzu-wen were also accused of being confederates, though the attacks on them were milder, so as not to detract from the criticisms leveled at their leader. The rapid rise and sudden fall of T'ao Chu (January 10, 1967) took on the meaning of a dramatic lesson aimed at "two-faced counterrevolutionaries." T'an Chen-lin was regarded as the moving spirit behind the "February adverse current" in favor of "revising the verdicts," or in other words a movement in favor of protecting disqualified leaders, restoring them to office, and returning to a moderate political line; for a few years his name was execrated by the supporters of the Cultural Revolution.

On several occasions, anniversaries were used as pretexts for revealing documents of great importance in the history and life of the Party. On May 16, the circular issued by the Central Committee to condemn the *February Outline Report* of P'eng Chen (see Chapter 29) was published. The twenty-fifth anniversary of the *Yenan Talks on Literature and Art* in 1942 was celebrated and commented on from the point of view of the struggle between two concepts, that of Mao Tse-tung concerned with serving the proletariat, peasants, and soldiers and looking to them for inspiration, and that of his enemies who, on the supposition that class struggle had already disappeared, wanted to make art and literature the property of the people as a whole. On May 23, Ch'en Po-ta pointed out that many Communists who were faithful to the Party insofar as organization and ideology were concerned still remained attached to bourgeois art and literature. "The economic base of society has changed, but art, as part of the superstructure serving the base, is still a serious problem today," as he put it.[4] Ch'i Pen-yu, for his part, spoke of the recent struggle on the literary and artistic front, merging the notions of "people's army" and "cultural army," both of which ensured the defense of the dictatorship of the proletariat and of socialism.[5]

In Shanghai, Yao Wen-yuan supplied a few historical details on the personal role of Mao Tse-tung in literary debates.[6] In general, the press as a whole in May was full of articles of the greatest interest in terms of the history of contemporary Chinese literature. A festival of eight model plays, some old and some new, was held, and eight films described as "great poisonous weeds" were violently criticized; spectators were thus prevented from making mistakes in judgment and appreciation.[7]

It was not a suitable time for artistic manifestations, however; after the anniversary of the *Yenan Talks on Literature and Art,* the main political themes reappeared and with them the chief preoccupations of the moment: to halt disturbances, struggle against indifference, unite the "rebels" with a view to seizing power, and protect production. It is impossible to follow the evolution of the situation and the troubles within the immense Chinese framework minute by minute, but the ills attacking it can easily be diagnosed: anarchism, particularism, and economism were the most obvious.

Anarchism caused the leaders increasing anxiety because it had a paralyzing effect on politics and on the economy. It was condemned from a doctrinal point of view as an outbreak of bourgeois individualism that placed a higher value on the liberation of the individual than on the liberation of humanity; it received further condemnation on the grounds that it was an obstacle to the Cultural Revolution. As reported in the *People's Daily* on April 26, "Anarchism is looming up, dissolving the targets of our struggle and deflecting it from its normal direction."[8] The press as a whole took up the theme. Anarchism was primarily the result of the inability of the "revolutionary rebels" to gain a firm foothold everywhere and at every level. It varied in intensity and was generally tempered by the inherent characteristics of an ancient society that was accustomed to doing without authority in times of crisis and based its inner order on morality and customs, and also by the Chinese distaste for extremes. Where any other country would inevitably have slid into a state of generalized, relentless civil war, China fell back on the traditional reflexes of prudence and discretion.

As the months went by, the situation worsened dangerously. At the outset of the Cultural Revolution, the cadres of the Party, the administrative structures, and the industrial enterprises stayed in office and as far as possible continued their work, though under the criticisms of a minority of "revolutionary rebels." Clashes involving bloodshed did not occur until the "rebels," armed with megaphones, started to exert their missionary zeal within the units. Things gradually grew more serious. The "rebels" obtained allies within every organization, causing factional strife within the organizations and paralyzing them almost entirely. The official order extending the Cultural Revolution to the factories in December 1966 had brought increasing numbers of people into action. Simultaneously, in the places where the revolution developed or triumphed, its organizations proliferated, became more diversified, formed splinter groups, and created internal opposition so that the very advance of the revolution prevented its organizations from seizing power. The official press made ceaseless denunciations of "particularism" and the "mountain stronghold" mentality,[9] local egoism, and the ambitions of small units and their leaders. Ch'en Po-ta said, with justification, that the "small group" mentality had become a problem affecting the nation as a whole.[10] Yet at the same time, the Central Committee took the precaution of dissolving all nationwide organizations formed during the Cultural Revolution (February 12).

Alongside anarchism and particularism, economism, already attacked during the previous winter and condemned in the circular of January 11 (see Chapter 33) reappeared, more tenacious than ever. It became a formidable weapon in the hands of the enemies of the Cultural Revolution, and its evil effects were denounced daily by the press and the local radio stations. In Heilungkiang, a province with a revolutionary committee, the opposition managed to "lead astray" the workers, who violated discipline at work, left the workshops, and joined in the armed struggle, although the new officials tried to prevent a stoppage in the factories and fought to maintain the eight-hour day.[11] In Kwangtung, "bad elements" sabotaged production. In Kweichow, where the former leaders had encouraged laissez-faire, endangered the collective economy, and directed the urban economy in capitalist style, the struggle continued.[12] In Chekiang, peasants from some districts went to the towns "to take part in violent struggles." The enemies of the Cultural Revolution incited the peasants to ignore the work point system and encouraged the workers to ask for additional bonuses.[13]

In Shanghai, professional associations were created only to be dissolved, for their interests ran contrary to the general interest and encouraged a corporatist mentality.[14] In Honan, numerous meetings were held in the *hsien* of Wuchih, where supporters of Liu Shao-ch'i enlarged the area allocated for private plots of land, developed free markets, increased the numbers of small enterprises, and fixed production norms on the basis of the household.[15] In Heilungkiang, in Kweichow, at Tsingtao, and in Shantung, anarchism appeared to be stronger than all other currents. The anarchists were accused of attacking everyone without distinction, of setting up obstacles to the authority of the revolutionaries, and of following the example of Liu Shao-ch'i, "whose degenerate individualism amounted to reactionary anarchism."[16]

In each separate case, the complete confusion of the situation was clearly apparent. At Kweiyang, the Hung Hsing Tractor Factory was alternately directed by the "reactionary" line and the "revolutionary" line, each of which denounced the other in identical terms (April 18). In Hunan and in the province of Kirin, the reactionaries took on a "leftist" appearance as well. In Honan, where it had not been possible to develop the class struggle properly in many factories and mines, violent incidents occurred in Chengchow and Kaifeng in May and in Loyang in June. Casualties were reported even in the army, and the clashes were accompanied by acts of extreme cruelty (eyes torn out, shattered limbs, and the like). In Inner Mongolia, the army intervened and got the better of Ulanfu and his supporters.

The situation was far more dramatic in Szechwan than elsewhere. Numerous minor incidents occurred from the last months of 1966 on in various parts of the province (Chengtu, Ipin, Wanpin) involving supporters and enemies of Li Ching-ch'üan, member of the Central Committee and Party secretary for the Southwest. Li had the support of the armed forces of the Chengtu region (Commander Huang Hsin-t'ing, Second Political Commissar Kuo Lin-hsiang) and particularly of the 54th Army. On May 4, the first clash occurred, involving "revolutionary rebels" and workers in the No. 1 Textile Factory in Szechwan. More than 1,000 people were killed or wounded. On May 6, another more serious clash occurred with the workers of the No. 132 Textile Factory. The "industrial army," upholders of Li, stopped the fight, and left for the countryside, after capturing 400 rifles or automatic firearms. From there, it harrassed the "defenders of Chengtu." On May 19, 1,800 red guards were taken prisoner, thirty-four of whom were killed and then beheaded.

Li Ching-ch'üan was dismissed by an order from the Central Committee on May 7, 1967. Chang Kuo-hua, commander of the Chinese forces in Tibet, became first political commissar of the Chengtu Military Region, and Liang Hsing-ch'u took over the command.[17] Li Ching-ch'üan, having lost the support of the army, had to flee, and his arrest was reported a few months later. Serious disorders occurred in Chungking on June 5 and 7, and 170 members of the "August 31 Column" were killed.

Fighting also occurred at Kunming in Yunnan at the end of May and the beginning of June, at Changsha in Hunan, where several dozen people were reported killed on June 8, in the provinces of the Northeast and particularly at Changchun and Kiamusze.

Alarmed by these events, the Central Committee, the State Council, the Party's Military Affairs Committee, and the Cultural Revolution Group hastily issued an extremely energetic "Seven Point Circular" on June 6. State organizations alone had the power to carry out arrests and searches and to pass judgments; socialist property was to be protected everywhere by the masses; and physical violence was forbidden. The armed forces were responsible for ensuring that these measures were applied. It was no longer a question of "upholding the left" or any other faction, but first and foremost of preserving the country from disintegration.

Notes

[1] Mao Tse-tung was against taking the Paris Commune as an example; if applied to China as a whole, it would not allow for the election of competent political and administrative cadres, entailing a risk of widespread anarchy, and would be considered premature by all the nations in the socialist camp.

[2] See *People's Daily* (April 6, 7, 8 and 10, 1967).

[3] See the translation of an article in the newspaper *Ch'un Lei* (April 13, 1967) in *A Survey of China Mainland Press*, No. 3951 (June 2, 1967). The "renegades" included An Tzu-wen, Po I-po, and Yang Hsien-chen.

[4] *People's Daily* (May 23, 1967).

[5] *Ibid.*

[6] *Ibid.* (May 25, 1967).

[7] *Taking the Bandits' Stronghold, On the Docks, The Red Lantern, Shachiapang, Raid on the White Tiger Regiment, The Red Detachment of Women, The White-Haired Girl,* and the symphonic work *Shachiapang* were the eight model works. The "eight great poisonous weeds" were *The Town Which Knows No Night, The Lin Family Shop, A Thousand Li Against the Wind, The Two Families, The Life of Wu Hsün, The Burning Prairie, North of the Country, South of the River* and *February Spring.*

[8] The editorial "Down with Anarchism," *People's Daily* (April 26, 1967). See also "Anarchism is the Punishment of Opportunist Deviationists," *People's Daily* (May 11, 1967).

[9] A term dating from the Sino-Japanese War. Groups of resistance fighters cut off in the mountains tended to consider nothing but their own particular point of view.

[10]Declaration of January 24, 1967, at Peking University.

[11]Radio Harbin, May 9 and 10, 1967.

[12]Declaration by Huang Yu-jung, assistant director of the Political Department of the Ministry of Industry and Communications, May 1967.

[13]Radio Hangchow (June 12, 1967).

[14]"Discredit Corporatism," *People's Daily* (March 15, 1967), a reproduction of an article in the *Wen-hui pao* of Shanghai.

[15]Radio Chengchow (May 19, 1967).

[16]*Tsingtao Daily* (May 11, 1967).

[17]See "Decision of the Central Committee on the Szechwan Question," in *CCP Documents of the Great Proletarian Cultural Revolution (1966-1967)* (Hong Kong: Union Research Institute, 1968), pp. 434-38.

35 The Crisis of the Summer of 1967

In spite of its urgent tone and the new responsibilities it gave the army, "The Seven-Point Circular" of June 6 did not restore peace and order. On the contrary, the attitude of a few of the military leaders led to several incidents of the utmost gravity, amounting to a quasi-rebellion against Peking. The worst disorders of the summer of 1967 took place in Wuhan and Canton. Once these localized crises were over, and no doubt because of them, the Cultural Revolution took a firmer, more moderate turn; after National Day on October 1, when the watchword throughout the celebrations was the union of the revolutionary masses, the revolution embarked on a middle way, under the growing authority of Chou En-lai, and every effort was made, though not without difficulty, to maintain this over the years that followed.

The events in Wuhan

The Central-South region had for a long time been under the control of T'ao Chu, secretary of that regional bureau of the Central Committee. At first a rising star, he became a victim of the early months of the Cultural Revolution. In the spring of 1967, T'ao Chu lost his influence. His colleague Wang Jen-chung, first secretary for Hupei, remained at his post in spite of attacks from the most radical elements among the red guards. Wang was a veteran of the Long March, an alternate member of the Central Committee, deputy governor of Hupei since 1949, deputy mayor of Wuhan, and political commissar of the Wuhan military region; he had long had a firm foothold in the area. Because he was away from Wuhan when the events occurred and was himself in difficulty, he does not seem to have played a direct part in them; Ch'en Tsai-tao, the commander of the military region, was the man behind them. A native of Macheng in northeastern Hupei, he was also a militant of long standing. He had begun his revolutionary activities thirty years earlier in the Hupei-Honan-Anhwei (O-Yü-Wan) Border Region, under the leadership of Chang Kuo-t'ao, the deserter of 1938, and Hsü Hsiang-ch'ien, the former National Defense Minister who returned to grace during the Cultural Revolution.

The local leading group in Wuhan was powerful and strongly rooted among the masses; its civil and military powers were closely intermingled. It apparently had at its disposal several important mass organizations, one of which, "The Army of a Million Heroes," had, so its enemies said, the support of the army. The organizations of the "revolutionary rebels" had various names: "Workers of New China," "Peasants of New China," "Detachment 913," "Army of February 4," "Headquarters of Steel," and the like, which, as was the case elsewhere, shed little light on their orientation and importance.

Serious disturbances had already taken place in March. They began again in June, involving considerable bloodshed in the second half of the month, when, according to some reports, more than 200 people were killed.

The gravity of the July crisis has been proved by irrefutable official texts, in particular the "Letter from the Central Authorities to the Revolutionary Masses and Military Commanders of Wuhan" (July 27), but little is known of its fundamental causes. It may be simply that Hupei, and probably the entire military region of Wuhan, had become a stronghold of resistance to the Cultural Revolution in the widest sense, ignoring directives from Peking and particularly those concerning the setting up of revolutionary committees. It may be that events in Szechwan had repercussions in Hupei that encouraged the local leaders to adopt an attitude of intransigence.

Peking sent three important people to Wuhan (July 16) to sort out the difficulties, as a result, no doubt, of a brief visit by Chou En-lai (July 14). They were no less than Hsieh Fu-chih, minister of public security and chairman of the Peking Revolutionary Committee; Wang Li, member of the Cultural Revolution Group of the Central Committee, and Yü Li-chin, political commissar of the army air force and member of the army's Cultural Revolution Group.[1]

The three delegates failed utterly in their mission to negotiate. They were arrested during the night of July 19-20 by the "Army of a Million Heroes," with the support of elements of an independent division. Hsieh

Fu-chih was given relatively careful treatment, but the others got a rough handling from the crowd and were paraded through the streets wearing high hats, the sign of ignominy. The "Letter to the Authorities of the Central Region" merely said primly:

> Some individuals in charge of the Wuhan Military District, in open resistance to the proletarian line of Mao Tse-tung and the correct directives of the Military Affairs Committee, pushed the ignorant masses into opposing the Central Committee and the Cultural Revolution [Group]. In so doing, they were not afraid to use fascist and barbarous methods, attacks, kidnapping and brutality against the representatives of the Central Committee.[2]

In Peking a large mass protest demonstration was held against Liu Shao-ch'i and Ch'en Tsai-tao on July 21. Another even larger demonstration, aimed more directly at the Wuhan military authorities, took place on July 25. It was presided over by Lin Piao, and many members of the army took part.

Three days earlier, on July 22, Hsieh Fu-chih and his two companions were set free, possibly under threat of action from the navy and airborne units. They arrived in Peking on July 24 to a triumphant reception. It appears that General Ch'en Tsai-tao was himself persuaded to come to Peking and that both his visit and the liberation of the other three men were the result of mysterious compromises, many examples of which are to be found in Chinese history, such as the one following the Sian incident, negotiated by Chou En-lai in December 1936.[3]

As the happy outcome of the Wuhan affair coincided more or less with Army Day (August 1), numerous articles appeared explaining the nature of relations between the Party and the army, and the place of the army among the people. The *Hung ch'i* editorial of July 31 bore the apt title "The Proletariat Must Keep a Firm Hold on the Rifle" and recalled the evil role played by P'eng Teh-huai and Lo Jui-ch'ing, both described as "careerist" and "anti-Party," with P'eng called an upholder of the primacy of the machine over man. The *People's Daily* and Chief of Staff Yang Ch'eng-wu dwelt on the same themes. On August 12, the anniversary of the Eleventh Plenum, the theme of fidelity to Mao Tse-tung was added to the others. Then another campaign was launched, "Support the army, love the people" (*yung chün, ai min*), "a strategic slogan for pursuing the Cultural Revolution still further," as the *People's Daily* said on August 28, while the "bourgeois military line" upheld by Liu Shao-ch'i and Lo Jui-ch'ing,

Liu's agent in the army, was repudiated.[4] Chu Teh and Liu Po-ch'eng, both of whom had been absent from public life for some time, reappeared during the August 1 celebrations.

The political leaders of the Central-South region, T'ao Chu and Wang Jen-chung, were at first spared criticism, no doubt because they had shown disapproval of the events in July. Then a brisk campaign began against them. Wang Jen-chung was chiefly accused of having confused revolution in education and cultural revolution (September 14) and of having opposed the actions of the "revolutionary rebels." T'ao Chu, labeled a "despot of the South," "enemy of socialism," "dishonest man," and "pretentious careerist," received rougher treatment. In September, Yao Wen-yüan, known since the affair of *Hai Jui Dismissed from Office* as a redoubtable critic, and an increasingly influential member of the Cultural Revolution Group, made harsh attacks on two of T'ao's books, *Ideals, Integrity and Spiritual Life*, (1962) and *Thinking, Feeling, and Literary Talent* (1964).[5] T'ao Chu was accused of having criticized Mao Tse-tung by means of allusions and images (the sun has spots, its rays may burn), of spreading the revisionist literary line of Chou Yang, of being a despicable pragmatist, an "ultraleftist anarchist," a rotten idealist, and a renegade whose real nature was revealed when reflected "in the magic mirror of the thought of Mao Tse-tung."

In September, when these criticisms were being made, the Cultural Revolution took an extremely important turn. Serious incidents in Canton in August were largely responsible for this.

The Canton disturbances

The events in Canton were related more or less directly to those in Wuhan. Both towns lay in the same Central-South region, and both were consequently under the control of T'ao Chu and Wang Jen-chung. The red guard press in Canton later denounced the fact that the town authorities had been in contact with those of Wuhan about July 21. A tense situation had prevailed locally, however, since the preceding winter, because the "revolutionaries" made pugnacious attacks on the local leaders who, like those in Wuhan, had held office in the region for a long time.

Chao Tzu-yang, first secretary of Kwangtung, political commissar of the military region, and secretary of the secretariat of the Party's Central-South Bureau, had held important local posts since 1950. Tseng Sheng, a Cantonese educated in Australia and Hong Kong, had been active in the trade union movement, and, most important, was organizer and commander of the East River guerrilla fighters (the Kwangtung and Kwangsi Column); he was a former mayor of Canton and an extremely popular and important local figure, whose reputation was such that he was often chosen to lead delegations abroad. He was secretary of the Canton Party Committee. Li Kuang-hsiang, a less well known man, was head of the Public Security Bureau. The Canton Military Region had, since 1955, been under the command of Huang Yung-sheng, a native of Kiangsi who in a local situation of extreme difficulty (owing to the Cultural Revolution) had already shown himself to possess qualities of exceptional flexibility and firmness.[6] Huang was in Peking when the events took place, and his share in them is not known.

In Canton, as in other towns, the red guards embarked on a wave of destruction from August 1966 on, during which considerable damage was done to buildings in traditional style, including some temples.[7] Numerous eyewitness accounts of vandalism and childish cruelty on the part of the young who believed that they had found the way to "destroy the old and set up the new" reached Hong Kong and helped further alienate the Overseas Chinese from the new regime. It seems that the first serious incidents arose early in 1967, when the question of revolutionary committees began to be a reality and the regional military command felt briefly endangered. The left-wing elements accused the army, and in particular the public security forces, of a reign of "white terror" among the revolutionaries. In the space of a few days, 700 of them were denounced, 220 had to "wear a hat," and others were dismissed from their work under various pretexts. Chao Tzu-yang—his spokesman was Li Kuang-hsiang—was suspected of wanting to stop the Cultural Revolution by means of "black directives," fearing that the disturbances would paralyse the life of the city.[8]

The "revolutionary rebels" said that the press was still in the hands of "bourgeois power" after a year of Cultural Revolution. But since the beginning of the revolution, the red guards and "revolutionary rebels" had split into countless factions whose orientations were not clear and whose names often changed. To mention only a few, the "Red Flag Workers," the "August 1 Corps," and the "Red Guard Headquarters" represented currents of opinion supporting the Cultural Revolution and the Peking Cultural Revolution Group, while the "Soldiers of Doctrine," the "Poor Peasants of the Suburbs," and the "Red Headquarters," later organized into "Local Red Guard Headquarters" (*Ti-tsung* for short), seemed to be more hostile to them and looked to the army and the Party for support.

Chou En-lai, who made a short visit to Canton from April 14 to 18, had tried in vain to reconcile the various elements, giving his personal support to the commander of the military region. In June, the commander was again said to support T'ao Chu and Chao Tzu-yang. On July 21, at the height of the Wuhan crisis, armed fighting broke out, resulting in 400 killed and wounded among the "revolutionaries" of the "Red Flag," who had been attacked by the *"Ti-tsung."* The local Military Control Committee was accused of not taking the incident seriously, and some of its members were accused of using the policy of support for the left to further their own designs. Further complications arose, owing to outside interference and, among other things, to the personal rivalry between Chiang Ch'ing and Lin Piao; the situation deteriorated rapidly into one of instability and anarchy, with groups representing the different currents triumphing alternately, supported by elements from local armies or armies from the neighboring province of Hunan (41st, 43rd, and 47th armies).

Clashes became more numerous and more serious; firearms were frequently used. The battle of August 12, according to most estimates, resulted in 500 casualties, both killed and wounded; 150 were killed in an ambush at Hsinshih on August 20. Fighting was suspended briefly, then broke out again in various parts of the town, on August 27. Public services ceased to function, transport was paralyzed, and the prisons opened their doors. As in Wuhan the month before, it was incipient civil war. Although things did not return to normal, the tension eased slightly when a mission of fifteen representatives was sent from Peking. On August 31, Radio Canton announced that there would be a reorganization with a view to the formation of a revolutionary committee. This optimism turned out to be premature. New, serious clashes occurred in Canton and the surrounding area in September and October, in spite of an order to hand in all firearms issued to all factions on September 5.

On November 12, Peking approved the formation of a preparatory group, led by Huang Yung-sheng, for the establishment of a provincial revolutionary committee. The committee itself was not formed until February 21, 1968. On March 22, Huang Yung-sheng was appointed chief of staff of the People's Liberation Army, as successor to Yang Ch'eng-wu, who had fallen into disgrace.[9]

The situation remained unstable for a long time in Canton and in the provinces of Kwangtung and Kwangsi; further violence occurred (particularly at Liuchow and Wuchow) early in the summer of 1968.[10]

Radicalism and xenophobia

The crisis of the summer of 1967 coincided with a series of radical demonstrations both at home and abroad. The number of them and their variety bore witness to a recovery of influence on the part of the extremists of the Cultural Revolution, who were within a few months of being eliminated. A third campaign against Liu Shao-ch'i developed in June and July. Further "crimes" were added indiscriminately to those already listed against him: avowed defeatism in 1946, the influence of Bukharin on his ideology, admiration for Chinese traditional painting, and respect for Confucius, whom he described as a "great and wise man." Mme Liu Shao-ch'i had to make yet another self-criticism (June 28). T'ao Chu, Hsia Yen, and Lu Ting-yi, "that clown of history," received similar treatment.

The "revolutionary rebels" did not limit their criticisms to those whom they regarded as "revisionists"; they dared to attack those closest to the premier (Li Hsien-nien, Li Fu-ch'un) and even Chou En-lai himself. Then, still more rashly, they attacked members of the army as well. The consequences of all this will be described later.

The extreme left wing found an unexpected sphere of action in the Ministry of Foreign Affairs, which it took over for more than a week, beginning on August 3, 1967.[11] Minister Marshal Ch'en Yi was accused of practicing "revisionist" diplomacy and of showing too much friendship toward the "French leading clique"; he had to make a new self-criticism on July 20, on August 7, and yet again on August 10 and 11, in front of an audience of 15,000 people.

Both at home and abroad, the outburst of xenophobia in August strongly recalled the most striking incidents in what was by then half-forgotten history. The affair of the Soviet cargo boat *Svinsk*, held up for more than a week in Dairen, was brought to an end after a threatening telegram from Kosygin. The Chinese ships that entered the ports of Venice and Genoa with their hulls and rigging covered with quotations and photographs of Mao Tse-tung were putting on a highly provocative act, composed of a mixture of puerility and willful fanaticism, for the benefit of the Italian authorities. The incident was continued in Peking, where the Italian commercial representative was subjected to a public trial.

In spite of the debt of hospitality they owed the Swiss, the Chinese protested to Berne over Swiss willingness to admit young Tibetan refugees into the country. Serious incidents involving Chinese residents and members of Chinese diplomatic missions occurred in Burma, Cambodia, and Indonesia. But it was the burning of the British office in

Peking on August 22 and the maltreatment of the members of the British mission that revealed the extent of the disorder in international relations. The subject lies beyond the scope of this work, though it should be pointed out in passing that the crisis died down without the Chinese contesting the British presence in Hong Kong, which from a military and legal point of view is as indefensible as the Portuguese presence in Macao; Chinese realism in the field of trade prevailed over all verbal excesses.

Notes

[1]The dates of the visits of these people vary slightly from one source to another.

[2]Several detailed accounts exist of the misadventures of the Peking envoys in Wuhan. One of the most highly colored of them, from a Wuhan red guard paper, is to be found in English in the *Survey of China Mainland Press*, No. 4048 (October 26, 1967). See also No. 4095 in the same collection (January 9, 1968).

[3]Ch'en Tsai-tao and Niu Hai-lung, commander of an independent division, and some of their subordinates, were called on to give an explanation to the Central Committee on July 26.

[4]See in particular the editorials in the *People's Daily* on August 4, 8, 11 and 28, 1967, and "The Great Chinese People's Liberation Army: Safe Pillar of Our Proletarian Dictatorship and Great Proletarian Cultural Revolution," *Hung ch'i* (August 20, 1967).

[5]See *People's Daily* (September 8, 1967).

[6]It should be noted that the Canton Military Region includes the three provinces of Kwangtung, Kwangsi, and Hunan and does not coincide with the Central-South Region.

[7]The famous monument of Yellow Flower Hill (Huang Hua Kang) to the memory of the seventy-two revolutionary martyrs of the 1911 revolution was disfigured.

[8]See among other texts No. 10 of the paper *Combat of January 25*, published in Canton on June 9, 1967; translated in *Joint Publications Research Service*, No. 423 (September 12, 1967).

[9]On the role played by Huang Yung-sheng in Canton and in the Canton Military Region, see the well-documented study by Jurgen Domes, "Generals and Red Guards," *Asia Quarterly*, Nos. 1 and 2 (1971).

[10]Among the most interesting studies on the situation in Canton is the article by Liao Fang-yu in the Hong Kong periodical *Ch'un chiu (Spring and Autumn)* Nos. 269 and 270.

[11]This "seizure of power" was carried out by the "June 16 Corps" of the Foreign Languages School, inspired or led by Yao Teng-shan, former chargé d'affaires in Indonesia, who had been expelled from Djakarta in April 1967.

36 Toward an Easing of the Situation

The turbulent summer was followed by a calmer autumn. The "September 13 Directive," issued jointly by the highest levels of the state, the army, and the Party, urged the masses to give priority to the harvest; the press redoubled its exhortations to continue the "great alliance" and denounced extreme "leftism." The mission of the army was enlarged, and just before the National Day Mao Tse-tung went on a rapid trip to the provinces, of limited scope but spectacular impact, which lent authority to the new development. For the moment, it seemed that the Cultural Revolution was over and that the Party was about to resume its traditional role and appearance. The illusion lasted until the end of the year.

The themes of the press and the radio clearly reflected the existing problems and gave some idea of the countermeasures taken. The first problem was the breakup of the unity of the proletariat, a breakup which had chiefly benefited the "revisionists" by preventing the "seizure of power" in the factories or by facilitating the "seizure of power" by factions deeply hostile to the Cultural Revolution. *Hung ch'i,* the doctrinal journal of the Party, did not hesitate to write in large characters on the first page of its fourteenth issue: "No fundamental conflict exists within the working class. A working class directed by the proletariat has even less reason to split into two large hostile organizations."

The second problem—often a consequence of the first—concerned the implementation of the "great alliances" that were essential to the " 'three-in-one' combination" and the formation of revolutionary committees. The subject gave rise to a profusion of articles that were extremely revealing as to the real situation in the provinces.[1] Some of them again provided instructions for forming the alliances on the basis of work and production units.

There was also more emphasis on the rehabilitation of cadres, who had already been shown more consideration in the circular of February 12, 1967, which asked the masses not to take action against cadres and Party members. Articles to this effect proliferated, became more urgent in tone, and more than before were based on the thought of Mao Tse-tung. Once again, 95 percent of the cadres—the classic figure for some time—were declared "good or relatively good." The need to establish good relations between old and new cadres—the latter a product of the Cultural Revolution—was emphasized, as well as the need for good relations between the cadres and the masses.[2]

A third problem arose from the intransigence of the "extreme left groups" who opposed both a return to order and the action of the army; they called for a purge of the latter, basing their claim on the rebellion of Wuhan. This no doubt explains why several extreme leftists were removed from the Cultural Revolution Group during the summer and autumn. The most prominent of them were Kuan Feng, Mu Hsin, and Wang Li, and in the following year Ch'i Pen-yü. These "two-faced perpetrators of sedition" were reported to have been imprisoned, along with Lin Chieh, one of the leaders of the "May 16 Corps," whose members included the most virulent of the extremists. They were all described as "false partisans of the left."

The struggle against the "right" continued as steadily as ever. Here the aim was to avoid the possibility of a countercurrent like that of the month of Thermidor,[3] which would have been damaging to the balance Chou En-lai was trying to maintain. The National Day editorial of the *People's Daily* on October 1 gave a firm, detailed account of the middle way.

Numerous practical measures were adopted to help restore a calmer atmosphere. The authorities appealed to the different factions to surrender their arms. Trials and executions were reported. Criminality and the black market were repressed with increased severity. Primary and secondary schools and higher educational establishments reopened.[4] The official propaganda organs launched new watchwords: "Combat self-interest and repudiate revisionism" (*t'ou-sse pi-hsiu*). All revolutionaries had to be united against Liu Shao-ch'i and his supporters, and individual or clan egoism had to be eliminated, thus removing the two major obstacles preventing the systematic organization and development of the Cultural Revolution.

Meanwhile, the army was entrusted with a double mission in the affairs of the nation. First, it was to supervise the operation of the administrative and economic hierarchies. A second, more political mission was to enhance the spirit of the Cultural Revolution by helping its authentic representatives. The new mission of the army was summarized in the formula known as "the three support and two military" (*san-chih liang-chün*), which appeared in the circular of October 17, 1967, of the Party's Military Affairs Committee.[5]

The "three support" concerned the left, industry, and agriculture, and the texts let it be understood that in each case it was an active support which could lead to more or less direct control. "Support the left" quickly came to mean giving energetic encouragement to the "great alliance" and making further efforts to propagate the thought of Mao Tse-tung in all sections of society. The two military tasks referred to the army's responsibilities for national security and for military instruction, which was given in all important sectors, and particularly in the schools.

The "three support and two military" gave legal sanction to the de facto situation, which in many fields was also the de jure one. Mao's directive of March 7, 1967, (revealed on March 7, 1968) had entrusted the army with the political and military education of students in higher education, secondary schools, and the second cycle in primary schools. The ostensible reason for this was to prepare heirs to the revolution, "so that the Party and the state would not change color."[6]

Although little information is available yet as to how far the civil apparatus was penetrated by the military, the importance of the army was borne out by the privileged treatment its members received from Mao Tse-tung. On September 26, he appeared before several thousand of them, and this practice, which became a more or less regular occurrence, was given wide coverage each time. The political role of the army and the fact that it constituted a major obstacle to the continuing of the revolution aroused hostile reactions from the extreme left, as already reported; the "May 16 Corps" was denounced by Chou En-lai on September 17. The premier condemned the slogan "Remove a handful from the army," which was liable to cause anxiety to the entire military hierarchy and precipitate the whole country into a state of hopeless anarchy by removing the means of action that was its last resort. Chou En-lai also accused the "May 16 Corps" of wanting to separate the Central Committee and the Cultural Revolution Group.[7] The Wuhan affair and the events in Canton had completely changed the situation and the prospects of the Cultural Revolution, and Chiang Ch'ing had to repudiate the most compromising of her friends. The Cultural Revolution Group, which had considerable power in the press and in cultural and student circles but much less influence in the army and the world of workers and peasants, started to go into a decline.

The quick visit of Mao Tse-tung to a few large towns in North, Central-South, and East China (including Shanghai, Nanchang, and Wuhan) in the last week of September provided justification for the watchwords and directives issued on National Day on October 1. A few days later, when in Wuhan with an Albanian mission, Chou En-lai echoed the trend toward moderation, making little effort to disguise the gravity of future problems, whether in the field of revolution or of production.

In October, Hsieh Fu-chih, an authorized spokesman if ever there was one, made an encouraging speech on the future role of the Party. On December 7, *Wen-hui pao* remarked that red guards should help recruit new members. On December 28, the same newspaper asked, "What sort of Party will be rebuilt?" The writer considered the strengthening of the Party to be a task for the present. Preparations should be made for the entry into the Party of elements chosen from among the "revolutionary rebels," and for the expulsion of worn-out, inactive members. Three days later, in the New Year's editorial, the *People's Daily* defined the main tasks for 1968: strengthen the structure and quality of the Party, the unity between the army and the people, and the study of the works of Mao Tse-tung. In fact, it is now known that on November 27, while appearing to consult the masses, the Central Committee of the Party and the Cultural Revolution Group had sketched the general aspects and the mission of the Ninth Congress; some people thought it would be called in the first half of 1968.[8]

The year 1967 ended with a moderate program, too hastily noted by some. The Cultural Revolution had stopped short in the face of the problems stirred up by its progress. During the summer, it had brought the country within an inch of civil war and had seriously affected production, as the drop in exports showed. It was time to withdraw from the edge of the precipice, though maintaining appearances as far as possible. It was thought that the Party would be purged and rejuvenated, and as such would become the nucleus of the revolution once more, and that the Ninth Congress would shortly ratify its renewal.

With the artificial speeding up of the formation of revolutionary committees, the first months of 1968 seemed to confirm these forecasts. This probably made no allowances for the opposition, which shortly became even more apparent at the base than at the summit. In the spring of 1968, the situation once more became extremely complex; the new structures were unstable, and, although they did not altogether disappear, the fulfillment of hopes for restoring peace seemed to be further away than ever.

Notes

¹See in particular the *People's Daily* of September 18 and the *Wen-hui pao* (Shanghai) of September 20. See also the *People's Daily* of October 19, 1967, on the implementation of the great alliance by professions and units.

²See *People's Daily* (October 21, 1967), and the instructions issued by Mao Tse-tung after his trip in Central and Eastern China, in *CCP Documents of the Great Proletarian Cultural Revolution (1966-1967)* (Hong Kong: Union Research Institute, 1968).

³July 1794, fall of Robespierre (tr.).

⁴Decision of the Central Committee, October 14, commented on in an editorial in the *People's Daily* on October 25 (text of the decision to be found in *CCP Documents of the Great Proletarian Cultural Revolution*). The teaching in the universities was limited in scope and experimental. The decision of October 14 had little more effect than the directive of March 7 preceding it, of which it was a reminder.

⁵Chinese text and English translation in *CCP Documents of the Great Proletarian Cultural Revolution*. The formula appeared before the circular.

⁶See *CCP Documents of the Great Proletarian Cultural Revolution* for a text of the directive of March 7.

⁷English text in *Survey of China Mainland Press*, No. 4066 (November 24, 1967).

⁸See Chinese text and English translation in *CCP Documents of the Great Proletarian Cultural Revolution*.

37 The Multiplication of Revolutionary Committees and the Twelfth Plenum of the Eighth Central Committee (January –November 1968)

The most outstanding feature of the early months of 1968 was probably the rapid formation of numerous revolutionary committees. The army was largely responsible for this; its political and educational functions were extended still further, and a somewhat unsuccessful attempt was made to associate the workers in the same activities. The committees appear to have been troubled for a long time by instability, partly owing to the persistent rivalries within the group of leaders in Peking, and partly to the philosophy of the Cultural Revolution, which was based on the principle of permanent disputation at every level in the hierarchy. At the beginning of the summer and during the summer, "polycentrism" and the tendency to create "independent kingdoms" were denounced more frequently than before and at higher levels. The Cultural Revolution was progressing but was not yet sufficiently established to be halted or suspended. The *People's Daily* of July 31 commented that victory would not be won until revolutionary committees existed everywhere, at all levels in the hierarchy, and above all not until they were firmly consolidated and had adequate experience.

"All China is red"

On January 1, 1968, six provincial revolutionary committees existed out of the twenty-nine planned. Committees had been formed in Tsinghai and Inner Mongolia, in addition to those created in Shansi, Kweichow, Heilungkiang, Shantung, Shanghai, and Peking during the previous spring; they were all heterogeneous and precarious and did not usually include similar committees at lower levels in the hierarchy. In January, three important committees were set up in Kiangsi (January 5), Kansu (January 24), and Honan (January 27); three more emerged during the next month, in Hopei (February 3), Hupei (February 5), and Kwangtung (February 21), and three more in March, in Kirin (March 6), Kiangsu (March 23), and Chekiang (March 24). The Hunan revolutionary committee was established on April 8 and that of the Muslim autonomous region of Ninghsia set up on April 10. Others came later, in Anhwei (April 18), Shensi (May 1), Liaoning (May 10), and Szechwan (May 31). Almost every region of China then had its provincial committee, except for the autonomous regions of Tibet and Sinkiang, and the Chuang autonomous region in Kwangsi; Yunnan, with its largely heterogeneous population; and Fukien, where many armed forces were deployed owing to its position opposite Taiwan.

These committees, founded to order, should be regarded, like the preceding ones, with numerous reservations as to their representative character, authority, and effectiveness. It is noticeable in many cases that their chairmen or vice-chairmen were local military leaders (from military regions or districts). It was obvious everywhere that the army had virtually enforced their formation. Each committee had several dozen members (the Honan revolutionary committee had 155 members) and represented many currents of opinion, bringing together extremely different kinds of people—former cadres, new activists, delegates of the masses (workers, employees, poor and lower middle peasants), and army cadres. The Party, which had become fragmented, no longer directed in the work of assemblies or similar bodies at the different levels, as it had in the past.

Sufficient time had not always been allowed for consolidating the "great alliance" during this accelerated process. The press repeatedly denounced the "factional spirit of bourgeois origin" of various groups wanting to be given more importance than others on the grounds of their "three pretensions": numbers, order of precedence, titles and functions of their representatives.[1] The study and living application of the works of Mao Tse-tung were naturally given a pride of place among their duties. Their other tasks consisted mainly of recommendations to their members to go among the masses as often as possible, to share in their work, and to behave like true "revolutionary rebels."

From April on, official sources carried new instructions from Mao Tse-tung. They called for simplified and unified committee composition and action, for the removal of surplus layers of administration, for cuts in staff in accordance with the formula "a few soldiers but of good quality," and for the formation of teams of leaders who were imbued with revolutionary spirit and closely linked with the masses. As in the case of the "Proletarian Headquarters" (that of Mao Tse-tung and Lin Piao), prompt and total obedience was to be given to the revolutionary committees, insofar as they represented "unified" power.[2]

The reconstruction of the Party, already under consideration at the end of 1967, had not been forgotten, as was borne out by the attention now devoted to the proletariat, whose advance guard the Party was. The thought of Mao Tse-tung was to be propagated in schools by teams of workers, and Mao Tse-tung himself reaffirmed that the proletariat must take the lead. Provincial newspapers wrote on the subject and at Wuhan a meeting of workers at Hanyang suggested the creation of instruction courses on the "rectification" of the Party.[3]

The situation in Peking, as in the provinces, was extremely confused. In March, Chief of Staff Yang Ch'eng-wu, Commander Fu Ch'ung-pi of the Peking garrison, and Political Commissar Yü Li-chin of the air force, one of the survivors of the Wuhan affair, were all eliminated simultaneously in Peking. The departure of Yang Ch'eng-wu, who was replaced by Huang Yung-sheng, the strong man of Canton, was probably partly due to the fact that Chiang Ch'ing disliked him (he had made the mistake of trying to have some of her supporters arrested), but other factors were also involved—his collusion with the left-wing extremists who had been pushed out of the Cultural Revolution Group a few months earlier and, above all, his personal ambition.[4]

Liu Shao-ch'i and Teng Hsiao-p'ing still seemed to retain their credit among many cadres at the base, though the latter kept quiet. Redoubled attacks were made against the former president of the Republic, against bourgeois influence, which was likened to that of the Kuomintang, and against a brand of syndicalism that favored "well-being and production" and was liable to confuse all classes. "Polycentrism" was denounced more violently than ever, as were economism and the indifference of the masses who thought it dangerous to take part in political life. Fighting broke out in April in several provinces (Shensi, Liaoning, Szechwan, Chekiang, Kwangtung, and particularly Kwangsi), and executions of counterrevolutionaries became more frequent. The editorial of the *People's Daily* on May 1 was vague, lacked optimism, and spoke of the vigilance needed to face the last round of the struggle. A provincial radio broadcast refuted the theory that "the situation is in complete obscurity"; the title alone provides food for thought. Right-wing opportunism was apparently under attack, rather than left-wing extremism. At the beginning of the year and during the spring it showed itself by a kind of return of the countercurrent of February 1967, proposing to "revise the verdicts" against the victims of the Cultural Revolution and dislocate the revolutionary committee. This, as Chou En-lai admitted, caused disturbances in Peking.[5]

The great image of Mao Tse-tung was once more displayed as a rallying symbol. The expression of it was the "three loyalties" campaign—to Mao's person, his thought, and his line. the need for obedience to the "Proletarian Headquarters of Chairman Mao and Vice-Chairman Lin Piao" was recalled. More than ever, it was the army that was expected to support the revolutionary committees and public order and to seize the final victory. The situation was summarized in the bold image in the headlines of *Chieh-fang-chün pao* (July 31, 1968): "The Gun Commanded by the Thought of Mao Tse-tung, Keystone of the Proletarian Dictatorship." Several hundred thousand red guards entered the army, strengthening it and helping to restore calm in the towns. Others were asked to join with the proletariat and the peasantry because, in spite of their original role, they could no longer aspire to carry the revolution through to the end.[6] A few days later (August 25), Yao Wen-yuan caused a stir by his article in *Hung ch'i*, "The Working Class Must Take the Lead in Everything," which defined the preoccupations and program of the moment. His most outstanding points were a further condemnation of the "many centers" theory and of "independent kingdoms," a new affirmation of the leading role of the working classes, a recapitulation of the instructions of Mao Tse-tung entrusting the leadership in education to the workers in the towns and to the peasants in the countryside, and an attack on the "chattering" of intellectuals, "which the workers and soldiers would rapidly bring to an end." Yao Wen-yuan ended by listing the steps that should follow the Cultural Revolution: the formation of revolutionary committees, campaigns to criticize and clean up, consolidation of Party organizations, simplification of administrative structures, reform of rules, dispatch of sedentary personnel to units at the base.

A change in course had been made. The red guards, whose mistakes were once more acknowledged by Chiang Ch'ing,[7] while Mao Tse-tung himself reproached them vehemently for their errors (July 28), withdrew; mass organizations were dissolved so as not to hamper the new revolutionary committees; pride of place was given to the workers, albeit theoretically; and the army gave them its support. In a speech on September 7 marking the creation of the last two revolutionary committees, Chou En-lai drew up a provisional balance sheet of the Cultural Revolution and stressed the need "to unify our knowledge, our advance, and our acts."[8]

Parallel to this, a fresh definition of the organization and the new tasks of education began to emerge (see Chapter 40). This was another step toward a return, if not to former institutions, at least toward a more peaceful atmosphere and more regular political and administrative structures. The Party quickly regained importance in the life of the nation.

The Twelfth Plenum

On October 11, the Twelfth Plenum of the Eighth Central Committee, enlarged by the inclusion of the Cultural Revolution Group and representatives of the provincial revolutionary committees, opened in Peking. It lasted until October 31.

The "great, glorious, and just" Party had come out victorious from the struggle for power waged by the two lines. The mobilization of millions of revolutionaries had made it possible to eliminate the "bourgeois" headquarters of Liu Shao-ch'i. The latter was expelled from the Party forever and dismissed from all his posts in the state. The "February adverse current" of 1967 and the "sinister wind" of the spring of 1968 had been overcome. The general conditions required for convening the Ninth Congress were fulfilled. The result was to be a Party regenerated by "fresh blood from the proletariat."

Meanwhile, the campaign against Liu Shao-ch'i and his chief supporters in the provinces resumed once more throughout China with unprecedented violence, to act as a justification for class struggle, which ought to continue, as *Hung ch'i* said in its fifth issue, quoting Lin Piao:

> The chief characteristic of life within our Party is that it is struggle, not peace or compromise. Our Party must engage the struggle within itself in order to become a firm, powerful, progressive Party, full of vigor for the fight.

As the editorial of the *People's Daily* of November 24 also said, the history of the struggle between the two lines must be studied conscientiously, and the great revolutionary masses must be made aware of it. Moreover:

> It can be said that throughout the development of the Chinese revolution, at each crucial moment and over every important problem, a bitter struggle invariably took place between the proletarian revolutionary line represented by Chairman Mao Tse-tung and the bourgeois reactionary line represented by Liu Shao-ch'i.

The Chinese Communists have shown such a habitual contempt for truth that it is reasonable to withhold judgment on this vital point in their history.

Notes

[1]For examples of this, see the *Chekiang Daily* (January 16, 1968) and the *Honan Daily* (January 8, 1968).

[2]Obedience to the "Proletarian Headquarters" was the subject of three new instructions in July; see *People's Daily* (August 5, 1968).

[3]On August 15 and 16, the press published extracts from recent instructions of Mao Tse-tung on this. See also the article by Yao Wen-yüan quoted below in this chapter.

[4]Yang Ch'eng-wu was severely criticized by Chou En-lai, K'ang Sheng, and Ch'en Po-ta: Ch'en Po-ta called him "a little clown turning somersaults over a beam." They all linked him with the left-wing extremist group (Wang Li, Kuan Feng, Ch'i Pen-yü). Lin Piao denounced his conspiratorial activities and his personal ambition; Chiang Ch'ing denounced his action against the Cultural Revolution Group; other, more complicated explanations were also given.

[5]See the declaration of March 21, 1968, by Chou En-lai, given in the *Survey of China Mainland Press*, No. 4166 (April 29, 1968), and in *Joint Publication Research Service*, No. 45823 (July 1, 1968).

[6]See daily papers of August 18, 1968.

[7]*People's Daily* (September 10, 1968).

[8]The Yunnan revolutionary committee was formed on August 13, that of Fukien on August 19, that of Kwangsi on August 26, and those of Sinkiang and Tibet on September 5.

38 The Ninth Congress and the Renewal of Party and State Structures (1969 –1971)

The promises of the Twelfth Plenum were quickly carried out. The Ninth Congress met at last in Peking, eight years late, from April 1 to 24, 1969. The Chinese Communist Party emerged from it completely transformed. The Ninth Congress was attended by 1,512 representatives who, instead of being elected by members of the Party, were chosen by "democratic consultation," as "blind faith in elections is a conservative idea."[1] The delegates were appointed after discussions between the revolutionary committees and the masses, which meant that the masses gave their approval to the candidates proposed by the committees. The former Party committees, with the exception of those of the army, seem to have had a secondary role in these appointments. An exceptional procedure provided for by the 1956 constitution made it possible to enroll particularly deserving individuals in the Party immediately, with no probationary period. It seems to have been widely applied.

The principal documents available at present for gauging the importance of the changes and the situation at the time are the political report of Lin Piao (April 1), the final communiqué (April 24), the new Party constitution, and the composition of the Central Committee and the Political Bureau.[2]

The new Party

As regards the Party and institutions, the Party was to some extent rehabilitated for good, because its role as "the core of leadership of the

Chinese people" was reaffirmed. It was, however, organized around the thought and will of one man alone and around his faction.

Previously the highest institutions of the Party and particularly the Central Committee comprised all those who had distinguished themselves during the Kiangsi period and the Long March. Various trends were represented. Former personal enemies of Mao Tse-tung, like Wang Ming, Li Li-san and, after 1959, Chang Wen-t'ien and P'eng Teh-huai (who had in fact ceased to be dangerous and served as negative examples) were not excluded. Carefully graded currents of opposition, which were occasionally and at least partially taken into account while openly or secretly condemned as "leftist" or "rightist," ran through it.

The Ninth Congress saw the end of this relative diversity in the organizations at the summit and the end of a Central Committee, which was thereafter composed of unknown people and newcomers. It need hardly be said that the Political Bureau and its Standing Committee revealed that the criterion of loyalty to Mao Tse-tung, and to a lesser extent to Lin Piao—respectively chairman, and vice-chairman and appointed successor—carried more weight than any other.

The Standing Committee was cut down from seven to five members. All of them—Mao Tse-tung, Lin Piao, Chou En-lai, Ch'en Po-ta, and K'ang Sheng—were both the theorists and prime movers of the Cultural Revolution, with the reservation that Chou En-lai had long since mastered the art of skillfully accommodating doctrine to circumstances. Hemmed in as he now was by the powerful personalities of the chairman and the vice-chairman of the Party and by two unshakable dogmatists, and deprived of some of his collaborators, who had been removed from the Political Bureau, he had to act with the utmost care.

The Standing Committee had considerable power in the new Party, for in the terms of Article 9 of the new constitution it was responsible for setting up "a number of necessary organs, which are compact and efficient . . . to attend to the day-to-day work of the Party, the government, and the army in a centralized way." The relations of the state with the Party and the army were to depend on this directorate of men who were dissimilar but equally determined.

The sixteen other full members of the Political Bureau and the four alternate members were listed in these categories no longer by order of precedence but according to the number of strokes composing the character for each surname, a method giving them complete equality. They seemed unlikely to interfere with the "five." Some were related to Mao Tse-tung and Lin Piao: their wives, the son-in-law or the nephew of the former.

Others were distinguished figureheads who were often old men, like Chu Teh and Tung Pi-wu, the vice-president of the Republic, or people whose devotion to Mao Tse-tung and Lin Piao had been shown by the Cultural Revolution, particularly at the level of provincial organizations. The strong personalities of former days, like Ch'en Yün, Li Fu-ch'un, Ch'en Yi, and Hsü Hsiang-ch'ien, had all disappeared, as had the victims of the recent events: Liu Shao-ch'i, Teng Hsiao-p'ing, P'eng Chen, P'eng Teh-huai, Ho Lung, Li Ching-ch'üan, and T'an Chen-lin, whose names recalled past struggles and often past glories.[3]

The new Party was organized around the thought and person of Mao Tse-tung; it had eliminated all who opposed him, whether because of their origins or their motives, particularly Liu Shao-ch'i and his supporters. It appeared coherent as regards leadership, though perhaps not entirely homogeneous. Theorists like Ch'en Po-ta and K'ang Sheng, practical men like Chou En-lai, and soldiers like Lin Piao and Huang Yung-sheng were united by their loyalty to Mao Tse-tung and their early adherence to the Cultural Revolution, which some of them had prepared, but they were completely different in temperament, in experience, and in their political orientation. Perhaps regarding these differences as a possible source of danger, the Ninth Congress was careful to name Lin Piao officially as the successor to Mao Tse-tung, a wise but excessive precaution sanctioning the primacy of a single man over the Party both in the present and the future and combining in his person the Party, the army, and a monopoly in the interpretation of Mao's thought, which had become "the Marxism-Leninism of our time."[4]

Membership on the Central Committee was enlarged to 170 full members and 109 alternate members. More than 60 percent of the members of the old committee were dropped from the new one, which was nevertheless twice as large. Out of a total of 279 full and alternate members only fifty-three had belonged to the former committee.[5]

About forty soldiers were full members (almost a quarter of the committee). The army was less fully represented among the alternate members, many of whom were young activists, workers, or scientists like Ch'ien Hsüeh-shen, the missile specialist. The Secretariat of the Central Committee was no longer mentioned. No details were given of the departments of the committee and their office-holders.

Although renewed at the top, the Party was neither renewed nor reorganized at its lower and middle levels. Delegates had been chosen for the congress, but the task of rebuilding the hierarchy as a whole had been postponed. It was already obvious, however, that replacing election by selection worked in favor of the young activists, to the detriment of the militants of long standing. The procedure also made it possible to stress class origins and to prepare the way for the proletariat to take over a Party that had for too long been under the leadership of intellectuals alone. It also ensured a majority for the prevailing faction at little cost.

The spirit of the Party changed as much as its composition. Its chief mission was to maintain and strengthen the revolutionary flame. The aim no longer was to "develop the national economy in a planned way," still less to "satisfy to the maximum extent the material and cultural needs of the people," as the 1956 constitution put it, but to bring about "the complete overthrow of the bourgeoisie," to lead "the proletariat and the revolutionary masses in the fight against the class enemy," and to practice the "theory of permanent revolution."[6] It should be pointed out once more that the study of "Mao Tse-tung thought" prevailed over all other ideological obligations, and even over the concept of the "practice of China's revolutionary struggle" mentioned in the 1956 constitution. Over and above the doctrinal pretensions of Mao Tse-tung himself, this emphasis should be seen as a sign of the determination to unite the Chinese people behind a national version of Marxism-Leninism and of course to provide more solid support for the propagation of the Maoist revolutionary message throughout the world.

The 1969 Party differed profoundly from that of 1956 on one vital point—its position and role within the state. Over the country as a whole, the revolutionary committees remained, for a time at least, the organs of "unified leadership," as confirmed by Lin Piao in the third section of his report of April 1. Articles 59 and 60, creating "leading Party members' groups" in all organizations of administrative bodies or mass associations comprising more than three members disappeared. This put the Party apparatus out of touch with the various levels of organizational apparatus and meant that it had no authority over them. At all middle and lower levels everywhere, the influence of the Party could make itself felt through people alone and no longer through the system. This situation lasted for many months more; the Party was purged, renewed, and rebuilt at every level in its hierarchy, just as it had been at the level of the Central Committee. The reasons why this work is barely finished today will become apparent later on.

The report of Lin Piao

The political report of Lin Piao is the other important text of the Ninth Congress, besides the new Party constitution. Basing all he said on the thought of Mao Tse-tung and magnifying the struggle between the two lines, Lin Piao expounded on the origins of the Cultural Revolution and justified it, placing the fundamental text, "On the Correct Handling of Contradictions among the People," in a new context within the historical development of the struggle against constantly recurring revisionism and attacking Liu Shao-ch'i (and scarcely anyone else) with unprecedented violence:

> [Liu Shao-ch'i and his gang] covered up their counterrevolutionary political records, shielded each other, colluded in doing evil, usurped important Party and government posts, and controlled the leadership in many central and local units, thus forming an underground bourgeois headquarters in opposition to the proletarian headquarters headed by Chairman Mao.

Lin Piao also put forward the tactics chosen by Mao Tse-tung, an attack on counterrevolutionary culture and opinions, followed by a mobilization of the whole people, who were then launched on a great political revolution. He gave a rapid outline of the most important episodes of the Cultural Revolution, its ebb and flow, the tests of strength between the two lines, and the internal struggles of the revolutionary movement during the summer of 1967 and the spring of 1968 (right-wing and extreme left-wing factions). He then set the general tasks and the political principles that ought to inspire them. The tasks, which fell within the general context of "struggle-criticism-transformation," were still considerable: "Therefore, it is wrong to speak lightly of the final victory of the revolution in our country; it runs counter to Leninism and does not conform to facts."

The passages on the consolidation and reconstruction of the Party probably furnish more new material than the rest. They explain the Cultural Revolution as a vast purge and a supreme attempt to ensure that the "proletarian" nature of the revolution did not yield to a revisionist bourgeois mentality. Here he quoted Mao Tse-tung:

> A human being has arteries and veins through which the heart makes the blood circulate, and he breathes with his lungs, exhaling carbon-dioxide and inhaling fresh oxygen, that is, getting rid of the stale and

taking in the fresh. A proletarian Party must also get rid of the stale and take in the fresh, for only thus can it be full of vitality. Without eliminating waste matter and absorbing fresh blood, the Party has no vigor.

Relations with other countries were treated according to the usual clichés. Although American imperialism inevitably came under attack, and the revolutionary movements which understood better than ever that "political power grows out of the barrel of a gun" were praised to the skies, the harshest treatment of all was reserved for the social-imperialism of the Soviet leaders: "We firmly believe that the proletariat and the broad masses of the people in the Soviet Union with their glorious revolutionary tradition will surely rise and overthrow this clique consisting of a handful of renegades."

As was to be expected, there were many denunciations of the "armed provocations" by the Russians on the Chinese borders, the Russo-American "collusion" to isolate China and "determine the destiny of the world," and the danger of a large-scale conventional or nuclear war of aggression. Lin Piao's report ended on the theme of unity in triumph; no important revelations were made, and the true facts were disguised beneath the purple veil of an ideology renewed by the thought of Mao Tse-tung.

He concluded by stating that although the Ninth Congress had been a "congress of unity and a congress of victory," the Great Proletarian Cultural Revolution ought not to come to a halt. The final communiqué recommended that it should be continued in various ways, for the congress held that it was essential to (1) develop the great mass movement for the living study and application of the thought of Mao Tse-tung throughout the country, eliminate the influence of the counterrevolutionary revisionist line of Liu Shao-ch'i, and achieve unity in thinking, policy, plan, command, and action; (2) continue to rely on the masses and carry on "struggle-criticism-transformation"; (3) send the intellectuals to be reeducated among the poor and the lower middle peasants; and (4) struggle against erroneous left- and right-wing tendencies. This is precisely what later happened.

Internal developments between the Ninth and the Tenth congresses

From the Ninth Congress until the Tenth Congress (August 1973), four main trends can be traced in Chinese national life: (1) an effort to restore normal political life centered around the rebuilding of the Party, though without abandoning the principles and certain aspects of the behavior of the Cultural Revolution; (2) an attempt to put the economy in order and get it going once more without allowing politics to give way to it; (3) an endeavor to instill life into education and culture, both understood in the new "proletarian" sense, as opposed to domination by "bourgeois intellectuals"; and (4) the gradual assertion of a new foreign policy founded on growing independence from the socialist camp as a whole and on the Chinese claim to ideological leadership of the world revolutionary movements, which had been "betrayed" by the leaders of the Soviet Union. Only the first of these tendencies will be considered in this chapter (see also Chapters 40, 41, and 44-47).

The rebuilding of the Party in the presence of the masses was slow and laborious, in spite of the publication of important articles on doctrine. It was relatively easy to set up the various elements composing it, but it was hard to know who should lead them, and what influences would appear in the new organization. In May and June, the leftists, "who are above the masses," were considered more dangerous than the rightists, "who do not need the masses." Appeals for unity, reconciliation, consolidation, and revolutionary discipline became more and more urgent. The reintegration of intellectuals and cadres was speeded up. During the summer, and again at the beginning of 1970, the anarchists "who suspect and reject everything" became the chief worry; they had to be dealt with by force or persuasion. Constant attacks were made on those who were indifferent, those who gave up the fight, those who thought that everything had been said and that nothing was left to criticize, those who considered the Party useless, and those who no longer dared obey for fear that their discipline might be considered reactionary.

The cadres were urged to form closer links with the masses, to take over the leadership of them, to help them express themselves, and to set up a rotation system allowing a third of the cadres at a time to share in manual work: "Just as a sword rusts if not whetted, or still water stagnates, once cadres become detached from manual work, they tend toward re-visionism."[7]

It was thought that work methods ought to be reviewed, and an extremely important text was devoted to this.[8] The familiar hydra of bureaucracy, subjectivism, and formalism was combatted. In November, a "four perfections campaign" was launched, inviting everyone to excel, after the fashion of the army, in political and ideological life, in working style, in military instruction, and in the organizing of daily life.

The struggle against the persisting influence of Liu Shao-ch'i did not come to a halt. It took on a more doctrinal aspect, and attacks were made on his "six black theories": "extinction of class struggle," "docile tool," "retrograde masses," "joining the Party to take over leadership," "peace within the Party," and "fusion of general and private interests." The supposed veneration of Confucius and Mencius shown by Liu Shao-ch'i was quoted again as proof of his desire to go "back to old things."[9]

Occasionally, and especially in July 1969, rumors of disturbances came from the western provinces, and particularly from Taiyuan, the capital of Shansi; the calls for unity suggest these incidents were in fact serious.[10]

In the spring of 1970, the tone at last became a little more optimistic, and signs of the rebuilding of the Party at the basic level began to appear here and there. "Advanced elements" emerged from certain revolutionary committees, though nobody dared call them Party committees. These committees gradually appeared, however, generally at the primary level. A few district (*hsien*) committees were created at the beginning of the summer of 1970. Their role went beyond that of a purely ideological advance guard but did not yet appear to include the direction of administrative organizations, as the *People's Daily* of January 6, 1970, wanted. The instructions given by Mao Tse-tung in July still called for unity, the rehabilitation of 95 percent of the cadres, and an end to the criticism of those who had already admitted their mistakes.[11] The primacy of the Party was affirmed in the justification of the Cultural Revolution, which was in reality "a vast movement, open to all, for consolidating the Party, on an unprecedented scale."[12]

The Communist Youth League slowly began to be formed once more, parallel to the Party. This dealt a last blow to the red guards, who from then on were mentioned only on rare occasions.

References to the calling of a new National People's Congress began to be made; it was announced at the Second Plenum of the Ninth Central Committee held at Lushan from August 23 to September 6, 1970, though exact dates were not given. The same session restated the watchwords of the Ninth Congress, particularly that of the unity "necessary for obtaining even greater victories."[13] It also began work on a draft state constitution, which was quickly reported from Taiwan. As was only to be expected, it reflected the same spirit as the Party constitution, placing Mao Tse-tung above all else, but treated the problem of production relations in the countryside with the utmost care.[14] The great tension of the Second Plenum will be described later; the extent and the effects of this were apparent a few months later.

The need to complete the rebuilding of the Party before the convening of a Fourth National People's Congress, which was to be responsible for adopting a new constitution or modifying the old one, resulted in the formation of the first provincial Party committees at the end of 1970. That of Hunan, the native province of Mao Tse-tung, was the first; it was formed on December 4, 1970. Others followed quickly: Kiangsi, Kwangtung and Kiangsu (all on December 26), Shanghai (January 10, 1971), Liaoning (January 13), Anhwei (January 21), Chekiang (January 28), Kwangsi (February 16), Kansu (February 17), Shensi (March 5), Honan (March 8), Tsinghai (March 11), Peking (March 15), Kirin (March 24), Hupei (March 28), Fukien (April 3), Shantung (April 5), Shansi (April 11), Sinkiang (May 11), Kweichow (May 14), Inner Mongolia (May 18), Hopei (May 20), Tientsin (May 26), Yunnan (June 3), Tibet (August 12), Szechwan (August 16), Hui Region of Ninghsia (August 18). When Heilungkiang announced the formation of its committee on August 19, every province had one.

The proceedings were the same in every case: "democratic consultations" to choose between 800 and 1,000 delegates for the provincial congress and nomination of a committee of fifty to 100 members, of a standing committee of ten to thirty members, and of a first secretary and two to four secretaries and assistant secretaries. The same speeches were given on the same themes: mass movement for the study of the thought of Mao Tse-tung, of the history of the "struggle between the two lines," and of the latest doctrinal texts; criteria for the choice of cadres; the union of the "three generations"; and the progress of production.[15] The new provincial first secretaries were almost always "heads of leading groups" of the Party and leading figures (chairmen or vice-chairmen) of revolutionary committees. The army still played an important part, particularly in the earliest committees, where it supplied two-thirds of the first secretaries and 60 percent of the secretaries as a whole; the rest were former cadres (more than 30 percent) and people who moved up during the Cultural Revolution (less than 10 percent).

Below the provincial level, the rebuilding of the Party under the new constitution seems to have been slow. If reports from Taiwan are to be believed, by February 1971 only 149 districts out of a total of more than 2,000 had formed Party committees, and a year later the figure amounted to slightly more than half of the total. Primary committees also seem to have been very slow to emerge. It was relatively easy to set up provincial or district committees, because the "democratic consultations" were eventually cut down to a few representatives from different categories, but the same was not true when the "masses" were directly involved in professional or territorial contexts. Each person knew all the others, while the humiliations, tensions, and conflicts of the Cultural Revolution had not yet been forgotten; coexistence among members of extremist tendencies was for a long time as forced and unstable as it had been during the days of the "great alliance" or the "three-in-one" combinations. Many details are still lacking today, making it impossible to give an accurate, certain picture of the physiognomy of the Party at the lower levels. While this laborious work of rebuilding the provincial and local apparatus was going on, various distinguished leaders disappeared one after the other, proving that serious differences in views and personal rivalries persisted at the summit.

The first to vanish was Ch'en Po-ta, whose Cultural Revolution Group had ceased to exist, while its last members, Chiang Ch'ing and K'ang Sheng, became much more self-effacing. Later, official documents revealed that he had experienced his first difficulties as early as the Ninth Congress, for which he had prepared a political report that the Central Committee rejected and replaced with the one eventually presented by Lin Piao. In August 1970, at the Second Plenum of the Ninth Central Committee, Ch'en Po-ta, supported by Lin Piao, apparently advocated a radical line opposed by Mao Tse-tung and Chou En-lai. After being attacked again in December 1970 (North China Conference) and above all in April 1971 (at the meeting known as the Meeting of the Ninety-Nine) Ch'en Po-ta was eliminated for good; the Tenth Congress dismissed him as a "Kuomintang anti-Communist, a Trotskyist renegade, and a revisionist secret agent."

The Second Plenum also saw the beginning or the aggravation of a major crisis between Mao Tse-tung and Chou En-lai on the one hand, and Lin Piao and the military leaders of the Political Bureau on the other, which, although it was not openly admitted, directly concerned the succession to Mao Tse-tung and the nature of the regime. On the first point Mao, without deliberately questioning the choice of his heir, refused to make provision for the office of president of the Republic, which, either before his disappearance or after it, would have fallen to Lin Piao. For similar reasons, he also rejected the flattering "genius theory" put forward, obviously with ulterior motives, by the vice-chairman of the Party. In this way he enabled Chou En-lai to recover some of the ground lost at the Ninth Congress and guided both Party and state in a less automatic, more collegiate direction. At the same time he also sanctioned the adoption of a moderate political line represented by the premier. The second point concerned the gradual restoration of direct Party control over the army, which had temporarily displaced the Party before helping with its reconstitution while inserting large numbers of army men in the Party, particularly at the provincial level. The decline of Lin Piao, which pleased many regional military leaders, either because they were suspicious of the radicalism he represented or simply because they owed unconditional loyalty to Mao Tse-tung, contributed to this delicate operation.

At the Second Plenum Lin Piao and his supporters seem to have rapidly abandoned their attempt to take a firm stand and Mao Tse-tung found himself maintaining appearances. The session ended in a draw, but an artificial truce was used to cover up a hidden struggle that remained unknown to the outside world, until it was suddenly resolved at the end of the summer of 1971.

On September 13, 1971, at about 2:00 A.M., a Chinese plane (Trident No. 256) crashed at Undar Khan in the Mongolian People's Republic, 500 or 600 kilometers from the frontier. Nine people in all, including Lin Piao, his wife Yeh Ch'ün, and his son Lin Li-kuo (assistant commander of the Chinese air force) died in an attempt to flee to the Soviet Union. On the same day, the chief of the general staff, General Huang Yung-sheng, air force Commander Wu Fa-hsien, Director of the Logistics Department Ch'iu Hui-tso, and navy Political Commissar Li Tso-p'eng were arrested, never to be seen again. These events were known in part, and partially suspected, then gradually half admitted by some of the leaders; they were not officially confirmed until August 1973, at the time of the Tenth Party Congress. Chou En-lai reported:

> However, during and after the Ninth Congress, Lin Piao continued with his conspiracy and sabotage in spite of the admonitions, rebuffs, and efforts to save him by Chairman Mao and the Party's Central Committee. He went further to start a counterrevolutionary coup d'état, which was aborted, at the Second Plenum of the Ninth Central Committee in August 1970. Then in March 1971 he drew up a plan for an armed counterrevolutionary coup d'état entitled *Outline of Project "571,"* and on September 8 he launched the coup in a wild attempt to assassinate our great leader Chairman Mao and set up a rival Central Committee. On September 13, after his conspiracy had collapsed, Lin Piao surreptitiously boarded a plane, fled as a defector to the Soviet revisionists in betrayal of the Party and country, and died in a crash at Undur Khan in the People's Republic of Mongolia.

The study of the documents available today, which came from the mainland by way of Taiwan, leave room for doubt as to the strict veracity of accounts of a plot to murder Mao, either organized personally by Lin Piao or merely inspired by him.[16] On the other hand, Lin's son and a few other officers may conceivably have voiced, in somewhat schoolboy terms, intentions they never had the time or the courage to carry out. The fact is that Lin Piao and Chou En-lai, since the Second Plenum, had confronted each other in a struggle for power; the questions of political orientation and choice of men were only the chief aspects of it. Mao Tse-tung had deep commitments to his appointed successor and appears to have hesitated for a long time, then tried to maintain an impossible balance between the two, before making a final choice and leaning toward Chou En-lai. Lin Piao could no longer count on the group consisting of Chang Ch'un-ch'iao, Yao Wen-yüan and Chiang Ch'ing, for they were so closely linked to Mao that they had withdrawn their support from their former leader Ch'en Po-ta. The fall of the latter, after a long career as Mao's privileged collaborator, and the fate of Liu Shao-ch'i provided ample warning. Lin Piao found himself in complete isolation and was forced to fade gradually into the background, while waiting to be evicted for good. The "Meeting of the Ninety-Nine" in April 1971, called by the Central Committee, probably lost him the active support of the chief military leaders, who had to make self-criticisms because they had supported Ch'en Po-ta; the reorganization of the North China military command had no doubt weakened his position in the capital.

After August 1, 1971 (Army Day), Lin Piao made no further public appearances; his name no longer figured on official occasions, and his position was no doubt such that he could put up no resistance to what the "Project 571" called "a gradual, nonviolent coup d'état." From August 15 to September 8, Mao Tse-tung went on a long trip through the provinces to discredit his national defense minister in the eyes of the provincial leaders, the majority of whom, as has been reported, were members of the army.[17] This was apparently the bitterest blow of all. A few days later, perhaps after a last dramatic confrontation with the Central Committee or the Political Bureau, Lin Piao attempted to escape the ignominious fate in store for him.

Over the next two years, Chou En-lai put all his efforts into consolidating his victory, patiently and carefully. He reconstituted the apparatus of the state at the summit and simplified it. At the intermediate levels, various people in office suspected of sympathy toward Lin Piao were dismissed. About a dozen provincial Party committees were affected to a varying extent, though the position and influence of the representatives of the army changed little. A long campaign aiming to "criticize revisionism and rectify working style" and attacking Lin Piao by means of Liu Shao-ch'i continued; at the same time, important cadres who had been violently attacked during the Cultural Revolution resumed some of their former responsibilities or reappeared. Two examples of this were Teng Hsiao-p'ing, who became deputy premier again, and T'an Chen-lin. Both had long been associated with Liu Shao-ch'i by the red guards and "revolutionary rebels." The return of these men gave hope and appeared almost as a conditional promise to many fallen cadres, winning for Chou En-lai the cooperation and support of many experienced members of the old Party, who still retained their influence.

Step by step, the radicalism of the Cultural Revolution seemed to be growing more attenuated; this evolution even affected the image of Mao Tse-tung. As a figure, he rose higher above normal humdrum events, while the cult surrounding him became less obsessive and fervent. A campaign began to study the philosophical utterances in his thought, which had otherwise been confined for too long to the "three constantly read articles," whose tone was moralizing rather than political.[18] The classics of Marxism-Leninism were all reprinted, as though to reestablish and ratify, both at home and abroad, the historical continuity linking Marxism, Leninism, and the thought of Mao Tse-tung, an aspect that had become somewhat blurred by the Socialist Education Movement and the Cultural Revolution. The aim was also perhaps to lessen in advance the psychological, ideological, and possibly political effects that would inevitably follow the death of the giant-like figure who had inspired and led the Chinese revolution for more than forty years. "If the Taishan were to crumble away, to what should I lift my eyes?" as his disciple Tze Kung asked the dying Confucius.

Balance sheet of the Cultural Revolution

It is impossible to draw up a limited and provisional balance sheet of the Cultural Revolution by reference to its aim rather than its general effects on China as a whole without going back to its causes. Seen in perspective and in the light of the considerable material amassed since 1966, it seems clear that the chief if not the sole cause of the revolution lies in Mao's determination to launch the Chinese revolution again, giving it the utmost intensity and extending it evenly to every domain of national life, making it total and irreversible for each individual just as much as for society.

The determination of Mao Tse-tung was based first of all on his opposition to political and economic tendencies considered dangerous from an ideological point of view and consequently reprehensible even if they served production efficiently. In this sense, the Cultural Revolution amounted to a conflict in line affecting simultaneously the defense and development of the Chinese revolution throughout China. The evil tendencies ascribed to Liu Shao-ch'i ("The Chinese Khrushchev") arose from a general line described as "neorevisionist" and thought to lead back eventually toward capitalism.

In fact, remaining within the limits of classical Marxism-Leninism, the "Liu Shao-ch'i line" gave priority to economic development over pure ideology. To do so, it needed organization, order, discipline, and strong leadership from the Party. With the centralization of all efforts as its aim and byword, the line had to handle carefully the intellectuals and technicians it needed, substituting the notion of "the whole people" for that of class struggle.

Everything arises from this fundamental opposition. Mao Tse-tung said so himself in January 1962 and again in August of the same year during the two working sessions of the Central Committee before the Tenth Plenum:

> If classes and class struggle were forgotten and if the dictatorship of the proletariat were forgotten, . . . then it would not be long, perhaps only several years, or a decade, or several decades at most, before a counterrevolutionary restoration on a national scale would inevitably occur, the Marxist-Leninist Party would undoubtedly become a revisionist party, a fascist party, and the whole of China would change its color. Comrades, please think it over. What a dangerous situation this would be![19]

The Cultural Revolution appeared as a conflict between two lines; it also appeared as a struggle for power, in that Mao Tse-tung wanted to resume sole leadership of the Party and state. He had not lost control of the leadership, and no one openly disputed his role, but the central and local apparatus no longer responded with the same flexibility and docility as before. Principles rather than men were involved in the struggle—the principle of autocratic leadership supported by the masses and that of collegiate leadership supported by the Party.

After 1949, Mao Tse-tung steadily speeded up the rhythm of social and economic changes, thus creating the conditions for a growing opposition within the Party and outside it. Each time opposition arose, he got the better of it, dominating the situation by the sheer force of his prodigious personality. Without giving full credence to the slogan, "The whole life of the Party has been a struggle between two lines," it does seem that opposing attitudes existed. They were represented by familiar names ranging from Kao Kang to Liu Shao-ch'i and included P'eng Teh-huai and others. The overly hasty switch to cooperatives, the Hundred Flowers, the people's communes, and the Great Leap Forward, were all fought against, hopelessly and unsuccessfully, by prominent people and important groups. The situation after the Tenth Plenum was no longer quite the same. The renewal of class struggle, purges and the prospect of further "leaps forward" worried the moderates, who had just seen their point proved by the failure of the "three black years" and the recovery resulting from the readjustments and the granting of "small liberties." They constituted the majority in the central, regional, and local Party apparatus and answered its impulses less and less, or else ignored them, though remaining ostensibly obedient—"submissive by day and rebellious by night," as the Chinese expression goes. Support from highly placed leaders also became stronger. If Lin Piao is to be believed, in 1964 Liu Shao-ch'i "came out and repressed the masses, shielded the capitalist-roaders in power. . . ."[20]

In the autumn of 1965, when the conflict was considered inevitable, Mao Tse-tung used the Wu Han affair to begin it and, as a last resource, resolved it by appealing to the masses:

> In the past we waged struggles in rural areas, in factories, in the cultural field, and we carried out the Socialist Education Movement. But all this failed to solve the problem because we did not find a form, a method, to arouse the broad masses to expose our dark aspect openly, in an all-around way and from below.

Lin Piao, reporting this, added: "Now we have found this form—it is the Great Proletarian Cultural Revolution."[21]

When Mao found that the majority of the Party and its affiliates (the Communist Youth League, trade unions) and the majority of the state apparatus could not be aroused, he had to make the masses bypass them and carry out a real coup d'état against socialist legality in order to overcome the obstacle.

The Cultural Revolution was imposed by circumstances, but it also owed much to Mao's individual ideological vision. The theory of contradictions, that of permanent revolution, and the mass line all found a perfect testing ground. Similarly, certain traits of personality and temperament in Mao Tse-tung and his life history emerged clearly. But above all, the Cultural Revolution corresponds to Mao's determination to make of the Chinese revolution a movement that was irreversible locally and an example for the rest of the world. The former leading classes had been destroyed, but their influence persisted. As Lenin put it, the old society left its body rotting in the middle of the new one; "bourgeois," "petty-bourgeois," and even feudal tendencies remained or were reborn. The phenomenon was particularly serious in China because of the basic materialism of the race, the powerful "family egoism," and the strength of the entirely original culture, which had continued without a break over thousands of years. The question of "successors" worried Mao, and he frequently referred to it.

The dangers incurred by the Chinese revolution were demonstrated by the development of the Soviet Union after the Twentieth Congress of its Communist Party. Lenin led the proletariat to win power, but he did not succeed in making it a final victory. Mao Tse-tung continued his work on this point, widening Marxism and making it reach a "newer, higher stage." By doing this, Peking took over from Moscow the leadership of modern revolutionary movements and consolidated its ideological positions and its means of action in foreign policy. Mao remained faithful here to China's age-old vocation to act as an example. The intention was to replace the cultural message of the old days with the revolutionary message, thereby leaving a lasting influence on the human race.

On the basis of these targets, the most positive achievement of the Cultural Revolution was to have halted policies leading indirectly to a decollectivization of land and to farming on a family basis. It is easy to see how a development like this, affecting 80 percent of the Chinese population, could destroy the authentic revolutionary spirit both in the individual and in society as a whole, put serious difficulties in the way of further collectivization based on mechanized agriculture, and perhaps, in the long run, as Mao Tse-tung feared, endanger the nature of the regime. Although the situation in agriculture remained mediocre, the time thus saved made it possible to apply a policy of far-reaching technical improvement in an attempt to attain the outputs laid down by the twelve-year plan, without producing any basic modification in collective structures and their operation.

The struggle for power ended in victory for Mao Tse-tung—that is, in the elimination of Liu Shao-ch'i and then, under more obscure conditions, in that of Lin Piao. Mao has moved back to the "first line" again, becoming the supreme judge once more, but—and more will be said of this in the concluding chapter—he has brought about an abnormal situation in institutional matters, shattered the myths that create unanimity among the people, and provoked serious political instability from which, even eight years later, China had not yet recovered.

Far from becoming a model and an irreversible process, the example set by the Chinese suffered from the events and their consequences. No "new man" emerged. The image of Mao was weaker from the viewpoint of the world outside, and had shrunk to the national frontiers. The avowed intention of making the Cultural Revolution a cyclic phenomenon, whereas the development of states requires peace, order, and planning, throws more and more doubt on the seriousness of Maoist vision, making it seem that of an old leader lagging behind the times, who has lived too far beyond his own era to be able to understand the new and has confused the past with the future.

Notes

[1] "Absorbing Fresh Blood from the Proletariat," *Hung ch'i*, No. 4 (1969).

[2] The Hong Kong periodical *Ch'un Chiu* published the two speeches by Mao Tse-tung on April 1 and 14, but these interesting and probably faithfully reproduced texts cannot be considered official.

[3] The members of the Political Bureau were, in order of precedence, Mao Tse-tung, Lin Piao, Chou En-lai, Ch'en Po-ta, K'ang Sheng, then according to the number of strokes composing the character of their surnames: Yeh Ch'ün, (Mme Lin Piao), Yeh Chien-ying, Liu Po-ch'eng, Chiang Ch'ing (Mme Mao Tse-tung), Chu Teh, Hsü Shih-yu, Ch'en Hsi-lien, Li Hsien-nien, Li Tso-p'eng, Wu Fa-hsien, Chang Ch'un-ch'iao, Ch'iu Hui-tso, Yao Wen-yüan, Huang Yung-sheng, Tung Pi-wu, Hsieh Fu-chih. Alternate members: Chi Teng-K'uei, Li Hsüeh-feng, Li Teh-sheng, Wang Tung-hsing. Hsieh Fu-chih died on March 26, 1972.

[4] Chapter 1 of the Party constitution says: "Mao Tse-tung's thought is the Marxist-Leninism of an era in which imperialism is heading for total collapse and socialism is advancing to worldwide victory."

[5] 169 full and alternate members of the Eighth Central Committee still remained just before the Ninth Congress; 116 were dropped from the Ninth Central Committee.

[6] Some clauses of the 1969 Party constitution, and particularly the one enabling a member to appeal directly to the Central Committee, were deliberately intended to maintain the revolutionary spirit as opposed to "bureaucratism."

[7] *People's Daily* (November 20, 1969).

[8] "Pay Attention to Work Methods," *People's Daily* (November 5, 1969).

[9] See "Ghost of Confucius's Shop and Actual Class Struggle"; English text in *Peking Review*, No. 50 (December 12, 1969).

[10] See English text of the proclamation of the Central Committee (July 23) in *China Quarterly*, No. 40 (October-December 1969), pp. 172-73.

[11] See the press of July 4, 1970.

[12] *Hung ch'i*, No. 7 (1970).

[14]Slightly modified, this draft (an English version is in *Issues and Studies*, Taipei, December 1970) was used as the basis for the State Constitution of January 17, 1975.

[15]On this subject see the editorial "Victory of the Line of Chairman Mao as Regards the Rebuilding of the Party," *People's Daily* (January 30, 1971).

[16]The most important of these are the texts known as *Chung-fa*, Nos. 4 and 12, available in English in the Taiwan periodical *Issues and Studies*, May and September 1972. They were documents issued by the Party to its members down to the provincial and military region levels for use during the campaign of struggle "against crooks of the type of Liu Shao-ch'i"; they are an interesting example of the way in which the leaders gradually filter information, both to preserve their dignity and to avoid ideological and political shocks.

[17]The remarks and speeches made by Mao Tse-tung during his trip are contained in the document *Chung-Fa*, No. 12.

[18]"On Practice," "On Contradiction," "On the Correct Handling of Contradictions Among the People," "Speech at the Chinese Communist Party's National Conference on Propaganda Work," "Where Do Correct Ideas Come From?" See in particular *Hung-ch'i*, No. 6 (July 1972).

[19]Lin Piao, "Report to the Ninth National Congress of the Communist Party of China" (April 1969).

[20]*Ibid.*

[21]*Ibid.*

39 The Tenth Congress and the Internal Political Situation; The Fourth National People's Congress

The long-awaited Tenth Congress eventually met in Peking from August 24 to 28, 1973, regularizing, from an institutional point of view at least, the situation created by the elimination of Ch'en Po-ta, Lin Piao, and the chiefs of staff. From this perspective, it looks like a personal success for Chou En-lai and his policy, and possibly also like a compromise on the succession to Mao Tse-tung.

The Tenth Party Congress

The Tenth Congress was attended by 1,249 delegates, all of whom were chosen rather than elected. They nominated a Central Committee differing little from the former one. Regular members of the Central Committee increased in number from 170 to 195, and alternate members from 109 to 124. About thirty members of the old committee, from all categories, were missing from the new one; instead, several distinguished victims of the Cultural Revolution reappeared, such as Teng Hsiao-p'ing, T'an Chen-lin, Wang Chia-hsiang, Li Ching-chüan, Li Pao-hua, and Ulanfu.

At the summit, Mao Tse-tung remained chairman of the Central Committee and the Political Bureau, though this time his successor was not named. Five vice-chairmen were appointed instead of one as before; they were, in order of precedence: Chou En-lai, Wang Hung-wen, K'ang Sheng, Yeh Chien-ying, and Li Teh-sheng. The Standing Committee, which had been reduced to three by the elimination of Lin Piao and Ch'en

Po-ta, was brought up to nine: the chairman, the five vice-chairmen, and Chu Teh, Chang Ch'un-ch'iao, and Tung Pi-wu.[1]

The new Political Bureau had twenty-one permanent and four alternate members as before, and was largely new (eight new members, among them three former alternate members and four new alternate members).[2] The members of the army who had disappeared were not replaced by others. Chou En-lai and his closest collaborators (Li Hsien-nien, Yeh Chien-ying), the so-called Shanghai group (Chang Ch'un-ch'iao, Yao Wen-yüan), the veterans (Chu Teh, Tung Pi-wu), and the first secretaries of various provinces (soldiers like Ch'en Hsi-lien and Hsü Shih-yu or civilians like Hua Kuo-feng and Chi Teng-k'uei) all represented different currents of opinion, whose relations, little known in detail, appear intricate and fluid.

No unknown figure emerged in the new team apart from Wang Hung-wen, a new member of the Central Committee in 1969 who was promoted directly to the post of vice-chairman, just after Chou En-lai. He was supposedly of proletarian origin, an activist who made a name for himself during the Cultural Revolution by his action among the workers in Shanghai, and a young man (under forty). Many considered him the archetype of the second generation, created and trained for power, the virtual successor of Chou En-lai and, one day, of Mao Tse-tung himself. His brilliant rise inevitably inspired various hypotheses. One was that he was entirely loyal to Chiang Ch'ing and deeply hostile to Chou En-lai. Another described him as a cadre singled out by the premier and destined to lead the nation. Yet another was that the choice of Wang Hung-wen was a temporary and fragile compromise, intended to keep Chang Ch'un-ch'iao and Yao Wen-yüan from becoming vice-chairmen of the Party. All these views were based on uncertain information or on arguments that were too theoretical to allow a categorical judgment to be made.

The Tenth Congress changed the Party constitution to some extent; Wang Hung-wen introduced the new statutes, stressing the continuation of revolutionary cycles, the lasting nature of the "two-line struggle," and, at the same time, the strengthening of centralized leadership by the Party and by its committees, the "training of successors for the revolution," and the need to "be open and aboveboard" and "not to intrigue and conspire." The individual articles of the constitution were intended to reflect the same revolutionary dynamism as those of 1969 but no longer went to the same extremes when referring to the thought of Mao Tse-tung (see Chapter 38). His thought was no longer considered as above or beyond Marxism and

Leninism but as an extension of both. It did not aspire to be the last and exclusive expression of them.[3]

The report of Chou En-lai

Chou En-lai explained the reasons and circumstances of the fall of Lin Piao and Ch'en Po-ta, just as Lin Piao had done for Liu Shao-ch'i at the Ninth Congress (see Chapter 38). Then, in a somewhat disconcerting way, he wove the themes of unity, vigilance, and past and future struggles into his speech. He rejoiced at the soundness of a Party 28 million strong ("Our Party has not been divided or crushed"), which had grown stronger and seen "Chairman Mao's Marxist-Leninist line" develop still further. In spite of all these assurances, he laid great emphasis, like Wang Hung-wen, on the continuation of "a two-line struggle" already half a century old, and called on revolutionaries to go "against the tide" if need be and not to be afraid of finding themselves alone, faced by deviationist tendencies which are hard to perceive, as one tendency often covers another.[4]

These were unexpected words from someone putting forward a truly moderate line and, what is more, accusing the most obviously "leftist" factions (those of Lin Piao and Ch'en Po-ta) of wanting to install "a feudal-comprador-fascist dictatorship." Were they a reflection of the political hypocrisy that was essential to obtain the endorsement of Mao Tse-tung and the Central Committee for the text, or of the linguistic conventions and artifices of old China and the totalitarian regimes, or of the supreme realism so often shown by Chou En-lai, including during the period of the Cultural Revolution? Above all, they bore witness to the infinite versatility of a man always ready to make the necessary sacrifice to the illusion his words created, while retaining what was most important in the things themselves.

Chou En-lai concentrated his remarks almost entirely on domestic politics and on Sino-Soviet relations. He barely touched on the national economy, merely mentioning the usual slogans, all more than ten years old, such as "take agriculture as the foundation and industry as the leading factor," "walking on two legs," "self-reliance, hard struggle," "learn from Taching in industry and from Tachai in agriculture." He ended his report by stressing once more the need to "strengthen the centralized leadership of the Party" and its committees and to train "millions of successors to the revolutionary cause of the proletariat" by the union of three generations.[5]

He called for unity and sacrifices to attain "a bright future," though by a "tortuous road."

The last months of 1973 appeared to confirm the tortuousness of the paths of the revolution. Contrary to all expectations, the National People's Congress was not called and the proposal for a constitution published in 1970 seemed to have been abandoned. The highest military posts were still vacant; a succession of reshuffles in the command of the twelve military regions caused a clearer separation among the hierarchies at the provincial level and reduced the importance of the army there. Within the Party, Teng Hsiao-p'ing appeared to have been admitted to the Political Bureau, where his personality and experience as former general secretary strengthened the hand of Chou En-lai.

Far from producing a certain calm in the ideological realm, corresponding to the moderation and pragmatism of the economic field, the Tenth Congress launched "leftist" trends once more. These were to be found particularly at the higher levels in education and in culture in general. The spirit of the Cultural Revolution persisted in the universities; candidates for entry had to have spent two years doing work contributing toward production, while entrance examinations were concerned with revolutionary spirit and ideology rather than knowledge. Music, literature, and the arts had to be sheltered from Western influences.[6]

The campaign against Confucius

In August 1973 a campaign of criticism was launched against Confucius, on the initiative of Mao Tse-tung. It was artificially though directly linked with the criticism of Lin Piao; after first developing among the cadres, it became a real mass campaign, a "people's war," carried on at the level of the workers and peasants. Simultaneously, in opposition to Confucius, who was known as the defender of a slave-owning society that resisted the natural changes of history, the ancient Emperor Ch'in Shih Huang-ti was rehabilitated and set up as the founder of a unified empire, the supporter of the "legalists" and through them of a society of landowners more advanced that that which preceded it, and the promoter of a new practical culture, the opposite of the literary and aristocratic culture of the Ju.[7] The fact that the greatest subject of the whole of Chinese history was brought up for discussion astounded all observers and gave rise to endless interpretations based on numerous officially inspired texts.[8] Many people saw the campaign as a political operation against Chou En-lai and the factions who had shown a reserved attitude toward the Cultural Revolution. In any case, the way the campaign was launched, the fact that the subject dealt with the crucial problem of Chinese society, whether past, present or future, and the challenge held up by Lin Piao to Mao Tse-tung, who was denigrated as a latter-day Ch'in Shih Huang-ti ("Project 571"), left no doubt as to the origins of this strange movement. It was without question a characteristic expression of the will of Mao Tse-tung, in his persistent anxiety to change Chinese society radically and permanently. In this respect, the historical analogy with Ch'in Shih Huang-ti is inevitable, for the Ju's narrow views, obstinacy, and insubordination justified the emperor's thorough political and cultural revolution. The present anti-Confucian movement also corresponds to a desire to maintain the ideological conquests of the Cultural Revolution and to compensate for the concessions made at the basic level by a new drive for socialist education, providing food for the "criticism of Lin Piao and the rectification of working-style" (*pi-hsiu cheng-feng*), the current form of class struggle.

The Fourth National People's Congress and the new constitution

Apart from the continuation and extension of movement to criticize Confucius and Lin Piao and a further decline in the presence of the army in the provincial Party organizations (eight out of eleven commanders of military regions were transferred in January), the year 1974 lacked events of real importance. The following year, however, brought China a new constitution and strengthened the moderate trend represented by Chou En-lai and Teng Hsiao-p'ing.

The Fourth National People's Congress (2,885 deputies "elected through democratic consultation") met at last, ten years late, from January 13 to 17; Mao Tse-tung was away from Peking at the time. On January 17, it adopted a new constitution replacing the constitution of September 20, 1954 (see Chapter 10). Unlike the former constitution, which did not mention the Party, the new one makes no effort to maintain a democratic facade for the regime but does quite the opposite. Instead of being a "people's democratic state" as before, China is now a "socialist state of the dictatorship of the proletariat," which has intermingled and become one with the Party, whose ideology has been extended to everybody. Nevertheless, the 1975 constitution is in many ways conservative, perhaps the result of a compromise or of fear that it might alarm the peasants.

Consequently, when it redefines the three levels of ownership in the people's communes (communes, brigades, and teams), it affirms that the team, which is in fact the natural village, remains the basic accounting unit and allows for the customary private plots. Collectivization is maintained at the lowest and most acceptable level.

Change Ch'un-ch'iao was delegated by the Party to present the report on the revision of the 1954 constitution, which had been rendered unsuitable in part by the general development of China; he stressed the "protracted and complex nature" of class struggle under a socialist regime. The 1975 constitution consists of a preamble, four chapters, and thirty very brief articles.

The preamable underlines the Party's role as leader and points out that the persisting rivalry between the socialist and capitalist lines makes it necessary to continue the revolution under the leadership of the proletariat.

The first chapter recalls a few general principles: the leadership by the working class through the Communist Party (Articles 1 and 2), the importance of Marxism-Leninism-Mao Tse-tung thought, the "theoretical basis guiding the thinking of our nation" (Article 2), the practice of "democratic centralism" by all organs of state, and elections "through democratic consultation." As regards the economy, the first chapter recalls the socialist principle, "from each according to his ability, to each according to his work," points out the role of the team, and acknowledges the right to "engage in limited household sideline production" (Article 7) or certain individual, nonagricultural occupations (Article 5). In the field of culture and education, the principle of complete dictatorship by the proletariat over the bourgeoisie in the superstructure is reaffirmed (Article 12).

Chapter 2 defines the structure of the state. The National People's Congress is officially placed under the leadership of the Communist Party. It is elected for a term of five years, meets once a year (Article 16), and its duties are to amend the constitution, make laws, and, on the proposal of the Party's Central Committee, to appoint the premier and the members of the State Council, or, in other words, the government. It also gives its approval to the plans for the national economy and the budget (Article 17). Its Standing Committee convenes the Congress, interprets laws, enacts decrees, dispatches and recalls diplomatic representatives abroad, receives the diplomatic representatives of foreign states, and ratifies and denounces treaties (Article 18). The office of president of the Republic no longer exists. The chairman of the Central Committee of the Party commands the armed forces (Article 15).

The State Council is the Central People's Government. It determines and carries out the administrative measures of the state (Articles 19 and 20).

At the level of the provinces and the municipalities directly under the central government, the people's congresses are also elected for five years. The people's congresses in the prefectures (*ti ch'u*), municipalities (*shih*), and districts (*hsien*) are elected for three years. People's congresses in people's communes and towns (*chen*) are elected for two years. At all these different levels, affairs are conducted by permanent revolutionary committees responsible to the people's congress at the corresponding level and to the organ of state at the level just above them (Articles 21-23). Similar arrangements are applied to the autonomous regions, departments, and districts inhabited by minority nationalities (Article 24).

The Supreme People's Court remains, but the Supreme People's Procuratorate has disappeared. The new constitution gives a political slant to justice and puts it into the hands of the people by prescribing the application of the "mass line" in inquiries and judgments and, in "major counterrevolutionary criminal cases," the mobilization of the masses (Article 25).

Chapter 3 deals with the fundamental rights and duties of citizens and states that they have the right to vote and stand for election at the age of eighteen. The right to strike is acknowledged, which is an innovation compared with 1954. Mao Tse-tung is responsible for this, and it should be interpreted as an impediment to excessive bureacracy.

Chapter 4 deals merely with national emblems and the capital. It contains no new arrangements compared with the old constitution.

Chou En-lai's report

The report on government activities presented by Chou En-lai to the Fourth National People's Congress reiterated the political and ideological themes of the moment: justification of the Cultural Revolution, which was a struggle against the bourgeoisie and the "bourgeois headquarters" of Liu Shao-ch'i and Lin Piao, the need to study Marxism-Leninism-Mao Tse-tung thought, the training of successors and theorists, unity of the people, and the strengthening of the leadership of the Party and its committees at the various levels. The main interest of the report lies in its references to the economy, or to be more accurate, to the economic ambitions of the regime. Economic achievements are given in terms of percentage increases over production for 1964, with no reference to firm figures. On the other hand, the premier laid much stress on the need to "accomplish the comprehensive modernization of agriculture, industry, national defense, and science and technology before the end of the century, so that our national economy will be advancing in the front ranks of the world." In this respect, Chou En-lai said that the first ten years would be crucial and he went on to announce that a long-range ten-year plan, as well as several five-year and annual plans, would be drawn up. He listed the priorities once more as agriculture, light industry, and heavy industry, giving "full play to the initiative of both central and local authorities under the state's unified planning."

The premier's report devoted considerable space to foreign policy, but this did not depart from the lines laid down several times after 1968. The Soviet Union was denounced vigorously, though the attacks left room for a relative appeasement over the frontier question; the United States was handled with tact; and the international economic crisis and the danger of a new world war were magnified.

The new government

The first session of the Fourth National People's Congress provided the opportunity for appointing the new government officially; many of its members were in fact already in office. Chou En-lai remained premier and strengthened his moderate trend by appointing Teng Hsiao-p'ing as deputy premier and chief of general staff, by confirming in office Marshal Yeh Chieh-ying as minister of national defense and Ch'iao Kuan-hua as foreign minister, and by nominating various experts in technical branches. Nevertheless, although Wang Hung-wen, Chiang Ch'ing, and Yao Wen-yuan were missing from the new government, Chang Ch'un-ch'iao became second deputy premier and head of the army's General Political Department. The representatives of the "radical" trend (sometimes known as the "Shanghai group") were not excluded.

The new National People's Congress elected Marshal Chu Teh, the ninety-year-old former commander-in-chief of the Red Army, as its chairman and as chairman of the Standing Committee.

The Second Plenum of the Tenth Party Congress, which was held from January 8 to 10, 1975, elected Teng Hsiao-p'ing as one of its vice-chairmen, no doubt to replace Li Teh-sheng.

The domestic situation in 1975 and the first four months of 1976

The first ten months of 1975 were notable for a certain degree of immobility, which may be explained by the age of Mao Tse-tung and the poor health of Chou En-lai, who spent most of this period in the hospital. A widespread movement for the "study of the theory of dictatorship by the proletariat," based on the action of millions of "theorists" who had been trained during the previous year or two among the workers and peasants and grouped in teams, filled in the time during the wait for the succession. The dangers of an evolution toward revisionism were still denounced actively and frequently. Even so, judging by an editorial by Chang Ch'un-ch'iao (April 1, 1975), apparently in reply to another by Yao Wen-yüan dealing mainly with the dangers arising from the threatening persistence of the "bourgeois right" (March 1, 1975), the prevalent attitude was one of caution.[9] Outbreaks of political and social unrest in a few towns (Hangchow in Chekiang) and in some sections of the economy (the railways) helped provide justification for this caution.

At the top, the fact that "radical" elements join the "moderates" in the exercise of power suggests that joint efforts are going into the collective leadership of the Party. Still, since the summer the divergent tendencies have increasingly come to the fore, especially in the area of education. It is here that the radicals are particularly influential and attempt to maintain a revolutionary ambience and to apply revolutionary methods.

Chou En-lai died on January 8, 1976. To everyone's surprise, Teng Hsiao-p'ing did not succeed him in the post of premier. In the weeks that followed his death, a furious press campaign was mounted against Teng Hsiao-p'ing, though his name was never mentioned. The message was familiar: a return once more to the revisionist "line," and end to "bourgeois" and "capitalist tendencies." On April 5, on the occasion of China's Memorial Day, a demonstration in memory of Chou En-lai developed into a manifestation of widespread violence. This was in the Square of Heavenly Peace in the very heart of Peking. Was this provocation manipulated by the "radicals," or, on the other hand, was it an initiative of followers of Teng Hsiao-p'ing? We don't know the answer. Hurriedly, on April 7, the Politburo passed two resolutions in the name of the Central Committee. The first named Hua Kuo-feng premier and deputy premier of the Party, a position in which he replaces the "radical" Wang Hung-wen. The second resolution deprived Teng Hsiao-p'ing of all his positions in the Party and in the state, and reduced him to the role of a simple Party member. Thus, a newcomer took the honored place of Chou En-lai.

Succession was decided by a compromise, doubtless imposed by Mao Tse-tung. Hua Kuo-feng looks like an interim solution. We know little about his life: he hails from Hunan, is fifty-four years old, had a career as provincial administrator, and served as minister of public security (February 7). We can only guess whether he will display Chou En-lai's outstanding talents. Clearly, nothing has really been solved in the general area of the locus and division of power. "Moderates" and "radicals" continue to hang on to their positions of power and influence in both Party and state. The hour of truth will perhaps not come for China before the disappearance of Mao Tse-tung. This hour is postponed by the compromise that has just been engineered, but we do not know how long it can prevent violent and completely unpredictable clashes between the Party factions.

Notes

1The last three are given in stroke order, corresponding to our alphabetical order.
2The Political Bureau constituted by the Tenth Congress was as follows: Mao Tse-tung, Chou En-lai, Wang Hung-wen, K'ang Sheng, Yeh Chien-ying, Li Teh-sheng, plus Chu Teh, Chang Ch'un-ch'iao, and Tung Pi-wu; and then, not in order of precedence: Wei Kuoch'ing, Liu Po-ch'eng, Chiang Ch'ing, Hsü Shih-yu, Hua Kuo-feng, Chi Teng K'uei, Wu Teh, Wang Tung-hsing, Ch'en Yung-kuei, Ch'en Hsi-lien, Li Hsien-nien, Yao Wen-yüan. Alternate members: Wu Kuei-hsien, Su Chen-hua, Ni Chih-fu, Saifudin.
3Mao Tse-tung spoke at the Ninth Congress, though he does not appear to have done so at the Tenth. If this is true, it reflects uncertainty in the ideological and political fields.
4The Party made every effort to prove that the trends represented by Lin Piao and Ch'en Po-ta, as in the case of Liu Shao-ch'i before them, were "apparently leftist, but in reality rightist."
5The union of the three generations was a creation of the Cultural Revolution. Until then the Party had concentrated its efforts on ideological persuasion of people under the age of fifty.
6Western classical music (particularly Sonata No. 17 by Beethoven) was attacked harshly, perhaps because Chiang Ch'ing wanted to maintain a monopoly for her revolutionary operas.
7Scholars and disciples of Confucius.
8Among the first texts were Yang Jung-kuo, "Confucius, A Thinker who Stubbornly Upheld the Slave System," *Peking Review*, No. 41 (October 12, 1973), and the self-criticism by the well-known historian Feng Yu-lan in *Kuang-ming jih-pao* (December 3, 1973).
9See the *People's Daily* of March 1, 1975, "On the Social Basis of the Lin Piao Anti-Party Clique," by Yao Wen-yüan, and the issue of April 1, "On Exercising All-Around Dictatorship over the Bourgeoisie," by Chang Ch'un-ch'iao.

40 The Economy 1962 –1976

When it put into practice the slogan "Politics takes command of the economy and revolution comes before production," the Cultural Revolution not only interrupted the process of readjustment that had begun in 1962 but at times temporarily paralyzed some sectors of industry. The third five-year plan, which apparently aimed at an annual growth of about 11 percent in industry and about 4 percent in agriculture, began in silence on January 1, 1966, and was scarcely mentioned again until the unobtrusive announcement of its completion.

The disorganization following the Great Leap Forward resulted primarily from an almost total lack of planning and from rhythms of work that totally discounted wear and tear on men or material and brought production into a frenzied state of anarchy. The disorganization arising from the Cultural Revolution resulted from the debility of technical ministries and executive bodies in charge of enterprises. These were under attack from red guards and "revolutionary rebels" and were accused of curbing the masses and imposing their own scientific or technical authority, itself borrowed from abroad. When the Cultural Revolution was taken into the factories, the workers split into opposing or rival groups, and the increasing time devoted to politics detracted from the working hours devoted to production and led to absenteeism. Some clashes resulting from such disputes caused damage to equipment, as in the case of the oil refineries at Lanchow. Here and there, strikes and wage claims made their appearance, inspired by the trends toward "economism," particularly during the hard year of 1967. Railway transport was severely disturbed at times, above all in the autumn of 1966 when 13 million red guards from the provinces converged on Peking.

The effects of the situation were abundantly reflected in the publications of the "revolutionary rebel" groups. They were partially acknowledged by Chou En-lai and by editorials in the *People's Daily,* which called with increasing urgency for production to be taken in hand again.[1]

Thanks to the action of Chou En-lai, to the fact that qualified financial and economic specialists had been maintained in office (Li Hsien-nien, Li Fu-ch'un), and to the intervention of the army, most of the key sectors of the economy—steel mills, oil refineries, coal mines, and transport—were protected. An appeal to the working class to shoulder its responsibilities, an extension of its participation in management, and the clashes on the Sino-Soviet border in the spring of 1969 also helped set the economy in order, particularly those industries concerned with national defense. It is worth pointing out, however, that Lin Piao scarcely mentioned the economy at the Ninth Party Congress. An outline of an economic policy did not emerge until the autumn of 1969, and it was still extremely tentative in spite of the announcement that a fourth five-year plan would be launched on January 1, 1971. A few statistics were published in 1972 and 1973, but at the Tenth Congress Chou En-lai said little more than had Lin Piao at the Ninth (see Chapter 39).

Agriculture

None of the main sectors of the national economy looked properly healthy, though agriculture was apparently less affected by the recent events than the rest and more liable to make progress. The beneficial results of the readjustments of 1959-1961 still made themselves felt over the years that followed. The more exaggerated aspects of the Socialist Education Movement and the Four Clean-ups Movement (*szu ch'ing*) encountered widespread inertia on the part of cadres and masses for, after ten years of collectivization, class struggle no longer held much meaning. On the other hand, the easing of controls and the freedom allowed for local initiative, as already mentioned, seem to have resulted in various more liberal practices (renting of land, fixing of quotas on a family basis).

As far as possible, except in the immediate area of large towns, the peasantry appears to have been left outside the Cultural Revolution at first. The continuation of the Socialist Education Movement in the countryside, as provided for by "The Sixteen Points" of August 8, 1966, had kept the red guards away from the peasants. In all events, the red guards were not numerous enough to carry out widespread and thorough action among a huge scattered population of peasants whose first concern was to provide for themselves. The student, the worker, and even the cadre could leave his place of work to "rebel" and "exchange experiences," but those who tilled the land were more than ever tied to their only means of survival.

The instructions issued on December 4, 1967, a year later than those of December 15, 1966 (see Chapter 33), contributed no new elements to the situation and reflected an increase in caution, for they forbade both "seizures of power" at the level of production teams and conflicts among the masses and treated the cadres more circumspectly. In the villages, the Cultural Revolution was intended to nip in the bud spontaneous movements toward decollectivization (though some occurred even so), to eliminate a few individuals who had gone too far in the direction of capitalism, and to act as a support for the ideological and political struggle being waged against Liu Shao-ch'i and his "revisionist" line in agriculture.[2]

From 1960 on, agricultural methods had started to benefit from new departures in industry: artificial fertilizers and insecticides were more abundant, seed was steadily improving, and small agricultural implements were better and in larger supply. Owing to a more rational development, hydraulic engineering was beginning to control, at least partially, the most extensive, sudden, and unpredictable effects of the monsoon climate. Nevertheless, weather was still largely responsible for good or bad harvests and made for a high coefficient of uncertainty in statistics. Specialists consequently differ widely in their opinions; as far as grain was concerned, four of them gave figures of 175, 190, 190, and 200-210 million tons for the 1966 output.[3]

The most cautious sources set production for 1967 at approximately 190 million tons and at approximately 180 million tons for 1968, whereas several others put it at more than 200 million tons. The following figures are given for 1969, by varying sources, in millions of tons: Soviet experts and some American experts, 190; a few American experts, 210; those most favorable toward China, 230.

In 1970, official sources began issuing firm figures once more. The grain output was given as 240 million tons in 1970 and 250 million in 1971, with a drop to 240 million again in 1972, and a rise to 250 million again in 1973. The figure for 1974 was close to 270 million tons, and some 274 million tons of grain were produced in 1975. The Chinese still maintain the validity of the targets of the twelve-year plan (1956-1967), though it is now eight years in arrears and the figures achieved are 100 million tons short of the objectives. The twelve-year plan concentrated on increasing output and divided China into three zones: North China (north of the line formed by the Yellow River and the Tsinling Mountains in Shensi), 3 tons per hectare; Central and East China (between the Yellow River and the Huai River), 3.75 tons per hectare; South and West China (south of the Huai and the Tsinling Mountains), 6 tons per hectare. This average is now attained in six provinces only, Chekiang, Kiangsu, and Kwangtung, and in the territories of the three special municipalities, Peking, Tientsin, and Shanghai. Elsewhere these figures are equalled only in the most privileged districts, amounting to about 800 out of a total of more than 2,135. No exact figures are available for cotton production, which still seems to be having difficulties.[4]

The continued importation of large quantities of Canadian, Australian, and now American wheat and the appeals for the storage of grain by both families and collectivities suggest that the situation is still difficult and that great differences exist among the provinces, while the state granaries are far from full. Several studies reveal that China has regularly imported between 4 and 5 million tons of wheat or wheat flour a year since 1961 and the failure of the Great Leap Forward.[5] According to more recent information, imports amounted to 7.7 million tons in 1973 and about 7 million tons in 1974. These purchases of wheat, only very partially balanced by exports of rice, impose a heavy burden in hard currency for a developing country anxious to build up its means of production; they total about $400 million, representing between 20 and 30 percent of total imports, depending on the year.

No details are known as to the volume of foodstuffs in reserve. In view of the factors making for decentralization during the Cultural Revolution, it seems reasonable to think that the question is now more than ever in the hands of the provinces. The leaders appear to be intensely conscious of the problem; their appeals for larger supplies of grain take on a pleading tone at times and are based on the needs "to be ready for a possible war and to face natural calamities." Everything suggests that state reserves ran out during the disturbances of the Cultural Revolution.[6] Nor are details available as to the average share of each consumer, for the total numbers and characteristics of the Chinese population have not been announced since the last census in 1953.[7]

A more detailed, matter-of-fact agricultural policy emerged after the Ninth Congress. It was based on both ideological stimuli and material incentives—the latter insofar as it did not aim to change rural socioeconomic structures in the countryside or production relations (as previously noted, Article 7 of the 1975 constitution was thoroughly reassuring in this respect). On this latter point much was said on the subject of the "history of the two lines" in the countryside.[8] The "criminal" views of Liu Shao-ch'i, who was "ready to restore capitalism," were invariably compared with the enthusiasm, lack of self-interest, and creative initiatives of the peasants. The spirit of Tachai reigned again and with it the tendency to pay on the basis of a monthly wage. Even so, the general trend was toward caution and modesty, and references to a new Great Leap Forward in agriculture had virtually disappeared. With a few exceptions, accounting was carried out at the lowest possible level—that of the production team—where it was most readily understood by the masses. Although a campaign to follow the example of Tachai at the *hsien* level was started in October 1975, the leaders appear to have realized that the salvation of China and Chinese agriculture lay in raising output by gradually substituting modern ways and techniques for old ones and by introducing varieties of rice and wheat already widely used in other parts of Asia to bring about the "green revolution."

Industry

Japanese and Russian experts, as well as many Western experts, estimated that industrial output for 1967 fell by 15 percent to 20 percent compared with that of 1966 (or, to put it more accurately, 1962) instead of rising by 11 percent, the annual increase apparently forecast by the third five-year plan. A further 10 percent fall occurred in 1968. A slight recovery seems to have been apparent in 1969, or perhaps at the end of 1968, in the most vital sectors, which were more closely supervised and easier to control. This fall in production was mentioned by Chou En-lai when he acknowledged on February 2, 1968, that the targets of the 1967 plan had not all been reached; he later said the same thing of the first three months of 1968.[9] Lin Piao for his part admitted a decline, though in his view the political advantages of the Cultural Revolution amply compensated for this.

Starting in 1969, the appeals to promote production became more and more urgent, showing real anxiety, judging by the tone of the editorial of the *People's Daily* of February 21, 1969, "Grasp the Revolution and Promote Production to Win New Victories on the Industrial Front." A unified national plan was quickly announced for 1969; economic themes took on renewed importance in 1970, and in 1971 the fourth five-year plan was launched.

No reliable statistics are available for industry for the bad years of 1967 and 1968, but a definite falling off seems to have been registered in the output of steel (average estimates put production at 10 million tons) and coal (average estimates give figures below 200 million tons), though the output of chemical fertilizers (between 7 and 9 million tons) and oil (approximately 12 million tons) does not seem to have suffered.

Chou En-lai is the source of a few official statistics in 1970:[10] steel, 10 to 18 million tons (average production over the previous five years); oil, 20 million tons; coal, 300 million tons (in 1970); fertilizers, 14 million tons (target for 1975: 30-35 million tons); cotton fabric, 8,500 million meters.

In 1971 the recovery and progress of Chinese industry were confirmed, with an increase of 18 percent over 1970, but only one firm figure was given, that of steel output (21 million tons), in the *People's Daily* of December 31.

In 1972, further progress was announced; steel production rose to 23 million tons, oil to 26 million tons of crude oil, and fertilizers to 17 million tons.

These figures increased again in 1973; steel output rose to 26 million tons, and, according to a remark made by Chou En-lai to the Japanese premier in January 1974, oil output amounted to 50 million tons of crude oil. According to 1975 estimates, 1974 production was in the region of 25 million tons of steel, 65 million tons of oil, 400 million tons of coal, and 25 million tons of fertilizers.

Transport

On the whole, transport remained inadequate for a country the size of China. Owing to the lack of steel and funds, railways developed little. About 42,000 kilometers of track existed altogether. Technical progress was slow and commercial yield remained mediocre.[11] Road transport was badly hampered by the high cost of production, by the fact of a young and weak motor industry (a total of 400,000 to 500,000 vehicles), and by limited fuel resources. 670,000 kilometers of roads were suitable for motor vehicles, according to an official figure.

The merchant fleet was estimated by Lloyds in 1975 at 2,828,000 gross registered tonnage; although shipyards were beginning to produce vessels of 15,000 to 20,000 tons, they were still far behind Japan and Taiwan. In the last few years, the Chinese have ordered or bought large numbers of ships from abroad so as to be independent of foreign flags. Inland waterways cover a total of 147,000 kilometers, and traditional craft (junks and sampans) are still widely used.

Air transport was still mediocre within the country and had developed little internationally. The broadening of Chinese foreign policy has encouraged Peking to open a few international lines, particularly to Europe and Japan, and to renew aging equipment.[12]

Foreign trade

All statistics and estimates reflect the decline in foreign trade after 1966 (see Table 40.1). It is generally reckoned at 10 or 12 percent in 1967 and 1968; a slight rise was apparent in 1969. The years of the Cultural Revolution are similar to those that preceded the striking drop of the period between 1961 and 1964.

Table 40.1
Foreign trade in 1960 and 1965-1969 (millions of dollars)

Year	Exports	Imports	Total
1960	2,075	1,931	4,006
1965	2,187	1,813	4,000
1966	2,452	1,939	4,391
1967	1,887	1,920	3,807
1968	1,858	1,762	3,620
1969[b]	1,980	1,893	3,873[a]

Source: Figures quoted by Jan Deleyne in *The Chinese Economy*.

[a] Approximate figure.
[b] The figures for 1970 are probably 10 percent higher than those for 1969.

In 1970, Chinese foreign trade ($4,246 million: $2,063 million in exports and $2,183 million in imports) almost reached the level of 1959. It continued to rise in 1971 ($4,611 million: $2,364 million in exports and

$2,247 million in imports) and again in 1972 ($5,716 million: $2,948 million in exports and $2,768 million in imports).

In 1973, the total was above $9,800 million, and in 1974 it passed the $12,000 million mark. The last two figures are, to some extent, affected by the devaluation and the fluctuations of the dollar. It should also be emphasized that the Chinese balance of trade displays a tendency toward deficits, with the amount varying between $500 million and $1,000 million per year.

Japan, Hong Kong, Western Europe, and, recently, the United States have been China's principal trade partners since the deterioration of the close political relations between China and the U.S.S.R. and the other members of the socialist camp. China imports mainly steels, machine tools, and wheat. Agricultural goods and by-products, textiles, and minerals, including oil, are the main exports.

China's foreign trade is still somewhat weak. For a number of reasons, it seems improbable that it will develop at a rapid pace. On the other hand, it will continue to rely on imports for a great deal of industrial equipment and transportation vehicles.

The movement toward a new economic policy

Economic themes regained importance in the second half of 1969; an economic policy which was at least partially new took shape, particularly in 1970. In spite of the announcement of the fourth five-year plan (1971-1975), and of the fifth five-year plan (1976-1980), no single document has yet appeared treating the policy in full, but its chief characteristics may be garnered from several texts and from examples found in the press.

1. Priorities are the same as they were during the readjustment period of 1961. The stress is still on agriculture and on the sectors of light industry working for it. Heavy industry will not be sacrificed, however, and although it no longer has the priority the first and second plans gave it, the formula of the years from 1961 to 1966, "Take agriculture as the foundation and industry as the leading factor," retains its force.

2. Since the large enterprises of heavy industry and the most technologically advanced branches of industry constitute the backbone of all future development, they will undergo careful planning and will generally remain in the hands of the state. But large numbers of small and medium-sized enterprises (coal, iron and steel, cement, engineering, electrical power stations) must be set up on the initiative of local collectivities, as well as by

the state. They will provide the nuclei for future large enterprises.[15]

3. A strong tendency exists toward financial and administrative decentralization and toward the geographic dispersal of industry. It mainly concerns light industry, which is easier to create and yields quicker returns, but the development of local units of heavy industry is under consideration and will lead to the formation of small autonomous local industrial systems. Instead of encouraging the people's communes to go in for industry on a large scale as in 1958, the aim now is to set up industries at the provincial or the *hsien* level, while the communes—with a few exceptions—are to retain only a few workshops to meet some of their own needs. This policy is justified in view of the reduction in area and economic functions of the communes after the readjustments of 1959-1961 but is hard to apply in a poor country which is still behind in the technical field.

4. A tendency toward economy and austerity also exists. Because China has more than ever to be "self-reliant," it must be as thrifty as possible, make the best of its resources, and "work hard," fearing "neither hardship nor death." However, to make up for some of the excesses in the propaganda accusing Liu Shao-ch'i of showing too much reverence for foreign methods, these are pronounced acceptable as long as they are closely linked to Chinese realities: "Foreign things must serve the nation."

5. The recovery and rehabilitation of the cadres in general inevitably affects cadres belonging to the administrative and technical sectors of the economy more than others. Managerial methods are consequently becoming more pragmatic. The Charter of Anshan with its five principles (priority for politics, leadership by the Party, mass movements, participation by cadres in production and by workers in management, technical revolution), proposed by Mao Tse-tung on March 22, 1960, in systematic opposition to the Charter of Magnitogorsk, is still one of the doctrinal texts; in fact, practices very like the old ones are in use, with the same men in authority, supposedly reeducated by the poor and lower middle peasants and by the workers. Renewed attacks on the theories of Sun Yeh-fang, whose notions of profit and of the importance of the law of value in planning are periodically condemned under their various disguises, and attacks on the persistent tendencies toward "economism" in general, show that there is no question of going any further. The obligation to continue the class struggle in the economic field is often reasserted; lack of self-interest is the prime virtue of the present. The working class must achieve both an "ideological breakthrough" and a "technical breakthrough" at the same time.

As Chapter 39 reported, Chou En-lai, in his speech to the Fourth National People's Congress, stressed the need for decisive progress during the next ten years to enable China to become a modern nation in every field. The target calls for an effort toward more rigorous planning, and above all, for the sort of more moderate political behavior likely to stimulate production, even at the expense of the revolutionary spirit.

Notes

[1] Declarations by Chou En-lai of October 9, 1967, February 2 and April 7, 1968, and the editorial of the *People's Daily* of February 21, 1969, for instance.

[2] Among other important texts see "Struggle Between the Two Roads in China's Countryside." *People's Daily* (November 23, 1967).

[3] Robert Michael Field, "How Much Grain does Communist China Produce?," *The China Quarterly*, No. 33 (January-March 1968).

[4] The twelve-year plan fixed the cotton output at 600 kilograms per hectare in North China and 750 kilograms per hectare in South China. China has recently bought cotton from the United States.

[5] See in particular Feng-hua Mah, "Why China Imports Wheat," *The China Quarterly*, No. 45 (January-March 1971), and Audrey Donnithorne, *China's Grain: Output, Procurement, Transfers, and Trade* (Hong Kong: Economic Research Center of the Chinese University of Hong Kong, 1970).

[6] Chou En-lai told Edgar Snow in 1970 that grain reserves amounted to about 40 million tons, but this figure seems to correspond to the quantity claimed by the state each year through taxation or purchase of quotas intended for redistribution or resale; the 40 million tons are not strictly speaking "reserves."

[7] See John Aird, "Population Policy and Demographic Prospects in the People's Republic of China," *People's Republic of China: An Economic Assessment* (Washington, D.C.: Joint Economic Committee of Congress, 1972). According to the various methods of assessment noted by John Aird, the Chinese population was estimated at between 915 and 918 million inhabitants in 1974. In 1973, Chou En-lai and several other Chinese officials mentioned an annual rate of increase of about 2 percent. The leaders today admit to a population of 800 million, but various experts in demography estimate the 1975 population to be somewhere between 830 and 930 million.

[8] See "The Road Forward for China's Socialist Agriculture," *Peking Review*, No. 7 (February 13, 1970).

[9] See p. 481. Chou en-lai said much the same thing in his conversation with Edgar Snow in December 1970.

[10] Interview with Edgar Snow in December 1970.

[11] The importing of French and German hauling stock made it possible to improve traffic on some lines in mountainous areas.

[12] Civil aviation uses Russian (Tupolev 104, Hyushin 18) and British (Viscount, Trident) aircraft and has just bought five Ilyushin 61 and ten American Boeing 717.

[13] Figures quoted in *The China Quarterly*, No. 56 (October-December 1973), p. 811. Other sources give slightly differing figures.

[14] The share of the European socialist camp was 75 percent during the first five-year plan, and this fell to about 15 percent during the Cultural Revolution; it has been increasing again since 1970

[15]"China's Road of Socialist Industrialization,"*Hung ch'i*, No. 10 (1969); English version in *Peking Review*, No. 43 (October 24, 1969), and "Orientation of China's Socialist Commerce," *Peking Review*, No. 50 (December 11, 1970).

41 Education and Culture, the Press, and Religion 1962 –1976

Education

From 1962 until all teaching in universities and institutes of higher education ceased on July 26, 1966, both the spirit and the system of education changed little in spite of the Socialist Education Movement. This, plus the slowing down of industrial production, brought large numbers of students back to the countryside and no doubt created a state of unrest still more apparent at the end of the secondary school cycle. On the other hand, the method of recruiting students (a stiff university entrance examination) and the curriculum remained the same and the teachers retained their authority. Full-time schools and schools combining study and work for production remained entirely different types of institutions; this was one of the criticisms later aimed at Liu Shao-ch'i.[1]

After 1960, however, official statistics no longer gave information on the numbers of students and secondary school pupils, on the respective importance given to different subjects, or on the "half-work, half-study" system in practice (see Chapter 27).

The "first shot of the Cultural Revolution" rang out on May 25, 1966, at Peking University, as has been described in Chapter 30. The appearance of the wall newspaper of Nieh Yuan-tze inspired Mao Tse-tung to launch this catchword, which was false when applied to the Cultural Revolution as a whole but full of meaning in the case of education and intellectual training. The flood tide that rushed in through this breach was to submerge the whole ancient academic structure in a moment. Many years were needed to build up a new one; the task is still unfinished today.

On June 13, the Central Committee and the State Council, ostensibly in reply to demands from students, announced their intention of abolishing the system of university entrance examinations, held to be "feudal" and "bourgeois." Shortly afterward, the universities halted admissions for six months so that the students in higher education institutions and in the second cycle of secondary education could devote themselves to the Cultural Revolution and so that new types of teaching and examinations (curricula, materials, methods) could be prepared. This measure was later prolonged for six months—in fact, until the autumn of 1970, at least in the case of higher education.

Meanwhile the tenth of "The Sixteen Points" of August 8, 1966, laid down the aims and the spirit of future reforms. Education was to serve the proletariat and to be combined with productive work. Courses were to be considerably shortened. Classes were to be improved and simplified, and subjects were to be redefined. Students were to be prepared for work in industry and agriculture and trained to "approach military questions."

These prospects did not prevent universities and secondary schools from entering a phase of far worse confusion than that already experienced since June. After inflicting degrading humiliation on their teachers and taking the violence into the streets, red guards and student "revolutionary rebels" split into rival factions; hard fighting broke out frequently between rival groups from the same establishment, or between groups from different units, often involving casualties. When the winter slowed down the demonstrations and marches presided over by Mao Tse-tung in Peking and the "exchanges of experiences" among the provinces, the leaders began to take things in hand again, for the students had fulfilled their political role for the time being. Students and secondary school pupils were asked to go back to their institutions "to study and make revolution there," to prepare the reform of the educational system and to receive military training. The army gave its support to these arrangements, quoting examples from history in justification, with the ostensible aim of creating reserve troops.[2] Contemporary documents, particularly the instructions of March 7, 1967, revealed a year later, all suggest that general education was almost entirely sacrificed to ideological training—or, in other words, to the study of "Mao Tse-tung thought." Efforts were made to get back to normal, however: Cultural Revolution committees were formed to organize the life of and to control each institution; most cadres and teachers were reinstated, though a few were eliminated; violence was forbidden; state property was protected and repayment demanded for damage caused.[3] These various measures appear to have been ineffective and many students seem to have been reluctant to go back to their universities. This situation, and the general trend toward a return to order, which was obvious after the crisis in the spring and summer, made the leaders undertake a new and serious attempt to get both students and teachers back to their posts and simultaneously to advance the revolution in education. An extremely firm circular published on October 14, bearing the stamps of the Central Committee, the State Council, the Military Affairs Committee, and the Cultural Revolution Group, was completed up to a point by the circular of December 7, 1967.[4]

It was becoming increasingly obvious that the universities, like the masses, were unable to get themselves organized politically (formation of revolutionary committees) or educationally. Consequently the army had to take charge here, as it did in so many other fields, to get the system going again. As well as fulfilling its normal task of spreading the thought of Mao Tse-tung and giving military training, it had to help with all the necessary reorganization and readjustments, and doubtless with setting up and carrying out the curriculum, which was in any case limited to revising basic subjects. According to the Hsinhua agency, it had already done this in 834 primary schools and 385 secondary schools in Peking. In several provinces, teaching seemed to be getting under way again.

On July 21, 1968, Mao Tse-tung entered the lists and issued basic instructions summarizing the rules to be applied to the rebuilding of education:

It is still necessary to have universities; here I refer mainly to colleges of science and engineering. However, it is essential to shorten the length of schooling, revolutionize education, put proletarian politics in command and take the road of the Shanghai Machine Tools Plant in training technicians from among the workers. Students should be selected from among workers and peasants with practical experience, and they should return to production after a few years' study.[5]

A few days later, on the morning of July 27, as though to prepare the way for the important article published by Yao Wen-yüan on August 25, a team of workers and fighters from the army made a "grandiose" entry into Tsinghua University to finish off "the sovereign empire of the intellectuals." A few days later, in token of his approval and encouragement, Mao Tse-tung sent the team the "precious" present of a basket of mangoes; this gesture became an important element in the folklore and symbolism of the Cultural Revolution. Yao Wen-yüan stated that the reform of education must be carried out by the proletariat in urban schools and by poor and lower-middle peasants in country schools. Workers' propaganda teams would work in conjunction with army propaganda teams to ensure necessary changes, see that education did not once more fall under the domination of "bourgeois intellectuals," and create a proletarian education system associating theory with practice. In the immediate future, "great alliances" had to be imposed on the students, as they were necessary for the formation of revolutionary committees. The students do not seem to have been pleased to see the teams of workers, who themselves were not overly enthusiastic about their task; this was the case in Shensi and Tsinghai.

The May 7 cadres' schools began to proliferate in the middle of 1968. They were so called because they perpetuated the spirit of the instructions addressed by Mao Tse-tung to Lin Piao on May 7, 1966, in which he said that the army must become a great revolutionary school and set an example in this for all branches of the administration and for schools and enterprises. Mao Tse-tung wrote:

> The People's Liberation Army should be a great school. In this school our army should study politics and military affairs, raise its educational level, and also engage in agriculture and side occupations and run small or medium-sized factories to make products for its own needs or for exchange with the state against equal values.[6]

The development of the May 7 cadres' schools involved sending hundreds of thousands of cadres to the countryside to undergo ideological reeducation by the poor and lower-middle peasants.

No great events occurred in the universities in 1969, though a few uncertain projects emerged here and there for schools intended to act as models.[7] The situation as a whole was still extremely disorganized, and the mingling of students with workers, peasants, and soldiers gave rise to endless practical and psychological difficulties. Several million young intellectuals, with diplomas from secondary or higher educational establishments, were sent from the towns to the countryside; there were more than ten times more of them than during the ten previous years, according to the press of May 6, 1969.

The need to renew an aging student population, which had been completely sacrificed from a professional point of view during three years of political agitation, and the wish to bring workers and peasants into the universities as teachers and pupils, made 1970 an important year. A whole issue of *Hung ch'i* (No. 8, July 21, 1970) was devoted to education, and classes seemed to have begun again on an experimental basis in most universities.

It was still impossible to give an overall view of the new system of education, though it seemed likely, as the principles were still intangible, that there would be some return to former practices. The general trends are relatively easy to define on the basis of a few examples quoted by the press.

The ascendancy of politics resulted in an enrollment limited to young people "of good social origins," who had been introduced or approved, in the case of secondary and higher education, by representatives of the "masses." The practice of concentrating all responsibility in the person of one director had at least partially disappeared, and groups belonging to the community were put in charge. All courses devoted considerable time to "Mao Tse-tung thought," to criticism (regarded as a permanent form of class struggle), and to manual work; teams of workers were constantly present throughout the academic structure, to take over leadership in ideology. Everything was done to ensure that the workers and peasants would retain permanent control of public education.

All educational establishments at every level had to have close ties with production and day-to-day realities. If need be, they took over a production unit (a farm or a workshop). In many cases, enterprises entrusted schools with the general and professional training of their personnel, except where the enterprises themselves had assumed responsibility for the neighboring schools.

Primary and secondary education was to be decentralized as far as possible. Administration, finance, admissions, and examinations were to be in the hands of collectives, which were to manage them in an open way. In the countryside, the production brigade, supervised by the commune, took charge of primary schools.[8] This arrangement, which would benefit the state financially, would also maintain frequent contact between poor and lower-middle peasants on one hand, and pupils and teachers on the other, ensuring that the latter were subordinated to the former in every respect. It would also provide the brigades and communes with good cadres, because they could hold back capable pupils who had previously been sent on to secondary and higher education establishments, and could prevent children attending school from severing spiritual links with their illiterate or little-educated elders.

In theory, secondary schools came under the control of the commune, as far as administration and teaching were concerned, while their courses were adapted to meet the needs of the commune. It is not clear how the powers were shared between state and commune.

The outline of higher education was still not properly defined, and practices seemed to vary considerably from one establishment to another. The essential elements of the curriculum, in addition to politics and military instruction, were science, mathematics, technology, and foreign languages. Social science was inextricably entangled with political criticism and comprised the history of the struggle between the two lines and attacks on the "authorities," such as Chou Yang, T'ien Han, Hsia Yen, and Yang Han-sheng.[9] Theoretically, no student could enter the university or an establishment of higher education without having spent two years working on production or serving in the army.[10]

In each of the three branches of education, courses appear to have been shortened, but this question, like that of the age of entering school, seems closely tied up with the question of adult entry into schools and universities. Like the questions of syllabi, methods, and the choice of basic textbooks and manuals, it is still at the experimental stage. At the moment, the cycles last five, four, and three years, at the primary, secondary, and higher levels, respectively, as against the former six years for each.[11]

The official press has reported that many students, among them 3,000 at Peking University, were recruited from among workers, peasants, and soldiers during the second half of 1970. As the commentators said, this provided reinforcement, guaranteeing the great victory of the thought of Mao Tse-tung in the field of education.[12] A generation of new intellectuals, "proletarian" in origin and ideology, was being formed.

Many questions, such as the problem of leadership and the position of the Party and the Communist Youth League within education, have not yet been answered. The "half-work, half-study" system, after falling into disfavor because it created two categories of education as in capitalist countries and because Liu Shao-ch'i was supposed to have been behind it, apparently still has supporters. Decisions regarding the nature and length of courses, the choice of textbooks, and the rules for organization and administration need some coordination on a national scale. This will probably take several years and will inevitably reflect economic considerations.

It should be emphasized that, in the eyes of Mao Tse-tung, the problem of education is the major problem of Chinese society. If society is to undergo a radical and irreversible transformation, the needs of politics must come before all else. This is the only way to abolish classes and class struggle for good and make it no longer necessary to send vast numbers of townspeople periodically to the countryside; it is the only way to get cadres and workers to share the same attitude to such an extent that they can become virtually interchangeable apart from their speciality, which would then be only a modest part of their activities. This would mean that the producer was no longer subject to production and that man could take his place in a world made for him, not for his machines. The sad thing is that this doctrine, which is conceivable in a postindustrial age able to put it to the test, has arisen in a preindustrial society, less capable than any other of ignoring economic realities on account of its rapidly increasing population.

Culture

The period between 1962 and 1971 witnessed a progressive and eventually total revision of the cultural policy hitherto followed by the Party. Traditional and Western cultures were rejected, as was the socialist culture drawing inspiration from the Soviet Union; the line defined by Mao Tse-tung at Yenan in May 1942 in his two talks at the Yenan Forum on Literature and Art was considerably expanded upon and hardened. This period also saw the repudiation and disappearance of the culture of the transitional phase from the May Fourth Movement of 1919 to the Socialist Education Movement; this phase also embraced the League of Leftist Writers and the authors of the 1930s, and filled the gap until a new generation of intellectuals born of the regime could take over.[13]

A "proletarian" culture was destined to replace that of "the people as a whole." It was to be centered around the thought of Mao Tse-tung and the study of scientific and technical subjects. Mao's attitude in this is reminiscent of one of the first Neo-Confucian reformists, the great viceroy Chang Chih-t'ung; he advocated "Chinese learning for the fundamental principles, Western learning for practical application,"[14] two proposals that may turn out to be as irreconcilable at the end of this century as they were at the end of the last.

The doctrine was asserted over and over again on different occasions, including anniversaries (particularly that of the Yenan Forum), the restatement of historical problems (the comparison of the slogans "Literature of national defense" and "Literature of the masses in the service of the national revolutionary war"), the struggle between the two lines, and criticisms of authors and literary works. Various concepts or theories that the intellectuals of the Party had not entirely thrown off, such as "individualism," "the community of human nature," and the absence of need for class struggle and the dictatorship of the proletariat, which lead straight to capitalism, were also condemned.

The Socialist Education Movement had limited the activities of those circles interested in literature, art, and the social sciences; the Cultural Revolution eliminated these people professionally and sometimes physically. The first to be hit were novelists, playwrights, and poets. Lao She, Ts'ao Yü, Sha Ting, and Ou-yang Shan followed in the footsteps of Wu Han, Teng T'o, and Liao Mo-sha. Lo Kuang-pin, co-author of *Red Cliff*, was assassinated by "revolutionary rebels." Chou Yang, T'ien Han, and Hsia Yen suffered heavier and more frequent criticism than all the rest. The historian Chien Po-tsan, who had already been attacked in 1966 by Ch'i Pen-yü and others (and by Mao Tse-tung himself), was relentlessly attacked for his interpretations of the progress of history.[15] Hou Wai-lu, one of the early revolutionary intellectuals, a former student in France who had rendered countless services to the Party, was denounced as "an old anti-Communist," "a flatterer of Chiang Kai-shek," "an adorer of America," "who had been parading for a long time beneath the mask of an authority on the history of Marxism."[16] Li Shu, editor of the periodical *Historical Studies*, was accused of having rejected the class viewpoint in history and was eliminated.[17] The only ones to weather these stormy times were Fan Wen-lan, who died in July 1969, Mao Tun, and Kuo Mo-jo, who is an archaeologist rather than a historian.

Members of scientific and technical circles were, for obvious reasons, less prone to political constraints or in any case easier to rehabilitate; their isolation makes it difficult to obtain details of their personal situation and working conditions.[18]

The Cultural Revolution wrote nothing on the blank page of proletarian culture, at least in the field of literature and the arts. A few socialist dramas, operas, or ballets, brought out before 1966, were revised, and a little music was written; Chiang Ch'ing discovered unexpected links between the piano and the revolution. Popular genius, already closely confined within the limits imposed by the thought of Mao Tse-tung, fell silent. The Cultural Revolution has so far led to a widespread elimination of culture and to complete barrenness.

It is perhaps not inappropriate to point out here that, in many fields, particularly those of art and the theater, the old culture for the elite served the masses infinitely better, by offering them examples of high quality, which artisans and artists spread among the entire people.

The daily press and publishing

In the summer of 1966, the Cultural Revolution brought complete sterility to the daily press and to publishing, with the exception of the abundant but ephemeral publications of the red guards, the *People's Daily* and its variations in the provinces, the newspaper *Kuang-ming jih-pao, Red Flag* (which was suspended and appeared at irregular intervals for a time), and, above all, the reprinting of the works of Mao Tse-tung on a gigantic scale. For several years, his works were the only things to be found in the bookshops; the twentieth century has offered few examples of such an astonishing spectacle, even in the Soviet Union. A scanty supply of books and periodicals is beginning to reappear now, alongside translations of Marx, Lenin, and Engels, interspersed with edifying novels here and there, supposedly born of the spontaneous creativity of the workers and peasants. There is no question of returning to the period before 1962 and the Socialist Education Movement; the Emperor Ch'in Shih Huang-ti who "had books burned and scholars buried" is officially considered more progressive than Confucius.[19] But signs exist that suggest the debate is still going on and the break with the past is not yet irrevocable.

Religion

China had been without Chinese or foreign gods since the desecrations and confiscations of the last week of August 1966. The Peking mosque was opened in 1971 for a short ceremony for Moslem diplomats. Buddhist temples and Christian churches are still shut. The only exception to this is the liberation of Msgr. Walsh, the American bishop of Shanghai, which may be linked with the silence observed by Peking when Pope Paul VI visited Hong Kong in November 1970.[20] It seems justifiable to hope that the new departure in Chinese foreign policy will bring China to reconsider the importance of the religious factor, particularly of Islam and Buddhism in African and Asian countries, and consequently among some of its own ethnic minorities.

Notes

[1] See the report by Chou En-lai to the Third National People's Congress, December 21 and 22, 1964.

[2]Circular of December 31, 1966, issued by the Central Committee and the State Council. See *CCP Documents of the Great Proletarian Cultural Revolution (1966-1967)* (Hong Kong: Union Research Institute, 1968), p. 150.

[3]Circular of February 19, 1967, and instructions of March 7, 1967, in *CCP Documents of the Great Proletarian Cultural Revolution*, pp. 321 and 343. English text of the March 7 instructions is in the daily news bulletin published by the Hsinhua Agency.

[4]See *CCP Documents of the Great Proletarian Cultural Revolution* and *People's Daily* (October 25, 1967).

[5]This declaration was not published until a year later, in the *People's Daily* of July 22, 1969. English version in *Peking Review*, No. 31 (August 1, 1969).

[6]*Peking Review*, No. 20 (May 16, 1969).

[7]Steelworks schools at Penki (Liaoning), Lishu (Kirin), and the school for cadres at Liuho (Heilungkiang).

[8]See the *People's Daily* of November 14, 1969, and May 12, 1969; the latter reference concerns the district of Lishu in the province of Kirin.

[9]See *Kuang-ming jih-pao* (January 15, 1970) and *Hung ch'i*, No. 1 (1970).

[10]According to the press, between 1970 and 1972, a total of 200,000 students were admitted to higher education after having been peasants, workers, or soldiers; 153,000 students were admitted under identical conditions in 1973. See *Peking Review*, No. 39 (September 18, 1973).

[11]In many cases, the rule also appears to be five, five, and three years.

[12]See *Hung ch'i*, No. 3 (1971).

[13]On the first effects of the Socialist Education Movement on cultural circles, see Chapter 27.

[14]Chang Chih-t'ung, *Exhortation to Study*. See Ssu-yu Teng and J. K. Fairbank, *China's Response to the West* (New York: Atheneum, 1967), p. 164.

[15]At the beginning and the end of this campaign respectively, see *Red Flag*, No. 4 (1966), and *Kuang-ming jih-pao* of January 15, 1971.

[16]*People's Daily* (November 22, 1966).

[17]*People's Daily* (October 23, 1966).

[18]It goes against the grain to have to read the declaration of the distinguished geologist Li Szu-kuang, who is now dead, on the powerlessness of scientific thought without the help of Mao Tse-tung.

[19]See in particular the *People's Daily* (September 28, 1973) and *Hung ch'i*, Nos. 10 and 11 (1973).

[20]Services are said to have begun again on a limited scale in one of the churches in Peking at the end of 1971.

42 Military Policy 1962 –1976

Military institutions in the strictest sense of the term changed little between 1962 and 1976, though the spirit behind them changed enormously.[1] This was due first of all to the influence of Lin Piao, who wanted to do away once and for all with the "professional" trends encouraged by his predecessor P'eng Teh-huai; then to the circumstances; and later to necessity. During the Socialist Education Movement, the role of the army was to set an example; after its direct intervention in the disturbances of the Cultural Revolution in January 1967, its role became that of a guardian. From then on extremely close spiritual links were formed between the army and the rest of the nation, while a state of complete interdependence grew up between the political, administrative, and economic hierarchies on one hand, and the military hierarchy on the other. This inner development was entirely in harmony with the evolution of China's National Defense policy once the country had gradually reassumed political and military independence with regard to the Soviet Union, using ideological reasons as a pretext.

The starting point of this twofold development was Lin Piao's article: "Forward under the Red Banner of the General Party Line and the Military Theory of Mao Tse-tung." All the ideas that were to be in the forefront over the next few years were already there: close links between the general line and the military line, the permanent nature of class struggle and the vital necessity of maintaining it within the army, the primacy of ideological and political work, intensive participation by the army in the activities of the masses and in production, the use of "democratic" methods, including large debates and big-character wall newspapers (*ta-tzu pao*), the defensive orientation of strategy, combining large units of the army operating from modern bases and innumerable militia units acting over the territory as a whole. The People's Liberation Army was, as Lin Piao said in the words of Mao Tse-tung, "an army of a new type."

The characteristics of this new army gradually became clearer, particularly after the Tenth Plenum in September 1962. The "four priorities"—man, political work, ideological work, and living ideas—dominated all military activities. In all circumstances the works of Mao Tse-tung had to be taken as the supreme instructions. The cadres had to go to the basic level, to create "four-good" companies; the best leaders and soldiers were to have the posts of responsibility. Vigorous military instruction was to consist largely of technical training, close combat, and night fighting.

A considerable effort was started and continued to ensure that the army was directed by the Party. The structure of the army's General Political Department was reinforced, and closer links were forged between the department and the local Party committees.[2] The four conferences held between October 1961 and January 1966 on political work in the army all stressed that, at all levels, those in command should be in complete submission to political instructions. At the last of the conferences, presided over by Hsiao Hua, the successor to Marshal Lo Jung-huan (who died in 1963), the point was made with such energy that foreign observers concluded that a powerful opposition group—the one led by Lo Jui-ch'ing—had been opposed and overcome.

The army began to take on extraprofessional duties, to propagate the thought of Mao Tse-tung and make known the details of its own organization and methods; at the same time, it became more democratic internally. Military ranks, dress uniforms, and even the emblem recalling the date of foundation were abolished on June 1, 1965. All wore the same insignia, consisting of a red star on a soft cap and red collar bands. On August 1, 1965, former marshal Ho Lung wrote an important doctrinal article, "The Democratic Tradition in the People's Liberation Army," exalting the "three democracies" in the army: democracy in politics, in economics, and in military affairs.

From 1965 on, possibly because of the escalation of warfare in Vietnam, concepts of defensive strategy were affirmed more clearly. They were expressed more fully in an article published by Lin Piao on September 3, "Long Live the Victory of the People's War," which caused a considerable stir. His main point was that the theory of people's war, formulated by Mao Tse-tung on the basis of scientific analysis and verified by the experience of the anti-Japanese war, retained all its validity. Lin Piao summarized the main points, citing first the primacy of politics: "Politics is the commander, politics is the soul of everything. Political work is the lifeline of our army." He then recalled that Mao Tse-tung had raised guerrilla warfare to the level of high strategy, putting it first, though without denying the value of mobile warfare when circumstances allowed. Lin Piao upheld the doctrine and outlined it himself:

> In order to annihilate the enemy, we must adopt the policy of luring him in deep and abandon some cities and districts of our own accord and in a planned way, so as to let him in. It is only after letting the enemy in that the people can take part in the war in various ways and that the power of a people's war can be fully exerted.

The need to retreat was subordinated to the need to attack: "Attack is the pivot of all our strategy and tactics." The same strategy could be applied on an international scale to the entire revolutionary movement:

> Taking the entire globe, if North America and Western Europe can be called the "cities of the world," then Asia, Africa and Latin America constitute the "rural areas of the world". . . . In a sense, the contemporary world revolution also presents a picture of the encirclement of the cities by the rural areas.

He described Mao's theory of people's war as having "the characteristics of our epoch" and as "a common asset of the revolutionary peoples of the whole world."

Like Mao Tse-tung, Lin Piao made light of nuclear weapons, holding that "imperialism" could not resort to them without being "isolated in the extreme," and adding, though without dwelling on the point, that "others" also possessed them.

In fact, the regime has chosen to get ready for people's war and nuclear war. To supply an army on the scale of that of the United States or the Soviet Union with modern conventional weapons was both costly and slow, in view of the weakness of China's industrial economy and the impact of the failures of the Great Leap Forward.

People's war and the nuclear deterrent may be explained chiefly by the increasingly rapid deterioration in Sino-Soviet relations from 1965 on. As a consequence of its independence in foreign policy, Peking had to undertake a total revision of its military policy, which could no longer rely invariably on Soviet logistical support and nuclear defense. In view of the poor quantity and quality of China's equipment in the fields of artillery, armor, engineering, and aviation and the fact that it had barely begun to produce atomic weapons, Peking's only possible strategy was a general concept of defense based on people's forces spread across the territory and capable of "submerging" the invader in a "vast ocean" of guerrilla fighters. This policy is far more reflective of deliberate political isolation and obvious economic inadequacy than it is of a military doctrine drawn from the frequently mentioned experience of the years before 1949.

From 1965 on, developments in the war in Vietnam seemed to justify the direction of Chinese military policy. If a war broke out, China would become another Vietnam. The press, the radio, and the cinema diligently spread this image among the population and abroad. But—and this appeared a paradox—the more the danger increased in Vietnam, the more the Chinese maintained their independence with regard to the socialist camp as a whole. They refused to fall into line with anyone else or to share in any measures likely to lead to an intervention, for they would inevitably bear the brunt in this case, as the United States and the Soviet Union each considered the other as a sanctuary. From 1969, the Sino-Soviet clashes on the Ussuri River led the Chinese to pay more attention to conventional heavy weapons (artillery and tanks) suitable for use in highly localized fighting, but their military policy remained unaltered in its general lines. It was reaffirmed on the forty-fourth anniversary of the founding of the army, celebrated on August 1, 1971: "Our preparedness against war is exclusively for the purpose of defense. We will not attack unless we are attacked; if we are attacked, we will certainly counterattack. This is our consistent just stand."[3]

Chinese military policy today is in careful harmony with the realities of a retarded economy and a geographical situation of great potential danger. In this respect, in spite of their attitudes and verbal excesses, the Chinese have remained true to their ancient tradition of pragmatism.

On the whole, the People's Liberation Army accepted the evolution imposed by Mao Tse-tung and Lin Piao in the autumn of 1959, and, except in the case of Lo Jui-ch'ing, outbreaks of dissidence were short lived and resulted from the political circumstances, not from a military line differing from the official line. The exaggerated importance allowed to ideological education or production compared with military training, the virtual substitution of moral determination for material means, and the decline of the commanding hierarchy's credit and authority compared with that enjoyed by the political instructors and commissars resulted in discontent and other very understandable reactions. But none of these reactions appears to have grown into the real "professionalism" that developed in 1954 and for some years after. Authentic professionalism would have implied adhering to a doctrine based on the use of modern units whose composition, fire power, and mobility were comparable to those of similar Western and Russian units, giving a secondary role to guerrilla warfare and priority to nuclear weapons. If China had chosen to follow this line, it would have needed considerable logistical support of high quality from the Russians, which would have led to a readjustment of Sino-Soviet relations in every respect. The "professionalists" would inevitably have been either convinced or potential "revisionists" at the same time. P'eng Teh-huai fell into this category, as did Lo Jui-ch'ing.

In view of his post as chief of staff, Lo Jui-ch'ing had to state his position clearly when the Americans stepped up their numbers in Vietnam to 500,000 men. Lo was a man of strong personality, as determined as P'eng Teh-huai and faithful to the Party above all else; he came into open disagreement with Mao Tse-tung shortly after the difficult working session of the Central Committee in September-October 1965.[4] Lo's dismissal, like that of P'eng Teh-huai five or six years earlier, does not appear to have caused extensive uneasiness within the army, which seems to have accepted the military line upheld by Lin Piao without any internal crisis. The concept of people's war had been familiar to all since its origins. As an "armed organization responsible for executing the political tasks of the revolution," the army's mission had been just as much to stir up, mobilize, indoctrinate, and control the population as to fight. After an interlude of Soviet inspiration, it came back to its true tradition. The army and the people were one once more.

Preparation for people's war, as redefined by Lin Piao, involved, even in peacetime and quite apart from the Socialist Education Movement and the Cultural Revolution, some measure of intervention in civilian institutions on the part of the army and its cadres. This intervention enormously strengthened the army's prestige throughout the nation, heightening patriotism without creating too much tension with the civilian hierarchies, for many of their important members had received their basic training from the army and the cadres were used to cooperating with the army in times of difficulty. For senior army cadres, all of whom still belonged to the first generation of the Red Army, people's war was a fundamental element in the military theory, both past and present, of Mao Tse-tung. Mao had come to power by means of the army, but the army owed him everything. He brought it into existence, giving it its political and moral foundations, and its doctrine. He healed its growing pains, enlarged it from a few hundred to several million men, and led it to victory in 1949. The army remained faithful to the dogma of his infallibility. As far as it is possible to judge today, the disappearance of Lin Piao, Chief of Staff Huang Yung-sheng, and other military leaders during the summer of 1971 does not seem to have had any irreparable effects on the basic loyalty of the army to its creator.

Developments within the armed forces

The Cultural Revolution furnished ample information on the army's intervention in politics, economics, and culture, but revealed much less about its internal transformation.[5] On the whole, the changes seem to have affected its leaders and numbers, rather than its main structures and equipment or the quantity and composition of its large units. Supplies of nuclear weapons had reached a high level, both in quantity and quality.

The basic principle of the law of July 30, 1955, on compulsory military service does not seem to have been questioned, though slight changes have come about in the way it is applied during moments of tension, either at home or abroad. Overall numbers appear to have grown by between 500,000 and 800,000 men, due to the increase in extramilitary tasks performed by the army, the strengthening of the Sino-Soviet frontiers, and the taking in hand of the red guards, many of whom were absorbed into the People's Liberation Army. The total figure, which may be a temporary one, may be set at 3.5 million men; this can probably be accounted for by the fact that units have been brought up to a war footing, and does not correspond to an increase in the numbers of armies and divisions.

The general structure appears to be the same. The Party's Military Affairs Committee, headed by Party Chairman Mao Tse-tung, is still the supreme authority, but since the disappearance of Lin Piao its exact composition and true role are no longer known.[6] In 1975, Marshal Yeh Chien-ying became minister of national defense, a post that had been vacant for some time, while Teng Hsiao-p'ing was appointed chief of general staff, a post he is said to have lost in March 1976. After the elimination of Hsiao Hua early in 1968, the army's General Political Department was without a head until the appointment of Li Teh-sheng, then commander of the Anhwei Military District and chairman of the Anhwei Revolutionary Committee. When in 1975 he became commander of the Shenyang Military Region in Manchuria, Li was succeeded by Chang Ch'un-ch'ao.[7]

Throughout the Cultural Revolution important changes in leadership occurred constantly, affecting the commanders of the different arms or services, military districts and regions, and the commanders of large units. Political considerations often constituted the main factor governing such choices. They arose from the wish to strengthen the influence of certain people (particularly Lin Piao) and the need to take into account local situations, which were often tricky. It should be noted here that both the revolutionary committees and the Party, which was in the process of reconstitution, included a large proportion of army personnel. After the disappearance of Lin Piao, the proportion of the military in the central organizations of the Party and the state was substantially cut down, but considerable numbers of them remained in provincial organizations. Not until 1974 or 1975 did the army regain the position it had held just before the Cultural Revolution.

Few changes are noticeable in the numbers, composition, and equipment of armies and divisions.[8] The doctrine governing the use of large units also seems to have changed little, in spite of the return to favor of people's war. In the event of war, these units, instead of spreading out among the masses, would be employed in the static or mobile defense of the vital points and chief axes of the territory, while guerrilla warfare would be entrusted to the militia of the towns and communes.

The air force and the navy appear to have progressed little. Both are still chiefly dependent on materiel acquired in the Soviet Union, which is now difficult to maintain correctly due to lack of spare parts. The air force has evolved a modern fighter plane, the F 9, with a better performance than the MIG 19 and MIG 21 (which are still in service), has produced TU 16 bombers, and still has several hundred Il 28. Most estimates give an average figure of 3,500 aircraft. The navy has about forty submarines (including one or two that can be equipped for missile launching and one nuclear submarine that is still in the planning stage) and has improved the rocket firing power of its small surface vessels. The cost of equipment, China's technical and technological backwardness, the clear inferiority of the Chinese air force and navy to its Soviet and American counterparts, and the strategy of defense in depth, based on support from the masses, combine to give the air force and navy a secondary role in comparison to non-conventional weapons and the ground forces.

The troops under the control of the minister of public security, which were long treated with distrust, possibly because of the reputation of former minister Lo Jui-ch'ing, have been thoroughly reorganized. The militia has apparently come back into favor after a long eclipse that may have been the result of political events and also possibly of excesses on the part of local leaders. It is impossible to enumerate the public security forces accurately, for although they are theoretically inexhaustible, they depend on the availability of arms and officers. On the assumption that each of the 70,000 people's communes has a company of at least 150 men, a likely total of 10 million militiamen is obtained, which probably rises to 12 million if the militia in the towns and factories, each of which has one company, are included. The militia represents the reserve force for the army, a dependable element in case of domestic unrest; it is also the nucleus at the center of moral and patriotic mobilization. Its roles in strategic defense on land and as the preserver of the social structure in the context of nuclear attack on China, deserve to be assessed. No important texts are available today to enable this to be done with any accuracy.

Nonconventional weapons

The major military event of the period between 1962 and 1976 is naturally the appearance of Chinese nuclear and thermonuclear weapons and of medium-range missiles, and also the launching of four earth satellites. The dates of the Chinese tests—seventeen atomic or thermonuclear explosions had occurred by October 27, 1975—show how rapid progress has been. The first atomic explosion took place on October 16, 1964, and was followed by eight others. The first thermonuclear bomb was tested on June 17, 1967, and four tests were carried out, including the explosion of a 3-megaton hydrogen bomb on October 14, 1970. The four earth satellites went into orbit on April 24, 1970 (173 kilograms), March 3, 1971 (221 kilograms), July 26, 1975, and November 26, 1975. In the space of six years the Chinese progressed from a 13-kiloton atomic device to a 3-megaton hydrogen bomb, and they have also, apparently, evolved tactical nuclear weapons.

Numerous experts have tried to evaluate the present Chinese military potential and to forecast their rate of progress. For this, Russians and Americans use observations collected by their satellites to analyze radioactive fallout and to measure waves. The Russians say little, but in 1971 the Americans reckoned that the Chinese already possessed about twenty medium-range rockets (with a range of between 1,100 and 2,800 kilometers), and that by 1973 they also possessed an operational intercontinental rocket and would have twenty or so of them by 1975.[9] China will thus have a striking force, but it is of relatively small value compared with those of superpowers as long as the country has not been immunized by the possession of an adequate retaliatory force. The latter may be achieved by about 1980. Some analysts think that China will be extremely vulnerable until then because its progress will render it more liable to preventive action on the part of the Americans or the Russians, particularly if China persists in its refusal to join in present or future negotiations for disarmament.

Without dwelling any longer on these prospects or possible events after 1980, it is quite clear that if China were to acquire an intercontinental nuclear deterrent force or a medium-range nuclear force larger than the latter, the basic elements of its foreign policy in East Asia would undergo rapid and far-reaching changes. Since the security of all Asian states is at stake, the result may be a search for collective arrangements that will bring about a new balance. On the other hand, China's nuclear and missile capabilities may free the large countries that are scientifically and financially capable of building up supplies of nuclear or thermonuclear weapons (Japan and India) to adopt new policies, inspiring simultaneously a realignment of the second- and third-rank nations bordering on the Pacific and Indian oceans. The general evolution of Chinese military policy, China's progress in the field of modern weapons, and its attitude toward the disarmament question are by far the most important subjects for reflection that the country has to offer us today.

Notes

[1] See Chapter 14 on military institutions and Chapter 21 for details on the replacing of P'eng Teh-huai by Lin Piao.

[2] A ruling on political work in the army came into use in March 1963.

[3] *Hung ch'i*, No. 9 (1971) and daily press of August 1, 1971; English version in *Peking Review*, No. 32 (August 6, 1971).

[4] Lo Jui-ch'ing tentatively expressed his theories in an article entitled "For the Anniversary of Victory over German Fascism! For the Struggle to the End Against American Imperialism!", *Hung ch'i*, No. 5 (May 5, 1965). He laid more stress on the role of the Soviet army than on that of the guerrilla fighters and emphasized people's war much less than did Lin Piao in the article briefly analyzed above. See also Lo Jui-ch'ing, "The People Defeated Japanese Fascism and Can Certainly Beat American Imperialism" (September 3, 1965). Lo Jui-ch'ing was rehabilitated in 1975, though he has not to date been given an important post.

[5] See Chapter 14 for details on military organization in general and the chapters on the Cultural Revolution for the virtually permanent role of the army in it.

[6] Marshals Yeh Chien-ying, Hsü Hsiang-ch'ien, and Nieh Jung-chen are, in order of precedence, vice-chairmen of the Party's Military Affairs Committee.

[7] Yang Ch'eng-wu, the former temporary chief of staff at the beginning of the Cultural Revolution has been rehabilitated and is now one of the seven or eight assistants to the chief of general staff.

[8]About forty armies, consisting of 120 infantry divisions (about 12,000 men each) and about twenty other specialized large units: armored and artillery units, airborne troops, and so on.
[9]Declaration made by the Pentagon on August 5, 1971. The declarations made early in 1971 by President Nixon and by Defense Secretary Melvin Laird in February 1972 mentioned the same prospects but gave fewer details. For a more recent review of the situation, see Harry Geller, "Nuclear Weapons and Chinese Policy," *Adelphi Papers,* No. 99 (London: International Institute for Strategic Studies, 1973), and "The Military Balance 1974-1975" (London: International Institute for Strategic Studies, 1975).

43 Foreign Policy 1966 –1976 (1): General Development

From the summer of 1966 until just before the Ninth Congress in April 1969, Chinese foreign policy was to a large extent paralyzed by the Cultural Revolution. The image of China abroad had already been dimmed by the lack of proportion and failure of the Great Leap Forward; the Cultural Revolution, totally unexpected, confusing, and often excessive, tarnished it still further. Chinese interests suffered as a result, and the damage as regards some of the neighboring states (Cambodia, Burma, Japan, and Nepal) would have been irreparable if Chou En-lai, with his usual skill and realism, had not saved the situation at the last moment.

At the end of 1968, and particularly in 1969 and 1970, a partial return to order at home and important changes in affairs in Asia and the world at large brought new vigor to foreign policy, reorienting it to a large extent, as was borne out by various declarations and attitudes indicating its general outline. Although those in charge of it refused to admit as much, it resembled that of a future superpower, aiming at counteracting the feared bipolar dominance of the United States and the Soviet Union and ready to mobilize all the nations of the world—neutral countries, those linked by treaties to the United States, or those of the socialist camp—for this purpose.[1]

Several events of great importance took place in 1971. The announcement that President Nixon would visit Peking before May 1972, closely followed by Peking's replacement of Taipei in the United Nations on October 25, 1971, gave China a place in world affairs at the highest level. International opinion was divided between those who hoped to get China to take part in working for peace and those who feared that Peking's new prestige would lead it to greater revolutionary intransigence. Mysterious events within the country during the same months added to the general uncertainty. Eventually, the elimination of Lin Piao was gradually acknowledged, confirming and ensuring a new departure, attributed by all to his rival Chou En-lai, who was applying "the line of Chairman Mao Tse-tung in foreign policy."

The momentary eclipse of Chinese foreign policy between 1966 and 1969 was due mainly to the urgency and importance of internal problems. The prime movers of the Cultural Revolution devoted all their energies to winning back power and rebuilding the image of the Chinese model of revolution. They seem to have had different views as regards foreign relations (whether governments or Communist Parties); the red guards and "revolutionary rebels" also intervened, with the result that the foreign minister briefly lost control of his ministry (August 1967). Ch'en Yi's self-criticisms, marked by restraint at first, and the sack of the office of the British chargé d'affaires in Peking were episodes in a long struggle between radical and more realistic tendencies.[2] The former appear to have come to the surface several times before the decline of the Cultural Revolution Group.

As was to be expected, the Cultural Revolution produced criticisms of the foreign policy of Liu Shao-ch'i and his supporters. The former president of the Republic was accused, generally speaking, of having wanted to practice a policy of appeasement toward revisionists, imperialists, and reactionaries and of having sought to reduce China's support for revolutionary movements elsewhere. The accusations were summed up in a slogan, "Peace with the imperialists, reactionaries and revisionists; less help for the revolutionary movements in all countries" (*san ho i shao*).

The first important declaration on foreign policy during this period was made by Chou En-lai, speaking at the Albanian Embassy on November 29, 1968. The chief source of anxiety and the main direction followed by the Chinese leaders were outlined clearly and concisely: "We must unite with all the peoples oppressed by American imperialism, Soviet revisionism, and their lackeys to form a great united front to frustrate the criminal plot of American imperialism and Soviet revisionism aiming to share out the world between them."

China put up ceaseless opposition to the sharing of power between the two states and to Soviet-American collusion, which had been worrying Chinese leaders since the Twentieth Congress of the Communist Party of the Soviet Union. Too weak in the military and economic fields to qualify as a superpower, and in any case unable to assume such a title without arousing the same mistrust and anxiety as other states whose ambitions it condemned, Peking tried to introduce into its state relations the Chinese doctrine of support for revolutionary movements and for national liberation movements. In his appeal, the premier called on every people, regardless of its regime. As Chou En-lai had said in a similar declaration in 1963, it was no longer a question of coming out in favor of equality between nations, or of making distinctions between different "intermediate zones," but of getting the least powerful to unite, with China showing them the way.

In this defensive but defiant attitude, China wanted to use all possible means of action abroad. Doctrinal intransigence was more of a necessity than ever. The long-range weapon of ideology, skillfully handled, must reach every region of the planet, and by the violence of its formulas make up for the inadequacies of its resources for action (economic, financial, and military aid).

As soon as the People's Republic could enter the United Nations without making overly large compromises it should do so, for there it could exercise its influence more usefully on the countries of the Third World, while trying to increase their representation and their role. As a permanent member of the Security Council, Peking would be sure of playing a direct part in the handling of all important international questions. This particular aim was attained sooner than expected.

China also had to acquire as soon as possible a maximum of modern military equipment, in terms of nuclear or thermonuclear weapons, for no independent foreign policy in the fullest sense could exist without them.

The revival in Chinese foreign policy at the end of 1968 was also due to various new factors, or factors that had come to the fore again. The Cultural Revolution exalted the ideological claims of Mao Tse-tung to the highest degree; he had become "the Lenin of our time." The transposition of this phenomenon on to the political plane had to be carried out as quickly as possible on a worldwide scale. It severed the last links between the Soviet Union and China; each regime was following a different development, both as regards ideology and as regards institutions and the spirit behind them. The break, soon revealed by the serious frontier incidents on the Ussuri River, encouraged China to behave like a great power that was free to make its own choices, use its own methods, and win a suitable audience in the world for its interests. The new departure in Sino-American relations in 1971 arose from this emancipation in Chinese foreign policy. To take part in international affairs, China had to introduce a new balance in its diplomatic relations, theoretically maintaining an equal distance from Moscow and Washington. Then, having acquired more space in which to maneuver, it would have to show more flexibility and initiative in its relations with foreign countries. Peking would have to make the fullest possible use of international contradictions to isolate the chief enemy of the moment.[3]

China could not fail to realize that a policy in the most general sense of the term was taking shape or being reborn in East Asia. Where the powers each pursued their own interests, or at best adopted parallel attitudes, clearly defined groups were being formed. The "Far-Eastern question" was gradually giving way to the "balance of power in Asia," reminiscent of the balance of power in Europe before 1939. The main parts in this would be played by the United States, the Soviet Union, Japan, China, and India.

A number of events illustrating this development during the years between 1969 and 1976 will be dealt with in the next four chapters: (1) the Nixon Doctrine stated at Guam on July 26, 1969; its chief characteristics were the progressive withdrawal of American troops from Southeast Asia, logistical support, and, if the need arose, intervention by the air force and the navy to help allies of the United States; (2) the political and even military rebirth of Japan, as a result of its powerful economic expansion; (3) persistent Russian interest in South and Southeast Asia (India, Indonesia), and the Soviet inclination to organize a collective system of security in Asia against China,[4] and (4) beginnings of economic and technical collaboration in Siberia between the Russians and the Japanese; attempts to establish military contacts.

The report given by Lin Piao at the Ninth Congress of the Chinese Communist Party (April 1, 1969) confirmed Chou En-lai's declaration of November 29, 1968.[5] It contained identical denunciations of the vain attempts of "American imperialism" and "social-imperialism," who "collude and at the same time contend with each other" and who "act in coordination and work hand in glove in opposing China, opposing Communism, and opposing the people." Inevitably in the circum-stances—the incidents on the Ussuri had occurred the month before and the invasion of Czechoslovakia the previous year—the Chinese national defense minister aimed his harshest attacks at the "Soviet revisionist renegade clique" whose turn it was to be described as a "paper tiger." Examples were cited to show the contrast between the peaceful inclinations of the Chinese leaders and the theory of "limited sovereignty" that "social-fascism" wanted to impose on the nations of the socialist community. Speaking with more clarity and urgency than Chou En-lai, Lin Piao launched an appeal to the nations of the world: "All countries and peoples subjected to aggression, control, intervention or bullying by U.S. imperialism and Soviet revisionism, let us unite and form the broadest possible united front and overthrow our common enemies!" He ended with a quotation from Mao Tse-tung which had the ring of an incantation: "The people of all countries are rising. A new historical period of struggle against U.S. imperialism and Soviet revisionism has begun."

A year later, on May 20, 1970, the coup d'état of March 18 in Cambodia and America's military support of General Lon Nol led Mao Tse-tung to reach beyond Indochinese and Sino-American questions to pass judgment on the situation in the world as a whole: "The danger of a new world war still exists, and the people of all countries must get prepared. But revolution is the main trend in the world today."[6] This message, encouraging the utmost intransigence in revolution, was enough to confirm Peking in the role for which it vied with the Kremlin. Even so, its violent words were not enough to disguise a concern for caution, fully justified by China's vulnerability and military weakness. It aroused anxiety and alarm in the world at large, though this was quickly forgotten when signs of a rapprochement between the United States and China became apparent.

President Nixon's declaration of July 26, 1969, announced a thorough revision of American policy in the world as a whole, but particularly in Asia, along with the one on Vietnam issued on November 3 of the same year. Both were naturally carefully analyzed in Peking. In the long run, they meant a return to the Vietnam status of the ten years from 1954 to 1964. The danger that China might be forced into a military intervention receded. Russian military assistance for Hanoi would become less necessary, and Moscow's political influence would diminish. China alone would be able to dominate the Indochinese question and would be a determining factor in settling it.

The new Nixon policy would possibly reopen a series of questions on which no progress had been made since the Korean War and President Truman's declaration on June 27, 1950. The Sino-American contention in Asia at least could be discussed. The Chinese had often called for it; they had nothing to lose and much to gain in the case of Taiwan, Korea, Japan, or their representation in the United Nations. In a worldwide context, they now had the opportunity to become involved in the affairs of the superpowers and to win certain obvious advantages, while being able to confuse the situation more effectively than they had been able to do over Vietnam. After a last crisis, provoked by the military intervention of the South Vietnamese in southern Laos and in the direction of North Vietnam (February-March 1971), events took their natural course.

The sudden visit of Henry Kissinger, personal adviser to President Nixon, to Peking (July 9-11, 1971) and the announcement that the president would go there before May 1972, started a new era in world politics, to be centered in the future around three main poles of attraction: Washington, Moscow, and Peking. China suffered from economic weakness and internal handicaps, but its size, its progress in the field of nuclear development, and its ideological independence had given it superpower status. Peking's admission to the United Nations three months later was the natural outcome of this rise, which the Americans, whether involuntarily or deliberately, had just precipitated.

President Nixon's visit to Peking (February 21-28, 1972) cleared the way for the Chinese to pursue an active foreign policy, the first evidence of which was the return to peace in Vietnam. The visit of Japanese Premier Kakuei Tanaka (September 25-30, 1972) removed the obstacle formed by nearly a century of tension, invasion, and war; economic exchanges proliferated and political adjustments were made—essential preliminaries to the search for a new balance of the four powers (the United States, the Soviet Union, China, and Japan) in East Asia.

Although an improvement was noticeable on some secondary points, relations with the Soviet Union were still of overriding importance for the Chinese; their foreign policy as a whole was subordinated to this. This explains the policy toward Vietnam enabling the Americans to pay more attention to the sensitive areas of the Near East and Europe. The Chinese policy of encouraging the political and military construction of Europe, "the key to the strategical rivalry between the United States and the Soviet Union," as Chou En-lai said at the Tenth Congress, and in practice openly favoring a Europe turned toward the Atlantic, should also be understood in this light.

On the threshold of 1976, the People's Republic of China was advancing rapidly toward its destiny as a world power.

Notes

[1]From 1970 on, China resumed and increased its grants of economic aid to foreign countries (the Third World and Communist countries). Between 1953 and the end of 1971, this aid was estimated at $5,600 million, about $3,700 million of which was reported to have been used by the end of 1971. See Leo Tansky, "Chinese Foreign Aid, An Economic Assessment," in Congress of the United States of America, Joint Economic Committee, *People's Republic of China: An Economic Assessment* (Washington, D.C.: U.S. Government Printing Office, 1972).

[2]See Chapter 35. Marshal Ch'en Yi, who died on January 6, 1972, was forced to make a particularly harsh self-criticism on March 6, 1968. Chou En-lai said on September 2, 1967, that in August power had been seized at the Foreign Ministry by "revolutionary rebels" from the Foreign Languages Institute.

[3]See, on this last point, the article "A Powerful Weapon to Unite the People and Conquer the Enemy," *Hung ch'i*, No. 9 (1971), which develops the historical and ideological justifications for this policy. See also, in the political report presented by Chou En-lai to the Tenth Congress, the interesting passage making the distinction between "collusion" and compromise between Soviet revisionism and American imperialism and "the necessary compromises revolutionary countries make with imperialist countries," and the corresponding quotation from Lenin.

[4]Security system denounced by Chou En-lai on July 14 and 30, 1969, "Down with the Collective Security of the New Tsars." The Chinese also attacked the projected arrangements between the Russians and the Americans for setting up an antimissile network, aimed toward China.

[5]On the report of Lin Piao in general, see Chapter 38.

[6]These two sentences were the subject of a long commentary on January 1, 1971 (*People's Daily* and *Hung ch'i*). English version in *Peking Review*, No. 1 (January 1, 1971).

44 Foreign Policy 1966 –1976 (2): Indian Subcontinent, Arab States, Africa, Latin America

The Indian subcontinent

India

Although they did not involve major military clashes, as in 1962, or the threats of direct intervention of 1965, Sino-Indian relations remained bad and were punctuated by various incidents such as the one involving the second secretary of the Indian embassy in Peking, K. Raghunat, who was accused of espionage because he read posters put up by the red guards (June 13, 1967), and the attack on the Chinese embassy in New Delhi (June 16, 1967). Later, a few skirmishes or outbreaks of artillery fire occurred at the Nathu Pass near the Sikkim frontier (September 11, 1967). The brief Indo-Pakistani war in December 1971 over the Bangladesh question provoked tension, but this did not reach the stage of fighting.

The Chinese acrimoniously and ironically combed the Indian press, which was open and liberal, for all suitable details that might support permanent criticisms of the Indian government, the Congress Party, and the pro-Soviet Communist Party. Difficulties in the food supply, social disturbances, revolts of the Assam tribes (Mizos, Nagas, and Kukis), the struggle of the "untouchables," and even the private life of Mrs. Indira Gandhi became the subject of articles and editorials that sometimes verged on insult. The Chinese naturally showed the most hostility on the subject of Indian foreign policy and the Naxalite rebellions.

The Indian government was openly accused of having acted as the instrument for Russo-American aggression against China. As regards relations with Moscow, it was pointed out that much had been made of Alexei Kosygin's visit to New Delhi in January 1968 and of that of the Indian national defense minister to Moscow, that Russian military materiel had been supplied to India (aircraft factories producing MIG 21 supersonic fighter bombers), and that India had granted port facilities to the Russian fleet in the Indian Ocean. As far as Indian-American relations were concerned, India was reproached for allowing the Seventh Fleet to use the Indian bases in the Andaman and Nicobar islands and for allowing an institute of seismology to be installed in Kashmir (for observing Chinese nuclear explosions, Peking said). The Indian government was accused at random of undermining the struggle of the Arab countries against Israel, of subscribing to "dirty deals" on the Near East question at the United Nations (the Delhi Conference, November 11-14, 1967), of giving help in the form of spare parts to the Israeli air force, and of encouraging a "two Chinas plot." As may be expected, India's annexation of Sikkim in April 1975 and its moral support for the Tibetan refugees, extending as far as the Human Rights Commission at the United Nations, were denounced on every possible occasion.

The Chinese were harshest of all as regards internal affairs. They condemned the "brutalities" of the government, "encouraged" by "surrendering" to the "renegade clique" of Dange and Namboodiripad in Kerala, West Bengal, and elsewhere, and urged the Indian people to reject parliamentary action and embark on the road of armed uprising as revealed by Mao Tse-tung. Peasant uprisings in Naxalbari and in several villages in the Darjeeling area were hailed enthusiastically; the *People's Daily* of June 5, 1967, contained an editorial entitled "Spring Thunder over India." Later (July 26) the same newspaper called on the Indian people to follow the example of the Naxalites and take up arms against exploitation by "Indian rats, American wolves, and Soviet foxes." The formation of the third Indian Communist Party, the Marxist-Leninist Indian Communist Party led by Kanu Sanyal, on April 22, 1969, received support from China, at least in theory. This new Party was weak, however, when compared with the Indian Communist Party and its left-wing offshoot, the Marxist Indian Communist Party, and particularly when compared with the whole range of Indian parties. This weakness, in conjunction with the new direction adopted by Chinese foreign policy, seemed to have led Peking to show more caution toward the entire Indian continent until the Bangladesh affair erupted and made China emphatically reaffirm its support for Pakistan (see below). The treaty of peace, friendship, and cooperation between India and the Soviet Union signed on August 9, 1971, in New Delhi was a direct consequence of the Chinese position.

The treaty was an unqualified success for Soviet policy in Asia; Chou En-lai regarded it as a retort to President Nixon's projected visit to Peking. It quickly proved its efficiency by forestalling Chinese military reactions when Bangladesh was invaded. Chinese diplomatic reactions, in the context of the United Nations, which was still new to them, were, like those of the Americans, rapidly cancelled out by a series of Soviet vetoes.

Chinese relations with India remained at a standstill until 1976, when ambassadors were exchanged once more. The present relatively moderate attitude is probably due to the Chinese fear that India will give in to Soviet solicitations, with a view to a collective security pact in Asia, and will accept more Russian military aid. Brezhnev's last visit to New Delhi, on November 26, 1973, was barely mentioned by the Peking press, which also reacted with great composure to the news of the first "peaceful" Indian nuclear explosion (May 16, 1974). Lastly, the Chinese showed great satisfaction at the overthrow of Mujibar Rahman in Bangladesh, and they quickly recognized the Dacca regime (August 31, 1975).

Pakistan

The Cultural Revolution did not interrupt the friendship between China and Pakistan, which was maintained by frequent exchanges of political, economic, and military missions. The foreign minister of Pakistan visited Peking in August 1968; he was followed in November by army Commander in Chief General Mohamed Yahya Khan, who succeeded Ayub Khan as president in April 1969. In July 1969, a government delegation, led by Lieutenant General Nur Khan of the air force, visited China. In June 1970, it was the turn of the commander of the air force (Air Marshal Abou Rahim), and in September 1970 of the commander in chief of the navy. On November 10, 1970, General Yahya Khan returned to Peking as head of state. The joint communiqué issued on this occasion stressed the "deep, all-round development" of the friendship between the two countries.[1]

Chinese missions to Pakistan were fewer and less dazzling. The major ones were led by Kuo Mo-jo to East Pakistan (March 11, 1970) and by Fang Yi, deputy minister of trade. In addition to substantial military aid, the Chinese gave Pakistan modest financial help, which was nevertheless useful to a country heavily in debt owing to military expenses entailed by hostility toward India.[2] Relations along the frontier were facilitated by the completion of a road from Sinkiang to Pakistan across the Karakorum (March 1971).

A striking demonstration of the true extent of the solidarity between China and Pakistan came when East Pakistan moved to secede and become Bangladesh. The Chinese never considered their own principles on support for peoples fighting for national liberation or the existence of revolutionary elements in Bengal sympathizing with Peking (the Awami National Party). The conflict was regarded as an attempt to break the national unity of Pakistan, and as a serious interference in Pakistan's internal affairs; the Indians were accused of encouraging the rebels and were threatened with intervention along the border. In its anxiety to counterbalance India adequately, China, instead of behaving like a revolutionary country, acted like a great state protecting its essential interest, which was to maintain the divisions on the Indian subcontinent. This policy met with failure when Bangladesh won independence and official recognition. On the other hand, the introduction of a further complication in the Indian subcontinent may prove helpful to Chinese-inspired revolutionary action in the long run.

Nepal

On July 1, 1967, Nepal experienced side effects of the Cultural Revolution. Violent anti-Chinese incidents occurred in Katmandu, but good relations were restored almost immediately. The Nepalese continued to state their policy of nonalignment and their "lack of faith in military blocs and pacts."[3] A few missions were sent to Peking, among them a delegation from the Panchayat.[4] The Chinese appeared much less reserved by comparison. They voiced loud approval of all events separating Nepal still further from India (withdrawal of men staffing Indian military control posts along the northern border). They condemned the "blackmail" practiced by India when negotiations were under way to renew the 1960 Sino-Indian trade and transit treaty, which expired in October 1970 and was eventually replaced by another signed on August 13, 1971. Numerous courtesies were exchanged, for instance on the fiftieth birthday of the king of Nepal, or the occasion of the wedding of the heir apparent, at which Kuo Mo-jo represented the Chinese government. Chinese aid continued (the hydro-electric power station of Sunkosi, and the Pokhara road, finished in 1972), and further trade agreements were signed in 1968 and 1971. The presence of Nepalese Communists in Peking was not enough to cast a shadow over relations between the two states, which were composed of patience on the Chinese side and a policy of carefully calculated balance between India, the Soviet Union, the United States, and China on the part of Nepal. The death of King Mahendra (January 31, 1972) did not change the situation and the new sovereign, King Birendra, made an important state visit to Peking in December 1973 and to Szechwan in June 1976. A later Sino-Nepalese agreement (February 1975) provided for the construction of a road more than 400 kilometers long between Pokhara and Surkhet.

Ceylon (Republic of Sri Lanka)

After some tension in August 1967, when crew members from Chinese ships staged propaganda demonstrations in the port of Colombo, as they did elsewhere, Sino-Ceylonese relations returned to normal and developed in both economic and commercial fields.[5] The pro-Chinese orientation of the Communist Party of Ceylon (Secretary N. Sammugathasan) and the revolt of Ceylon's "People's Liberation Front" in March 1971 are possible sources of mistrust and uneasiness in the relations between the two countries, even though both countries, for different reasons, do their best to avoid this possibility.[6] State visits were exchanged in 1972 and 1973, and both sides reaffirmed the need to keep the great powers away from the Indian Ocean, which should remain a "peace zone."

The Near East and North Africa

After the Six Days' War in June 1967, all Chinese political action in the Near East was centered around the conflict between Israel and the Arab states. The Chinese immediately took up the cause of the Arabs, and above all the Palestinians, against Israel, which was "upheld by American and British imperialism." But they quickly shifted their attacks to the Soviet Union, which they accused of "ignominious betrayal" of the Arab cause; of hatching, with the United States, "a sinister conspiracy for a fraudulent political solution"; and of preparing a "Near-Eastern Munich" with American help. The prime object of Chinese policy in this hypersensitive part of the world became to oust Soviet influence. Peking steadily encouraged the various Palestinian movements, particularly the most extremist of them, to continue a relentless and uncompromising struggle, which should be both "patriotic" and "revolutionary," publicizing their acts of resistance and sabotage. Palestinian missions were given official receptions in Peking, and "Palestine weeks" were organized there.[7] Military aid was given to the El al-Fatah commandos in the form of light weapons. When they were crushed by the Jordanian army, the Chinese government voiced a loud protest (September 21, 1970).

On the other hand, United Nations efforts to reestablish peace were resisted, often in the coarsest terms. The Soviet five-point plan, the Jarring mission, and the Rogers mission gave rise to insulting comments and were denounced as frauds. The conduct of the moderate Arab states was treated with reserve or plain suspicion. Kuo Mo-jo, a man of secondary political rank, was sent to represent China at the funeral of Colonel Nasser. "It is to be hoped," said the Chinese on this occasion, "that the people of the United Arab Republic will transform their sorrow into strength and carry their struggle against American-Israeli aggression right through to the end."

The Near East was eminently suitable ground for Chinese propaganda. Everything was to be found there: the application of the Chinese theory of just wars, an easy denunciation of Russian "pusillanimity," a demonstration of American hostility toward the Arabs, and evidence of collusion between the Russians and Americans, made inevitable by a prudent approach. All this presented no danger of complications, for China was far away and professed to be impartial. Chinese efforts produced negative results, however, for the Islamic faith is an insuperable obstacle to Marxism-Leninism of whatever origin. For a long time, Chinese aid was ridiculously small compared with Soviet economic and military aid; the best area for China in this respect was still East Asia. Renewed hostilities involving Israel, Syria, and Egypt in the autumn of 1973 gave Peking another opportunity to show its support for the Arab nations, and especially for the Palestinian organizations, but also to reveal its lack of power. No Chinese veto at the Security Council impeded U.N. action, and the two superpowers were free to act as they wished in this most sensitive area of the world.

China continued to give aid to the Yemen (Arab Republic of the Yemen) and began to help the People's Democratic Republic of Southern Yemen after its creation on November 30, 1967. The foreign minister visited Peking on September 17, 1968, and was followed by the premier (August 1-13, 1970). Both visits were accompanied by economic and technical agreements. Chinese medical help was sent, and an extensive network of roads was built. The rebels of Dhofar, whose movement had begun in the summer of 1965, becoming the "Popular Front for the Liberation of Oman and the Arab Gulf" in 1968, received material help and moral support.

Diplomatic relations were opened with Kuwait on March 29, 1971. The differences arising between the Arab oil-producing countries and their customers were followed closely and retold with the help of extremely crude propaganda, for China can act with impunity here, as its low consumption of oil and plentiful reserves make it independent.[8]

Relations between China and the other Islamic countries of the Near and Middle East were uneventful. Turkey (August 5), Iran (August 16), and Lebanon (November 10, 1971) opened diplomatic relations with China, for it was difficult to defer them any longer. A modest economic arrangement was concluded with Syria. Relations with Afghanistan were less good, for it was suspected of having wanted to attack the unity of Pakistan, which was an ally of China and sorely tried by the loss of Bangladesh (the Pushtunistan and Balushistan questions), and of having pro-Russian sympathies. Iran (the empress and the premier visited Peking in September 1972, and Chi P'eng-fei went to Teheran in 1973) is becoming the privileged partner in this part of Asia.

On the African continent, Sino-Tunisian relations went through a crisis in late September 1967, ending in the recall of Chinese diplomatic personnel. Relations with the other North African countries were normal;[9] they become closer in the case of Mauritania, whose president, Mokhtar Ould Daddah, visited China (October 20-24 1967), while several missions were exchanged later.[10]

The Sudanese head of state, General Gaafar al-Nimeiry, was entertained in Peking on August 6, 1970. When the pro-Communist *putsch* occurred in Khartoum the following year (July 19, 1971), the Chinese sacrificed ideology to political interests yet again—or, more accurately, to their anti-Soviet action in the Third World; they supported the Sudanese government and condemned the "coup d'état clique." A Sudanese mission led by the national defense minister went to China in August, and a protocol on economic and technical cooperation, including a loan of $35 million, was signed on August 24, 1971.[11]

The African states

The Chinese kept in close touch with developments in Africa through various African and Afro-Asian organizations or conferences. All movements of rebellion aiming at decolonization or having revolutionary tendencies were approved and sometimes helped, from those in the Portuguese territories or in South Africa to those in Eritrea, Zaire (formerly the Democratic Republic of Congo) and Cameroon. At the same time, all possible means were used to fight Soviet influence, as in the Near East. As the Hsinhua Agency said on July 4, 1967, summarizing their criticisms, "Soviet Aid to African Countries is Zero." Because the Chinese were ill at ease in the Afro-Asian People's Solidarity Organization, where Russian influence was stronger than theirs, and did not take part in the conferences of nonaligned countries, they instead made extensive use of the Afro-Asian Journalists' Association, whose secretariat, directed by Mr. Djawoto, was in Peking.

At the end of the Cultural Revolution and when it entered the United Nations, China paid increasing attention to state relations; diplomatic links were established with regimes whose ideology was very unlike that of China, and consequently the aid granted to some dissident movements was cut down or stopped altogether. Tanzania and Guinea seem today to be the most solid bases of Chinese diplomacy in Africa. The agreement signed with Tanzania and Zambia on September 5, 1967, for the building, at high cost, of a 1,600-kilometer railway line from Dar es Salaam to Lusaka (work on it was begun on October 26, 1970, and was finished in 1976), made a great impression on international observers. It was known that other arrangements already existed (Sino-Tanzanian Navigation Company, factories turning out agricultural tools and textiles, and medical aid), and secret military agreements were also suspected.[12] When Tanzanian President Julius Nyerere visited Peking in June 1968 (he went there again in March 1974), he maintained his political distance, saying with careful humor that Sino-Tanzanian friendship was a "friendship between very unequal equals" and did not make his country a satellite of China.

Guinea, where anticolonialism was expressed more violently than elsewhere, received support for all statements by its president, particularly in November 1970 during the affair of the Portuguese mercenaries.[13] China and Guinea exchanged military and trade missions. Chinese technicians began a project for a railway line from Guinea to Mali, and the Independence Palace in Conakry, built by China, was inaugurated in 1967. Congo (Brazzaville) was still given limited Chinese technical aid.[14] Ethiopia recognized China on December 1, 1970, and Emperor Haile Selassie was given a magnificent reception in Peking (October 6-10, 1971). A loan of $85,937,500 was granted to Ethiopia during the visit. General Mobutu, the president of Zaire, went to Peking in January 1973 and again in December 1974. There he found support for his nationalism, for "Africa belongs to the great African peoples," as Chou En-lai said, while Mobutu's

"positive neutralism" was also approved. His regime, which Mao Tse-
tung admitted he had wanted to overturn at considerable cost, was instead
granted a loan of $100 million and generous technical aid in the field of
agriculture. By the end of 1975 all the African states, except the Ivory Coast
and the Central African Republic, had established or reestablished
diplomatic relations with China; some of them had been granted large
loans.[15]

Latin America

No outstanding events occurred in relations between China and Latin
America during the three or four years of the Cultural Revolution. Tension
mounted briefly between China and Cuba at the end of 1966, but then
lessened, in spite of the fact that the Cubans tended to draw closer to the
Soviet Union than to China.

In January 1971, China and Chile, under President Allende's leadership,
established formal diplomatic relations and the Chinese gained an official
footing on the South American continent. Peru (November 2, 1971),
Mexico (February 14, 1972), Argentina (February 19, 1972), and Brazil
(August 16, 1974) followed Chile's example. The tragic death of President
Allende was regretted by Peking but did not entail a break with Santiago,
which scandalized those with Maoist sympathies. The visit to Peking of
Mexican President Luis Echeverria led the Chinese to sign the articles of
the Treaty of Tlaltelolco forbidding the presence of nuclear weapons in
Latin America, which was an important departure from their position on
disarmament in general.

As is to be expected, the Chinese still make full use of the issues in dispute
between Washington and the South American capitals. The question of
enlarging fishing limits to 200 nautical miles, which was raised by the
states bordering on the South Pacific, has aroused Chinese interest and
gained their support.

Chinese propaganda directed at revolutionary movements in Latin
America has so far produced only moderately good results. Pro-Chinese
groups exist in each country, but their membership is small and they suffer
from an instability that is accentuated by local political habits.[16]

Notes

[1]Ali Bhutto led an important mission on a visit to Peking from November 6 to 8, 1971, but this unplanned trip was linked with the Bangladesh crisis. Its results underlined once more the fact that, under a profusion of words, Chinese foreign policy remained faithful to its traditional realism. Mr. Bhutto visited Peking again in May 1974 and May 1976. The Chinese in their turn sent several missions to Pakistan.

[2]As of 1975, this amounted to $60 million granted in 1965, though a loan of $200 million was granted by China in November 1970.

[3]Declaration by the foreign minister, March 11, 1970.

[4]The local parliament, which has no political parties, as all authority is in the hands of the sovereign.

[5]Agreement of February 9, 1970, for the building of textile mills, with loans granted in September 1970. A further loan of 150 million rupees (about $25 million) was agreed to by the Chinese at the end of April 1971—that is, after the rising of the People's Liberation Front.

[6]The Chinese are reported to have condemned the "Ceylon Guevarists" in a letter that they do not seem to have made public. China's large purchases of rubber from Ceylon are an important element in their mutual relations. Mrs. Bandaranaike visited Peking in June 1972.

[7]Yasser Arafat went to Peking in March 1970, followed by Houni Younes in August. The Palestine Liberation Organization is permanently represented in Peking.

[8]In 1969, the total world oil production was 2,130 million tons, of which China produced and consumed 20 million. On "The Dirty Oil War in Which Social-Imperialism is Taking Part," see *People's Daily* (March 15, 1970).

[9]Algerian Foreign Minister Bouteflika visited Peking in July 1971. President Boumedienne went there in February 1974. Several visits have been exchanged by military delegations.

[10]The Chinese granted a long-term loan to Mauritania amounting to $21,875,000 in May 1971.

[11]Another Sudanese delegation, led by Vice-President Khalid Hassan Abbas, went to China in December 1971 and a loan of $35,742,187 is reported to have been granted to them.

[12]Supplies of Chinese aircraft and the building of missile observation bases.

[13]See the declaration of November 25, 1970, by the government of the People's Republic of China.

[14]Congolese Premier Alfred Raoul visited Peking in October 1969 (when a new agreement for economic and technical cooperation was signed) and in July 1970. President Marien Ngouabi went to Peking in July 1973.

[15]Equatorial Guinea (formerly Spanish) (October 20, 1970), Nigeria (February 10, 1971), Cameroon (March 26, 1971), Sierra Leone (July 29, 1971), Togo (September 19, 1971), Senegal (October 6, 1971), Dahomey (December 1972), Madagascar (November 1972), Mauritius (April 1972), Chad (November 30, 1972), Ghana (March 1972), and Gabon (April 20, 1974). Dahomey, Madagascar, and Togo received the largest economic and financial aid—approximately $46, $50, and $48 million, respectively. Official visits between China and African countries are so numerous and frequent that it is no longer possible to note them all.

[16]For a source of information on these groups, see Chapter 22 note 26.

45 Foreign Policy 1966 –1976 (3): Japan, Korea, and Southeast Asia

Japan

The continuation in power of the Sato government after the elections of December 27, 1970, the prospect of a partial American withdrawal from the West Pacific, from which the Japanese stood to gain, and the rhythm of expansion of the Japanese economy and its effects abroad all contributed to worsen the political climate between Peking and Tokyo. From 1967 on, and often in outspoken terms, the Chinese constantly denounced Japanese militarism, which they considered renascent and ready to provide support for a strategy of encirclement of China. They tried to forestall this possibility by improving relations with North Korea and, depending on the circumstances or the time, by stressing their attempts either to exert pressure or to seduce in the commercial field, and by doing their utmost to win over members of Japanese political circles who disapproved of too close links between Tokyo and Washington. Sato's departure and the arrival of Kakuei Tanaka, who visited Peking in September 1972 a few months after President Nixon, brought about a rapid and radical development of the situation. Normal diplomatic relations were quickly established between the two states, while trade became even more brisk.

No change occurred in the break with the Japanese Communist Party led by Kenji Miyamoto; the forming of a dissident, pro-Chinese party on November 30, 1969, had no doubt made it final.

The Chinese launched their harshest attacks against the personal policy of Eisaku Sato and that of his Foreign Minister, Kiichi Aichi, and his defense minister, Yashuhiro Nakasone; the last two remained in office until the reshuffle of the summer of 1971. They were all accused of having maximum political ambitions for Japan, of being ready to act as the accomplices of the Americans, who were willing to use Asians to fight other Asians, or of the Russians, who wanted to encircle China under the pretext of organizing collective security in Asia. To put it more exactly, the Chinese reproached the Sato government with indefinitely prolonging the American military presence in Japan. That presence was authorized by the Japanese-American mutual security treaty of 1960, which could have expired on June 22, 1970, but was automatically renewed. The withdrawal of American troops from Okinawa as laid down by the agreement of June 17, 1971, was described as a false withdrawal, and Chou En-lai accused Sato of wanting to make the whole country into a new Okinawa. With some justification, the Chinese suspected the Japanese of wanting to maintain the political and military status quo in South Korea, Taiwan, the Malacca Straits, and Southeast Asia as a whole, in the interests of their security, and of being ready to take over at least partially the U.S. role in this part of the world. As they put it, the Asian and Pacific Council attended every year by the foreign ministers of several countries in East Asia provided the framework for a future "counterrevolutionary" military alliance supported by Washington. The idea of collective security, "sinister trash in the wrappings of regional economic cooperation," was under consideration by Japan and the Soviet Union; the Russians explained their views in April 1969.

Japanese military expansion was condemned in many articles and commentaries accompanied by figures taken from Nakasone's plans or declarations. The increase in the budget and in the numbers of armed forces in Japan, the fact that the Japanese air force was probably superior in quality to that of the Chinese, while the military laboratories certainly were, and the possibility that Japan could acquire nuclear weapons in record time if need be worried the Chinese. They would not be satisfied by the defensive nature of Japanese rearmament, or by Tokyo's signing of a treaty on the partial prohibition of nuclear tests; instead they noted every scrap of evidence, no matter how small, of the "rebirth" of Japanese militarism. The suicide of the writer Mishima according to the traditional rites of *seppuku* (November 1970) was put to extensive use.

Chinese anxiety about Japanese economic expansion was also frequently voiced and, for the moment at least, appears to have had more justification than that just described. The differences between the economic potentialities and the rates of growth of the two countries are striking. The Chinese pointed out that Japanese industry was eight times more powerful than it had been before World War II. They noted that Japanese investments in Southeast Asia had increased from $300 million beteen 1945 and 1963 to $2,200 million between 1963 and 1967, and were expanding as far away as Latin America, where by the end of 1969 they amounted to $513 million, compared with $121 million in 1965.[1] Japan had acquired control of foreign trade in various countries in Asia, such as South Korea and Indonesia; its share in South Korean trade was 21 percent in 1960 and 40 percent in 1966, and in Indonesia it had increased from 17 to 30 percent over the same period. The Chinese made a realistic estimate of Japan's vast needs in raw materials over the years to come. Their anxiety about plans for collaboration between Japan and the Soviet Union increased and was mingled with bitterness, for the collaboration would have affected regions ceded by China to the tsars at the time of the Unequal Treaties.[2]

Similarly, the discovery of oil deposits in the sea bed of the archipelago stretching from Japan through Ryukyu to Taiwan resulted in stern Chinese warnings to the Japanese, the South Koreans, and the Taiwan Chinese.[3] When the Tiaoyutai islands were included in the territory of Okinawa given back to Japan, it provoked anti-Japanese and anti-American reactions in both Peking and Taipei.

The chief weapon used by the Chinese leaders was the attraction of the Chinese market and above all its prospects. While denouncing the Sato government and its expansionist policy of a return to a new "East Asian co-prosperity sphere," they opened the door still wider to trade with Japan, which in fact they could not do without. The economic conjuncture resulting from the loosening of links with the socialist camp and realistic calculations accompanied by demands in puerile terms made trade increase in 1970 to $822,700,000 or 32 percent more than in 1969.[4] Almost a quarter of Chinese trade is now with Japan, which is a relatively low figure when compared with that for trade between Japan and Taiwan, which is almost identical.

During the relative calm that followed the Cultural Revolution, many prominent people in Japanese politics (the Liberal Democratic Party and the opposition parties) went to Peking; an association was formed in the Diet for the reestablishment of diplomatic relations between the two countries (December 9, 1970).[5] The evolution of American policy, as borne out by Henry Kissinger's surprise visit to Peking, caused momentary embarrassment to the Sato government, which fell into line with Washington's attitude, but its overtures met an extremely cold response from Chou En-lai (November 1971). A new chapter of supreme importance for the history of Japan and East Asia opened with the visit of Kakuei Tanaka, the new Japanese premier, to Peking (September 25-30, 1972).[6] It seems likely that the Chinese, when the time comes, will try to obtain Japan's cooperation in China's development, while simultaneously guarding against the nuclear rearmament of Japan, and, if possible, removing it from American and above all from Soviet influence. Meanwhile, the difficulties involved in drawing up a Sino-Japanese peace and friendship treaty, under discussion since the end of 1974, show that Japan is in an awkward situation, caught between Moscow and Peking.

The mediocre relations between the Japanese and Chinese Communist Parties were long a by-product of the mediocre relations between Peking and Tokyo. Starting in the summer of 1966, the Chinese Communist Party relentlessly denounced the "revisionism" of the Japanese Party, going so far as to expel its two representatives in Peking.[7] The rapprochement between the Japanese Communist Party and that of the Soviet Union in 1971 and the foundation of a "Japanese Communist Party (Left)" announced in January 1970, which was formed out of various small left-wing groups that held a congress from November 2 to 30, 1969, confirmed a break between the two Parties, which was in fact five years old. The reasons for it probably lie in the extreme doctrinal intransigence of the Chinese Communist Party and the desire for independence on the part of the Japanese Communist Party, whose problems are those that arise in the context of a highly industrialized and intellectual society.

Korea

Identical fears of the rebirth of Japanese power and its possible consequences for Taiwan and South Korea brought about a rapprochement between China and North Korea after a cool period lasting several years. This development became apparent in 1969; its first outward demonstration was Chou En-lai's visit to Pyongyang from April 5 to 7, 1970, just before the extension of the mutual security treaty between Japan and the United States. The main theme was the condemnation of Japanese militarism and its dangers. After a long diatribe against its resurrection, the communiqué of April 7 said in conclusion: "Both parties consider that American and Japanese reactionaries intensify aggression and provocations to war more and more and that, faced with this situation, it is imperative for the Chinese and Korean peoples to unite against the common enemy. . . ."

The Chinese and the North Koreans also stated their anxiety about the security of the three countries of Indochina and their interest in the development of revolutionary struggles in every country in the world. The Soviet Union and the socialist camp were not mentioned in the speeches of April 5 and 7, and the North Koreans made only a very brief reference to the Cultural Revolution. Relations between the two parties and ideological relations remained unchanged, but state relations (including military relations) were definitely improved and the outline of a sort of united East Asian front, to oppose Japan and the United States, began to emerge.

Concrete signs of friendship and cooperation grew more numerous. The twentieth anniversary of the Korean War was celebrated with due pomp in Peking, in the presence of Pak Sung Chul, deputy premier and foreign minister. The theme of solidarity among Asian peoples was elaborated once more. Three months later, the twentieth anniversary of the entry of the Chinese "volunteers" into North Korea was celebrated and an impassioned speech was delivered by Chinese Chief of Staff Huang Yung-sheng.

Relations between Peking and Pyongyang improved steadily over the following months; the Chinese gave their support whenever an incident occurred between the two Koreas, various economic agreements were drawn up, missions were exchanged frequently, and the Chinese were more active in making their presence felt at the periodic meetings at Panmunjom. When the Nixon Doctrine and the visit of the American president to Peking appeared likely to modify the situation in Northeast Asia, North and South Korea responded by opening careful and restricted talks with a view to preparing the unification of the whole peninsula (communiqué of July 4, 1972), with Chinese approval. When the negotiations appeared to be coming to a halt, the Chinese began a new campaign against Seoul and supported Pyongyang's intransigent attitude.[8] This versatility was due to their wish to counter Russian influence in North Korea, whether in state interests or ideology. As the real prospects of reunification are slender, this attitude is easy to maintain.

The Korean question was, naturally, seriously affected by the American withdrawal from Vietnam and by the absence of any U.S. reaction to the achievement of Communist control over the Indochinese states. As Japanese security is also involved, Japan and the United States maintain their support for South Korea, even at the price of formal concessions, such as the dissolution of the United Nations command.

Burma

The Cultural Revolution put the exemplary nature of Sino-Burmese relations severely to the test. On June 26 and 27, a few overly zealous Chinese teachers provoked incidents that sparked violent reactions. The Chinese claimed that more than fifty of their compatriots had been killed in Rangoon. As a result, all Chinese experts were withdrawn; General Ne Win became a "fascist reactionary" and a "new Chiang Kai-shek" once more; and leaders of the Burmese Communist Party (White Flag), among them Thakin Ba Thein Tin, first deputy chairman of the Central Committee, reappeared in Peking. The Chinese gave wide publicity and considerable encouragement to the Burmese Communist Party, which fell into line with the ideology of Peking. The assassination of its chairman, Thakin Than Tun (September 24, 1968), attributed to Ne Win and the revisionists, was deplored and given wide coverage (March 20, 1969), as were the deaths of Thakin Zin and Thakin Chit, the president and general secretary, respectively, of the Burmese Communist Party, both of whom died fighting in March 1975. The thirtieth and thirty-fifth anniversaries of the Party were celebrated ostentatiously, and the successes of the Burmese guerrilla fighters were underlined by the press. The Chinese knew better, however, than to force the Ne Win government thoughtlessly to turn to the West or the Soviet Union, as had happened in the case of India.

In the summer of 1971 (August 6-12), General Ne Win was invited to pay a "friendly, unofficial" visit to China, where he was received by Chairman Mao Tse-tung. No final communiqué was issued, and Chou En-lai made a somewhat lukewarm comment on the improvement of Sino-Burmese relations: "We are pleased to note that over the last two years relations between our two countries have returned to normal, our governments have exchanged ambassadors, and trade between the two countries has developed," while showing only moderate optimism as to the future. It seems reasonable to deduce from this that General Ne Win remained faithful to the line followed by all Burmese governments and jealously maintained Burmese neutrality. The August 1975 visit of the Burmese foreign minister to Peking and that of General Ne Win, which took place in November, have apparently not changed the situation for either side.

Indonesia

Sino-Indonesian relations, after being suspended as a result of the incidents of the spring of 1966 and the autumn of 1967 in Djakarta, remained at a standstill. The Chinese continued their attacks on the Suharto government, accusing it of "selling" the country to American imperialism by accepting capital investment, by exporting strategic raw materials (oil, copper, nickel, and bauxite) and by allowing air force bases to be installed. Soviet penetration of Indonesia, in the form of deferred repayments and military aid for the struggle against the revolutionaries, was denounced for the same reasons and still more violently than American penetration.[9]

Peking then launched repeated incitements to revolt by supporting the resurrection of the Indonesian Communist Party (PKI). After 1967, once it had made its self-criticism and condemned the opportunism of former Secretary-General D. N. Aidit (August 17, 1966), it began to follow the same direction as the Chinese revolution and started a series of small guerrilla operations. The PKI, or at least its pro-Chinese faction, sent a permanent delegation to Peking, headed by Jusuf Adjitorop. In April 1969, the Indonesians denounced the nationality treaty of 1955. The Chinese found it hard to react, for large numbers of Overseas Chinese were in Indonesia and their position was precarious; China's maneuvers had to be verbal rather than concrete in nature.[10] Peking's policy of a more open attitude toward the world has not yet become apparent in Djakarta. The violent anti-Communism of the Indonesian government and Peking's desire to contrast its support for revolutionary struggles with the "treason" of the Soviet revisionists do not encourage it. If, however, Southeast Asia as a whole begins to lean toward neutrality as a result of the relations between the United States and China and the effects of recent events in Indochina, China's more open attitude is likely to become manifest in Indonesia also.[11]

Malaysia

Malaysia, under the leadership of Tunku Abdul Rahman, was one of the main targets for Chinese propaganda. It was described as an "instrument of neocolonialism" supported by British troops but was under attack from within by the Malay Communist Party, whose few members were keen fighters and owed total allegiance to Peking. From time to time, the racial animosity between the Malay community and resident Chinese gave rise to rioting, the chief victims of which were the Chinese communities. In

Chinese eyes the establishment of diplomatic relations with Moscow in November 1967 and the visit of the trade mission led by Patolichev in February and March 1968 were proofs of Soviet covetousness toward Malaysia. The prospects of the neutralization of Southeast Asia, the desire not to allow such a prosperous region, 40 percent of whose population was Chinese, to fall under Russian and Japanese influence, and finally a more auspicious local situation once Abdul Razak had come to power in September 1970 brought a Sino-Malaysian rapprochement in the economic field. In May 1971, a Malaysian trade delegation went to Peking and in August a delegation from the People's Republic of China went to Kuala Lumpur for the first time. These visits prepared the way for political developments that were speeded up by events in Vietnam. In May 1974, Prime Minister Abdul Razak went to Peking and diplomatic relations were established between Peking and Kuala Lumpur; the policy of peaceful neutrality advocated by Kuala Lumpur was encouraged. The Chinese, however, still give discreet support to the Malay Communist Party.

Singapore

In March 1975, Singapore Foreign Minister S. Rajaratnam went to Peking to expand economic cooperation between the two countries; this has not yet been extended to the political field, although Premier Lee Kuan-yew went to Peking in May 1976.

Thailand

For many years, the nature of the Thai government, its modest but direct interventions in the war in Laos, Cambodia, and Vietnam, and the fact that the Americans were allowed to build and use six or seven air force and naval bases on its territory constituted insurmountable obstacles to a rapprochement between Peking and Bangkok. On their side, the Chinese gave warm encouragement to the Thai Patriotic Front created on January 1, 1965, in which the leading role was taken over early in 1968 by the Thai Communist Party, which had been in existence for some time but was still weak. In December 1968, it published a ten-point program bringing it strictly into line with the Chinese Communist Party; a Supreme Command of the Thai People's Liberation Army appeared at the same time. This army began to organize sabotage and guerrilla operations on a modest scale, with limited success.

The outcome of the war in Indochina, the American tendency toward disengagement, and the official support given by Peking to the Thai revolutionaries all combine now to create anxiety within the country, which had long been protected by the resistance of its neighbors. This explains the attempt of the government of General Thanom to strengthen its position by reverting to a relatively flexible military dictatorship (November 17, 1971). Its fall in October 1973 probably facilitated a rapprochement between Bangkok and Peking. After various official contacts, Prime Minister Kukrit Pramoj, went on a visit to Peking, where a joint communiqué announcing the opening of diplomatic relations was signed on July 1, 1975. Several questions have not yet been settled between the two states (American military presence, the nationality of residents of Chinese origin, the activities of pro-Communist guerrilla fighters, and the like).

The Philippines

The Philippines have nothing in common with China, for they are close to Thailand in their policy on international alignment and their share in the war in Vietnam. Peking has adopted an attitude toward Manila similar to its attitude toward Bangkok. It tends to exaggerate the importance of the small Philippine Communist Party reconstituted in December 1968, and of the new people's army, which became active again in the summer of 1969 after a long eclipse. The geographical position of the Philippines and their close economic and military association with the United States made it seem unlikely that China would carry much weight in the destiny of the country. The collapse of South Vietnam and Cambodia, however, led Manila rapidly to follow the example of the Americans and the Japanese. In September 1974, Mme Marcos made a preliminary visit to Peking to prepare for an official visit by President Marcos, which took place in June 1975 and resulted in the opening of normal diplomatic relations (June 9).

ASEAN and SEATO

The general evolution of the situation in Indochina inevitably helped to strengthen the links binding Thailand, the Philippines, Malaysia, Singapore, and Indonesia in the Association of Southeast Asian Nations (ASEAN), created in 1967; it prompted them to turn to a policy of neutrality, with the official encouragement of Peking, so as to exclude or limit the influence of the Soviet Union and the United States.

Similarly, SEATO (the Southeast Asia Treaty Organization), created in Manila in 1954 and weakened by the withdrawal or nonparticipation of France and Pakistan, is in the process of disappearing. In some respects ASEAN, which fits the current situation better, can take on part of its legacy.

The three states of Indochina

After the first Geneva conference in 1954 the Chinese were always careful to make a clear distinction between the case of Vietnam and that of Laos and Cambodia. When Laos assumed neutrality as a result of the second Geneva conference (1961-1962), this underlined the distinction, although the existence of the Ho Chi Minh Trail in the east of the country and the maintenance of a Pathet Lao zone destroyed its meaning to some extent. Cambodia, headed by Prince Sihanouk, loudly proclaimed its neutrality, which did not, however, prevent it from providing sanctuary for the South Vietnamese National Liberation Front and for regular units from North Vietnam.

The coup d'état in Cambodia on March 18, 1970, destroyed these appearances, giving back full significance to the expression "Indochinese war," which had been out of use for fifteen years; Peking from then on wanted to involve the "three Indochinese peoples" in the same war, though it was careful not to provide Laos and Cambodia with military help on a scale liable to overturn the situation and provoke the United States to retaliate more strongly still. These new developments incited the Chinese to make their influence more widely felt in this part of the world, to the detriment of the Soviet Union. They were careful to ensure a state of harmony in relations between North Vietnam and the Laotian and Cambodian revolutionary movements and to prevent North Vietnam from assuming the dominant role over the other two. The development of their foreign policy after 1969 led the Chinese to come around gradually to a return to peace and to cooperate, at least indirectly, in its achievement. China signed the Paris agreements on Vietnam (January 27, 1973) and gave its approval to the later arrangements between the different factions in Laos. Cambodia was the only country not included in this general movement; in its case, China still gave firm support to Prince Sihanouk.

The situation as a whole was quickly thrown into confusion after the fall of Saigon and Phnom Penh in the spring of 1975.

Vietnam

From the end of 1966 until the death of President Ho Chi Minh on September 3, 1969, nothing important occurred to affect Chinese policy toward Vietnam. The Chinese naturally recognized the Provisional Revolutionary Government of the Republic of South Vietnam, created on June 10, 1969, and continued to give economic and military support to the effort of the North Vietnamese, encouraging them to maintain an attitude of the utmost intransigence. The Chinese relentlessly denounced the "tricks" of the American peace proposals, objected in advance to any intervention whatsoever by the United Nations, opposed the convocation of a new Geneva conference, and ignored the Paris talks, which opened on May 13, 1968. They also spoke out against Soviet-American "collusion," even in their official messages to Hanoi, contending that it supposedly encouraged the transfer of American military means from Europe to Vietnam but actually excluded the Soviet Union from the "antiimperialist front." At times tension between China and the Soviet Union, combined with disturbances due to the Cultural Revolution, delayed the transport across China of Russian military materiel to Tonkin, as well as Chinese deliveries.[12]

Visits were exchanged less frequently at the summit. The Chinese did not want to find themselves involved in action undertaken in Vietnam by the socialist camp as a whole. Although such joint action was unlikely, it would bring them into total subordination to the Soviet Union. The Vietnamese, for their part, were worried by the nature and scale of the Cultural Revolution and were uncertain as to its final outcome. Because they were determined above all to retain the indispensable material aid given them by the Russians, they appear to have been reserved and careful in their relations with Peking.[13]

The death of Ho Chi Minh, whose personality had enabled North Vietnam to keep at an equal distance from Peking and Moscow, brought the first change. Chou En-lai arrived in Hanoi on September 4, 1969, the day after Ho's death, and was followed by a large delegation led by Li Hsien-nien on September 10. When Kosygin came to Tonkin, honoring the last wish expressed by the late president of North Vietnam, the Chinese and the Russians made a further attempt at a rapprochement and later opened bilateral talks in Peking (see Chapter 47).

The situation created in the Lao Dong Party—where pro-Chinese and pro-Russian currents of opinion acquired more freedom of expression— the redoubled American military effort, and the active foreign policy adopted by China once more combined to make Vietnam regain full importance. In October, Premier Pham Van Dong of North Vietnam, and Nguyen Huu To, chairman of the Presidium of the Central Committee of the South Vietnamese National Liberation Front, went to Peking; an agreement for Chinese economic and military aid had been concluded there the month before. The communiqué signed by Chou En-lai and Pham Van Dong on October 25 condemned the "Vietnamization" of the war and stated again that the unconditional withdrawal of American troops and the settling of the Vietnam question by the Vietnamese themselves was the only "just way" to end hostilities. Mao Tse-tung was quoted again, "The 700 million Chinese people provide a powerful backing for the Vietnamese people; the vast expense of China's territory is their reliable rear area," affirming the stability of the Chinese situation.

The coup d'état of General Lon Nol in Cambodia on March 18, 1970, and the destruction of the supply bases of the South Vietnamese rebels in Cambodian territory modified the political and military situation in the peninsula as a whole and led Peking to take a more direct part in events. The Chinese quickly took in Prince Sihanouk, inciting him to form a "Government of National Union" on May 5, and pressed his case with other states, particularly North Korea.

A few days earlier, on April 24 and 25, 1970, "at the instigation of Prince Sihanouk," a summit conference of the Indochinese Peoples had been held "in the Laos, Vietnam, and China border area"—in fact near Canton— attended by four delegations claiming to represent the "peoples" of Cambodia, Laos, and the two Vietnams. The joint communiqué merely developed the customary themes of mutual solidarity and support "according to the wishes of the interested parties," based on mutual respect, and acknowledged the validity of the Geneva agreements of 1954 and 1962. On April 28, the Chinese government endorsed the communiqué in a declaration repeating its substance and adding the usual references to the "powerful support" and "militant friendship" of 700 million Chinese.

On May 20, Mao Tse-tung himself made a formal declaration stating his "warm" support for the joint communiqué and extending this support to all the peoples in the world, including those of North America, Europe, and Oceania. His true meaning was conveyed by one short passage: "The danger of a new world war still exists, and the peoples of all countries must get prepared. But revolution is the main trend in the world today."[14]

The Soviet Union was not mentioned by name in any of these texts, as if to indicate that it was permanently excluded from the peninsula. The respect due to the interests of North Vietnam and also the political testament of the late President Ho Chi Minh prevented an open denunciation of the Russians.

After the declaration of May 20, when American and South Vietnamese troops had left Cambodia, when the Nixon policy of gradual withdrawal had begun to take effect and operations had been slowed down or suspended, the Chinese had fewer opportunities to make resounding statements on events in Vietnam. Economic aid, exchanges of missions, and the celebration of various anniversaries maintained a climate of friendship that increased Chinese influence in Hanoi, though without making it predominate.[15]

At the end of 1970, fears of renewed American bombing of North Vietnam brought the Chinese government to reaffirm its principle of support for Hanoi, recalling its adherence to the ten main points and eight subsidiary points of the South Vietnamese National Liberation Front.

The last crisis came when the South Vietnamese army entered Laos by Route 9 (Tchepone area) in February 1971. The main target was the temporary or permanent destruction of the Ho Chi Minh Trail, but the ambiguous terms of various American or South Vietnamese statements gave observers to understand that the intention was to push on into North Vietnamese territory; Chou En-lai and Marshal Yeh Chien-ying made a hasty visit to Hanoi (March 5-8, 1971). It was a relatively unnecessary show of solidarity, for the risk of escalation was small. Nevertheless, China more than ever before voiced fears as to its security: "The U.S. expansion of its war of aggression to Laos and Cambodia has turned Indochina into one battlefield," as the joint communiqué put it, and added firmly, but somewhat vaguely:

> Should U.S. imperialism go down the road of expanding its war of aggression in Indochina, the Chinese people are determined to take all necessary measures, not flinching even from the greatest national sacrifices, to give all-out support and assistance to the Vietnamese and other Indochinese peoples for the thorough defeat of the U.S. aggressors.

Five months later, the rapid secret visit of Henry Kissinger, the adviser to President Nixon, to Peking, created a new, larger context for the Indochinese question and a completely new psychological climate. The possibility of a future settlement could be viewed with far more optimism once the obstacles to relations between China and the United States had been removed. On the other hand, the thaw in Sino-American relations became one of several elements in the diplomatic game shortly to be started by the Chinese to implant their influence in East Asia as a prelude to replacing that of the United States. Peking was faced with the task of protecting its national interests without incurring the many accusations it had aimed at the Soviet Union and without sullying the image of China in the eyes of the world's revolutionaries. Helped by the lassitude of both camps and by the fact that the Russians gave priority to their relations with the Americans, the Chinese were wholly successful in this delicate maneuver. The Paris agreements of January 27, 1973, were hailed by Foreign Minister Chi P'eng-fei as "the promise of a détente in Indochina and in the Far East as a whole." The "Geneva spirit" of 1954 seemed to reign once more.

The attack launched by Hanoi and the Provisional Revolutionary Government against South Vietnam in April 1975, in spite of the Paris agreements, probably received no encouragement from the Chinese, though they could not help applauding when it succeeded. Its success was the beginning of new Sino-Vietnamese relations, insofar as Vietnam, reunified and at peace, can dispense with Chinese aid to a larger extent and shows a tendency to extend its influence to its weak Cambodian and Laotian neighbors (or even further) and, in so doing, rivals Peking. The ideological quarrel between Moscow and Peking, the persisting dispute over various islands, underlined by the Paracels incidents in January with South Vietnam, and the fate of the large Chinese communities in Vietnam are all elements of future disagreement, which will be difficult to settle.

Laos

Until the Indochinese conflict spread to Cambodia, the situation in Laos was fairly stable; the Chinese merely demanded a halt to the U.S. air force operations in Laos and the withdrawals of Thai units from the north bank of the Mekong River.[16]

From March 1970 on, the Pathet Lao won firmer Chinese support by coordinating their action with that of the North Vietnamese and trying to reopen negotiations with Vientiane; at the same time they brought considerable pressure to bear on the Plain of Jars and the middle valley of the Mekong. No great changes occurred in the political and strategic situation in 1970. An attitude of mutual restraint was observed toward Laos. The Chinese attitude remained cautious until the South Vietnamese attack on Tchepone in February 1971, when they sent Chou En-lai to Hanoi, as mentioned earlier. Meanwhile, a Chinese declaration of February 12, 1971, referred mainly to Laos, stressing the point that the invasion constituted a serious threat to China.

Although Chinese support for the Pathet Lao was unobtrusive, because they were more directly involved with the North Vietnamese and also because Laotian neutrality had been officially recognized at Geneva on July 23, 1962, by China and all the other powers present, events in 1970 and 1971 had probably increased Peking's influence on the Pathet Lao leaders.[17] It was in China's interest to practice a policy of nonintervention openly and to maintain as far as possible the existence of a friendly Laos, capable of standing up to pressure from both Vietnam and Thailand. In this respect, future Chinese policy may have something in common with past French policy. Meanwhile, Peking gave official support to the agreements drawn up on February 21 and September 14, 1973, between the royal government of Vientiane and the Pathet Lao, as a first step toward national unity, which in the new international context appeared both possible and desirable. The government changes of August 1975 advanced this unity; the Pathet Lao are the ones who really benefit from this, and they will soon be the only ones to do so. They will find themselves in an awkward position between Hanoi and Peking.

Cambodia

The first, most serious strain in relations between China and Cambodia occurred in September 1967. Prince Sihanouk had already been irritated by new disturbances on the part of the Khmer Communists, when to his even greater annoyance Chinese propaganda inspired by the Cultural Revolution appeared through the channels of the Sino-Cambodian Friendship Association and certain local newspapers. His petulance led him to take extreme measures both at home and abroad. Cambodian diplomats in Peking were recalled, but there was no break in diplomatic relations between the two countries. When Chou En-lai intervened personally, Sihanouk went back on his decision, but for a time he leaned toward the

United States, particularly because the Americans were quick to recognize the frontiers claimed by Cambodia. Diplomatic relations were reestablished between Phnom Penh and Washington on June 11, 1969, having been interrupted in May 1965.

The coup d'état of March 18, 1970, rapidly put an end to Cambodia's experiment in neutrality, which the Chinese had taken care to maintain except for the incidents during the Cultural Revolution, and Peking was forced to draw up a new policy. It was based on winning Sihanouk back forthwith; he arrived in Peking on March 19. A Khmer government in exile and a National United Front of Kampuchea (FUNK) were formed there, and the Chinese made constant use of these for promoting a front including all the Indochinese peoples, initiated at the summit conference of April 24 and 25 near Canton. A brief, powerful military incursion of American and South Vietnamese forces into eastern Cambodia on April 30, whose purpose was to destroy North Vietnamese sanctuaries and save Phnom Penh, fused all three wars into one.[18]

Although the supporters of Prince Sihanouk, apart from his temporary allies, the Red Khmers, made few appearances during the next few years in the areas affected by the war in Cambodia, the Peking leaders constantly brought him to the fore, in the context of their Indochina policy and their plan to form an Asian front to oppose a new association between Japan and the United States and a rapprochement between the Japanese and the Russians. The visit of Prince Sihanouk to Pyongyang (July 1971), his presence at many national and international functions, and the courtesy shown to his family and himself are all part of this. While the Russians and the Americans hoped that Cambodian neutrality would limit Peking's influence in the Mekong valley, the Chinese were getting ready to establish their influence for their own benefit, through Prince Sihanouk. The end of the Lon Nol government revealed fairly dramatically that the real power within the country was in the hands of the Red Khmers. Since then, the Chinese have tried to save face by showing great consideration for Prince Sihanouk, who is still head of the Royal Government of National Union of Cambodia and for their interests by giving a resounding welcome to the representatives of the new power and especially to Khieu Samphan, deputy premier of the Cambodian government (in April 1974, and particularly in August 1975). It seems likely that this ambiguous situation will go on until it is clarified after the retirement of Prince Sihanouk.

Although it is obviously too early to form an opinion as to the future of the states of Indochina and Southeast Asia, it is likely that China will try to make this area into a region that is politically divided, militarily weak and insignificant, economically prosperous, and reserved to Peking's influence. China's proximity, its particular weight, the network of Overseas Chinese, and the highly diverse nature of the countries involved should make the task easier. It remains to be seen whether the United States and the Soviet Union will abandon to Chinese ambitions a region whose position is of considerable value in the air and sea strategy already taking shape in the Indian Ocean, the crossroads of the world's greatest sea routes.

Notes

[1]According to the Chinese, exports of Japanese capital amounted to $1,260 million for the year 1969 alone; "Down with the Resuscitated Japanese Militarism," *People's Daily* (September 3, 1970).

[2]The Japanese share in the development of Siberia would have consisted in building harbors and electric power stations, and exploiting several mines and the forests. Trade between Japan and the Soviet Union amounted to about $700 million in 1969, which was the same as Sino-Japanese trade for the same year.

[3]A liaison committee for oil research in the area was created in Seoul on November 12, 1970.

[4]The joint communiqué signed on March 1, 1971, by representatives of the China-Japan and the Japan-China trade missions calls for reflection, in that it shows how attitudes inherited from the old imperial court persist. It also shows signs of childishness in terms of modern diplomacy.

[5]Sheldon W. Simon has written several studies on the difficult relations between the Japanese and Chinese Communist Parties between 1966 and 1968; see "Maoism and Inter-Party Relations; Peking Alienation of the Japanese Communist Party," *The China Quarterly*, No. 35 (July-September 1968).

[6]See the important joint communiqué issued on September 26, 1972.

[7]The manifesto of the new Japanese Communist Party was analyzed in *Peking Review*, No. 1 (January 2, 1970).

[8]The Chinese also upheld the North Korean proposal to secure membership of the United Nations for one confederate Korea, rather than two separate states of Korea.

[9]In April 1967, Soviet loans to Indonesia amounted to a total of $1,200 million, according to the Chinese.

[10]In 1973, it was reported that 1.2 million Chinese have Indonesian nationality, 1.1 million are stateless, and 250,000 have Chinese nationality.

[11]China supported Indonesia and Malaysia in their action against an international status for the Malacca Straits.

[12]Particularly in March 1967 and May 1968.

[13]Le Than Nghi, deputy premier of North Vietnam, went to Peking in July 1968 and in August 1969. The Chinese sent nobody to Hanoi until the death of Ho Chi Minh in September 1969.

[14]"Peoples of the World, Unite and Defeat the US Aggressors and All Their Running Dogs!"

[15]Agreements on economic and military aid of May 25, 1970, and February 15, 1971.

[16]According to the Laotian government, no operational units from Thailand existed in Laos, only instructors.

[17]The Laotians, like the Cambodians and the Vietnamese, sent a delegation to the Twenty-Fourth Congress of the Communist Party of the Soviet Union in March 1971.

[18]President Nixon set out the justification for this intervention in his speech of April 30, 1970.

46 Foreign Policy 1966 –1976 (4): United States, Western Europe, International Organizations, Disarmament

The United States

The search by both parties for a real dialogue to prepare for negotiations between China and the United States probably dates back to the end of November 1968 or the beginning of 1969. Several unexpected events thwarted the realization of this secret wish and postponed its announcement until the spring of 1971.

In November 1968, the Chinese indicated that they were willing to resume the Warsaw talks between Chinese and American ambassadors. The election of Richard Nixon as president of the United States, the deterioration of Sino-Soviet relations, and the more open foreign policy decided upon at the end of the Cultural Revolution made the step logical and appropriate. In 1956 and 1961, in periods of reduced internal tension, the Chinese had proposed meetings with the Americans at the foreign minister or summit level. The proposals hardly bound them at all, because the real concessions had to be made by the opposite party, but they were useful for propaganda purposes—an example of Chinese "goodwill" as opposed to American intransigence.

The 135th meeting, scheduled to take place on February 20, 1969, more than a year after the previous one (January 10, 1968), was cancelled, partly because of the defection of Liao Ho-hsü, the Chinese chargé d'affaires at the Hague, to the United States, partly also because of political questions at home, and, as some observers thought, because Nixon had expressed a somewhat negative attitude toward China in his inaugural address (January 29, 1969).

The Chinese desire to use the threat of a Sino-American rapprochement in the talks opened in Peking on October 20, 1969, with the Soviet Union eventually made the Chinese change their mind. The 135th Sino-American session was held on January 20, 1970. It took place at the Chinese embassy in Warsaw, not on Polish territory, which aroused great interest in the West. Were the Chinese going to stop behaving like "lone wolves," in the 1963 expression of Adlai Stevenson, the American delegate to the United Nations, and had the Americans abandoned their strategy of containment?

The fragile hopes born of the 135th meeting was almost immediately dashed by the coup d'état in Cambodia on March 18, 1970. The tense situation that followed, the apparently belligerent attitude adopted by Peking, combined with one of determined support for Prince Sihanouk, resulted in the cancellation of the 136th meeting, planned for May 20. Mao Tse-tung chose that day for his resounding statement on the continuing danger of war, adding: "But revolution is the main trend in the world today."

Once the March crisis was over, Washington quickly made several reassuring advances and statements; various trade restrictions disappeared, several categories of American citizens were given permission to go to China, and this was then extended to all citizens. The dialogue had been interrupted and had to be started again. Washington, encouraged by certain circles and specialists, appeared to be determined to take bold steps. The disturbances of the Cultural Revolution were over; China was clearly making progress in the nuclear field; and the break between China and the Soviet Union was proving irreparable. In his message of February 25, 1971, on the state of the world, Nixon devoted much space to China, stressing the need to enlarge contacts with Peking, suppress the pointless obstacles separating China from the United States, and take its legitimate national interests into account, all of which was bound to please the Chinese leaders.

The Chinese had to adjust themselves to the end of the Indochinese war, now a foreseeable possibility. The withdrawal of American troops continued, and the resulting military disengagement led to far-reaching political modifications in Southeast Asia. It was essential to ensure China's participation in the new balance of power about to develop in East Asia, for it was liable to be more dangerous and more lasting than the old. The Americans for the moment held all the keys to the problems involved— Southeast Asia, Taiwan, Japan, Korea, and the United Nations—as Mao Tse-tung said to Edgar Snow. The need to impress and worry the Russians, with whom negotiations were still at a standstill, was as real as ever.

Once more the month of March nearly cancelled out all the efforts on either side. But a mere few weeks after the crisis of Tchepone and Chou En-lai's solemn warning at Hanoi, a huge step was taken toward a rapprochement. On April 14, when he greeted the American table tennis team, which had been invited to visit Peking with several other teams after the world championships in Japan, Chou En-lai made some highly significant remarks:

> A new page has been turned. A new chapter has been opened in the relations between our two peoples. Your visit to China has opened the door to friendly contacts between the peoples of the two countries.

On April 23 American Secretary of State William Rogers echoed these words, enlarging upon them: "I think it was the Prime Minister of the People's Republic of China who said that it was a new page in our relations. We would hope that it becomes a new chapter, that there will be several pages to follow."[1]

The Americans added a series of declarations and a few revelations to these first remarks. Some of the earliest ones were aimed at fixing the starting points for future discussions, or at reassuring those worried by such an apparently sudden development. Most of them were circumspect, like that made by President Nixon on April 29: "What we have done has broken the ice. Now we have to test the water to see how deep it is."[2] Other statements were frankly reticent, like that made by the State Department spokesman Charles Bray on the international status of Taiwan, which had been in suspense since 1945. A few more measures were taken to remove points of friction, such as the lifting of the embargo on various strategic products and the bringing to a halt of drilling for oil in the Tiaoyutai Islands.

On July 15, President Nixon astounded the world by announcing on American television that he would go to Peking before May 1972. He also revealed that his adviser on international affairs, Henry Kissinger, had just paid a forty-eight-hour visit to Peking from Pakistan (July 9-11). China announced the news simultaneously but with more restraint, and either because the Chinese wanted to show in advance that their line throughout the negotiations would be a hard one, or because it was necessary for propaganda, they continued to attack some aspects of United States policy in Asia just as before. Then, on the Chinese side at least, silence returned to the diplomatic front and persisted until August 29, when Peking reacted very sharply to a statement made by William Rogers on the representation of two Chinese states in the United Nations (August 2).

Two months later, Kissinger made a second visit to Peking from October 20 to 25, and Peking's well-timed entry into the United Nations cleared a major obstacle from the horizon of Sino-American relations. Washington and Peking found themselves adopting similar attitudes, particularly in the Security Council, toward the Indian subcontinent. On November 30, the White House announced that President and Mrs. Nixon would visit China (Peking, Shanghai, and Wuhan) from February 21 to 28, 1972.

The visit happened as planned. The atmosphere surrounding the guests at their reception was one of reserve and strict courtesy at first; it subsequently became almost familiar, if not friendly. The joint communiqué published at the end of the visit set forth differences on which the attitude of either side was unyielding, but on the American side it acknowledged the principle of Chinese political unity and to a large extent committed the fate of Taiwan to the continent:

> The United States acknowledges that all Chinese on either side of the Taiwan Strait maintain that there is but one China and that Taiwan is a part of China. The United States government does not challenge that position. It reaffirms its interest in a peaceful settlement of the Taiwan question by the Chinese themselves.

It seems probable that, beyond the specific questions mentioned or omitted by the communiqué, the Americans and the Chinese made a tentative sketch of what East Asia could become. Perhaps this was behind the remark Nixon made as he left Shanghai: "This week has changed the world."

After two or three years of ups and downs, an open dialogue had been established at the summit, and would, according to the terms of the communiqué, take on a conventional form. For the first time since 1950 the expression "world politics" regained its full meaning.

Several visits by Henry Kissinger to Peking in 1972 (June) and 1973 (February and November) no doubt helped to speed up the development of various specific questions (and first of all those arising from a return to peace in Indochina) and prepare for a new order in Asia and the world as a whole. The communiqués, similar to the one published at the end of the presidential visit (communiqué of February 29, 1972) were so vague that they did not allow for much beyond purely personal interpretations. An important step toward building up regular bilateral relations was made when liaison bureaus with diplomatic privileges were set up in both capitals in May 1973; scientific exchanges increased and trade relations also developed.

The resignation of President Nixon was received with discretion and, no doubt, regret. The establishment of Communist control over South Vietnam, in spite of the Paris agreements signed by Peking, did not produce lasting tension between the United States and China; President Ford visited Peking in November 1975. Although the Chinese periodically denounce American hegemony, particularly in front of international organizations, they nevertheless give it tacit encouragement where it can usefully checkmate the Russians. As in the heyday of their alliance with the Russians, but in reverse, the Chinese are trying to thwart the détente between East and West by arousing the mistrust of the Americans. It seems likely that this consideration, combined with security needs, will dominate relations between Peking and Washington for a long time, in spite of the vast ideological gap between the two capitals.

Western and Mediterranean Europe

China had long thought of Western and Mediterranean Europe in terms of separate states, taking advantage now and then of the region's lack of political and economic unity and occasionally stressing the contradictions attributed to the decline of capitalism and the rivalries inherent in imperialism. This attitude was quickly modified when, anxious to create as many obstacles as possible to hamper the influence and the expansion of the superpowers, above all the Soviet Union, China began to encourage the development of a united Europe. Exhortations and warnings were issued together. "We have supported the European Community in our official documents and in speeches at the United Nations," as Chou En-lai said to one of his visitors.[3] A few months later, in a speech to a Dutch delegation, he added: "History shows us that peoples who allow themselves to grow weaker bring unhappiness upon themselves!" This attitude made the Chinese show great hostility toward the Conference on European Security and Cooperation, which opened in Helsinki on July 3, 1973, and ended on August 1, 1975. The Chinese desire to keep as many of the Russian armed forces as possible in the West, coupled with the fear of seeing Europe undergoing a definitive, tacit division into two zones of influence, one Russian and one American, explains the growing Chinese interest in the Mediterranean countries. Cordial diplomatic relations were established with Italy (November 6, 1970), Greece (June 5, 1972), Spain (March 1973), and Malta, whose prime minister, Dom Mintoff, obtained a loan of $44 million when he visited Peking in April 1972 and January 1975. The incidents in Cyprus, which occurred shortly after a visit by Archbishop Makarios to Peking, aroused sharp attacks on the Soviet Union. "Give the Mediterranean back to the Mediterranean peoples" became a familiar slogan in Chinese propaganda.

A Chinese ambassador was accredited to the European Economic Community on September 15, 1975. The prospects of cooperation between China and Europe are unlikely to grow until a political and military Europe is born, but it is perhaps a suitable time for the members of the EEC to begin a common study of the facts, the means, the advantages, and the future risks entailed.

Great Britain, Canada, Australia, and New Zealand

Hong Kong, though a British colony and leased territory, is still Chinese in geography and population and as such could not escape the tumult of the Cultural Revolution. In May 1967, the left-wing unions launched agitation which Peking was bound to back, but this received little local support. The disturbances went on until the beginning of the winter, involving about twenty victims, material destruction, partial strikes, bomb scares, and frontier incidents; the financial losses entailed were heavier for the Communists than for the British.

The attitude of firmness and calm on the part of the British authorities, who intended to continue to carry out their responsibilities at least as long as the Chinese did not mean to take Hong Kong back under their sovereignty, and the importance of the colony for the economy of China as one of Peking's chief trading partners and sources of foreign currency combined to good effect. The situation became normal, and prosperity returned in 1968.[4]

The situation in Hong Kong inevitably had rapid repercussions in Peking at the level of state relations. The powerlessness of Marshal Ch'en Yi, subject to attacks and pressure from the red guards, and the temporary seizure by the latter of the Foreign Ministry itself precipitated matters. What had begun as a tense situation, with exchanges of notes at a diplomatic level, developed into outbreaks of violence and the fire on August 23, 1967. The coolness and composure of the British mission—particularly of Chargé d'Affaires Donald Hopson—and of the Foreign Office in its request that the Chinese adopt a "more acceptable" attitude saved the relations between the two countries, which had been in existence since January 1950. As a result, other unfortunate affairs (the detention of British journalists, ship's captains, and engineers) were gradually settled as time passed.[5]

The development of Sino-American relations and above all the recognition of China by other Commonwealth countries led the British and the Chinese to exchange ambassadors; their relations then acquired full meaning from a legal and practical point of view. This change was made on March 13, 1972. The visit of Sir Alec Douglas Home to Peking in October 1972 appears to have ensured the survival of Hong Kong for some time to come.

After several years of hesitation and negotiations lasting for eighteen months, Canada eventually recognized the Peking government on October 13, 1970. The Chinese sent their foremost diplomat, Huang Hua, to Ottawa, no doubt mindful of the prospect of future relations between China and the United States and of admission to the United Nations. Canadian Prime Minister G. E. Trudeau went to China in October 1972.

Australia opened relations with Peking on December 21, 1972; Prime Minister Gough Whitlam visited Peking in October 1973. New Zealand recognized China in December 1972.

France

In his radio and television broadcast on August 10, 1967, General de Gaulle justified his foreign policy by the need for world peace, referring in somewhat melancholy terms to China: "This is why we have objectively established contacts with Peking, though the immediate benefits may not be obvious."

Several incidents had in fact cast a shadow over relations between France and China since the beginning of the Cultural Revolution; clashes occurred between Chinese students and the French police outside the Soviet Embassy in Paris (January 27, 1967) and the Richard incident occurred in Peking (February 1, 1967).

The events of May 1968 in France were praised and given full support in China by the press and by mass organizations. Rallies were held in Peking and six other towns to back up the "just struggle" of the French students and the workers on strike, who were described as "glorious successors to the Paris Commune," and to shower insults on the "betrayal" of the French Communist Party and the Confédération Générale du Travail.[6] The

French government became the "French dominating group" guilty of "criminal violence" and "bloody repressions"; economic losses were carefully enumerated. De Gaulle and French institutions were not spared; "de Gaulle is peddling the rubbish of elections in honeyed terms," reported the Hsinhua News agency on July 3. These are merely a few examples.

Relations between France and China—as was the case with China's relations with other countries—were more serene in 1969. The retirement of the president of the Republic on May 5 was greeted neither by insults nor regrets. Several private and official visits were exchanged in 1970 and 1971, though they brought no real changes in the situation. Cultural relations between the two countries were at a standstill; they resumed gradually in 1973, with the exchange of a few students. Trade figures remained low.[7] The Chinese did not disown the actions of left-wing groups and gave a friendly reception to their representatives.

In September 1973, President Georges Pompidou was entertained in Peking with great courtesy. Various points on which the policy of the two countries converged, such as the importance attached to independence and national sovereignity and "the right not to allow oneself to be disarmed" were stressed by both sides. Toasts and communiqués revealed that Chinese and French points of view were in disagreement on certain important questions. "Détente, agreement, and cooperation," said Pompidou on the subject of Europe. Chou En-lai replied that the détente was superficial, thinking of the Soviet Union, and the fundamental attitudes of the two men were equally different. When Pompidou spoke of the "weight of wisdom and reason of two ancient peoples," the Chinese premier retorted by stressing his "faith in the younger generation" and in the "rapidly flowing current of history."[8] Their exchange confirmed the limitations of a political dialogue that was at least temporarily unable to produce far-reaching modifications in the respective positions of the two states. All that could be expected was an increase in exchanges of views, in mutual understanding, and in economic and cultural contacts; even this much needs considerable time.

Teng Hsiao-p'ing's visit to France (May 13-16, 1975) gave the Chinese a chance to speak out against the illusion of détente and to encourage political unity in Europe, but did not appreciably change relations between France and China.

Austria, Belgium, West Germany, the Netherlands, and Portugal

Austria (May 26, 1971), Belgium (October 25, 1971), and West Germany (October 11, 1972) all opened diplomatic relations with China. The Netherlands raised its office to the status of embassy on May 18, 1972. Portugal, the last state to have large colonies in Africa, did not participate in the movement before the revolution of April 1974. The declaration of diplomatic recognition, which the Portuguese then made, was ignored by the Chinese, who were following the upheavals in Portugal closely and denounced Russian intrigues in Lisbon. The Chinese are also extremely active in some of the movements for the liberation of Angola and Mozambique, with the aim of removing them from Soviet influence, which was regarded as "an element of division in the revolutionary struggle of the African peoples." As of 1976, the fate of Macao, which was apparently going to be linked with that of Hong Kong right to the end, remained unchanged.

The United Nations

Once contacts had been reestablished between China and the United States in July 1971, thanks to the efforts of Henry Kissinger, the question of the admission of China to the United Nations entered a new phase. The theory of "two Chinas" could no longer be defended and the Americans only put it forward to cover their retreat and make their ally, Nationalist China, accept the inevitable.

On October 25, at its twenty-sixth session, the General Assembly of the United Nations voted to seat Peking and exclude Taiwan (motion proposed by Albania), by seventy-six votes for, thirty-five against, and seventeen abstentions. The Chinese delegation to the twenty-sixth Assembly took its seat a few days later.[9] Chinese gradually entered all the organizations under the control of the world organization. Its representatives used the new platform to state the general policies of their government and also to make harsh attacks on the "collusion" of the superpowers, the myth of détente, which was merely "the cover-up for a desperate struggle to acquire nuclear superiority and dominate the world" and "an illusion and an invention to lull the vigilance of the peoples to sleep."[10] At the Economic Commission for Asia and the Far East, the Chinese attacked the Russian proposal for a collective security pact in Asia. They supported the developing countries everywhere, particularly as regards the exploitation of raw materials and rights to the sea (boundaries of territorial waters and fishing zones). In spite of all this, the Chinese did not question the fundamental structure of the United Nations or its methods. They paid their contribution toward expenses and supplied administrative personnel, including a general undersecretary of political affairs and decolonization (Tang Ming-chao).

Disarmament

On June 15, 1971, during the Twenty-Fourth Congress of the Communist Party of the Soviet Union, Moscow invited the other four nuclear powers (United States, Great Britain, France, and China) to hold a conference on nuclear disarmament. The Chinese refused on July 30, 1971, the day before their Army Day, and took the opportunity to reaffirm the principle of equal rights for all countries in the world and their condemnation of the Moscow Treaty on the Nonproliferation of Nuclear Weapons (July 25, 1963) and the Strategic Arms Limitation Talks (SALT). They also restated their position, already known for some time: (1) the complete prohibition and total destruction of nuclear weapons; (2) the commitment not to be the first to use nuclear weapons; and (3) the calling of a summit conference of all the peoples of the world to discuss the total ban on and total destruction of nuclear weapons. They also called on the United States and the Soviet Union to make a joint declaration, or separate declarations, not to be the first to use nuclear weapons and to destroy all nuclear bases installed in countries other than their own. On November 24, 1971, the Chinese delegation to the United Nations used much the same terms to reject a Russian proposal to hold a world disarmament conference.

Like the French, the Chinese refused to take part in the interminable Geneva conference on disarmament. They did not sign the agreement forbidding the use of biological and toxic weapons of April 10, 1972, or the Stockholm agreement on environment of June 16, 1972.

Chinese propaganda launched violent attacks, as was to be expected, on the Soviet-American agreement concluded in Moscow on May 26, 1972, on strategic arms limitation. They also attacked the agreement on preventing nuclear war signed in Washington on June 22, 1973. As Nixon and Brezhnev met on both occasions, their task was made easier.

Chinese progress in the field of missiles and satellites and the broadening of their diplomacy have not led the Chinese to relax their fundamental position on disarmament. This was affirmed in reaction to the Moscow treaty of July 25, 1963, stated in their declaration of July 31, 1963, and repeated on October 16, 1964, when they carried out their first nuclear explosion (see Chapter 24).

Notes

[1]Statement by Secretary of State Rogers (in answer to a question) at his news conference on April 23, 1971; text in *The Department of State Bulletin* 64, No. 1663 (May 10, 1971): p. 575.

[2]Statement by President Nixon (in answer to a question) at his news conference on April 29, 1971; text in *The Department of State Bulletin* 64, No. 1664 (May 17, 1971): p. 630.

[3]Interview with the General Director of the Agence France-Presse (May 16, 1973). The Russians took up the remarks and accused China of "pushing the NATO bloc to undertake ill-considered activities against the USSR from a position of strength" (Moscow, Agence France-Presse, May 26, 1973).

[4]In 1969, exports from mainland China to Hong Kong amounted to $449.8 million, 10 percent more than in 1968; Jan Deleyne, *The Chinese Economy.*

[5]The detention of the completely innocent journalist Anthony Grey in reprisal for the conviction of Chinese journalists in Hong Kong is an apt example of the maladjustment of the Chinese to the principles and practices of modern law. The account given by the engineer George Watt, arrested in Lanchow, also illustrates this.

[6]See *People's Daily,* (June 6, 1968).

[7]Less than $200 million on an average until 1973.

[8]Speech of September 14, 1973.

[9]Head of delegation Ch'iao Kuan-hua; permanent representative Huang Hua.

[10]Declaration by Ch'iao Kuan-hua on October 2, 1973.

47 Foreign Policy 1966 –1976 (5): The Socialist Bloc

From the beginning the Cultural Revolution was noticeably anti-Soviet in tone. Because it was directed against domestic "revisionists," it was logical, in view of ten years of steady deterioration in Sino-Soviet relations, to attack also the foreign "revisionists" who were thought to have inspired them. Numerous incidents occurred during the summer of 1966. On several occasions, huge yelling crowds laid siege to the Soviet embassy for days at a time. Citizens of the Soviet Union or of Eastern European countries— diplomats, journalists, and experts—were badly molested, while the police looked on in apparent indifference. On August 23, the Chinese Foreign Ministry made it known that it no longer considered itself responsible for the safety of foreigners entering the Soviet Embassy and rejected all notes of diplomatic protest from Moscow. To make the already threatening atmosphere even more somber, it accused the Soviet Union of collusion with India and Japan. In November, the return of Chinese students from Russia gave rise to large demonstrations, and accounts of the "persecutions" they had suffered were given wide coverage in the press for several days running.

Incidents were most violent and distressing in January and February 1967, when the families of the Russian diplomats were evacuated from Peking. The pretext was a clash in Moscow on January 25, 1967, in front of the Lenin Mausoleum between the Russian police and a group of sixty-nine Chinese students on their way back from France and Finland. The incidents stopped abruptly when the Soviet Union sent a note in the form of an ultimatum, threatening to ensure the protection of its own citizens (February 9). Other minor affairs cropped up over the year, as at Shenyang

(June 11), Dairen (August 13), and in Moscow (December 25). The main incidents were various noisy controversies inspired by current events such as developments in Vietnam and the Brezhnev-Johnson meeting at Glassboro. No important doctrinal texts were published.

The first half of 1968 was relatively calm, filled with small incidents, mutual accusations of aspiring to world hegemony, of secret agreements with the United States, of the betrayal of Vietnam, or of the refusal to allow organized joint action there. The Soviet invasion of Czechoslovakia on August 20 provided new, choice material for an ideological quarrel that was wearing thin.

Peking made extensive use of the event, which fully justified all its accusations of "great power chauvinism" and was remarkably useful in furthering the Chinese cause among other Communist Parties. Officials and the press used stronger language than ever before against "social imperialism." Chou En-lai, speaking at the Rumanian Embassy on August 23, Ch'en Yi at the Korean Embassy on September 9, and Chou En-lai once more at the Albanian Embassy on September 29 made lengthy denunciations of the "abominable crime," though they still reproached the Czechs for their "revisionism." The Warsaw Pact was described as "antisocialist" and "aggressive," and its aims were denounced as imperialistic and "comparable to NATO's." Chou En-lai thought that the world had just entered a "new historical period," one of struggle against American imperialism and Soviet revisionism; the appeal he launched two months later to the peoples of the world has already been mentioned (Chapter 42). In October, the new chief of general staff, General Huang Yung-sheng, gave "strong" support to the Albanians, who were worried by the Russian invasion of Czechoslovakia, and also accused the Soviet Union of concentrating troops along the Chinese frontiers. Chou En-lai took this up and complained of deliberate violations of Chinese air space. The slogan "Make preparations for war" was heard everywhere. The climate of Sino-Soviet relations worsened so quickly that some outside observers, alarmed by the precedent in Czechoslovakia, began prophesying war.

In 1969, the two nations came face to face on the frontier. The year opened with an article in *Hung ch'i*, meagre in content but expressed in extremely insulting terms: "The Blood of Heroes and the Fear of Renegades." It dealt with the affair of the monument of Orzhonikidze, where an inscription in memory of the Chinese who had fought for the Russian Revolution had been obliterated by the Russians; it also tried to prove that an opposition existed in the Soviet Union, consisting of members of a clandestine "Marxist-Leninist" Party. In the preceding

October, *Hung ch'i* had published a pamphlet attributed to a "Stalin group," which attacked the "higher castes," who were described as a "tumor feeding on the people and seizing it by the throat." More frequent and harsher criticisms dealt with the situation within the Soviet regime.[1] The Russian press reacted in a similar way; at the time of the incident on Chen Pao (Damansky) Island in the middle reaches of the Ussuri River (11:00 A.M. on March 2), the atmosphere was very bad indeed (see Map No. 5). The Chinese laid ambush to a Russian company making a routine patrol of the island, which is disputed territory, though it is uninhabited and at times under water. Thirty-eight were killed and fourteen wounded, for the patrol was off its guard. The local Soviet commander retaliated with an attack using artillery and tanks, causing similar casualties in the opposite camp.

Peking made immediate and wide use of the incident. The next day, huge demonstrations took place at Shenyang and in Peking, and then in towns throughout China; 150 million people took part. An article appeared, shortly to become a classic, entitled "Down with the New Tsars," claiming Chinese sovereignty over the contested island, even under the terms of the "unequal treaty imposed on the Chinese people in 1860 by Tsarist Russian imperialism," and accused the Russians of premeditation:

> The armed provocation by the Soviet revisionist renegade clique against our country is a frenzied action it has taken out of the need of its domestic and foreign policies at a time when it is beset with internal and external difficulties and landed in an impasse.[2]

In fact, without looking into the details of the event or its legality, it looks as if the Chinese, by suddenly deciding to open fire on Soviet patrols, which they had previously avoided or asked to retire, bore a good deal of responsibility for the incident. Whatever happened later, the surprise tactics gave them the initial advantage. Their primary motivations probably lay in the upcoming Ninth Congress, which was intended to be the "Congress of Unity," in their corresponding desire to focus on a concrete case that could be easily explained and documented by painful historical memories (the "new Tsars"), and in the ideological struggle being waged against "revisionists within and without." Further disgrace would be heaped on the supporters of Liu Shao-ch'i, while the patriotism of all would be awakened, to serve the thought of Mao Tse-tung. In any case, in the excitement of the Cultural Revolution, all unexpected incidents (initiatives by soldiers in a local context or clashes between

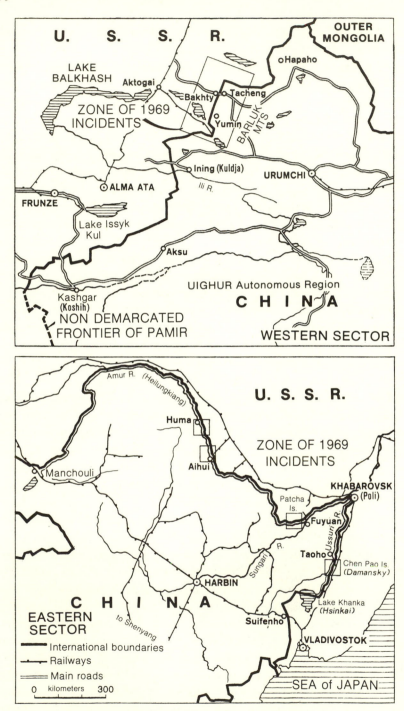

Map 5   Sino-Russian frontiers

patrols) would unfailingly find firm support in Peking and in China as a whole.

Unlike the earlier one, the March 15 incident at the same place was apparently provoked by the Russians to discourage the Chinese from any further actions, while arousing patriotic indignation to equal that in the enemy camp, and possibly to make the West aware of the danger the Chinese represented. It was well planned and was reported to have caused 800 casualties among the Chinese, as compared with sixty among the Russians, whose equipment on hand was clearly superior to that of the Chinese.

Four or five more smaller clashes occurred during the spring and summer at other points on the frontier, in the Bakhty region of Kazakhstan on May 3, at Tacheng north of Yumin in the Barluk mountains (northwestern Sinkiang) on June 10, on Patcha Island in the Amur (Heilungkiang) on July 8, and at Tiehlieketi near Yumin on August 13. In each case, the Chinese reacted less vigorously than they had at the time of Chen Pao. The incidents ceased soon after, or at any rate were no longer mentioned, for Kosygin went to Peking on September 11 as a consequence of the death of Ho Chi Minh, and negotiations between Russian and Chinese deputy foreign ministers Alexei Kuznetsov and Ch'iao Kuan-hua opened on October 20 in Peking.

Just before the dialogue between the two countries resumed, Peking tried to define its position clearly in a declaration on October 7. In spite of supposedly "irreconcilable" differences in basic principles, the Chinese government was determined to obtain a peaceful settlement of the frontier problem or at least to preserve the status quo. It also proposed that the troops of both countries break contact in the contested areas. Although the Chinese affirmed that they did not demand the restitution of territory seized by Tsarist Russia by "iniquitous" treaties, they wanted the negotiations to cover the whole of the frontier question.[3]

As of late 1975, negotiations have been going on for six years in Peking without any apparent results apart from a lessening of local tension.[4] They have not put an end to the political and ideological controversy, which has inspired countless texts.

State relations, and particularly economic relations, weathered the storm, though they were still considerably reduced. When the Ussuri crisis was almost at its height, the Conference on Navigation of Frontier Rivers was held at Khabarovsk (June 13 to August 8, 1969) and Heiho (July 10 to December 19, 1970); sessions were held in each following year. The year 1970 was one of controversies and "preparation for war"; the Chinese underlined this by ostentatiously building urban air raid shelters and by asking that food be stockpiled in the countryside, but no serious incidents occurred. Ambassadors were exchanged in the autumn; Tolstikov was sent to Peking and Liu Hsin-ch'üan to Moscow. In 1971, trade figures tripled as a result of new agreements.[5]

During the next two years, while still rejecting Chinese "slander" and refusing to yield on ideological or territorial issues, the Russians made unsuccessful approaches aimed at restoring peace, twice going so far as to suggest the conclusion of an agreement not to resort to force (January 1971 and June 1973).[6] The Chinese did not take this up, and the political reports to the Ninth and Tenth Party Congresses were as violent and insulting as ever, as has already been described. At the Tenth Congress, however, Chou En-lai affirmed once more that disagreement on basic issues ought not to prevent normal state relations, as prescribed by the Five Principles of Peaceful Coexistence, and that frontier questions should be settled peacefully by means of negotiations "carried out beyond the reach of all possible threats." In view of the greater strength of the Soviet Union and the anxiety of the Chinese not to jeopardize their position in the socialist camp, from which the Russians were thinking of expelling them, Chou En-lai was bound to show some restraint.

Setting aside the chronology of events, let us look into the substance of the quarrel. Peking's criticisms can be summarized under several headings, whose tone suggests that the disagreements were becoming increasingly political in nature. In foreign policy, the Chinese opposed the world mission assumed by the Soviet Union (which they associated with a sharing of power with the United States), the Soviet vocation in Asia, and the Russian claim to lead the socialist camp. The Russian slogan, "We will go wherever the interests of the Soviet Union require us to go," was in their eyes identical with President Eisenhower's declarations on U.S. responsibilities toward the rest of the world. It was the expression of an unacceptable "super-imperialism," and led to "nuclear despotism" accompanied by pacts that were swindles compared with real disarmament.[7]

Soviet Asian policy, no matter what form it took, was condemned out of hand, whether it concerned the continent as a whole or bilateral relations between states. Projects for organizing collective security systems, signs of economic expansion, movements of naval units in Asian waters were all taken as evidence of hostile intentions toward China, aimed at immobilizing and encircling China.[8] Relations between the Soviet Union and Indonesia were described as "a friendship sullied with blood."[9] Several texts revealed the "ruthless exploitation" of the Mongolian people, and it has already been shown how closely the Chinese followed the Russian rapprochement with Japan and India and Russian efforts to replace the United Kingdom in the Indian Ocean.

Within the socialist world, the doctrine of "limited sovereignty" of states, the "plundering" of their resources under the guise of economic integration, and the role of Comecon were attacked more often than anything else. The Chinese attacked Soviet "neo-colonialism," "naval despotism," and Soviet spying activities throughout the world, particularly in China (affairs of January and March 1974). Their attacks were more frequent and more violent than ever in 1975, possibly because of the progress, or at least apparent progress, of the détente between Moscow and Washington. Difficulties within the Soviet Union were constantly highlighted, such as the policy toward ethnic minorities ("USSR Peoples' Prison" was the title of an article in the *People's Daily* on July 4, 1969), the failure of the development of the Altai Mountains, economic failures, mismanagement, absenteeism among the workers, and the decline in morality.

Ideology was less important in the Chinese campaign against the Soviet Union. Even so, the theory of an "international alliance among the workers and peasants" was questioned and described as "social-colonialist rubbish";[10] a long doctrinal article was published to mark the centenary of the birth of Lenin ("Leninism or Social Imperialism"); another appeared on the centenary of the Paris Commune (March 18, 1971); and in the cultural field Stanislavsky was attacked.

The Sino-Soviet crisis of 1969 and the international Communist movement

The World Conference of Communist and Workers' Parties, held in Moscow from June 5 to 17, 1969, three months after the serious armed clashes on the Ussuri River and six weeks after the Ninth Congress of the Chinese Communist Party, was a partial failure for the Russians as regards their relations with China.[12] In his speech on June 8, Brezhnev reproached the Chinese for their armed provocations, their territorial claims, their appeals to the Russian people to rebel against their government, their rejection of "scientific Communism," and their pretension to impose the thought of Mao Tse-tung on the whole world. He had the backing of the French and Polish Communists, but the Italians (Enrico Berlinguer) and the Rumanians (Nicolae Ceausescu), who supported equal rights for all parties with no central leadership, opposed him. The final resolution did not condemn China. Yugoslavia, Albania, Cuba, North Vietnam, and North Korea did not attend the conference. Peking showed moderation in its reaction but continued to attack the Soviet Union alone. The Chinese question has developed little since then within the international Communist movement, in spite of a rapprochement between Peking and Washington; the situation reflects the embarrassment and wait-and-see policy of the Soviet Union.[13]

Relations between China and Eastern Europe

The more open policy of the Chinese, apparent in 1970 and borne out by the return of most Chinese ambassadors to their posts and their desire to unify all possible opposition to the Russians within the socialist camp, led the Chinese to tighten their links with Albania, develop their contacts with Rumania, and put their relations with Yugoslavia on a normal basis. The Albanians were reliable ideological allies of the Chinese, and echoes of the Cultural Revolution were heard in Albania. Thanks to them, the Chinese gained a slight foothold in the Mediterranean and the Balkans, and Chinese economic aid acted as a demonstration. In Chinese public opinion, ill informed as to the true world situation, the friendship with Albania took on a significance out of all proportion to reality; its importance was blown up still further by frequent exchanges of missions of all kinds.[14]

Relations between Peking and Bucharest were already good and were improved by Chou En-lai's visit to Rumania (June 16-24, 1966) and by Rumanian Premier Ion G. Maurer's visit to China (July 3-4, 1967); the worries that the Czechoslovak crisis inspired in Bucharest helped them progress still further. The Rumanians still put the unity of the socialist camp above all else and were careful not to allow the Chinese to put them in an awkward position, but they made unmistakably friendly gestures toward them. Peking and Bucharest exchanged numerous official visits of state and Party representatives, with forceful declarations on the usual themes of independence and national sovereignty. The Chinese allocated large loans to the Rumanians.[15]

Relations between China and Yugoslavia were at best mediocre after 1958 for ideological reasons; the Chinese regarded Yugoslavia as the oldest and purest example of modern revisionism and excluded it from the socialist community. After confirming diplomatic relations to the level of chargés d'affaires for more than ten years, the two countries exchanged ambassadors in May 1970. In June 1971, Foreign Minister Mirko Tepavac went to Peking, a perfect illustration of how in this part of the world, as elsewhere, the interest of the state has priority over ideology, and resistance to the Soviet Union is of more importance than principles. Links between the two countries were strengthened by the visit of Yugoslav Premier Dzemal Bijedic to Peking in October 1975.

The Chinese were insulting in the extreme as regards Czechoslovakia, describing it as "a colony of the Soviet empire" and its new leaders as a "clique of puppets," "slaves grovelling at the feet of the new tsars." They sent an ambassador to Prague nonetheless. A similar attitude prevailed toward Poland, East Germany, and Hungary—states whose obedience to Moscow left no room for divisive maneuvers, at least for the time being.

Thus between 1966 and 1976, the fears born of the invasion of Czechoslovakia by Russian troops; the incidents on the Ussuri, whether deliberately provoked or coincidental; the reconciliation of Washington and Peking; and the Soviet-Cuban intervention in Angola combined to worsen, and at times nearly rupture, the already severely strained Sino-Soviet relations. The United Nations has often been the theater for confrontations whose violence has shocked the world. More and more, ideological differences are blurred by the opposition between the two countries, which have been stated in short slogans: the Russians speak of "totalitarian nationalism"; the Chinese held that Moscow's interests in socialism are restricted to Soviet revisionism. Periods of greater or lesser tension will probably alternate in the future, depending on the international situation, specific issues, or the arrival of new leaders on either side, but China has, without any doubt, embarked for good on a new, authentically and entirely national road. It will not return to the socialist camp except to take over its leadership.

Notes

[1] See, for example, an article of February 23 on the restoration of capitalism in Soviet agriculture.

[2] English text of the Hsinhua Agency bulletin (March 3, 1969).

[3] Apart from the question of "unequal treaties," particularly those of Aigun (May 28, 1838), Peking (November 14, 1860), and St. Petersburg (February 12, 1881), the dispute involved about 600 islands in the Ussuri and Amur valleys, and 20,000 square kilometers in the nondemarcated Pamir region inhabited by Tadjiks.

[4]Various indications suggest that, since a return to ideological unity was impossible, the Russians wanted to settle the entire ideological dispute, including a new realignment on the part of the Chinese. The Chinese, anxious to retain complete freedom of action and avoid a worsening of the military conflict, merely wanted local arrangements. Although the Chinese said they were prepared to base negotiations on the existing treaties, they probably wanted to make the Russians admit that the treaties concerning the present Sino-Russian frontiers were "unequal treaties." For the former Chinese position on this point, see *People's Daily* (March 11, 1969), for a note from the Foreign Ministry entitled "Chen Pao Island Has Always Been Chinese Territory."

[5]The 1971 agreement provided for exchanges amounting to 120 to 130 million rubles. An agreement was signed on July 16, 1973, opening a direct Chinese airline to Moscow.

[6]Declaration of Brezhnev at Tashkent, September 24, 1973.

[7]The draft treaty to denuclearize the sea bed tabled at Geneva on October 7, 1969, was denounced for the same reasons as the Moscow Treaty of July 25, 1963.

[8]"New Measures of the New Tsars for their Expansion in Asia," *People's Daily* (September 3, 1969).

[9]*People's Daily* (September 1, 1969).

[10]*Ibid.* (August 28, 1969).

[11]*Ibid.* (April 22, 1970).

[12]The eighteen Parties that met in Moscow in March 1965 (see Chapter 25) decided that another Communist world conference should be called, following those held in 1957 and 1960. After many difficulties, a consultative committee met in Budapest on February 26, 1968. The world conference, originally fixed for November 25, 1968, was postponed until June 5, 1969, owing to events in Czechoslovakia.

[13]On this question in general, see François Fejtö, *L'Héritage de Lénine* (Paris: Casterman, 1973).

[14]The most important missions on the Chinese side were led by Chou En-lai, Chief of General Staff Huang Yung-sheng (December 1968), and the head of the army's General Political Department, Li Teh-sheng (August 1971), and on the Albanian side by Mehmet Shehu (April 1966) and General Begir Balluku (January 1967).

[15]The most important visit was that of Nicolae Ceausescu and Ion Maurer to Peking, from June 1 to 9, 1971. Rumanian Foreign Minister Radulescu, went to Peking in March 1971 and obtained a loan of $244 million for his country.

Conclusion

> For the empire is a powerful and weighty
> thing which cannot be carried away in a
> gust of words.
>
> *A. de Saint Exupéry, Citadelle*

Balance sheet of a generation

The regime is now of age; yet it would be dishonest not to admit at the start that, in spite of this, we do not have a sufficient grasp of its assets and liabilities to enable us to evaluate them, let alone pass judgment on them. Its history shows that China even now is a nation in a category of its own; it is of little or no use to try to apply modern laws of political science and economy here. Forty centuries of historical continuity and isolation in a completely developed world that China dominated with ease by the sheer weight of its size, culture, and political genius explain the survival of this entirely original society and a national and individual psychology of such a singular brand. The Middle Ages are in contact with the world of today in China. Mao Tse-tung—and he is no exception in this—was eighteen when the Manchu dynasty collapsed and his basic intellectual education was already completed. Both he and Liu Shao-ch'i have enjoyed quoting the classics, and Ch'en Yi, in a moving self-criticism, admitted to the red guards that Confucius and Mencius were present in his thoughts alongside Communism and bourgeois ideas.

The old and the new worlds are mingled in the apparatus of both Party and state. This is made obvious on official occasions, as, for example, when the vice-president of the Republic, formerly a scholar under the Empire, his colleague Mme Sun Yat-sen, former warlords and ex-Kuomintang generals mixed with first and second generation Communists. The same is true for society as a whole; characteristics of the old and new cultures are juxtaposed like colors in a prism, or merge in one individual.

The present shows, as did the past (this notion is linked with the preceding one), that China has an irresistible tendency to reject or sinicize all foreign examples suggested to or imposed on it and to fall back on or discover the Chinese way in every field. This is often an illusory or hazardous undertaking, but the idea in itself is essential to China, for it is in line with the country's habits, its concrete forms of thought, and above all with its immense pride.

It is common knowledge that China today is just as closed to the outside worlds as was imperial China. The fundamental data needed to plot an accurate graph of the development of a nation are lacking. Population figures, which in the case of a country tyrannized by its demography and living barely above subsistence level are of such vast importance, can only be calculated to the nearest 50 million. The deepest strata of society are inaccessible to the outsider.

Since 1966 this uncertainty has spread to political institutions and their workings. That they are out of order is clear enough, but many of the causes are not apparent, any more than are the rivalries and struggles for influence revolving around the figure of Mao Tse-tung.

Mao Tse-tung, permanent, giant-like and supreme, personifies the unknown. He is the incarnation, not only of the Chinese revolution, but of "Marxism-Leninism in our era." For the moment, he is still the chief factor in Chinese domestic and foreign policy, the figure behind the initiatives that turned aside from the main current of history to launch the country in completely unexpected directions, such as the Hundred Flowers and the Great Leap Forward, the people's communes and the Cultural Revolution. He prevents all choices and bars the way, while trying to get his successors (and with them the country he has molded with his own hands) to start on a way of no return, in line with his own philosophy.

The study of contemporary China is still encumbered by a heritage of too many preconceived ideas and approximate, often exaggerated mental pictures going straight back to the eighteenth century. For the missionaries, the philosophers, and the curious of that time, China contained no marvels and was the most well-organized and virtuous empire on earth. The monolithic aspect of its politics, ideology, and culture, both then and now, combine to encourage belief in an apparent state of harmony, disguising practices that are either tolerated or necessary and enable the true nature of human relationships to pass unnoticed. The Chinese world is quite different from the one revealed by official texts or guided tours.

Equally, the Western scalpel is ill suited to the dissection of Chinese events and attitudes. Our scrupulous care in linking our acts and our words and our demanding logic bring us to make justifiable mistakes regarding China. Numerous examples could prove that Chinese statesmen accept a considerable difference between the principles they are obliged to state and the pragmatism of their conduct, a fact that the West finds disturbing. The old, frequently denounced Confucian hypocrisy was due to the ability to accept opposites easily, rather than to a deliberate failure in morality.

With the charisma of Mao Tse-tung, the prodigious mutation attempted after 1949 was helped by two series of factors, one affecting institutions in the strict sense and the other the features of the Chinese people and society. Unlike its predecessor, the Kuomintang, the Communist Party possessed a highly ramified control system reaching down to the roots of society and capable of organizing or transforming everything at every level and in every field. It acted like a lever, which China had consistently lacked until then, to lift the country above its past. The Party imposed the establishment of new structures. By means of a complete monopoly of the press, whose function was to educate first and inform afterward, through its skill in instigating and leading impressive mass campaigns, it awakened individuals and groups to a predetermined political life and hastened the development of individual and collective habits and mentality.

In its undertakings the Party was helped not only by the circumstances described in the first chapter, but also by the absence of all obstacles other than family and village traditions. The numerical weakness of the bourgeoisie, the ignorance of any form of political democracy, the lukewarmness and rarity of religious feelings, the habit of subordinating the individual to the family or clan group, a numerous and uncommitted younger generation, and the adaptability of the people all contributed greatly to facilitate the Party's action.

It would be unjust, even so, not to emphasize the complexity of the task; China's vast expanse and huge population give an adequate idea of this.

Before 1949 all problems were crystallized in one, which was to win power by combining, simultaneously or alternately, political action and war. This overriding necessity required those in command merely to make realistic tactical choices and to create a centralized yet flexible leadership. The rest was achieved by unity in doctrine, and those executing the commands needed only to be disciplined and full of energy and to have faith in their mission.

After 1949 everything had to be done at once. The Party and the regime (both full of newcomers) had to be made to retain their revolutionary enthusiasm; rapid economic development had to be ensured, which was all the more urgent in view of the dangerous rise in population brought about by the restoration of peace and order at home. The masses had to be given a useful and modern education, while a transformation had to be operated in the beliefs, prejudices, and habits of a society traditionally hard to handle, both because its numbers were vast and because it was chiefly rural and scattered. The country had to be made secure from the outside world without endangering its national independence, while its individual vocation as leader of the world revolution had to be ensured without severing ideological and political links with the socialist camp. When, as during the years from 1949 to 1957 and 1962 to 1966, a certain degree of harmony was achieved among these simultaneous aims, China went through periods of political stability and economic progress, and its influence could be felt abroad. When, on the other hand, exaggerated importance was given to one factor alone, the result was always a serious lack of balance, bringing with it disastrous effects. This was the case during the Hundred Flowers campaign, the Great Leap Forward, and the Cultural Revolution.

Achievements in the political field

As at the time of the greatest dynasties, the regime restored political unity, which had been disintegrating since the beginning of the last century and had ceased to exist for part of the present one. The great tradition was renewed with all its beneficial consequences at home and its former brilliance abroad. Behind the revolutionary verbosity, the "Chineseness" was more real than ever.

The new unity appeared to be solid. Even the great crises, the economic crisis of the Great Leap Forward and the serious political crisis of the Cultural Revolution, including the Lin Piao affair, do not seem to have shaken it much, beyond introducing a relative degree of decentralization, which is possibly all to the good. The ideological break between Moscow and Peking must have upset many socialist consciences, but it did not provoke any outstanding defections (except for that of Wang Ming) or intolerable inner tensions.

The ship has managed to weather the storm mainly through the personal authority of Mao Tse-tung, the growing feeling of nationalism, and the help of the army. What is going to happen, though, when the "great helmsman" now more than eighty, lets go of the tiller?

Clearly the China of 1976 is no longer that of 1965. The crisis of state institutions lasted nearly ten years, until the formulation of the January 1975 constitution. These institutions—staffed by people of diverse and often rival origins (former cadres who have been rehabilitated, cadres coming from the mass, army cadres)—no longer have the coherence, experience and prestige of the former ones.

The unity of the Party, maintained with great care until 1966, is an idea that was abandoned and even fought against for several years. Today the Party is again reputedly corrupted by a "bourgeois and capitalist" tendency—that of Teng Hsiao-p'ing and his supporters. The official history is no longer the record of Communists working together in a spirit of brotherhood for the revolution and the building of socialism, but above all that of a permanent battle between two lines; as such it is widely taught. The Chinese have watched their most respected leaders and the most admired among their military chiefs being accused of heinous crimes, described as having wormed their way into the Party in order to work there for the Kuomintang and to bring China back to capitalism, or suspected of conspiring with foreign countries; several of them were dishonored in their private lives. The purge began with Liu Shao-ch'i, who by virtue of his office as president of the Republic and his title of first vice-chairman of the Party was second only to Mao Tse-tung and regarded as his successor, and included most of the old cadres of the Central Committee and the Party apparatus in the provinces. As happened in the French Revolution, the purge hit the lenient—the "Indulgents" and then the extremists—the "Enragés"—members of the Cultural Revolution Group, going as far as Ch'en Po-ta, its chairman. Before Lin Piao or with him, a minister of National Defense, several marshals, and four heads of staff were suddenly eliminated. Mao Tse-tung revised his judgment, though he never dared admit as much, when he rejected his "closest comrade-in-arms," his appointed successor, and the expounder and depositary of his thought. He has just recently supported the elimination of Teng Hsiao-p'ing, whom Chou En-lai had, with his agreement, appointed to succeed him as premier, and it is Hua Kuo-feng who benefits from his favor.

None of the great figures in the Party, except Mao Tse-tung, and to a lesser extent Chou En-lai, escaped being spattered and sullied. The victims often had to take a direct part in campaigns highly insulting toward themselves and join in accusation meetings where respect for the older generation, the builders of New China, vanished. The frequent, urgent appeals for unity now show that this was the chief victim of the events. But paradoxically, every effort is made to reconcile this unity with the pursuit of the class struggle within the Party.

At the time of the most flagrant mistakes of the Hundred Flowers or the Great Leap Forward, the infallibility of the Party was a dogma, its leadership being invariably "correct." Economic difficulties were put down to natural hazards, the ill will of the Soviet leaders, or sometimes to badly informed cadres, or to counterrevolutionaries, former landlords, and rich peasants. Today former heads of departments in the Central Committee or regional or provincial Party secretaries—those reinstated being classed alongside those expelled—are accused of errors and sabotage. Mao Tse-tung and the late Chou En-lai who, as chairman of the Party and premier, were truly responsible for events, are the only ones to escape blame and the law of self-criticism, as though sanctified by some saving grace.

It is an acknowledged fact that the Party ceased to exercise its authority in the autumn of 1966, and, except for its core, disappeared early in 1967 when the first revolutionary committees were created and entrusted with "unified" power. The Central Committee (in fact the Political Bureau and its Standing Committee) shared its powers with the Military Affairs Committee and the Cultural Revolution Group of Ch'en Po-ta and retained only partial authority over the State Council.

At the primary level, the Party no longer intervened organically, but simply by means of those of its members who were still revolutionary enough and had enough force of character to impose themselves. The same was true of the Communist Youth League, which had suffered from the "little generals of the revolution," and the trade unions, which have just reappeared.

The Ninth Congress and Tenth Congress wanted to put the Party back in command and tried to recreate it with a new constitution and a spirit that was more revolutionary than ever. If this task turns out to be slow, uncertain, difficult, and downright painful for many of those involved, it will be because of constant human problems and also because it is made harder by the collapse of authority and discrediting of the Party. The collapse and discredit are a serious phenomenon, much more serious in China than in any other socialist country. After 1949, the Party embodied the power of the state; it had been preceded by thirty or forty years of no power at all or by political disunity between the imperial and Communist orders. The Chinese were not taken in by the constitutional facade of the state. The Party laid down the general line from time to time, made or ratified decisions at every level, and expressed its indignation or enthusiasm on a local or national scale at will. The grave reversals of the "three black years" had lessened its influence, but it was still supreme and irreplaceable. Its self-effacement in the summer of 1966 quickly gave way to the effacement of all authority. Within a few months, the erosion of the Party's position led to a state of semi-anarchy and to the call to the army.

Imperial China, and still more Republican China, went through periods during which government and administration went into temporary eclipse. In such periods, the traditional order enabled the old society to look after itself at the level of the family and the village. The solid foundations of morality and customs and the primitive subsistence-level economy allowed the society to come through the crises, not unscathed, but without being destroyed. The Communist regime rapidly eliminated this old state of harmony almost entirely, breaking down the natural framework and setting up that of production instead, acting within the teams and brigades of the people's communes.

It seems that the Cultural Revolution, by raising once more, at least partially, the question of authority at the very roots of society, also raised that of production relations, creating the possibility of a solution—some degree of political and economic emancipation in relation to the Party and an increase in the real share of the masses in determining their own fate. In view of the size of the rural population, this would be an event of great import. If the Party does not quickly rediscover a solid unity on all levels, the regime is likely to have great difficulty in carrying out its agricultural policy as a whole, and possibly also in maintaining real collectivization, for the efficiency of the latter was questioned by many near the summit after the failure of the Great Leap Forward. In this case, the Cultural Revolution, which was a struggle for power, an ideological confrontation, and above all a conflict of political lines centered on the countryside, would have failed to attain its chief target. This observation acquires further importance in light of the theory held by some observers who think that Communism in China is maintained by the centralized, authoritarian form it has taken rather than by its content.

Achievements in the economic field

In twenty-six years, the new regime, though sometimes verging on disaster, has undeniably accomplished meritorious work in the economic field. In spite of steady growth in numbers, a population that was once subject to frequent famines now has assured means of survival. A fair system of food distribution has been introduced. Heavy industry has grown up and been implanted in new areas. Light industry, which was already well developed in 1949, has become still more varied, making further progress. Peak industries have been created. For a vast, poor country whose resources are not evenly distributed from a geographical point of view, with no real scientific and technological tradition and inadequate means of transport, this is no mean achievement.

The priority placed on politics, the voluntarism of Maoist thought (real "leftist adventurism"), the vain search for a unique method of development, and the shortage of qualified economists have sometimes precipitated China into dead ends. The general line has been punctuated with zigzags, and the clock has occasionally had to be put back at considerable cost; much time has been lost as a result.

The twelve-year plan for agricultural development, the keystone of the construction of socialism and the chief source of financing for it, was not achieved. According to the most optimistic hypotheses, China produced some 274 million tons of grain in 1975, when it ought to have harvested 350 or 400 million in 1967, and, according to the promise given by Ch'en Po-ta, fed 600 million more Chinese.

In the industrial sector, the plan was to catch up with England in 1972. That year has come and gone, and England, with a twelfth of China's population and a twentieth of its territory, is still far ahead of China; the leaders have forgotten the race and the challenge.

Now, both urged on and hampered by its vast population and held back by fruitless searches for shortcuts to modernization, China can no longer wait or make mistakes. It has been left to itself, and the question is whether it still has time to achieve the economic momentum needed to put it out of reach of the effects of a demographic explosion that may have gotten out of hand. China's entire future and at least part of ours depend on the same question. By definition, history cannot forecast future events, but it has proved that China has not stood by its bet as to its growth and that it has not yet emerged from its backward condition; it is still moving along the take-off runway.

The social, educational and cultural fields

The most far-reaching changes effected by the regime belong, beyond all doubt, to the social and educational domains. The old family order represented by the family and the village, founded on a moral code of Confucianist inspiration with the addition of a few superstitions, has been replaced by a socioeconomic organization of a collective type based on a revolutionary and socialist moral code, and an effort is being made to reduce family relationships merely to ties of affection. The regime has done all in its power to make altruism—at times relentless—take over from the solidarity inherent in ties of blood. The individual has been emancipated from his family so as to be reintegrated in the group, and through it, subordinated to the Party. Willing or unwilling, he has had to acquire a political awareness; his horizons have been enlarged to take in the nation as well as the village; and he has been given a new, though prefabricated picture of the world outside. His life has consequently taken on new dimensions and a new meaning.

The setting up of some sort of new system of values had been necessary because the 1911 Revolution had interrupted the natural order and emptied individual destinies of their meaning, whereas until then they had been justified by the continuum of the family. The philosophy of existence came into question just as much as the problem of living standards and more than the Western notion of the quality of life. A comparable situation might be the replacement of Christian values by secular morality in nineteenth-century Europe. It bears no more than a resemblance, however, and perhaps things are only beginning in China. Where the Party, by demanding servile obedience, strove to transpose the fundamental explanation, conferring a long-lasting quality on the social group rather than on the family, the Cultural Revolution caused things to develop secretly, though perhaps in depth. The notion of rebellion and the ardent encouragement to criticize cadres and those in authority may be the beginning of a change in the relations between the central power and the society; it may sow the seeds of independence of judgment, of liberty of thought, and eventually of a true individualism. Here again the future depends on whether or not the Party fully regains its authority.

In terms of quantity, the Chinese Communists have done prodigious work in education. School attendance figures as high as 70 or 80 percent, the proliferation of technical schools, the development of adult education, and the contribution of the press toward the popularization of science and its applications all bear faithful witness to this. In terms of quality, the Party has linked the curriculum with the needs of development and discouraged the traditional inclination to study arts; it has done away with the age-old prejudices held by the intellectual, the learned scholar cut off from real life, toward the cadres and manual workers and has opened education to the most humble sections of society. Many of the benefits, however, were unfortunately offset, in this field as in many others, by the errors of the general line, the unchanging priority given to politics and class sectarianism.

The lack of a national tradition in the organization of education, the refusal to accept Western and even Soviet schemas, and the circumstances already described, led after 1966 to a state of chaos whose effects have been temporarily attenuated by the low rate of growth in industry but will inevitably be serious in the long run. The severest reproach deserved by the system, particularly since the Cultural Revolution, is that it merely trains instruments to serve society, while the sole mission of the individual is to transform society. A balance could probably be struck between the old elitist Confucian formula, "The scholar is not a utensil,"[1] and the needs of a society in the process of development. It would allow man and humanistic studies to persist and bind China again to the best in its traditions.

Here the problem becomes one of culture and of the personality of China among the nations. A few frail clues suggest that some leaders are gradually waking up again to the value of their cultural legacy, at least as regards the preservation of architectural monuments and works of art that have survived the sectarianism of leftist leaders and the fanaticism of the red guards. Have they perhaps become aware of the value of the past and of the imaginary past of China? Have they heard the warning of the poet?

> All the countries whose legend is lost
> Will be condemned to die of cold. . . .[2]

The new man

The regime has started to change the way in which the individual thinks and expresses himself, just as much as his social and political environment or his vision of his country and the world. The transformation of the script (disappearance of the literary language and development of an everyday language more relevant to life itself), a more logical and stricter style—as used by the press, totally under Marxist influence—help to reduce the traditional Chinese lack of precision. Time and accuracy are not treated with as much disrespect as before. On the other hand, as the absolute criteria are not those of reason and common sense but those of an intolerant, intangible ideology, inevitably giving justification to the conclusions of the masses against those of the individual, work is sterilized as soon as it leaves the domain of pure science or technical subjects. The thinker and the humorist have no place in a society where the days of scholasticism have returned, and where mental restrictions alone can save the functioning of the intellect. Traces of the old Chinese spirit have not altogether disappeared, however. Subtlety, the gift of allusions, the art of play-acting, of inflating words, of reasoning by means of analogy, the coexistence of opposites, and the sinicization of concepts are all to be found in the language, that of both the red guards and their elders. It is hard to measure the extent of the damage done and just as hard to say how long it will be before a uniform, elementary, and fanatical type of man emerges, indistinguishable from the mass of the people and no longer needing any forms of expression beyond the ready-made formulas imposed by the ideology.

The moral traits are more clearly defined. To all appearances at least, the regime has wrought miracles in this domain. The absolute uprightness, purity, and austerity of public morals, the civic sense which had become one with the loyalty to Mao Tse-tung and the Party (until 1966 at least), the spirit of sacrifice, the patriotism, and the respect and love for the army, which for centuries had been discredited, strike even the least observant onlooker. It is hard to say whether these are the consequences of constraints in a society organized from top to bottom for the mutal supervision of its members, of a national consciousness that is extolled every day, or of the conformity of a basically malleable people. The three explanations can be combined. Father Huc, who wrote with some justification, "The life of the Chinese is materialism in action," would probably be astounded. If he were to look closely, he might perhaps recognize the Chinese of his times in them, by considering their characteristics rather than their moral traits.

In spite of the intolerance that can be turned on to order and his sincere or feigned outbursts of revolutionary passion, the Chinese of today still appears to have retained his essential qualities and failings: moderation and inclination to compromise rather than violence, patience and endurance, strong inner will hidden beneath a courteous gentleness, a lack of fatalism replaced by an optimistic, gay, and brave resignation, a sense of humor (though chances of using it have become rare and dangerous), and above all a boundless self-respect which can survive any amount of criticism and self-criticism, and which, like that of poor Ah Q, the immortal character created by Lu Hsün, has to justify itself to itself to save its face.

As to the rest, the Chinese is still about as sober, frugal, thrifty, and industrious, though not truly dynamic, as he always has been. He will presumably remain so, as long as the older generations have not disappeared, and as long as his material environment remains the same; until now, his dwelling, his food, his means of transport, and his tools have scarcely changed. The great difference between the present and the pre-Communist era is the levelling-out in living conditions. Today, as yesterday, apart from a few large industrial centers, China is a vast nation of farmers, still close to the past as regards their agricultural means and methods. Collective organization, resisted by the peasants as soon as it goes beyond a certain point and becomes unacceptable (the readjustment of the people's communes in 1958 is a striking example of this), has not yet prevailed against the old realities.

China before the nations

Less than thirty years after the abolition of the Unequal Treaties, China rose to a position in the world as a result of several factors—its vast area, the size of its population, its early achievements in nuclear weapons, the messianic quality of its revolutionary message, its nationalism, which had made it stand out against Moscow's leadership, and the exceptional personality of Mao Tse-tung.

International opinion already considered China a first-class power. President Nixon predicted that in the near future it would be one of the centers of decision on the planet, while the Russians claimed it aspired to become not only the political center of the world, but its military and technical center as well.[3] These exaggerated statements arise either from a desire to seduce in the diplomatic field, or from hostile propaganda; whatever the case, they bear witness to an astounding rise. This is probably the most certain and the greatest result attained by the regime.

In this respect, the Chinese Communists, and particularly Mao Tse-tung and Chou En-lai, deserve all the more admiration, for this picture of the new China is for the moment based on little more than fiction. The country's poverty, its mediocre economic capacity, still mainly directed to feeding its people, its tiny share in world trade, the setbacks in its development, and the monumental errors in leadership are plain for all to see.

In foreign policy, China has not yet achieved its main aims. Peking waited twenty-two years before being admitted to the United Nations; it has not yet been able to take back Taiwan, reassert its influence over the belt of former tributary states in Southeast Asia, correct its frontiers with the Soviet Union, or neutralize Japan. It has suffered a serious defeat in its policy toward Indonesia and Pakistan and has met only limited success in its action in the Near East, and, with one or two exceptions, in its policies toward the African states. On the other hand, China's schemings have worried some states and its value as an example has dwindled in all eyes.

The friendship and confidence accorded to China by governments and nations are enough to help forget its economic weakness, its domestic disorders, its failures in foreign policy, and its refusal to comply with the diplomatic practices acknowledged everywhere. The country's current status abroad arises from the prestige enjoyed by traditional China and from the international situation, rather than from the present regime.

China is regaining its former position because it is to some extent renewing its links with the most authentic traditions of its civilization and greatness, though it does so without admitting as much. After more than a hundred years of mutual misunderstanding and contempt and incidents followed by military expeditions, the China of the great dynasties and the great emperors of the eighteenth century is emerging once more and the old currents of admiration are welling up again.

The appearance of a wiser China after the mysterious and worrying Cultural Revolution has somewhat relieved the anxiety of other nations and made them greet Peking with renewed hope. China's presence in world politics ensures that one of the key pieces in the building of peace can be fitted back into the puzzle. The country also benefits from the alarm felt by many nations who, like it, want to maintain their identity and are faced with the possibility of being stifled politically and economically by the two superpowers in the new organization of the world. In this respect, the nation is both reassuring and frightening. China is reassuring because the two great powers are no longer completely alone, and because, in spite of its weakness, China can make things awkward for them and hamper their military and naval dispositions on the Asian continent or in the Pacific. China is worrying because it proves in its turn that the world has entered the era of giant nations. It is to be hoped, in view of this, that China will help speed up the formation of true unity in Europe.

Although China can no longer aspire to its age-old tradition and become the center and model for the world, it is, even so, taking on an important role in the world of the future. All Chinese, as they look at Mao Tse-tung, no doubt feel this and are proud of it.

At the close of this second volume of the history of the Chinese Communist movement and regime, it inevitably comes to mind that time and ruptures have already thrust nearly all those mentioned out of the way. With the death of Chou En-lai in 1976, only Mao Tse-tung, the greatest among them, remains, but he is an old man and those around him are minor figures or newcomers.

The old Party has gone and with it the China of the early Communists; the masts of the new China are already disappearing over the horizon. Another China is near. Mao Tse-tung and Chou En-lai have spent their last years preparing its arrival, the former by ensuring that China will always be lit by the torch of revolution, and the latter by making it take its place among the realities around it, and among its own realities.

It is to be hoped that their successors will leave room in the synthesis they are creating for the spiritual and moral heritage of the ancient China. At a time when the "finite" world is looking for a new culture and trying to shape the features of the man of tomorrow, it would indeed be a tragedy if the only civilization to survive the ages were to founder before its eyes.

Notes

[1] With only one use.
[2] Patrice de La Tour du Pin, *La Quête de Joie* (Paris:Gallimard, 1939).
[3] See the Soviet Journal *Kommunist*, No. 12 (August 1968), referring to various Chinese statements, although not citing specific ones.

Bibliography

Western publications

So many varied works have been written on the People's Republic of China that the main purpose here is to give the reader a carefully selective bibliography intended to provide reliable basic information on each category of questions. Books are therefore listed under the following headings:

(a) Reference works, bibliographies, selected biographies, directories
(b) Specialized publications in Western languages, translations from Chinese press
(c) Maps and atlases, geographical works
(d) General works
(e) Ideology and doctrine
(f) Domestic policy
(g) Economics and population
(h) Culture, education, the press, publications, religion, ethnic minorities
(i) National defense
(j) Foreign policy

Each of these headings includes a limited number of works. These deal only with the period from 1949 to 1975, are usually the result of studies and research of lasting value, and contain numerous useful references. With a few exceptions, reports written from a journalistic point of view, travel books, books of limited scope, or highly specialized works do not appear in the list.

Articles in newspapers or reviews are too numerous and too scattered to be catalogued. The most widely accepted ones appear in the specialized publications listed below.

It is abundantly clear that, as far as the study of China is concerned, the United States is well ahead of all other countries, as regards the quantity of works produced, their variety, and their scientific value. The European countries are well behind, in spite of a few excellent works. Works in Russian are not included in this bibliography.[1]

(a) Reference works, bibliographies, selected biographies, directories

BERTON, PETER and WU, EUGENE. *Contemporary China, a Research Guide.* Stanford, Calif.: Stanford University Press, 1967.

BERTON, PETER A. M. *Soviet Works on China: a Bibliography of Non-Periodical Literature, 1946-1955.* Los Angeles: University of Southern California Press, 1959.

BOORMAN, HOWARD, *et al.*, eds. *Biographical Dictionary of Republican China.* 4 vols. New York and London: Columbia University Press, 1967-1968.

CHEN, NAI-RUENN. *The Economy of Mainland China, 1949-1963: A Bibliography of Materials in English.* Berkeley and Los Angeles: University of California Press, 1963.

CLARK, ANNE B. *A Checklist of Bibliographies and Reference Tools on Communist China for the Use of the Center for East Asian Studies.* Cambridge, Mass.: Center for East Asian Studies, 1961.

ELEGANT, ROBERT. *China's Red Masters: Political Biographies of the Communist Leaders.* New York: Twayne, 1951; London: Bodley Head, 1962.

HOOVER INSTITUTION. *Chinese Periodicals and Newspapers.* Stanford, Calif.: the Hoover Institution, 1973.

HSÜEH CHUN-TU. *Revolutionary Leaders of Modern China.* New York: Oxford University Press, 1971.

[1]The Centre de Recherche et de Documentation sur la Chine Contemporaine de l'Ecole des Hautes Etudes en Sciences Sociales, 54 Boulevard Raspail, Paris, has a library with about a hundred periodicals and 15,000 books or microfilms in Chinese, Western languages, or Russian on modern China. The Centre gives priority to teachers and students of Chinese engaged in research.

HUCKER, CHARLES O. *China: A Critical Bibliography*. Tucson, Ariz: Arizona University Press, 1962.

JOURNAL OF ASIAN STUDIES, THE. *Bibliography of Asian Studies* (annual publication). Ann Arbor, Mich.: The Association for Asian Studies. Between 1936 and 1940, the publication was called *Bulletin of Far Eastern Bibliography*.

KLEIN, DONALD W. and CLARK, ANNE B. *Biographic Dictionary of Chinese Communism (1921-1965)*. 2 vols. Cambridge, Mass.: Harvard University Press, 1971.

LUST, JOHN. *Index Sinicus: A Catalogue of Articles Relating to China in Periodicals and other Collective Publications, 1920-1955*. Cambridge, England: Heffer, 1964.

PERLEBERG, MAX. *Who's Who in Modern China*. 2 vols. Hong Kong: Vaughan, 1955.

STATE STATISTICAL BUREAU. *Ten Great Years*. Peking, 1969.

UNION RESEARCH INSTITUTE. *Who's Who in Communist China*. 2 vols. Hong Kong: 1969.

WALES, NYM. *Red Dust: Autobiographies of Chinese Communists as Told to Nym Wales*. Stanford, Calif.: Stanford University Press, 1952.

WU YUAN-LI, ed. *China: A Handbook*. New York: Praeger, 1973.

YIN, HELEN and YIN YI-CHANG. *Economic Statistics of Mainland China, 1949-1957*. Cambridge, Mass.: Harvard University Press, 1960.

YUAN TUNG-LI. *China in Western Literature*. New Haven, Conn.: Yale University, Far Eastern Publications, 1958.

Note: Other books coming under this heading, and bibliographies in Russian and Japanese, are included in BERTON and WU, *Contemporary China: a Research Guide*, which is a work of fundamental importance for research.

(b) Specialized publications, translations from the Chinese press

English (periodicals)

Asia Quarterly. Brussels.

Asia Profile. Hong Kong. First issue August 1, 1973.

Asian Survey. Berkeley, Calif.: University of California, Institute of International Studies. First issue March 1, 1961, when it succeeded the *Far Eastern Survey* (1932-1961). Monthly.

The China Quarterly. London: Congress for Cultural Freedom until January-March 1968; Contemporary China Institute, School of Oriental and African Studies, London University, since April-June 1968. First Issue January 1, 1960. Quarterly.

China News Analysis. Hong Kong. First issue August 1, 1953. Weekly.

China Report. New Delhi. Bimonthly.

Far Eastern Economic Review. Hong Kong. First issue October 1, 1946. Weekly.

Issues and Studies. Taipei, Taiwan. Monthly.

Journal of Asian Studies. Ann Arbor, Mich.: The Association for Asian Studies. First issue November 1, 1941, when it succeeded the *Far Eastern Survey* (1932-61). Quarterly.

Translations into English

The United States Consulate General in Hong Kong has been publishing extensive translations of the Chinese press (daily papers and periodicals) since 1950, which are easily available to research students. The main series are: *Survey of China Mainland Press, Selections from China Mainland Magazines, Current Background, Extracts from Chinese Mainland Publications*. They contain indexes and chronological tables.

The Joint Publications Research Service has been publishing translations of materials from China or on China since 1957.

The Union Research Institute in Hong Kong publishes translations as well as more important works.

Various English-speaking countries, and in particular the United States, have translation services or services to monitor the Chinese radio. These publications occasionally form part of more general organizations, such as the International Arts and Sciences Press, New York, which has a series devoted to China (IASP Translation Journals).

Translations into French

The *Bulletin de Liaison pour les Etudes chinoises en Europe*, published by the Ecole en Sciences Sociales des Hautes Etudes forms a useful link among research students and gives information on their work. The series entitled *Extrême-Orient*, published by *La Documentation française*, the

Mondes Asiatiques (formerly *France-Asie*), and the periodical *La Nouvelle Chine* (appearing every two months) are partly or wholly concerned with China.

The *Revue Bibliographique de sinologie,* an extremely erudite periodical, devotes little space to modern China.

Various institutions belonging to the universities occasionally produce joint publications of materials for use in the study of the Far East today.

(c) Maps and atlases, geographical works

Apart from maps belonging to widely known series available in bookshops, the following may also be consulted:

War Office map (1/4,000,000), China, Mongolia, Central Asia, Northern India.
World Air Map (1/1,000,000).
CIA Atlas (U.S. Department of Commerce), 1959.
Postal Atlas of China (in English and Chinese).
International Boundary Study, The Geographer, U.S. Department of State.

CRESSEY, G. B. *Land of the 500 million.* New York: McGraw-Hill, 1955.
JEN YU-TI. *Geography of China.* Peking: Foreign Languages Press, 1965.
LATTIMORE, OWEN. *Inner Asian Frontiers.* London: Oxford University Press, 1940.
NAGEL (guide books). *China.* Geneva, 1968.
SHABAD, THEODORE. *China's Changing Map.* Rev. ed. New York: Praeger, 1972.
TRAEGEAR, T. R. *A Geography of China.* Chicago: Aldine, 1965.
TREGEAR, T. R. *An Economic Geography of China.* New York: American Elsevier, 1970.
WANG KIUN-HENG. *Précis de géographie de Chine.* Peking: Foreign Languages Press, 1959.

(d) General works

BARNETT, A. DOAK. *China After Mao.* Princeton, N.J.: Princeton University Press, 1967.
BARNETT, A. DOAK, ed. *Chinese Communist Politics in Action.* Seattle: University of Washington Press, 1969.

BARNETT, A. DOAK. *Uncertain Passage, China's Transition to the Post-Mao Era.* Washington: The Brookings Institution, 1974.

CENTRE D'ETUDES DE POLITIQUE ETRANGERE. *Aspects de la Chine.* Vol. 3. Paris, 1962.

CHEN, THEODORE H. E. *The Communist Regime (Documents and Commentary).* New York: Praeger; London: Pall Mall, 1967.

CH'EN, JEROME. *Mao and the Chinese Revolution.* London and New York: Oxford University Press, 1965.

CHUNG, HUA-MIN and MILLER, ARTHUR C. *Madame Mao: A Profile of Chiang Ch'ing.* Hong Kong: Union Research Institute, 1968.

FEUERWERKER, ALBERT, ed. *Modern China.* Engelwood Cliffs, N.J.: Prentice-Hall, 1964.

GRAY, JACK. *Modern China's Search for a Political Form.* London and New York: Oxford University Press, 1969.

GRAY, JACK and CAVENDISH, PATRICK. *Chinese Communism in Crisis: Maoism and the Cultural Revolution.* New York: Praeger; London: Pall Mall, 1968.

GUILLAIN, ROBERT. *Dans trente ans la Chine.* Paris: Seuil, 1968.

GUILLERMAZ, JACQUES. *La Chine Populaire.* 7th rev. ed. Paris: Presses Universitaires de France, 1976.

———.*A History of the Chinese Communist Party, 1921-1949.* London: Methuen; New York: Random House, 1972 (Second rev. French ed. 1975, 2 vols.).

HARRISON, JAMES P. *The Long March to Power: A History of the Chinese Communist Party, 1921-72.* New York: Praeger; London: Macmillan, 1972.

HO PING-TI and TSOU TANG, eds. *China in Crisis.* 2 vols. Chicago: University of Chicago Press, 1968.

HSÜ KAI-YU. *Chou En-lai: China's Gray Eminence.* Garden City, New York: Doubleday, 1968.

ILLIEZ, PIERRE, *Chine Rouge, Page Blanche.* Paris: Julliard, 1973.

KARNOW, STANLEY. *Mao and China.* New York: Viking, 1972.

KIRBY, E. STUART, ed. *Contemporary China.* 6 vols. New York: Oxford University Press, 1956-1964.

KUO PING-CHIA. *China: New Age and Outlook.* New York: Knopf, 1956.

LEWIS, JOHN WILSON. *Leadership in Communist China.* Ithaca, N.Y.: Cornell University Press, 1966.

LEWIS, JOHN WILSON, ed. *Party Leadership and Revolutionary Power in China.* London: Cambridge University Press, 1972.

LI TIEN-MIN. *Chou En-lai.* Taipei, Taiwan: 1970.

LINDBECK, JOHN, ed. *China: the Management of a Revolutionary Society.* Seattle: University of Washington Press, 1972.

MARCUSE, JACQUES. *The Peking Papers.* London: Barker, 1968.

MYRDAL, J. *Report from a Chinese Village.* New York: Pantheon, 1965.

PEZEU-MASSABUAU, JACQUES. *La Chine.* Paris: Colin, 1971.

RICE, EDWARD E. *Mao's Way.* Berkeley and Los Angeles: University of California Press, 1972.

RICHARDSON, WILLIAM, ed. *China Today.* New York: Maryknoll, 1969.

ROY, DAVID TOD. *Kuo Mo-jo: the Early Years.* Cambridge, Mass.: Harvard University Press, 1971.

SCALAPINO, ROBERT A., ed. *Elites in the People's Republic of China.* Seattle: University of Washington Press, 1972.

SCHRAM, STUART R. *Mao Tse-tung.* New York: Simon and Schuster, 1966.

TANG, PETER S. H. *Communist China Today.* 2 vols. New York: Praeger, 1957-1958.

TEIWES, FREDERICK C. *Provincial Party Personnel in Mainland China, 1956-1966.* New York: Columbia University, East Asian Institute, 1967.

TOWNSEND, JAMES R. *Political Participation in Communist China.* Berkeley and Los Angeles: University of California Press, 1967.

TSOU TANG and HO PING-TI. *China's Heritage and the Communist Political System.* Chicago: University of Chicago Press, 1968.

TUNG, WILLIAM. *The Political Institutions of Modern China.* The Hague: M. Nijhoff, 1964.

WALKER, RICHARD. *China Under Communism, the First Five Years.* New Haven, Conn.: Yale University Press, 1955.

WILSON, RICHARD. *Anatomy of China: An Introduction to One Quarter of Mankind.* New York: Weybright and Talley, 1968.

(e) *Ideology and doctrine*

CARRERE D'ENCAUSSE, HELENE and SCHRAM, STUART R. *Le Marxisme et l'Asie, 1833-1964.* Paris: Colin, 1965.

CARRERE D'ENCAUSSE, HELENE. *L'U.R.R.S. et la Chine devant les révolutions dans les sociétés préindustrielles.* Paris: Hachette, 1970.

CH'EN, JEROME. *Mao Papers: Anthology and Bibliography.* London: Oxford University Press, 1970.

CH'EN, JEROME. *Mao.* Englewood Cliffs, N.J., and London: Prentice-Hall, 1969.

COHEN, ARTHUR. *The Communism of Mao Tse-tung.* Chicago: University of Chicago Press, 1964.

COHEN, JEROME A, ed. *Contemporary Chinese Law.* Cambridge, Mass.: Harvard University Press, 1970.

COHEN, JEROME A. *The Criminal Process in the People's Republic of China, 1949-1963.* Cambridge, Mass.: Harvard University Press, 1968.

DITTMER, LOWELL. *Liu Shao-ch'i and the Chinese Cultural Revolution: The Politics of Mass Criticism.* Berkeley and Los Angeles: University of California Press, 1974.

GARAUDY, ROGER. *Le Problème chinois.* Paris: Seghers, 1967.

GRAY, JACK. *Modern China's Search for a Political Form.* London and New York: Oxford University Press, 1969.

HSIUNG, JAMES CHIEH. *Ideology and Practice: the Evolution of Chinese Communism.* New York: Praeger; London: Pall Mall, 1970.

JOHNSON, CHALMERS A. *Ideology and Politics in Contemporary China.* Seattle: University of Washington Press, 1973.

LEWIS, JOHN WILSON. *Leadership in Communist China.* Ithaca, N.Y.: Cornell University Press, 1966.

LIU SHAO-CH'I. *The Collected Works of Liu Shao-ch'i.* 3 vols. Hong Kong: Union Research Institute, 1968-1969.

MAO TSE-TUNG. *Selected Works.* 4 vols. Peking: Foreign Languages Press, 1961-1965. (*Note*: Some texts written after 1949 have been published in separate booklets by the Foreign Languages Press.)

PYE, LUCIAN. *The Spirit of Chinese Politics.* Cambridge, Mass.: Massachusetts Institute of Technology Press: 1968.

SCHRAM, STUART R. *The Political Thought of Mao Tse-tung.* Rev. ed. New York: Praeger; London, Pall Mall, 1969.

SCHRAM, STUART R. ed. *Mao Tse-tung Unrehearsed. Talks and Letters: 1956-1971.* Harmondsworth, England: Penguin, 1974.

SCHURMANN, F. H. *Ideology and Organization in Communist China.* Berkeley and Los Angeles: University of California Press, 1966.

SCHWARTZ, BENJAMIN I. *Communism and China: Ideology in Flux.* Cambridge, Mass.: Harvard University Press, 1968.

SOLOMON, RICHARD. *Mao's Revolution and the Chinese Political Culture.* Berkeley and Los Angeles: University of California Press, 1971.

UNION RESEARCH INSTITUTE. *Index to Selected Works of Mao Tse-tung.* Hong Kong, 1968.

URBAN, GEORGE, ed. *The Miracles of Chairman Mao, 1966-1970.* London: Stacey, 1971.

WHYTE, MARTIN KING. *Small Groups and Political Rituals in China.* Berkeley, Los Angeles, and London: University of California Press, 1974.

YU, FREDERICK T. C. *Mass Persuasion in Communist China.* New York: Praeger; London: Pall Mall, 1964.

(f) Domestic policy

BARNETT, A. DOAK, ed. *Chinese Communist Politics in Action.* Seattle: University of Washington Press, 1969.

BARNETT, DOAK A. *Cadres, Bureaucracy, and Political Power in Communist China.* New York and London: Columbia University Press, 1967.

BAUM, RICHARD and TEIWES, FREDERICK C. *Ssu-Ch'ing: The Socialist Education Movement of 1962-1966.* Berkeley: University of California Center for Chinese Studies, 1968.

BENNETT, GORDON A. and MONTAPERTO, RONALD N. *Red Guard: The Political Biography of Dai Hsiao-ai.* New York: Doubleday, 1971.

CHEN, C. S. ed. and RIDLEY, CHARLES P., trans. *Rural People's Communes in Lienchiang.* Stanford, Calif.: Hoover Institution Press, 1969.

CHIEN YU-SHEN. *China's Fading Revolution, Army Dissent and Military Divisions, 1967-1968.* Hong Kong: Centre for Contemporary Chinese Studies, 1969.

DUTT, V. P. and DUTT, GARGI. *China's Cultural Revolution.* London: Asia Publishing House, 1970.

ESMEIN, JEAN. *The Chinese Cultural Revolution.* New York: Doubleday, 1973.

FAN, K. H. *The Chinese Cultural Revolution: Selected Documents.* New York: Monthly Review Press, 1968.

FOKKEMA, D. W. *Report from Peking.* London: Hurst, 1970.

ZHELOKHOVSTEV, A. *La Révolution Culturelle vue par un Sovietique.* Paris: R. Laffont, 1968.

KLOCHKO, MIKHAIL. *A Soviet Scientist in China.* New York: Praeger, 1964.

LEYS, SIMON. *Les Habits Neufs du Président Mao.* Paris: Editions Champs Libre, 1971.

MACFARQUHAR, RODERICK, ed. *The Hundred Flowers.* New York: Praeger, 1960.

MACKERRAS, COLIN and HUNTER, NEALE. *China Observed.* New York: Praeger; London: Pall Mall, 1968.

MU FU-SHENG. *The Wilting of the Hundred Flowers*. New York: Praeger, 1963.

PYE, LUCIAN. *The Authority Crisis in Chinese Politics*. Chicago: University of Chicago, Center for Policy Study, 1967.

ROBINSON, THOMAS W., comp. *The Cultural Revolution in China*. Berkeley and Los Angeles: University of California Press, 1971.

SNOW, EDGAR. *The Other Side of the River*. New York: Random House, 1962.

UNION RESEARCH INSTITUTE. *Chinese Communist Party Documents of the Great Proletarian Cultural Revolution (1966-1967)*. English and Chinese text. Hong Kong, 1968.

UNION RESEARCH INSTITUTE. *The Case of P'eng Teh-huai 1959-1968*. English and Chinese text. Hong Kong, 1969.

UNION RESEARCH INSTITUTE. *Documents of the Chinese Communist Party Central Committee, September 1966-April 1969*. Vol. 1. Hong Kong, 1971.

VOGEL, EZRA F. *Canton under Communism: Programs and Politics in a Provincial Capital, 1949-1968*. Cambridge, Mass.: Harvard University Press, 1969.

(g) *Economics and population*

BUCHANAN, KEITH. *The Transformation of the Chinese Earth. Perspective on Modern China*. London: Bell, 1970.

BUCK, J. L., DAWSON D., OWEN, L., and WU YUAN-LI. *Food and Agriculture in Communist China*. New York: Praeger, 1966.

CHAO KUO-CHÜN. *Agrarian Policy of the Chinese Communist Party 1921-1959*. London and New Delhi: Asia Publishing House, 1960.

CHEN, NAI-RUENN and GALENSON, WALTER. *The Chinese Economy under Communism*. Chicago: Aldine; Edinburgh, Edinburgh University Press, 1969.

CHEN, NAI-RUENN, comp. *The Economy of Mainland China 1949-1963: A Bibliography of Materials in English*. Berkeley, Calif.: Social Science Research Council, Committee on the Economy of China, 1963.

CHENG CHU-YUAN. *Economic Relations Between Peking and Moscow, 1949-1963*. New York: Praeger; London: Pall Mall, 1964.

CHENG CHU-YUAN. *Communist China's Economy 1945-1962. Structural Changes and Crisis*. South Orange, N.J.: Seton Hall University Press, 1963.

CHOU, KANG. *Agricultural Production in Communist China 1945-1965.* Madison: University of Wisconsin Press, 1970.

CONGRESS OF THE UNITED STATES OF AMERICA, JOINT ECONOMIC COMMITTEE. *China: A Reassessment of the Economy.* Washington, D.C.: U.S. Government Printing Office, 1975.

CONGRESS OF THE UNITED STATES OF AMERICA, JOINT ECONOMIC COMMITTEE. *People's Republic of China: An Economic Assessment.* Washington, D.C.: U.S. Government Printing Office, 1972.

DELEYNE, JAN. *The Chinese Economy.* Translated by Robert Leriche. London: Deutsch, 1973; New York: Harper Torchbooks, 1974.

DONNITHORNE, AUDREY. *China's Economic System.* New York: Praeger, 1967.

DUMONT, RENE. *La Chine surpeuplée—Tiers monde affamé.* Paris: Seuil, 1965.

DUMONT, RENE. *Révolution dans les campagnes chinoises.* Paris: Seuil, 1957.

ECKSTEIN, ALEXANDER. *Communist China's Economic Growth and Foreign Trade.* New York: McGraw Hill, 1966.

————.*The National Income of Communist China.* Glencoe, Ill.: The Free Press, 1962.

GALENSON, WALTER and LIU TA-CHUNG, eds. *Economic Trends in Communist China.* Chicago: Aldine; Edinburgh: Edinburgh University Press, 1968.

HO PING-TI. *Studies on the Population of China, 1368-1953.* Cambridge, Mass.: Harvard University Press, 1959; London: Oxford University Press, 1960.

HOLLISTER, WILLIAM W. *China's Gross National Product and Social Accounts 1950-1957.* Cambridge, Mass.: Massachusetts Institute of Technology, 1958.

HSIAO, KATHERINE HUANG. *Money and Monetary Policy in Communist China.* New York: Columbia University Press, 1971.

HUGHES, T. I. and LUARD, D. E. T. *The Economic Development of Communist China, 1949-1960.* London: Oxford University Press, 1961.

ISHIKAWA, SHIGERU. *National Income and Capital Formation in Mainland China (an Examination of Official Statistics).* Tokyo: Institute of Asian Economic Affairs, 1965.

KING, FRANK H. H. *A Concise Economic History of Modern China 1840-1960.* New York: Praeger, 1968.

KLEIN, SIDNEY. *Politics Versus Economics: The Foreign Trade and Aid Policies of China.* Hong Kong: International Studies Group, 1968.

KUO, LESLIE T. C. *The Technical Transformation of Agriculture in Communist China.* New York: Praeger; London: Pall Mall, 1972.

LI CHOH-MING. *The Statistical System of Communist China.* Berkeley and Los Angeles: University of California Press, 1962.

LI CHOH-MING. *Economic Development of Communist China.* Berkeley and Los Angeles: University of California Press, 1959.

LIU, T. C. and YEH, K. C. *The Economy of the Chinese Mainland: National Income and Economic Development, 1933-1959.* 2 vols. Princeton, N.J.: Princeton University Press, 1965.

MAH FENG-HWA. *The Foreign Trade of Mainland China.* Edinburgh: Edinburgh University Press, 1969; Chicago: Aldine, 1971.

MENGUY, MARC. *L'Economie de la Chine Populaire.* 2d ed. Paris: Presses Universitaires de France, 1971.

MIYASHITA, TADO. *The Currency and Financial System of Mainland China.* Tokyo: Institute of Asian Economic Affairs, University of Washington Press, 1966.

PERKINS, DWIGHT H. *Market Control and Planning in Communist China.* Cambridge, Mass.: Harvard University Press, 1966.

PERKINS, DWIGHT H. *Agricultural Development in China 1369-1968.* New York: Aldine, 1969.

PRYBYLA, JAN. S. *The Political Economy of Communist China.* Scranton, Penn.: International Text Book, 1970.

RICHMAN, BARRY M. *Industrial Society in Communist China.* New York: Random House, 1969.

SCHRAN, PETER. *The Development of Chinese Agriculture, 1950-1959.* Urbana: University of Illinois Press, 1969.

WALKER, KENNETH R. *Planning in Chinese Agriculture; Socialisation and the Private Sector 1956-1962.* Chicago: Aldine; London: Cass, 1965.

WILLMOTT, W. E. *Economic Organization in Chinese Society.* Stanford, Calif.: Stanford University Press, 1972.

WU, YUAN-LI. *The Economy of Communist China: An Introduction.* New York: Praeger, 1965.

——— .*An Economic Survey of Communist China.* New York: Bookman Associates, 1956.

——— .LING H. C., and WU, GRACE HSIA. *The Spatial Economy of Communist China: A Study of Industrial Location and Transportation.* New York: Praeger, 1962.

YANG, C. K. *Chinese Communist Society: The Family and the Village.* Cambridge, Mass.: Massachusetts Institute of Technology Press, 1965.

YIN, HELEN and YIN YI-CHANG. *Economic Statistics of Mainland China, 1949-1957*. Cambridge, Mass.: Harvard University Press, 1960.

(h) Culture, education, the press, publications, religion, ethnic minorities.

BUSH, RICHARD C., JR. *Religion in Communist China*. Nashville and New York: Abingdon, 1970.

CHEN, THEODORE H. E. *Thought Reform of the Chinese Intellectuals*. Hong Kong: Hong Kong University Press, 1960.

DIENY, JEAN-PIERRE. *Le Monde est à vous: La Chine et les livres pour enfants*. Paris: Gallimard, 1970.

DUFAY, FRANÇOIS. *L'Etoile contre la Croix*. 1961.

FEUERWERKER, ALBERT and CHENG, S. *Chinese Communist Studies of Modern Chinese History*. Cambridge, Mass.: Harvard University Press, 1961.

FOKKEMA, D. W. *Literary Doctrine in China and Soviet Influence, 1936-1960*. The Hague: Mouton, 1965.

DE FRANCIS, JOHN. *Nationalism and Language Reform in China*. Princeton, N.J.: Princeton University Press, 1950; London: Oxford University Press, 1951.

FRASER, STEWART E. *Education and Communism in China. An Anthology of Commentary and Documents*. London: Pall Mall, 1971.

GOULD, SIDNEY. *Sciences in Communist China*. Washington, D.C.: Bailey, 1961.

HSIA, C. T. *A History of Modern Fiction, 1917-1957*. New Haven, Conn.: Yale University Press, 1961.

HSIA, TSI-AN. *The Gate of Darkness: Studies of the Leftist Literary Movement in China*. Seattle: Washington University Press, 1968.

HUANG SUNG-K'ANG. *Lu Hsün and the New Culture Movement of Modern China*. Amsterdam: Djambatan, 1957.

LANG, OLGA. *Pa Chin and his Writings: Chinese Youth Between the Two Revolutions*. Cambridge, Mass.: Harvard University Press, 1967.

LEFEUVRE, JEAN, S. J. *Shanghai, les enfants dans la ville*. Paris: Castermann, 1962.

MONSTERLEET, JEAN. *Sommets de la littérature chinoise contemporaine*. Paris: Domat-Montchrestien, 1953.

NUNN, G. RAYMOND. *Publishing in Mainland China*. Cambridge, Mass.: Massachusetts Institute of Technology Press, 1966.

ORLEANS, LEO A. *Professional Manpower and Education in Communist China.* Washington, D.C.: National Science Foundation, 1961.

PRICE, R. F. *Education in Communist China.* New York: Praeger, 1970.

PRŮŠEK, JAROSLAV. *Studies in Modern Chinese Literature.* Berlin: Akademie-Verlag, 1964.

RIDLEY, CHARLES, GODWIN, PAUL and DOOLIN, DENNIS. *The Making of a Model Citizen in Communist China.* Stanford, Calif.: The Hoover Institution Press, 1971.

TING YI. *A Short History of Modern Chinese Literature.* Peking: Foreign Languages Press, 1959.

WU YUAN-LI and SHEEKS, ROBERT B. *The Organization and Support of Scientific Research and Development in Mainland China.* New York: Praeger, 1970.

(i) National defense

BUESCHEL, RICHARD M. *Communist China's Air Power.* New York: Praeger, 1968.

CHENG, J. CHESTER. *The Politics of the Chinese Red Army: A Translation of the Bulletin of Activities of the People's Liberation Army.* Stanford, Calif.: The Hoover Institution, 1966.

CHIEN, YU-SHEN. *China's Fading Revolution: Army Dissent and Military Divisions, 1967-1968.* Hong Kong: Centre of Contemporary Chinese Studies, 1969.

GITTINGS, JOHN. *The Role of the Chinese Army.* London and New York: Oxford University Press, 1967.

GRIFFITH, SAMUEL B. *The Chinese People's Liberation Army.* New York: McGraw-Hill, 1967; London; Weidenfeld & Nicolson, 1968.

HUCK, ARTHUR. *The Security of China.* London: Chatto & Windus, 1970.

JOFFE, ELLIS. *Party and Army: Professionalism and Political Control in the Chinese Officer Corps 1949-1964.* Cambridge, Mass.: Harvard University Press, 1965.

RHOADS, EDWARD J. M. *The Chinese Red Army 1927-1963: An Annotated Bibliography.* Cambridge, Mass.: Harvard University Press, 1964.

WHITSON, WILLIAM W., ed. *The Military and Political Power in China in the 1970s.* New York: Praeger, 1972.

WHITSON, WILLIAM W., and HUANG CHEN-HSIA. *The Chinese High Command: A History of Communist Military Politics, 1929-71.* New York: Praeger, 1973.

(*j*) *Foreign policy*

BARNETT, A. DOAK. *Communist China and Asia: Challenge to American Policy.* New York: Harper, 1960.

BARNETT, A. DOAK, ed. *The United States and China: The Next Decade.* New York: Praeger, 1970.

BOORMAN, H. L., ECKSTEIN, ALEXANDER, MOSELEY, PHILIP and SCHWARTZ BENJAMIN. *Moscow-Peking Axis: Strength and Strains.* New York: Harper, 1957.

BOYD, R. G. *Communist China's Foreign Policy.* New York: Praeger, 1962.

CLUBB, O. EDMUND. *China and Russia: The Great Game.* New York: Columbia University Press, 1971.

COHEN, JEROME ALAN. *The Dynamics of China's Foreign Relations.* Cambridge, Mass.: Harvard University Press, 1970.

DALAI LAMA. *My Land and My People. The Autobiography of H. H. the Dalai Lama.* Edited by David Howarth. London: Weidenfeld & Nicolson, 1962.

DEUTSCHER, ISAAC. *Russia, China and the West: A Contemporary Chronicle 1953-1966.* London: Oxford University Press, 1970.

DULLES, FOSTER RHEA. *American Policy Towards Communist China: The Historical Record, 1949-1969.* New York: Crowell, 1972.

DUTT, VIDYA PRAKASH. *China's Foreign Policy, 1958-1962.* New York: Asia Publishing House, 1964.

FAIRBANK, JOHN KING. *The United States and China.* Rev. ed. Cambridge, Mass.: Harvard University Press, 1972.

FEJTÖ, FRANÇOIS. *Chine-U.R.S.S., de l'alliance au conflit: 1950-1972.* Paris: Editions du Seuil, 1973.

FLOYD, DAVID. *Mao Against Khrushchev: A Short History of the Sino-Soviet Conflict.* New York: Praeger; London: Pall Mall, 1964.

GITTINGS, JOHN. *Survey of the Sino-Soviet Dispute: A Commentary and Abstracts from the Recent Polemics, 1963-1967.* London and New York: Oxford University Press, 1968.

GRIFFITH, WILLIAM. *The Sino-Soviet Rift.* Cambridge, Mass.: Massachusetts Institute of Technology Press, 1969.

HALPERN, A.M., ed. *Policies Towards China: Views from Six Continents.* New York: McGraw-Hill, 1966.

HINTON, HAROLD C. *China's Turbulent Quest: An Analysis of China's Foreign Relations since 1945.* Rev. ed. Bloomington: Indiana University Press, 1972.

HINTON, HAROLD C. *The Bear at the Gate: Chinese Policy-Making Under Soviet Pressure.* Stanford: Stanford University Press, 1971.

JOHNSON, CECIL. *Communist China and Latin America, 1959-1967.* New York and London: Columbia University Press, 1970.

JOHNSTON, D. M. and CHIU, HUNG. *Agreements of the People's Republic of China 1949-1967, a Calendar.* Cambridge, Mass.: Harvard University Press, 1968.

LAMB, ALASTAIR. *The China-India Border.* London: Oxford University Press, 1964.

LARKIN, BRUCE D. *China and Africa, 1949-1970.* Berkeley and Los Angeles: University of California Press, 1971.

LONDON, KURT, ed. *Unity and Contradiction: Major Aspects of Sino-Soviet Relations.* New York: Praeger, 1962.

MACFARQUHAR, RODERICK. *Sino-American Relations, 1949-71.* New York: Praeger, 1972.

MAXWELL, NEVILLE. *India's China War.* New York: Random House, 1971.

MEHNERT, KLAUS. *Peking and Moscow.* Translated by Leila Vennewitz. New York: New American Library, 1964.

MERTENS, PIERRE and SMETS, PAUL F. *L'Afrique de Pékin.* Brussels: Amibel, 1966.

MOORSTEEN, RICHARD and ABRAMOWITZ, MORTON. *Remaking China Policy.* Cambridge, Mass.: Harvard University Press, 1971.

PURCELL, VICTOR. *The Chinese in South-East Asia.* 2d ed. London: Oxford University Press, 1965.

RICHER, PHILIPPE. *La Chine et le Tiers monde.* Paris: Payot, 1971.

ROSE, LEO EUGENE. *Nepal: Strategy for Survival.* Berkeley and Los Angeles: University of California Press, 1971.

YOUNG, KENNETH T. *Negotiating with the Chinese Communists: the United States Experience, 1953-1967.* New York: McGraw-Hill, 1968.

ZAGORIA, DONALD S. *The Sino-Soviet Conflict, 1956-1961.* Princeton, N.J.: Princeton University Press, 1962.

Publications in Chinese

Generally speaking, the mainland Chinese sources used in this volume consist of official texts, editorials, reports, or articles from the daily press or periodicals, and of collections of documents or monographs. Virtually no serious works exist on the history of the Party or the regime in general. The large amounts of materials appearing at certain moments (during the Four

Histories Movement, for example) cannot be obtained, with a few exceptions, and are usually not published. The men regarded as the accepted historians of the Party or of Mao Tse-tung (Hu Ch'iao-mu and Li Jui, for instance) were eliminated during the Cultural Revolution.

The Peking authorities—their strictness here varies from one moment to another—do not allow works of basic importance, specialized periodicals, or provincial newspapers to leave the country. During the Cultural Revolution and its aftermath from 1966 on, the publication of anything apart from booklets aimed at spreading the thought of Mao Tse-tung virtually ceased.

This situation made research carried out abroad, particularly in Taiwan, Hong Kong, the West, Japan, and the Soviet Union, gain much more importance. Biographies and collections of documents have abounded during the last few years, and several of them are mentioned in the text of this book. These works are based on old or indirect sources and are sometimes, like those of the mainland itself, colored by propaganda and must be used with care.

For these reasons, because of limited space, and above all because this book is intended primarily for readers who know no Chinese, or who are just beginning to study it, the Chinese section of the bibliography is confined to the most ordinary and easily accessible publications and reference works. Specialists are invited to consult, when necessary, more selective bibliographies or the Chinese sources mentioned in the Western works mentioned above.[2]

General bibliographies

Ch'üan-kuo hsin shu-mu (*National Bibliography*). Peking.

Ch'üan-kuo tsung shu-mu (*Cumulative National Bibliography*) (annual). Peking.

Chung-hua min-kuo ch'u-pan t'u-shu mu-lu (*National Bibliography of the Republic of China*). Taipei. (In two languages.)

The Monthly List of China Books. Taipei.

---

[2]The selections of works by Mao Tse-tung in their various forms have not been mentioned in the bibliography. The most complete and outstanding of them is probably the one being compiled at the moment by a group of Japanese students of Chinese under the direction of Professor Takeuchi Minoru; it has almost been completed. The title is *Mao Tse-tung chi* (*Collected Works of Mao Tse-tung*); it will run to ten volumes.

Writings by other Chinese theorists are so scattered that they cannot be listed in a general work. There is considerable work to be carried out here in the way of collecting texts and reviewing them, both within China and abroad.

Annual directories and miscellaneous collections

Jen-min shou-ts'e (People's Handbook). Peking. (Last published in 1965.)
Hui-huang ti shih-nien (Ten Glorious Years). *Wei-ta ti shih-nien (Ten Great Years)*. Peking: Foreign Languages Press, 1959.
Fei-ch'ing nien-pao (Yearbook of Chinese Communism). Taipei.
Chung-hua jen-min kung-ho kuo t'iao-yüeh chi (Collected Treaties of the People's Republic of China). Annual collection.
Chung-kung chün-shih wen-chien hui-p'ien (Collected Documents on Military Affairs 1950-1954). Hong Kong.
Chung-yang jen-min-cheng-fu fa-ling hui-p'ien. (Compendium of Laws and Decrees of the Central People's Government). Peking (1949-1954).
Chung-hua jen-min kung-ho-kuo fa-kui hui-p'ien (Compendium of Laws and Regulations of the People's Republic of China). Peking. (Sequel to the above. Two issues a year, beginning in September 1954).

Biographies

Several series of selected biographies concerning mainland China have been published in Hong Kong, Taiwan, and Japan, and several of the Hong Kong and Taipei periodicals listed below often include biographical articles. Two selections will be mentioned here:

Chung-kung jen-ming-lu (Biography of Chinese Communists). Taipei, 1967.
Huang Chen-hsien, Chung-kung chün-jen chi (Chinese Communist Soldiers).

Periodicals

Two daily newpapers, *Jen-min jih-pao (People's Daily)* and *Kuang-ming jih-pao (Daily Light)* are allowed to leave China at the moment, along with *Hung-ch'i (Red Flag)*, which until October 1958 was entitled *Hsüeh-hsi (Study)* and is theoretically published twice a month.

Apart from these three, *Hsin-hua yüeh pao (New China Monthly)*, now called *Hsin-hua pan-yüeh-k'an (New China Semi-Monthly)*, is the most useful publication for research students.

The list below gives the chief periodicals available until 1966, some of which at least may be found in specialized libraries. Over the last year or two a number of periodicals have begun to appear or reappear, and some, such as *Li-shih yen-chiu,* are once more available in the West.

Hsin chien-she (New Construction). Monthly.
Hsin kuan-ch'a (New Observer). Twice a month.
Jen-min chiao-yü (People's Education). Twice a month.
Jen-min wen-hsüeh (People's Literature). Monthly.
Li-shih yen-chiu (Historical Studies). Twice a month.
Min-tsu t'uan-chieh (Solidarity of Nationalities). Monthly.
Shih-chieh chih-shih (World Knowledge). Twice a month.
Ti-li chih-shih (Geographical Knowledge). Monthly.
T'ung-chi kung-tso (Statistical Work). Twice a month.
Cheng-fa yen-chiu (Studies in Government and Law). Quarterly.
Ching-chi yen-chiu (Economic Studies). Monthly.

A great many periodicals in Taiwan deal with questions relating to the People's Republic of China. Only the most important are given here.

Chung-kung yen-chiu (Studies on the Chinese Communists), formerly *Fei-ch'ing yen-chiu.*
Fei-ch'ing yüeh-pao (Communist Monthly).
Wen-ti yü yen-chiu. English version: *Issues and Studies.*

Several periodicals in Hong Kong deal with the continent, particularly: *Chan Wang (Look),* monthly; *Ch'un ch'iu (Spring and Autumn),* twice a month; *Tsu-kuo yüeh-k'an (Fatherland),* monthly; and *Ming-pao,* monthly. They occasionally publish texts or selections of documents.

Political secrecy, concern for propaganda, and the scattered and varied nature of sources create immense complications for the researcher or bibliographer when it comes to identifying, tracking down, and above all obtaining working documents. In every country, a considerable effort still needs to be made to create a modern approach to the study of Chinese, carried out by students with qualifications in several different fields, particularly political economy and scientific and technical subjects, who have access to the necessary documents and source materials.

Index

Note: The following abbreviations have been used in this index: C.C., Central Committee; C.C.P., Chinese Communist Party; C.P., Communist Party; C.R., Cultural Revolution; G.L.F., Great Leap Forward; S.E.M., Socialist Education Movement.